Management Accounting

PEARSON
Education

We work with leading authors to develop the strongest
educational materials in accounting, bringing cutting-edge
thinking and best learning practice to a global market.

Under a range of well-known imprints, including
Financial Times Prentice Hall, we craft high quality print
and electronic publications which help readers to
understand and apply their content, whether studying
or at work.

To find out more about the complete range of our
publishing, please visit us on the World Wide Web at:
www.pearsoned.co.uk

Management Accounting
Analysis and Interpretation

Cheryl S. McWatters Ph.D. CMA
University of Alberta

Jerold L. Zimmerman Ph.D.
University of Rochester

Dale C. Morse Ph.D.
University of Oregon

FT Prentice Hall
FINANCIAL TIMES

An imprint of **Pearson Education**
Harlow, England • London • New York • Boston • San Francisco • Toronto • Sydney • Singapore • Hong Kong
Tokyo • Seoul • Taipei • New Delhi • Cape Town • Madrid • Mexico City • Amsterdam • Munich • Paris • Milan

Pearson Education Limited

Edinburgh Gate
Harlow
Essex CM20 2JE
England

and Associated Companies throughout the world

Visit us on the World Wide Web at:
www.pearsoned.co.uk

First published 2008

© Pearson Education Limited 2008

The rights of Cheryl McWatters, Jerold Zimmerman and Dale Morse to be identified
as authors of this work have been asserted by them in accordance with the Copyright,
Designs and Patents Act 1988.

All rights reserved. No part of this publication may be reproduced, stored in a retrieval
system, or transmitted in any form or by any means, electronic, mechanical, photocopying,
recording or otherwise, without either the prior written permission of the publisher or
a licence permitting restricted copying in the United Kingdom issued by the Copyright
Licensing Agency Ltd, Saffron House, 6–10 Kirby Street, London EC1N 8TS.

All trademarks used herein are the property of their respective owners. The use of
any trademark in this text does not vest in the author or publisher any trademark
ownership rights in such trademarks, nor does the use of such trademarks imply
any affiliation with or endorsement of this book by such owners.

Materials from the Certified Management Accountant Examinations, Copyright © 2008 by the
Institute of Certified Management Accountants are reprinted and/or adapted with permission.

ISBN: 978-0-273-71247-3

British Library Cataloguing-in-Publication Data
A catalogue record for this book is available from the British Library

Library of Congress Cataloging-in-Publication Data
A catalog record for this book is available from the Library of Congress

10 9 8 7 6 5 4 3 2 1
12 11 10 09 08

Typeset in 9/12.5 pt Linoletter by 73
Printed and bound by Graficas Estella in Graficas Estella, Navarra, Spain

The publisher's policy is to use paper manufactured from sustainable forests.

Supporting resources

Visit **www.pearsoned.co.uk/mcwatters** to find valuable online resources

For instructors

- A comprehensive solutions manual, providing answers to all the questions in the text
- PowerPoint slides that can be downloaded and used as OHTs
- An extensive testbank of multiple-choice questions and further graded questions in application of knowledge and in problem solving

Also: The Companion Website provides the following features:

- Search tool to help locate specific items of content
- E-mail results and profile tools to send results of quizzes to instructors
- Online help and support to assist with website usage and troubleshooting

For more information please contact your local Pearson Education sales representative or visit **www.pearsoned.co.uk/mcwatters**

Preface

To remain competitive in a dynamic environment, organizations must adapt and respond to major environmental forces, including technological change, globalization and customer preferences. We present management accounting within an analytical framework for organizational change to underscore how organizations must adapt to create organizational and customer value.

A central aim of this book is to provide students with an understanding and appreciation of the strengths and limitations of an organization's accounting system, enabling them thereby to be critical users of the system. Whether students pursue professional careers in accounting or in other areas of management, they will interact with accounting systems. In all organizations, managers rely on management accounting systems to provide information to deal with changes in their operating environment. In some instances, managers use this information for making planning decisions; in others, managers rely on the accounting system for information with which to measure performance, information which influences the behaviour of management and staff. Management accounting contributes to the creation of organizational value through its dual roles of generating information for improved decision making and providing mechanisms to control organizational members.

Conceptual framework

The conceptual framework organizes our thinking about the organization's accounting system and provides a basis for analysing proposed changes to the system. We rely on this framework to demonstrate that management accounting is an integral part of the organization's strategy and not simply a selection of computational topics. Organizational value is linked closely to having the appropriate management accounting system. Our use of a conceptual framework reinforces our view that management accounting is understood best when it is integrated into the 'big picture'. Management accounting concepts are not used in isolation but rather as part of the organization's strategy. We draw upon the concept of opportunity cost as a basis for decision making and organizational theory to reinforce the role of accounting as a control mechanism.

Trade-offs

We emphasize throughout the text that one accounting system cannot fulfil all the demands placed on it to provide information for planning decisions and to control organizational members to achieve organizational goals. As elsewhere in life, trade-offs exist. An accounting system that privileges control purposes is likely to be less effective for planning purposes. Use of the system for one purpose comes at the cost of reduced effectiveness for the other. Accounting systems are not free goods and we stress the need for managers to be alert to their trade-offs, costs and benefits. For example, costing systems for inventory valuation are not adequate for other purposes, such as a make-or-buy decision. However, some books leave the impression that one system can be used for multiple purposes as long as adequate adjustments are made. We prefer to highlight that these adjustments are not costless. For example, recent advanced manufacturing techniques, such as JIT, TQM and activity-based management (ABM), are presumed to improve the organization's ability to make planning decisions, but proponents and textbooks frequently do not address how their implementation affects the use of the system for organizational control.

Logical sequence

An important distinction between this text and others is that the chapters build on each other. The first chapter presents the conceptual framework that we incorporate throughout the text. Chapter One also identifies the trade-offs that exist among the different uses of an accounting system. The next four chapters focus on strategy and planning decisions. Chapters Six and Seven examine strategy and problems of organizational control. The following chapters highlight planning and control issues by developing our theme of the trade-offs that exist when using an accounting system for making planning decisions and control purposes. Chapter Fourteen explores the role of management accounting in a dynamic environment. We introduce recent management innovations, with the caveat that organizations should adopt such approaches when they align with their strategic and environmental context.

Acknowledgements

This Pearson edition has provided a further opportunity to develop our pedagogical approach and to improve the text's goals to encourage critical thinking and to link management accounting to the broader organizational context. This edition also highlights that the organizational context is both local and global. Feedback from students and instructors has enabled us to improve the book's accessibility and readability. We have included, when appropriate and helpful, real-world illustrations to bring concepts from the theoretical to the practical level. Many of these examples result from conversations with colleagues and students who challenged us to present conceptual material in ways that were readily understood by users without extensive training in accounting. Others stem from our everyday experience and interactions with the organizational world around us.

In preparing this edition, I have had the luxury of study leave to review and reflect on both longstanding and current issues in management accounting and other management disciplines. Students, other instructors and research colleagues have listened to my ideas and offered insights with which to refine arguments and analyses. My co-authors have left me much liberty to present topics that reflect my own thinking yet maintain the integrity of our individual theoretical perspectives. In particular, my colleague, Jerry Zimmerman, has provided me with critical and constructive comments which have led to greater clarity and an improved manuscript. I truly appreciate his confidence in my ability to present concepts and topics in a way that harmonizes our viewpoints.

The opportunity to revise this text results from the interest in and enthusiasm for our conceptual approach provided by our publisher. I appreciate very much the support of our colleagues at Pearson Education, in particular Matthew Smith whose positive attitude and dedication to the project were exemplary. Philippa Fiszzon and Linda Dhondy did a grand job in providing editorial and production assistance.

Lastly, to my husband John, who encouraged me to take on this project, I offer my thanks for his on-going support and his acceptance of the trade-offs that my focus on this book has required.

Cheryl S. McWatters

Note: Permission has been received from the Institute of Certified Management Accountants to use questions and/or unofficial answers from past CMA examinations.

Learning objectives – bullet points at the start of each chapter show what you can expect to learn from that chapter, and highlight the core coverage.

Running case study – a real-world case study runs throughout each chapter, highlighting key management accounting issues, and discussing them in both practical and theoretical terms.

Numerical examples – at frequent intervals throughout each chapter, there are numerical examples that give you step-by-step workings to follow through to the solution.

Concept reviews – these short questions, integrated throughout each chapter, allow you to check your understanding as you progress through the text. They comprise discussion questions requiring you to review or critically consider topics you have just considered.

CHAPTER **EIGHT**

Budgeting
(Planning and control)

Learning objectives

1 Use budgeting for planning purposes.
2 Use budgeting for control purposes.
3 Identify the conflicts that exist between planning and control in the budgeting process.
4 Describe the benefits of having both short-term and long-term budgets.
5 Explain the responsibility implications of a line-item budget.
6 Identify the costs and benefits of budget lapsing.
7 Develop flexible budgets and identify when flexible budgeting should be used instead of static budgeting.
8 Explain the costs and benefits of using zero-base budgeting.
9 Create a master budget for an organization including sales, production, administration, capital investment and financial budgets.
10 Create pro-forma financial statements based on data from the sales, production, administration, capital investment and financial budgets.
11 Use spreadsheets to analyse monthly cash flows. (Appendix)

Mother Goose Child-Care Centre

Mother Goose Child-Care Centre (MGCC) is a not-for-profit organization that provides child care and pre-school education to children in the Selly Oak Ward in the city of Birmingham. MGCC rents space in a neighbourhood building, where both the child care and pre-school programmes are housed along with MGCC's administrative offices.

The child-care programme is for children between six months and three years of age. MGCC charges £600 monthly per child for eight hours of child care every weekday. MGCC's child-care centre is open 12 months of the year. A licensed and certified staff provides a structured set of activities tailored to the ages of the children; one assistant is required for every four children. The child-care centre has a capacity of 30 children.

The pre-school programme is four hours per day, either morning or afternoon, for nine months. Each session has a capacity of 40 children from three to five years of age. The programme costs £450 per month per child. MGCC requires one pre-school teacher for every eight children. A qualified nurse is always on call for both the pre-school and the child-care programmes.

A ten-member Board of Directors oversees and supervises the operations of MGCC. The Board of Directors hires the manager of the child-care centre, the head teacher of the pre-school programme and the office manager. The child-care manager and the head teacher hire their staff, plan their programmes and are responsible for the financial operations of their programmes. The office manager has a secretary and bookkeeper, who prepare monthly bills for users of the facility, monthly financial reports for the Board of Directors, purchase supplies and are responsible for collecting and disbursing funds.

The financial year of MGCC is from 1 July to 30 June. Prior to its beginning, the office manager asks the child-care manager and head teacher to prepare budgets to plan for the coming financial year. MGCC cannot spend more than its revenue, so the budgeting process is very important for planning the new school year. While not profit-driven, MGCC strives to create value for parents by providing quality programmes that adhere to government standards and best practices for early childhood education. This strategy ensures that organizational value is created in terms of MGCC's continued attractiveness and viability as an educator and child-care provider.

---

about the profitability of the organization's different components. If segment reports were not included in external reports, investors would not be able to discern if a highly profitable segment is offsetting an unprofitable one.

Numerical example 9.7

The Green Corporation makes two products: chemex and citrol. The corporation has two product lines. A separate manager is responsible for each division. The Chemex Division sells 50 tonnes of chemex on the open market for £10,000 per tonne. Also, 20 tonnes of chemex are transferred to the Citrol Division. The Citrol Division sells 100 tonnes of citrol on the open market for £20,000 per tonne. The Chemex Division has variable costs of £5,000 per tonne and fixed costs of £200,000. The Citrol Division has variable costs of £8,000 per tonne, excluding the cost of chemex. The fixed costs of the Citrol Division are £400,000. The central administration allocates £100,000 of fixed costs to the Chemex Division and £500,000 of fixed costs to the Citrol Division. Calculate the profit of the two divisions, using the market price as the transfer price of chemex.

Solution

	Chemex division (£)	Citrol division (£)
Revenues		
Open market sales	500,000	2,000,000
Internal sales of chemex	200,000	
Variable costs		
Internal purchase of chemex		(200,000)
Other variable costs	(350,000)	(800,000)
Contribution margin	350,000	1,000,000
Fixed costs	(200,000)	(400,000)
Profit before allocated costs	150,000	600,000
Allocated costs	(100,000)	(500,000)
Divisional profit	50,000	100,000

If all the central administration costs have been allocated, Green Corporation's profit is the sum of the profit of the two divisions, or £150,000.

In *Numerical Example 9.7*, the allocated costs, fixed costs and internal sales are reported separately in the segment reports of the two divisions. These costs and sales are highlighted to provide managers with additional information for decision making. For example, allocated costs might be eliminated for performance evaluation purposes, if the allocated costs are not controlled by, or affect the behaviour of, the divisional manager. Reporting each division's contribution margin allows a manager to ignore fixed costs when making incremental planning decisions. Internal sales should be highlighted to identify interactions among the divisions. These interactions provide important information when considering the elimination of or changes in one of the divisions.

Segment reporting is just one of the end results of the transfer-pricing and cost allocation process. Product costs are another result. The next chapter describes different methods of allocating costs to products.

Concept review

1 What is the purpose of segment reporting?
2 How do transactions with other units of the organizations affect segment reports?

Chapter summary – each chapter ends with a 'bullet point' summary. This highlights the material covered in the chapter and can be used as a quick reminder of the main issues.

Organizational analysis – integrated throughout the text, these illustrative examples highlight the practical application of accounting concepts and techniques by real businesses, emphasising the importance of management accounting in the organization.

Key terms summary – at the end of each chapter, there is a listing of all the key terms, recapping the most important points in that chapter. Each key term appears emboldened when it first appears in the chapter.

Self-study problem – at the end of each chapter you will encounter one of these questions, allowing you to attempt a comprehensive question before tackling the end-of-chapter assessment material. To check your understanding and progress, solutions are provided at the end of the problem.

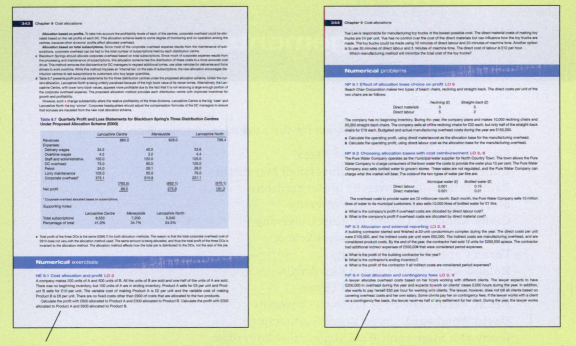

Numerical exercises – similar to the Numerical examples in the body of the chapter they are clearly identified in terms of learning objectives and concepts addressed.

Numerical problems – longer than the preceding Exercises, the problems combine numerical computations, analysis and interpretation with the concepts learned in the chapter.

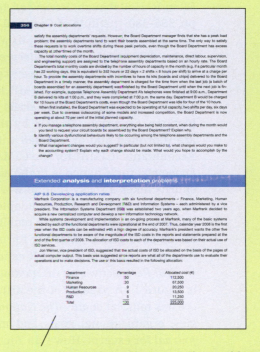

Analysis and interpretation problems – these comprehensive questions reinforce the text's framework for organizational change. They require the reader to develop critical thinking skills and to write short essays presenting analyses. Many of the problems do not have one single correct answer, but instead are designed to contain multiple dimensions demanding a broad management perspective.

Extended analysis and interpretation problems – the final set of exercises in each chapter require the reader to combine analysis and interpretation with numerical computations within the broader context of organizational change.

Acknowledgements

We thank the following reviewers for their valuable comments on the book:

Shahzad Uddin, University of Essex
Philip G.M.C. Vergauwen, Universiteit Maastricht
Paul Marambos, University of Hertfordshire
Martin Quinn, Dublin City University
Cathy Knowles, Oxford Brookes University
Jodie Moll, Manchester Business School
Verna Care, Brunel University
Roland Kaye, University of East Anglia
Ronnie Patton, University of Ulster
F.H.M. Verbeeten, RSM Erasmus University
David Woodward, University of Southampton
Jenny van Sten-van't Hoff, Hogeschool Rotterdam

We are grateful to the following for permission to reproduce copyright material:

Jeffrey Hyde for 'Robots Don't Get sick or Get Paid Overtime, but Are They a Profitable Option for Milking Cows?', by Jeffrey Hyde, James W. Dunn, Annette Steward, and Ellen R. Hollabaugh, *Review of Agricultural Economics*, Volume 29, Number 2 (2007), pp. 366–380; Institute of Certified Management Accountants (ICMA) for reproduction of CMA examination questions and unofficial answers, which have been adapted to make: AIP *(Analysis and Interpretation Problem)* 1-18, NP *(Numerical Problem)* 2-2, NP 5-11, AIP 7-20, NE *(Numerical Exercise)* 8-1, NP 8-7, NP 8-15, NP 9-7, AIP 9-2, AIP 9-6, AIP 9-7, NP 10-23, AIP 10-8, NP 11-8, NP 11-14, NE 12-7, NP 12-1, NP 12-4, NP 12-9 and AIP 12-7. Materials from the Certified Management Accountant Examinations, Copyright © 2008 by the Institute of Certified Management Accountants are reprinted and/or adapted with permission; Chartered Institute of Management Accountants (CIMA) for the CIMA Code Of Ethics For Professional Accountants; *The Economist* for 'Change is in the air', 20 January 2007, p. 76 and 'A maker of ice-cream churns takes a rocky road to world domination' (2007) Vol. 384, No. 8542, 18 August, pp. 55–6, which have been adapted respectively under the headings 'Organizational analysis: Japan's DoCoMo's mobile phone services' and 'Organizational analysis: Ice cream goes global'; Elsevier for our Figure 3.2 'Examples of Police Incident/Activity Analysis' from P.M. Collier, 'Costing police services: The politicization of accounting', *Critical Perspectives on Accounting*, Volume 17, No. 1, January 2006, pp. 57–86, where it is Figure 1 on page 67 of the article; Terrence Belford for 'Note-by-note progression creates musical chain', *The National Post*, 20 October 1999 (on which AIP 1.19, Strategies, organizational goals and management accounting is based); *The Wall Street Journal* for excerpt 'How Can You Beat High Cost of College? Become a Professor', by Steve Stecklow, April 15, 1997, pg A1, and for excerpt 'Brokerage Firms Are Raising Fees As Trading Falls', by William Power, December 18, 1990, pg C19. Reprinted with permission of *The Wall Street Journal*, Copyright © 2008 Dow Jones & Company, Inc. All Rights Reserved Worldwide.

Getty Images: Page 3, Spencer Platt; Page 37, Forrest Anderson, Time & Life Pictures; Page 77, ColorBlind Images; Page 115, Justin Sullivan; Page 149, Martin Brigdale; Page 185, Maria Teijeiro; Page 217, Alan Powdrill; Page 265, David Buffington; Page 311, Somos/Veer; Page 361, Neil Lukas; Page 413, Inti St Clair; Page 451, Alistair Berg; Page 501, Grant V. Faint; Page 549, Getty Images.

Alamy Images: Page 7, Kevin Foy; Page 13, David Levenson; Page 14, Rolf Adlercreutz; Page 18, Corbis Super RF; Page 39, Photofusion Picture Library; Page 41, David R. Frazier Photolibrary, Inc.; Page 45, imagebroker; Page 56, Eric Nathan; Page 60, Carsten Reisinger; Page 79, Hornbil Images; Page 84, Jochen Tack; Page 90, Darren Matthews; Page 94, bildagentur-online/begsteiger; Page 116, Richard Levine; Page 119, Les Gibbon; Page 124, Stefan Sollfors; Page 131, stock_wales; Page 137, David R. Frazier Photolibrary, Inc.; Page 153, Trevor Smithers ARPS; Page 157, Iksung Nah; Page 163, David Bowman; Page 169, Derek Croucher; Page 187, David Hancock; Page 189, Super-Stock; Page 194, Corbis Premium RF; Page 204, Pier Photography; Page 219, M. A. Battilana; Page 231, Ferruccio; Page 236, imagebroker; Page 267, Larry Lilac; Page 271, The Flight Collection; Page 312, Ian Miles-Flashpoint Pictures; Page 314, Rob Wilkinson; Page 324, mediacolor's; Page 332, The Garden Picture Library; Page 363, nagelestock.com; Page 365, Kitt Cooper-Smith; Page 379, Andrew Fox; Page 414, Niall McDiarmid; Page 418, Peter Stone; Page 455, Jeremy Sutton-Hibbert; Page 469, Digital Vision; Page 505, Alex Segre; Page 514, Rob Walls; Page 522, Greg Wright; Page 551, Kevin Foy; Page 552, Art Kowalsky; Page 557, Motoring Picture Library; Page 565, JUPITERIMAGES/Brand X; Page 570, JUPITERIMAGES/Brand X; Page 571, Oleksiy Maksymenko.

In some instances we have been unable to trace the owners of copyright material, and we would appreciate any information that would enable us to do so.

Management Accounting

CHAPTER ONE

Organizations and accounting

Learning objectives

1 Explain how technological change, globalization and customer preferences can affect an organization and its management accounting system.

2 Identify strategies for achieving customer value.

3 Describe features of organizations that promote decisions to achieve organizational goals.

4 Explain the critical role played by management accounting in making planning decisions and controlling managers to create organizational value.

5 Identify the trade-offs that exist in using information for making planning decisions, control and external reporting.

6 Identify the roles of different types of management accountants.

7 Recognize the role of judgement and ethics in making management accounting choices.

DVD Stores

Three years ago when Kathy Johnson approached Nadja Joshi about investing in a DVD shop, Nadja was not very excited. But Kathy persisted. She explained to her friend that shops don't have to pay for DVDs until they are sold. Any unsold DVDs are returned to the producer of the DVD. Therefore, no initial investment is required for inventory and no risk of unsold inventory exists.

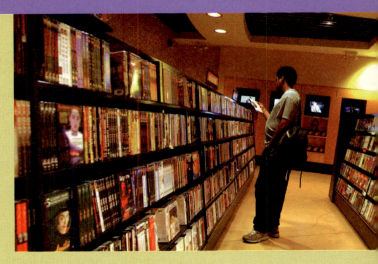

Kathy's initial business strategy was to have low mark-ups on DVDs and attempt to sell large volumes. Kathy also wanted to support local recording artists by reserving some shelf space for their DVDs. She had noticed the quick replacement of compact discs with the DVD format.

Kathy eventually convinced Nadja to invest £30,000 along with her own £30,000 to form a partnership. Kathy would receive an annual salary of £20,000 for managing the shop and the remaining profits would be shared equally. Nadja would not be involved in management. They were also able to borrow £100,000 from the bank and leased space in the centre of town for their shop, which they called DVD Store. After sales exceeded expectations, they opened two more outlets in regional shopping centres. Kathy and Nadja also hired managers to operate these two regional shops.

With the growth of the business, problems have begun to arise. Sales have not been as high as expected at one of the regional shops and the other appears to suffer from considerable shoplifting. Competition in the retail DVD business has increased with a high street chain opening a megastore near one of the regional shops. In addition, the Internet has become an important factor. Customers search and buy from Internet retailers like Virgin Megastores (www.virginmegastores.co.uk), HMV (www.hmv.co.uk), and CDZone (www.cdzone.co.uk). Potential customers also are downloading music and movies from file-sharing sites.

These new competitors have hurt sales. Kathy and Nadja must make some decisions to revise their strategy and operations and adapt to the increased competition. They realize that the shops must be much more sensitive to their customers and operate more efficiently, but they aren't sure exactly what to do.

MANAGEMENT ACCOUNTING IN A CHANGING ENVIRONMENT

Management accounting helps create **organizational value** through better decision making and management of the members of the organization. For example, managers use information on costs to make decisions on products and services. Also, management accounting information is used to evaluate the performance of a manager. Management accountants bring an integrating perspective to the organization's strategic and financial decisions.

Management accounting includes the design and use of information within organizations. Previously management accounting focused on financial information, such as the cost of a product or the revenues generated by a unit of the organization. But selecting and analysing non-financial information, such as the time required to make a product, the percentage of defective products or the number of on-time deliveries, has become an important part of management accounting. Non-financial information supplements financial information by providing a broader understanding of the organization, which can lead to better decisions.

Management accounting is not composed of a fixed set of rules. Organizations have different goals and are composed of different members; therefore no universal rules of management accounting exist. Management accounting must adapt to each organization.

Management accounting is not a static process: it adapts to organizational change. Three major forces cause organizations to evolve: changes in technology, globalization and customer preferences. Organizations that fail to adapt to these forces will not be able to survive in the long run. Organizations must meet the needs of other stakeholder groups beyond those of their customers. For example, the goals of shareholders and employees also must be satisfied to maintain the organization's viability.

Organizations depend on management accounting to provide information in a dynamic environment. If the evolution of the management accounting system lags behind the evolution of the organization, the system will act as an anchor preventing the organization from successfully dealing with a changing environment. Organizations must adapt to changing environments and management accounting must adapt to a changing organization. Therefore, the study of management accounting is a study of a process, not a study of a set of procedures. The process of management accounting is linked to organizational characteristics, which are constantly changing. To understand management accounting, you must understand organizations and the forces that affect them.

The following sections describe the three major forces – technological change, globalization and changing customer mix and preferences – which affect organizations. Organizations have chosen to adapt to these forces in different ways. Some of these adaptations, such as total quality management (TQM) and just-in-time (JIT), have become commonplace. These adaptations and others are described in the following sections. In identifying and understanding these changes in organizations, we can appreciate the role and process of management accounting.

■ Technological change: information and communication technologies

Technology has dramatically changed the way we live. Information technologies, transportation systems, food technology and medical and scientific discoveries affect the way we work, eat and play. Organizations have been similarly influenced by technological change and will be continually influenced by breakthroughs in the future. For example, consider how the Internet has changed our lives.

Today people take information and communication technologies for granted. Many devices that we use daily rely on micro-chips and software to operate correctly. Today's electronic treadmills take your pulse as you run, adjust the pace to your heart rate, and inform you of speed, distance, calories and carbohydrates burned. Global positioning systems route you quickly to your destination. Upon arrival, you can take photographs that can be published instantly on the Internet or transmitted over mobile phones.

Information acquisition and dissemination

The information and communication technology industries have revolutionized the way organizations operate. Organizations can communicate with their members, suppliers and customers through devices such as the Internet, mobile phones and personal digital assistants (PDAs). Information on changing demand for products and demographics is easily accessible. In addition, computers can manipulate information and simulate different scenarios to allow organizations to make better predictions of the future. Restaurants use electronic pagers to inform customers that their table is ready or waiters that food orders are ready. Airlines use instant messaging to update passenger flight itineraries.

Information and communication technologies take care of many of the tasks traditionally performed by humans. For example, eBay prepares dispatch labels and invoices. The eBay Selling Manager software tracks a seller's inventory. As a result, eBay sellers do not have to hire personnel to do the administrative tasks. Instead, they can focus on what they do best: selling. Air travellers today do work traditionally performed by airline company personnel. Airline companies rely on the customer for booking flights, choosing seats, as well as for checking in.

Advanced technologies allow organizations to make better quality products more efficiently through automation and precise operations. Manufacturing firms use **computer-assisted manufacturing (CAM)** and **computer-assisted design (CAD)**. CAM allows organizations to make products through programmed machines. Programmable machines perform welding in the manufacture of cars and insert components in a circuit board in the electronics industry. CAD allows engineers and designers to create new product ideas using three-dimensional plans. Car manufacturers like BMW and airplane manufacturers like Airbus and Boeing rely heavily on CAD.

All of these technologies make a firm's products more reliable and safer. The production processes are more efficient as well; fewer mistakes are made in producing goods, which lowers production costs significantly. Advanced technologies also enable firms to deliver their products and services timely and reliably. This creates value for customers – they get higher quality products at lower prices. Being able to download a new tune now, instead of having to go into town and search for the DVD, makes a big difference to the customer who prefers novelty to sound quality.

Information and communication technology systems are often highly integrated. The sale of a book, an insurance policy or a flight via the Internet will update the relevant company databases instantly. Managers can use this up-to-date information for planning purposes and for monitoring the execution of their company's strategy. This creates organizational value – the benefits received by various stakeholders from their investment in the firm.

The BCM (Boots Contract Manufacturing) Kosmetik GmbH's production facility in Dietzenbach, Germany, for example, uses such an integrated approach to the manufacturing of its cosmetics. Employing **computer-integrated manufacturing (CIM)** BCM Kosmetik has tied its reporting system to its marketing and scheduling systems to provide current production and inventory information. The systems feed data into a database that many users can access simultaneously. Using real-time information,

Customer value and organizational value

Throughout this text, we use the terms 'customer value' and 'organizational value'. Understanding these important concepts is critical to applying the topics covered throughout the text.

'Customer value' is the benefit received by the customer from a product or service relative to its cost. The following example illustrates this rather abstract definition. Suppose you are looking to purchase a particular MP3 player that sells for £155. But you really like this particular MP3 player; therefore, you would be willing to pay £160. You buy this model for £155 and get value of £160. So we would say that you, as the customer, have received £5 of value.

'Organizational value' is the benefit received by various stakeholders from their investment in the organization. Suppose you start a business by investing £25,000 and borrow another £10,000 from the bank. The total investment is £35,000. After a couple of years of making profits, you can sell the firm for £48,000 as the buyer realizes that the business has good prospects to continue to make profits. We would say that you have created £13,000 of organizational value from running the business.

employees can continually monitor quality, and react quickly to design changes and market demand. The system also is linked to the firm's regulatory obligations, as cosmetics are subject to government regulation.[1]

To be successful, organizations must recognize the advantages of greater access to information. A survey of financial executives indicated that many accounting systems are not adapting rapidly enough to new technology. Of the financial executives surveyed, 80 per cent indicated that their company's accounting system produced useful data too slowly and inefficiently. Firms were required to adapt to meet the demand for real-time information and production. For example, GlaxoSmithKlein, a large pharmaceutical firm, installed software to reduce the time to make certain budgeting comparisons from two to three weeks to two to three days.[2]

E-business and the Internet

Firms that existed before the Internet era often had trouble in transforming their businesses to operate online. An airline company, such as EasyJet, had an advantage over its older rivals, such as KLM-Air France and British Airways. EasyJet adopted the Internet almost from its inception, operating an integrated system. This strategy enabled it to adjust prices quickly to the dynamics of supply and demand, plan flights more efficiently and grow quickly. Traditional airlines interacted with their clients mainly through travel agents. Adopting the Internet was a challenge for them, as they had to add Internet sales to existing retail channels. This change meant opening up their reservations systems to the public, and integrating and co-ordinating web-based sales with sales from agents. These changes impeded their ability to compete.

Other so-called bricks-and-mortar shops, such as US-based bookshop Borders and UK-based HMV outsourced their Internet sales to their main rival Amazon.[3] However, in 2006, HMV admitted to having underestimated the growth of Internet sales, and decided to reverse the deal with Amazon.[4]

---

[1] www.taylor.com/industry/case_studies.php (accessed 6 May 2006).
[2] *The Wall Street Journal*, 2 February 1995, B2:5.
[3] *The Wall Street Journal*, 28 April 2003, 'When Worlds Collide'.
[4] *The Financial Times*, 10 May 2006, 'HMV wrestles back online bookshop from Amazon'.

Kevin Foy/Alamy

Self-service kiosks and Internet check-in enable airlines to improve efficiency, reduce costs and increase capacity to adjust quickly to customer demand.

■ Globalization: low costs, efficient operations, JIT and TQM

Globalization is the integration of national economies into a single international economy. Although trade and monetary barriers continue to exist between many countries, globalization has been a major force affecting business organizations in the past 40 years. In 1970, almost all cars and televisions purchased in Europe were made there. Today, however, most of the televisions and many of the cars purchased in Europe come from elsewhere. A simple examination of the tags on the clothes you are wearing indicates the extent of globalization. Shoes are made in Singapore, T-shirts in Guatemala, digital phones in China, jeans in South Korea and handbags in Italy. Many products contain parts produced in many different countries. Financial markets and ownership also extend across national borders. Economic problems in one country frequently ripple around the world. The financial crisis in Southeast Asia in 1999, the burst of the Internet bubble in 2000, and the surge in demand for commodities originating from China and India had a global impact. Multinational organizations with operations in multiple countries are commonplace. As well, the Internet has created an international marketplace. With the reduction of tariffs from the establishment of the European common market and treaties such as the North American Free Trade Agreement (NAFTA), business organizations must consider the whole world as a source of competition, a source for parts and an opportunity for new customers.

Low costs

To be successful in a global economy, business organizations must provide their products and services at a lower cost than their competitors. With the advent of the Internet, consumers can easily compare prices for different products and services. No longer will businesses be able to sell products at high prices without offering a corresponding product or service.

With global competition limiting the prices that can be charged to customers, organizations will have to find ways to control the cost of creating products and services. One approach to reducing costs is to shift labour costs to developing countries with lower labour rates. This procedure may cause temporary hardships and job losses, but an organization (and each individual) must continually reassess its comparative advantage in a global economy in order to survive. Although the global economy threatens those organizations and individuals unable to adapt, consumers in the current global economy enjoy the greatest diversity of products at the lowest prices and highest quality in the history of the world.

Efficient operations

Seeking out places with lower labour costs is one way to reduce product costs. However, shifting production to take advantage of lower labour rates does not necessarily result in the lowest cost. Firms must also examine the efficiency of their low-cost workers compared to that of other workers who command higher wage rates. If higher paid employees can work more efficiently, organizations prefer to use labour that is more expensive. These workers are often more productive. Even if they are paid more, employing them can lower overall costs. One of the basic theories of economics states that workers should be paid based on their productivity.

To improve efficiency and lower the cost of providing products and services, organizations must continually re-evaluate their processes. Re-engineering refers to modifying work processes within the organization to operate more efficiently, often by adopting new technologies or streamlining existing processes.

Just-in-time (JIT)

Just-in-time (JIT) is a process of providing products on demand. JIT allows some organizations to operate more efficiently and at a lower cost. Manufacturing organizations using JIT make a product when an order is received, rather than make it in advance and hold it until it is sold or discarded. With JIT, customers should no longer have long waits for delivery of the product. To make JIT work, the organization must design systems from order entry to delivery that operate efficiently and immediately. Many firms that offer goods via the Internet apply JIT systems: customers do the order entry accurately at a time convenient for them. A fully completed order then triggers all the activities required to deliver the products in a timely fashion. JIT is designed to eliminate or reduce activities that do not provide value to customers. JIT reduces inventory by making the product only when ordered, there is no wasted product due to obsolescence or lack of demand. Financing costs of the inventory are lower. Moreover, the costs of warehousing and holding inventories are reduced. Dell uses JIT and the Internet to deliver quickly tailor-made laptops to a global customer base with a minimal inventory requirement. Littlefuse, a US-based producer of fuses, turned 930 square metres of warehouse space into an assembly area by adopting JIT.[5]

JIT works by supplying the product quickly only when demanded. If customers have to wait, they will go elsewhere for the product. Organizations are able to shift to JIT, in part, because of technological changes. For example, the advent of bar-coding and the instant reporting of sales to grocery-store suppliers allowed supermarket chains such as ASDA, Carrefour and Sainsbury's to hold less inventory, and offer customers lower prices. RFID (radio frequency identification) chips make tracking inventory much easier. JIT frequently is used with other advanced manufacturing

---

[5] *The Economist*, 1 July 2006, 'Lean and unseen'.

techniques such as CAM. CAM allows manufacturers to shift production quickly to accommodate changes in demand. The design of Toyota's automated plants reduces the time of changing over from making one type of car to another.

JIT is also used in service organizations. For example, gourmet food shops prepare orders on demand for delivery to the customer or take away. Food is fresher and less wasted if not prepared in advance.

Total quality management (TQM)

Total quality management (TQM), sometimes referred to as 'Six Sigma', has formalized the move to a customer orientation. TQM is a philosophy of continually lowering costs and improving the provision of services and products to customers. Quality is defined by the customer and designed into the product. TQM involves everyone within the organization. The shift to TQM means that the organization seeks to improve continually its operations, internal processes and customer services. Many firms adopt both JIT and TQM jointly, as the two share a number of common principles.

■ Customers: value chain analysis

Organizations must continually monitor technological change and global competition, but unless they identify and meet customer preferences, all is for naught. Creating **customer value** by fulfilling their desires is critical to the success of an organization. If customers want pistachio gelato and you supply vanilla, your sales will suffer and some other organization will step in to supply pistachio. Organizations must continually seek to add value to customers by adapting to changing customer preferences. For example, eBay has created an entire market for auctioning low-cost collectibles. Value chain analysis, along with TQM, help an organization have a customer focus.

Value chain analysis

Value chain analysis is associated with both JIT and TQM. The basic concept is to look at what the organization does through the eyes of the customer. Organizations do many things, but from a customer perspective, only some activities provide value to the customer. Those activities are called the value chain. A typical value chain might be:

Research and development → Design and engineering → Production →
    Distribution → Customer service

Any activities that are not on the value chain are considered **non-value-added activities**. Non-value-added activities do not provide value for customers. Examples of non-value-added activities include the moving and storing of products and many administrative tasks. Elimination of non-value-added activities allows the organization to save resources and sell its products and services at a lower price without reducing the value to customers.

■ Adapting to a changing environment

Organizations and their management accounting systems must adapt to a rapidly changing environment. In this section, the impact of technological change, globalization and customer preferences have been outlined. In addition, procedures for dealing with these external forces have been introduced. Computer-integrated manufacturing (CIM), just-in-time (JIT), total quality management (TQM) and value chain analysis are methods that take advantage of technological changes and allow an organization

Figure 1.1 Framework for organizational change

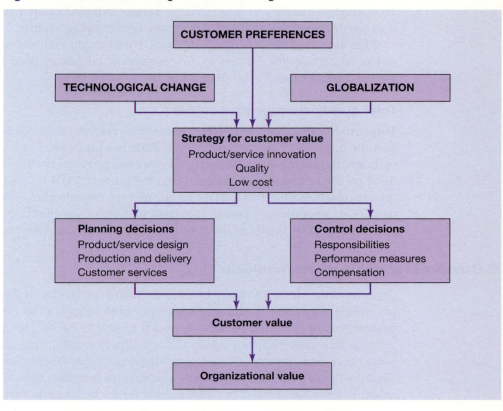

to compete and meet customer demand. These procedures are reviewed in subsequent chapters and other procedures are introduced. We'll see that the success of an organization is closely tied to having the appropriate procedures and management accounting system.

This chapter develops a framework, outlined in Figure 1.1 to describe how organizations must change to adapt to technological change, globalization and customer demand. The framework highlights that an organization's planning and control decisions must be consistent with its strategy. This model does not include all factors that affect an organization. For example, other approaches to organizational analysis and behaviour emphasize decision making, human resources, leadership and power. Each model provides insights into the complex nature of an organization. The framework in this book focuses on how organizations make decisions and control behaviour (and the trade-off between the two) such that organizational value is created. The remaining sections of Chapter 1 describe how the organization adapts and the role of management accounting therein.

Concept **review**

1 Why is management accounting an evolving process?

2 How can new technologies affect an organization?

3 What is the impact of globalization on an organization?

4 Why is meeting customer demand so critical for an organization?

DVD Stores (continued)

Kathy knows she must be aware of technological innovations that may make in-shop sales of DVDs obsolete. Most important is the need to adapt to the Internet and digital music platforms. She also has identified some innovations that will help in operating her business. Bar-coding of the DVDs allows for inventory tracking by Kathy and the suppliers of the DVDs. Also, anti-theft magnetic tapes help reduce shoplifting.

Globalization is now affecting Kathy's business. On the one hand, through the Internet, retailers across the world suddenly have become her competitors. On the other hand, if Kathy uses the Internet, the whole world could become her market.

Kathy is also concerned about her customers. Although her stores sell DVDs for low prices, she has ignored other aspects of customer satisfaction. Are customers finding the DVDs they want? Do customers receive friendly service? Should more LCD and plasma screens be mounted so that customers can more easily preview DVDs? Does she need to sell the software and hardware to use digital formats?

Kathy realizes that her sales goal and her goal to help local artists are dependent on having satisfied customers. She is considering implementing a customer survey to discover what they want and restructuring the organization to recognize the importance of customers. She plans to attend an upcoming seminar on TQM to learn more about making the organization more sensitive to customers.

STRATEGY FOR INCREASING CUSTOMER VALUE

Customers receive value from purchasing the products and services of an organization. If the value the customers receive is less than the price they pay for the product and/or service, they will not make the purchase. Therefore, an organization must offer its products and services at a price less than the value placed on them by the customer. At the same time, the organization must be able to provide the product or service at a cost less than the price in order to sustain itself. For example, if customers value DVDs at €17 each, DVD stores must sell them for less than €17, say €16, and be able to buy them for €15. (The difference between the sales price and the purchase cost represents the margin on each DVD. The larger the margin, the more organizational value is created.) To make matters more complex, the organization must accomplish this task in a world of technological change and globalization.

Organizations develop strategies by looking at the opportunities and threats posed by technological change, globalization and customer preferences. New technology offers opportunities to be more efficient and competitive, but also threatens to make the existing technology of the organization outdated. Globalization provides the threat of new competitors entering an organization's market, but a global economy provides the greater opportunities of expanding markets for an organization's products or services. Changing customer preferences provide opportunities to develop new products and services, but threaten the success of existing products and services.

At the same time, organizations must recognize their own strengths and weaknesses, given the existing and proposed characteristics of the organization. Personnel skills, access to capital, location, brand awareness and loyalty, and organizational structure all help to determine the strengths and weaknesses of the organization.

Given the existing and potential strengths and weaknesses of the organization and the opportunities and threats of the environment, an organization must decide how to create **customer value**. Organizations generally follow one of the following three strategies: innovative product/service design, high-quality products and services, or low-cost production. These strategies reflect the key variables that provide customer value.

■ Innovative product/service design

Some organizations focus on using changes in technology and customer preferences to introduce new innovations or designs that add customer value. For example, Apple's innovative iPod design captured a large segment of the MP3 player market. Being the 'first mover' requires an organization to have excellent marketing and design skills. The marketing function is critical in identifying customer trends and niches that have not been previously identified. At the same time, an organization needs a good design team to take advantage of new technologies and meet changing customer demand.

By beating other global competitors to the market with a new product or service, an organization, such as Apple, can reap temporarily the rewards of adding customer value before profits are diluted due to price competition. Obtaining patents can lengthen the time of profitable opportunities for a new product, but other organizations will soon find ways to make similar products.

The strategy of competing through innovative product/service design is higher risk, but offers large profit opportunities. Certain brand-name drug companies typically compete through innovative product design. They spend considerable amounts on research and development for new remedies for diseases. When successful, a new drug can be very profitable, but if a drug company cannot continually develop new drugs, the company will have to invest in a different strategy to survive.

■ High-quality products and services

Some organizations follow the strategy of providing high-quality products and services to achieve customer value. 'High quality' in this case means delivering a product or service that conforms to the specifications of the design and meets or surpasses the expectations of the customer. High quality does not necessarily mean making a product with greater functionality than other products. A five-bedroom house is a different product than an apartment, yet both can be of high quality if they meet the specifications of what the customer expected. Moreover, one customer can perceive two five-bedroom houses differently in terms of quality, due to other features such as size, layout, landscaping and location.

Successfully achieving a high-quality strategy requires that the organization pay considerable attention to the details of manufacturing and service provision. It must be aware of customer expectations and develop procedures to ensure that each product and service satisfies, and even surpasses, those expectations. For example, Internet-banking firms must offer customers highly reliable, secure and easy-to-use network connections.

■ Low-cost production

Another strategy to compete in a global economy is to be the low-cost producer of a product or service. Low-cost retailers, such as ASDA, ALDI and Tesco, can sell at lower prices than their competitors. By offering the products and services at a lower price, these organizations create customer value.

To be a low-cost producer, an organization must operate very efficiently. Low-cost producers cannot afford to have numerous non-value-added activities. At the same

David Levenson/Alamy

ASDA is one of many low-cost retailers which offer products at reduced prices, creating value for customers who prefer low cost to other product attributes.

time, low-cost producers cannot completely sacrifice quality. Customers will still expect a certain quality level.

Generic drug manufacturers are examples of low-cost producers. They spend very little on advertising and expect to be successful by charging lower prices for drugs than brand-name drug companies do. Most grocery chains and drug stores, such as Carrefour in France and Boots in the UK, have their own private label brands. These products compete with name brands, and can sell at lower costs because of savings on advertising.

■ Strategies and management accounting

Whether an organization chooses to create customer value through innovation, high quality or low cost, management accounting plays an important role. Strategies require planning and implementation, both of which are supported by management accounting. Management accounting methods should differ, however, depending on the strategy chosen. Certain management accounting methods promote innovation, while others promote quality or low-cost production. Matching management accounting methods with a strategy is critical to the success of the organization. The role of strategy in achieving customer value is incorporated in the framework for organizational change in Figure 1.1 (earlier).

DVD Stores (continued)

Kathy needs a strategy to adapt to the opportunities and threats from changes in technology, globalization and customer demand. An examination of her own weaknesses has indicated that she has neither sufficient funds for major capital investments nor the technical expertise to develop new methods of recording or distributing DVDs. Kathy's strengths come from knowledge of local customers and recording artists. She decides not to expand her retail shops, but focus on excellent customer service in her existing ones. Better customer service will help to increase sales, especially at the weaker regional shop. In addition, she believes that the sale of music DVDs can be expanded through an Internet site and digital downloads dedicated to local artists. This Internet strategy would reduce the need for a major input of capital.

Concept review

1 What is customer value?

2 How can an organization create customer value?

ORGANIZATIONS AND DECISIONS

Organizations are groups of individuals who have joined together to perform particular tasks to achieve particular goals. Organizations include schools, businesses, clubs, religious groups, hospitals and governmental bodies. Organizations are formed because groups of individuals can perform particular tasks more easily than individuals operating alone can.

An organization performs tasks to achieve goals. The goals of an organization reflect the interests of its **stakeholders**. The stakeholders of the organization include any parties that are affected by the organization: owners, creditors, employees, customers and society. Typical goals might include providing cash or non-monetary benefits to the owners, maximizing profits, satisfying customers, improving the welfare of members of the organization, and providing services to society. To survive, however, an organization must receive sufficient resources through sales, donations or other means to support its expenditures.

To achieve these goals, an organization must continually adapt to a changing environment. Decisions must be made that will lead to customer value. This section describes how an organization makes decisions to achieve customer value and meet its goals.

H&M sales representatives are responsible for selling goods to customers but cannot offer substantial price discounts. Managers must be consulted and approve these decisions.

Rolf Adlercreutz/Alamy

■ Organizational structure

Although organizations form to achieve goals not easily achievable by individuals, not all individuals within the organization will agree on how the organization should operate. Organizations have formal or informal structures that describe how decisions are made. An organization's structure is composed of three related processes: (1) assigning responsibilities, (2) measuring performance, and (3) rewarding individuals within the organization.

Assigning responsibilities

The first component of the organizational structure determines the responsibilities of the different members of the organization. These responsibilities define the duties that a member of an organization is expected to perform. The responsibilities of a particular individual within an organization are specified by that person's job description. Customer sales representatives in high street stores such as Zara and H&M typically have the responsibility to sell products to customers, but cannot offer substantial discounts on prices. A manager must be called for that decision. A division manager may have the responsibility to set prices on products, but not the responsibility to borrow money through issuing debt. The responsibility to issue

Figure 1.2 Partial organizational chart of a corporation

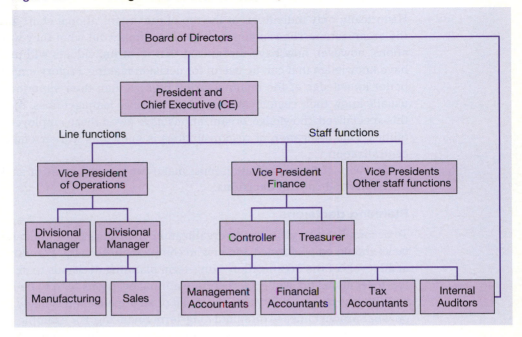

debt is usually retained by the president or the board of directors. The organizational chart in Figure 1.2 represents the structure in a traditional firm. This type of organizational chart is frequently used to provide a hierarchy of responsibilities. As firms adopt advanced manufacturing technologies, they often develop alternative organizational structures and charts which reflect these new management approaches.

Performance measures

Organizations must also motivate individuals to perform their duties consistent with the goals of the organization. Individuals have their own goals, which are not necessarily congruent with the organization's goals. To motivate individuals within the organization, it must have a system for measuring performance and rewarding individuals. **Performance measures** are direct or indirect measures of output of individuals or groups of individuals within the organization. Performance measures for a salesperson could include total sales and customer satisfaction based on a survey of customers. Performance measures for a manufacturing unit could include number of units produced, their cost and percentage of defective units.

Rewards

Performance measures are extremely important because rewards are generally based on them. Rewards for individuals within organizations include wages and bonuses, prestige and greater responsibilities, promotions and job security. Since rewards are based on performance measures, individuals and groups are motivated to act to influence the performance measures. Therefore, the performance measures influence the direction of individual and group efforts within the organization. A poor choice of performance measures can lead to conflicts within the organization and derail efforts to achieve organizational goals. For example, measuring the performance of a call-centre representative on the number of calls she takes per day will encourage her to reduce the time spent per customer, and potentially reduce the quality of the services she provides.

■ Decision making within an organization

Historically, only individuals at the top of the organizational chart made decisions for the organization. The remaining employees simply did what they were told. Organizations, however, now have recognized that most individuals within the organization have knowledge that can be useful for decision making. Factory employees often have better knowledge of the manufacturing process than their superiors do. Salespeople usually know their customers better than the sales manager does. To take advantage of this specialized knowledge, organizations have given these employees more responsibilities. This delegation of responsibilities is known as worker empowerment or decentralization.

Members of the organization must make two general types of decisions: **planning decisions** and **control decisions**.

Planning decisions

To accomplish the goals of the organization, managers must make decisions on what tasks should be performed and how to complete those tasks. Planning decisions occur at all levels of the organization. Long-term planning decisions tend to be made by the top-level managers while short-term planning decisions tend to be made by individuals with less responsibility. The chairman of an organization is likely to make decisions on what product lines to offer and long-term financing. For example, in 2004, Nokia reorganized its structure into four business groups: Mobile Phones, Multimedia, Enterprise Solutions and Networks. Once that decision was made, division managers at Nokia decided for each division the specific products and services to be provided. Lower-level managers at Nokia made further decisions on staffing, warehousing, selling, and purchasing procedures.[6]

Planning decisions revolve around activities in the value chain. These activities include the choice and design of products or services to be provided, the activities necessary to make and deliver the products and services, and other customer service choices. But managers make other types of planning decisions.

Control decisions

The managing, motivating, and monitoring of individuals within the organization is called control. The purpose of control is to encourage members of the organization to work towards the goals of the organization. Due to diverse individual preferences, organizational goals and those of individual members usually do not coincide. For example, most organizations set the goal to maximize profits. Maximization of profits, however, may mean more hours of overtime for employees, which may not be in their best interests.

The organizational design and the assignment of responsibilities help to control decisions made by members of the organization. For example, a purchasing manager is constrained to follow specific rules in making a purchase and can only make purchases above a specified amount with approval from a superior.

Control also encompasses the choice of performance measures and a reward system. Performance measures and rewards based on those performance measures are used to motivate members of the organization.

Organizations also control members through monitoring. Monitoring includes the direct observation of members of the organization to verify that they are performing their duties correctly. For example, telemarketing companies routinely record all

---

[6] www.nokia.com/AI4136002?newsid=918690 (accessed 22 January 2007).

telephone conversations or supervisors randomly monitor calls. Monitoring could also be performed indirectly by observing the output of an individual. For instance, the monitoring of sales staff frequently includes comparing their sales targets to actual sales, as well as tracking the sales margin. To motivate sales staff to provide the customer with what is preferred, some retailers monitor sales returns. These sales reports become part of the performance measurement system. For instance, sales people often receive commissions. Sales teams also may be rewarded based on store or product-line performance.

A university's examinations and grades are a control system with which students are familiar. Grades and examinations are performance measures that provide students with incentives to work hard.

■ Framework for organizational change

The first three sections of this chapter are summarized in the framework for organizational change in Figure 1.1 (earlier). In the framework, technological change, customer preferences and globalization are all external forces that affect an organization. The organization must adapt to these forces by developing a strategy for creating customer value. These strategies include developing innovative products or services, providing superior quality or generating products and services at a lower cost.

To implement the strategy, the organization must make both planning and control decisions. Planning decisions are choices of activities that will add value to the customer (value chain). These activities include designing products and services, making and delivering products and services at low prices, and providing additional customer services. These decisions should be consistent with the strategy chosen by the organization.

To ensure that the strategy is implemented as planned, control decisions must also be made. These control decisions include the assignment of responsibilities within the organization and the selection of performance measures and compensation packages.

With appropriate planning and control decisions, the organization will create value for customers. If customers find value in what the organization offers, the organization can succeed and the various stakeholders of the organization will receive value from their investment in the organization.

The framework for organizational change is the basis for analysing organizations. Each chapter contains an example of organizational analysis (see Research In Motion, for example, later in this chapter). The analysis relates the organization's strategic choices with planning and control implementation decisions. Management accounting supports and directs the planning and control implementation decisions, while recognizing the organization's strategic choices. More specifically, the following questions are addressed.

At a strategic level:

■ What are the opportunities and threats that exist in the business environment with respect to technological change, globalization and customer preferences?
■ What are the strengths and weaknesses of the organization in creating customer value through innovative products/services, high quality and/or low cost?

At the implementation level:

■ What activities should be implemented to achieve the strategy and create organizational value?
■ How should the organization assign responsibilities, measure performance and compensate employees to motivate them to make decisions consistent with the strategy?

The framework for organizational change is also used to integrate management accounting topics in this book. The role of accounting in the framework is described in the next section.

Organizational **analysis**

Research In Motion

Research In Motion Limited (RIM) was founded in 1984 and had an initial public offering (IPO) in which it sold shares to the general public in 1997. The company develops innovative, wireless solutions for the mobile communications market, enabling users to take advantage of wireless connectivity in a seamless way. Through its products and services, customers can access e-mail, telephone, text messaging, the Internet and intranet applications. For example, Cambridge County Council adopted RIM's Blackberry to improve its services to its citizens, such as ambulance crews, while ensuring privacy and data security.

Corbis Super RF/Alamy

The Blackberry's innovative technology and design have resulted in brand awareness and customer loyalty, enabling RIM to capture the global market for wireless communications.

An analysis of RIM indicates a focus on new technologies and research and development to create and maintain innovative products and services. RIM relies on a customer base extending from the corporate sector to the individual user. RIM also enters into strategic partnerships with carriers such as cable suppliers, and Internet portals (e.g. Google and Yahoo) to expand its offerings and customer base. The short product life cycles in this market requires RIM to introduce enhanced applications and products on an on-going basis. RIM, however, also must be concerned about competition. Although the company had a first-mover advantage in the market, other competitors, such as Apple, offer similar devices. RIM is trying to grow as quickly as possible and create brand awareness and loyalty to discourage competitors. Advertising reinforces its brand image with testimonials and frequent case studies of satisfied users. To grow rapidly, it has forged a number of strategic alliances with both suppliers and carriers around the globe.

The role of management accounting in implementing this strategy is to measure, analyse and communicate the costs and benefits of the different services offered by RIM. This process is difficult because many costs (such as research and development) are incurred now with potential benefits to follow in the future. Rapid growth and intense competition makes it more difficult to project revenues and costs in a reliable manner. Growth has been rapid with sales revenue of $6.6 million in 1997 to over $2 billion in fiscal 2006. Fiscal 2006 also saw RIM's subscriber base nearly double to about 5 million users worldwide.

Management accounting assists in establishing a system of assigning responsibilities, measuring performance and compensating employees. Performance measures used by the company are growth-oriented, which is consistent with its current strategy. Important non-financial metrics are the number of and growth in subscriber accounts. RIM also tracks its gross margin percentage, net warranty expense (given its focus on quality), and cost savings due to changes in its product mix and supply chain leverage. Employee compensation includes share options, which encourage employees to focus on long-term company growth and organizational value.

Source: www.rim.net

DVD Stores (continued)

Kathy realizes that she has not had time to consider carefully the organizational structure of DVD Stores. She begins by examining the responsibilities that she has delegated. At present, managers control the daily operations of their respective regional shops. The managers also make their own inventory decisions because Kathy believes that they have a better understanding of their own customers' preferences. Kathy currently uses total sales as a performance measure, and frequently visits the regional shops to verify that appropriate in-shop marketing and shelf space are reserved for local artists. The reward system for the managers, however, is not based on any performance measures. Managers are paid £25,000 whether sales are high or low. Kathy decides that a bonus based on sales will provide additional incentives for managers. To develop operations and sales on the website, Kathy will have to hire another manager who has the requisite technical expertise. The manager will be evaluated on the number of visits to the site, music downloads and total sales. Kathy must also consider the possible impact of her Internet business on sales in her current locations. Perhaps there is a way to include this impact in the revised organizational structure.

Concept **review**

1 Why do organizations form?

2 What are the three basic processes of an organization's structure?

3 How do planning and control decisions help achieve an organization's strategy?

THE ROLE OF ACCOUNTING

Accounting plays an integral part in assisting an organization to achieve its goals. In addition, it is an important aspect in the development of economies. Developing economies are finding that transparency in organizations is critical to attracting external investors and growth. Transparency is achieved through accounting/control processes that provide assurances that the organization and the economy are operating appropriately.

Accounting traditionally identifies events affecting the organization. It also measures and communicates those effects in monetary terms. For example, the purchase of a building by the organization is measured by the cash outlay for the building. A sale on credit is identified as a receivable for the organization and measured in terms of the money owed to the organization. Since all the events are measured in a common monetary unit, such as the euro or pound sterling, accounting systems aggregate the effect of different events and make comparisons. Accounting reports communicate accumulated accounting data to organizational managers and to external users such as shareholders and government regulators.

The role of management accounting in today's organization goes well beyond recording the monetary amounts of past events. The ability to satisfy user needs, especially through the provision of forward-looking information, is necessary. To fulfil this role, specifically the information demands of managers and external users, management accountants must ensure that the accounting system encompasses non-financial information such as production data, consumer demand forecasts, customer satisfaction statistics, service calls and industry benchmarks. By integrating financial and non-financial data, the accounting system can provide more comprehensive information to better serve its users.

Figure 1.3 The accounting system serves different purposes

	Role	Users	Decisions	Preferred characteristics
A c c o u n t i n g s y s t e m	Management	Internal managers	Planning Control	Measure inputs and outputs Timeliness Identify responsibility Forward-looking
	Financial	Shareholders Creditors Other external users	Investment Credit	Verifiable Measure organizational value Measure risk of organization Consistent with GAAP
	Tax	Taxing authorities	Tax liability	Verifiable Measure past income

Different parties use accounting information related to the organization. Figure 1.3 describes the different roles of the accounting system of the organization. Management accounting involves the use of accounting information by managers to help achieve the organization's goals. Managers receive this information in the form of reports such as sales reports, inventory reports, budgets and monthly operating reports. Management accounting provides information for two general functions: making planning decisions and control. Accounting allows for better planning decisions through more knowledge of the problem. Managers use accounting for control through influencing members of the organization to make decisions that are consistent with the organizational goals. Preferred characteristics of management accounting include accurate measures of multiple inputs and outputs of the organization, timeliness, identification of responsibility and the capacity to be forward-looking.

The accounting system must also meet the requirements of constituents outside the organization. **Financial accounting** is used to report to investors, creditors and other interested parties outside the organization. These parties are primarily interested in information for making investment and credit decisions. Preferred characteristics of financial accounting include verifiability, measures of organizational value, measures of organizational risk, and consistency with financial reporting regulations, known as generally accepted accounting principles (GAAP).

Tax accounting is used to calculate income taxes and report to government taxing authorities, such as the UK's HM Revenue & Customs, Canada's Revenue Agency or the US Internal Revenue Service (IRS). Taxing authorities prefer accounting to be verifiable and to measure past income consistent with tax regulations.

Financial reporting and income tax reports are not the primary focus of this book. Nonetheless, management accounting cannot ignore reporting to external parties, especially when numbers from the accounting system are used for both external reporting and for planning decisions and control.

■ Use of accounting for making planning decisions

Planning decisions are made to help an organization achieve its goals. Increased knowledge about the impact of a decision on the organization allows managers to make more informed choices. For example, the forecast of sales is used to determine the amount of product to be manufactured. If a customer survey is performed, a more accurate sales forecast will lead to better production decisions.

Management accounting is not the only source of information to improve decision making. Information about customer tastes and the political, legal and competitive environment also leads to better decisions within an organization. The advantage of management accounting information is the conversion of events into a common unit of measure, the monetary unit. Conversion of events into monetary amounts allows managers to compare the impact of various decisions on the organization. The decision to adopt advanced manufacturing technologies or to continue manual operations can be analysed by converting both events into monetary outlays and comparing the monetary outlays of each alternative. Non-financial information also is often useful, such as the impact of different alternatives on the welfare of employees. New manufacturing methods may improve or harm employee welfare, especially if adoption leads to the need for fewer workers overall.

The manner in which management accounting is used to improve planning decisions depends on the strategy of the organization. The initial chapters (2 to 5) of this book focus on accounting methods that support planning decisions.

Use of accounting for control decisions

Management accounting assists in control by helping align the interests of the members of the organization with the goals of the organization. The members of the organization are motivated to achieve organizational goals through a reward system. Rewards are based on achieving sufficiently high performance measures. Some performance measures are based on accounting numbers. For example, managers of divisions are commonly evaluated based on the accounting profits of the division. Non-accounting performance measures and direct observation (monitoring) of members also are used to evaluate and reward the members of the organization. Management accounting reports often include non-accounting measures of performance such as customer satisfaction and product defect rates.

Management accounting also helps to assign responsibilities to control members of the organization. Limits on actions by managers frequently are based on accounting numbers. For example, a salesperson may have the right to grant credit to a customer only up to £1,000. The communication of these responsibilities often occurs through management accounting documents such as the budget.

Designing a system to align the interests of the members of the organization with the goals of the organization is not an easy task. Chapters 6 and 7 focus on control issues, and Chapters 8 to 14 look at the combined use of management accounting for making planning decisions and for control.

The emergence of management accounting

Management accounting has emerged in parallel with the adaptation of the organization to its environment. While management accounting procedures can be traced to medieval times or earlier, the Industrial Revolution marked a turning point in their development. The Industrial Revolution and subsequent decades brought changes in the nature of organizations. These changes required new methods for planning and control. For example, in the eighteenth century, Josiah Wedgwood was motivated by dynamic economic and market conditions to re-examine his business methods. He began to use cost data to calculate production expenses, evaluate economies of scale and to control worker performance at his pottery works. In the nineteenth century, management accounting became more important as firms confronted environmental factors little different from those faced today: technological change, competition and customer tastes. Technological change, such as improved communications and transportation networks, shortened operating cycles and decision-making horizons. Technological innovations intensified competition, as customers grew accustomed to the availability of cheaper, mass-produced goods.

Organizations were increasing the size and scope of their operations. Most business firms were small and operated by family members or by a small ownership group. But as firms grew larger to take advantage of new and costly technology, such as steam engines, families could not afford the necessary capital investments to do so. Many turned to outside investors and professional managers. The delegation of decision making to managerial employees meant changes in management and operating methods, as organizations dealt with the differing interests of shareholders, managers and workers.[7]

Many of today's management accounting techniques were refined and adapted in the nineteenth and early-twentieth century. British textile and iron mills grew by combining the various processes for cloth and iron production, often integrating vertically to reap the benefits from economies of scale. For example, Boulton and Watts combined operations to reduce its reliance on sub-contractors in the manufacture of steam engines. Operating departments were treated as separate entities and evaluated in a manner similar to profit centres. This data allowed managers to compare the cost of conducting a process inside the firm versus purchasing the process from external vendors. The growth of railways and the rise of steel production encouraged the development of costing systems to report production yield (inputs per ton of output), the cost impact of changes in input mix and production methods, along with the return on capital invested.

Retailers also adapted accounting techniques to control operations in a growing mass market. H.G. Selfridge opened his London store in 1909 after amassing a personal fortune in the US merchandising sector. Selfridge adapted the methods of US merchandisers such as Marshall Field's where he had worked and risen to the executive ranks. These methods included gross-margin (revenues less cost of goods sold) and stock-turn ratios (sales divided by inventory) used to measure and evaluate performance.

Across the Atlantic, similar developments took place. Firms such as Du Pont Powder Company and General Motors devised innovative performance measures to control their growing organizations.[8] US developments also reflected the fact that multi-divisional firms had to manage activities over greater distances compared to their counterparts in the UK and Europe where organizations were not as geographically dispersed.

In the twentieth century, management accounting was heavily influenced by external considerations. Government intervention and wartime economies affected management accounting techniques and systems, as firms adapted to production shortages and changes in market demand. Many organizations developed their management accounting in parallel with their engineering and production systems. Income taxes and

---

[7] J.R. Edwards and E. Newell (1991) 'The Development of Industrial Cost and Management Accounting before 1850: A Survey of the Evidence', *Business History*, XXXIII (1), pp. 35–57; and C.S. McWatters (1995) 'Management Accounting and the Calvin Company', *Accounting, Business and Financial History*, Vol. 5, No. 1, pp. 39–70.

[8] S. Paul Garner (1954) *Evolution of Cost Accounting to 1925*, Montgomery, Ala.: University of Alabama Press; and A.D. Chandler (1977) *The Visible Hand*, Cambridge, Mass.: Harvard University Press.

financial accounting requirements frequently took precedence over management accounting.

In recent decades, the impact of rapid technological change, globalization and customer preferences has caused managers to question whether many current management accounting procedures are still appropriate. In order to succeed, the organization must implement an appropriate strategy supported by an appropriate management accounting system. Therefore, changes in management accounting reflect the firm's strategic efforts to create organizational value.

The history of management accounting illustrates its emergence and adaptation in response to changing organizational circumstances. Management accounting provides information for planning decisions and control. It is useful for assigning responsibilities, measuring performance and determining rewards for individuals within the organization. As other parts of the organizational structure adapt and change, it is not surprising that management accounting evolves in a parallel and consistent fashion.

DVD Stores (continued)

Kathy has not paid much attention to the accounting system of DVD Stores. When she started the first shop, she purchased software for her personal computer to record expenditures and cash receipts. At the end of the year, she hired a local accounting firm to generate financial statements and complete tax forms. The financial statements are sent to Nadja Joshi, her partner, and the bank that made the loan. As long as sales were strong, Kathy did not worry about using the accounting system for managing the shops. But sales have declined and Kathy is thinking about how she can make better decisions. In particular, she must decide how to operate her new website and digital platform to make them profitable.

Concept review

1 What are the differences between management accounting and financial accounting?

2 How does management accounting support planning decisions?

3 How is management accounting used for control decisions?

4 What has caused management accounting procedures to evolve over time?

TRADE-OFFS IN USING ACCOUNTING FOR MULTIPLE PURPOSES

Figure 1.3 (earlier) describes a single accounting system that generates accounting numbers for multiple purposes. But one accounting system is unlikely to be appropriate for all the different purposes of internal and external users of accounting. For example, a manager might like to know the cost of developing and maintaining the organization's web page versus hiring an external webmaster, but a creditor would want to know the impact of the method chosen on cash flows available to pay interest.

Since a single accounting system will not provide appropriate information for all decisions, trade-offs must be made among the different roles for accounting. This theme of trade-offs among different uses of accounting information is referred to throughout this book. Examples of these trade-offs are discussed next.

■ Trade-off between making planning decisions and control

Managers generally have specialized information that is useful for making planning decisions. To make the best planning decision, the person with the best information about a choice should make the decision. But there is the problem of motivating the individual to make decisions consistent with the goals of the organization. For example, a computer specialist may be the best-informed individual on the relative qualities of different computers. If the computer specialist is given the responsibility to purchase a computer for the organization, she may choose the most powerful and expensive equipment available. Having the most expensive computer may not be in the best interest of the organization, if the organization has a better use of cash elsewhere.

Instead of delegating responsibility to the manager with specialized knowledge, the organization could request the manager to communicate the specialized knowledge to higher level managers, who would make decisions using the transferred information. But the communicated information could also be used to evaluate the manager with the specialized knowledge. Knowing that any information a manager communicates can be used for evaluation purposes might cause the manager to alter the information and make it less useful for making planning decisions. For example, an information-systems manager might know how to modify the existing computer network to improve its response time. This information would be useful for upper management in making investment decisions for a new network. However, the information-systems manager is evaluated based on network response time. The manager can modify the network to achieve response-time goals more easily, but upper management's knowledge of this modification would eventually lead to higher expectations about the manager's performance. The use of information to reward the information-systems manager inhibits the communication of information useful for planning decisions.

■ Trade-off between making planning decisions and external reporting

External reporting is prepared for users outside the organization. Current regulations set forth by financial accounting, tax and securities regulators in many countries specify the use of historical costs to measure the value of most organizational assets. The historical cost of an object is its acquisition price or the value of resources used to acquire the object. For example, land purchased 10 years ago for £70,000 may now have a market value of £200,000, but the land is still recorded at £70,000 in the financial reports. No gain due to the increase in market value is recognized in financial or tax reports until the land is sold.

An advantage of using historical costs is their objective nature. Historical costs depend less on the subjective judgement of managers because they reflect actual transactions. Outside investors, creditors and tax authorities generally prefer accounting numbers that are not susceptible to manipulation by managers. Nonetheless, historical costs are not necessarily the costs that managers should use for decision making within the organization.

Managers of organizations often make planning decisions. Estimates of future costs are useful for these planning decisions. Historical costs are only a good estimate of future costs if the economic, competitive and operational environments have remained the same. For example, the historical cost of a gold watch is not a very good estimate for making another gold watch if the cost of gold or the wages of watchmakers have changed. Therefore, financially reported (historical cost) numbers should be used with care for planning as they can lead to inappropriate decisions.

■ Trade-offs between control and external reporting

If a financial report based on historical costs is the only available method of evaluating managers, managers will work to affect the financial report. But maximizing profit based on historical costs may not be consistent with the shareholder goal of maximizing shareholder value. For example, research and development (R&D) expenditures, which increase the value of the organization, are an immediate expense under International Financial Reporting Standards and local (e.g. UK; US and Canadian) GAAP, and reduce present profit figures. By cutting R&D, managers increase current profit at the expense of future profits. If the R&D activity creates value for customers and shareholders in the long run, the focus on short-term financial reports may conflict with long-term strategies.

To achieve the goals of the organization through control, performance measures should be closely associated with those goals. Financial reports based on historical costs may not be closely linked to the goals of the organization and could lead to dysfunctional behaviour by members of the organization.

■ Multiple accounting systems

Implementing multiple accounting systems could resolve the trade-offs existing among the various uses of an accounting system. Separate accounting systems could be established for making planning decisions, control and external reporting. The problem with this solution is the cost of establishing multiple systems. Many small organizations have the resources for only a single accounting system. Regulators and banks often require financial reports; therefore, the financial accounting system may be the only accounting system that is available within the organization. Larger organizations, however, might have two or more accounting systems for different purposes.

Multiple accounting systems sometimes can be confusing. With multiple accounting systems, items may be reported at different costs. One accounting system might report that a particular division made profits of £6.2 million and the other accounting system reports its profits at £5.8 million. Managers will be forced to spend time reconciling the differences. Remember the old proverb: 'A man with one watch knows what time it is. A man with two watches is never sure.'

An accounting system with only monetary measures is not the only source of information to assist in making planning decisions and control. Planning decisions are likely to be based, at least partially, on non-monetary factors. For example, planning decisions to achieve goals such as employee satisfaction would use employee surveys as an information source. Control could also be implemented using non-monetary performance measures. For example, a manufacturing manager could be evaluated based on the percentage of defective units produced.

This book recognizes that most organizations do not have separate accounting systems for different purposes, and trade-offs will exist in using accounting numbers for different types of decisions. The trade-off between making planning decisions and control is a primary focus of this book.

Concept review

1 Why does the use of accounting numbers for both planning decisions and control lead to trade-offs?

2 Why might historical costs from financial reports be inappropriate for making planning decisions?

3 Why might the profit number in financial reports be inappropriate for evaluating managers?

DVD Stores (continued)

Kathy Johnson wants to estimate future cash flows to determine if she can expand DVD Stores to the Internet without going to the bank. These plans require accurate estimates of future sales, but Kathy is worried that the managers of the shops will provide her with low estimates of future sales if she rewards them based on beating their forecasts. The managers will want to establish a low benchmark, so that bonuses for high sales and earnings can be achieved easily.

In deciding how to expand to the Internet, Kathy must estimate the cost of creating a website. Because she has never attempted such a project, her current financial accounting system provides no information on necessary expenditures to sell on the Internet. Therefore, the financial accounting reports are not relevant. Kathy must acquire more data about website design to make the decision.

Kathy realizes that her strategies would be more successful if strong links existed between these goals and the performance measurement and reward system. She decides that an initial step would be to compensate her shop managers based on the accounting profit generated from their respective shops. But her shops managers are young and looking for other work opportunities. She is worried that they aren't concerned about the long-term interests of DVD Stores. Kathy recently visited one of the regional shops and found customers grumbling about not enough staff available to provide customer service. When she approached the manager about this problem, he responded that he had cut the number of sales positions to reduce costs and improve profits. Kathy is concerned that customers will not return to any of the DVD Stores if they are disappointed with service at this regional shop. Therefore, she decides to perform customer surveys as an additional performance measure to be used jointly with accounting profit to reward the managers.

MANAGEMENT ACCOUNTANTS IN ORGANIZATIONS

Management accountants are responsible for the accounting system within the organization. As discussed previously, the accounting system should be designed to assist in making planning and control decisions, and in financial and tax reporting. The management accounting function in small organizations is normally performed by a bookkeeper who records transactions. An outside accountant often assists in the creation of financial statements and tax returns. The emphasis on financial reporting means that managers may not have relevant information easily available for planning purposes. Control is unlikely to be as important because the manager making the decisions is likely to be the owner.

In larger organizations, someone is normally assigned the responsibilities of a management accountant. That person usually is called the **controller**. The controller assists managers in making decisions and reports to the chairman or chief executive (CE). The controller is delegated responsibility for the communication and implementation of an organization's accounting policies and procedures, and acts as both consultant to and evaluator of other parts of the organization. The controller may also have assistant controllers who carry out specialized accounting and reporting duties. The functions of the controller are distinct from those of the treasurer who deals primarily with financial concerns such as investments, financing, banking and credit policy. Controllers are more than just compilers of information; they are members of senior management and strategic planning teams and act as interpreters and advisors. Controllers are expected to provide analytical insights and to add value to the management process.[9]

---

[9] R. Colman (2005), 'Creating the go-to team', *CMA Management*, June/July, www.managementmag.com// index.cfm/ci_id/2324/la_id/1.

In large corporations, the controller often reports to the vice president of finance rather than to the CE (see Figure 1.2 earlier). Larger corporations also have an internal audit department. The internal audit department is concerned with the organization's control system. Its role is to ensure that financial and operating assets are used efficiently and appropriately to achieve organizational objectives. The **internal auditor** monitors the various divisions and departments of the corporation to determine if prescribed operational procedures are being followed. To maintain its independence and profile, the internal audit department often reports directly to the CE and the board of directors.

ETHICS AND MANAGEMENT ACCOUNTING

Management accountants apply professional judgement in deciding how to establish and operate accounting systems within an organization. The potential trade-offs that exist because of the multiple uses of accounting systems make the management accountant's judgement even more critical. The management accountant frequently confronts decisions that affect the welfare of people inside and outside the organization. The process of determining standards and procedures for dealing with judgemental decisions affecting other people is known as **ethics**.

Ethics do not give a specific answer to a problem, but suggest a process in dealing with the problem. When faced with an ethical dilemma, the management accountant should gather sufficient information. Conflicts often disappear when sufficient information comes to light. The management accountant should then determine how stakeholders are affected. Too often crises arise when the effect on some individual or group is forgotten or ignored.

For example, suppose a controller finds inventory items that are outdated by newer models. The old inventory items can only be sold below their historic cost. Their sale or write-down will cause a reported loss on the accounting statements and will harm the chances of the divisional employees obtaining a bonus. The controller could simply ignore the old inventory; however, there is a cost to keep the goods in storage. Although recognition of the loss associated with the old inventory may harm the current employees, other parties would be harmed by continuing to ignore it. The owners would have to continue to pay storage costs, and bonuses of future employees may be affected if the loss is postponed. Once the impact on all the parties is examined, the controller will have more information to make a judgement.

A code of ethics assists the management accountant in making judgement decisions. Organizations frequently have a code of ethics that deals with standard problems facing the management accountant. This code of ethics reinforces the organization's control system to reduce the risk of unacceptable behaviour. Organizations also develop their own ethical commitments and standards that reflect their operating environment and culture. Moreover, ethical standards will differ across countries and the management accountant must be alert to the possibility that such differences may result in ethical dilemmas. An ethics control system provides guidance in decision making and a framework for accountability.[10]

With operations in the North Sea, Asia and the Americas, Talisman Energy Inc. recognized that employees often faced ethical dilemmas which were open to a number of

---

[10] The Society of Management Accountants of Canada has a number of sources to provide guidance on codes of ethics and ethics strategies. See *Management Accounting Issues Paper*, 'Codes of Ethics, Practice And Conduct', 1999; *Management Accounting Guideline*, 'Implementing Ethics Strategies Within Organizations', 1999; *Management Accounting Handbook*, Standard 6200, Ethics Control Systems, 2002.

different interpretations. Along with its written Policy on Business Conduct and Ethics, Talisman introduced an e-learning ethics awareness programme in 2005 to provide information regarding potential ethical issues, to review ethical expectations in a number of areas including human rights, bribery, community relations and environmental stewardship, and to outline resources available to resolve such issues when they arose. The training is also an important mechanism to provide a corporate-wide approach to ethical issues across the firm's global operations.[11] The establishment of ethical standards is an important tool to help organizational members make appropriate choices.

Various professional bodies of management accountants also have a code of ethics. For example, the Chartered Institute of Management Accountants (CIMA) has prescribed a set of ethical standards (see the box).

CIMA Code of Ethics for professional accountants

1 **Integrity:** A professional accountant should be straightforward and honest in all professional and business relationships.

2 **Objectivity:** A professional accountant should not allow bias, conflict of interest or undue influence of others to override professional or business judgments.

3 **Professional competence and due care:** A professional accountant has a continuing duty to maintain professional knowledge and skill at the level required to ensure that a client or employer receives competent professional service based on current developments in practice, legislation and techniques. A professional accountant should act diligently and in accordance with applicable technical and professional standards when providing professional services.

4 **Confidentiality:** A professional accountant should respect the confidentiality of information acquired as a result of professional and business relationships and should not disclose any such information to third parties without proper and specific authority unless there is a legal or professional right or duty to disclose. Confidential information acquired as a result of professional and business relationships should not be used for the personal advantage of the professional accountant or third parties.

5 **Professional behaviour:** A professional accountant should comply with relevant laws and regulations and should avoid any action that discredits the profession.

Source: www.cimaglobal.com/cps/rde/xchg/live/root.xsl/cimaethics15.htm (accessed 22 January 2007).

This code of ethics is not sufficient to solve all ethical problems, but it provides a framework for the management accountant. In the case of the controller who found the old inventory, the integrity section of the code of ethics suggests that the decision to recognize the loss immediately is consistent with the communication of unbiased information. Additionally, current employees should not be held responsible for the loss because old inventory reflects a decision in prior years to produce extra inventory.

In a global market, and with a trend to delegate decision making to lower levels of the organization, organizations often implement ethics programmes to ensure that employees understand how ethics relates to the organization's core strategies. Management accountants provide advice and support for the implementation of ethical policies and strategies, especially given their role in decision making and control.[12]

---

[11] www.talisman-energy.com/cr_online/2005/social-ethical_business_conduct.html (accessed 15 December 2006).

[12] The Society of Management Accountants of Canada (1999) *Management Accounting Guideline*.

The Chartered Institute of Management Accountants (CIMA), the Society of Management Accountants of Canada (SMAC), and the Institute of Management Accountants (IMA) in the US also administer programmes that qualify certified management accountants (CMAs). Applicants must pass examinations in management accounting and in the related fields of economics, finance, financial accounting, organizational behaviour and decision analysis. CIMA, the SMAC and the IMA work together with other international partners to foster the profession's role in the global marketplace.

Concept review

1 Describe the roles of controllers and internal auditors in organizations.
2 Why should management accountants have a code of ethics?

SUMMARY

1 Explain how technological change, globalization and customer preferences can affect an organization and its management accounting system. Technological change offers opportunities for new products and services and more efficient methods of operations. Globalization forces organizations to be more concerned about their customers and operating efficiently. Customer preferences continually change. Organizations and their management accounting systems must adapt to these changes.

2 Identify strategies for achieving customer value. Customer value can be achieved through innovative product/service design, quality and low cost.

3 Describe features of organizations that promote decisions to achieve organizational goals. To achieve organizational goals, organizations must assign responsibilities, measure performance and compensate members of the organization.

4 Explain the critical role played by management accounting in making planning decisions and controlling managers to create organizational value. Management accounting improves planning decisions by providing decision makers with more information to make better decisions. Management accounting also supports control by assisting in the assignment of responsibilities and establishing performance measures to motivate individuals.

5 Identify the trade-offs that exist in using information for making planning decisions, control and external reporting. Using the same accounting system for making planning decisions, control and external reporting leads to trade-offs. Employees will bias information used for planning purposes if the information is also used as a benchmark for measuring performance. External reports will similarly be affected if also used to evaluate performance.

6 Identify the roles of different types of management accountants. Controllers are responsible for the accounting systems within the organization. Internal auditors monitor members of the organization to determine if prescribed procedures are being followed.

7 Recognize the role of judgement and ethics in making management accounting choices. The management accountant must use judgement in resolving trade-offs arising from different uses of accounting information. This judgement should recognize the effect of decisions on all involved parties. A code of ethics assists the management accountant in making decisions.

KEY TERMS

Computer-assisted design (CAD) Use of computers for designing new products.

Computer-assisted manufacturing (CAM) Use of programmable robots to assist in the manufacturing of products.

Computer-integrated manufacturing (CIM) A manufacturing plant with all its systems linked by computer networks and databases.

Control decisions Use of information to influence members of the organization to make decisions that are consistent with organizational goals.

Controller The person within an organization responsible for the accounting system.

Customer value The benefit received by the customer from a product or service relative to its cost.

Ethics The process of determining standards and procedures for dealing with judgemental decisions affecting other people.

Financial accounting The accounting system used to report to investors, creditors and other interested parties outside the organization.

Globalization The integration of national economies into a single international economy.

Internal auditor A person within the organization who monitors various divisions and departments of the organization to determine if prescribed operational procedures are being followed.

Just-in-time (JIT) Process of providing products and services at the time they are needed.

Management accounting The accounting system used within the organization to help the organization achieve its goals.

Non-value-added activities Activities in an organization that do not benefit the customers of the organization.

Organizational value The benefit received by various stakeholders from their investment in the organization.

Performance measures Direct or indirect measures of the actions of individuals or groups of individuals within the organization.

Planning decision The selection of activities to help the organization attain its goals.

Tax accounting The accounting system used to calculate taxable income and report to government taxing authorities.

Stakeholders Parties that are affected by an organization.

Total quality management (TQM) A philosophy of continually lowering costs and improving the provision of services and products to customers.

Value chain The sequence of critical organizational processes to satisfy customers of the organization.

Analysis and interpretation problems

AIP 1.1 Using accounting for making planning decisions LO 4

The owner of a small software company felt that his accounting system was useless. He stated, 'Accounting systems only generate historical costs. Historical costs are useless in my business because everything changes so rapidly.'

a Are historical costs useless in rapidly changing environments?
b Should accounting systems be limited to historical costs?

AIP 1.2 Goals of a corporation LO 2

A finance professor and a marketing professor were recently comparing notes on their perceptions of corporations. The finance professor claimed that the goal of a corporation should be to maximize the value to the shareholders. The marketing professor claimed that the goal of a corporation should be to satisfy customers.

What are the similarities and differences in these two goals?

AIP 1.3 Accounting and control LO 4,6

The finance director of a small university is complaining about the amount of work that she is required to do at the beginning of each month. The institution's principal requires the director to submit a monthly report by the fifth day of the following month. The monthly report contains pages of financial data from operations. The finance director was heard saying, 'Why does the principal need all this information? He probably doesn't read half of the report. He's a professor of Slavic languages and probably doesn't know the difference between a cost and a revenue.'

a What is the probable role of the monthly report?
b What is the director's responsibility with respect to a principal who doesn't know much accounting?

AIP 1.4 Control and internal auditors LO 6

A large diversified company hired a recent accounting graduate as an internal auditor. He was thrilled by this opportunity. The company trained him to provide assistance to the managers of the various divisions in achieving the goals of the organization. He would be able to learn about many different aspects of the business in the role of an internal auditor as he rotated among the various divisions. The internal auditor position seemed to be an ideal position that would lead to early advancement in the company. His first outing to a division, however, was not particularly successful. The managers of the division barely tolerated his criticism of their operating processes. Instead of being perceived as a person helping the organization achieve its goals, he was shunned by the divisional managers.

a Why were the divisional managers not appreciative of the internal auditor?
b How could the organization improve the role of the internal auditor?

AIP 1.5 Financial reporting and ethics LO 7

The chairman of the company has come to the finance director at the end of the financial year. He says, 'We've had a pretty bad year. Sales have been off, but I think we'll do better next year. Can you do something about the annual financial report to make us look a little better and get us through until next year? Otherwise, I might get fired.'

a What can the finance director do to make the annual financial report look better?
b What other factors should the financial director consider in responding to the chairman?

AIP 1.6 One Cost System Isn't Enough LO 5

Robert S. Kaplan in 'One Cost System Isn't Enough' (*Harvard Business Review*, Jan–Feb 1988, pp. 61–66) states:

> No single system can adequately answer the demands made by diverse functions of cost systems. While companies can use one method to capture all their detailed transactions data, the processing of this information for diverse purposes and audiences demands separate, customized development. Companies that try to satisfy all the needs for cost information with a single system have discovered they can't perform important managerial functions adequately. Moreover, systems that work well for one company may fail in a different environment. Each company has to design methods that make sense for its particular products and processes.
>
> Of course, an argument for expanding the number of cost systems conflicts with a strongly ingrained financial culture to have only one measurement system for everyone.

Critically evaluate the preceding quote.

AIP 1.7 Tax reporting and accounting systems LO 5

Tax laws in Japan tie taxable income directly to the financial statements' reported income. A Japanese firm's tax liability is the net income as reported to shareholders multiplied by the tax rate. In contrast, with a few exceptions, UK, Canadian and US firms can use different accounting procedures for calculating net income for shareholders (financial reporting) and income for calculating taxes.

Given these differences in the tax laws between for example, the UK, Canada, the US and Japan, what effect would you expect these institutional differences in tax laws to have on internal accounting and reporting? Why is it essential for management accountants to keep aware of and comment on tax policy and its effects?

AIP 1.8 Making planning decisions and financial reporting LO 5

The controller is complaining to her friend about the crazy requests that come from the top managers. 'The CEO has requested that I calculate product costs to include research and development and selling costs. Doesn't he know that according to GAAP, research and development and selling expenditures are expensed during the period incurred and are not product costs.'

Evaluate the controller's comments.

AIP 1.9 Role of the divisional controller LO 6

The Arjohn Corporation is a multi-divisional firm. Each division has a manager who is responsible for division operations. The controller for each division is assigned to the division by the corporate controller's office. The division controller manages the division's accounting system and provides analysis of financial information for the division management. The division manager evaluates the performance of the division controller and makes recommendations for salary increases and promotions. However, the final responsibility for promotion evaluation and salary increases rests with the corporate controller. Each division of Arjohn is responsible for product design, sales, pricing, operating costs and expenses, and profits. However, corporate management exercises tight control over the financial operations of the divisions. For example, corporate management must approve all capital expenditures above a very modest amount. The method of financial reporting from the division to corporate headquarters provides further evidence of the degree of financial control. The division manager and the division controller submit to corporate headquarters separate and independent commentary on the financial results of the division. The corporate management maintains that the division controller is there to provide an independent view of the division's operations.

Arjohn Corporation's dual reporting systems for decisions may create problems for the division controller.

a Identify and discuss the factors that make the division controller's role difficult in this type of situation.
b Discuss the effect of the dual reporting relationship on the motivation of the division controller.

AIP 1.10 Responsibilities, information, and performance measures LO 3

Steve Johnson sells sportswear for a wholesaler to retail shops. Retail shops like to have 30 days to pay after receipt of the goods. Unfortunately, retail shops often have financial difficulties and fail to make timely payments and in some cases no payments at all. Steve's manager, who has never visited the retail shops, makes the decision whether to require collection on delivery (COD) or allow the store to pay in 30 days. Forcing the store to make payment on delivery often deters the shop from making a purchase. Steve, who visits each store, argues that he should have the right to make the decision on allowing for payment within 30 days.

a How would the wholesaler benefit from Steve making the decision to allow for payment within 30 days?
b What types of performance measures should be used for Steve, if he is not given the responsibility to allow for payment within 30 days?
c What types of performance measures should be used for Steve, if he is given the responsibility to allow for payment within 30 days?
d Should Steve be evaluated on increased sales or the level of uncollectible accounts receivable? What are the trade-offs between these two measures?

AIP 1.11 Global competition LO 1

Peter Jensen has opened a small business making handcrafted guitars. His guitars sell for around £4,000 apiece and he only sells about 30 each year. When warned about potential competition from a producer in another country, Peter said, 'I'm not worried about global competition. Although my guitars are very expensive, I work hard to satisfy my customers. My guitars have an exclusive name that customers are willing to pay for. I will never be a low-cost producer.'

Should Peter worry about global competition and change his business?

AIP 1.12 The role of managers LO 3

The activities of managers can be categorized as either planning or control. Label each of the following manager activities as either a planning decision or a control activity.

a Choosing a price for a product.
b Explaining to an employee how to operate a machine.
c Deciding which supplier of a part to use.
d Congratulating the engineering department for a wonderful design.
e Planning a building site for a new factory.
f Asking an employee to provide service to a customer.
g Creating a new process for manufacturing.

h Deciding how to finance a new project.

i Keeping track of the hours worked by the employees.

AIP 1.13 Total quality management (TQM) LO 1

The owner of a jewellery shop has just heard about TQM as a way of managing. The owner sees no reason to invest any further in TQM. As he told a friend, 'TQM may be relevant for some of the cheap jewellery shops in town, but I only sell the highest quality diamonds and jewellery. I am already the top quality jewellery retailer in town. TQM has nothing further to offer me.'

Evaluate the comments of the jewellery shop owner.

AIP 1.14 Computer-aided manufacturing (CAM) LO 1

CAM welding machines can be programmed to make different types of welds. Software is inserted into the machine to change the welding pattern. The Kipling Box Company makes steel boxes that require only one type of weld. The president of the company is trying to decide if the company should invest in a CAM welding machine.

What are the advantages and disadvantages of investing in the CAM welding machine?

AIP 1.15 Just-in-time (JIT) LO 1

A hospital administrator has just read a book about JIT. She feels that JIT is a good idea for manufacturing companies, but doesn't think that JIT would be of much use to a service organization.

Describe how JIT could be used in a hospital.

AIP 1.16 Computer-integrated manufacturing (CIM) LO 1

Many top-level managers do not understand CIM. Only a small percentage of conversions to CIM began with top-level managers. The push for CIM usually begins with shop-floor engineers.

What are the advantages of implementing a change from the top versus the bottom of the organization?

AIP 1.17 International and domestic differences LO 1

A manager of a fashion designer and manufacturer in Milan was heard to say, 'I don't understand all the fuss about studying international business. We are already international; as is Europe. We sell domestically, but most of our trade is with the countries around us. Despite the fact that the language of fashion is universal, we speak English, French, German and Spanish. We also have to deal with multiple taxing authorities. Inflation is like changing exchange rates, both raise comparability problems. Since we have been successful in Europe, I have no doubt we will be successful globally.'

How would you respond to this manager?

Extended **analysis** and **interpretation** problems

AIP 1.18 Ethical behaviour LO 7

FulRange Inc. produces complex printed circuits for stereo amplifiers. The circuits are sold primarily to major component manufacturers, and any production overruns are sold to small manufacturers at a substantial discount. The small-manufacturer market segment appears very profitable because the basic operating budget assigns all fixed production expenses to the major manufacturers, the only predictable market.

A common product defect that occurs in production is a 'drift' that is caused by failure to maintain precise heat levels during the production process. Rejects from the 100 per cent testing programme can be reworked to acceptable levels if the defect is drift. However, in a recent analysis of customer complaints, Scott Richardson, the cost accountant, and the quality control engineer have ascertained that normal rework does not bring the circuits up to standard. Sampling shows that about one-half of the reworked circuits will fail after extended, high-volume amplifier operation. The incidence of failure in the reworked circuits is projected to be about 10 per cent over one-to-five years' operation.

Unfortunately, there is no way to determine which reworked circuits will fail, because testing does not detect this problem. The rework process could be changed to correct the problem, but the cost-benefit analysis for the suggested change in the rework process indicates that it is not feasible. FulRange's marketing analyst has indicated that if the problem is not corrected, it will significantly affect the company's reputation and customer satisfaction. Consequently, the board of directors would interpret this problem as having serious negative implications on the firm's profitability.

Richardson has included the circuit failure and rework problem in his report that has been prepared for the upcoming quarterly meeting of the board of directors. Due to the potential adverse economic impact, Richardson has followed a long-standing practice of highlighting this information.

After reviewing the reports to be presented, the plant manager and his staff are upset and indicate to the controller that he should control his people better. 'We can't upset the board with this kind of material. Tell Richardson to tone that down. Maybe we can get it by this meeting and have some time to work on it. People who buy those cheap systems and play them that loud shouldn't expect them to last forever.'

The controller calls Richardson into his office and says, 'Scott, you'll have to bury this one. The probable failure of reworks can be referred to briefly in the oral presentation, but it should not be mentioned or highlighted in the advance material mailed to the board.'

Richardson feels strongly that the board will be misinformed on a potentially serious loss of income if he follows the controller's orders. He discusses the problem with the quality control engineer, who simply remarks, 'That's your problem, Scott.'

a Discuss the ethical considerations that Scott Richardson should recognize in deciding how to proceed in this matter.
b Explain what ethical responsibilities should be accepted in this situation by each of the following: controller, quality control engineer, and plant manager and staff.
c What should Richardson do in this situation? Why?

(CMA adapted)

AIP 1.19 Strategies, organizational goals and management accounting LO 2,3,4

In 1993, Wayne Albo found an opportunity to enter the record store business. Wayne Albo was a Canadian chartered accountant (CA) and specialist in mergers and acquisitions. He was also an experienced business evaluator. Through his Calcorp Group of companies, he dealt with a base of clients who had businesses that they were looking to sell or expand. As a result, Albo was on a first-name basis with numerous entrepreneurs. That year, a friend called Albo with a proposition. One of his clients had died suddenly, leaving behind a chain of record stores. The individual had not planned for any successors to carry on the business. There were 13 stores, in small cities, with sales of about $4 million (CDN) per year. Although Albo was making a good living as a consultant, he decided to take the plunge and enter into the record-store market.

Albo could see the potential for profits. Record stores in smaller cities did not face the same amount of competition, as did stores in Montreal, Toronto and Vancouver. Secondly, the customers were generally older than those in the teen-driven big city market were. Thus, customers had more disposable income, and demand was more stable. Finally, some of the 13 stores were exclusive sites in smaller shopping malls; these permitted higher profit margins.

Once Wayne Albo became the owner of a record-store chain, numerous opportunities popped up. A&A, another record chain, went bankrupt; Albo picked up a dozen new locations from amongst the A&A stores. When the owner of National Record Stores in Winnipeg died, Albo (with the help of Working Ventures, a labour-sponsored investment fund) purchased the chain of 35 stores, along with its wholesale division, warehouse and experienced administrative staff. With Working Ventures as an equity partner, and cash flow generated from his existing stores, Albo began a Canada-wide buying spree. He purchased a chain of 17 stores owned by Top Forty, and then 80 stores run by Rock Entertainment.

Albo recognized that technology was changing rapidly. He believed that web-based record stores soon would be his competitors. Although his own company, Ave Entertainment, did not have the necessary expertise or experience to enter that market, Albo knew of two young entrepreneurs, David Cubitt and Bill Birss, who did. In 1989, Cubit and Birss had started a mail-order catalogue business in the basement of a suburban home. With their mail-order marketing, they had brought a huge selection and competitive pricing, usually reserved for urban centres, to rural communities. They later introduced the 'warehouse outlet' concept to the music industry. Their next step was to launch a website, under their name CD Plus (www.cdplus.com). This website enabled them to put their 65,000-title catalogue on line. The website also features interviews, articles, reviews, and links to artist Web pages.

Through a share swap, Albo acquired the bricks-and-mortar stores, the website, and the 'CD Plus' name. In the summer of 1999, Albo brought in Leo Sienna, a veteran of the food distribution business, as president and CEO of CD

Plus. The bricks-and-mortar locations provided millions of dollars of inventory to online shoppers, with a quick turn-around time. In addition, a decade of experience in record sales was transferred to the online market. CD Plus' strategy was to add value to the customer through a large selection, competitive pricing, and favourable exchange rates for US customers. The Internet opened up global markets to the '100% Canadian' company.

By 2000, CDPlus.com Inc. had 150 stores across Canada, generated over $150 million (CDN) in sales per year, and was a publicly traded company. CD Plus had added partnerships with ZapYou.com (video games) and DVD Warehouse Inc. Any webmaster could become a CD Plus Partner by placing CD Plus' banner on her own website. She would earn a 5 per cent commission on every sale originating from her site. CD Plus would do all the work – processing the order, shipping the product, and handling the customer service and billings. CD Plus also offered a wholesaling service, through its operations in Burnaby, BC.

In 2004 CD Plus de-listed and became part of the Entertainment One Income Fund. In May 2005, CD Plus purchased KOCH Entertainment of the US to further expand its market reach. It now had operations in the CD, DVD and Video Game market.

a Refer to the framework for organizational change in Figure 1.1. Using this analytical framework, outline why and how CD Plus adapted to its environment, and its strategies to achieve customer value.

b What is the role of management accounting in supporting the firm's strategy to create organizational value? In discussing this question, consider both the financial and non-financial information that CD Plus would find useful.

Sources: Based on Terrence Belford, 'Note-by-note progression creates musical chain', *The National Post*, 20 October 1999; www.cdplus.com/cdplus300/ws/new/index.asp; www.cdplus.com/shop

CHAPTER TWO

Measuring and analysing activity costs

(Planning)

Learning objectives

1. Use differential costs and benefits to assist in cost-benefit analysis.

2. Identify and measure opportunity costs for making planning decisions.

3. Ignore sunk costs for making planning decisions.

4. Use cost-benefit analysis to make information choices.

5. Determine how activity costs vary with the rate of output.

6. Calculate marginal and average costs.

7. Approximate activity costs using variable and fixed costs.

8. Use account classification, the high-low and regression methods to estimate variable and fixed costs.

Jones and McLean, Chartered Accountants

The firm of Jones and McLean, Chartered Accountants (CAs), provides consulting, auditing and tax services for its clients. Being a small firm, Jones and McLean competes on the basis of customized services at reasonable cost. Its reputation is important and results from providing quality services to high-profile clients such as corporations and local agencies. The clients' annual financial reports are audited by Jones and McLean to determine if the financial statements are not misleading and follow generally accepted accounting principles. In performing the audit, the firm of Jones and McLean checks the accuracy of the financial statements by examining items such as receivables, inventory and fixed assets, and their corresponding documentation. Much of this work is performed just after the completion of the client's financial year, which is often 31 December. Therefore, January and February are very busy audit months.

The firm of Jones and McLean also completes tax returns for its clients. Tax returns should be sent to HM Revenue & Customs within one year after the end of the financial year for business clients and by 31 January for individual clients. Taxes, however, must be paid before tax returns are due, thus the firm prefers to file all tax returns on a timely basis to assist clients with cash-flow planning. Therefore, January to March, and the first part of April, are busy months for tax work at Jones and McLean.

The advisory services provided by Jones and McLean include advice on management information systems, product development and executive compensation. Clients demand consulting services more evenly throughout the year, compared to the demand for audit and tax services.

The firm of Jones and McLean consists of 10 CAs: two partners (Mary Jones and Ed McLean), two managers and six professional staff. All the CAs can perform audits, prepare tax returns and provide advisory services, but at least one partner must check the work for each client. The administrative staff includes five clerks. The two managers and six professional staff members receive annual salaries with no overtime pay. The CAs generally incur considerable overtime during the first four months of the year and take longer vacations during other times of the year to compensate for the overtime. The administrative staff is paid on an hourly basis with a 40 per cent increase for overtime. They generally work one hour for every two hours of work by CAs. Other costs of operating the office include rent, utilities, computing equipment and network services, photocopiers and office supplies. Once all revenues and expenses for the year are finalized and the yearly profit is determined, the partners share the net profit between them according to the terms of their partnership agreement.

The firm of Jones and McLean has been asked to audit the local Metro Housing Association (MHA). The MHA has a financial year end on 30 June, so much of the audit work must be done in July and August. The initial audit of the MHA will require more CA time than subsequent audits because Jones and McLean would have to learn about the accounting systems and management processes of the MHA. Audits are awarded on a competitive basis. Based on the fees paid in previous years and the bids of competing firms, MHA officials have told Jones and McLean that MHA will pay a maximum of £15,000 for the audit services. Jones and McLean must decide if the £15,000 fee is sufficient to accept the audit. While the revenue figure of £15,000 is known, the partners need information about the costs to determine if the audit contract would be profitable.

MAKING PLANNING DECISIONS

Chapter 1 describes the dual roles of management accounting in providing information for making planning decisions and for control to create organizational value. This chapter focuses on making planning decisions. Planning decisions are both long-term and short-term in nature. These decisions are linked to the organization's strategy and value chain. Typical planning decisions made within an organization include:

- What customers should the organization target and satisfy?
- How should the organization finance its operations?
- What products or services should the organization provide?
- What activities should be used to provide the products or services?
- What method should be used to price products or services?

The criteria for making these decisions depend on the strategic mission of the organization. The aspects of a decision that will help the organization to achieve its goals are called benefits. For example, the strategic mission of TimeBank (a UK national volunteering charity) is to motivate a new generation of citizens to give time through volunteering in areas that fit with individual interests and talents. Its website contains information on volunteer opportunities, recruitment campaigns and voluntary organizations. The website is consistent with its strategic goals and would be considered a benefit. Benefits, however, are seldom achieved without a cost. The cost of a decision is the use of organizational resources to achieve a benefit. The cost of TimeBank's website includes the cost of researching, writing and updating the information, along with the technical demands to maintain the site and its related databases.

Decisions should be made after a careful analysis of benefits and costs. The benefits and costs to the organization, however, may be different than the benefits and costs to the manager within the organization who is making the decision. Managers may have goals different from the organization, and will tend to make the decision that leads to the greatest net benefit to them. The problem of control is to motivate the managers to align their individual goals with the organizational goals. Control problems are taken up again in Chapter 6. In Chapters 2 to 5, we assume the goals of the managers and the organization to be the same.

■ Using cost-benefit analysis

Cost-benefit analysis is the process of analysing alternative decisions to determine which decision has the greatest expected benefit relative to its cost. We all informally use cost-benefit analysis in making day-to-day decisions. For example, a common

Photofusion Picture Library/Alamy

Riding your bike is cheaper and environmentally friendly yet less convenient than driving your car – especially in traffic. Cost-benefit analysis assists in evaluating your options.

decision may be whether to ride your bicycle or drive your car to lectures. The benefit of riding a bicycle is more exercise, but the cost is a longer travel time and possibly the need to take a shower after arriving at university. The benefit of driving is a shorter commute time, but the cost is the petrol, payment of parking fees or fines. Some uncertainties also exist. For example, the probability of rain, an accident or a traffic jam should affect the expected benefits and costs of travelling to university. To make a decision, you identify, measure and compare the expected benefits and costs of each alternative and choose the alternative with the greatest net benefit (total benefits less total costs). Managers should use cost-benefit analysis to make planning decisions, but the benefits and costs are not always easily identified and measured.

One method of avoiding the measurement of all the benefits and costs of each alternative is to compare only those costs and benefits that differ among the alternative decisions. The difference in benefits is known as the **differential benefit** and the difference in costs is known as the **differential cost**. A comparison of the differential benefits and costs will lead to the same decision as a comparison of all the benefits and costs because the remaining costs and benefits are not affected by the decision. For example, in 2005 HMV (the music store) had to decide whether or not to launch its own digital music service. This move was a possible strategic response to the decline in in-shop sales and the entry of market competitors offering digital downloads. The differential benefit of launching the digital service was the increased sales from Internet traffic, and the improved quality of customer information gathered from the Web. The differential cost of launching the service was the cost of building this technology into existing websites, the cost of hiring extra staff to maintain the service, the cost of purchasing new computer hardware and software, and the potential impact of the digital sales on other music formats. HMV should have launched the website provided the differential benefit exceeded the differential cost. The remaining benefits and costs generated by HMV were irrelevant to the website decision, since they were the same whether it decided to launch the digital service or not.

Numerical **example** 2.1

The manager of Kemp Sports must decide whether to rent only mechanical or only manual stringing machines for the squash racquets that it manufactures. A mechanical stringer can string 60 racquets per hour and requires one operator. A manual stringing machine can string 10 racquets per hour and each machine requires one operator. The rental cost for a mechanical stringing machine is £100 per hour and the rental cost of a manual stringing machine is £10 per hour. The cost of electricity for a mechanical stringer is £8 per hour. Labour cost is £9 per hour. Kemp must produce 120 squash racquets per hour to meet customer demand. To produce 120 racquets, either 2 mechanical or 12 manual machines are required. The other manufacturing processes are not affected by the choice of stringing machines.

Solution

The rest of Kemp Sports is not affected by the choice of stringing machines and the revenues will be the same with a sufficient number of stringing machines (two mechanical or 12 manual). The decision, therefore, hinges on the differential costs of the two types of machines. The differential costs for each type of machine are:

Type of cost	Manual method	Mechanical method	Difference
Rent	12 × £10 = £120	2 × £100 = £200	−£80
Labour	12 × £9 = £108	2 × £9 = £18	+£90
Electricity		2 × £8 = £16	−£16
Totals	£228	£234	−£6

The manual method results in lower costs and is the preferred choice. This decision, however, overlooks possible qualitative costs and benefits of this choice, such as the effect on quality and employee morale.

Even with differential costs and benefits, not all costs and benefits can be easily identified and measured when performing cost-benefit analysis.

■ Problems in identifying and measuring benefits

The benefits of making a particular decision depend on the goals of the organization. The achievement of some goals is not easily identified and measured. For example, most automobile dealerships have the goal of customer satisfaction. When you purchase a new vehicle, you receive a survey from the dealership asking you if you are satisfied with your new car and the services provided. Since many buyers never return these surveys, the measurement of customer satisfaction is not necessarily accurate.

Benefits to organizations are often measured in terms of cash inflows. Yet the cash inflow from a decision is not always known and must often be estimated. For example, the benefit of introducing a new product would be estimated by forecasting future sales. These cash inflows occur in the future; therefore some uncertainty in measurement will exist. Also, cash flows from different time periods should be adjusted for the time value of money before they are accumulated. The time value of money is discussed in Chapter 13.

While the Air France-KLM merger resulted in reduced costs and improved global competitiveness, many costs and benefits are intangible or difficult to measure with certainty.

Not all the benefits of a decision have immediate monetary implications. Benefits, such as training and development, a better work environment and increased employee satisfaction, are difficult to identify and measure in financial terms. These benefits have monetary consequences in later years.

In 2003, Air France and KLM announced a merger to create the Air France-KLM group with an emphasis on co-ordinating its flight operations instead of completely integrating the two airlines. In making this decision, the executives of each airline attempted to measure the benefits of the merger. Some benefits are obvious. A merged airline would bring reduced maintenance costs through combined services and greater bargaining power with suppliers, including aircraft purchases. Other benefits, however, are less direct. By merging, the new airline group had access to two airport hubs, Amsterdam Schipol and Paris-Charles de Gaulle. It also had a wider range of routes to offer passengers. The executives also believed that a merger would secure a competitive advantage over its rivals, enabling the new firm to become both a pan-European market player and a global industry leader. These benefits are more difficult to measure. The costs of this merger are discussed below.

■ Problems in identifying and measuring costs

Costs are the use of organizational resources. Costs are easy to identify and measure when cash is the resource being used. For example, the purchase price of a new laptop computer is easily identified and measured in monetary terms. Some costs, however, do not have immediate or obvious monetary implications. For example, requiring employees to work overtime may adversely affect employee morale and have long-term cost implications, such as increased staff turnover and greater difficulty in attracting new employees.

Measuring the cost of using non-cash resources is also a problem. For example, what is the cost of using raw materials in inventory? Possible answers include the purchase price (historical cost), the current market price or the future replacement cost. What is the cost of using the current labour pool or facilities? Once again, numerous possible answers exist. The next section introduces the concept of opportunity cost to answer these questions.

In the case of Air France-KLM, some cost estimates are not easy to calculate. The two airlines had different organizational cultures. Each was strongly identified as the national 'flag' carrier. It would be difficult to estimate the impact of the merger on staff morale and on the citizens of France and the Netherlands, especially as it could become an emotional issue for both staff and passengers. Information technology systems and reservation systems needed to be integrated. Yet determining accurately the cost to do so is not straightforward, given the complex nature of these systems and the potential downside if the integration were delayed or poorly achieved.[1]

---

[1] Air France-KLM Merger; address by Jean-Cyril Spinetta, Nyenrode European Business Forum, 23 February 2006.

■ Opportunity costs

Using the resources of an organization, whether the resource is cash, inventory, buildings or employee time, is a cost to the organization. It is a cost to the organization because once the resource is used for one purpose it cannot be used for another. If cash is spent to outsource cleaning services, it cannot be used to hire a new employee. If a building is used to house the assembly division, it cannot be used by the marketing department or sold to another party. If an employee is designing a product, that employee cannot be selling the product to customers at the same time. Cost is defined as the use of resources. The measurement of costs is based on the forgone opportunities of using those resources for other purposes. The size of the forgone opportunity of using a resource is the **opportunity cost**.

We use opportunity costs to make decisions every day. For example, the opportunity cost of accepting a job is forgoing the opportunity to do something else with our time. If our best alternative to working is playing golf, the opportunity cost of working is the forgone opportunity to play golf. If the opportunity to play golf has a value greater than the benefits of working, we will choose to play golf. Another example is the opportunity cost of attending an early morning lecture. The forgone opportunity is being able to sleep later. Also, the opportunity cost of taking in a movie is the forgone opportunity of using the time and money for another activity. In each case, a decision to use a resource prevents the resource from being used for another purpose.

The concept of opportunity cost is consistent with cost-benefit analysis. Opportunity costs provide a means of measuring the cost of a particular decision. The costs of each alternative decision should be identified and measured in terms of the forgone opportunity of using the resources for other purposes.

■ Measuring opportunity costs

The forgone opportunity of using a resource is the opportunity cost to an organization. If a decision involves the use of many different resources, the opportunity cost of using each resource should be measured in monetary terms. The opportunity cost of using each resource is then added and the total opportunity costs are compared with the benefits derived from the decision.

Cash is an organizational resource that is frequently expended to perform different activities. Cash is used to purchase materials, hire employees and pay utility bills. Any proposed activity that requires the outlay of cash is incurring an opportunity cost, since cash can be used for many other purposes. The measurement of the opportunity cost of using cash in the short run, however, is simply the face value of the cash expended. For example, if a proposed activity requires the purchase of £100 of strawberries, the opportunity cost would be £100.

Measuring the opportunity cost of using non-cash resources is slightly more complicated. To measure the opportunity cost, the next best use of the resource should be identified. Forgone opportunities of using a resource include selling the resource or using it for another activity. Generally, however, a similar resource can be purchased, so the use of the resource does not necessarily prevent the other activities from occurring. For example, raw materials can be replaced with further purchases, additional machines and buildings can be bought, and more employees can be hired.

If the next best use of the resource is to sell it, the sales price of the resource is the opportunity cost of using the resource. For example, suppose you are debating whether or not to keep this book as a reference after the course is over. The opportunity cost of keeping the book is the re-sale price you would receive at a used bookstore.

If the use of the resource means that additional resources must be purchased for other activities, the cost of replacing the resources is the opportunity cost. For a new-car dealership, the forgone opportunity of selling a car is the inability to sell the same car to another customer. But the dealership can buy another car from the manufacturer or from another dealer. Therefore, the opportunity cost of selling a new car is the cost to acquire another vehicle.

In general, the opportunity cost of using a non-cash resource is either its sales price or its replacement cost. Under the unusual circumstances where a resource cannot be replaced and is critical for another activity, then the loss in organizational value of not being able to perform the other activity is the opportunity cost. For example, the time of an employee who has specialized knowledge of the organization's computer network is limited. This knowledge cannot be easily replaced by hiring another employee. If the employee has no free time, assigning her to perform routine network maintenance prevents her from performing some other activity, such as evaluating system security. The opportunity cost to the organization of using the employee's time for one activity is the loss in value caused by not being able to undertake the other.

The following numerical examples illustrate the identification and measurement of opportunity costs.

Numerical **example** 2.2

Doris Wheaton has 10 bags of cement in her garage. The bags cost £4 per bag last year when they were purchased. The store now sells the cement for £5 per bag but does not take returns. A neighbour, however, told Doris he would buy the cement from her for £3 per bag if she did not want them. Doris is considering using the cement to make a patio.

a If Doris uses the 10 bags of cement to make her patio and has no other use for the cement, what is the opportunity cost of using the cement?
b If Doris must also rebuild her front steps (which requires 20 bags of cement), what is the opportunity cost of her existing 10 bags of cement?

Solution

a If Doris has no other use of the cement, the next best alternative to using the cement for the patio is to sell the cement. She can sell the cement to her neighbour for £3 per bag for 10 bags, or £30. Therefore, the opportunity cost of using the cement is £30.
b Using the cement for the patio means that the cement must be replaced to make the front steps. The replacement cost of £5 per bag for 10 bags, or £50, is the opportunity cost of using the 10 bags of cement for the patio.

Numerical **example** 2.3

Clean Copy Centre has hired a permanent employee to operate a copy machine for large jobs. The permanent employee is paid £7 per hour whether or not copy jobs must be performed. Temporary help can be hired for £8 per hour.

a What is the opportunity cost per hour of using the permanent employee to copy a job if there is no other work for the employee to perform?
b What is the opportunity cost per hour of using the permanent employee if the employee could be working on another copy job that would generate a value of £6 per hour of work?

→

c What is the opportunity cost per hour of using the permanent employee if the employee could be working on another copy job that would generate a value of £10 per hour of work?

Solution

a If there is no alternative use of the employee's time, the opportunity cost of using the employee is £0 per hour.

b The cost of hiring a temporary employee (£8/hour) is greater than the increased value of performing the other work (£6/hour). Therefore, the organization will not hire the temporary employee. Using the permanent employee prevents the employee from performing the other work and generating a value of £6 per hour. Under these circumstances, the opportunity cost of using the employee is £6 per hour.

c The cost of hiring a temporary employee (£8/hour) is less than the increased value of performing the other work (£10/hour). Therefore, the organization will hire the temporary employee if the permanent employee does not have time. Using the permanent employee on another activity causes the copy centre to hire a temporary employee. The opportunity cost of using the permanent employee is the cost of hiring a temporary employee, or £8 per hour.

Numerical **example** 2.4

An importer rents a building for storage. The rental cost is £1,000 per month. Presently, the importer occupies only half of the building space. She could sub-let the remaining space for £300 per month. She is considering a new line of products to import that would take up the remaining space. What is the opportunity cost of using the building to add the new line of products?

Solution

The opportunity cost is the forgone opportunity to sub-let the remaining space, or £300 per month.

Numerical **example** 2.5

Your firm registered the Internet web domain name (URL) www.uniwork.org.uk and has signed up with a reliable web-hosting service. For £300 per year, it has the exclusive right to use this URL. You plan to use the website to post job openings for recent university graduates. You expect this business to generate revenues of £120,000 per year and expenses of £30,000 per year. Before starting the business, another company offers to buy your URL and service for £110,000 per year.

a What 'cost' does the accounting system assign to the URL and hosting service?
b What is the opportunity cost of the URL?

Solution

a The accounting system assigns a cost of £300 per year to the URL.
b If you start the business, the opportunity cost of the URL is the £110,000 you forgo by not selling it.

The identification and measurement of opportunity costs may appear cumbersome and difficult, but *opportunity costs are the appropriate costs for making planning decisions*. In most cases, the opportunity cost of using a resource is either the purchase price or selling price of the resource being used. In a competitive market with full information and no transaction costs, purchase and selling prices converge to the market price or value of the resource. Therefore, the market price of a resource is a reasonable approximation of the opportunity cost of using the resource. The following section describes sunk or historical costs, which are generally poorer approximations of opportunity cost.

■ Sunk costs and historical costs

Sunk costs are costs that have already been incurred and cannot be changed no matter what action is taken. Given that sunk costs are costs incurred in the past, they are the same for all possible alternatives in the present and the future. Therefore, sunk costs are irrelevant for cost-benefit analysis. Ironically, we often find ourselves including sunk costs when making decisions. For example, many people use the purchase price originally paid for their home to determine the listing price when they decide to sell. Other people stay to the final minutes of a soccer match to 'get their money's worth', even though the weather has turned miserable and the home team is down by three goals at half-time.

The historical cost of a resource reflects the cost at the time of its acquisition. When a resource is acquired, the historical cost is usually a close approximation of the opportunity cost because it reflects the market value at that time. Except for somewhat arbitrary write-downs (depreciation and amortization), however, the historical cost of the resource remains the same as long as the resource is held by the organization. The historical cost does not change with changes in market value. The historical cost of a resource becomes a sunk cost following the purchase of the resource.

The ticket cost is sunk once purchased, yet fans often remain at the stadium to get their money's worth.

Financial reporting to outside investors is based on historical costs. Most internal accounting reports also use historical costs. The popularity of historical cost accounting reports might appear surprising. Although the historical cost approximates the opportunity cost of a resource at the time of purchase, the historical cost is a sunk cost subsequent to the purchase and should not be used for planning purposes. Given potential deviations between historical costs and opportunity costs, we might question why historical cost accounting has survived. In the last century, regulations may have been partly responsible for its survival. Financial reporting requirements around the world are based on historical costs. Yet the demand for opportunity costs (market values) by external parties for making planning decisions (for example, investment decisions) might have some effect on regulations.

Another reason for the continued popularity of historical costs is their use for control decisions. Verifying the actions of managers is an important part of control. Historical costs generally are more useful than opportunity costs for control, as they reveal the past actions of managers. These costs are easily verifiable and less subject to managerial discretion. These features are usually important when performance is being measured by historical costs. Thus, historical cost data can be utilized to motivate and reward managers.

Situations exist when historical costs are used to make planning decisions. Historical costs or simple adjustments to these figures might be reasonable approximations of opportunity costs. If the environment does not change very much from the time of the resource acquisition, the historical cost might remain a close approximation of the opportunity cost. Using rules of thumb to approximate opportunity costs, such as increasing historical costs by expected price inflation, might also be effective.

The problem for managers is to determine when to use historical cost numbers as reasonable approximations and when to expend additional effort to determine the opportunity costs, which are more closely approximated by the market value.

Numerical **example** 2.6

Paul Wong is struggling to assemble his new home theatre system. He has spent five hours thus far on the chore and estimates that at this rate, he will complete the assembly in two more hours. Joan Jimenez walks into the room and informs Paul that he is doing it the hard way. She describes a simpler approach that will take only one hour to disassemble the work that he has done over the past five hours and re-assemble the system completely. What should Paul do?

Solution

Paul should follow Joan's advice because the remaining time to completion is less. The five hours of work that he has performed is a sunk cost.

Jones and McLean, Chartered Accountants (continued)

The firm of Jones and McLean has two alternatives: (1) accept the offer to audit the MHA or (2) reject the offer to audit the MHA. Mary Jones and Ed McLean will presumably make the decision that benefits the firm the most, but they may not be in complete agreement on the firm's goals. Mary prefers to travel to Italy in the summer, while Ed needs extra money to pay for his daughter's university expenses. This type of conflict is a control problem. It may be partially resolved by adjusting the partners' method of sharing the profits that the firm generates and by altering their respective workloads. In this chapter, we assume that Mary and Ed both want to increase the long-term profitability of the firm.

To Jones and McLean, the immediate cash benefit of auditing the MHA is the £10,000 fee. But there could be other benefits that are less obvious. For example, by performing the audit, Jones and McLean could be in the position to acquire similar audit engagements. The learning that will occur in auditing the MHA could be applied to these other contracts. Accepting the audit also provides the firm with the option of continuing to audit the MHA in the future. If another accounting firm audits the MHA this year, Jones and McLean are not likely to have the opportunity to undertake the audit in the near future. Firm reputation also would be enhanced by having the MHA as a client.

In deciding whether to accept or reject the MHA audit, Jones and McLean should determine the opportunity costs of using materials, labour and facilities, and ignore sunk costs. The materials such as computer forms and paper will all be replaced, so the replacement cost should be used for the opportunity cost. The seasonal nature of the auditing business means that the firm of Jones and McLean has excess labour and capacity during the summer months. The opportunity cost of using the CAs, who are paid an annual salary, would be reduced employee morale from lost free time. Their annual salary, however, is a sunk cost. The clerical staff is paid on an hourly basis, so any increased clerical staff hours from the MHA audit creates an opportunity cost equal to the additional hours times the wage rate, or 1.4 times the wage rate if overtime is incurred. Overtime may be avoided by hiring temporary help. The costs of the facilities appear to be sunk costs. The rent has already been paid and the equipment has already been purchased. There will be some costs of learning how to perform the audit. Utility costs might increase slightly if the engagement is accepted. If Jones and McLean accept this audit engagement, the firm also forgoes the opportunity to take on other contracts that might prove more profitable.

Concept **review**

1 How does the use of differential costs and benefits help in performing cost-benefit analysis?
2 Why are some costs and benefits difficult to measure?
3 What should be considered in determining the opportunity cost of using a resource?
4 Why should sunk costs be ignored for planning purposes?

THE BENEFIT AND COST OF INFORMATION

Cost-benefit analysis, as described in this chapter, applies to all types of planning decisions. One planning decision is whether to choose to gather further information before making another planning decision. The manager may ask for another accounting report or a marketing survey. How should the manager make the decision to obtain further information? Once again, a cost-benefit analysis is appropriate. If the benefit of further information is greater than the cost, the additional information should be produced or purchased. The problem is measuring the cost and benefit of the information.

The cost of more information includes the cost of acquiring, modifying, communicating and analysing the information. Resources, including cash and employee time, are used in the process. Each of these resources has an opportunity cost.

The benefit of information comes from improved decisions. If reading the *Financial Times* (FT) leads to better investment decisions, then the FT has a benefit. If reading the FT does not change any decisions, then the FT has no benefit as an information system. The differential benefit of new information is the difference between the expected benefit of making a decision with the new information and the expected benefit of making the decision with existing information. For instance, you can choose an MBA programme without further information. But information on the quality and nature of alternative MBA programmes would be beneficial in deciding which one is best for you.

Consider, for example, Ken Hwang who is choosing amongst MBA programmes for the upcoming year. Ken believes that an MBA degree will increase his future career opportunities, as well as his salary. He has been accepted into two schools, Cranbrook and Oakridge. Both charge similar tuition fees. However, the two MBA programmes differ on other dimensions. Cranbrook delivers its full-time programme over 12 months, while Oakridge offers flexible, part-time studies. Faculty reputation, class size and international focus are other areas in which they differ. While Ken prefers small classes, he considers faculty reputation and international experience to be more important. Therefore, he will make his final choice based on an analysis of these two factors. Ken does not have much time to decide or much money for an extensive search. He plans to visit the websites of both programmes for further information, as an Internet search is low cost and timely.

The particular decision being made also affects the benefit of additional information. A weather report is unlikely to have much value when selecting an investment, but is likely to improve the choice of whether to have a picnic or when to plant a field of barley. In doing a cost-benefit analysis for information choice, the decision context must be known. Information that improves more than one decision is likely to be more valuable. Firms that choose to purchase only one management accounting system should select the system that provides the greatest benefit for a large number of decisions. The ability of a management accounting system to satisfy the demands of many users increases its benefit.

Numerical **example** 2.7

A pharmaceutical firm is about to mix a batch of a drug. There is a one-in-five chance of the batch failing due to bacterial contamination. This risk can be reduced to one in seven if a £5,000 diagnostic test is performed first. If the batch is started but scrapped due to the bacterial contamination, the loss to the firm is £25,000. Should the firm spend the £5,000 on the test?

Solution

If the firm does not spend the £5,000 to gather information about the presence of the bacteria, the expected loss is $1/5(-£25,000) + 4/5(£0)$, or $-£5,000$. If the firm spends the £5,000, the expected loss is $1/7(-£25,000 - £5,000) + 6/7(-£5,000)$, or $-£8,572$.

The expected loss when the test is undertaken is greater than the expected loss of not performing it. Therefore, the test should not be performed as the expected benefit from gathering this additional information exceeds the expected cost.

Concept **review**

1 What is the cost of information?

2 What is the benefit of information?

Jones and McLean, Chartered Accountants (continued)

The firm of Jones and McLean has the option of gathering more information before deciding to audit the MHA. Further study may provide more accurate estimates of hourly requirements for the audit and a better measure of the cost of the audit. While it would be preferable to obtain information from other firms that have experience of auditing associations and not-for-profit organizations, competitors are not willing to divulge this confidential information. Instead, Jones and McLean could examine its previous audit work to estimate the cost. It could project the audit cost by developing different estimates and weighting the probability of each. These different estimates also could outline the worst-case and best-case scenario to assist the partners in assessing the uncertainties involved. Additional study will be costly, however, and should not be performed if the results of the study will not affect the decision. Further information should be obtained only if the expected benefits of an improved decision are greater than the cost of the information.

ACTIVITY COSTS AND THE RATE OF OUTPUT

The operation of an organization can be divided into activities. These activities are tasks performed by the organization to help achieve its goals. Activities may include designing products, accounting, purchasing materials, hiring employees, making product parts and responding to customer queries. In the first chapter, specific activities that added to customer value were identified as the value chain of an organization. By adopting an appropriate strategy for customer value and activities linked to this strategy, customer preferences can be met and organizational value created.

Activities are units of work within the organization that are the subject of cost-benefit analysis. An organization must decide whether and how to engage in a particular activity. For example, an organization must decide whether to advertise a certain product on television, on the Internet or not at all.

Making planning decisions with respect to activities requires knowledge about their benefits and costs. In this section, we examine the cost characteristics of activities. Activities use a variety of resources and are, therefore, costly to perform. In general, the cost of the activity is related to the intensity of the performance of the activity. For example, surveying 60 customers is more costly than surveying 10. The relation between activity costs and the rate of output of the activity (for example, the number of customers surveyed) can be described by stages. These stages include the cost of initiating activities, the cost of activities at normal rates and the cost of activities when exceeding capacity. While our focus is on the rate of output, Chapter 3 illustrates additional ways to capture activity costs.

■ Costs of initiating activities

Certain costs must be incurred before activities can begin. These start-up costs may include the purchase of materials, machines and facilities, the hiring of employees, and designing and planning the activity. For example, a typical activity performed by an organization is the payment of wages to employees. The activity must be designed to record hours worked, determine deductions and distribute pay cheques. Employees in the payroll department must be hired and trained. Equipment must be purchased. These start-up efforts must occur even if the organization has only a few employees to pay. Therefore, the cost per payroll cheque issued could be very high if only a few are issued.

In summary, the cost per output of an activity is generally quite high for the first few units of output. This high cost per unit reflects the start-up costs of initiating activities.

Costs of activities at normal rates

Once the activity is designed, sufficient equipment has been purchased, training is complete and employees have learned to perform the activity, an activity achieves a normal rate of operation. In the example of the payroll activity, considerable costs are incurred to initiate the activity. But once several payroll cheques have been processed and issued, considerable learning has taken place. At that point, further cheques can be issued more efficiently. The cost per additional cheque issued would probably be relatively small.

Cost of activities when exceeding capacity

The normal rate of an activity is not constrained by the size of the facility, equipment or employees. **Capacity** is a measure of the constraints on activities. Capacity constraints include the physical size of the facility, the number of machine hours available and employee time. When the rate of output of an activity reaches capacity, the activity no longer operates as efficiently. Additional costs arise because limitations in facility size cause congestion. Extra equipment might have to be purchased, or existing equipment might become overused and additional maintenance costs incurred. Also, employees might have to be paid overtime. An organization can increase capacity for an activity, but the cost of buying a new facility or hiring and training a new set of employees might be high, especially if the firm must do it quickly. Therefore, the cost of additional output when exceeding capacity is greater than under normal operations.

Graphical analysis of activity costs and the rate of output

The common characteristics of how costs change with increased output of an activity during a period of time are graphed in Figure 2.1. The curve represents total cost of the activity at different rates of output. The total activity costs might rise sharply at low rates of output (point A) because of start-up costs. Activity costs then increase moderately when normal operating rates are achieved (point B). When output rates near

Figure 2.1 A non-linear cost curve

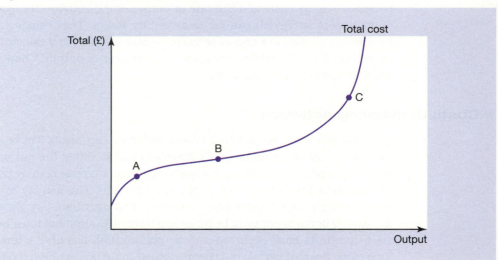

capacity (point C), total costs begin to rise sharply again due to congestion and other capacity-related costs.

Marginal and average costs

The **marginal cost** of an activity is the cost of producing one more unit of output, given the existing rate of output. The marginal cost of the activity is the slope of the total cost curve in Figure 2.1 at each rate of output; the steeper the slope, the higher the marginal cost. The marginal cost is highest at very low output rates (point A) and output rates near capacity (point C). The marginal cost is lowest at normal operations (point B) between these extreme rates of output.

The marginal cost is useful in making decisions about small changes in output rates of activities. Given a particular rate of output, the marginal cost represents the cost of another unit of activity output or the cost savings of one less unit of activity output. In the case of the payroll activity, the marginal cost would be the cost of issuing one more payroll cheque (or the cost savings of issuing one less cheque), given a specified level of payroll cheques being issued.

The **average cost** per unit of activity is calculated by dividing the total activity costs by the number of units of output. For the pattern of total costs in Figure 2.1, the average cost per unit is very high at low levels of output but declines as output increases. The average cost per unit only increases as output nears capacity.

The average cost per unit is commonly calculated by organizations. For example, a firm might calculate the average cost of issuing a payroll cheque by summing all the costs related to payroll and dividing by the number of cheques issued. This figure does not reflect the cost of issuing additional payroll cheques, as it includes the initial start-up costs which will not be incurred again if additional cheques are issued. Therefore, the average cost should not be used in decisions to make small adjustments to the rate of output.

Numerical example 2.8

Beechcraft Aircraft Refinishing specializes in the refurbishment of small aircraft. The company estimates the following total costs for painting aircraft in one month:

Number of aircraft	Total cost (£)
10	100,000
20	150,000
30	190,000
40	220,000
50	250,000
60	280,000
70	320,000
80	370,000
90	470,000
100	600,000

a What is the marginal and average cost for each level of output of the painting activity?
b The company is currently painting 80 aircraft per month. A small regional airline would like to bring in 10 aircraft for painting this month. The airline is willing to spend £90,000 for the paint job. Should Beechcraft accept this additional job?

Solution

a

Number of units	Total cost (£)	Marginal cost (£)	Average cost (£)
10	100,000	100,000	100,000
20	150,000	50,000	75,000
30	190,000	40,000	63,333
40	220,000	30,000	55,000
50	250,000	30,000	50,000
60	280,000	30,000	46,667
70	320,000	40,000	45,714
80	370,000	50,000	46,250
90	470,000	100,000	52,222
100	600,000	130,000	60,000

b The company should not accept the offer because the marginal cost of painting 10 additional aircraft is £100,000. The average cost of £52,222 should not be used for this decision.

Jones and McLean, Chartered Accountants (continued)

Before auditing Grove City, the firm of Jones and McLean would have to learn about specific requirements related to association audits and also acquaint itself with the MHA's accounting system. These start-up costs would make the audit of the MHA more costly than if Jones and McLean were already performing audits of similar not-for-profit organizations.

If Jones and McLean accept too many of these audit engagements, the firm could find itself nearing capacity in terms of office space and support personnel. Increased congestion and delays would impose costs on the other services provided by the firm. These congestion costs would be a cost of accepting too many audits.

Concept review

1 Why are opportunity costs of making the first few units of a product or service likely to be relatively high?

2 Why should capacity be a factor in determining opportunity costs?

3 What type of decisions should use marginal costs?

4 Why is the average cost inappropriate for some decisions?

APPROXIMATIONS OF ACTIVITY COSTS

Activity costs are not always easy to estimate. The activity cost curve in Figure 2.1 requires estimates of the opportunity cost of using resources to perform the activity at different levels of output. Such estimates are difficult to measure, so managers often use approximations. One approximation is to use the market value of resources for the opportunity cost. Chapter 3 further examines activity costs in terms of whether the costs are associated directly or indirectly with an activity. In addition, the total activity costs can be approximated using fixed and variable costs.

Figure 2.2 Fixed and variable cost approximation of activity costs

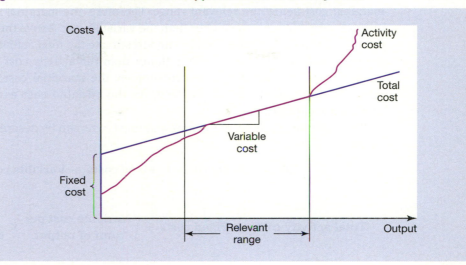

Fixed costs

An approximation of Figure 2.1 using straight lines is provided in Figure 2.2. The approximation assumes that there is a cost of setting up and starting operations called a **fixed cost** (intersection of the cost axis in Figure 2.2). Fixed costs do not change with the rate of output. Fixed costs include the cost of using the facilities, purchasing machines, hiring and training employees, and using other resources that do not change with the rate of output.

Variable costs

Once the fixed costs of an activity are incurred, there are additional operational costs to produce output for the activity. The costs that increase with the rate of output are called **variable costs**. In Figure 2.2 the linear representation of total activity costs assumes that the variable cost of each additional unit is constant over all rates of output. The **variable cost per unit** is the slope of the line in Figure 2.2. Variable costs include the cost of using additional labour, materials and other resources to increase the output of the activity.

Relevant range

In Figure 2.2, the straight line is the fixed and variable cost approximation of the total activity costs. The line most closely approximates the activity costs in the range of normal operations. This range is called the **relevant range**. The relevant range encompasses the rates of output where the combined fixed and variable costs are close approximations of the total activity costs. The slopes of the total activity cost curve and the fixed and variable cost curve are about the same, therefore the variable cost per unit is a close approximation of the marginal cost. In the relevant range, the variable cost can be used to estimate the cost of additional units of output of the activity.

For output quantities below the relevant range of output, the total fixed and variable costs tend to overestimate activity costs. The fixed and variable cost curve is flatter than the activity cost curve, implying the variable cost per unit underestimates the marginal cost below the relevant range. Therefore, the marginal cost of the first few units of output tends to be higher than the variable cost. Above the relevant range, the total fixed and variable costs tend to underestimate the total activity costs. Once again, the fixed and variable cost curve is flatter than the activity cost curve, implying the variable cost per output unit underestimates the marginal cost above the relevant range. The marginal cost is greater than the variable cost as the rate of output approaches capacity.

The total costs in terms of variable and fixed costs can be described by the following equation:

$$\textbf{Total activity costs } = \textbf{ Fixed costs } + \textbf{ Variable costs}$$

or

$$\textbf{Total activity costs } = \textbf{ Fixed costs } + \left(\begin{array}{c} \textbf{Variable cost per} \\ \textbf{unit of output} \end{array} \times \begin{array}{c} \textbf{Number of} \\ \textbf{units of output} \end{array} \right)$$

Numerical example 2.9

Jackson Company makes computers. One activity in assembling the computer is to test it before it leaves the manufacturing plant. The company estimates that the annual fixed costs to purchase testing equipment, use space in the plant and train employees are £100,000. The variable costs of labour and electricity to do the testing are £10 per unit. What are total expected costs if the company tests 5,000 computers per year? What are total expected costs if the company tests 7,000 computers per year?

Solution

Total expected costs to test 5,000 computers per year is the sum of fixed costs (£100,000) and variable costs (£10/test × 5,000 tests = £50,000), or £150,000. Total expected testing costs if Jackson Company tests 7,000 computers per year is the sum of fixed costs (£100,000) and variable costs (£10/test × 7,000 tests = £70,000), or £170,000.

Jones and McLean, Chartered Accountants (continued)

For Jones and McLean, the fixed cost of performing an association audit is learning the regulations on auditing these entities and also learning the specific details of their accounting systems. The partners estimate these fixed costs to equal £8,000. The £8,000 will be sunk, hence irrelevant, when determining the cost to perform additional association audits in the future.

Jones and McLean estimate variable costs in terms of CA time. These variable costs include the cost of using supplies and clerical help, and the cost of motivating the CAs to work during the summer. The partners estimate that the variable cost per hour of CA time for all these costs is £90/hour. They also estimate that the MHA audit will require 100 hours of CA time. Therefore, the total estimated cost of auditing the MHA is £8,000 + (100 hours × £90/hour), or £17,000.

If Jones and McLean perform only one such audit (MHA) this year, the £15,000 revenue would not cover the £17,000 cost of performing the audit. If Jones and McLean perform more association audits this year, however, most of the fixed costs related to doing them would already have been incurred. Therefore, Jones and McLean must decide whether to audit more associations than just the MHA.

Jones and McLean must also consider the option to audit the MHA next year. If some of the fixed costs of auditing the MHA this year will not be incurred next year, the trade-off between losing money this year and making money in subsequent years should be compared. The partners should read Chapter 13 on discounting future cash flows to make this type of comparison.

Concept **review**

1 How does a fixed cost change with the rate of output?

2 What do variable costs approximate?

ESTIMATION OF ACTIVITY COSTS THROUGH THE IDENTIFICATION OF VARIABLE AND FIXED COSTS

Fixed and variable costs can be used to estimate the total cost of an activity. However, estimating activity costs through fixed and variable costs is often difficult and prone to error. This section describes two methods: the account classification and high-low method. The Appendix at the end of this chapter describes a method using regression analysis.

■ Estimating variable and fixed costs through account classification

Accounting aggregates costs within different categories called accounts. For example, all maintenance costs may be aggregated within a single account, or all electricity costs may be aggregated within a single account. The costs in these accounts are treated as if they were all the same and had predictable relations with the output of different activities. For example, the costs in the electricity account are assumed to be similar and have predictable relations with different activities such as accounting and machining. In the case of the accounting department, the major use of electricity is for lighting. The cost of electricity for lighting is not likely to change much with the output of the accounting department, which could be described in terms of number of transactions recorded or hours of work performed by accountants. Under these circumstances, the cost of electricity would be considered fixed with respect to accounting. In the case of machining, the major use of electricity is the operation of the machines. The more the machines operate, the more electricity is used. The cost of electricity for machining is likely to change with the change in output of machining, which could be described in terms of machine hours or number of units machined. Under these circumstances, the cost of electricity would be considered variable with respect to machining.

The account classification method assumes that each cost account associated with the activity of interest can be identified as either fixed or variable with respect to the

Figure 2.3 Classifying accounts as fixed and variable

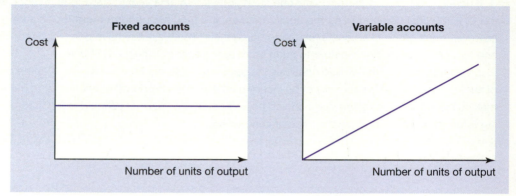

output of the activity. If the costs of an account do not change with the output level, the account is classified as fixed. If the costs of an account increase proportionally with the units of output of an activity, the account is classified as variable. Figure 2.3 demonstrates the fixed and variable relation.

In reality, few cost accounts can be described as either exactly variable or exactly fixed with respect to an activity. Costs generally are mixed in that they tend to curve, instead of being linear as in Figure 2.3. The account classification method, however, requires the identification of cost accounts as either fixed or variable.

Once the cost accounts are classified as fixed or variable, all of the costs in each category are aggregated. The total costs of the fixed cost accounts are the fixed costs of the activity. The total costs of the variable cost accounts are divided by the expected units of output of the activity to determine the variable cost per unit.

The advantage of knowing the fixed costs and variable cost per unit of an activity is the ability to estimate costs given different levels of output of the activity. Each additional unit of output should increase costs by the variable cost per unit until capacity constraints become a factor.

How waiting staff costs are classified reflects a restaurant's strategy. Fixed staffing levels might denote quality, but at higher cost than if staffing fluctuated with demand.

Eric Nathan/Alamy

Numerical **example** 2.10

Topper Restaurant is trying to estimate the cost of providing a meal using the account classification method. The manager estimates the following costs for serving 20,000 meals during the next year:

	£
Food	40,000
Waiting staff	80,000
Supervisory staff	60,000
Facility rental	50,000
Equipment	10,000

a What are the fixed costs and the variable costs per meal?

b What are the estimated costs, if 30,000 meals are prepared?

Solution

a Supervisory staff, facility rental and equipment are all fixed costs. Waiting staff may be fixed or variable and food is variable. If waiting staff is fixed, fixed and variable costs would be calculated as follows:

Fixed costs (£):		Variable costs (£):	
Waiting staff	80,000	Food	40,000
Supervisory help	60,000		
Facility rental	50,000		
Equipment	10,000		
Total	200,000	Total	40,000

Variable costs/meal = £40,000/20,000 = £2/meal.

If waiting staff is variable, fixed and variable costs would be calculated as follows:

Fixed costs (£):		Variable costs (£):	
Supervisory help	60,000	Waiting staff	80,000
Facility rental	50,000	Food	40,000
Equipment	10,000		
Total	120,000	Total	120,000

Variable costs/meal = £120,000/20,000 = £6/meal.

b If 30,000 meals are prepared, the estimated costs include fixed costs of £200,000 and variable costs of £2 × 30,000, or total costs of £260,000. Alternatively, if waiting staff is considered a variable cost, the estimated costs include fixed costs of £120,000 and variable costs of £6 × 30,000, or total costs of £300,000.

■ Using the high-low method to fit historic cost data

Attempting to classify accounts as fixed or variable and to estimate the future cost of each account requires considerable judgement and errors are possible. Another method of estimating the variable and fixed costs is to look at the past costs of the activity. The analysis of past costs will provide an approximation of estimated fixed and variable costs, if the following conditions hold:

1 *Past costs reasonably approximate future costs.* If operational procedures and prices have not changed too much, then past costs should closely approximate future costs.

2 *Several periods of past cost data at different output levels exist.* If the activity is new or recently developed, the analysis of past data will not work.

3 *The future output level is within the range of the past data.* If more units of output of the activity are expected in the future than in the past, the past data will not reveal potential capacity constraints.

4 *The costs of each activity can be separately identified.* All the costs can be traced to the activity.

If these conditions are satisfied, a graphical analysis of past costs and output levels will provide an estimate of the fixed and variable costs of the activity. Figure 2.4 shows a

Figure 2.4 Estimating fixed and variable costs

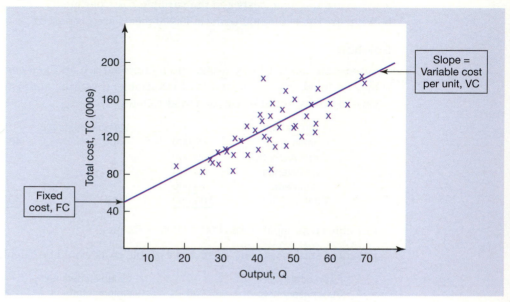

graph of historical costs and the output level for many different periods. The pattern of data points indicates a positive relation between the output of the activity and the total cost of the activity. The problem is to find a line that can closely approximate the data.

One method of drawing the line is to connect the points representing the highest and lowest output of the activity. This approach is called the high-low method and is represented by the line in Figure 2.4. The slope of the line is the variable cost per unit and the intersection on the y-axis (zero output of the activity) is the fixed cost.

To estimate the variable cost per unit and fixed cost mathematically, the highest and lowest points can be used to determine the equation of the line. The estimated variable cost per unit is the difference between the total activity cost at the highest output level and the total activity cost at the lowest output level *divided by* the difference between the highest output level and the lowest output level. The estimated fixed cost is the total activity costs at the lowest output level *minus* the per-unit variable cost times the lowest output level.

The fixed cost also can be estimated by using the difference between the total activity costs at the highest output level and the per-unit variable cost times the highest output level. Either method will generate the same estimate.

In Figure 2.4, the lowest output level is 18 units with an activity cost of £90. The highest output level is 69 units with an activity cost of £200. The variable cost per unit is:

$$\frac{\text{Difference in costs}}{\text{Difference in output}} = (\pounds 200 - \pounds 90)/(69 - 18) = \pounds 2.16/\text{unit}$$

The fixed cost is:

$$\frac{\text{Total cost at}}{\text{the lowest output}} - \left(\frac{\text{Variable cost}}{\text{per unit}} \times \frac{\text{Lowest}}{\text{output level}}\right) = \pounds 90 - (\pounds 2.16/\text{unit} \times 18 \text{ units})$$

$$= \pounds 51.12$$

The accuracy of activity cost estimates using historic costs depends on whether the economic and operating conditions of the past will continue into the future. Estimating costs outside the range of historic output is also a concern. In Figure 2.4, the historic output level was between 18 and 69 units. The cost of making 80 units may be much higher than indicated by the line in Figure 2.4. The maximum output may be 69 units, with any further production requiring increased capacity.

Numerical **example** 2.11

Mighty Peg plc makes hand-crafted cricket bats. The company has used the same traditional manufacturing procedures for many years and the prices of the willow wood and labour have remained relatively stable. The following data are historic costs of making the bats:

Year	Number of bats produced	Historical costs (£)
2002	10,000	110,000
2003	13,000	120,000
2004	11,000	105,000
2005	15,000	125,000
2006	17,000	125,000
2007	13,000	115,000
2008	16,000	130,000

a Estimate the variable cost per bat and the fixed costs using the high-low method.

b Using the estimates of fixed and variable costs, estimate total costs if planned production is 14,000 bats.

Solution

a The lowest output was in 2002 and the highest output was in 2006. Using those two data points, the variable cost per bat is:

$$(£125{,}000 - £110{,}000)/(17{,}000 - 10{,}000) = £2.14 \text{ per bat}$$

The fixed cost per bat using the 2002 data is:

$$£110{,}000 - (£2.14 \text{ per bat} \times 10{,}000 \text{ bats}) = £88{,}600$$

b The estimated costs of 14,000 bats are fixed costs of £88,600 plus variable costs of (£2.14 per bat × 14,000 bats), or £29,960. Therefore, total estimated costs are £88,600 + £29,960, or £118,560.

In this chapter, fixed and variable costs are defined as costs that are fixed or vary with the rate of output of an activity. These activities are the building blocks of the organization. An organization performs a variety of activities to provide products and services that create customer value. In Chapter 5, we will see that the cost of products and services also can be viewed through the framework of fixed and variable costs. Fixed costs are those costs that are incurred to start making units of the product or service. The variable cost per unit is the cost of making another unit of the product or service.

Concept **review**

1 How is account classification used to estimate fixed and variable costs?

2 How is the high-low method used to estimate fixed and variable costs?

Organizational **analysis**

Online securities trading with Barclays Brokers, E*Trade, Selftrade and TD Waterhouse

In 1986, deregulation of the UK securities market brought major changes to the City of London and the London Stock Exchange. The elimination of ownership restrictions resulted in the acquisition of many stock-exchange members by foreign and domestic financial firms. To maintain its status as a world leader in international finance, the City quickly focused on innovation and global talent to remain competitive. The 'Big Bang' of October 1986 also eliminated fixed minimum dealing commissions on securities trades. Before deregulation, minimum commissions on securities trades were set. Once free from regulation, brokers were free to set their own commission rates. The industry could now compete to add customer value through offering a low-cost service. Savvy investors and routine traders, who did not want the advice and research provided by the major brokerage firms, could now execute trades with much lower commission fees.

However, the largest impact on brokerage commissions came with the arrival of Internet trading to execute securities trades. Thanks to the Internet, firms began to compete more on price, frequently offering free trades or cash bonuses to lure clients. As well, brokerage houses now have global reach. Canada's TD Waterhouse uses its knowledge of discount brokerage to promote its services to traders who demand reliability, low commissions and the ability to maintain a well-diversified portfolio through access to its research services.

With Internet trading, new competitors have entered the marketplace. Two of these new market competitors, E*Trade and Selftrade, operate entirely online. Each company competes through service innovation by developing new methods of trading, accessing accounts and providing research online. Quality in terms of accurate trade execution and confidentiality is another way to add customer value. Differences in services and quality, however, are difficult to maintain because other companies can quickly duplicate these efforts. For example, Selftrade focuses on low, flat fees and its award-winning service; E*Trade points to its lower prices relative to its major competitors. Therefore, purely online brokerage houses compete extensively by offering low commissions on securities trades. Given low barriers to entry and the resulting increased competition, online trading provides traders with a low-cost way to buy and sell shares.

Barclays Stockbrokers, a division of Barclays Bank Group, is a full-service brokerage house. Barclays has been in the banking business for over 300 years with more than 100,000 employees in its global operations. Barclays Stockbrokers offers multiple services including estate planning, investment banking, foreign exchange trading, investment research, and trade execution. Online brokerage houses, however, are an alternative to its trading services, thus its entry into the online market enables the firm to retain customers who might switch from its full-service offerings to seek alternative services from competitors. Its online trading also builds on Barclays' early entry into online banking in 1997.

E*Trade, Selftrade, Barclays and TD Waterhouse all attempt to add customer value through different pricing strategies. E*Trade offers tiered pricing with the more trades executed per month, the lower the fixed fee per trade. Selftrade provides trade executions at a fixed fee for all trades, no matter the size or number. Barclays emphasizes the scope of its services (trade execution, financial advice, reports and banking privileges) with account structures matched to investor risk preferences and experience. TD Waterhouse seeks to compete through its superior customer service, user-friendly website and international brand awareness. Each of these strategies is designed to add value to different types of customers. Organizational value, however,

Carsten Reisinger/Alamy

Websites play a key role in information dissemination, be it e-trading, selecting a career or seeking volunteer opportunities, such as those available at TimeBank.

also must be achieved. As the market matures, market differentiation is increasingly important. Low cost is only one factor that customers consider and many are willing to change firms to take advantage of greater convenience, added services, special offers and incentives.

What variable and fixed cost structures for securities trade execution are likely to exist in these companies to be consistent with their market and pricing strategies?

How will the changes in the structure of commission fees affect the ability of both old and new competitors to implement a successful strategy in the long run?

Source: 'Advantage London, or back to deuce? How the big bang made a city boom', *The Independent* online edition, 20 October 2006; http://news.independent.co.uk/business/analysis_and_features/article1905002.ece, (accessed 3 February 2007). Websites: http://uk.etrade.com; www.selftrade.com; http://stockbrokers.barclays.co.uk; www.tdwaterhouse.co.uk

SUMMARY

1 Use differential costs and benefits to assist in cost-benefit analysis. Differential analysis identifies the costs and benefits that vary across alternative decisions. Only differential costs and benefits are relevant for decisions, as all other factors are the same for each possible decision.

2 Identify and measure opportunity costs for making planning decisions. Opportunity cost is defined in terms of alternative uses of a resource. The size of the forgone opportunity of using the resource is the measure of the opportunity cost.

3 Ignore sunk costs for making planning decisions. Sunk costs are costs that have already been incurred. Sunk costs are not relevant for planning decisions.

4 Use cost-benefit analysis to make information choices. More information should be gathered, if the benefit of improved decision making is greater than the cost of the information.

5 Determine how activity costs vary with the rate of output. The cost of the first few units of output of an activity tends to be quite high. At normal production levels, the cost of further units of output tends to be lower. When the activity nears capacity, the cost of additional units of output tends be higher.

6 Calculate marginal and average costs. The marginal cost is the cost of one more unit of output, which is the slope of the total cost curve. The average cost is the total cost of the activity divided by the number of units of output.

7 Approximate activity costs using variable and fixed costs. Approximating costs by fixed and variable costs assumes that there is a cost to initiate the activity, which is the fixed cost. Subsequent units of the activity output are assumed to cost the same amount per unit, which is the variable cost per unit.

8 Use account classification, the high-low and regression methods to estimate variable and fixed costs. The account classification method identifies fixed and variable costs by categorizing different cost accounts. The high-low and regression methods use historic outputs and costs to estimate fixed and variable costs.

KEY TERMS

Average cost The total costs of production divided by the number of units produced.

Capacity Measure of constraints on the operation of an organization.

Cost-benefit analysis The process of making decisions by comparing the costs and benefits of alternative choices.

Differential benefit The difference in benefits of two alternative decisions.

Differential cost The difference in costs of two alternative decisions.

Fixed cost The cost of initiating production, which does not vary with the number of units produced.

Marginal cost The additional cost of producing one more unit given a certain level of output.

Opportunity cost The forgone opportunity of using a resource for another purpose.

Relevant range The range of output levels over which variable costs are reasonable approximations of opportunity costs.

Sunk cost A cost that has already been incurred and cannot be changed.

Variable cost The variable cost per unit times the number of units produced.

Variable cost per unit The variable cost per unit is an approximation of the marginal cost using fixed and variable costs.

APPENDIX
Using regression to estimate fixed and variable costs

The high-low method described in the chapter is a method to estimate fixed and variable costs. The high-low method may result in poor estimates if the high and low points represent extreme or unusual levels of operating activity. Regression analysis is a statistical method of drawing a line that is more accurate. Regression analysis identifies a line that minimizes the summation of the squared deviations of all the historical cost data points from the regression line.

The following data from *Numerical example 2.11* is used to demonstrate fitting a line with regression analysis.

Year	Number of bats produced	Historical costs (£)
2002	10,000	110,000
2003	13,000	120,000
2004	11,000	105,000
2005	15,000	125,000
2006	17,000	125,000
2007	13,000	115,000
2008	16,000	130,000

These data are inputted into a computer program that performs regression analysis. The historical costs are the dependent variable or the variable to be estimated. The number of bats is the independent variable or the variable which will be used to estimate costs. The output of any regression software program looks like the following:

	Coefficient	Standard error of coefficient	t-ratio
Constant	75,611	9,161	8.25
Number of bats	3.165	0.6648	4.76
Adjusted R^2 = 0.783			

The estimate of the constant coefficient is an estimate of fixed costs equal to £75,611. The coefficient on the number of bats is the variable cost per bat equal to £3.165. The remaining information of the output provides indications of how well the regression line represents the historical costs for different levels of output.

The adjusted R^2 is a measure of how well the number of bats explains the costs. If all the plotted points in Figure 2.5 were aligned in a straight line, knowing the number of bats would determine the costs. If the regression line closely represents the cost data, then the adjusted R^2 approaches 1. The adjusted R^2 of 0.783 is quite high, indicating that the regression line is a close approximation of the historical cost data for different levels of output. An adjusted R^2 of 0 would indicate that no association exists between the number of bats and costs. An adjusted R^2 near zero also indicates that the measures of the variable cost per unit and the fixed costs are not very accurate.

Figure 2.5 **Estimating fixed and variable costs, Mighty Peg plc, 2002–2008**

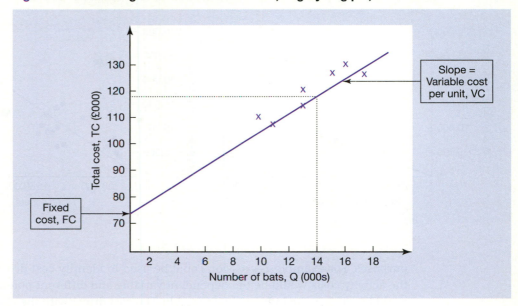

The standard errors of the coefficient indicate how confident we should be in the estimates of the fixed cost and variable cost per unit. In general, there is approximately a 95 per cent chance that the true fixed cost estimate and the true variable cost per unit is within 2 standard errors of their estimates. Therefore, there is a 95 per cent probability that the true fixed cost is within the range of £75,611 + (2 × £9,161), or £93,933, and £75,611 − (2 × £9,161), or £57,289. The variable cost per unit is within £3.165 + (2 × £0.6648), or £4.4946, and £3.165 − (2 × £0.6648), or £1.8354.

The *t*-ratio can be used to determine the probability that the fixed cost and variable cost per unit are different than 0. This information is not particularly useful in this situation, as we would expect those costs to be greater than 0.

The estimated fixed cost and per-unit variable cost allow for the estimation of costs given planned production. If planned production next year is 14,000 bats, the expected costs given the regression line are:

	£
Fixed costs	75,611
Variable costs (£3.165/bat × 14,000 bats)	44,310
Total estimated costs	£119,921

Although regression provides a more objective method of fitting historical cost data, it is susceptible to the same problems as the high-low method. In particular, regression assumes that the process that generated the historical costs is the same process that will be used in the estimation period.

Regression is only valid for estimating costs within production levels experienced in the past. For example, the previous range of bats produced was 10,000 to 17,000. Estimates of costs of producing more than 17,000 bats may be influenced by capacity constraints. Regression analysis, however, assumes that variable costs per unit are constant at all levels of output, and does not recognize capacity constraints. It also assumes that the relation between costs and levels of output is a straight line.

Due to these problems, regression analysis is not commonly used to estimate the fixed cost and the variable cost per unit. However regression could be used for other

Figure 2.6 Total costs of hiring personnel as a function of number of personnel and total assets

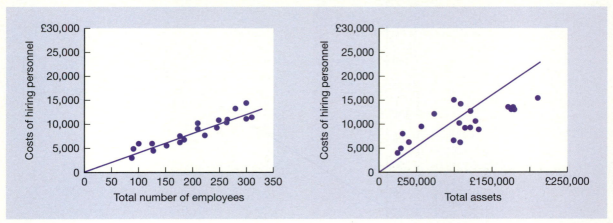

purposes. For example, regression could be used to identify cost drivers. In this case, the activity costs would be the dependent variable and different potential cost drivers could be tried as the independent variable. The cost driver with the closest association (highest R^2) with the activity cost would be the cost driver used by the organization for that activity. For example, Figure 2.6 provides graphs describing the relation between the costs of hiring personnel and two different possible cost drivers: total number of personnel and total assets. The total number of personnel is more closely associated with the cost of hiring personnel and has a higher adjusted R^2. Therefore, the total number of personnel provides a more accurate cost driver for tracing the indirect costs of hiring personnel to different cost objects.

Self-study problem 1

Identifying opportunity costs

In the US, athletics play a major role on many university campuses. At Western University (WU), athletic scholarships are a key mechanism in WU's strategy to attract star athletes. These scholarships average $15,000 per student annually. Due to budget cutbacks, the university administration believes that it can no longer afford them. The Athletics Department is arguing that the cost of dropping athletic scholarships will be high. Competitive teams are known to generate donor revenues and publicity. Without the scholarships, the athletic teams will not be competitive and WU might be dropped from the Big-17 Conference. This conference includes major university teams that attract as much interest as the premier teams in the country. Ticket revenues will drop by 10 to 20 per cent. Alumni will not provide as many donations. Currently, alumni give several million dollars per year to WU, and these funds help the university to offset cutbacks in government funding. Since many of the athletes are on partial scholarships, WU might also lose the remaining tuition. The average tuition fees are $25,000 per year. WU will get less media attention, especially in the sports pages of newspapers, on television and the Internet.

What are the benefits and opportunity costs of providing athletic scholarships?

Solution

The arguments of the Athletics Department reveal benefits of having athletic scholarships, especially as part of WU's strategy to attract star players. Competitive teams are one way to attract donors and publicity. These benefits, however, are difficult to measure. For example, donations and ticket revenues are likely to be higher with more competitive teams. Publicity will probably be higher, but the value of this publicity is difficult to measure. The value of being in an athletic conference depends on the quality of the other institutions in the league. Being in the premier league, for example, gives those institutions a certain amount of prestige, which is difficult to value. Athletes on partial scholarships also pay some tuition.

These benefits should be offset against the opportunity costs of having athletic scholarships. What are the forgone opportunities of providing scholarships? The opportunity cost of any cash payments to athletes for books, housing and food can be measured directly. However most of the scholarship is the waiving of tuition fees and providing free education to the athletes. The opportunity cost depends on whether providing free education to athletes prevents a tuition-paying student from attending WU. If the university is at capacity and the athlete takes the place of a tuition-paying student, the forgone opportunity is the lost tuition. In the case of WU, this amount is $25,000 per student. If WU is not at capacity, the forgone opportunity is the marginal cost (approximated by the variable cost) of educating an additional student. The variable cost of educating a student (additional materials, grading, etc.) might not be very high, as most costs at a university are fixed (such as faculty and staff salaries).

Self-study problem 2

Approximating opportunity costs with variable and fixed costs

Frank Choi, the president of Trace Products, understands product costs, but he feels that estimating opportunity costs for his gold ore processing plant is difficult. Instead, he tells his controller to worry only about fixed and variable costs. The controller estimates that the variable cost of processing gold ore is £1,000 per tonne of gold ore. The fixed costs are £50,000.

a What is the estimated cost of processing 60 tonnes of gold ore?
b What is the danger of approximating activity costs with variable and fixed costs?

Solution

a The estimated cost of processing 60 tonnes of gold ore is:

$$(60 \text{ tonnes} \times £1,000/\text{tonne}) + £50,000 = £110,000.$$

b The danger of estimating opportunity costs with variable and fixed costs is being outside the relevant range. In the relevant range, the estimates from variable and fixed costs should be fairly close to the opportunity cost. If output levels are extremely low or near capacity, however, the fixed and variable cost estimate tends to differ from the opportunity cost.

Numerical exercises

NE 2.1 Cost-benefit analysis and differential costs LO 1

The owner of a garden maintenance shop has a request for cutting and trimming a yard. If the owner does the job himself, he estimates that it will take 3 hours to complete. If he calls a temporary worker to do the job, it will take 4 hours to complete. In either case, the transportation costs and the wear on the machinery should cost £5 for the job. The owner values his time at £10 per hour and pays the temporary worker £6 per hour.

Should the owner do the job himself or have a temporary worker do the job?

NE 2.2 Identifying opportunity costs and avoiding sunk costs LO 2, 3

Raw materials on hand originally cost £4 per pound. They can be replaced for £6 per pound, and can be sold for £5 per pound.

a What is the opportunity cost of using the raw materials if they will not be replaced?
b What is the opportunity cost of using the raw materials if they can also be used in another product?

NE 2.3 Identifying opportunity costs LO 2

What is the opportunity cost of an employee's time if she is paid £12/hour, cannot be replaced and could be generating £4 of profit on another project?

NE 2.4 Opportunity costs and rates of output LO 5, 6

Determine marginal and average costs for the following data. Also identify start-up costs and capacity constraints.

Number of units	Total costs (£)
1	25
2	40
3	52
4	62
5	72
6	82
7	100
8	130

NE 2.5 Approximating activity costs LO 7

The fixed cost of trucking a load of potatoes is £50. The variable cost is £0.50 per kilometre. How much is the estimated cost of trucking a load of potatoes 500 kilometres?

NE 2.6 Fixed and variable costs LO 7

An Italian ski manufacturer has determined that the fixed cost of making slalom skis is €1,000,000 and the variable cost is €100 per pair of skis. During normal operations the firm plans to make 20,000 pairs of skis.

a What is the expected cost of making 20,000 pairs of skis?
b What are the expected costs of making 30,000 pairs of skis using the fixed and variable costs?
c Why might the variable and fixed costs be poor predictors of costs when 30,000 pairs of skis are made?

NE 2.7 Fixed, variable and average costs LO 6, 7

Midlands University is trying to decide whether to allow 100 more students into the university. Tuition is £5,000 per year. The director of finance has determined the following schedule of costs to educate students:

Number of students	Total costs (£)
4,000	30,000,000
4,100	30,300,000
4,200	30,600,000
4,300	30,900,000

The current enrolment is 4,200 students. The vice-chancellor of the university has calculated the cost per student in the following manner: £30,600,000/4,200 students = £7,286 per student. The vice-chancellor was wondering whether Midlands should accept more students if the tuition is only £5,000.

a What is wrong with the vice-chancellor's calculation?
b What are the fixed and variable costs of operating Midlands University?

NE 2.8 Fixed and variable costs LO 7

Chen Industries is planning to build a computer chip factory to make 10,000 chips per month. The company has two different options in manufacturing the chips. A CAM approach will cause fixed costs to be equal to £1,000,000 per month and variable costs of £20 per chip. A more manual approach will cause fixed costs of £500,000 per month and variable costs of £50 per chip.

Which method should the company use to minimize costs?

NE 2.9 Opportunity costs LO 2, 3

Emily Stewart must decide whether to repair a fence around her garden or pay someone £300 to do it for her. If Emily repairs the fence, she could use some leftover fencing materials from a previous job. Those materials cost £60, but she cannot sell them and has no other use for them. In addition she would have to buy additional materials that would cost £100. Emily estimates that she would spend 15 hours purchasing the materials and repairing the fence. If she did not do the repairs herself, she could spend the time playing tennis. She values her tennis-playing time at £10 per hour.

Should Emily make the fence or pay someone else to do it for her?

NE 2.10 Opportunity costs LO 2

Ken Morrow is returning from a thrilling accounting class. As he passes the student union building, he thinks about visiting the video games lounge. For £5 he could play the video games for 1 hour. The best alternative to playing video games is to study for his accounting exam. One more hour of studying should raise his grade from a B+ to an A−. The higher grade would give Ken an opportunity to get a higher paying job. Ken estimates that the higher grade is worth about £200 in job opportunities.

What is the opportunity cost of playing the video games for an hour?

NE 2.11 Variable and fixed costs LO 7

The school newspaper editor estimates that the fixed cost of an edition is £5,000. The variable cost is 3p per copy.

a What is the projected cost of an edition if 3,000 copies are produced?
b What is the projected cost of an edition if 5,000 copies are produced?

Numerical problems

NP 2.1 Differential costs and revenues LO 1

A grocery retailer is deciding how to use a particular space in the store. One option is to lease a freezer to put in the space and sell a variety of ice cream treats. The ice cream treats should generate annual revenues of £10,000 but will reduce revenues from other ice cream sales by £2,000 annually. The freezer leases for £1,000 per year, the electricity for the freezer should cost £500 per year, and the cost of the ice cream treats will be £5,000 per year. The other option is to rent shelving for £500 per year and sell artisan bakery goods from a local bakery. The revenues from the bakery items should be £7,000 per year and their cost should be £3,000. Selling the artisan bakery goods should not cause any other loss of revenue. Other costs are the same for the two options.

What should the grocery retailer do with the space?

NP 2.2 Differential, variable and fixed costs LO 1, 7

Darien Industries operates a cafeteria for its employees. The operation of the cafeteria requires fixed costs of £4,700 per month and variable costs of 40 per cent of sales. Cafeteria sales are currently averaging £12,000 per month.

Darien has an opportunity to replace the cafeteria with vending machines. Gross customer spending at the vending machines is estimated to be 40 per cent greater than current sales, because the machines are available at all hours. By replacing the cafeteria with vending machines, Darien would receive 16 per cent of the gross customer spending and avoid all cafeteria costs.

A decision by Darien Industries to replace the cafeteria with vending machines will result in a monthly increase (decrease) in operating income of how much?

(CMA adapted)

NP 2.3 Differential costs and revenues LO 1

A hardware store is considering opening on Sunday. The differential cost of paying for salespeople and utilities is £1,000 per Sunday. Sales on Sunday are expected to be £10,000. The sales price of an item is determined by taking the purchase price of the item and adding 20 per cent.

a If sales on Sunday do not affect sales the rest of the week, should the hardware store open on Sundays if the goal is to increase profit?
b Should the hardware store open on Sundays, if 60 per cent of the sales on Sundays would have occurred on other days of the week at the hardware store?

NP 2.4 Opportunity cost of space LO 2

JP Max is a department store carrying a large and varied stock of merchandise. Management is considering leasing part of its floor space for £72 per square metre per year to an outside jewellery company that would sell merchandise. Two areas are being considered: home furnishings which occupies 1,000 square metres and electronics which occupies 1,200 metres. These departments have annual profits of £64,000 for home furnishings and £82,000 for electronics.

Considering all the relevant factors, which department should be leased and why?

NP 2.5 Opportunity cost of using materials LO 2, 3

Emrich Processing is a small processor of custom stainless-steel parts. Customers send new and used stainless-steel parts to Emrich for cleaning in various acid baths to remove small imperfections or films on the surface. These parts are used in a variety of applications, ranging from nuclear reactors to chemical and medical applications. Depending on the foreign substance to be removed, Emrich chooses the acid-bath mixture and process.

Such chemical cleaning operations require highly skilled technicians to handle the dangerous acids. Regulations of the Environment Agency (EA) and the Health and Safety Executive (HSE) are closely followed. Treatment of the part with other chemicals in the proper chemical bath results in a benign waste solution. This waste solution can be disposed of via the city sewer system.

On 12 May, Emrich ordered a 50-litre drum of a specialty acid known as GX-100 for use in a 15 May job. It used 25 of the 50 litres in the drum. The 50 litres cost £1,000. GX-100 has a shelf life of 30 days after the drum is opened, before it becomes unstable and must be discarded. Due to the hazardous nature of GX-100 and the other chemicals that Emrich uses, it works closely with Environ Disposal, a company specializing in the disposal of hazardous wastes. At the time of ordering the GX-100, Emrich anticipated no other orders in the May–June time period that could use the remaining 25 litres of GX-100. Knowing it would have 25 litres remaining, it built £1,000 into the cost of the job to cover the cost of the GX-100 plus an additional £400 to cover the cost of having Environ dispose of the remaining 25 litres.

On 1 June, a customer called and asked for a price bid for a rush job to be completed on 5 June. This job will use 25 litres of GX-100. Emrich is preparing to bid on this order.

What cost amount for the GX-100 must be considered in preparing the bid? Justify your answer.

NP 2.6 Opportunity cost of using display space LO 2

Home Auto Parts is a large retail auto-parts store selling the full range of auto parts and supplies for do-it-yourself auto-repair enthusiasts. Annual store sales are £5 million. The store is arranged such that there are three prime displays in the store: front door, checkout counters and end-of-aisles. These display areas receive the most customer traffic and contain special stands that display the merchandise with attractive eye-catching posters. Each display area is set up at the beginning of the week and runs for one week. Three items are scheduled next week for special display areas: Ensea Oil, windshield wiper blades and floor mats. The table below provides information for the three promotional areas scheduled to run next week:

Planned displays for next week

Item	End-of-aisles Ensea Oil	Front door Wiper blades	Cash register Floor mats
Sales price	69p/can	£9.99	£22.99
Projected weekly volume	5,000	200	70
Unit cost	62p	£7.99	£17.49

Based on past experience, management finds that virtually all display-area sales are made by impulse buyers. To increase customer traffic to the store, the special display items are not advertised. The display items purchased do not reduce the sales of similar items in the store, because people attracted to the displays did not enter the store to buy these items. The display items are extra purchases by consumers attracted by the exhibits.

After the above table is prepared, but before the store manager sets up the display areas, the distributor for Armadillo car wax visits the store. She says her firm wants its car wax in one of the three display areas and is prepared to offer the product at a unit cost of £2.50. At a retail price of £2.90, management expects to sell 800 units during the week if the wax is on special display.

a Home Auto has not yet purchased any of the promotion items for next week. Should management substitute the Armadillo car wax for one of the three planned promotion displays? If so, which one?

b A common practice in retailing is for the manufacturer to give free units to a retail store to secure desirable promotion space or shelf space. The Armadillo distributor decides to sweeten the offer by giving Home Auto 50 free units of car wax, if it places the Armadillo wax on display. Does your answer to question **a** change?

NP 2.7 Opportunity cost of time LO 2

The Indo Corporation is considering leasing a private jet to fly between the corporate offices in Copenhagen, Denmark and the firm's main plant in Lisbon, Portugal. The commercial carrier has one flight leaving Copenhagen each morning and one returning flight departing Lisbon in the afternoon. Ten executives take this seven-hour (one-way) trip every day and 10 make the return flight each day. A recent study showed that business travellers are unable to work while travelling. The average salary (including fringe benefits) of an executive is €200,000. On average, they work 2,500 hours per year. Round-trip airfare on the commercial carrier averages €500.

Two alternative private jets are available for leasing. The following table summarizes various operating statistics for the two jets:

Model	Number of seats	One-way flight time (hrs)	Total daily operating cost (€)
Lx-0100	10	6	5,100
Lx-0200	7	4	5,200

The leased plane will duplicate the existing commercial carrier's scheduled departure times. The Lx-0200 cannot make more than one round trip a day.

Which alternative air transportation should the firm undertake? (Show calculations.)

NP 2.8 Marginal and average costs LO 5, 6

Allan Brothers Company has designed a machine for sorting tomatoes. The machine is able to detect bruises on a tomato. Bruised tomatoes are used for making tomato sauce. The tomatoes without defects are shipped to grocery stores. Managers at Allan Brothers are uncertain of the demand for these sorting machines, but have estimated the following opportunity costs of making different numbers of the machines:

Number	Total costs (£)
1	100,000
2	150,000
3	190,000
4	220,000
5	250,000
6	280,000
7	340,000
8	400,000
9	500,000

a Prepare a table showing how the marginal cost of sorting machines varies with the number of machines manufactured.
b Why does the marginal cost increase after six machines?
c What is the average cost of making five sorting machines?
d If the sorting machines can be sold for £70,000, how many machines should be produced?

NP 2.9 Cost behaviour patterns LO 5

For each question below, draw a graph that depicts how costs vary with volume. Completely label each graph and axis.

a The Medford plant operates 40 hours per week. Management can vary the number of workers. Currently, the plant has 200 workers being paid a rate of £10 per hour. The plant is near capacity. To increase output, a second shift of 40 hours per week is being considered. To attract workers to the second shift, a 20 per cent wage premium will be offered. Plot total labour costs as a function of labour hours per week.
b The Bristol plant has a contract with the Northern Gas Company to purchase up to 150 million cubic metres of natural gas monthly for a flat fee of £1.5 million. Additional gas can be purchased for £0.0175 per cubic metre. The Bristol plant manufactures aluminum cans. One thousand cans require 10 cubic metres of gas. Plot total gas costs as a function of can production.

NP 2.10 Variable and fixed costs LO 7

The MedView brochure refers to a new radiology imaging system that MedView rents to private clinics for £18,000 per month. A 'scan' refers to one imaging session that is billed to patients at £475 per scan. Each scan requires that the patient receive a chemical injection, and exposing and developing an X-ray negative. MedView claims that 45 scans per month are sufficient to cover the cost of renting the machine plus any additional variable costs.

What variable cost per scan is MedView assuming in calculating the 45 scans per month amount?

NP 2.11 Opportunity costs LO 2, 3

Trinity Church has been asked to operate a homeless shelter in its parish hall. To operate a homeless shelter, the church would have to hire a full-time employee for £1,200 per month to manage the shelter. In addition, the church would have to purchase £400 of supplies per month for the people using the shelter. The space that would be used by the shelter is rented on occasion for wedding parties. The church averages about 5 wedding parties per month at a rental fee of £200 per party. Utilities are normally £1,000 per month. With the homeless shelter, the utilities will increase to £1,300 per month.

What is the opportunity cost to the church of operating a homeless shelter in the parish hall?

NP 2.12 Average, variable and fixed costs LO 6, 7

A university has 5,000 students, but a capacity of 6,000 students. The fixed cost of operating the school is £1,000,000 per month. The variable cost is £100 per student per month.

a What is the average cost per student of operating the university given 5,000 students?
b What is the cost of adding 50 more students?

NP 2.13 Average, variable and fixed costs LO 6, 7

A soccer ball manufacturer plans to make 100,000 balls per year. The following annual costs are estimated:

	£
Utilities	10,000
Machines	50,000
Administration	100,000
Marketing	120,000
Labour	200,000
Materials	150,000
Total	630,000

Labour and materials are variable costs and the remaining costs are fixed.

a What are the annual fixed costs of making soccer balls?
b What is the variable cost per soccer ball?
c What is the average cost per ball?
d If the manufacturer is operating normally and not near capacity, what is the expected cost of making 1,000 more balls?

NP 2.14 Fixed and variable costs LO 7

Oxcam University has been asked to host a professional rugby game at the campus playing field. The athletic director must estimate the opportunity cost of holding the event at the university. The only other sporting event scheduled for the university that evening is a fencing match that would not have generated any additional costs or revenues. The fencing match can be held at the local high school, but the rental cost of the school gymnasium would be £200. The athletic director estimates that the professional rugby game will require 20 hours of labour to prepare the field. Clean-up depends on the number of spectators. The athletic director estimates the time of clean-up to be equal to 2 minutes per spectator. The labour would be hired especially for the rugby game and would cost £8 per hour. Utilities will be £500 greater if the rugby game is held at the playing field. The professional rugby team would cover all other costs.

a What is the variable cost of having one more spectator?
b What is the opportunity cost of allowing the professional rugby team to use the playing field if 10,000 spectators are expected?
c What is the opportunity cost of allowing the professional rugby team to use the playing field if 12,000 spectators are expected?

NP 2.15 Estimating with fixed and variable costs LO 7

Based on the last few years of operations (when he made between 1,000 and 15,000 units), Will Jones calculated that the fixed cost of making his sole product is £400,000 and the variable cost per unit is £200.

a If Jones expects to make 18,000 units, what is his expected cost in the next year using the fixed and variable costs?
b What are two dangers of using the fixed and per-unit variable cost, as calculated, to estimate next year's costs?

NP 2.16 Estimating variable and fixed costs through account classification LO 8

Beadco Company sells necklaces of beads and is trying to determine the costs of working with each supplier. One supplier of ceramic beads operates in Kenya. During the year, the supplier is expected to sell Beadco 1,000,000 beads at a cost of £0.10/bead. The year's supply of beads is normally sent in a container, which costs £5,000 to ship to the company in Liverpool. With 1,000,000 beads, the container is only half full. There would be no additional freight charges if the container were full. To make the order with the Kenyan company, Beadco must send a purchasing agent to Kenya. The cost of the trip including the salary of the purchasing agent is £10,000. The processing of the purchase order also requires the use 20 hours of personnel time, which includes time spent by the accountant and the treasurer. The average cost per hour for these personnel is £50. When the beads arrive, each bead must be inspected for quality and breakage. An inspector who is paid £20/hour can inspect 1,000 beads per hour.

a What is the fixed cost per bead of working with the Kenyan supplier if 1,000,000 beads are purchased?
b What is the variable cost per bead purchased from the Kenyan supplier?
c If 1,500,000 beads were purchased, what would be the total costs of purchasing from the Kenyan supplier?

NP 2.17 Identifying variable and fixed costs using the high-low method LO 8

A Belgian manufacturer of tennis balls is noted for making all its tennis balls exactly the same. The manufacturer, however, is less certain about its costs. It has not changed its operating methods in the past ten years, and the cost of labour and raw materials has remained about the same. The manufacturer has had the following costs and output during the past ten financial years:

Year	Costs (€m)	Number of balls (m)
1999	20	50
2000	25	75
2001	30	105
2002	28	100
2003	32	110
2004	23	80
2005	35	120
2006	31	115
2007	36	118
2008	22	90

Plot this data.

a Identify the highest and lowest output levels.
b Using the high-low method, estimate the fixed costs of making tennis balls.
c What are the variable costs per ball?
d If the manufacturer expects to make 112 million balls, what are the expected costs in the coming year?
e Why would it be more difficult to estimate the expected costs, if the manufacturer expects to make 150 million balls?

NP 2.18 Using regression to estimate fixed and variable costs LO 8

Use the data in NP 2.17. Estimate the fixed and variable costs per unit.

NP 2.19 Estimating sales LO 4, 7

A Christmas tree retailer is trying to estimate demand for Christmas trees before ordering inventory for the season. The trees are purchased from the supplier for £10 and sold for £25. Fixed costs of operating the Christmas tree lot are £100. Based on prior experience, the Christmas tree retailer estimates that there is a 0.5 probability that 80 trees can be sold and a 0.5 probability that 100 trees can be sold. Any unsold trees must be discarded at a cost of £2 each.

a Should the retailer order 80 or 100 trees to maximize the expected profit?
b How would a survey that provides more precise demand for Christmas trees add value to the retailer?

NP 2.20 Changing variable costs with rate of output LO 5, 7

Air Bus Manufacturing estimates that the variable cost per unit of making 5 or less buses per month is €150,000 per bus. The variable cost per unit of making 6 to 25 buses per month is €100,000. Also, the variable cost per unit of making more than 25 buses per month is €200,000. There are no fixed costs using this method of analysing costs.

a How does each level of output relate to the concepts of start-up costs and capacity?
b What is the estimate of fixed costs at the normal level of operations?

Analysis and interpretation problems

AIP 2.1 Variable and fixed costs LO 7

Fast Lab operates four X-ray film-developing labs in central London. The four labs are identical: They employ the same production technology, process the same mix of films, and buy raw materials from the same companies at the same prices. Wage rates are also the same at the four labs. In reviewing operating results for November, the newly hired assistant controller, Matt Paige, became quite confused over the numbers:

	Lab A	Lab B	Lab C	Lab D
Number of rolls processed	50,000	55,000	60,000	65,000
Revenue (£000s)	£500	£550	£600	£650
Less:				
Variable costs	(195)	(242)	(298)	(352)
Fixed costs	(300)	(300)	(300)	(300)
Profit (Loss)	£5	£8	£2	(£2)

Upon further study, Matt learned that each plant had fixed overhead of £300,000. Matt remembered from his management accounting class that as volume increases, average fixed cost per unit falls. Lab D had much lower average fixed costs per roll than labs A and B. Matt, therefore, expected lab D to be more profitable than A and B. But the numbers show just the opposite.

Write a concise but clear memo to Matt that will resolve his confusion.

AIP 2.2 Opportunity costs and executive share options LO 2

A large public accounting firm, reporting findings of a survey on corporate directors' compensation, remarked, 'Since there are usually greater growth rates in smaller companies, share options offer directors a good chance at investment appreciation at no cost to the company.'

A share option has the following characteristic. Suppose one three-year share option is granted to a director at today's share price of £10. Then, at any time over the next three years, the director can buy one share from the company at £10. If next year the share price rises to £14, the director can exercise the option by paying £10 to the company and receiving one share. The share then can be sold in the market for £14, thereby realizing a £4 gain.

Critically evaluate the *quoted* sentence.

AIP 2.3 Opportunity cost of using inventory LO 2

Increased demand, security fears, depleted oil reserves and production cut-backs all contributed to an increase in the world price of crude oil to record levels. In 2006, for example, the market price reached $74 per barrel for UK-traded Brent crude. This increase was a threefold gain in three years and an 18 per cent increase during the year. The average market price in 2002 had been just $25 per barrel.

At one point after a quick surge in the price of crude, the major oil companies raised the retail price of refined oil products, even though these products were manufactured from oil purchased at the earlier, lower prices. The media charged the oil companies with profiteering and price gouging. Quick to respond, outraged politicians promised immediate investigations.

Critically evaluate the charge that the major oil companies profited from the rapid increase in the market price. What advice would you offer their management?

AIP 2.4 Differential costs of a new product LO 1

Indurin Company manufactures Syndex, a popular drug for headaches. Recently, Indurin has been subject to increased competitive pressure as other pharmaceutical firms have developed and marketed new products. The chief executive of Indurin is considering the introduction of Syndex Plus. Syndex Plus will be a new drug targeted to consumers who prefer extra-strength medications. He wants a prediction of the additional profit that this new drug will generate. In his management accounting course, he learned that he should compare incremental revenues with incremental costs. He has determined that the total expected sales of Syndex Plus equals incremental revenues, as there were no previous sales of Syndex Plus. The incremental costs are the additional costs necessary to make Syndex Plus. Extra space and labour are available; therefore these costs are expected to be very low.

When asked to compute the expected costs, the finance director asked, 'What about the effect of introducing Syndex Plus on the sales of Syndex?' The chief executive replied, 'Irrelevant! The decision to introduce a new product should only be based on a comparison of incremental costs and revenues.'

Evaluate the chief executive's decision rule.

AIP 2.5 Opportunity cost of attracting industry LO 2

The Itagi Computer Company based in Japan is looking to build a CD-ROM manufacturing facility in Europe. Itagi Computer is concerned about the safety and well-being of its employees and wants to locate in a community with good schools. The company also wants the manufacturing plant to be profitable and is looking for subsidies from potential communities. Subsidies are often an effective way to entice new businesses to locate in the region and create jobs for citizens. Many communities, especially those with high unemployment, use this strategic incentive.

Bienville has not been very well since the shoe factory closed due to intense competition from imports. City officials have been working on a deal to encourage Itagi to locate in Bienville. Itagi officials have identified a 20-hectare undeveloped site. The city has agreed tentatively to buy the site for Itagi at a cost of €50,000. Also, the city will not require Itagi to pay any property taxes on the factory for the first five years of operation. The property-tax deal will save Itagi €3,000,000 in taxes over the five years. This deal was leaked to the local newspaper. The headlines the next day were: 'Bienville Gives Away €3,000,000+ to Japanese Company'.

a Do the headlines accurately describe the deal with Itagi?
b What are the relevant costs and benefits to the citizens of Bienville of making this deal?

AIP 2.6 Opportunity cost of using military forces LO 2, 3

The National Audit Office has costed recent peacekeeping and military operations by the UK military in other countries. The calculation is based on the cost of paying and supplying personnel, movement of material and personnel to the problem area, depreciation on equipment, and armaments used. Newspaper accounts indicated that some of these actions provided training for personnel and the acquisition of new high-tech equipment. These articles also questioned if military spending in areas where no domestic threat existed could not have been allocated more usefully to international development or climate change.

How would you calculate the opportunity cost of using military forces?

AIP 2.7 Historical costs approximating opportunity costs LO 2

Maverick Productions organizes rock concerts. Last year, the company rented the local sports grounds for a rock concert that included the Rolling Rocks. The concert was a big success and Maverick Productions made £10,000 on the concert. This year, Maverick Productions is planning to bring the Rolling Rocks back to town for another concert. The company plans to rent the professional soccer stadium, which is larger, but it still plans to use the same ticket agency and vendors. Maverick Productions has detailed accounting records of the revenues and costs of the previous Rolling Rocks concert and would like to use these accounting records to make plans for the concert this year.

a What are some of the advantages and disadvantages of using the past concert accounting records to make estimates of the costs and benefits of the concert this year?
b Are there ways of adjusting the past accounting records to make them better predictors of costs and benefits?

AIP 2.8 Cost-benefit analysis of information LO 4

A DVD manufacturer feels that he needs better information on the quality of DVDs that the plant is producing. He is considering purchasing a scanning machine that would identify defects in the DVD as it is being produced. The scanner would have to be operated full time by an employee.

What factors should the manufacturer consider in determining the costs and benefits of the scanning machine?

AIP 2.9 Classifying costs as fixed and variable LO 7

The city water department is responsible for supplying water to the city. Water is pumped from deep wells to reservoirs, chlorine is added, and the water is piped to the different customers in the city. The pumps only operate when the reservoirs decline to a certain level. The reservoirs are located on the highest part of the city, so gravity can be used to establish water pressure for the city users. Pipes will frequently break due to age, so the city water department maintains a maintenance department. The water department has the following accounts to record costs:

Maintenance	Billing and collection
Power (for the pumps)	Salaries of top managers
Rent	Chemicals

If litres of water consumed by the city are treated as the output of the water department, describe each of the accounts as either fixed or variable. How would you describe each of these accounts if customer services or production activities were used instead?

AIP 2.10 Identifying processes performed by an organization LO 2, 4

The Department of Accounting of the University of New North Wales is responsible for teaching the accounting classes at the university. The accounting department is analysing what it does. The purpose of the analysis is to operate more efficiently and allocate responsibilities among the professors. The accounting department is also thinking about hiring an administrator to perform certain activities that do not require the specific skills of the professors.

a What are the general activities performed by an accounting department?
b What activities could an administrator perform instead of a professor?
c How could the costs of the different activities be measured?

AIP 2.11 Estimating costs using past data LO 8

A business consulting firm recently has begun to construct interactive web pages for 10 of its clients. The consulting firm foresees considerable future demand for website and web page construction, but is uncertain whether it can compete in this area. To compete successfully, the consulting firm must be a low cost producer of these sites. The firm decides to gather extensive cost data for each of the 10 jobs that it has already completed. The firm also knows the number of web pages produced for each client.

a How can you use regression to estimate variable and fixed costs of constructing web pages?
b What insights about how the firm can compete in the construction of web pages do estimates of the variable and fixed costs provide?
c What problems exist in using the data to estimate variable and fixed costs?

AIP 2.12 Estimating costs with varying levels of output LO 5, 6

The Fantastic Software Company offers customer support to users of its software via the telephone and on line. The telephone service is located in one room, with space and telephone lines for 5 service representatives who provide advice and technical support over the telephone. Each representative can handle up to 20 calls per day.

a Describe the cost structure of the customer-support activity, if the measure of output is calls handled per day.
b What is the nature of the marginal costs?

AIP 2.13 University tuition benefits LO 2

The following is from a *Wall Street Journal* article:

> Joseph Mercurio has two children at Boston University, which now charges $21,970 per year for tuition. But he doesn't worry about the cost, because his employer picks up the tab.
>
> That perquisite is even better than it first appears, because it is tax-free. He estimates he would have to earn $80,000 in pretax income to cover his kids' tuition. 'It's a benefit of enormous value to me,' he says.
>
> . . . So how does he get such an unusual perk? He is executive vice president at Boston University, one of hundreds of colleges and universities that subsidize the cost of education for employees' children, and sometimes spouses.
>
> Colleges have long argued they need the benefit to retain and recruit valuable employees who might otherwise be lured to competing institutions or more lucrative jobs in the private sector.
>
> . . . It cost the University of Pennsylvania $7 million last year to send employees' children to Penn and other schools. For Stanford University, the bill is at least $4.5 million, up from $3.5 million four years ago.
>
> . . . some schools are now discussing cuts in their benefit programs.

. . . To make up an expected $1 million annual decline in federal subsidies, Case Western recently cut its tuition benefit for employee children who attend its graduate schools to 50% from 100%.'

Source: Steve Stecklow, 'How Can You Beat High Cost of College? Become a Professor', *Wall Street Journal*, 15 April 1997, p. A1. Reprinted with permission of *The Wall Street Journal*, Copyright © 2008 Dow Jones & Company, Inc. All Rights Reserved Worldwide.

a Critically evaluate the statement, 'It cost the University of Pennsylvania $7 million last year to send employees' children to Penn and other schools.'

b Do you think that Case Western made a wise decision to cut its tuition benefits for employee children?

Extended **analysis** and **interpretation** problem

AIP 2.14 Opportunity costs

Alex MacDonald was saddened when he heard of the death of his uncle, but was shocked when he heard that he had inherited a 1,000 acre farm, Ullapool Pasture, located in the Scottish highlands. The farm currently has a house, out-buildings to house hired help and a barn. The inheritance also includes 500 head of sheep. When Alex arrives in Scotland to check on his inheritance, he finds the buildings and fences in need of repair. The manager of the farm greets Alex with a handshake and the financial statements from the end of the most recent financial year, which was about three months ago. The accounting report includes only a balance sheet and a profit and loss statement:

Ullapool Pasture
Balance Sheet
31/12/08

Assets		*Liabilities*	
Cash	£2,000	Mortgage	£200,000
Equipment	100,000		
Buildings	184,000	*Owner's equity*	
Accumulated depreciation	(52,000)	Owner's share	34,000
Total assets	£234,000	Total liabilities and equities	£234,000

Ullapool Pasture
Profit and Loss Statement
for the year 2008

Sale of sheep	£50,000
Cost of supplies	(10,000)
Manager's salary	(15,000)
Depreciation	(10,000)
Interest on mortgage	(20,000)
Net loss	(£5,000)

Alex looks a little worried after seeing the financial statements. He is relieved, however, when he notices that the sheep were not on the balance sheet. 'Well, at least there is some additional value on this farm that is not recorded in the financial statements,' he says.

The manager replies, 'We decided not to report the sheep as an asset because the number varies throughout the year and we're never sure exactly how many sheep are out there. I'd like to keep working for you, but my feeling is that you should sell this place. A neighbour is willing to buy the place for £300,000. I think it is a good offer and you should accept it.'

Alex is reluctant to accept the offer without further investigating the operations of Ullapool Pasture.

a How does the offer to buy Ullapool Pasture provide a benchmark for Alex?
b How should Alex use the balance sheet and profit and loss statement to value Ullapool Pasture?
c If Alex decides to continue operating Ullapool Pasture as a sheep farm, how should he decide on the appropriate number of sheep to raise?

CHAPTER THREE

Measuring and analysing product costs

(Planning)

Learning objectives

1. Identify activities of the organization related to the different products and services of the organization.

2. Treat products as cost objects for the purpose of making product-mix and pricing decisions.

3. Estimate the direct costs of a product or service.

4. Identify different levels of indirect product costs.

5. Trace indirect product costs using a cost driver.

6. Use activity-based costing to estimate the cost of a product or service.

7. Recognize costs and benefits of using activity-based costing.

8. Estimate product costs using a single cost driver.

Bended Knee Skateboards

Bended Knee Skateboards has been operating for five years. The company has two products: a flat skateboard sold to large discount chains and a moulded skateboard sold to specialty shops. Bended Knee has been successful in recent years with the popularity of skateboarding, but its management must make some decisions about changing the products manufactured, the prices of products, the manufacturing processes, suppliers and customers.

A skateboard is constructed much like plywood. Thin layers of wood veneer are glued together with the grain of the wood of adjacent layers going in opposite directions. This alternating pattern gives the skateboard strength and some flexibility. The layers of wood veneer of the flat skateboard are glued and squeezed together using a flat press. Ten flat skateboards can be pressed at once, so the flat skateboards are normally produced in batches of 10. The moulded skateboards are pressed in individual moulds. Because there are five moulds, the moulded skateboards are made in batches of five. The moulded skateboards also have a layer of plastic glued to the bottom of the skateboard to allow the skateboard to slide when the rounded bottom comes in contact with rough surfaces. Both types of skateboards use the same polyurethane wheels and axle assemblies, which are purchased from another company and attached at Bended Knee Skateboards. The flat skateboards are painted with a single colour, while the moulded skateboards are multi-coloured with a variety of designs.

Bended Knee Skateboards is owned by Geoff Williams, who also manages the company and designs new products. Geoff has hired four managers for the following departments: administration, purchasing, production and marketing. The cost accounting system has separate accounts for the cost of operating each of the departments and the cost of materials and labour used to make the skateboards. Geoff has projected the following costs for next year given the assumption that 50,000 flat skateboards and 5,000 moulded skateboards will be produced and sold:

	£
Materials	60,000
Labour	300,000
Administrative	90,000
Purchasing	50,000
Production (excluding labour and materials)	210,000
Marketing	100,000
Total expected costs	810,000

Bended Knee Skateboards has competitors making similar skateboards. They sell flat skateboards to large discount stores for £15 and moulded skateboards to specialty shops for £25. Projected revenues for Bended Knee Skateboards at those prices are:

	£
Flat skateboards: (50,000 units at £15/unit)	750,000
Moulded skateboards: (5,000 units at £25/unit)	125,000
Total expected revenues	875,000

ACTIVITIES AND PRODUCT COSTS

Organizations are composed of a variety of activities. These activities are the building blocks of an organization's effort to provide products and services. In deciding which products and services to offer, managers also must decide on the series of activities necessary to provide those products and services. For example, manufacturing organizations must make decisions on design, engineering, acquisition of raw materials, personnel, manufacturing processes, inventory warehousing, transportation, marketing and customer service.

Activities consume resources, such as materials and employee time, and, therefore, cause costs. Since activities create the products or services that an organization provides, activity costs are the basis for estimating product costs. For example, digital scanning of court documents is an activity in a law office that is part of the cost of providing legal services.

A simple approach to estimating a product's cost is to aggregate all of the activity costs associated with that particular product. A problem arises, however, when an activity supports multiple products. For example, the janitorial services in a manufacturing plant support all of the products made in the plant. To estimate the individual product costs, some method for dividing activity costs among the products that the activity supports must be used. This chapter describes methods of tracing activity costs into product costs. Product-cost information is important for making planning decisions. Before we consider methods of tracing activity costs into product costs, we examine how product costs are used for making product-mix and pricing decisions.

ESTIMATING PRODUCT COSTS FOR PLANNING DECISIONS

In making planning decisions, the costs and benefits of different decisions must be estimated. For example, the decision to purchase a computer network for an organization is based on the estimated costs and benefits associated with each possible network system. The comparison of estimated costs with estimated benefits helps managers identify the best choice for the organization. Management accounting assists in this process through estimating the benefits and costs associated with each decision.

The first step in the cost estimation process is to decide what item of the organization to cost. The item to be costed, called the **cost object**, depends on the decision being made. The primary cost objects described in this chapter are the products or services provided by the organization. But cost objects also may include sub-units of the organization, customers, suppliers and time periods. Each of these cost objects is related to different planning decisions. The cost of using suppliers and the cost of customers are described in the next chapter. The cost of sub-units in organizations is important in evaluating managers of the sub-unit and is discussed in Chapter 7. Cost associated with a time period is a subject covered in financial accounting.

The cost of using resources to provide a product or service is called the **product or service cost**. For example, the cost of developing, writing and producing a computer game is the product cost of the computer game. The computer game is the cost object. For simplification, the term 'product cost' is used in this book for both product and service costs. The procedures for estimating service costs are the same as the procedures for estimating product costs.

Estimating the cost of a product or service is useful in making decisions about what products or services to provide and determining a price for those products and services.

The overall objective is the creation of organizational value by providing products and services at a price to meet customer preferences. These planning decisions can be improved with better estimates of product costs.

THE PRODUCT-MIX DECISION

The role of organizational managers is to help the organization achieve its goals. Most organizational goals, from satisfying customers to generating a profit for owners and/or shareholders, are related to the products and services that organizations provide. Managers of organizations must decide which products and services add both customer and organizational value. Customer value occurs if the price of the product is less than the benefits the customer derives from the product. Organizational value occurs if the price of the product is greater than the product cost.

An organization is usually established to provide a certain product or service. But as the organization evolves, other products and services are frequently offered. For example, a bakery may start by making bread, but later might decide to branch into pastries. Microsoft started by writing operating systems, but now has a wide variety of software, games, hardware and related server systems. The organization's product mix continually evolves, as new opportunities arise and competitive pressures affect existing products and services.

The choice of what products and services to offer is known as the **product-mix decision**. For example, Nestlé's Foods, headquartered in Switzerland, must decide what food products to offer in its global markets. Products vary from country to country and not all products are offered in each. For example, Nescafé coffee is familiar from Bulgaria to China. Yet the coffee beans selected, roasting method, strength and packaging vary considerably depending on local tastes.

The product cost provides information to managers useful in making the product-mix decision. The organization with a higher product cost for a particular product will be at a competitive disadvantage. If a computer chip manufacturer makes a chip that costs £150, the firm is at a competitive disadvantage if a competitor currently makes a comparable chip for £100. For example, Dell Inc. dropped its digital music player line, as it was not competitive in this market segment. Dell continues to be a major supplier of corporate and personal computer systems, and has expanded into other areas of IT and network services where the company has competitive advantage.

An organization must continually analyse its existing and new products or services to determine whether it has a comparative advantage in offering them. On the one hand, an organization may identify a service which it can provide at a low cost due to its having special skills. Microsoft has personnel who have an intimate knowledge of the Windows operating system. This advantage allowed Microsoft to integrate an Internet browser into Windows at a low cost. A low-cost provider of services has a comparative advantage over its competitors and is likely to include that service in its service mix. On the other hand, a high-cost producer is

Hornbil Images/Alamy

Nestlé uses cost and revenue data to decide which products to offer in different markets around the globe, while catering to local tastes and preferences.

unlikely to continue to include that product or service in its mix, unless some other benefits exist in offering it.

The ultimate decision on choosing the set of products to offer (the product mix) is based on a comparison of the benefits of the product with the costs of providing the product. If the benefits exceed the costs, a product is included in the product mix. The benefits of the product usually are measured in terms of revenues generated from sales. But an organization must consider other benefits of having a product. For example, having a particular product in a product mix may be important to sales of other products. Automobile dealerships want a wide variety of products to give customers a comprehensive selection. If dealerships limited their inventory to only the most profitable models, customers would be less likely to shop there. Restaurants feature varied menus to attract repeat customers who might prefer steak and champagne for dinner, but only order a sandwich at lunch. Often there are cost advantages of offering multiple products. With economies of scope, an organization can offer two products more cheaply than two separate organizations offering one product each. A product's benefits also are related to the employees of the organization. Dropping a product from the product mix can result in the laying off of employees. Managers must deal continually with ethical issues related to the welfare of both employees and owners. Most of the problems and examples in this text focus on revenues as the primary benefit of having a product or service, but other intangible benefits should be considered.

■ Pricing decision

Part of the product-mix decision is based on the demand for the product or service. If the price of the product or service is too high, consumers will not buy it. If the price is too low, making and selling the product will reduce organizational value. Determining the price of a product or service is another important planning decision that managers must make.

As we will see in Chapters 4 and 5, the pricing decision is complicated and affected by customer value and competition. But product costs are also used to make pricing decisions. The product cost serves as a lower boundary in making a pricing decision. If products and services are sold below their cost, then organizational value will decline.

Bended Knee Skateboards (continued)

Geoff Williams of Bended Knee Skateboards is considering a change in its product mix and prices. Currently, about 91 per cent of the skateboards it produces are flat and 9 per cent are moulded. The current prices for these skateboards reflect competitors' prices, but Geoff Williams feels that by lowering the price, he could sell more skateboards. Before making these decisions, however, Geoff must determine the cost of each type of skateboard. If the cost of one of the models is greater than the competitors' prices, then Geoff should drop that skateboard from the product mix. If the cost of one of them is less than the competitors' prices, then Geoff has some flexibility to reduce the price of that skateboard to increase sales. Unfortunately, the present accounting system gives no indication of the cost of either type of skateboard. Also, Geoff is not sure that the company is operating very efficiently. Even if he could determine the costs of his products, he may be able to reduce the product costs further by cutting costs. Before he can identify cost-cutting opportunities, however, he must gain a better understanding of the operating activities at Bended Knee.

For planning purposes, activities are divided into those that support only one product and those that support multiple products. Activities that are associated with only one product generate costs that are **direct product costs**. Direct product costs can be easily traced from the activity to a single product. **Indirect product costs** occur because activities support more than one product, and cannot be traced easily to a single product. In the next two sections, we examine some characteristics of direct and indirect product costs.

Concept **review**

1 What is a cost object?
2 How does the product cost help support the product-mix decision?

Bended Knee Skateboards (continued)

The accounting system of Bended Knee Skateboards presently identifies costs by departments (administration, purchasing, production and marketing). Although these departments represent general activities in the organization, Geoff Williams needs more detailed information about sub-activities. For example, the production activity is composed of the following sub-activities: warehousing and handling raw materials, cutting, gluing, setting up moulds, painting and assembly. Of these sub-activities, the warehousing and handling of raw materials and the setting up of moulds are identified as non-value-added. Therefore, Geoff should focus his cost-cutting efforts on those activities, but he is still not sure of the costs of each of them.

DIRECT PRODUCT COSTS

Activities that are only associated with one product create direct product costs. No problem exists in tracing those activity costs to a particular product, but the costs must still be measured. Direct product costs are commonly associated with either the use of material resources or labour. Categorizing direct product costs as material or labour allows managers to analyse the components of the product cost.

Materials used to make a product are called **direct materials**. Direct materials also are referred to as raw materials. The labour used to make the product or to provide a service is also a direct cost of the product or service, and is called **direct labour**. Direct labour consists of the cost of the time that workers spend producing the product or service. It excludes the cost of training or being idle. For example, the direct cost of making an oak chair includes the cost of direct materials (the cost of the oak and finish used to make the chair) and the cost of direct labour (the cost of the labour used to cut, sand, assemble and finish the chair). Most service organizations, such as law firms, have direct labour costs but few direct material costs.

Although direct product costs can be traced easily to the product, the management accountant still needs assistance in estimating direct costs. If the product or service has been provided previously, the historical cost usually is of some use in estimating future direct costs. Nevertheless, the management accountant should consult with engineers, suppliers and personnel managers for information on estimating direct costs.

To determine the cost of direct materials, the management accountant must obtain a list of the required raw materials and parts necessary to make the product. In manufacturing settings, engineers are normally consulted for this information. Purchase prices must then be obtained for each material and part. The management accountant can estimate direct material prices by surveying suppliers and asking for bids for certain items. For example, to estimate the direct material costs of building a house, a contractor using the architect's plans must identify all the materials necessary to build the house. The contractor then goes to suppliers to determine the price of each item. The estimated direct material cost of the house is determined by multiplying the quantity of each piece of material in the house times its respective price.

To estimate the cost of direct labour, engineers and other experts are usually consulted to determine the hours of labour necessary to complete the product or provide the service. If the product or service is currently being offered, the labour time required can be measured directly. Adjustments should be made, however, for improvement through learning. Normally, the first time products are made or services provided, direct labour time will be longer. Once the employees have gained experience, the labour operations can be performed more quickly. The cost of direct labour also requires estimates of labour rates – usually provided by a personnel manager in a larger organization.

Numerical **example** 3.1

To determine the direct cost of making a sandwich, Ben's Deli uses the following estimates:

Item	Quantity per sandwich	Purchase price
Meat	100 grams	£4.00/kg
Roll	1	£1.20/dozen
Mustard	15 grams	£0.04/30g
Pickles	15 grams	£0.06/30g
Labour	1 minute	£6/hour

Calculate the direct cost of making a sandwich.

Solution

The direct cost is determined by multiplying the quantity of the different items necessary to make a sandwich times its respective price. Some debate exists about whether the labour of the cook is a direct cost of making a sandwich. If the cook were also cooking other food at the same time, the labour would be an indirect cost of making a sandwich.

Item	Quantity per sandwich	×	Purchase price	=	Cost
Meat	100 grams		£4.00/kg		£0.40
Roll	1		£1.20/dozen		0.10
Mustard	15 grams		£0.04/30g		0.02
Pickles	15 grams		£0.06/30g		0.03
Labour	1 minute		£6/hour		0.10
Total direct cost/sandwich				=	£0.65

Concept **review**

1 What is the difference between direct and indirect product costs?

2 How are direct product costs commonly classified?

3 Describe methods of estimating direct product and service costs.

Bended Knee Skateboards (continued)

Geoff Williams of Bended Knee Skateboards estimates the direct materials and direct labour of the two types of skateboards. The direct materials include the thin sheets of wood veneer, glue and the polyurethane wheels and axle assemblies. The moulded skateboards also require a plastic sheet. To estimate the cost of these direct materials, Geoff goes to the various suppliers to obtain price information for the coming year. Each skateboard requires two sets of wheels and axles. The quantity of the remaining materials per skateboard is more difficult to estimate. Geoff examines usage of the sheets of wood veneer, sheets of plastic and glue in the previous year. By cutting the veneer more carefully and using more experienced employees, Geoff figures he can reduce scrap and spoiled units. These improvements should reduce the quantity of materials per skateboard by 5 per cent. Geoff decides that estimating glue costs per skateboard is too difficult and decides to treat the cost of glue as part of indirect production costs.

To estimate direct labour costs, Geoff uses the wage rates on the recently signed labour contract. To determine the amount of time necessary to make each type of skateboard, he uses a stopwatch to time workers. Assuming that learning will take place, Geoff estimates that the time to complete a skateboard in the coming year will be 7 per cent less than his current observations. The calculation for direct materials after incorporating the scrap improvements is:

Flat skateboard

Materials	Quantity	Price (£)	Cost (£)
Wood veneer	$1m^2$/unit	$0.02/m^2$	0.20/unit
Wheel assemblies	2/unit	0.44 each	0.88/unit
Total direct materials			1.08/unit
Direct labour	0.5 hours/unit	10/hr	5.00/unit
Total direct costs			6.08/unit

Moulded skateboard

Materials	Quantity	Price (£)	Cost (£)
Wood veneer	$1m^2$/unit	$0.02/m^2$	0.20/unit
Wheel assemblies	2/unit	0.44 each	0.88/unit
Plastic layer	1/unit	0.12 each	0.12/unit
Total direct materials			1.20/unit
Direct labour	1 hour/unit	10/hr	10.00/unit
Total direct costs			11.20/unit

Geoff compares these direct costs with his competitors' prices of £15 for the flat skateboard and £25 for the moulded skateboard. In both cases, the direct costs are less than the competitors' prices, so there is no immediate need to drop a product. There may even be an opportunity to lower prices and still make a profit. But Geoff knows that the direct costs are only part of the picture. He must also estimate the indirect costs of his products.

INDIRECT PRODUCT COSTS

Indirect product costs occur because some organizational activities support multiple products. Indirect product costs also are called **overhead costs**. Since indirect product costs cannot be easily traced to specific products or services, the estimation of indirect product costs is likely to be more difficult and uncertain than the estimation of direct product costs.

Accounting reports to external parties cannot be relied upon to estimate indirect product costs. They are based on generally accepted accounting principles (GAAP) and treat some indirect costs, such as research and development (R&D) and marketing costs, as **period costs** rather than product costs. The rationale for treating R&D and marketing costs as period costs is the difficulty in measuring the future benefits of those activities. Yet R&D and marketing are part of the cost of developing and delivering a product to a customer. Also, the external accounting reports are based on historical cost, which may not be good estimates of future indirect costs.

To estimate the indirect costs of products, the management accountant must have a good understanding of the organization's operations. Knowing how different activities in the organization interact to create products allows the manager to more accurately trace indirect costs to products. To simplify the analysis of the different organizational activities, indirect product costs are divided into four types: unit-level, batch-level, product-level and facility-level.

■ Unit-level costs

Unit-level costs are indirect product costs that vary with the number of units produced of a product or service. Certain activities and their associated costs increase with the number of units produced. Machine usage is an example of indirect unit-level costs. The cost of operating a machine increases with the number of units produced due to wear on the machine parts. These indirect costs are proportional to the number of units of all products produced. The costs are indirect because the machine is used to make more than one product.

■ Batch-level costs

Often products are created in batches. A batch consists of multiple units of the same product that are processed together. As a batch moves through a manufacturing plant, adjustments to machinery, called set-ups, must be made to make the particular product in the batch. Services also are performed in batches. A DHL truckload could be considered a batch of packages to be delivered to different customers. Costs associated with batches are called **batch-level costs**. Batch-level costs are fixed with respect to the number of units in the batch up to capacity limits, but vary with the number of batches. An example of an activity which primarily generates a batch-level cost is an airplane flight. Many costs of an airplane flight do not vary with the number of passengers. The cost of the flight crew and the plane are fixed with respect to the number of passengers, up to the seating capacity of the plane. The cost of meals and beverages, however, is a unit-level cost since they vary with the number of passengers.

Manufacturing is frequently performed in batches to reduce the need to continually reset machines for different products. Once machines are set up for a batch run, multiple units can be manufactured without further set-up costs. The set-up activity to run the batch and its corresponding cost are common to all the units in the batch. The cost of the set-up activity is fixed with respect to the number of units in the batch.

DHL deliveries can be analysed as a batch-level cost, fixed in terms of capacity but variable in terms of loads and vehicles in service.

© Jochen Tack/Alamy

■ Product-level costs

Some activities benefit products as a whole, rather than individual units or batches of a product or service. For example, engineering and design efforts are common to all units of a particular product. Once the design and engineering activities have been completed for a particular product or service, no further engineering or design costs are incurred as more units or batches are made. Costs that are common to all the units of a product are called **product-level costs**.

Product-level costs are fixed with respect to the number of units and batches produced, but vary with the number of products. In the case of engineering and design activities, each new product incurs additional costs, so engineering and design costs vary with the number of products. In the case of airlines, creating flight service between different cities is a new product. The costs of obtaining gates and ticket counter space, and the cost of establishing ticketing, baggage and gate operations are all product-level costs.

■ Facility-level costs

Some activities are not related to any products or services, so costs cannot be traced to products. For example, the cost of a manufacturing plant cannot be traced to the many different products made within the facility. Also, the plant manager's salary is not associated with any particular unit, batch or product of the organization. Costs that cannot be identified with a particular unit, batch or product are called **facility-level costs**. Facility-level costs are fixed with respect to the number of units, batches and products or services produced. Facility-level costs are common to multiple products or services. Facility-level costs, however, vary with the size and number of facilities. In the airline industry, the cost of maintaining and operating the airline reservation system is a facility-level cost. The cost of the reservation system is reasonably fixed and does not vary with the number of flights or services between cities that the airline offers.

Recognizing whether an indirect cost is a unit-, batch-, product- or facility-level cost is important in understanding the relation between indirect costs and products and services. Japan's DoCoMo, presented later in the chapter, provides an example of how knowledge of the type of cost is important in making strategic choices about products and services. Activity-based costing, described later in this chapter, uses the level of indirect costs to trace indirect costs to products and services.

Concept **review**

1 What are indirect product costs?

2 Explain how indirect product costs are classified as unit-, batch-, product- and facility-level.

Bended Knee Skateboards (continued)

Geoff Williams categorizes the indirect costs of Bended Knee Skateboards as follows:

Support function	Level	Amount (£)
Administrative	Facility	90,000
Purchasing	Batch	50,000
Production		
Warehousing and handling	Batch	18,000
Cutting	Unit	50,000
Gluing	Unit	10,000
Setting up moulds	Batch	55,000
Painting	Unit	35,000
Assembly	Unit	42,000
Marketing	Product	100,000
Total		450,000

This categorization indicates that the tracing of indirect costs to the two types of skateboards is complicated. Splitting the indirect costs among the flat and moulded skateboards should recognize each of these levels of indirect costs.

TRACING INDIRECT COSTS USING A COST DRIVER

Although tracing indirect costs to different products appears to be problematic, a careful analysis of the activities that cause the indirect costs can provide some direction. Indirect product costs occur because an organization performs an activity which is related to multiple products. These activities are triggered by some event called a **cost driver**. A cost driver is the cause of the cost of an activity. For example, purchasing of raw materials is an activity used by many products. Purchasing costs occur because purchase orders are made. Therefore, a cost driver for purchasing costs could be the number of purchase orders. The more purchase orders that a product uses, the more purchasing costs it causes. The purchasing costs can, therefore, be traced to the different products based on how much of the cost driver (purchase orders) each product uses.

The procedure for tracing activity costs to different products through cost drivers is described in the following steps:

1 Identify the activities that generate indirect product costs.
2 Estimate the cost of the activities.
3 Select a cost driver for each activity.
4 Estimate the cost-driver usage by all of the products.
5 Calculate a cost-driver application rate.
6 Trace activity costs to each product.

■ Identify the activities that generate indirect product costs

The procedure for tracing activity costs to different products begins with identifying organizational activities that cause indirect costs. Indirect costs do not just happen. Something causes them, and the management accountant must discover those activities. Some activities, such as engineering and marketing, that cause indirect costs provide value to the customer. These activities are on the value chain. Other activities, called non-value-added activities, provide little value to the customer. These activities include moving products within the organization and setting up machines.

Identifying activities within the organization that cause indirect product costs requires considerable organizational knowledge. Management accountants cannot provide good estimates of product costs from the security of their offices. They must observe all the operations of the organization and how they interact.

Organizational **analysis**

Japan's DoCoMo's mobile phone services

Before the introduction of mobile phone number portability in late 2006, NTT DoCoMo controlled about 55 per cent of the Japanese mobile-phone market. With this regulatory change, Japanese consumers were now able to keep their mobile phone numbers when they switched from one mobile carrier to another. The ability to switch service provider with no change in telephone number was expected to encourage competition and reduce service rates. Yet, the rate of switching has been much less than that occurring in other countries where these 'churn rates' often reach 50 per cent of customers.

A number of reasons exist for the low level of switching. Japanese customers cannot retain the e-mail address linked to their mobile phone. Many people use their phones as much or more for e-mail as for telephone calls. Unlike in other markets, Japanese subscribers are not able to use their existing hand-set when switching services, as hand-sets are network-specific. Government controls also prevent the cost of hand-sets from being subsidized by the mobile operator. Moreover, if subscribers change services, they often find that they no longer have access to features such as games, mobile-TV and digital music. Customers are being lured to switch or stay with innovations such as loyalty programmes, discounts on increased phone usage and new handsets. Handsets now come in every size, shape and colour, with touch screens and even scented models. Music and entertainment services offered in conjunction with mobile services have improved. Even with new entrants and market mergers, competition remains intense, especially amongst DoCoMo and its main rivals, Softbank and KDDI. Yet, prices have not fallen as much as expected. Users appear to be willing to pay for innovative services and features.

The cost of providing a mobile phone call plays an important role in the turmoil surrounding the mobile phone market. Almost all of DoCoMo's mobile services are facility- or product-level activities. These activities include the establishment and maintenance of telecommunications networks, R&D and sales activities. Billing services could be considered at the batch-level, if service to each customer is perceived as a batch. But essentially no costly activities exist at the unit-level, except, for example, payment to television broadcasters for the use of their services. Therefore, the marginal cost of providing one more mobile phone call for an existing customer is small as long as the network has sufficient capacity. If the system is very busy, an additional call can delay other calls, reducing the customer's value of DoCoMo's service.

This product cost structure and the intense competition provide some interesting problems for DoCoMo in making pricing and other strategic decisions.

What are some creative ways for DoCoMo to compete? What types of acquisitions and alliances could help solidify DoCoMo's position in the mobile phone market?

Source: 'Change is in the air', *The Economist*, 20 January 2007, p. 76.

■ Estimate the costs of the activities

Once the activities are identified, the costs associated with each activity are estimated. These costs should include employee time and materials consumed by the activity. The activity may also incur utility and rental costs.

If purchasing is identified as an organizational activity causing indirect costs, all the costs associated with the purchasing activity are identified and estimated. Those costs would include wages of those working in the purchasing activity, supplies, travel to visit suppliers, the cost of computers, telephone and other utility costs, and cost of the space used by purchasing. All of these costs would be aggregated and treated as the cost of the purchasing activity.

■ Select a cost driver for each activity

After identifying the activities and estimating their costs, a cost driver is chosen for each activity. A cost driver causes or 'drives' the costs of an activity. The choice of the cost driver should recognize whether the activity causes unit-level, batch-level, product-level or facility-level costs. Unit-level costs should have cost drivers that vary with the number of units, such as direct labour hours, cost of raw materials or simply the number of units. Batch-level costs should have cost drivers that vary with the number of batches, such as number of purchase orders (for batches of parts), time to reset machines for new batches or simply the number of batches. Product-level costs should have cost drivers that reflect the proportion of the activity dedicated to the different products. For example, design hours could be used for design costs. Alternatively product-level costs could be divided equally among all of the products. Choosing cost drivers for facility-level costs is more problematic, as facility-level costs do not often vary with characteristics of products.

Cost drivers are ideal tracers of indirect activity costs when the usage of the cost driver is proportional to the activity costs. When proportionality exists between cost-driver usage and the indirect costs of an activity, each unit used of the cost driver

Figure 3.1 Proportionality of cost-driver usage and activity costs

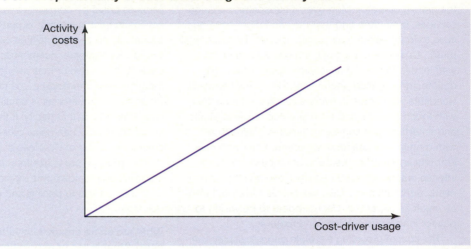

causes the same activity cost. Proportionality assumes that there are no fixed costs. Figure 3.1 depicts a proportional relation. Implicitly, this relation assumes that all indirect costs are variable with respect to the chosen cost driver.

Estimate the cost-driver usage by all of the products

Indirect product costs are generated by activities that support more than one product. The tracing of these activity costs to the different products is based on the usage of the cost driver of the activity. The more a particular product uses the cost driver, the more the activity costs are traced to the product. The problem is determining the cost of using a single unit of the cost driver. The estimate of the cost of using a single unit of the cost driver is calculated in the next section by dividing the total activity costs by the total usage of the cost driver by all products. Therefore, an estimate of the cost-driver usage by all products must be made. For example, if the number of purchase orders is selected as a cost driver for purchasing costs, the total number of purchase orders used by all products must be estimated.

Calculate a cost-driver application rate

The **cost-driver application rate** is used to trace activity costs to different products. To determine the cost-driver application rate for each activity, the estimated costs of each activity are divided by the total estimated usage of the respective cost driver. The ratio provides an estimate of the cost of using one unit of the cost driver.

For example, assume that the total estimated purchasing costs for all products are £500,000 and the total estimated number of purchase orders, the cost driver, is 20,000. Then the cost-driver application rate for a purchase order is £500,000/20,000 purchase orders or £25/purchase order. Each purchase order is estimated to cost £25.

Trace activity costs to each product

Once a cost-driver application rate has been calculated for an activity, the activity costs are traced based on the usage of the cost driver by each product and service. The cost-driver application rate is multiplied by the cost-driver usage of each product.

If a cost-driver application rate is estimated to be £25 per purchase order, a product that will use 10 purchase orders will be assessed (£25/purchase order) × (10 purchase orders), or £250. The £250 becomes part of the product cost.

Numerical **example** 3.2

A sunglass company manufactures three different products (Euro, Aussie, and Salsa) that use the same assembly line. To change production from one product to another, the machines on the assembly line must be reset. The activity of resetting the machines is estimated to cost €400,000 during the year. The estimated number of resets for each product is: Euro = 50; Aussie = 200; Salsa = 150. If the number of resets is the cost driver of the resetting activity, how should the resetting costs be traced to the three products?

Solution

The estimated resetting activity cost is €400,000. The number of resets is chosen as the cost driver. The estimated total cost-driver usage is 50 + 200 + 150, or 400 resets. The cost-driver application rate is €400,000/400 resets, or €1,000/reset. The resetting activity costs traced to the different sunglasses are:

Product	Estimated resets	Application rate (€)	Traced costs (€)
Euro	50	1,000/Reset	50,000
Aussie	200	1,000/Reset	200,000
Salsa	150	1,000/Reset	150,000
Total	400		400,000

More resetting costs are traced to the Euro model, since it uses more of the cost driver.

Concept **review**

1 What are the six steps in tracing indirect costs to products?

2 What is the preferred relation between the cost-driver usage and the activity costs?

ACTIVITY-BASED COSTING (ABC)

Most firms are finding that indirect costs are becoming a higher proportion of total product costs. Advanced manufacturing technologies and computing systems have increased the indirect costs of many organizations and, in many cases, have replaced direct labour. As the proportion of indirect costs to direct costs increases, firms are taking a closer look at how indirect costs are related to their different products. Without an accurate tracing of indirect costs to products, organizations are likely to make poor product mix and pricing decisions.

Indirect product costs occur because activities often support more than one product. The previous section outlines the procedure for tracing the cost of a single activity to different products. That procedure can be duplicated for other activities within the organization. Tracing the costs of different activities to products is the basis of **activity-based costing (ABC)**. By analysing the activities of the organization and how they relate to different products, organizations can estimate product costs more accurately. More accurate product costs can lead to better product-mix and pricing decisions.

ABC is a procedure to trace costs from activities to products. Additionally, the analysis of activities and their costs can lead to better decisions about cost-reduction opportunities, more efficient supplier relations, and more focus on added value to the customer.

Foot patrols often improve community relations but the link is not easy to discern. ABC models assist in selecting the appropriate mix of police activities.

Darren Matthews/Alamy

For example, in public sector organizations, governments and taxpayers expect value for money. Such organizations need to determine the best means to deliver services in an efficient, economical and effective manner. The Home Secretary requires the use of a national police activity-based costing model that assists local police authorities to trace costs and link costs to outcomes. Figure 3.2 provides an indication of the activities involved in policing. Police authorities attempt to match required service levels with available resources, and compare outcomes and costs to performance benchmarks. Policing includes a wide variety of activities which makes it difficult to choose the appropriate mix of activities. Some activities are operational in nature and others are at the headquarters' (facility-sustaining) level. High visibility of the police on foot patrol may reduce crime, but this causal link is not always obvious. Policing requires surplus capacity to be ready for unforeseen events and the value of this extra capacity needs to be costed.

The complex nature of policing also makes it difficult to distinguish the cost driver, which causes the activity, from the cost object. The national police activity-based costing model uses police incidents and not policing activities as the cost objects. The national model will continue to evolve as police authorities gain further expertise with activity analysis. This knowledge can then be shared to improve police services in different contexts and settings.[1] Chapter 4 discusses this strategic use of ABC under the heading of activity-based management.

In this section, ABC is used to trace all of the activity costs to the different products. Activities that are dedicated to only one product involve no tracing difficulties, since they are direct product costs. The tracing of indirect product costs is more problematic. In the previous section, a number of steps are outlined to trace costs of activities that support multiple products. To complete the product cost-estimation process, those steps must be followed for each activity. The estimated cost of a product is the sum of the direct product costs and the indirect product costs traced from the various activities.

---

[1] P. M. Collier (2006) 'Costing police services: The politicization of accounting', *Critical Perspectives on Accounting*, Vol. 17, No. 1, January pp. 57–86.

Figure 3.2 Examples of police incident/activity analysis

	Crime	**Non-crime**	**Public reassurance**	**Other**
Incident	Violence against the person Robbery Domestic burglary Theft of motor vehicle Criminal damage Drug offences	Traffic Anti-social behaviour Public order Domestic disputes Missing persons Sudden deaths		
Incident-related activities		Travel Deal with incident Enquiries Searches Interviews Files Reports At court		
Non incident-related activities	Crime prevention Informants Prison interviews		Foot patrol Mobile patrol Community work	Briefings Firearms licensing Meetings Non-incident paperwork Supervision

Source: P. M. Collier (2006) 'Costing police services: The politicization of accounting', *Critical Perspectives on Accounting*, Vol. 17, No. 1, January, pp. 57–86. With permission from Elsevier.

Numerical **example** 3.3

A tree nursery is considering a change of product mix in its inventory. The manager wants to estimate the product cost of different types of trees. There are no activities that lead to direct costs. Indirect costs are identified and estimated for the following activities: watering, repotting (transferring trees to larger pots) and administration. Total estimated annual costs for each activity, the cost driver for each activity and the expected annual usage of each cost driver are as follows:

Activity	*Estimated costs (£)*	*Cost driver*	*Estimated usage of cost driver*
Watering	50,000	Number of trees	500,000
Repotting	100,000	Number of repots	200,000
Administration	75,000	Number of different types of trees	500

a What is the application rate for each of the activities?

b Given the choice of cost driver, at what level is each activity: unit, batch, product or facility?

c What are the estimated costs of 100 royal oaks, each of which requires one repotting each year?

Solution

a The application rate for each activity is calculated by dividing the estimated costs of the activity by the estimated usage of its respective cost driver:

Activity		Application rate
Watering	£50,000/500,000	£0.10/tree
Repotting	£100,000/200,000	£0.50/repot
Administration	£75,000/500	£150/type of tree

b Both watering and repotting are unit-level activities, since their cost drivers vary with the number of units. Administration is treated as a product-level activity, because each product receives the same indirect costs.

c The indirect costs traced to the 100 royal oaks are:

Activity	Application rate	Usage	Costs (£)
Watering	£0.10/tree	100	10.00
Repotting	£0.50/repot	100	50.00
Administration	£150/type of tree	1	150.00
Total annual indirect costs			210.00

The estimated cost per royal oak is £210/100 royal oaks, or £2.10/royal oak.

Numerical example 3.4

An online retailer of sports equipment located in France is attempting to determine the cost of the products that it sells over the Internet – in this case soccer balls. The company buys its products directly from manufacturers in batches and stores them at a central warehouse near Paris. The product is shipped to the consumer via DHL. The company incurs additional costs resulting from advertising to encourage consumers to visit the website, designing the website, purchasing, and general administration. The costs of the different activities and cost-driver usage are described in the following table:

Activity	Activity cost (€m)	Cost driver	Total usage of cost driver
Warehousing	1	Average € of inventory	€2m
Shipping	3	Direct material (DM) cost	€30m
Advertising	5	?	
Website			
General design	1	?	
Product-related	4	Number of Web pages	8,000 pages
Purchasing	2	Number of purchases	5,000 purchases
General admin.	1	?	

In addition to these activity costs, the company purchases €30m of products for resale.

a Why are there question marks for the selection of a cost driver for certain activities?

b What level of costs (unit, batch or product) are generated by warehousing, shipping, website product-related and purchasing activities?

c What are the cost-driver application rates for these activities?

d To determine the profitability of selling soccer balls via the Internet, the company wants to estimate the total product cost of the balls. The company plans to buy €500,000 of balls for resale. On average, the warehouse will hold €100,000 of balls in inventory. Soccer balls require 20 pages on the Internet and 10 purchases. What is the total estimated cost of selling the balls?

Solution

a The activities with question marks are not related to any particular product and could be considered facility-level costs. Tracing these costs may cause misleading product costs, as they probably do not vary with additional products. They are not included in the following analysis, but must be considered part of the total cost of the organization.

b Warehousing costs vary with the value of the inventory in the warehouse, so these costs would be unit-level. Shipping costs vary with direct material costs and would also be unit-level. Product-related website costs vary with the number of different products and are product-level. Purchasing costs are performed in batches and are batch-level costs.

c

Activity		Application rate
Warehousing	€1,000,000/€2,000,000	50% of Average Inventory in euros
Shipping	€3,000,000/€30,000,000	10% of DM cost
Website		
Product-related	€4,000,000/8,000	€500/page
Purchasing	€2,000,000/5,000	€400/purchase

d

Activity	Application rate	Soccer ball usage	Cost
Warehousing	50% of Average inventory	€100,000	€50,000
Shipping	10% of DM cost	€500,000	€50,000
Website			
Product-related	€500/page	20 pages	€10,000
Purchasing	€400/purchase	10 purchases	€4,000
Direct cost of soccer balls			€500,000
Total cost of soccer balls			€614,000

The estimated total cost of selling soccer balls via the Internet is €614,000.

■ Advantages of ABC

ABC seeks to improve the tracing of indirect costs to products by recognizing the different levels of activities that lead to indirect product costs. With each activity having its own cost driver, ABC can capture some of the complexity of indirect product costs.

ABC is most beneficial in estimating accurate product costs for organizations with multiple products and services. If a firm only has one product or service, no problem exists in tracing costs to different products or services.

ABC is also more beneficial in firms where products and services use overhead activities in different ways. If some of an organization's products require considerable engineering time and others require considerable machine time, these products use overhead activities differently. Also, high- and low-volume products tend to use overhead activities differently, especially if there are batch-level and product-level costs.

ABC is especially useful to organizations with a high percentage of indirect product costs. Many organizations now have indirect product costs that are greater than 50 per cent of total costs. When a large percentage of product costs are indirect, accurately tracing those costs to products becomes more important.

The usefulness of ABC in making planning decisions is not just limited to accurate product costs. ABC also assists managers in finding opportunities to reduce costs. The identification of activities that cause costs often reveals activities that are not value-added. These non-value-added activities are opportunities to reduce costs.

ABC can provide useful information on how the different overhead activities relate to the rest of the organization. **Activity-based management** is the process of analysing the management of the different overhead activities to enable the organization to provide both customer and organizational value by operating more efficiently. ABC is part of activity-based management, which is covered in the next chapter.

The installation of an ABC system in an organization requires considerable knowledge about how the different overhead activities are related to products. The process of implementing ABC forces organizational members to analyse and understand their organization better. This knowledge will be beneficial in making other planning decisions.

■ Problems with ABC

Although ABC has many advantages, it is not without problems, and does not always achieve a particularly accurate estimate of the cost of making a product. The accuracy of ABC depends on identifying and estimating the costs of the activities, and the relation of the cost driver to the costs of the activity. If cost-driver usage is not proportional to the cost of the activity, inaccurate estimates will occur. Cost-driver usage will not be proportional to activity costs if some of the activity costs are fixed with respect to the cost driver. For example, a company may decide to purchase an expensive testing machine to inspect different products. Inspection is an activity and the number of inspections could be used as the cost driver. The cost of the machine, however, is fixed with respect to the number of inspections. The variable costs of inspection may be quite low.

If activity costs have a fixed component with respect to the cost driver, ABC ignores the difference between the fixed and variable costs of an activity. In this case, the application rate reflects both the fixed and variable costs of the activity and will not accurately reflect the cost of additional use of the activity. In addition, ABC cannot resolve the problem of what to do with facility-level costs. Facility-level costs do not lend themselves to tracing to different products, since they are fixed with respect to the number of products and the number of units of each product produced.

ABC is costly to implement. An increase in the number of cost drivers increases the cost and complexity of the system. Allocating costs amongst cost drivers can be inaccurate, resulting in biased cost data. Managers may find it difficult to interpret the information to make decisions that are timely and accurate. Many measurements and observations must be made to

© bildagentur-online/begsteiger/Alamy

The banking sector uses ABC to meet the diverse needs of clients. ABC assists banks in determining their product portfolio and customer profitability.

implement ABC. However, these additional measurements and observations may also have control effects. For example, if engineering hours are used to trace engineering costs to products, engineering hours will be more carefully controlled. For example, research conducted in a Marconi plant in Portugal indicated that ABC was useful for pricing and investment decisions, but was not considered relevant at the production level. Also it was not linked to the performance measurement system.[2] Therefore, both planning decisions and control issues should be considered jointly in deciding whether to adopt ABC.

ABC must also be integrated with other reporting systems to increase its capacity to be used at the strategic level. A case study in a UK-based multinational bank revealed that ABC was comprehensive in its analysis of costs and products, but was not used at the strategic level to improve long-term planning decisions.[3]

ABC has a further limitation in that firms might equate improved costing methods with an improvement in the underlying activities. The focus on refining the accounting for indirect costs might overlook operating inefficiencies. For example, if indirect costs are caused by the holding of work-in-process inventories or an inefficient plant lay-out, the apparent costing improvement of the ABC system does not resolve the existing operational deficiencies. If managers naively consider the situation rectified due to the new costing system, they might not take the necessary steps to investigate and improve the layout and/or the production flow. These steps might reduce the indirect costs or eliminate them completely.

Concept review

1 How are product costs estimated using activity-based costing?

2 What are the advantages and disadvantages of activity-based costing?

Bended Knee Skateboards (continued)

Bended Knee Skateboards would like to estimate its product costs under ABC. The following indirect cost activities and cost drivers are identified. Also, activity costs, cost-driver usage and application rates are estimated:

Activity	Cost driver	Costs (£)	Cost driver usage	Application rate
Administration	Direct labour hours	90,000	30,000	£3/DLH
Purchasing	Number of orders	50,000	100	£500/order
Warehousing	Number of deliveries	18,000	150	£120/delivery
Cutting	Machine hours	50,000	5,000	£10/machine hour
Gluing	Labour hours of gluing	10,000	5,000	£2/gluing hour
Setting-up	Number of set-ups	55,000	6,000	£9.17/set-up
Painting	Litres of paint	35,000	1,000	£35/litre
Assembly	Hours to assemble	42,000	10,500	£4/hour
Marketing	Customer visits	100,000	80	£1,250/visit

→

[2] M. Major and T. Hopper (2005) 'Managers Divided: Implementing ABC in a Portuguese telecommunications company', *Management Accounting Research*, Vol. 16, pp. 205–229.

[3] K. Soin, W. Seal and J. Cullen (2002) 'ABC and organizational change: an institutional perspective', *Management Accounting Research*, Vol. 13, pp. 249–271.

The tracing of indirect costs to each product depends on the expected usage of the cost drivers by the two products. The tracing of indirect costs for each product is:

Activity	Application rate	Usage by flat skateboards	Applied to flat skateboards (£)	Usage by moulded skateboards	Applied to moulded skateboards (£)
Administration	£3/DLH	25,000	75,000	5,000	15,000
Purchasing	£500/purchase	30	15,000	70	35,000
Warehousing	£120/delivery	50	6,000	100	12,000
Cutting	£10/machine hour	4,000	40,000	1,000	10,000
Gluing	£2/gluing hour	4,500	9,000	500	1,000
Setting-up	£9.17/set-up	5,000	45,833	1,000	9,167
Painting	£35/litre	500	17,500	500	17,500
Assembly	£4/hour	8,000	32,000	2,500	10,000
Marketing	£1,250/visit	40	50,000	40	50,000
Total			290,333		159,667

The indirect cost per unit using ABC with these cost drivers is:

Flat skateboards	£290,333/50,000 units =	£5.81/unit
Moulded skateboards	£159,667/5,000 units =	£31.93/unit

With direct costs, the estimated costs of making each product are:

	Direct materials	Direct labour	Indirect costs	Cost/unit
Flat skateboards	£1.08	£5.00	£5.81	£11.89
Moulded skateboards	£1.20	£10.00	£31.93	£43.13

Using these product costs, the moulded skateboard that sells for £25 looks like a big loser. Geoff Williams, however, should not eliminate the moulded skateboards from the product list without some further investigation. The ABC method applied facility-level costs that are common to both flat and moulded skateboards. These costs will not necessarily be avoided if no more moulded skateboards are produced. The opportunity cost of making moulded skateboards should consider the alternative use of the facilities if moulded skateboards are no longer made. Also, some of the indirect costs may be sunk. In other words, they will be incurred whether or not moulded skateboards are made. These sunk costs should be ignored in making the product mix decision.

TRACING INDIRECT PRODUCT COSTS USING A SINGLE COST DRIVER

Under ABC, each activity that generates an indirect product cost should have its own cost driver to trace the activity's costs to the different products. By tracing indirect costs of an activity to different products and services, an organization can make more informed decisions, such as pricing and product-mix decisions. If these planning decisions are not sensitive to the accuracy of the estimate of indirect product costs, then using a single cost driver to trace all indirect product costs is often sufficient. For example, an organization is unlikely to be as concerned about tracing indirect costs to its products and services when indirect costs represent only a small percentage of total costs. Large discount retail stores, such as Aldi, have very large direct costs in the form of costs of purchasing merchandise. The indirect costs tend to be relatively small when compared to the direct costs, so the method of applying indirect product costs is not as important. Many professional services also have a cost structure that is dominated by direct costs. The costs in accounting and legal firms are primarily for professional personnel whose work can be directly traced to a particular client or service, such as an audit or legal case. Once again, the relatively small proportion of indirect costs makes the application procedure less important.

The benefits of ABC do not always outweigh the costs of ABC; therefore many organizations still use one or two cost drivers to trace all indirect product costs to the different products. The following steps describe the tracing process using a single cost driver. The process is the same as in ABC, except all the indirect costs are pooled together and only one cost driver is used.

■ Identify and estimate all of the indirect product costs

Before any indirect product costs can be traced, they first must be identified and estimated. The costs of all of the activities that support multiple products are included. Direct product costs are measured separately. In financial reporting to external parties, some indirect costs, such as R&D and marketing, are not traced to products and services. For making planning decisions, however, the cost of all indirect resources used by a product or service should be identified and estimated.

■ Identify a cost driver to apply indirect costs and estimate the usage of the cost driver for all products and services

Once the total indirect product costs are estimated, a single cost driver must be chosen. The cost driver should reflect the cause of the indirect costs. This cost driver could be related to the process of making the product or providing the service. For example, the number of direct labour hours used for each product or service is a possible cost driver. Or some physical characteristic of the product or service could be used as a cost driver such as the number of parts. As in the case of ABC, the cost-driver usage should approximate the cost of using the indirect resources. This link will be more tenuous, since all of the indirect costs are pooled together. It is unlikely that one cost driver can be found that is proportional to all of the indirect costs.

The cost driver should be easily measurable because once chosen, the amount of the cost driver used by each product or service must be estimated. The total estimated cost-driver usage is the sum of the estimated usage of the cost driver by each of the organization's products and services. For example, if the number of machine hours is the cost driver, the number of machine hours used by all of the organization's products and services must be estimated.

■ Calculate the application rate

Once a single cost driver is identified to trace indirect costs to different products or services, calculate the application rate by dividing the total estimated indirect costs by the total estimated usage of the cost driver across all products or services. For example, suppose the estimated indirect costs for a computer repair shop are £50,000 for 2,500 repair jobs. The management accountant could apply them equally to each repair job by using an application rate of £50,000/2,500 repair jobs, or £20 per repair job. This procedure, however, would not recognize that some repair jobs are simple, and that the indirect cost of working on those computers is lower than the indirect cost of working on more complex repair jobs. If the number of direct labour hours, cost of parts added or number of hours in the shop are used as cost drivers to apply indirect costs, the indirect cost of working on a computer may be more closely approximated. If direct labour hours are used to apply indirect costs and the 2,500 service jobs require an estimated 5,000 direct labour hours, the application rate would be £50,000/5,000 direct labour hours, or £10 per direct labour hour.

■ Apply indirect costs to the various products and services

Once the application rate is calculated, the estimated indirect costs are traced to the different products and services based on the estimated usage of the cost driver. In the computer repair shop example, an application rate of £10 per direct labour hour is estimated. A repair job that requires 5 direct labour hours would have £50 of estimated indirect costs, or £10 per direct labour hour (the application rate) times 5 direct labour hours (the cost driver).

Each product or service will receive a portion of the indirect costs based on the estimated usage of the cost driver by that product or service. This procedure will partition all of the expected indirect costs to the products and service.

Numerical **example** 3.5

The Cascade Cleaning Service in Fallbrook provides cleaning services for commercial buildings. The company cleans three different buildings:

	m^2	Estimated hours of cleaning time
Anderson Office Building	100,000	8,000
Carla's Pizza	10,000	6,000
Town Hall	90,000	6,000
Total	200,000	20,000

Cascade Cleaning Service has the following estimated indirect costs:

	£
Supplies	50,000
Administration	50,000
Total	100,000

Apply these indirect costs to the different buildings using both square metres and estimated hours of cleaning time. Which application procedure is better?

Solution

If square metres are used, the application rate is £100,000/200,000m², or £0.50 per m². Using this application rate, the application of estimated indirect costs follows:

	m^2	Application rate (£)	Estimated indirect costs (£)
Anderson Office Building	100,000	0.50	50,000
Carla's Pizza	10,000	0.50	5,000
Town Hall	90,000	0.50	45,000
Total applied costs			100,000

If estimated hours of cleaning are used, the application rate is £100,000/20,000 hours, or £5.00 per hour of cleaning. Using this application rate, the application of estimated indirect costs follows:

	Estimated hours	Application rate (£)	Estimated indirect costs (£)
Anderson Office Building	8,000	5.00	40,000
Carla's Pizza	6,000	5.00	30,000
Town Hall	6,000	5.00	30,000
Total applied costs			100,000

Insufficient evidence is available to determine which application procedure is better. The goal is to apply indirect costs to approximate the costs of using the indirect resources. The cost of using supplies probably is associated more closely with the hours of cleaning time, although the cost of floor wax could be associated more closely with the square metres of floor space. The administrative cost may be fixed and common to all the cleaning jobs and does not represent a cost of providing a specific cleaning job. The administrative costs would have to be analysed more carefully to determine if they represent costs of individual cleaning service jobs. If not, the administrative costs should not be applied to the different cleaning service jobs to estimate indirect costs.

Concept **review**

1 How are indirect product costs traced to different products and services using a single cost driver?

2 What are some problems in tracing indirect product costs using a single cost driver?

Bended Knee Skateboards (continued)

Bended Knee Skateboards could trace indirect costs by many different types of single cost drivers. Two possible cost drivers are the number of units and the number of direct labour hours. The total indirect costs are estimated to be £450,000. The number of units is estimated to be 50,000 of flat boards and 5,000 of moulded boards, or a total of 55,000 units. Therefore, the application rate by number of units equals £450,000/55,000 unit, or about £8.181818 per unit. With this application rate, the indirect costs would be traced in the following manner:

	Number of units	Application rate (£)	Traced costs (£)
Flat skateboards	50,000	8.181818	409,091
Moulded skateboards	5,000	8.181818	40,909
Total traced costs			450,000

Based on this tracing of indirect costs, the estimated cost per unit of the two types of skateboards is:

	Direct materials (£)	Direct labour (£)	Indirect costs (£)	Cost/unit (£)
Flat skateboards	1.08	5.00	8.18	14.26
Moulded skateboards	1.20	10.00	8.18	19.38

Bended Knee Skateboard also could apply indirect costs using the estimated number of direct labour hours. Each flat skateboard uses an estimated 0.5 hours of direct labour and each moulded skateboard uses an estimated 1.0 hours of direct labour. A total of (0.5 hours/unit) × (50,000 units), or 25,000 hours, are expected to be used for the flat skateboard and (1 hour/unit) × (5,000 units), or 5,000 hours, are expected to be used for the moulded skateboard. Therefore, a total of 25,000 hours + 5,000 hours, or 30,000 direct labour hours, are expected to be used. The application rate would be £450,000/30,000 hours, or £15/hour. Using this application rate, the indirect costs would be applied in the following manner:

	Units	Number of hours	Application rate (£)	Traced costs (£)	Traced costs per unit (£)
Flat skateboards	50,000	25,000	15	375,000	7.50
Moulded skateboards	5,000	5,000	15	75,000	15.00
Total traced costs				450,000	

→

Based on this tracing of indirect costs, the estimated cost per unit of the two types of skateboards is:

	Direct materials (£)	Direct labour (£)	Indirect costs (£)	Cost/unit (£)
Flat skateboards	1.08	5.00	7.50	13.58
Moulded skateboards	1.20	10.00	15.00	26.20

Geoff Williams is very confused by these results. Using the number of units to trace indirect costs, both the flat skateboard with a £15 sales price and the moulded skateboard with a sales price of £25 are profitable. After this analysis, Geoff is suspicious of using a single cost driver to trace indirect costs. In fact, his analysis of the unit-, batch-, product- and facility-level costs indicate that a single cost driver will not trace indirect costs accurately.

SUMMARY

1 **Identify activities of the organization related to the different products and services of the organization.** The activities of the organization are linked either directly or indirectly to the different products and services of the organization.

2 **Treat products as cost objects for the purpose of making product-mix and pricing decisions.** Estimating the cost of a product allows managers to estimate the profitability of the product and whether to include that product in the product mix.

3 **Estimate the direct costs of a product or service.** Direct product and service costs are divided into direct labour and direct materials. Estimates of direct labour costs can be made by estimating the labour time required to make a product or service and multiplying that labour time by the estimated wage rate of labourers. The direct material cost is estimated by determining the necessary parts and materials and multiplying by their respective prices. The labour rates and price of materials are intended to approximate the opportunity cost of using the labour and materials.

4 **Identify different levels of indirect product costs.** Indirect product costs are unit-level if they vary by the number of units; batch-level if they vary by the number of batches; product-level if they vary by the number of products; and facility-level costs if they vary by the number and size of facilities.

5 **Trace indirect product costs using a cost driver.** Indirect costs are traced to products using the following steps: (1) identification of activities, (2) estimation of cost of activities, (3) selection of cost driver for each activity, (4) estimation of total usage of the cost driver, (5) calculation of cost-driver application rates, and (6) application of indirect activity costs based on usage of the cost drivers.

6 **Use activity-based costing to estimate the cost of a product or service.** Activity-based costing identifies activities that cause indirect costs and cost drivers that can be used to trace those activity costs to different products and services. An application rate is calculated for each cost driver to apply the indirect costs.

7 **Recognize costs and benefits of using activity-based costing.** Activity-based costing recognizes that indirect costs vary with different levels of operations. Indirect costs also have different causes and appropriate cost drivers are chosen to reflect these differences. Activity-based costing does not adjust for fixed opportunity costs and presumes that indirect costs vary with usage of the cost driver.

8 **Estimate product costs using a single cost driver.** With a single cost driver, all indirect product costs are lumped together to calculate an application rate. All indirect product costs then are traced based on the usage of the single cost driver.

KEY TERMS

Activity-based costing A process of identifying activities that cause indirect costs and choosing cost drivers to apply those indirect costs to different products and services.

Activity-based management A process of analysing the management of the different overhead activities to enable the organization to provide both customer and organizational value by operating more efficiently.

Batch-level costs Indirect costs that are associated with the number of batches of a particular product or service.

Cost driver The cause of the cost of an activity.

Cost-driver application rate The ratio of the total activity cost divided by the total expected usage of the cost driver of the activity.

Cost object An item to be costed for decision-making purposes.

Cost of goods sold (Numerical Example 3.6) The historical cost of products sold as reported in the profit and loss statement.

Direct labour Labour costs that can be identified with a specific product or service.

Direct materials Parts and raw materials of a product.

Direct product costs Costs that can be directly traced to a specific product.

Facility-level costs Indirect costs that are common to multiple products and services.

Indirect product costs Costs that are associated with more than one product.

Overhead costs Indirect costs of products or services.

Period costs Costs that are associated with periods of time, rather than products, for reporting to external parties.

Product or service cost The forgone opportunity of using resources to provide a product or service.

Product-level costs Costs associated with a product, but not with a particular unit or batch of the product.

Product-mix decision A decision on the types and proportions of products and services to offer.

Unit-level costs The costs associated with individual units of a product or service.

APPENDIX
Product costs and financial reporting

The product costs reported in financial reports are not necessarily the product costs that are estimated through ABC or other methods for management decisions. Managers are concerned about all of the costs related to the product from research and development to customer service. Financial reporting practices dictated by generally accepted accounting principles (GAAP), in the UK, Canada and the US for example, require that certain costs be treated as a cost of the period rather than a product cost. Period costs or expenses are assigned to the period of time in which they were incurred. Research and development, marketing and general administrative costs are period costs rather than product costs for financial reporting purposes. They become expenses of the period in which the expenditure occurred.

An additional expense of the period is the cost of the products sold during the period. The product costs of products sold are called **cost of goods sold**. The product costs of products not sold are treated as an asset and called inventory. Inventory costs only become cost of goods sold when the inventory is sold.

A major financial reporting issue is to determine whether a cost is a period cost or a product cost. If a particular cost is determined to be a period cost, it must be expensed immediately. If the cost is a product cost, then it becomes an expense of the period in which the product is sold, which could be in subsequent years. Managers often have preferences on whether a particular cost is treated as a period or product cost for financial reporting purposes, due to the potential influence of financial reports on shareholder wealth, management compensation and taxes. For internal planning decisions, however, managers prefer a product cost estimate that encompasses all aspects of making and delivering the product or service.

The typical profit and loss statement of a financial report of a company begins with revenues, which reflects the sales of the period. The cost of goods sold and other period expenses then are deducted from the revenues to determine net profit.

Numerical example 3.6

The Watermark Book Shop opens on 1 January 2008. During the year, the book shop purchases £500,000 of books. The freight charges to have the books delivered are £50,000 and are treated as product costs. Over the year, the book shop has the following other costs, which are treated as period costs:

	£
Rent	12,000
Advertising	30,000
Salaries	80,000

Watermark Book Shop has revenues of £800,000 during 2008 and has 20 per cent of its books unsold at the end of the year. Prepare a profit and loss statement for the book shop for 2008.

Solution

The freight charges are treated as product costs, therefore total product costs during the year are £550,000. Since 80 per cent of the books are sold during the year, the cost of goods sold is 80% × £550,000, or £440,000. The remaining product costs (20% × £550,000, or £110,000) remain as an asset called inventory. The period costs are completely expensed during 2008.

Watermark Book Shop
Profit and Loss Statement
Year 2008

	£
Revenues	800,000
Cost of goods sold	(440,000)
Rent	(12,000)
Advertising	(30,000)
Salaries	(80,000)
Net profit	238,000

Financial reports treat time periods as the cost object. Revenues through the revenue recognition principle and expenses through the matching principle are traced to different time periods. Making the period of time the cost object is not consistent with any specific internal planning decisions. The increased value or income of the organization achieved during a particular time period can be estimated by tracing costs and revenues to that particular period. This measure provides information to external users about the value of debt and ownership shares of the organization, and also provides information for owners to evaluate senior managers. For internal purposes, however, a measure of period profit only gives an indication of how well the existing organizational strategy is working. A loss during a period may indicate the organization needs to re-examine its strategy.

Numerical exercises

NE 3.1 Identify direct and indirect costs of activities LO 1, 3, 4

The Uplands Athletic Club estimates the cost of the following three departments: Aquatics, Court Sports and Aerobics/Weight Room. These departments had the following direct costs:

Aquatics: £200,000   Court Sports: £100,000   Aerobics/Weight Room: £100,000

In addition, estimated indirect costs for all three departments related to locker rooms and central administration costs were £200,000. These costs tend to be proportional to the department costs.

What are the total costs of each of the departments?

NE 3.2 Product costs and financial reporting (Appendix)

Albert Short buys model airplanes for £1 apiece and sells them for £2 apiece. In addition, it incurs administration expenses that are treated as a period expense. Albert Short began operations in 2006.

What is the profit for 2006, 2007 and 2008 given the following data?

Year	Units sold	Units purchased	Administration expenses (£)
2006	10,000	12,000	5,000
2007	25,000	30,000	10,000
2008	30,000	35,000	12,000

NE 3.3 Estimate direct product costs LO 3

What are the direct costs of a rugby ball that requires €0.20 of leather, €0.01 of string, and 5 minutes of labour at €6 per hour?

NE 3.4 Use single cost driver to trace indirect costs LO 5

The total expected overhead of a machine shop is £200,000. The overhead is traced using machine hours as a cost driver. The estimated machine hours for all products are 10,000 hours.

How much overhead is traced to a product that requires 20 machine hours?

NE 3.5 Use activity-based costing to trace indirect costs LO 6

Novex Corporation wants to trace costs to its customers through ABC. The following activities and costs are traced using cost drivers:

Activity	Expected cost (€)	Cost driver	Expected usage of cost driver
Advertising	200,000	Sales	€2,000,000
Customer Service	80,000	Number of calls	10,000 calls
Accounting	140,000	Number of customers	2,000

What is the indirect cost of a customer who buys €20,000 of Novex's products and makes 20 calls to customer service?

NE 3.6 Costs for product-mix decisions LO 2

A farmer has an extra plot of ground for growing organic vegetables. She has the choice of planting carrots or onions. The plot would produce 500 kilograms of carrots and 1,000 kilograms of onions. The carrots sell for £0.17/kg and the onions sell for £0.11/kg. The carrot seeds cost £10 and the onion sets (similar to seeds) cost £40. Both carrots and onions require £50 of labour for tilling, weeding and harvesting.

What should the farmer plant on the acre?

NE 3.7 Costs associated with periods (Appendix)

A new hardware shop buys £340,000 of inventory during the year. The store sells all the items for 40 per cent greater than their costs. At the end of the year, the cost of inventory not yet sold was £40,000. The payments to the suppliers of the inventory are considered product costs, but all other costs are treated as period costs. Those costs include £15,000 for rent, £6,000 for utilities, and £60,000 for salaries.

What is the profit for the period?

NE 3.8 Estimating direct product costs LO 3

The Wooden Chair Company makes walnut and oak chairs. The cost of walnut is £2.40 per metre and the cost of oak £3.00 per metre. The controller of the Wooden Chair Company estimates that both walnut and oak chairs use 10 metres of wood. The cutting, assembling, and finishing of both walnut and oak chairs require 3 direct labour hours. Labour costs are £8 per hour.

What are the direct product costs of walnut and oak chairs?

NE 3.9 Estimating direct service costs LO 3

A CA firm is estimating the direct service costs of performing an audit. The firm estimates that the audit will require 5 partner hours, 20 manager hours and 50 assistant hours. The estimated opportunity costs of using these people are £150 for partners, £80 for managers and £40 for assistants.

What is the direct service cost of performing the audit?

NE 3.10 Estimating application rates LO 4

Suppose engineering is identified as a product-level, indirect cost activity and the number of hours engineers devote to each product is used as a cost driver. Engineering costs are €100,000. Product A uses 700 hours and product B uses 300 hours for a total of 1,000 engineering hours. There are only two products.

What is the application rate for engineering costs? How is this rate applied to products A and B?

NE 3.11 Estimating indirect product costs using a single cost driver LO 5, 8

A sheet metal wholesaler purchases sheet metal and cuts and bends the sheet metal to the specifications of its customers. The cutting and bending require the use of large, expensive machines. Since most of the indirect costs are related to these machines, the manager of the company decides to apply indirect costs based on the number of machine hours required to meet customer specifications. The manager estimates that total indirect costs for the next period will be £100,000 and the machines will be used a total of 2,000 hours.

a What is the application rate for indirect costs?
b What is the applied indirect cost of a job that requires 4 hours of machine time?

Numerical problems

NP 3.1 Product-mix decision LO 2

John Jitters, owner of the Virtual Buzz Coffee House, is having a fit. Many customers have expressed disappointment that the Virtual Buzz does not serve espresso hot chocolate. Currently, Virtual Buzz serves both espresso and hot chocolate separately, but not together. The espresso sells for £0.75 per shot and costs £0.40 to make. The hot chocolate sells for £1.75 per mug and costs £0.50 to make. If John were to make espresso hot chocolate, he would sell it for £2.50, but it would cost £1.40 per mug to make. Monthly sales of espresso and hot chocolate are currently 3,000 shots and 300 mugs, respectively. Based on customer responses, John estimates that he could sell 500 mugs of the espresso hot chocolate per month, but his sales of hot chocolate would be cut in half. John does not feel that his other beverage sales will be affected.

Should John add espresso hot chocolate to his product mix?

NP 3.2 Relating costs to time periods (Appendix)

Euromaster Artworks buys and sells paintings. During March, the company had the following paintings (with their costs) in inventory. Some of the paintings have been sold and the sales price is also reported.

Painting	Cost (€)	Sales price (€)
Van Goof	30,000	50,000
Rembranch	20,000	Not sold
Angelomichael	10,000	40,000
Gogone	25,000	Not sold
Monnay	13,000	10,000
Picatto	3,000	7,000

Euromaster Artworks also has the following period costs during March: rent – €3,000, salaries – €10,000, utilities – €1,000, insurance – €500.

What is the profit for Euromaster Artworks during March?

NP 3.3 Estimating direct service costs LO 3

Southampton Bank provides house loans for the region. Customers seeking a loan to buy a house initially talk to a loan officer who gathers the appropriate information about the customers. The bank then hires a local appraiser to evaluate the home being purchased. The customer and appraisal information is then sent to the vice president of the bank to make the final decision on the home loan. If both the bank and customer agree on the conditions of the home loan, the bank sends its lawyer to the closing of the house sale with the appropriate documents. Once the bank loan is implemented, a loan maintenance officer receives and records the monthly payments and sends the cheques on to the treasurer, where they are deposited in the bank. The average time spent on a house loan by each of these employees and their hourly wages are as follows:

Employee	Time (hours)	Wage rate/hour (£)
Loan officer	2.0*	15
Appraiser	3.0*	40
Vice president	0.5*	80
Lawyer	2.0*	70
Loan maintenance officer	4.0/year	20
Treasurer	1.0/year	30

*Only in the first year of the loan

a A decision to make the loan is made by the vice president. The loan officer and appraisal work has been completed already. What is the cost of a loan application that has been turned down?

b If the loan is accepted, the remaining labour costs are incurred. What is the average direct labour cost of an accepted loan in the first year?

c What is the average direct labour cost of an accepted loan in the second year?

NP 3.4 Estimating indirect service costs using a single cost driver LO 4, 8

A car repair shop applies overhead to different service jobs using direct labour hours. The manager estimates that total indirect costs will be £30,000 and total direct labour hours will be 2,000.

a What is the application rate for indirect costs?

b If a service job requires 5 direct labour hours, how much indirect service costs will be applied to that service job?

c If direct labour costs £10 per hour, what would be the total service costs of a service job that requires 6 direct labour hours and requires £100 of parts?

NP 3.5 Activity-based costing LO 6

Collins Sheet Metal Shop is considering adding a metal dry box for rafts to its product mix. The metal box requires 20 square metres of 0.35cm aluminum. The cost of the aluminum sheet metal is £5 per square metre. Direct labour on the box is estimated to be 5 hours at £10/hour. The following activities, their cost drivers and application rates are expected to be used in making the new box:

Activity	Cost driver	Application rate	Usage per dry box
Bending	Number of bends	£0.20/bend	20 bends
Drilling	Number of holes	£0.10/hole	30 holes
Welding	Number of centimetres	£0.30/cm	100 centimetres
Marketing	Number of products	£50/product	Marketed as 1 product
Accounting	Number of sales	£5/sale	Sold individually

Collins Sheet Metal is making 10 of these dry boxes. What is the expected cost per dry box?

NP 3.6 Estimating product costs LO 8

A tennis racquet manufacturer makes several kinds of tennis racquets. At the start of the year, the manufacturer estimates overhead to be equal to €4 million. The overhead is applied to tennis racquets based on direct labour costs, which are estimated to be €2 million in the coming year. Direct material costs are estimated to be €3 million.

a What is the application rate for the manufacturer?
b What is the product cost of a batch of 1,000 racquets that use 200 direct labour hours at €10 per hour and €5,000 of direct materials?

NP 3.7 Multiple cost drivers LO 6

A manufacturing firm has the following expected overhead costs, cost drivers and expected cost-driver usage:

Overhead item	Cost driver	Expected cost (£)	Expected cost-driver usage
President's salary	Number of products	100,000	100
Personnel dept.	Direct labour hours	80,000	8,000
Machine set-ups	Number of batches	50,000	250

What is the indirect cost of a product that uses 100 direct labour hours and requires 5 batches to make 100 units?

NP 3.8 Cost of a bank service LO 2, 6

First Midlands Bank is a large, multi-branch bank offering a wide variety of commercial and retail banking services. First Midlands determines the cost of various services to provide information for a variety of decisions.

One set of services is a retail loan operation providing residential mortgages, car loans and student college loans. At a branch bank, an applicant files a loan application. The branch manager is responsible for completing the loan application. From there, the loan application is sent to the loan-processing department, where the applicant's prior credit history is checked. Here, a recommendation is made whether to approve the loan or not, based on the applicant's credit history and current financial situation. This recommendation is forwarded to the loan committee of senior lending officers who review the file and make a final decision.

Thus, there are three stages to making a loan: application in a branch, the loan-processing department and the loan committee. Mr and Mrs Jones visit the High Street branch and file an application for a residential mortgage. The following information about each stage of processing the Jones' loan application is available:

- *High street branch bank.* The branch manager spends one hour taking the application. The branch manager spends 1,000 hours per year of her total time taking loan applications, and the remainder of her time providing other direct services to customers. Total overhead in the high street branch is budgeted to be £259,000 excluding the manager's salary. It is traced to direct customer services using the branch manager's time spent providing direct customer services. The branch manager's annual salary is £42,600.
- *Processing department.* The processing department budgets its total overhead for the year to be £800,000, which is traced to loans processed using direct labour hours. Budgeted direct labour hours for the year are 40,000 hours. Direct labour hours in the processing department cost £18 per direct labour hour. The Jones' loan requires 5 direct labour hours in the loan-processing department.
- *Loan committee.* Ten senior bank executives comprise the loan committee. The loan committee meets 52 times per year, every Wednesday, all day, to approve all loans. The average salary and benefits of each member of the loan committee is £104,000. The loan committee spends 15 minutes reviewing the Jones' loan application before approving it.

For costing purposes, all employees are assumed to work eight-hour days, five days per week, and 52 weeks per year.

Calculate the total cost of taking the application, processing and approval for the Jones' mortgage.

NP 3.9 Exterior house painters LO 3

Your company, Day-Glo Painting, has just finished its first year of operation. During its first year of operation, you painted the exterior of 20 houses in pink with purple trim. Although the first few homeowners were unsure about the colours and threatened to sue the company, the pink and purple houses are now becoming a fad and are quite popular. The profit and loss statement for the company during the first year is:

Day-Glo Painting
Profit and Loss Statement
Year of 2008

	£
Revenues	120,000
Direct labour (£20/hour)	(75,000)
Paint	(20,000)
Rental of painting equipment	(5,000)
General administration	(10,000)
Profit	£10,000

The direct labour of painting and cost of paint vary with the square metres of surface area painted. During the year, the company painted 400,000m^2 of surface. In addition, direct labour, but no significant paint, is used to paint the trim around doors and windows. Painting trim takes an hour per 20m of trim. During 2008, the company painted 40,000m of trim.

The second year is just beginning. The time and cost of labour, the cost of paint per litre, and the cost of rental and general administration are expected to be the same in the second year. Day-Glo Painting is bidding to paint a house that has 25,000m^2 of surface area and 3,000m of trim.

a What is the cost of paint per square metre of surface?
b What is the cost of direct labour per metre of trim?
c What is the cost of direct labour per square metre of surface?
d What is the rental and administration cost of painting the house?
e What is the total cost of painting the house?

NP 3.10 Product cost with multiple cost drivers LO 4, 5, 6

Neptune Corporation is planning on making 1,000 units of toy planets. The planets use £1 of raw materials per unit and 10 minutes of direct labour at £12 per hour. The manufacture of the 1,000 planets also uses the following overhead cost drivers:

Cost driver	Application rate	Usage in making toy planets
Machine hours	£20/machine hour	100 machine hours
Number of set-ups	£200/set-up	3 set-ups
Raw material cost	£0.20/£1 of raw materials	£1,000 of raw materials
Number of products	£4,000/product	1 product

a Describe each of the cost drivers as representing unit-level, batch-level, product-level or facility-level costs.

Machine hours _____   Number of set-ups _____

Raw materials cost _____   Number of products _____

b What is the average cost per unit for making toy planets?

NP 3.11 Comparing single cost drivers with ABC LO 6, 7, 8

A road contractor has been using kilometres of road constructed as a cost driver. Based on last year's costs, he estimates that he can build a kilometre of road for £3 million. The county has recently asked him for an estimate to build 20km of road.

Before making his bid based on his £3 million/km estimate, he goes to his accountant for advice. The accountant has analysed last year's costs very differently. She has divided last year's costs into different activities and chosen a cost driver and measured its usage last year. Her estimates are as follows:

Activity	Costs (£m)	Cost driver	Cost driver usage
Surveying	10	Hours	200,000 hours
Excavating	200	Tonnes of earth moved	2,000,000 tonnes
Bridges	120	Number of bridges	60 bridges
Grading	80	Number of km	200 kilometres
Gravel	30	Tonnes of gravel	750,000 tonnes
Paving	160	Number of km	200 kilometres

The costs from last year appear to be good estimates of costs in the coming year.

The 20km of county road up for bid will require 30,000 hours of surveying, 300,000 tonnes of earth moved, 10 bridges and 80,000 tonnes of gravel.

a Allowing for a 10 per cent profit, what should be the road contractor's bid using the £3 million/km cost driver?
b What is wrong with using kilometres as a cost driver?
c Allowing for a 10 per cent profit, what should be the road contractor's bid using the multiple cost drivers suggested by the accountant?

NP 3.12 Using regression to choose cost drivers LO 5

During the past 10 months, the Arcade Corporation has had the following indirect costs. The Arcade Corporation is trying to determine a good cost driver for its indirect costs. The usage of two potential cost drivers, direct labour hours and machine hours, has also been recorded over the past 10 months.

Month	Indirect costs (£000)	Direct labour hours	Machine hours
1	3,200	5,000	3,000
2	3,600	5,100	3,400
3	3,800	5,400	3,500
4	3,500	5,200	3,300
5	2,800	5,000	2,900
6	4,000	5,500	4,000
7	3,500	5,100	3,400
8	3,700	5,400	3,800
9	4,200	5,700	4,200
10	2,500	4,500	2,600

Which cost driver is most closely associated with the indirect costs?

NP 3.13 Tracing activity costs to products LO 5

GMPK treats its administrative support group as an indirect cost for its three major services: auditing, tax and consulting. The estimated costs of the administrative support group are €300,000 for the year. The firm is considering the following cost drivers with the corresponding usage by each service.

Cost driver	Auditing	Tax	Consulting
Number of telephone calls	800 calls	100 calls	100 calls
Revenue in euros	€4 million	€4 million	€4 million
Hours working on projects	4,000 hours	4,000 hours	2,000 hours

a Which cost driver appears to reflect most accurately the costs of the administrative support group?
b How are the costs of the administrative support group traced using each cost driver?
c Why might GMPK decide to use a cost driver different than the cost driver that most accurately reflects the costs of the administrative support group?

NP 3.14 Activity-based costing LO 6

A dialysis clinic offers two services: haemodialysis (HD) and peritoneal dialysis (PD). HD requires patients to come to the clinic three times a week to receive treatment. PD allows patients to administer their own treatment daily in their own homes. The profit analysis of the two services are as follows:

	Total (£)	HD (£)	PD (£)
Revenues			
Total revenue	3,006,775	1,860,287	1,146,488
Analysed service costs			
Standard supplies	664,900	512,619	152,281
Episodic supplies	310,695	98,680	212,015
General overhead	785,825		
Unanalysed service costs			
Durable equipment	137,046	116,489	20,557
Nursing services	883,280	750,788	132,492

Activity analysis of the general overhead indicated the following costs, cost drivers and their usage:

Activity	Costs	Cost driver	HD usage	PD usage
Facility costs	£233,226	Square footage	18,900	11,100
Support staff	354,682	Number of patients	102	62
Communications	157,219	Number of treatments	14,343	20,624
Utilities	40,698	Kilowatt usage	563,295	99,405
Total	£785,825			

What is the profitability of the two services under ABC? Calculate the average cost per treatment using ABC.

Source: Adapted from 'Applying ABC to Healthcare' in *Management Accounting* (February, 1997).

Analysis and interpretation problems

AIP 3.1 Product-mix decision LO 2

Scoop's Ice Cream is a small company that makes its own premium ice cream and sells ice cream cones and cartons of ice cream in a retail space of the establishment. The company has been known for its 23 flavours of ice cream. The owner of Scoop's, however, is thinking of adding a 24th flavour: sticky toffee pudding. Sticky toffee pudding is a mixture of vanilla ice cream, raisins, hazelnuts and chunks of caramel toffee. Scoop's currently makes vanilla ice cream, but none of its other products use raisins, hazelnuts or caramel toffee.

What costs should be considered in deciding whether to add sticky toffee pudding to the Scoop's product mix?

AIP 3.2 Identifying direct costs of a service organization LO 3

Avanti Airlines is attempting to estimate the direct cost of flying a passenger from Bologna, Italy to Bordeaux, France. The estimation of direct costs is the initial step in determining a new pricing strategy for the firm. A careful examination of operations, however, indicates that very few costs can be traced directly to a specific passenger on a flight.

Identify the direct costs of servicing an airline passenger and how they could be measured.

AIP 3.3 Level of indirect costs LO 4

Describe the following activities as unit-level, batch-level product-level or facility-level.

a Sending lorry shipments of products to customers.
b Providing computer networking processing services for the office.
c Operating a machine to make products.

d Setting up machines to make different products.

e Applying for patents on products.

f Accounting for sales transactions.

AIP 3.4 Activity-based costing LO 6, 7

Indicate by putting a T or an F next to the statement whether you think it is true or false.

a ABC is likely to benefit multi-product firms more than single product firms.

b A move from a single unit-based cost driver to ABC is likely to shift overhead from low-volume products to high-volume products.

c ABC improves the tracing of direct costs to products.

d With ABC, all cost drivers should be correlated with the number of units of output.

e The application rate per cost driver is normally calculated at the end of the period.

AIP 3.5 Levels of indirect costs LO 4

A railway company is trying to decide how to charge its customers for carrying freight. A manager suggests the following would be a good measure upon which to base the price of transporting freight: multiply the weight in kilograms times the distance travelled in kilometres.

a What types of customers will the railway company tend to lose to other transport companies, if it decides to charge customers based on kilograms times kilometres travelled?

b Suggest a pricing system for freight based on the concept of activity-based costing.

AIP 3.6 Cost reduction LO 4

In 2007, Japan Airlines Group (JAL) announced a medium-term business plan with a focus on product competitiveness. Included in the plan are a decrease in the number of large aircraft, especially on international routes, and a reduction in aircraft types and cabin configurations. In the longer term, JAL plans to reduce the number of aircraft types from 9 to 5 or 6. The company, however, is not planning to decrease the number of airplanes in its fleet, only the composition of the fleet.

a How does the reduction in the number of large aircraft, different types of planes and cabin configurations lead to cost reductions?

b How does this action relate to the different levels of indirect costs?

Source: Based on 'JAL Group Announces FY2007-2010 Medium Term Revival Plan', www.jal.com/en/corporate/ (accessed 13 February 2007).

AIP 3.7 Costs of providing a service LO 3, 8

The Municipality of Progress is considering a reimbursement fee to recover costs of its Fire Authority in cases where the local court finds the parties responsible for the fire guilty of gross negligence. If the programme is successful, the municipality may extend it to all emergency services and be able to reduce the local council tax levy. Progress currently uses labour hours to trace costs to different services. The cost per labour hour is determined as follows:

	£
Annual salaries and benefits (12,480 hours)	225,000
Education and training	50,000
Property and liability insurance	40,000
Depreciation of building and equipment	65,000
Operating supplies	25,000
Utilities	20,000
Total annual costs	425,000

Cost per labour hour = £425,000/12,480 = £34.05/labour hour

The Fire Authority currently performs many services including: (1) fire fighting, (2) medical assistance, (3) hazardous waste removal, (4) rescuing pets, (5) search and rescue, (6) community service at local schools and the senior citizen centre, (7) training and (8) maintenance of equipment. The latter three activities account for over 80 per cent of the annual labour hours.

Is the fee of £34.05/labour hour an accurate measure of the cost of fighting fires due to gross negligence?

AIP 3.8 Relating activities to products LO 1

A fast-food restaurant is trying to determine the cost of its two services: counter-service/eat-in and drive-through/take-away. Describe the typical activities associated with a fast-food restaurant.

Which activities are common to both services and which activities are only related to one service?

AIP 3.9 Implementing activity-based costing LO 7

Critically discuss the following quotation:

ABC (activity-based cost) information, by itself, does not invoke actions and decisions leading to improved profits and operating performance. . . . For ABC systems to be effective, everyone in the company – from top management to operating personnel – must view them as cost management tools rather than as accounting tools. To achieve this objective, the accounting or finance department must relinquish ownership of these systems to the users. If accounting or finance fails to understand this key point, then ABC is unlikely to succeed. . . . While traditional systems are the property of accounting and are used to support the financial accounting process, successful ABC systems are owned by the functions and are designed to support the needs of cost management, not financial accounting. The result is a reduction in the role of accounting in the management of costs. '(M)ost companies that implement ABC systems run them in parallel to their financial accounting systems. Parallel systems remove the risk of compromising the cost management capabilities of ABC to accommodate financial accounting rules and regulations.'

Source: Robin Cooper, 'Look Out, Management Accountants,' *Management Accounting* (May 1996), pp. 20–21.

Extended **analysis** and **interpretation** problem

AIP 3.10 Pilot plant

The Bion Company has a Research and Development (R&D) building which is shared by three wire and cable groups: High Voltage, Medium Voltage and Low Voltage. Adjacent to the R&D building is a pilot plant, a small-scale production facility designed for limited runs of experimental and commercial products. The three groups rely on the pilot plant to produce samples of their formulations.

In the pilot plant, sample sizes vary from about 1,000kg to 10,000kg. The R&D groups, including the pilot plant, are run as cost centres. The pilot plant also takes on special production runs for external customers that are too small for a regular plant. The pilot plant consists of three combination blending/extruding machines, which produce pellets of compounded material. Unlike large commercial compounding machines, which can operate 24 hours a day, these machines are run for approximately 1,000 hours a year. In the past, the pilot plant has costed its jobs based on direct materials, variable machine time and allocated overhead. Overhead is allocated by machine time. A single plant-wide machine rate is calculated pooling all three machines. The overhead pool includes plant fixed costs plus the labour cost of the department.

Approximately 20 per cent of the machine technicians' time is spent performing general clean up and maintenance. Before each job, machine time is calculated by a computer program, which outputs feed rate and set-up parameters. Each product is scheduled to a specific machine based on its formulation. The cost schedule of each machine is shown below. Capacity represents the historic annual average capacity.

	Clean-up (hours/batch)	Capacity (kg/yr)	Variable cost (£/hr)	Operators
Machine 1	4	250,000	25	2
Machine 2	6	250,000	25	2
Machine 3	8	500,000	50	1

Fixed costs:	£200,000/yr
Labour costs: 1 manager	@£45,000/yr
6 technicians	@£30,000/yr

While formulations vary considerably, 90 per cent of the blends are either resin or flame-retardant magnesium hydroxide. These bulky materials normally are ordered one to two weeks ahead of time, and take up much of the floor space. The additives are quite standard and are kept in stock. Weigh-ups and general set-up are time consuming and vary from job to job: a formulation that requires seven additives takes considerably more time to prepare than a similar run with two additives. In the past, time spent on set-up was not tracked, but it is a simple matter for the chief operator to include these numbers with the run report. One of the technicians is not assigned to a particular machine, but is responsible for arranging stock on the floor. The manager spends most of his time scheduling runs and attending to administrative work.

In a typical job, total weigh-up time is the amount of labour time required to locate, prepare and mix the direct materials prior to inserting them in the machine.

Job #71302

		Composition and Direct Cost	
Sample run 5,000 kg:	90%	NCPE-0600, RESIN	£0.10/kg
	8%	KISUMA, FLAME RETARDANT	£0.12/kg
	2%	COMPOUND Z, ANTI OXIDANT	£0.14/kg
RUN ON MACHINE 1		250 kg per hr for 20 hours	
TOTAL WEIGH-UP TIME*		16 employee hours	

*Total weigh-up time is the amount of labour time required to locate, prepare and mix the direct materials prior to inserting them in the machine.

Required

a Calculate the cost of the sample run as charged to the Low Voltage department.

b What is wrong with this system? Construct an alternative costing system and describe its benefits.

c Re-calculate the cost of this run using this new system.

(Contributed by B. Graham, R. Mardsen, J. Quinn, P. Leparulo, N. Ahmed, and J. Vallandingham.)

CHAPTER FOUR

Managing activities
(Strategy and planning)

Learning objectives

1. Select a competitive strategy for an organization.

2. Use activity-based management to reduce the costs of an organization without affecting customer value.

3. Make trade-offs in the product life cycle to reduce overall product costs.

4. Use target costing as a method to select viable products and reduce product cost.

5. Estimate the costs of using different suppliers.

6. Use supply chain management to operate more efficiently and reduce costs.

7. Estimate customer profitability.

8. Make pricing decisions that maximize organizational value.

9. Explain why some organizations use cost-based pricing.

Dell Computer Corporation

As the individual behind Dell, Michael Dell is recognized for his vigilance in keeping Dell focused on the customer. Dell Computer Corporation designs, develops, manufactures, markets, services and supports a wide range of computer systems, including desktops, notebooks, network servers, peripherals and IT infrastructure software. From its base in Round Rock, Texas, Dell conducts operations and sells its products worldwide

through wholly-owned subsidiaries. Dell has seen many changes in its business and market since its initial days in 1984, when it operated from a bedroom in a university dormitory. Sales have gone from $6 million in its first year to almost $60 billion.

The successful implementation of Dell's strategy focused on profitability, liquidity and growth necessary to achieve organizational goals. Many external factors also affect Dell's business model. These factors include the general economic and business environment, the global demand for computing systems, and the level and intensity of competition in the computing industry. In an era of global markets and technological change, Dell has attempted to keep pace with changing customer preferences. For example, while many firms were only just beginning to confront the challenges of e-commerce, Dell had reacted swiftly to the Internet. Dell introduced online shopping in 1995, well before many competitors were thinking about the opportunity.

STRATEGIC DECISIONS

Organizations face two groups of planning decisions: strategic and short-term. Strategic decisions have long-term implications. Strategic decisions go beyond the confines of the organization and determine how the organization operates in a global economy. Strategies must consider the strengths and weaknesses of the organization and how the organization can take advantage of market opportunities. Market opportunities occur when an organization can add greater customer value relative to competing organizations. Strategic decisions are normally made by the leaders of the organization to provide focus and direction. This chapter focuses on strategic decisions and their management accounting implications.

Members of an organization must also make shorter-term planning decisions. Every day, managers must decide how many units of different products to make, how to use their scarce resources and how to modify activities to make the organization operate more efficiently. With short-term planning decisions, most of the organizational resources are fixed. In the short run, the organization will not be able easily to change the capacity of its facilities. Therefore, managers will have to make decisions based on using the existing space. Short-run decisions will also be required to adapt to minor changes in market conditions. Chapter 5 is devoted to short-term planning decisions.

In order for a strategy to be successful, an organization must continually adapt to customer preferences, and do so better than its competitors. In the first chapter, the critical success factors were defined as innovative product/service design, high-quality products and services, and low-cost production. Each of these strategies offers an opportunity to compete, but an organization must identify its comparative advantages before selecting a strategy.

Organizations that choose to compete through innovative design of products and services must excel at understanding their customers through marketing efforts. The organizations must be creative and fast-moving to meet the changing preferences of their customers. Excelling in design and engineering is critical. Changes in technology often open windows of opportunity, so organizations that compete through innovation are usually on the cutting edge of the technological revolution. Nokia, a world leader in mobile telephones, keeps ahead of the competition through constant innovation to offer the latest technology. Nokia's strategy is to introduce new products yearly, such as its early move into mobile phones with digital cameras and digital audio players, pre-empting other market players.

Amazon uses technology to make shopping easy; incentives, e-newsletters and 'free' shipping encourage repeat sales. Technology replaces bricks and mortar resulting in lower prices.

Organizations that choose to compete through the delivery of high-quality products and services must excel in manufacturing and the delivery of customer services. When customers contract with an organization, they expect products and/or services with specific characteristics. The delivery of products and services that do not meet those expectations will encourage customers to look for other suppliers. Alternatively, if customers can rely on an organization to consistently deliver products and services that conform to their expectations, the customer gains considerable value from repeat purchases from the organization. Amazon.co.uk, the Wal-Mart of the Internet, strives to meet customer expectations by using technology to determine customer preferences and to make these products readily available. One measure of success is the number of repeat customers. Repeat customers are encouraged to return through incentives, such as Amazon's membership programme which provides benefits, such as free shipping, for an annual fee.

Organizations that choose to compete through low-cost production excel through efficient operations. These organizations achieve lower production costs through a careful analysis of the different activities that they perform. Amazon.co.uk also competes through low-cost provision of goods and services. Compared to its bricks-and-mortar rivals, Amazon.co.uk offers lower prices due to lower investment in fixed costs, such as warehouses, instead of retail shops. Much of the remaining chapter examines ways to reduce costs through the analysis of activities.

Concept **review**

1 How do strategic decisions differ from short-run decisions?

2 What are the critical success factors to add customer value?

Dell Computer Corporation (continued)

Dell's value chain is customer-focused. The goal is to deliver the best customer experience through direct, comprehensive customer relationships, co-operative research and development with technology partners, custom-built computer systems and service and support programmes tailored to customer preferences. Recent concerns that Dell was losing its competitive edge in terms of the customer experience resulted in the launch of the 'Resolve in One' programme. This programme seeks to improve customer-service indicators such as call-centre waiting time, first-contact problem resolution and overall customer satisfaction.

Dell's value chain begins with the initial product design. Direct customer relationships provide Dell with a flow of information about its customers' plans and requirements. This market intelligence enables Dell to weigh customer preferences against Dell's products and services. The design stage incorporates this customer information to better understand end-users' needs and to deliver high-quality computer products and services tailored to meet those needs. Dell extends its direct relationship to its suppliers and strategic partners to ensure customer feedback is incorporated into their design and services.

ACTIVITY-BASED MANAGEMENT AND THE VALUE CHAIN

In Chapter 3, activities were analysed with the intent to determine product costs. Activity-based costing (ABC) was initially developed due to concerns that traditional accounting methods appeared to provide misleading product costs. ABC is an alternative way of tracing costs to products that, in some cases, leads to very different product costs. Improved product cost information alters either product prices or the product mix.

Activity-based management (ABM) extends ABC by analysing the management of activities, instead of simply retracing the costs of activities. The goal of ABM is to provide value to the customer and at the same time provide profit to the shareholders. ABM connects ABC to the strategy of the organization. To reap the potential benefits of ABM, organizations must integrate ABM with the organization's strategy to create customer value. If this integration does not take place, ABM implementation has often been less successful in providing improved information for decision making and control.

ABM achieves its twin goals of achieving customer and shareholder value primarily through the analysis of activities along the value chain. The value chain identifies those activities that affect the value received by a customer from purchasing the organization's products or services. Those activities that add value to the customer are called value-added activities. The value-added activities are described in the value chain of an organization. The value chain for the production of a motion picture would be:

Writing the script → The actors → Designing sets and costumes →
  Shooting the film → Editing → Advertising → Delivering the film to theatres

Each of the activities in the value chain is critical to the value derived by a customer viewing the film.

Another example of a value chain relates to the manufacture of oak chairs:

Design → Acquisition of materials → Cutting → Sanding → Assembly →
  Finishing → Marketing → Distribution → Customer service

Each of these activities is critical to making the oak chair and satisfying the customer.

Service organizations are likely to have different types of value chains. For example, a university might have a value chain that looks like this:

Research and development → Recruiting students → Teaching →
  Student services → Placement → Alumni relations

Research and development includes activities such as curriculum development, making teaching plans and acquiring knowledge for use in the classroom. Recruiting students involves writing informative brochures, marketing, soliciting applications and selecting qualified students. Teaching is the activity of communication and discovery in the classroom. Student services include other learning activities and advising. Placement involves helping students find employment. Alumni relations maintain communication with alumni. Each of these activities adds value to students, but is part of the cost of educating them.

Organizations also perform activities that are not on the value chain. These activities are called non-value-added activities. Non-value-added activities do not have any effect on customer value. For example, customers are not affected if products are moved from the manufacturing floor to inventory, if products remain in inventory for any length of time or if machines are set up for a production run. Also, many administrative activities have no direct effect on customer satisfaction. Each of these activities has a cost without any direct benefit to the customer. Therefore, the identification and measurement of non-value-added activities give some indication of cost-saving opportunities for an organization.

Activity-based management also implies a cross-functional approach to management rather than managing the functional areas such as manufacturing, engineering, finance, and customer service separately. Activities tend to be performed by employees of multi-functional teams. Activity analysis and the search for cost-reduction opportunities require input from employees from different functional areas. The use of multi-functional teams provides a means to foster information sharing and is consistent with ABM.

An analysis of activities through ABM should also include a comparison of how those activities are performed by other organizations. An organization should look at the 'best practices' of other organizations to establish a benchmark for evaluating its

Les Gibbon/Alamy

Every student has an opinion about university food. Many universities outsource food services, leading to lower costs and improved quality in some cases.

own practices. It then might choose to adapt these practices to its operations. Alternatively, the organization might determine that a particular activity can be performed better and at a lower cost by another organization. An opportunity, therefore, may exist to outsource the activity. **Outsourcing** is a decision to pay another organization to carry out certain activities. The decision to outsource an activity is based on the cost of performing the activity in-house versus the cost of paying an organization to perform the activity. Publishing companies, for example, may outsource editing and printing. Universities often outsource food, custodial services and bookstores. Organizations that outsource essentially all of their activities are called virtual organizations. Omnicom Group is an example of a virtual organization that provides marketing communications services to clients by acting primarily as a facilitator between the client and the service provider, rather than undertaking the work itself.

Organizational **analysis**

Omnicom Group Inc.

Omnicom Group Inc., through its wholly and partially-owned affiliates, provides a variety of marketing and communications services to clients worldwide. Omnicom offers its services in over 100 countries through a global portfolio of agency brands. With revenues of more than $10 billion, it is the largest firm in its peer group and recognized for its creativity and award-winning services. Omnicom's marketing and communications services include advertising in various media (e.g. the Internet, television, radio, newspaper and magazines),

customer relationship management (CRM), public relations, strategic media planning, direct and promotional marketing, and Internet and digital media development.

Omnicom delivers its services to clients through a virtual network of worldwide, national and regional independent agency brands. This virtual network enables Omnicom to provide clients with various services, such as interactive and mobile marketing, across its agencies and around the globe simultaneously. Omnicom Group's consistent maintenance of separate, independent agency brands enables it to represent competing clients.

Commissions charged on media billings are not uniform and are negotiated with the client. In accordance with industry practice, the media source typically bills the agency for the time or space purchased and the Omnicom Group bills its clients for this amount plus a commission. In many cases, fees are generated in lieu of commissions. Several different fee arrangements are used, depending on the client and individual agency. In general, fee charges relate to the cost of providing services plus a mark-up. Importantly, Omnicom outsources the major share of its business activities to its various subsidiaries and affiliates, operating as a facilitator between the client and the agency brand. Its own revenues are derived from the commissions earned on these outsourced services.

According to the trade journal, *Advertising Age*, Omnicom Group Inc. has consistently ranked as the largest advertising agency group worldwide. Why would an organization choose to outsource its advertising activity to Omnicom Group, instead of performing the activity in-house?

What advantages and disadvantages would the firm need to consider when selecting one alternative over the other?

Sources: *www.omnicomgroup.com*; Omnicom Group Inc. Form 10-K, 2006

The outsourcing decision should also consider quality and timely delivery. If outsourcing an activity means reduced quality control or late deliveries, the organization should reconsider its decision. Many European firms outsource certain activities to organizations in other countries because of lower costs. For example, call centres and technical support services are frequently established in other countries where staff and technical expertise are available at a lower cost. However, if lower costs are accompanied by reduced quality and slow delivery, these firms may be better off performing the activity in-house. The organization must evaluate the outsourcing decision in terms of its strategy to ensure that it does not put at risk activities critical to its success.

Outsourcing frequently presents ethical dilemmas. An example of this conflict can be found in the practice of many firms to outsource the preparation of income tax returns to firms in India. Lower labour costs for accounting professionals compared to salary rates in other countries makes India an attractive option for accounting firms. Firms can reduce their costs and focus on more lucrative work by contracting the preparation of tax returns to an Indian firm. Outsourced work may then reduce employment and training opportunities for local staff. The digital transmission and storage of tax documents could place a client's privacy and confidential information at risk. Another concern is the qualifications of staff in overseas locations, notwithstanding strong efforts to maintain high professional standards. These issues relate to the ethical responsibility of the accountant with respect to the client, including transparency in how accounting services are being provided. Finally, the ability to achieve higher profits through outsourcing is seen by many as the breaking of the social contract with local workers to provide well paid and secure jobs. Alternatively, firms argue that they need to be more efficient to compete in a global market. Governments have reacted to these arguments. For example, the US prohibits firms that have received a government contract from outsourcing this work outside the country.[1]

Numerical **example** 4.1

An Internet retailer of home furnishings purchases furniture from different manufacturers. The furniture is shipped to the company headquarters in Liverpool, where it is stored until sold. Then the furniture is shipped to the customer using

---

[1] R.G. Brody, M.J. Miller, and M.J. Rolleri (2007) 'Outsourcing Income Tax Returns to India: Legal, Ethical, and Professional Issues', *The CPA Journal* Online, www.nysscpa.org/cpajournal/2004/1204/perspectives/p12.html (accessed 20 February).

the company's lorry fleet. The activities, their costs, and the cost of best practices for the different activities are listed below.

Activity	Cost (£)	Cost of best competitor
Purchasing	5,000,000	6,000,000
Shipping to Liverpool	3,000,000	2,000,000
Receiving	500,000	600,000
Warehousing	2,000,000	2,000,000
Web page maintenance	800,000	600,000
Order processing	4,000,000	4,500,000
Shipping to customer	3,000,000	2,000,000

What activities are potential sources of cost savings?

Solution

Three of the activities are not on the value chain. Shipping to Liverpool, receiving those products and warehousing do not add value to the customer. Those activities could be replaced by having manufacturers ship directly to the customer. Therefore, the activity of shipping to the customer using its own fleet should be re-examined. Purchasing and order processing appear to be operating efficiently when compared to the cost of the best competitor, but web page maintenance is a potential source of cost savings either through improvement or outsourcing.

Concept review

1 How does activity-based management help an organization?

2 How does the analysis of activities lead to outsourcing?

Dell Computer Corporation (continued)

After the design has been completed, the next link in Dell's value chain is the actual production of the computer system. On-demand production of computer systems allows customers to 'design' the system to include the features and capabilities to match their specific requirements. Via the Internet or telephone, customers can configure the system that best matches their preferences at a price that represents fair value.

Once the computer is produced, the next stage is its delivery to the customer. Customers need not leave the comfort of their living rooms, as delivery via courier results in the product's arrival right at their doorsteps. The direct relationship continues after the sale, as dedicated account teams consisting of sales, customer service and technical personnel continue to support the customer's technology objectives.

Since Dell operates in a highly competitive industry with short product life cycles, the organization must eliminate activities that do not create customer and organizational value. Internal as well as external factors affect Dell's performance and both must be carefully monitored. One method to monitor and create organizational value is through the use of activity-based analysis and management.

For instance, Dell must effectively manage periodic product transitions and component availability; and develop new products based on new or evolving technologies and the market's acceptance of those products. Inventory control is necessary, as Dell must balance its inventory levels to minimize excess stock. The risk of obsolescence also is high, when product life cycles are short. Finally, activities are performed by individuals, and Dell must continue to improve its infrastructure (including personnel and systems) to keep pace with the growth in its overall business activities.

→

Dell analyses its various activities to determine which ones are essential to create shareholder and customer value. Some activities, such as carrying inventory, do not add value and possibly could be eliminated. Their elimination reduces costs and improves the company's bottom line.

COST REDUCTION

Cost reduction must be continually on the mind of managers of organizations. Low-cost production is one of the primary ways that organizations compete in a global economy. With strong competitive pressures, organizations have little control over prices. Therefore, an important way to improve profit is to decrease costs.

Activity-based management is one approach to reducing costs. The identification and reduction of non-value-added activities can increase profits by lowering costs. Also, outsourcing certain activities is another way to reduce costs.

In this section, two other cost-reduction approaches are examined: product life cycle and target costing.

■ Product life cycle

A strategic approach to making product-mix and pricing decisions and looking for cost reduction opportunities requires a broad perspective of the product and how it adds value to the customer. The **product life cycle** describes all the stages of supplying a product or service from its initial conception to the satisfaction of the last customer and the product's removal from the marketplace. The product life cycle recognizes that product costs are more than just the costs of making the product. An organization incurs considerable costs related to a product before the first unit is made. Additional costs also are incurred after the product is sold because of delivery costs and customer service. These costs are incurred over the whole life of the product, which may be as short as a month or as long as 50 years. High-fashion clothing, computers and electronic equipment tend to have very short product lives, since new innovations quickly cause existing products to be obsolete. Other products such as Weetabix have been around for many years, and are still popular.

The product life cycle begins with the initial planning and proposal stage. Organizational activities at this stage include marketing surveys to determine customer demand, analysis of demographics to evaluate customer characteristics, an analysis of competitors and an evaluation of the organization's strengths and weaknesses.

When a proposal is accepted, the product or service is designed and engineered. During the design and engineering process, comparisons are made with leading competitors' products and services. This process of comparing an organization's products and activities with those of other organizations is called **benchmarking**. The design stage is extremely important to the success of the product or service. Although the design and engineering activities themselves may not be very costly, the design and engineering stage pre-determines the major cost of providing the product or service. Once the design of the product or service is completed, most of the necessary raw materials, manufacturing activities and labour requirements have been determined.

The production stage is the stage of manufacturing or provision of services. Most of the product and service costs are incurred at this stage. Activities during the production stage include the acquisition of resources, setting up machines to manufacture the product, assembling the product and providing the service to the customer.

Once production begins, the organization must engage in distribution and customer service activities. An organization does not end its relationship with the customer at the time of the sale. Organizations should monitor customer satisfaction and obtain information on ways of improving the product or service. An organization should also support customers who are dissatisfied with the product or service through warranties and repairs to faulty products.

Each of these stages contains activities that are costly to perform. If the product life cycle is likely to be very long, a useful exercise in analysing the cost of a new product is to estimate the costs of the different stages over the life of the product. Occasionally companies forget to recognize the costs of initiating the product and the costs of customer service in estimating the cost of a product. Table 4.1 is an example of recognizing all of the costs over the product's life.

The costs of the later stages, however, are heavily influenced by the decisions made during the earlier stages. The planning and design stages commit the organization to most of the costs of providing a product or service. For example, the design stage determines the type of materials necessary to make the product. Unless the organization can find a cheaper supplier of materials, the cost of materials is committed at the time of product design. The cash outlays to buy the materials, however, are delayed until the production stage begins. Figure 4.1 shows the stages when product costs are committed and the stages when cash outlays are made.

Table 4.1 Costs of different stages in different years of the product life

Stage	2000 £	2001 £	2002 £	2003 £	2004 £	Totals £
Design	100,000	50,000				150,000
Marketing	20,000	40,000	100,000	30,000	10,000	200,000
Engineering	80,000	100,000	10,000	10,000		200,000
Production		100,000	800,000	700,000	100,000	1,700,000
Customer service			30,000	40,000	50,000	120,000
Total product cost						2,370,000

Figure 4.1 Product life cycle and costs

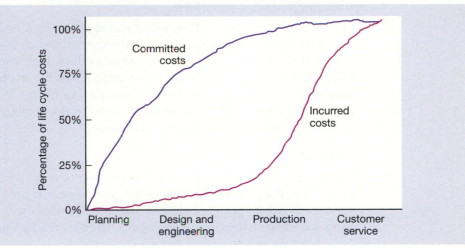

Since many product and service costs are pre-determined during the earlier stages of the product life cycle, management accountants should be involved. If management accountants become involved only during the production stage, their opportunities to influence the product or service cost through cost-saving decisions are limited.

Typical decisions related to the product life cycle involve trade-offs among its different stages. For example, more effort and cost at the planning stage can reduce the customer service costs. A well-planned product is more likely to satisfy customer demand and less likely to cause customer complaints and returned merchandise. Also, design and engineering efforts can reduce production costs. BMW spends considerable time and effort using three-dimensional designs for its automobiles. These three-dimensional designs are costly to prepare but reduce production costs because potential problems in the production stage can be identified much more easily than with two-dimensional designs.

The cost of the product to the customer does not end with its purchase. The customer incurs costs to operate, maintain and dispose of the product. Therefore, the seller of a product can add value to the customer by making the product less costly to operate, maintain and dispose of. For example, Apple Inc. is renowned for its user-friendly interfaces from its Mac to iPods. Trade-offs yielding overall cost reductions may involve reduced costs to the customer once the product is purchased. Most tyre shops are willing to accept used tyres when they are replaced, because their proper disposal is costly for the individual customer. The European Union has issued a number of directives dealing with the disposal of various products, including electronic goods, hazardous chemicals and medical equipment. Recycling and disposal costs are explicitly included by manufacturers in the cost of various products.

Stefan Sollfors/Alamy

Apple customers value the user-friendly design of its products. This design focus has enabled Apple to create brand recognition and loyalty in a competitive market.

Numerical **example** 4.2

SkiVite is in the process of designing and engineering a new snow ski especially suited for alpine conditions. Although the current design is acceptable, SkiVite is considering further design and engineering efforts that would cost the company €100,000. The engineering manager estimates that the improved design and engineering would reduce the cost of making a pair of skis by €11. SkiVite expects to make and sell 10,000 pairs of this new ski in the coming year. Should SkiVite spend the €100,000 to improve the ski's design?

Solution

Spending €100,000 in the design stage will save €11/pair × 10,000 pairs, or €110,000 in the production stage in the coming year. If production continues beyond the coming year, even greater production savings will occur. Therefore, the extra spending on designing and engineering benefits SkiVite.

■ Target costing

Target costing is a strategic management process for reducing costs at the early stages of product planning and design. Multi-disciplinary teams and group problem solving are key mechanisms to take full advantage of target costing techniques. The role of the management accountant within these teams is to ensure that the process includes a focus on financial management and product profitability.

With target costing, a product opportunity is identified first. The product opportunity is a description of all of the functional characteristics of the product. For example, a new car's functional characteristics would include engine size, wheelbase dimensions, interior and electronic components. At the same time, a selling price is identified that would make the model competitive in the marketplace. The product opportunity and the necessary functional characteristics are then turned over to the design and engineering department to determine if the product can be made at a sufficiently low cost to provide a profit for the organization. The target costing equation is as follows:

$$\textbf{Target cost } = \textbf{ Target selling price } - \textbf{ Target profit}$$

In target costing, the market determines the target selling price of products and little opportunity exists for the individual organizations to set prices. This process is often referred to as price-led costing, in contrast to cost-led pricing in which selling prices are based on the product cost plus a mark-up. Therefore, controlling costs is extremely important. The target profit is the profit margin that is required to provide an adequate return on the capital invested. It provides a measure of the opportunity cost of the capital invested in the product.

The target cost is frequently less than the initial cost estimate. The design is reworked and milestones established to reach the target cost. These milestones generally set a series of targets to be achieved over time instead of one-time targets that might prove impossible to attain. The iterative nature of the target costing process is important to maintain employee morale and prevent employee burn-out.

Target costing looks at all of the product costs in the product life cycle. The goal is to reduce the total product cost over time. The target costing process is a multi-functional team effort as trade-offs in cost reduction may be necessary. The organization does not want cost reduction in one area to be offset by cost increases in another. Using a concurrent design process, the team members can share their knowledge of design, marketing, manufacturing and purchasing such that the final product meets customer specifications. This approach provides opportunities for cost reduction at the design stage since the requirements of the entire product life cycle are recognized. Target costing reduces the risk inherent in a sequential design process in which one stage, such as manufacturing and marketing, can reject a product due to factors overlooked at an earlier step.[2]

Target costing has been common practice in Japan for many years. Toyota was one of the first companies to use the technique. Members of the sales division, who are closest to the customers and understand their preferences, identify cars with characteristics that are particularly attractive to customers. For example, dual-side air bags are a characteristic that most customers expect in the cars they buy. The sales staff establishes a price (say, €31,000) for such a car, and estimates the amount of sales for that model. Next, a profit per car (say, €2,000) is chosen to provide the necessary return to undertake the investment. A target cost (€31,000 − €2,000 = €29,000) is then determined to

---

[2] This section draws upon the Society of Management Accountants of Canada, *Management Accountants Standards,* Section 3400 (April 2002).

give Toyota the necessary profit. The company then seeks a design that will allow it to reduce costs without losing the functional characteristics. For example, the design team may find ways to re-design the manufacturing process or reduce the number of model-specific parts in order to reduce costs without affecting customer value. Target costing has allowed Toyota to reduce costs, but still manufacture high-quality cars.

Numerical **example** 4.3

The marketing department of Targa International identifies a new e-mail pager for which customers are willing to pay £300. Required features are an LCD screen, a keyboard and roller-wheel mouse. Targa's normal margin is 20 per cent of the sales price. What is the e-mail pager's target cost?

Solution

The margin is $0.20 \times £300$, or £60. Therefore, the target cost is $£300 - £60$, or £240. Targa must design an e-mail pager that can be produced at a maximum cost of £240. If Targa's current cost is greater than £240, then it can take steps to re-design its product and/or production process to reduce the cost without sacrificing customer value. If it cannot do so, then Targa will not be competitive in this market.

Concept **review**

1 How does an analysis of the product life cycle lead to lower costs?
2 What part of the product life cycle is extremely important in reducing costs using target costing?

Dell Computer Corporation (continued)

While Dell does not compete primarily on price, a key way to increase profits is to reduce costs, especially costs related to non-value-added activities. Customers do not receive value from inventory handling and storage, nor do they wish to bear the cost of obsolescent products. Therefore, building computers on demand translates into lower space requirements for inventory and lower investments in working capital.

This approach appears to be the model for sure success, yet it has not always been the case. At the end of the 1980s, Dell's sales and net income were growing at impressive rates. However, there was a downside to such rapid growth. To meet the increasing demand for its products, Dell purchased as many 256K memory chips as possible. Prices for memory chips were at their peak, but then chip prices decreased significantly. With the market introduction of 1 megabyte (MB) memory chips, Dell suddenly found itself with a surplus of expensive, obsolete chips.

Dell was forced to sell off the inventory, which decreased earnings. To compensate for the drop in earnings, Dell raised its prices. Its growth rate decreased, and its expansion into new countries lost momentum. After this experience, Dell analysed its inventory and purchasing activities. It adapted these activities to improve its inventory turnover and to utilize forecasting more effectively to reduce its overall cost of doing business. Dell has also suffered recently from the market savvy of competitors who view computers as entertainment systems, offer more stylish designs and have been quick to introduce computer processors from rival manufacturers. Dell's low-cost strategy has been forced to react to the innovation strategy being followed by its competitors. In a competitive market, customers demand both low-cost and innovative solutions.

Another way to reduce costs relates to Dell's direct customer relationship. This approach allows Dell to reduce the non-value-added costs of wholesale and retail networks. Dell's strategy differs from those of other computer firms, such as Hewlett-Packard and Toshiba, which compete by using both direct online sales and retail networks.

Outsourcing is another way to reduce costs. If Dell can outsource a product or service to an external supplier at a lower cost, it can eliminate one activity and concentrate on those that create organizational value. For example, the components in a Dell computer are produced by outside suppliers who deliver the parts as required. Outsourcing reduces the risk of carrying inventory and helps to reduce costs. Outsourcing does create other risks. For example, Dell suffers both loss of sales and market reputation when outsourced components fail. Faulty batteries shipped with Dell systems led to sales returns and warranty claims. In these situations, even when the supplier may be responsible, it is Dell's name that customers see on their failed computer.

Outsourcing also allows firms to focus on what they do best. For example, in late 2006, Dell and Altiris announced an agreement to co-develop the next generation of applications for integrated hardware and software management. The arrangement joins the complementary capabilities of world leaders in computing systems and systems management. The partnership with Altiris allows Dell to offer its customers improved information technology, while concentrating on value-added activities. The result should be better value for customers, which in turn should lead to improved organizational value for Dell.

SUPPLY CHAIN MANAGEMENT AND COSTS

Supply chain management focuses on the management of relations with other organizations. Each organization is a link in a supply chain. Products and services flow into the organization from external suppliers, and products and services flow out to customers.

Efficient interactions between different organizations in the supply chain have a substantial impact on reducing costs. The cost of parts and services from external suppliers is becoming a higher percentage of total costs, as organizations choose to outsource many of their activities. If an organization is looking for ways to reduce costs, interaction with suppliers is an obvious activity to examine given the proportion of costs related to suppliers.

Supplier and consumer organizations interact in many ways. Traditionally, consumer organizations look for suppliers of parts and services by requesting bids from supplier organizations. Most governmental organizations are required to go through a bidding process in selecting a supplier. The qualified supplier who submits the lowest bid is awarded the contract. The danger of this procedure, however, is that the lowest bidder is not always the cheapest supplier when other costs are considered.

■ Estimating the cost of a supplier

Suppliers affect an organization's costs in many different ways. The timeliness of the delivery of the parts or services affects costs. A late delivery can shut down an organization and be extremely expensive. The packaging of parts or products from suppliers also has an impact on costs. Some packaging is difficult to dismantle and dispose of. Ideally, an organization would like the supplier to package its parts or products so they are ready for immediate use without requiring unpacking and warehousing. Customers increasingly expect environmentally-friendly packaging. Suppliers must consider environmental impacts and disposal costs when designing packaging.

The quality of the supplier's products or services also has an effect on the costs of an organization. Even if an organization can return defective parts, the cost of inspecting and handling those defects can be large. A high-quality part is much easier to assemble and can reduce customer service costs because of reduced customer complaints.

Suppliers also affect purchasing costs. An organization incurs purchasing costs because purchase agents must contact and communicate with suppliers. Purchasing department staff must write purchase orders. Accountants must record transactions with suppliers and maintain supplier accounts. Accounts payable staff must prepare invoices for payment. Cheques need to be issued, frequently requiring the approval and signature of the organization's treasurer. Some suppliers require more purchasing costs than do other suppliers.

Treating the supplier as a cost object can help identify whether a supplier is truly a low-cost one. To determine the cost of a supplier, the costs related to delivery, inspection, warehousing, quality and purchasing must be added to the purchase price of the part or service. Activity costs through the use of cost drivers can be traced to different suppliers.

Numerical **example** 4.4

The Tip Top Computer Company is looking for suppliers of modems to ship with its computers. The company needs 10,000 modems and has sent out a request for bids from modem suppliers. The company recognizes that the cost of the modems goes beyond the purchase price. Some suppliers require more contact with the purchasing department, which costs the company £20 per contact. The suppliers also have different expected defect rates. Tip Top inspects all incoming modems and discovers about 60 per cent of the defective units. Defective units that are discovered through inspection are returned to the supplier at a cost of £10 per modem. The other 40 per cent are built into Tip Top computers. These undiscovered defective modems are sent to customers. When the customer discovers the defect, the cost to the company to replace the defect and provide the additional customer service is £100 per defect. The bids and expected purchase contacts and defect rates for the suppliers are:

Supplier	Bid/modem (£)	Purchase contacts	Percentage of defects (%)
A	10.00	50	1.00
B	9.75	40	2.00
C	10.50	80	0.50

Which supplier is least costly?

Solution

The number of defects discovered through inspection and by customers is as follows:

Supplier	Total defects	Discovered through inspection	Discovered by customers
A	0.01 × 10,000 = 100	0.6 × 100 = 60	0.4 × 100 = 40
B	0.02 × 10,000 = 200	0.6 × 200 = 120	0.4 × 200 = 80
C	0.005 × 10,000 = 50	0.6 × 50 = 30	0.4 × 50 = 20

The supplier costs are estimated as follows: Multiply the bid/modem times 10,000 to determine the cost of the modems; the purchase contacts times £50 to determine the cost of purchase contacts; the number of defects discovered through inspection times £40 to determine the cost of returns; and the number of defects discovered by customers times £200 to determine the cost of customer complaints:

Supplier	Cost of modems (£)	Purchase contacts (£)	Returns (£)	Customer complaints (£)	Total cost (£)
A	100,000	2,500	2,400	8,000	112,900
B	97,500	2,000	4,800	16,000	120,300
C	105,000	4,000	1,200	4,000	114,200

Supplier B has the lowest purchase cost, while Supplier C has the lowest defect rate. However, Supplier A is the lowest-cost supplier when overall costs are considered.

■ Working with suppliers to reduce costs

At first glance, a natural tension appears to exist between a supplier and a purchasing organization. Any change in the price of a part or service reduces the profit of one party and increases the profit of the other. Alternatively, the purchasing organization is the customer of the supplier and the supplier should be looking for ways to add value to its customers.

As seen in the previous section, the cost of a supplier is not solely determined by the price of the part or service purchased. Customers also receive value from innovative features and the quality of the product or service. To improve on the features and quality of the product or service supplied, the supplier must have knowledge of the customer's operations and expectations. Co-operation, therefore, is the key to successful relations between suppliers and customers.

Suppliers can reduce customers' costs by linking their computer systems together with electronic data interchange (EDI). When the customer's computer detects a need for more inventory, it sends a message directly to the supplier's computer. The supplier can then replenish the customer's inventory without having the customer go through the order process. Marks & Spencer uses EDI extensively to reduce the costs of ordering inventory. Business-to-business e-commerce allows organizations to interact over the Internet. Cisco Systems handles the majority of its orders via the Internet, with products being delivered directly to customers. FreeMarkets Inc. links suppliers and customers through online purchasing auctions. These auctions decrease purchase time and cost, and allow firms to monitor product availability on a global basis. Global marketplaces often increase quality since firms must compete on both quality and cost dimensions to retain their place in these online exchanges. These online auctions also benefit emerging markets. Mobile phone technology and the Internet link buyers and sellers in developing nations which previously did not have reliable communication networks. Small producers share real-time information to take advantage of market opportunities.

Receiving, inspection, warehousing, purchasing and dealing with defective parts are also costs of working with suppliers. Each of these costs can be reduced through co-operation with the supplier. For example, the supplier can work with the customer to determine the appropriate packaging and delivery locations to reduce receiving costs. If the supplier can guarantee quality levels, the customer can eliminate costs associated with defects and possibly inspection costs. Purchasing costs for the customer increase with multiple transactions and interactions with the supplier. These purchasing costs can be reduced through long-term relations with suppliers that eliminate the start-up costs of working with a new supplier.

Warehousing costs can be very high for organizations with considerable inventory. Inventory levels and, therefore, warehousing costs can be reduced with closer links to suppliers. Suppliers who have information about their customers' inventory levels can make timely deliveries to meet customer preferences, without inundating their customers with excessive inventory. Suppliers of grocery stores also use EDI and e-commerce to connect to the store's inventory information system so timely replenishment of the grocery store shelves can be made.

If an organization operates a just-in-time (JIT) system, its suppliers must have knowledge of the orders received by the organization. The suppliers must deliver parts and services on demand, because a JIT organization has minimal inventory on hand.

The discussion of supplier relations illustrates the importance of inter-organizational information systems. For suppliers to serve their customers appropriately, they need to have real-time access to their customer's inventory records. The sharing of inventory information with suppliers via EDI and business-to-business e-commerce is common practice.

Concept **review**

1 What activities add to the cost of working with a supplier?

2 How can an organization work with its suppliers to reduce costs?

Dell Computers Corporation (continued)

Like its competitors, Dell seeks to gain competitive advantage through supply chain management. By maintaining strong links with suppliers, Dell also develops co-operative, meaningful relationships with the world's most advanced technology companies. Working with these companies, Dell engineers manage quality, integrate technologies and design and manage system architecture. The goal is to deliver the right technology to its customers in a competitive time frame.

Supply chain management and build-to-order manufacturing processes enable Dell to work with its suppliers to create customer value. These activities allow Dell to rapidly incorporate new technologies and components into its product offerings. Supply chain management is enhanced through electronic links to its top suppliers. The results of these efforts contribute to an average of only five days supply in inventory.

CUSTOMER RELATIONS AND PROFITABILITY

The supply chain focuses on relations with both suppliers and customers of an organization. The previous section described relations with suppliers, but relations with customers also provide opportunities to reduce cost and add value to customers. In order to add value, organizations must know their customers, and be able to identify the most profitable ones.

In the past, most organizations believed any customer was a good customer. However, organizations now evaluate customers, and are finding that some customers are not as profitable as others. Why do customers differ? Some customers buy more than others. Some customers are farther away and require higher delivery costs. Some customers are chronic complainers or demand additional customer service. To evaluate customers, the different customers are treated as cost objects. Customer-related costs are compared with the benefits of having the customer. In some cases, the cost of having a customer is higher than the benefit. For example, drivers with a history of accidents tend to create greater costs for their insurance companies than the premiums that they pay. If so, the insurance company can refuse to provide insurance for those high-risk drivers or increase their premiums.

Some organizations might also attempt to educate customers to make them more profitable. For example, golf courses try to educate golfers on appropriate behaviour on the golf course. Slow play and damage to greens can be costly for the golf course, so most golf courses have rangers to encourage faster play and respect of the course.

A cost-benefit analysis of customers is useful to identify unprofitable customers, but should also reveal what type of customer is the most profitable. When the preferred type of customer is identified, marketing efforts can be focused on that group. Banks have found that extensive users of the bank's credit card are very profitable. Therefore, banks put considerable effort into recruiting new credit card holders. Barclays UK uses customer information to tailor products and services to customer profiles. For example, it tracks information on the use of the credit card over time, credit risk and payment patterns to determine which customers are the most profitable and to find ways to shift unprofitable customers to profitable ones. This focus on customer relationship management reduces customer attrition and improves customer acquisition.[3]

© stock_wales/Alamy

Bank management systems monitor credit-card usage and payment patterns. Evaluating risk and profitability enables banks to focus on target markets and eliminate non-profitable customers.

Numerical **example** 4.5

James Wilson, a contractor, purchases 1,000 windows annually from Clear Windows, a window manufacturer, for £120,000. The product cost of £80/window includes the cost of designing and manufacturing the windows, but does not include transportation or customer service. The cost to Clear Windows of delivering the 1,000 windows to James Wilson is £10,000. Employees at Clear Windows spend 80 hours a year taking orders, answering questions, and offering other assistance for James Wilson. The cost of using employee time is £20 per hour. What is the annual net benefit to Clear Windows of having James Wilson as a customer?

Solution

The benefit of having James Wilson as a customer is the revenue generated from sales or £120,000. The costs include:

Cost of goods sold (1,000 windows × £80/window)	£80,000
Cost of transportation	10,000
Cost of service (£20/hour × 80 hours)	1,600
Total costs of James Wilson as customer	£91,600

The net benefit is the benefit (£120,000) less the cost (£91,600), or £28,400.

---

[3] 'Barclays UK Consumer Finance Responds To A More Competitive Market', www.sas.com/success/barclaysuk.html (accessed 20 February 2007).

With customers providing differential net benefits to the organization, the organization may want to consider differential pricing. For example, customers purchasing large amounts of the product are likely to be more profitable. The organization could give price discounts for large purchases. The next section examines the pricing decision for an organization.

Concept **review**

1 What types of customers are most expensive?
2 How can an organization work with customers to make them more profitable?

Dell Computer Corporation (continued)

As noted by Michael Dell, 'From the start, our entire business . . . was oriented around listening to the customer, responding to the customer, and delivering what the customer wanted. Our direct relationship – first through telephone calls, then through face-to-face interactions, and now through the Internet – has enabled us to benefit from real-time input from real customers regarding product and service requirements, products on the market, and future products they would like to see developed. . . . While other companies had to guess which products their customers wanted, because they built them in advance of taking the order, we knew – because our customers told us before we built the product.'

Customers are good, but profitable ones are better. Dell has used its customer knowledge to analyse customer preferences and to determine what customers value and what they are willing to pay for. Direct customer contact allows Dell to maintain, monitor and update its database of information about customers and their current and future product and service needs. This information can be used to shape future product offerings and after-sales service activities.

Service and support activities are designed to fit specific customer requirements. Dell offers a broad range of activities through its own technical personnel and its direct management of specialized service suppliers. These services range from online and telephone support to on-site customer-dedicated systems engineers.

PRICING AND CUSTOMER VALUE

An important strategic planning decision for an organization is the pricing of its products and services. The pricing decision is complicated and requires knowledge of customers, knowledge of present and potential competitors, and knowledge of product costs.

Knowledge of potential customers is probably the most important and difficult aspect of the pricing decision. The products and services offered by the organization are intended to add customer value. Some customers, however, receive more value from the products and services than others do. For example, the value of an airplane ticket from Montreal to Paris is much higher to a businessperson going to Paris for an important meeting than it is to someone who is considering a vacation in France. Airlines offer tickets with certain restrictions and features, such as meals, lounge access and wider seats. Customers then can select the type of ticket and flight that provides them with the most customer value. Customers will only purchase the product or service if the value derived is greater than the purchase price.

An organization cannot make pricing decisions without considering its competition, both existing and potential. In a global economy, new competition can arise quickly and set lower prices because of lower labour or material costs. E-commerce reduces barriers to entry, providing global access to markets.

The product cost also is an important element in the pricing decision. The product cost serves as a lower boundary for the pricing decision. Products sold below their cost reduce organizational value.

■ Pricing to maximize organizational value

A primary goal of a business organization is to create organizational value. Therefore, identifying the price of a product that will maximize the value of the business is important. To determine the price that maximizes value, a manager must know the quantity demanded for the product or service at different prices. The quantity demanded at a given price reflects how many consumers derive value greater than the price. In general, the quantity demanded will rise if the price is lowered. Alternatively, fewer customers will purchase the product or service if the price is raised. The following schedule of quantities and prices for kayaks is a typical example of how the quantity demanded varies with price:

Kayaks sold	×	Price per unit (£)	=	Total revenue (£)
100		900		90,000
150		800		120,000
200		700		140,000
300		600		180,000
400		500		200,000
480		400		192,000
600		300		180,000

Notice that the number of units that can be sold increases with a decrease in price.

The maximum revenues are generated when a price of £500 per kayak is set and 400 kayaks are sold. But choosing the price that maximizes revenue does not necessarily maximize value. The product cost at different levels of output must also be estimated. If the variable cost per unit and fixed costs can be identified and measured, total costs at different levels of output are easy to estimate. In the kayak example, suppose that the fixed cost of making kayaks is £50,000 and the variable cost is £300 per kayak. Table 4.2 describes the total revenues, total costs and value added from making and selling different numbers of kayaks.

Producing 300 kayaks and selling them at a price of £600 per unit creates the highest value added for the organization. The choice of making 300 kayaks can also be made using **incremental costs** and incremental revenues. The incremental costs and revenues are the additional costs and revenues of making more units of a product or service.

Table 4.2 Revenues, costs and value added

Kayaks sold	Price (£)	Total revenue (£)	−	Total cost (£)	=	Added value (£)
100	900	90,000		80,000		10,000
150	800	120,000		95,000		25,000
200	700	140,000		110,000		30,000
300	600	180,000		140,000		40,000
400	500	200,000		170,000		30,000
480	400	192,000		194,000		−2,000
600	300	180,000		230,000		−50,000

The incremental revenue of increasing production from 200 kayaks to 300 kayaks is £180,000 – £140,000, or £40,000 while the incremental cost is £140,000 – £110,000, or £30,000. Therefore, making 300 kayaks is preferred to making 200 kayaks. The incremental revenue of increasing production from 300 kayaks to 400 kayaks is £200,000 – £180,000, or £20,000 while the incremental cost is £170,000 – £140,000, or £30,000. Therefore, moving beyond a price of £600 with the production of 300 kayaks causes incremental cost to be greater than incremental revenue, and is not preferred.

Economic theory states that the price-quantity combinations should be chosen where marginal cost equals marginal revenue. To determine the marginal cost and marginal revenue, however, total revenues and total costs must be estimated for each unit. Estimating revenues requires precise knowledge of consumers and competitors. Estimates of revenues tend to be rough approximations, and are usually not done on a unit-by-unit basis. In the kayak example, revenues and costs are estimated at price increments of £100 instead of on a unit-by-unit basis. Therefore, incremental costs and revenues are compared instead of marginal costs and revenues. Incremental costs are never equal to incremental revenues in the kayak example, but they are closest around the price of £600 and the output of 300 kayaks.

Numerical **example** 4.6

NetLaw networks computers in law firms. The hardware, software and other variable costs are €100,000 per installation. The fixed costs of operating NetLaw are €1,000,000. The president of NetLaw estimates the following levels of sales given different prices:

Price (€)	Expected sales
150,000	50
175,000	44
200,000	30
225,000	20

What price per installation should be set by the president to maximize the value of NetLaw?

Solution

The revenue and cost for the different levels of production are:

Price (€)	Expected sales	Total revenue (€)	Total cost (€)	Added value (€)
150,000	50	7,500,000	6,000,000	1,500,000
175,000	44	7,700,000	5,400,000	2,300,000
200,000	30	6,000,000	4,000,000	2,000,000
225,000	20	4,500,000	3,000,000	1,500,000

Installing 44 network systems for €175,000 apiece is the preferred strategy.

■ Pricing in a competitive environment

Organizations that choose to compete by offering innovative products and services face more difficult pricing decisions as no price currently exists for the new product or service. Competitors have yet to duplicate the product and service and the organization has some leeway in setting prices. Once competition enters the market, however, the organization has a much more difficult time differentiating its product from competing products. Flexibility in price-setting is reduced, since customers will switch to a competitor's product, if the product is priced too high.

With strong competition, the price of a product becomes squeezed between the cost of the product and the lowest price of a competitor. Therefore, the competitive advantage shifts to the lowest-cost producer. Organizations that produce at a high cost must consider eliminating the product from its product mix.

Numerical **example** 4.7

A textile manufacturer can make the following products: trousers, jeans, shirts, skirts and socks. The product costs of each item and competitor prices are listed below:

Product	Product cost (£)	Competitor price (£)
Trousers	10	15
Jeans	9	8
Shirts	6	9
Skirts	13	20
Socks	2	1

a What products should be in the product mix of the textile manufacturer?

b What is the possible range of prices that the textile manufacturer could offer for the products in the product mix?

Solution

a The textile manufacturer should not make products with a product cost higher than the competitor's price. Therefore, the company should only make trousers, shirts and skirts.

b The range of possible prices should be between the product cost and the competitor's price. Therefore, the prices should be in the following ranges:

Product	Price range (£)
Trousers	10–15
Shirts	6–9
Skirts	13–20

■ Cost-based pricing

The financial benefits of estimating customer value and the corresponding demand with different prices, and then choosing prices to maximize organizational value appear obvious. Yet, many businesses use only costs to make pricing decisions. A recent study of Australian and UK companies reported that firms viewed cost information as an important factor in pricing decisions, especially in intensely competitive markets.[4]

Cost-based pricing generally uses the average product cost as the base. A percentage is added to the product cost to cover period costs that are not included in the average product cost, and to provide a profit. Some businesses, such as grocery stores, use very low percentage mark-ups over the product cost. Other businesses, such as fine jewellery stores, set prices two or more times greater than their product costs. The choice of the mark-up percentage is based on the relative size of non-product costs, the ability to sell the product quickly and how competitors are pricing their products.

---

[4] C. Guilding, C. Drury and M. Tayles (2005) 'An empirical investigation of the importance of cost-plus pricing', *Managerial Auditing Journal*, Vol. 29, No. 2, pp. 125–137.

Numerical **example** 4.8

A grocery store marks up all items 10 per cent. The cost of a 7kg turkey is £20. At what retail price should the turkey be sold? A larger turkey is sold for £33. What is the turkey's cost?

Solution

The 7kg turkey should be sold at (1 + 0.10) × £20, or £22.
The cost of the larger turkey is £33/1.10, or £30.

Setting prices based on the product cost without consideration of customer value and demand could put businesses at a competitive disadvantage. An analysis of both product costs and the demand for products at different prices is necessary to maximize profit. The following reasons are often given for pricing based only on product costs: (1) difficulty in estimating customer value and, therefore, demand at different prices, (2) contracts and regulations, (3) long-run customer goodwill and (4) discouraging competition. Each of these reasons is discussed in the following sections.

Difficulty in estimating customer value

Many businesses have a difficult time estimating customer value and, therefore, demand for their product or service. The product or service could be new and the marketing group can provide little insight on customer demand or it may have numerous competitors whose reaction to a pricing decision is uncertain. A decision to lower prices may be followed by a similar decision by competitors, and not lead to increased sales. These types of complications make demand estimation very difficult and point out the importance of knowing your customer and competitors well.

The book market is one in which the competition between supermarkets, online retailers and independent booksellers has led to reduced prices for consumers. However, as supermarkets and discount sellers increase their share of the market, the result has been reduced availability of books, as large retailers prefer the latest, most popular titles, whereas independent stores might offer a greater range of books, including hard-to-find editions. Thus, the consumer may find that prices have dropped, but selection has decreased. It is difficult to estimate the market demand for a particular author or title, as consumer tastes change rapidly and a particular novel might be in fashion one week, but off the top-ten list the next. Mass retailers often do not have the market knowledge of the independent retailer who is closer to the customer. This example indicates the dilemma of estimating customer demand for a product at different prices and in a dynamic market where gains in market share might result in lower profits overall.

Contracts and regulations

Sometimes sales contracts are based on product costs. For example, a company may agree to build a hydro-electric dam for its costs plus 15 per cent. Contracts with the Ministry of Defence for complicated equipment commonly base price on product costs. Cost-based contracts are often used when the cost of the product is difficult to estimate before production begins. For example, estimating the costs of a new commercial jet is difficult, as much of the technology is untested. By not determining the price until completion, the supplier of the product or service is not forced to bear the risk of uncertain costs. The purchaser agrees to bear the risk by reimbursing the costs plus a certain amount for profit.

Regulated industries, such as utilities, also use cost-based pricing. Utilities are often monopolies. Monopolies have no competitors; therefore, they could set very high prices if not regulated. Regulatory boards allow these utilities to sell their service for a price that recovers the cost of the service and enough for a reasonable profit for the owners.

Long-run customer goodwill

Temporary reductions in supply or increases in demand allow organizations to set a much higher price than normal. For example, a shortage of petrol in the 1970s allowed retailers to set very high prices for petrol. Increased demand for play-off tickets during a winning season allows a professional sports team to charge a higher price for the tickets. Organizations with these temporary opportunities do not always adjust their prices to take advantage of excess demand. They recognize that at least some customers will not return to a business that raised prices during a shortage. Newly opened restaurants generally do not charge higher prices, recognizing instead the greater need for return customers in order to remain profitable once their novelty has faded. A long-run strategy that ignores short-run opportunities to raise prices may create the most value for the organization.

Discouraging competition

An organization has more flexibility in pricing a unique product or service. Customers do not have the opportunity to shift to a similar product, if the price is set too high. If organizations attempt to take advantage of the uniqueness of their product or service by setting a relatively high price, new market competitors will quickly introduce similar products and services to share in the success. However, a lower price with only a small mark-up on the product cost will discourage competitors from making similar products or services.

Cost as a lower boundary for price

Pricing decisions should consider both demand and the costs of providing a product or service. When demand is difficult to estimate, the cost of the product or service offers a lower boundary in making the pricing decision. Pricing a product below its cost reduces the value of the organization. The two exceptions to this rule are **lead-loss pricing** and **predatory pricing**. Lead-loss pricing is a strategy of selling a particular product at a price below its cost to lure customers, with the hope of selling other products. Grocery stores frequently have special prices for staple goods, such as butter and eggs, to lure people to the store. Once there, customers often are inclined to pick up the rest of their grocery needs. Predatory pricing is a strategy of selling a product at a price below its cost to drive out competition. Once competition is eliminated, the organization raises its prices to capture the benefits of being the sole supplier of the product. Predatory pricing is prohibited by the rules of the World Trade Organization (WTO) and the European Commission and is illegal in many countries. Organizations cannot set

Milk is frequently priced to entice customers into the grocery store. Once there, customers may pick up other needs, offsetting the special price for milk.

David R. Frazier Photolibrary, Inc./Alamy

prices below costs to eliminate competition. For example, in 2007, the European Commission upheld an earlier ruling that Wanadoo Interactive, part of France Telecom, had set its prices for high-speed Internet access artificially low to prevent competition. The Commission ruled that Wanadoo's prices had been insufficient to cover variable or full costs and fined France Telecom for this pricing strategy.

Concept **review**

1 What is the economic rule for selecting a price to maximize value?

2 How does a competitive environment affect the pricing decision?

3 Why is the product cost sometimes used as a base for pricing?

Dell Computer Corporation (continued)

The intensity of competition in the computer industry results in pricing pressures and the need to respond quickly to customer preferences. Dell is not considered to be the lowest-cost provider of computer systems. Instead, its flexible pricing strategy provides customers with the ability to create the system that matches their preferences and their pocketbook. Some features are considered necessary; while others might be optional or an indulgence, such as the best sound speakers to listen to DVDs while you surf the Internet. When building their computer, customers can trade off certain features to arrive at an acceptable price. As well, Dell's just-in-time system translates into less inventory risk and the ability to change prices quickly as market conditions dictate.

Striving to create customer value by providing what customers want, when and where they want it ensures that activities that add value are emphasized. The direct sales approach also eliminates the need to support an extensive network of wholesale and retail dealers, thereby avoiding typical dealer mark-ups. This strategy makes it easier for Dell to adapt to the marketplace and to offer more competitive pricing.

Sources: M. Dell with Catherine Fredman (1999), *Direct from Dell: Strategies That Revolutionized an Industry*, HarperCollins Publishers, Inc.; www1.dell.com; SEC Form 10-Q, FY07-Q1; SEC Form 10-K, 2006.

SUMMARY

1 **Select a competitive strategy for an organization.** The critical success factors to compete and increase customer value include offering innovative products and services, high-quality products and services, and low costs.

2 **Use activity-based management to reduce the costs of an organization without affecting customer value.** Activity-based management identifies the non-value-added activities as areas for potential cost reduction.

3 **Make trade-offs in the product life cycle to reduce overall product costs.** Most costs of a product are pre-determined by the design of the product. Improved designs can reduce the cost of manufacturing, delivering, maintaining and disposing of the product.

4 **Use target costing as a method of selecting viable products and reducing product cost.** With target costing, the product opportunity is identified first. Then a multi-functional team determines if and how the organization can offer the product and still make a profit.

5 **Estimate the costs of using different suppliers.** The cost of a supplier includes the cost of late delivery, inspections, unpacking, warehousing, purchasing and quality.

6 **Use supply chain management to operate more efficiently and reduce costs.** Supply chain management focuses on relations with both suppliers and customers. Co-operation and the sharing of information with both of these groups can reduce costs for all parties.

7 **Estimate customer profitability.** The cost of a customer includes the cost of the product or service sold to the customer plus the cost of customer service, freight charges and collection. These costs should be compared with the revenues from that customer to determine customer profitability.

8 **Make pricing decisions that maximize organizational value.** Organizational value is maximized when prices and quantity of output are chosen at the output level where the marginal cost is equal to the marginal revenue.

9 **Explain why some organizations use cost-based pricing.** Cost-based pricing may be used when customer value is difficult to estimate, contracts and price regulations are based on costs, and long-run customer goodwill and competition are factors.

KEY TERMS

Benchmarking The process of comparing an organization's products and activities with those of other organizations to determine best practices.

Incremental costs The additional costs of making more units of a product or service.

Lead-loss pricing A strategy of selling a particular product at a price below its cost to lure customers with the hope of selling other products.

Outsourcing A decision to pay some other organization to perform certain activities.

Predatory pricing A strategy of selling a product at a price below its cost to drive out competition.

Product life cycle The stages of supplying a product or service from its initial conception to the satisfaction of the last customer and the product's withdrawal from the marketplace.

Supply chain management The management of relations with other organizations.

Target costing A strategic management process beginning with the identification of a market opportunity and the design of a product or service to meet the market opportunity and also make a profit for the organization.

Numerical exercises

NE 4.1 Customer profitability LO 7
Applegate Farms is currently selling 100 dozen eggs monthly to the Jiffy Super Market for £0.50 per dozen. The manager at Applegate Farms estimates that the cost of feeding and caring for the chickens and collecting the eggs is £0.30 per dozen. Applegate Farms makes four deliveries a month to the Jiffy Super Market. Jiffy Super Market is located 5 kilometres from the farm. The manager of Applegate farms estimates the cost per kilometre for the truck and driver is £0.50 per kilometre.

Assuming no other costs are associated with selling to the Jiffy Super Market, what is the monthly profit generated by Applegate Farms from selling eggs to the Jiffy Super Market?

NE 4.2 Pricing LO 9
The Benson Shoe Company makes 100,000 pairs of shoes each year. The company has fixed costs of £200,000 per year and variable costs of £10 per pair of shoes. The company would like to have earnings 20 per cent greater than total costs.

What price should the company charge?

NE 4.3 Trade-offs in the product life cycle to reduce costs LO 3
WireOne makes mobile phones. It currently has plans to manufacture the AZZ01 model. By redesigning the case at a cost of £95,000, it estimates that it can cut the repair cost of warranty work by half when defective units are returned. WireOne expects to sell 300,000 AZZ01s in the first year. Two per cent of AZZ01s are expected to require warranty work if the case is not redesigned. The cost of repairing and returning a defective mobile is £33.50.

Should WireOne redesign the case of the AZZ01?

NE 4.4 Trade-offs in the product life cycle to reduce costs LO 3

Along with its existing models of mobile phones, WireOne currently has plans to manufacture the TEL99 model. By redesigning the phone's motherboard at a cost of £495,000, WireOne estimates that it can cut the phone's production cost by £0.72 per unit when defective phones are returned. It expects to sell 100,000 TEL99s in the first year.

Should WireOne redesign the TEL99's motherboard?

NE 4.5 Product life cycle costs LO 3

Based on customer demand and competition, an auto manufacturer has decided to offer a 100,000-kilometre warranty on all parts. Using current parts and production standards, the warranty will cost the company €100,000,000 per year. Using parts that last longer will cost €40,000,000 per year more and will reduce the warrant costs to €55,000,000 annually.

Should the firm use longer-lived parts?

NE 4.6 Target costing LO 4

Precision Timepieces has identified customers who would be willing to buy stopwatches with specific characteristics for £20 apiece. Precision wants a 20 per cent profit margin on anything that it makes and sells.

What is the target cost to achieve the 20 per cent profit margin on the stopwatches?

NE 4.7 Estimating customer profitability LO 7

Alpaca Products imports Peruvian sweaters and sells them wholesale. Lidla is a large retailer with 50 different warehouse stores across Europe. Alpaca normally purchases sweaters for €5 each and ships them via boat to Amsterdam for €0.50 apiece. Alpaca normally sells the sweaters for €10 apiece, but Lidla is considering the purchase of 1,000 sweaters and wants the price reduced to €8 each. Lidla also wants the 1,000 sweaters delivered in a month. Alpaca will have to air freight the shipment for €1,000. Lidla also expects Alpaca to put Lidla labels on the sweaters and ship them directly to the warehouse stores. The labelling will require 20 hours of labour at €10/hour. The shipping to the warehouse stores will cost €0.40 per sweater.

What is the profit to Alpaca of having Lidla as a customer?

NE 4.8 Estimating the cost of different suppliers LO 5

Warpco has asked for bids for making 1,000 mechanical arms. The Hand Company has offered to supply them for £10 each and the Elbow Company has offered to supply them for £11 apiece. If Warpco accepts the Hand Company offer, it will have to send a manager to Hand Company at a cost of £800 to check on the quality of production. Warpco will also have to test each mechanical arm delivered from Hand Company. Each test will cost £0.40. Warpco has already worked with Elbow Company and no quality checks would be necessary on its mechanical arms.

Which supplier should Warpco use?

NE 4.9 Using product life cycle for planning decisions LO 3

A nursery has the choice of planting trees in the ground or in pots prior to sale. The pots cost £5 each and potted trees must be watered 100 times per year. Trees that are planted in the ground must be watered 25 times per year. Each watering costs £0.05 in water and labour. When sold, the trees planted in the ground must be dug up with a backhoe. The total cost of digging up each tree and putting the roots in a burlap sack is £10 per tree. The average time between planting and selling a tree is two years.

Should the nursery use pots?

NE 4.10 Using product life cycle to reduce costs LO 3

The Xeron Computer Company is considering a design change that would reduce the weight of its high-end desktop computer by 2 kilograms. This design change would cost £300,000 to implement for all computers sold. The cost saving from this change is the reduced shipping cost. The company expects to sell 500,000 more of these computers. Shipping costs are approximately £1 per kilogram.

What should Xeron Computer do?

NE 4.11 Cost-based pricing LO 9

A bank loans money at 8 per cent annually. One way in which it generates cash is the sale of fixed-rate savings bonds. One-year savings bonds are sold in denominations of £1,000, £10,000 and £100,000. The processing cost of selling savings bonds is £50 for all denominations.

What interest rate should the bank offer its customers for each denomination if it wants to limit its costs to 7 per cent net of processing costs?

Numerical problems

NP 4.1 Estimating the costs related to suppliers LO 5

An automobile manufacturer has decided to outsource car seats. The manufacturer needs 20,000 seats. There are three manufacturers of car seats (Fast Co., Slow Co., and Steady Co.) who are asked to bid on the car seats. They have made the following bids:

	Fast Co.	Slow Co.	Steady Co.
Bid/seat	€100	€90	€105

The car manufacturer has more information on the suppliers, due to previous business with them. Each supplier has a different probability of having a late delivery and a defect. The car manufacturer uses a JIT system, so a late delivery causes the plant to shut down. The expected costs of each shutdown are €15,000. Defects are returned to the supplier, but the cost of dealing with the defect is €80 per defective seat. The number of defects and late deliveries expected from each manufacturer of the car seats for the 20,000-seat order are:

	Fast Co.	Slow Co.	Steady Co.
Number of defects	300	100	20
Number of late deliveries	10	25	0

Which supplier of car seats should the manufacturer use?

NP 4.2 Costs and revenues related to customers LO 7

East Midlands Bank has two types of individual customers who make sight deposits: university students and regular customers. For university students, the bank charges £0.10 per cheque. Regular customers get free cheque-related services. The bank earns 10 per cent on the customer deposits by lending the money to other clients, but pays the customers 5 per cent on deposits. Each type of customer costs the bank £20 in terms of accounting and mailing. The average university student deposit in East Midlands Bank is £300, while regular customers have average deposits of £1,000. University students write an average of 100 cheques per year.

Which type of customer is more profitable for the bank?

NP 4.3 Estimating the cost of suppliers LO 5

After an extensive cost-benefit analysis, Mercy General Hospital has made a decision to outsource its ambulance operations to a private company. The administration has narrowed down its decision to two companies that meet the initial bid specifications. Hell's Bells Company submitted a bid of £50,000 per year plus £30 per hour of actual emergency service. Just-In-Time Company submitted a bid of £100,000 per year plus £25 per hour of actual emergency service. Based on previous experience and trends, the administration expects between 12,500 and 15,000 hours of emergency service work during the next year.

a What is the range of costs of the two ambulance services?
b What other criteria should Mercy General consider in this decision?

NP 4.4 Optimal output levels LO 8

Measer Enterprises produces standardized telephone keypads. The firm operates in a highly competitive market in which the keypads are sold for £4.50 each. Due to the nature of the production technology, the firm can produce only between 10,000 and 13,000 units per month, in fixed increments of 1,000 units. Measer has the following cost structure:

	Rate of production and sales (£000)			
	10,000 units	11,000 units	12,000 units	13,000 units
Factory cost, variable	37,000	40,800	44,600	48,400
Factory cost, fixed	9,000	9,000	9,000	9,000
Selling cost, variable	6,000	6,600	7,400	8,200
Administration, fixed	6,000	6,000	6,000	6,000
Total	58,000	62,400	67,000	71,600
Average unit cost	£5.80	£5.67	£5.58	£5.51

At what output level should the firm operate?

NP 4.5 Pricing LO 8

Europark Entertainment is trying to decide what price to charge customers to enter its new amusement park. The cost of operating the park is fixed at €300,000 per day. All rides are free with the price of admission. The expected daily attendance depends on the daily admission fee. Management makes the following estimates:

Individual admission fee (€)	Expected attendance
10	20,000
20	15,000
30	12,000
40	10,000
50	7,000

a What is the marginal cost of another individual attending the amusement park?

b What price should Europark Entertainment charge for admission to maximize profit?

NP 4.6 Managing the supply chain to reduce costs LO6

FloorCare manufactures, packages and sells floor wax to hospitals. Lorry shipments of chemicals are delivered to FloorCare, which then mixes and packages the floor wax in containers of various sizes. FloorCare maintains an average daily inventory of £500,000 of one chemical, X7666, that is used in all of the floor waxes. This amount represents half a month's supply of X7666. At the beginning of each month the current supplier delivers £1 million of X7666 (200,000 litres) to FloorCare. The cost of in-bound freight (paid by FloorCare) is £2,300. To finance its inventory (including in-bound freight), FloorCare borrows money from the bank at 18 per cent per year.

A new supplier proposes to make daily just-in-time (JIT) deliveries of X7666. The cost per litre is £5.03, which includes the in-bound freight paid by the new supplier. The quality of X7666 from the new supplier is equivalent to that of the current supplier. The average daily inventory of X7666 with the new supplier's JIT deliveries is 5,000 litres.

a Should FloorCare switch to the new supplier?

b What other factors should FloorCare consider before switching to the new supplier?

NP 4.7 Cost-based pricing LO 9

A grocery store makes pricing decisions based on product cost. All other costs to operate the store are fixed at £800,000 per year. The average cost of inventory at the store is £1,000,000. The inventory turns over eight times a year.

a If prices are set at 12 per cent above cost, what is the profit of the grocery store for the year?

b What is the profit of the grocery store if turnover increases to 10 times per year and prices remain at 12 per cent above costs?

c What price mark-up is necessary for the company to have a £300,000 profit if inventory turnover is eight times per year?

Analysis and interpretation problems

AIP 4.1 Target costing and product mix LO 4

The Peter Paint Company makes water- and oil-based paints for houses. Recently, the firm has been investigating other opportunities. One possibility is producing 'finger paints' for children. Finger paints are considerably different than house paints, since they must be designed and produced to be easily washable. The marketing people at Peter Paint believe that there is an opportunity to enter this new market. They estimate that the company could sell 1 million units of finger paints annually for £1 per unit.

How should Peter Paint use this information in making a decision to add finger paints to its product mix?

AIP 4.2 Pricing decision LO 8

Internetco offers a wireless connection to the Internet in Edinburgh, Scotland. The wireless connection is achieved with a remote modem that sends and receives signals through a network of antennae located throughout the city. The network has already been established. The customer simply buys the remote modem from Internetco and then pays a monthly fee for the service. Internetco is attempting to decide what price to charge for the service.

What factors should Internetco consider in making the pricing decision?

AIP 4.3 Value chain LO 2

The FastBike Company manufactures bicycles and is trying to identify which activities are value-added and which activities are non-value-added. Describe each of the following activities as value-added or non-value-added:

a Engineering and designing the bicycle
b Storing the finished bicycles
c Moving the raw materials from the warehouse to the assembly area
d Assembling wheels to the frame
e Providing customer service.

AIP 4.4 Estimating profitability of customers LO 7

A bank spends considerable time in evaluating loan applicants. People come to banks to request loans to purchase houses, cars or for business reasons. The loan officers must analyse these requests to decide which applicants should be granted a loan.

a How does the process of evaluating a loan request relate to a cost-benefit analysis of customers?
b Rather than just making a decision to deny or grant a loan application, what other options do loan officers have in dealing with loan applicants?

AIP 4.5 Making decisions with respect to suppliers LO 5

In the US, no universal health care system, comparable to those in Canada, the UK and Europe, exists. US businesses often provide health insurance for their employees, but have found that doing so has become increasingly costly. One approach to contain these costs is the use of a health maintenance organization (HMO). An HMO agrees to cover the health costs of an organization's employees. In return, the organization pays a premium amount per employee. The HMO then contracts with doctors to provide the health services. Choosing an HMO, however, has been a real dilemma for organizations. Some questionable suppliers have entered this market and have offered services, been paid the premiums, and then have not provided the health services. In these cases, the organization still must cover the health expenses. Therefore, the HMO that provides the lowest bid is not necessarily the lowest-cost supplier of health services for employees.

a What other factors should the organization consider in choosing an HMO other than the bid price?
b What are other ways of contracting with HMOs to ensure quality health service for employees?

AIP 4.6 Pricing services LO 8

The following story appeared in the *Wall Street Journal* on 18 December 1990:

> Big brokerage firms, responding to the deep slump in stock-trading volume, are hitting investors with a round of commission increases. Merrill Lynch & Co., the nation's biggest brokerage firm, will raise by 5% the commission rates it charges individuals to buy or sell stocks on any order over $5,000. . . . It is the firm's first commission boost in $4\frac{1}{4}$ years, and the first for trades over $10,000 in 12 years. (There will be no change in commissions for trades under $5,000.)
>
> Merrill also will boost its handling charges, which cover the cost of processing and mailing transactions statements, to $4.85 a transaction from $2.35 . . . John Steffens, Merrill's executive vice president in charge of private-client businesses, said the firm has been considering raising commissions and fees for some time. 'We think [the increases] are justified based on a whole series of things, including postal-rate increases.'
>
> 'The deterioration in [trading] volumes has pressured a lot of firms to raise commissions to cover their infrastructure costs,' said Dean Eberling, a securities industry analyst.
>
> Earlier this year other brokerage houses, including discount firms raised commissions and fees.

Discuss the issues raised in this story.

(Reprinted with permission of *The Wall Street Journal*, Copyright © 2008 Dow Jones & Company, Inc. All Rights Reserved Worldwide.)

AIP 4.7 Customer profitability and customer service LO 7

First Union Corporation in the US uses 'Einstein', an in-house computer program, to rank customers based on their profitability. 'Profitable' customers keep several thousand dollars in their accounts, use bank clerks less than once a month and rarely make calls to the bank's customer call centre. 'Unprofitable' customers make frequent branch visits, keep less than a thousand dollars in the bank and call frequently. When a customer requests a lower credit card interest rate or a waiver of the bank's $28 bounced-cheque fee, the operator pulls up the customer's account. The computer system displays the customer's name with a red, yellow or green box next to it. A green box signals the call operator to keep this profitable customer happy by granting the request (within the limits of the operator's authority). Customers with red boxes rarely get what they want, in hopes they will go to another bank. This system is an example of how First Union estimates customer profitability to decide the level of service supplied to individual customers.

a What are some of the dangers to the bank of adjusting customer service to profitability?

b Are there ways to make less profitable customers more profitable?

Source: Adapted from R. Brooks (1999) 'Unequal Treatment', *Wall Street Journal*, 7 January, p. A1.

AIP 4.8 Pricing based on cost LO 8

Your company makes computer mouse pads. The mouse pads are popular gift items due to their registered use of sports team logos. The annual fixed costs of the mouse pads are £50,000 and the variable costs per unit are £1. The company president has asked you to choose a price for the mouse pads. A careful study of the competition indicates that a price between £3 and £5 would be appropriate. The president, however, wants to use a cost-based pricing system. She suggests a price that is 100 per cent greater than the average cost. You return to your office thinking that this type of pricing will be simple, but then you become confused in calculating the average cost and the corresponding price.

a What information is missing to calculate the average cost?

b What is the relationship between a price based on average cost and the quantity produced?

c What is the danger of using any type of cost to determine the price?

AIP 4.9 Choosing competitive strategies LO 1

For each of the companies listed below, identify whether its competitive strategy is:

a innovative product/service design

b high-quality products and services

c low-cost production

> **i** Apple Computer Inc.
> **ii** Aldi
> **iii** Dell Computer Inc.
> **iv** Shell Service Stations
> **v** InterContinental Hotels
> **vi** Nokia Mobile Phones
> **vii** eBay.co.uk
> **viii** Ryanair and easyJet Airlines

AIP 4.10 Identify non-value-added activities LO 2

Which of the following activities of a manufacturer do not add value?

> **i** Purchasing raw materials for production
> **ii** Inspecting incoming raw materials when received
> **iii** Shipping completed products to customers
> **iv** Set-up labour to prepare the machines for production
> **v** Labour used to produce products on the machine
> **vi** Labour to clean out the machine after production
> **vii** Cost of products scrapped during production
> **viii** Store partially completed products in warehouse until the next machining operation
> **ix** Labour to inspect the quality of finished products

AIP 4.11 Activity-based management and cost reduction   LO 2

A fast-food chain has produced a series of cost benchmarks for various activities within its restaurants. The local franchise of the fast-food chain has made the following cost comparisons for the different activities:

Activity	Local franchise cost	Food chain benchmark
Cooking	£0.50/meal	£0.52/meal
Taking orders and serving	£0.30/meal	£0.25/meal
Cleaning	£0.05/m^2	£0.05/m^2
Storage	£0.10/£1 of inventory	£0.11/£1 of inventory
Administration	£7,000/month	£6,500/month

On what activities should the local franchise focus its attention to cut costs?

AIP 4.12 Product life-cycle costs and activity-based costing LO 2, 3

Manitou Company is trying to reduce costs to remain competitive. Manitou uses ABC and one of the overhead activities is purchasing. The cost driver for purchasing is number of parts. Based on ABC, Manitou's product designers have decided to reduce the number of parts for each product to reduce costs. For example, a tool manufactured by the company was previously composed of 45 parts. After redesign the tool contained 40 parts.

Is this approach to cost savings successful?

AIP 4.13 Pricing and activity-based costing LO 1, 2, 9

The Mittelberg Paper Company purchases large rolls of paper from paper manufacturers. The company then cuts and packages the paper to meet the demand of small printing companies. The company uses ABC to determine the cost of the product and then charges the printing companies an additional 20 per cent for profit. The price calculation for a recent order looks as follows:

Activity	Application rate	Usage of cost driver	Cost (£)
Cutting	£5/cut	30 cuts	150
Packaging	£1/package	200 packages	200
Storing	£0.60/package	200 packages	120
Delivery	£4/kilometre	10 kilometres	40
Administration	£40/order	1 order	40
Total activity costs			540
Raw materials			300
Total cost			840
Profit 0.20 × £840			168
Price			1,008

The customer is not happy with the price and threatens to change suppliers.

How should the Mittelberg Company re-examine its activities, its relation with its customer and its pricing process?

AIP 4.14 Cost-based pricing LO 9

The major oil companies in the UK continue to be under close scrutiny regarding their pricing practices. They claim that they use cost-based pricing in charging their retail outlets for petrol. The retail outlets then pass on the costs of the petrol to consumers. The reason for the scrutiny is that the price of petrol varies considerably across the UK. Many filling stations, even if they sell branded petrol, are owned by independent retailers who establish their retail price based on the local market. Supermarket stations have a significant share of the market. Therefore, profit margins and retail prices reflect competition between these large stores and the small independent retailer. For instance, supermarket stations often provide fuel discounts for purchases made in their main store. Nonetheless, the price of the same brand of petrol can vary greatly with consumers in rural areas paying much higher prices than those in metropolitan areas do.

a Why do oil companies claim to use cost-based pricing?

b What information would be critical to verify that costs are the basis for price deviations around the UK?

AIP 4.15 Supply chain management LO 6

General contractors for building homes contract with the person wanting a new home to construct the house according to the architect's specifications, at a set price and by a specific date. The price may change if the purchaser of the new home wishes to alter the specifications of the house, or if there are contingencies due to unforeseen difficulties (such as dense rock excavation that was not apparent until the foundation was dug). The delivery date of the finished home may also change by agreement between the purchaser and the contractor. If the buyer is under some urgency to move into the house, the contract between the general contractor and the buyer may include penalties if the house is not completed in time. In summary, the reward to the general contractor is conditional on building the house to specifications, at a sufficiently low cost and on time.

The general contractor usually sub-contracts parts of the building to specialists such as excavators, electricians and plumbers. These sub-contractors have significant influence over the cost of the project and how quickly it is completed. Therefore, the reward structure of the general contractor depends on relations with sub-contractors.

Outline the various methods of working with and managing sub-contractors which will help make the general contractor profitable in the long run?

Extended **analysis** and **interpretation** problem

AIP 4.16 Heavy equipment strategic planning

Johnson Industries is a US manufacturer of heavy equipment used in road building, forestry and construction. Although the firm has been successful in these areas, it is looking to expand into other businesses. Farm equipment is considered a possibility. In particular, the company has designed a combine for harvesting wheat. The combine uses a rubber track rather than wheels as a means of locomotion. The rubber track has the advantage of less pressure on the soil and, therefore, less soil compaction. The track also has better traction on hilly fields. The track-driven combines, however, are more difficult to transport on major roadways.

Six varieties of wheat are grown in the US but they can be categorized generally as either winter or spring wheat. Winter wheat is planted in the late fall and is harvested in the spring. Spring wheat is planted in the spring and harvested in summer. The following table indicates the number of bushels of wheat grown in the top-10, wheat-growing states in 2007.

State	Number of bushels (millions)
North Dakota	393
Kansas	255
Montana	190
Washington	183
South Dakota	130
Idaho	117
Minnesota	104
Oklahoma	93
Colorado	76
Nebraska	73

The management of Johnson Industries estimates 5,000 new combines are sold each year in the US for the harvesting of wheat. Management has developed the following analyses of the competition and potential customers:

Analysis of competition: Two other major competitors currently offer product lines of combines. Jones Farm Equipment works through agriculture co-operatives and provides a low-cost line of combines with prices ranging from $150,000 to $250,000 each. Its combines have less capacity, power and longevity than does the product designed by Johnson Industries. The combines normally are serviced through the co-operatives.

Jordan Manufacturing produces a line of combines comparable to the machine designed by Johnson Industries in terms of capacity, power and longevity. Its combines currently do not have tracks, although rumours exist that the firm is thinking of such a product. Jordan Manufacturing has an extensive network of dealership and service units throughout the wheat-growing areas. Its combines sell for prices between $200,000 and $300,000 each.

Customer analysis: Customers for wheat combines fall into three major groups: 1) travelling crews who move from farm to farm to harvest wheat, 2) large agri-business farms, and 3) smaller privately-owned farms. The travelling crews need combines that are easy to transport. The agri-business farms and privately-owned farms purchase combines for use on their own farms. The agri-business farms tend to buy a combine almost every year and self-service their fleet of combines. The travelling crews must replace their combines every three to four years and depend on local dealerships to service their equipment. Smaller farms might buy a new combine every 10 years and also require local dealerships for service. Each group of customers purchases about the same number of combines each year.

The purchase of a combine is a major investment for all customers. Customers are very knowledgeable about the different functions and capabilities of the combine. They value capacity, power and longevity; however, they also are concerned about the comfort of the cab as combine operators work long hours during harvesting season. Customers have heard about Johnson Industries' track-driven combine and are curious about how well it will function.

In addition to the combine's functionality, the travelling crews and smaller farmers value service. If a combine breaks down during harvest, it is critical that it be fixed immediately. A very short window exists during which the harvest can take place. A combine that is out of service for a week might mean the loss of the entire crop.

Additionally, Johnson Industries has undertaken an analysis of its strengths and weaknesses. Its major strength is its reputation for high quality products in other heavy industries. It has an extensive set of dealerships located in US states with large construction projects and with population growth that stimulates the housing industry. Its major weakness is a lack of knowledge of the agricultural business. Although farmers recognize the Johnson brand name, they are uncertain about the firm's ability to offer farm equipment with the appropriate functions, capabilities and service. Johnson Industries does not have any international experience. Neighbouring Canada is one of the world's largest wheat producers and a potential market for combines produced in the US.

Johnson Industries estimates that the variable cost of making its combine will be about $150,000 per machine. Marketing and fixed construction costs are estimated to be $20 million annually. Service units will be self-sufficient if they are located in close proximity to a minimum of 40 Johnson combines.

a Describe a plausible strategy for Johnson Industries for the production and sales of its proposed combine.
b Outline a pricing strategy for the combine.
c Given the pricing strategy recommended in (b), what percentage of the market must Johnson Industries capture to make a profit?

CHAPTER FIVE

Short-term decisions and constraints

(Planning)

Learning objectives

1. Explain why short-term decisions differ from strategic decisions.

2. Estimate profit and break-even quantities using cost-volume-profit analysis.

3. Identify limitations of cost-volume-profit analysis.

4. Make short-term pricing decisions considering variable cost and capacity.

5. Make decisions to add or drop products or services.

6. Determine whether to make or buy a product or service.

7. Determine whether to process or promote a product or service further.

8. Decide which products and services to provide when there is a constraint in the production process.

9. Identify and manage a bottleneck to maximize output.

Tweedsmuir Hall Bed and Breakfast

In 1780, a wealthy London banker acquired Tweedsmuir Hall as his country estate. Located in the Lake District near Cumbria, Tweedsmuir Hall is by no means a small country cottage. The main house has six bedrooms and there is also a detached house for the caretaker on the property. Tweedsmuir Hall has remained in the family for several generations, but the current generation can no longer afford the upkeep of such a large estate property. The family has put Tweedsmuir Hall up for sale for £700,000.

Heather and Jesse Stuart live and work in central London and have always dreamed of an escape to the country. After reading the advertisement for Tweedsmuir Hall, they decided to rent a car and drive to the Lake District to take a look. They were thrilled with the beautiful oak interior, and thought that Tweedsmuir Hall would make a wonderful bed and breakfast. A local contractor was contacted to determine the cost of converting Tweedsmuir Hall into an upmarket bed and breakfast. The contractor has estimated that an additional £300,000 would be required to convert the main house into a bed and breakfast with six bedrooms, each with their own bathroom. The Stuarts figure that they could live in the caretaker house if they bought Tweedsmuir Hall.

Before purchasing Tweedsmuir Hall, the Stuarts make the following estimates of the costs of operating Tweedsmuir Hall as a bed and breakfast:

Interest on mortgage of £800,000 at 10 per cent	£80,000 per year
(The Stuarts would make a down payment of £200,000 on Tweedsmuir Hall and the remodelling.)	
Insurance	£5,000 per year
Property taxes	£10,000 per year
Utilities and maintenance	£8,000 per year + £5 daily per rented room
Breakfast (£3/person, 2 people per room)	£6 daily per rented room
Maid service	£15 daily per rented room

After completing this list of costs, the Stuarts are unsure of how to use them to make a decision.

Heather and Jesse check with other local bed and breakfasts and learn that their prices range from £75 to £150 per room. They are aware that the higher the price that they charge for rooms, the fewer rooms they will rent.

SHORT-TERM PLANNING DECISIONS

Strategic planning decisions, such as opening a chain of shops, have long-run implications for the organization. Strategic decisions involve the strengths and weaknesses of the organization and how it can compete in a global economy. Organizations make strategic planning decisions infrequently. Strategic planning is often tied to the budgeting process, which commonly occurs on an annual basis.

Alternatively, short-term planning decisions must be made on a daily basis. Managers make frequent decisions on production, price discounts, use of resources and modifications of activities. Minor changes in the product mix or price might also be made in the short term.

The defining characteristic of a short-term planning decision is the inability to change the capacity of the organization. New factories cannot be constructed in a few days, weeks or even months. Moreover, entirely new product lines cannot be designed and implemented in the short term. With short-run decisions, managers are limited to the use of existing long-term assets, such as buildings and equipment. However, in certain industries, global outsourcing allows companies to add capacity by outsourcing some non-strategic processes.

Managers make planning decisions by looking at the incremental effect of those decisions. Looking at incremental effects is appropriate in the short term, because much of the environment is fixed and will not be influenced by the decision.

To capture the incremental approach of short-term planning decisions, costs are divided into fixed and variable quantities. Fixed costs reflect the cost of the existing capacity of the activity or product. On the one hand, if the fixed costs already have been incurred, they are sunk and not relevant to the short-term planning decision. For example, property taxes are paid annually. Once paid, they are sunk until they are due next year. Variable costs, on the other hand, reflect incremental changes and become an important decision variable. This chapter examines short-term management decisions with fixed costs and capacity constraints.

Concept **review**

1 How do short-term decisions differ from strategic decisions?

2 Why are fixed and variable costs important in making short-term decisions?

Tweedsmuir Hall (continued)

Heather and Jesse estimate that their variable costs are £26 per room:

	£
Utilities and maintenance	5
Breakfast (£3/person and 2 people per room)	6
Maid service	15
Total variable costs	£26/room

COST-VOLUME-PROFIT ANALYSIS

Cost-volume-profit (CVP) analysis is a method used to examine the profitability of a product at different sales volumes. As more units of the product are sold, both revenues and costs increase. CVP provides an estimate of the change in profit with a change in units sold. CVP makes certain assumptions about revenues and product costs to simplify the analysis.

The first assumption is the partitioning of product costs into fixed and variable. Therefore, total product costs are equal to:

Total product costs = Variable costs + Fixed costs

$$(VC/\text{unit} \times Q) \quad + FC$$

where VC = Variable cost per unit
Q = Number of units produced and sold
FC = Fixed costs

By assuming that the total product costs are either fixed or variable, capacity constraints are not recognized. The variable cost per unit is assumed to be constant over all levels of production. For example, suppose a mobile phone costs £5 per month plus £0.10 per minute. The mobile's fixed cost is £5 and its variable cost is £0.10 per minute.

The second assumption is that all units of the product sell for the same price. Every customer pays the same price for the product, and the price remains the same no matter how many units are sold. The revenues generated from the sale of the product, therefore, are:

$$\text{Revenues} = P \times Q$$

where P = Sales price per unit

Under CVP, profit from the product is simply the revenues less the costs, and can be written using the following equation:

Profit = Revenues − Variable costs − Fixed costs

Using the previous assumptions, the profit equation for CVP analysis can be written as:

$$\text{Profit} = (P \times Q) - (VC/\text{Unit} \times Q) - FC$$

Re-arranging the profit equation yields:

$$\text{Profit} = [(P - VC/\text{Unit}) \times Q] - FC$$

The sales price per unit minus the variable cost per unit is called the **contribution margin per unit**. The contribution margin per unit is the increase in profit caused by making and selling one more unit of the product or service. The fixed costs do not change as additional units are made. For example, if the contribution margin of making a car is €5,000, selling 100 more cars will increase profit by €5,000 × 100, or €500,000. With its focus on the contribution margin per unit, CVP analysis is particularly useful in estimating the short-run profit impact of selling more or less units.

Numerical **example** 5.1

The variable cost of making electronic pagers is estimated to be £10 per pager. The monthly fixed costs to operate the facility are £100,000. Pagers sell for £25. What is the expected profit if 10,000 pagers are produced and sold? What would be the additional profit if 1,000 more pagers were produced and sold?

Solution

If 10,000 pagers are produced and sold, the expected profit is:

$$[(P - VC) \times Q] - FC = [(£25 - £10) \times 10,000] - £100,000 = £50,000$$

→

The profit from making 11,000 pagers is:

$$[(P - VC) \times Q] - FC = [(£25 - £10) \times 11,000] - £100,000 = £65,000$$

Therefore, the additional profit from selling 1,000 more pagers is £65,000 − £50,000, or £15,000. The additional profit from these additional sales can also be estimated by multiplying the per-unit contribution margin times the additional quantity:

$$[(P - VC) \times Q] = [(£25 - £10) \times 1,000] = £15,000$$

Tweedsmuir Hall (continued)

The Stuarts have re-evaluated their original cost estimates. They realize that the opportunity cost of purchasing and remodelling Tweedsmuir Hall should include not only the interest payment on the mortgage, but also the forgone interest earned on the £200,000 down payment. If that forgone interest is also at a 10 per cent rate, the opportunity cost of investing £1,000,000 in Tweedsmuir Hall is £100,000 per year. Therefore, the fixed costs per year of operating Tweedsmuir Hall as a bed and breakfast are:

	£
Opportunity cost of purchase and remodel	100,000
Insurance	5,000
Property taxes	10,000
Utilities and maintenance	8,000
Total fixed costs	123,000

Variable costs per room rented per day or room-day are:

	£
Utilities and maintenance	5
Breakfast	6
Maid service	15
Variable cost per room-day	26

As an initial estimate of profit, Heather and Jesse assume that they can rent rooms at £80 per night and operate at half of the capacity of Tweedsmuir Hall. Tweedsmuir Hall's capacity would be 365 days per years × 6 rooms, or 2,190 room-days. Half of that capacity would be 2,190/2, or 1,095 room-days. With variable costs of £26 per room-day the expected profit is:

$$= [(P - VC) \times Q] - FC = [(£80 - £26) \times 1,095] - £123,000 = -£63,870$$

Jesse and Heather are quite discouraged by this estimate.

■ Break-even analysis

CVP analysis can also be used for planning decisions with longer time horizons. In planning for an investment in a new product, information about the quantity of units that must be sold to break even or have zero profit is useful. If the organization cannot hope to sell enough units of the new product to break even, then the investment should not be made. **Break-even analysis** determines the sales level in units at which zero profit is achieved. Using variable and fixed costs to approximate product costs, the equation solves for the quantity of units at which profit is equal to zero:

$$0 = [(P - VC) \times Q] - FC$$
$$FC = (P - VC) \times Q$$
$$FC/(P - VC) = Q$$

The break-even quantity is simply the fixed costs divided by the contribution margin per unit. The Appendix at the end of this chapter outlines additional approaches to calculate the break-even quantity.

Numerical **example** 5.2

An ice cream vendor must pay £100 per day to rent her cart. She sells ice cream cones for £1 and the variable costs of making the cone are £0.20 per cone. How many ice cream cones must she sell per day to break even?

Ice-cream vendors face uncertain demand, inclement weather and competition. CVP is a quick way to evaluate different combinations of prices, quantities and costs.

Solution

The break-even quantity is:

$$FC/(P - VC) = £100/(£1 - £0.20) = 125 \text{ ice cream cones}$$

Break-even analysis can also be used to determine prices or target costs that are sufficient to cause zero profit. For example, the break-even equation can be solved for the price per unit.

$$0 = [(P - VC) \times Q] - FC$$
$$P = (FC/Q) + VC$$

Numerical **example** 5.3

A contractor can build 20 condominiums a year with a fixed cost of £1 million and a variable cost per condo of £50,000. At what price must the contractor sell the condos to break even?

Solution

$$P = (FC/Q) + VC = (£1,000,000/20) + £50,000 = £100,000/condo$$

Tweedsmuir Hall (continued)

Jesse and Heather clearly are not thrilled with their initial profit estimate. So instead of estimating profit given the expected number of room rentals, they decide instead to estimate how many rooms must be rented to break even. They keep their initial cost estimates of £123,000 of fixed costs and £26 of variable costs per room per day or room-day, but assume that the daily room rental rate will remain at £80 per room. The break-even quantity is:

$$FC/(P - VC) = £123,000/(£80 - £26) = 2,278 \text{ room-days}$$

This result is even more discouraging, since the break-even quantity is greater than the capacity of Tweedsmuir Hall, which is 2,190 room-days.

The Stuarts then decide to try to estimate a daily rental rate that will allow them to break even given a 50 per cent occupancy rate (1,095 room-days).

$$P = (FC/Q) + VC$$
$$\text{Rental rate} = (£123,000/1,095) + £26 = £138 \text{ per room-day}$$

This rental rate is within the range of rental rates charged by other bed and breakfasts in the district, but it provides no profit for Heather and Jesse. The Stuarts decide to use a rental rate of £150 per night in their remaining calculations. This rate is the highest one charged by any competitor in the area.

■ Achieving a specified profit

The profit equation also can be used to determine the necessary quantity of a product or service that must be produced and sold to achieve a specified target profit. Instead of setting the profit equal to zero, the profit can be set at a specified amount. Then, the profit equation can be used to solve for the required quantity of units produced and sold:

$$\text{Profit} = [(P - VC) \times Q] - FC$$
$$\text{Profit} + FC = (P - VC) \times Q$$
$$(\text{Profit} + FC)/(P - VC) = Q$$

The necessary quantity to achieve a certain profit is the sum of the profit and fixed costs divided by the contribution margin per unit.

Most firms are interested in the cash flow available, after paying income taxes. An extension of CVP analysis provides the number of units that must be sold to achieve a specified after-tax profit. The Appendix at the end of the chapter outlines the calculation of the necessary quantity to produce and sell to achieve a certain after-tax profit.

Numerical **example** 5.4

Suppose our ice cream vendor, who must pay £100 per day to rent her cart, wants to make £60 profit a day. She sells ice cream cones for £1 and the variable costs of making the ice cream are £0.20 per cone. How many ice cream cones must she sell per day to have a profit of £60?

Solution

The necessary quantity to have a profit of £60 is:

$$(\text{Profit} + FC)/(P - VC) = (£60 + £100)/(£1 - £0.20) = 200 \text{ ice cream cones}$$

Tweedsmuir Hall (continued)

Heather and Jesse realize that they cannot live on zero profit. To estimate an acceptable profit, the Stuarts examine their existing annual profit from working at their jobs in London. Presently their joint salaries are £100,000, but they pay £45,000 per year for their apartment. By living in the caretaker house at Tweedsmuir Hall, they will not have to pay rent, so the net forgone profit of buying Tweedsmuir Hall is £55,000. The Stuarts also value the intangibles of living in the country to be £25,000 per year. Therefore, Jesse and Heather believe that they would need a profit of at least £30,000 annually from Tweedsmuir Hall to make the investment comparable to their existing situation. The number of room-days that must be rented to achieve a £30,000 profit, if a daily rental rate of £150 is used, is:

$$(\text{Profit} + FC)/(P - VC) = (£30,000 + £123,000)/(£150 - £26) = 1,234 \text{ room-days}$$

Although this number is well below the total capacity of 2,190, Heather and Jesse are not sure that they can rent that many rooms, especially at a daily rate of £150 per room.

Graph of CVP analysis

CVP analysis can be represented easily by a graph. Figure 5.1 demonstrates the ice cream vendor's CVP problem. The total cost line is in the same form as the variable and fixed cost approximation of opportunity costs in Chapter 2. The fixed cost of £100 is the intercept of the vertical axis. The variable cost of £0.20 per ice cream cone is the slope of the total cost line. The total revenue line is a straight line that extends from the origin. The slope of the total revenue line is equal to the sales price of £1 per cone.

The break-even point occurs when total costs are equal to total revenues. Total costs equal total revenues at the point where the two lines intersect. The shaded area to the left of the break-even quantity represents the expected loss, if lower quantities are produced and sold. The shaded area to the right of the break-even quantity represents the expected profit, if higher quantities are produced and sold. From *Numerical example 5.4*, we see that if 200 ice cream cones are prepared and sold, a £60 profit will be achieved.

CVP analysis and opportunity costs

CVP analysis is used for planning purposes, therefore, the opportunity costs are the appropriate costs to measure. The cost of using non-cash resources to make the product should reflect the alternative use of that resource. Also, if the investment being

Figure 5.1 Cost structure for an ice cream vendor

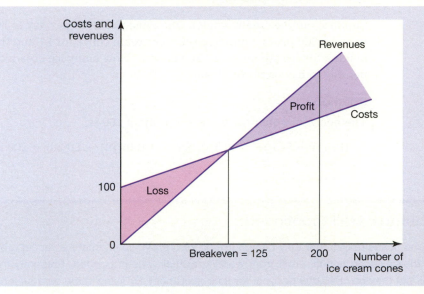

considered involves the long-term use of cash, the planning decision should recognize that there is an opportunity cost of using cash. If cash is borrowed, the interest expense should be included in the analysis as a fixed cost of the product. If the organization has available cash for a long-term investment in a product, the investment prevents it from receiving interest on the cash. That forgone interest is an opportunity cost. Therefore, CVP analysis should include the interest expense of borrowed cash plus the forgone interest of available cash used to make the investment.

Numerical **example** 5.5

Mariana Franca is thinking about buying a farm in southern Italy that costs €400,000. She can borrow €300,000 for the purchase at 10 per cent interest, but must use €100,000 of her own cash for the remainder. What is the annual cost of financing the investment in the farm?

Solution

External financial reports in the form of a profit and loss statement would only record the 10 per cent interest on the loan, 0.10 × €300,000, or €30,000 annually. CVP analysis, however, recognizes the forgone opportunity of using the €100,000 in cash to buy the farm. If the cash would have earned 10 per cent, the cost of financing for CVP analysis is 0.10 × €400,000, or €40,000 annually.

■ Limitations of CVP analysis

CVP analysis is simple to use. Activity costs are approximated using fixed and variable costs, while the sales price and variable cost per unit are assumed constant over all levels of output. These simplifications allow us to estimate profit by looking at the difference between two straight lines, as in Figure 5.1. Most likely, however, cost and revenue estimates are only reasonable approximations within a small range of output levels.

For most goods, including high-end athletic gear, the basic law of supply and demand applies – a lower price is needed to increase sales.

Approximating costs with fixed and variable costs

From Chapter 2, we learned that fixed and variable costs only approximate costs in an intermediate range of outputs. That range is the relevant range. At low levels of output, product costs are likely to be less than the sum of fixed plus variable costs. Also, as an organization nears capacity, product costs are likely to be higher than fixed plus variable costs. Therefore, CVP analysis should not be used at low levels of output or at output levels near capacity.

Assuming a constant sales price

In most markets, if you want to sell more units, you must lower your sales price. Assuming that you can sell very large quantities at a constant price is unrealistic. In CVP analysis, no explicit assumption of a constraint in production or sales is made. The assumption of a constant sales price is usually only accurate over a narrow range of output levels. For example, Reebok sells only a certain number of trainers at £100 per pair. If Reebok wants to sell more, it will have to lower the price.

Determining optimal quantities and prices

CVP analysis assumes that straight lines can represent costs and revenues. Therefore, the choices of quantity and price in CVP analysis are not determined by setting marginal cost equal to marginal revenue. As drawn in Figure 5.1, the marginal revenue (the slope of the revenue line) is always greater than the marginal cost (the slope of the cost line). The slopes of the two lines are not equal at any level of output. CVP analysis suggests that profit is maximized when an infinite number of units are produced. This result is absurd, given capacity constraints and the need to make price concessions to sell more units.

CVP analysis and the time value of money

CVP analysis is a one-period model. During a period of time, the revenues and costs are estimated for different levels of output. Products, however, may have a life cycle of many years. To accommodate a longer product life cycle, an assumption could be made that each intermediate time period is identical in terms of revenues and costs. If revenues and costs differ for different intermediate time periods, some method of trading off profit from different periods of time must be used. Large capital investments to make the product may adversely affect profit early in the product life cycle, but improve it in the latter stages of the product life cycle. Chapter 13 describes such a method to deal with multiple periods and to recognize the time value of money.

CVP analysis and multiple products

CVP analysis assumes that the fixed and variable costs of each product can be identified separately. However, most organizations provide multiple products, and some costs frequently are common to these products. For example, a mobile telephone manufacturer produces numerous models ranging from inexpensive, simple telephones to expensive, complex units. Under these circumstances, CVP analysis is not a very good planning tool, unless the multiple products can be considered as a 'basket' of goods. The 'basket' would contain a certain proportion of all the different goods provided by the organization, and would be treated as a single good.

For instance, a company that makes and sells bicycles and tricycles could consider its basket of products to be two bicycles and one tricycle. The price of the basket would be the sales price of two bicycles and one tricycle. The costs of the basket would include the fixed costs of the company plus two times the variable cost of the bicycle plus the variable cost of the tricycle. CVP analysis then could be used for the 'basket' of goods, as a single price and a single fixed and variable cost exist for the basket. This procedure only works, however, if the proportions of different products in the basket remain constant for all levels of output.

Numerical **example** 5.6

A company is considering buying a manufacturing plant that assembles personal computers and laser printers. The plant is expected to make and sell twice as many personal computers as laser printers. The factory has annual fixed costs, such as property taxes and insurance, of £5 million that are not identified with either the personal computers or the laser printers. The sales price and variable cost per unit of the personal computer are £250 and £100, respectively. The sales price and variable cost per unit of the laser printer are £200 and £75, respectively. How many units of personal computers and laser printers must be sold to break even?

Solution

To solve this problem a 'basket' of both goods must be established. The products are made and sold in a 2 to 1 proportion; therefore, the basket should contain 2 personal computers and 1 laser printer. The sales revenue of this basket is (2 × £250/personal computer) + (1 × £200/laser printer), or £700. The variable cost of this basket is (2 × £100/personal computer) + (1 × £75/laser printer), or £275. The break-even quantity of this basket is:

$$\text{Quantity} = (£5,000,000)/(£700 - £275) = 11,765 \text{ baskets}$$

The 11,765 baskets are equivalent to 23,530 personal computers and 11,765 laser printers.

The limitations of CVP analysis described in this section indicate that CVP analysis should be used with care. CVP analysis has the advantage of being simple, but should only be used as a rough planning tool. CVP analysis provides a manager with a quick approximation of the profit effect of an investment. Whether a manager wants to analyse the investment further depends on the cost of that analysis and the potential benefits of more accurate information.

Concept **review**

1 What is the basic profit equation for CVP analysis?
2 What is the purpose of performing break-even analysis?
3 What are the major assumptions of CVP analysis?
4 How does CVP analysis work with multiple products?

PRICING DECISIONS IN THE SHORT TERM

Chapter 4 describes strategic pricing issues. However, managers often face short-term pricing decisions. For example, a customer might request a discount on the price of a product. Or customers may give the organization a 'take it or leave it' offer to purchase a product. Customers are constantly pitting one supplier against another to get the best price. How do managers decide on a price when customers threaten to go to a competitor?

In Chapter 4, the product cost is described as the lower boundary for a pricing decision. The product cost includes all of the direct and indirect costs of designing, making and selling the product. To be profitable in the long run, the revenues generated from the sale of the product must be greater than the cost of all of the activities associated with the product. In the short run, however, some of the product costs are fixed and the variable cost per unit is the best estimate of the cost of making another unit of the product. Therefore, the result of any sales price greater than the per-unit variable cost is a positive contribution margin and greater profit for the organization.

Using the variable product cost as a base for pricing all of the units will lead to a loss, if fixed costs cannot be covered by revenue. On the one hand, an organization should not use the variable product cost for a short-term pricing decision, if production is at capacity and all the units can be sold at a higher price. On the other hand, if the organization has excess capacity and has a one-time opportunity to sell additional units to a customer at a price above the variable cost, the transaction will increase organizational value.

Numerical **example** 5.7

It's late at night and a customer arrives at a motel just off the M1 motorway. The customer has only £30 and tells the motel manager that he will take a room for £30 otherwise he will have to sleep in his car at the next motorway service area. The normal price of a room for the night is £70, but the motel is only 30 per cent full and very few new customers are expected that night. The variable cost of renting the room including linen, maid service and utilities is £20. The fixed cost of operating the motel is £1,000,000 per year. Should the motel manager take the customer's offer and rent the room for £30?

Solution

Given that the motel has excess capacity and will lose this customer if this one-time offer is refused, the motel manager should accept the offer. The contribution margin of the additional room rental is £30 − £20, or £10.

Concept **review**

1 What cost should be considered in making a short-term pricing decision?

2 How does capacity affect the short-term pricing decision?

Tweedsmuir Hall (continued)

Jesse is confused about using the variable cost to make a pricing decision. He asks Heather, 'Do you mean that if a customer arrives late at night and we have empty rooms that will not be filled, we should be willing to rent a room for as low as £26? Nobody rents rooms for that low a price. We'll lose money.'

Heather replies, 'The variable cost of renting one more room is £26. If we can rent it for £30, we make £4 more than if we don't rent it at all.'

Jesse is still not convinced. He provides another argument for not renting at such a low price: 'What if we rent a room to someone earlier in the day for £100 and then rent a room for £30 to a late arrival? What happens if they have breakfast together and they discover the price difference? Won't the person paying the higher rent be upset?'

Organizational **analysis**

Ryanair

Ryanair is a low-cost air carrier based in Dublin, Ireland. Ryanair was established in 1985, but grew rapidly in the 1990s with the de-regulation of the airline market. De-regulation of the airline industry led to increased competition and more choice for passengers. In 1996, the European 'Open Skies' agreement enabled airlines to compete freely across Europe. Passengers can now fly across Europe at low cost and with easy cost comparisons and bookings via the Internet.

One way in which airlines measure their operating performance is revenue per seat. Cheap fares decrease revenues, but operating their aircraft more efficiently may offset this loss. Ryanair focuses on the market segment seeking discount fares – passengers who are willing to trade off convenience and amenities for cost. Initially, Ryanair used only one type of aircraft, allowing it to increase the efficiency of its maintenance and servicing and to shorten its turnaround time at airports. As Ryanair expanded its operations, it added more aircraft to its fleet and new routes. In 2006, it carried over 40 million passengers with services in more than 20 European countries.

Food and beverages are offered for sale, and fewer flight attendants are used per flight. Ryanair also operates from smaller airports, such as Brussels Charleroi and London Stansted, which are less frequented and less costly. This strategy has made it possible for Ryanair to offer lower fares based on its lower operating cost. Yet, while passengers might appreciate low fares, Ryanair's emphasis on the bottom line has hurt its market image. Passengers complain about the high costs of on-board purchases, baggage restrictions and additional charges. Ryanair also faces increasing challenges from other low-cost airlines, including the UK-based easyJet.

The larger airlines might pose a threat to Ryanair, if they decide to compete in this market segment. However, larger firms, such as British Airways, find that the low-cost/low-service approach has not been as successful for them as for the smaller airlines, when seats are sold at a price near marginal cost. Cheap economy fares are costly in terms of decreased yield per seat. The industry also suffers from greater price pressure as a result of excess capacity. Business passengers are more lucrative, since they are less sensitive to price, and are more willing to pay for convenience and flexibility.

Ryanair must also deal with higher airport fees charged by government authorities and the renewal of its fleet of aircraft. Economic factors need to be monitored closely, as Ryanair passengers tend to be tourists and not businesspeople. In some markets, Ryanair must take into account that its competitors are railways and motor coaches, not other airlines. Replacing trains and buses with airplanes has also raised environmental concerns.

How might Ryanair and other low-cost carriers establish airfares? What threats do such pricing strategies face?

Why can some airlines offer low fares and be profitable, while other airlines find this approach infeasible?

How might an airline, such as Ryanair, use break-even analysis to determine if it should provide fewer or more flights in a specific market?

Sources: www.ryanair.com; www.easyjet.com; 'Ryanair – the world's least favourite airline', *The Guardian* Unlimited, 26 October 2006, http://business.guardian.co.uk/story/0,,1931871,00.html (accessed 26 February 2007); 'EasyJet predicts 50% growth in profits', *The Guardian* Unlimited, 7 February 2007, http://business.guardian.co.uk/story/0,,2007697,00.html (accessed 26 February 2007).

PRODUCT-MIX DECISIONS

Chapter 4 describes strategic issues surrounding the selection of products to offer. An organization should offer a product mix that reflects the organization's competitive advantage, whether it is innovation, quality or low-cost production. Modifications to the strategic product-mix decision must be made, given short-term changes in the market. For example, an organization might temporarily eliminate a product from its product mix due to a short-term price decrease. In this section, the following short-term decisions are examined: (1) the decision to add a product or service, (2) the decision to drop a product or service, (3) the decision to make or buy a product or service, (4) the decision to process a product further, and (5) the decision to promote a product or service. The analysis in each case examines the incremental impact of the decision on the profit of the organization.

■ The decision to add a product or service

When a product or service is added to an existing product mix, both costs and revenues will be affected. Costs will generally increase, because additional inputs such as direct labour and direct material are necessary to make the new product or service. Indirect costs also may increase, if additional indirect resources, such as supervisory costs and utilities, are used to make the new product or service.

An additional product also affects revenues. Revenues from selling the new product are added to the revenues of the existing products. But the new product might affect the revenues of the existing products. A new product might be an accessory of an existing product and increase the sales of the existing product. For example, designing new software for an existing computer should increase sales for both the computer and the software. A new product might also be a substitute for an existing product and replace the sales of the existing product. For example, an improved laundry detergent would probably reduce the sales of the firm's existing laundry detergents.

The decision to add a new product should be based on a comparison of the incremental costs and incremental revenues. If incremental revenues are greater than incremental costs, the new product should be added. For example, if our ice cream vendor is considering the sale of soft drinks, she should consider only incremental costs such as the cost of a special refrigeration unit and the cost of purchasing the soft drinks. Incremental revenues should include not only the sale of soft drinks, but also the effect on ice cream sales. If incremental revenues are greater than incremental costs, the ice cream vendor also should sell soft drinks.

Numerical **example** 5.8

The owner of a professional rugby union team and football stadium is considering renting the facility to a professional soccer team. The soccer team would need the stadium for eight games and would be willing to pay rent of £20,000 per game. The football stadium, which originally cost £20 million to build, can be converted from rugby to soccer and soccer to rugby at a cost of £12,000 per conversion. The cost of cleaning and the maintenance due to each soccer game is estimated to be £5,000 per game. Given the overlap of the rugby and soccer season, the stadium would have to be converted four times each year. Should the owner of the professional rugby union team rent the stadium to the soccer team?

→

Solution

The incremental revenues are 8 × £20,000, or £160,000. The incremental costs are (4 conversions × £12,000/conversion) + (£5,000/game × 8 games), or £88,000. The incremental revenues are greater than the incremental costs, so the rugby team owner should rent to the soccer team. The cost to build the stadium is sunk and irrelevant to the decision.

Tweedsmuir Hall (continued)

The Stuarts are considering adding a dinner service to the other services that they would offer at Tweedsmuir Hall. This service would be available to guests and non-residents. The kitchen and dining room are already available, so there would be no additional cost of using the facility. The incremental costs would include food, beverages and a cook. The incremental costs to provide 5,000 dinner meals annually are estimated to be £150,000. The average meal price is estimated to be £40. In addition, having a dinner service should increase room rentals (at £150 per room) by 200 rooms. Given this information, Jesse and Heather calculate the additional profit that the dinner service will generate:

	£
Incremental revenues:	
Meals (£40 × 5,000)	200,000
Additional room rental revenues (£150)(200)	30,000
Total incremental revenues	230,000
Incremental costs:	
Food, beverages and cook	150,000
Variable room costs (£26 × 200)	5,200
Total incremental costs	155,200
Excess of incremental revenues over incremental costs:	74,800

These additional estimated profits make the purchase of Tweedsmuir Hall much more appealing.

■ The decision to drop a product or service

Not all products and services are a success. Even previously successful products and services may outlive their popularity with customers. Competitors might introduce more attractive products or services which firms cannot offer. At some point, management must decide when to drop these products or services. When the product cost is estimated to be greater than the sales price of the product, the product should be dropped.

The product cost, however, is not always known and often is approximated using historical direct and indirect costs. The indirect costs are traced to the product through a cost driver. These indirect costs include overhead items, such as the supervisor's salary, that may not disappear if a product is dropped. In other words, not all of the estimated product costs are avoidable, if a product is eliminated. A manager should attempt to identify the **avoidable product or service costs** in making a decision to drop a product or service. If avoidable costs are greater than the revenue of a product, the product should be dropped from the product mix. This decision assumes that dropping the product from the product mix would not affect sales of the remaining products.

Numerical **example** 5.9

Based on the following information, a plastic pipe manufacturer is considering dropping a pipe that can handle high pressure from its product mix:

	€
Revenues from high-pressure pipe	100,000
Costs from high-pressure pipe:	
Direct material	(30,000)
Direct labour	(50,000)
Allocated overhead	(30,000)
Loss from high-pressure pipe	(10,000)

What factors should the manufacturer consider before dropping this product?

Solution

Direct costs are generally avoidable, but the allocated overhead might not be avoidable. If only half of the allocated overhead (€15,000) were avoidable, then revenues (€100,000) would be greater than avoidable costs (€95,000). Another factor to consider is any alternative use of the space, labour and machines presently devoted to making high-pressure pipes. If an alternative use of those resources exists, managers should consider the profit forgone from those alternative uses as part of the opportunity cost of making high-pressure pipes. Also, managers should consider the effect of dropping the high-pressure pipe on the demand for its other products.

■ The decision to make or buy a product or service

Porsche represents luxury in sports cars. While Porsche designs and manufactures its cars, most parts are outsourced to other firms, subject to strict quality standards.

David Bowman/Alamy

Porsche AG designs and manufactures luxury sports cars. But most of its vehicle parts are made by other companies. Porsche AG imports these parts from all over the world and then assembles the cars in Germany. Why does Porsche AG not make all of the various parts itself? Also, many companies have decided not to perform their own payroll, customer service, IT support or tax accounting. They hire other companies to perform these functions. Why is there a reluctance to undertake these activities themselves?

Organizations must determine what they can do themselves and what they should pay other organizations to do. This outsourcing decision is described in Chapter 4. The basis for this decision should be a comparison of the costs of providing the product or service in-house with the cost of purchasing the product or service from an external supplier. Holding quality constant, if the cost to purchase the product or service is lower than cost to provide the product or service within the organization, then the organization should outsource.

The problem once again is identifying the costs. If the product or service is currently provided in-house, identification of avoidable costs is important. If an organization decides to use an outside supplier, indirect costs traced or allocated to a product or service are not always avoidable.

Alternatively, if an outside supplier is currently providing the product, the incremental costs of providing the product in-house should be identified when considering in-house production.

Make-or-buy decisions involve other factors than immediate cost implications. Using outside suppliers gives an organization less control over quality and timely delivery. However, outside suppliers often have the expertise and machinery to provide the product at a lower cost than the organization can.

Some organizations, like Porsche AG, have taken outsourcing (the use of outside suppliers) to an extreme. Apple Computers concentrates on in-house hardware and software design, as it competes by offering innovative products. The manufacturing process is outsourced, but Apple's competitive edge is maintained through its focus on the design process.[1]

■ The decision to process a service or product further

Another decision related to the product mix is whether to process a product further and sell a more refined product. For example, wooden furniture may be sold unfinished, without stain or paint, or already stained or painted. Also, a restaurant may choose to serve food buffet style or hire staff to serve the food directly at the table. The decision to process further is based on a comparison of the incremental costs and incremental revenues of further processing. If the incremental revenues are greater than the incremental costs, the product should be processed further.

Numerical **example** 5.10

A sporting goods shop is deciding whether to sell bicycles assembled or unassembled. An unassembled bicycle is purchased by the shop for €100 and can be sold unassembled for €200. To assemble a bicycle requires 30 minutes of labour time. Labour costs €16 per hour. If the shop assembles the bicycle, it sells for €210. At a price of €210, the number of assembled bicycles sold would equal the number sold unassembled. Should the bicycle be assembled by the shop or sold unassembled?

Solution

The incremental revenues are €210 − €200, or €10. The incremental costs are the cost of assembly, 1/2 hour × €16 per hour, or €8. The incremental revenues are greater than the incremental costs, so the bicycle should be assembled by the shop. Note that the shop's purchase cost of €100 is irrelevant to the decision. Once it purchases the unassembled bicycle, the €100 is a sunk cost.

Tweedsmuir Hall (continued)

Heather and Jesse have thought of another way to make Tweedsmuir Hall bed and breakfast more profitable. Instead of making breakfast and dinner for guests, they could have the breakfast and dinners catered. By using a catering service, £100,000 in remodelling costs could be saved because the kitchen would not

---

[1] 'Apple's Blueprint for Genius', *BusinessWeek* online, 21 March 2005, www.businessweek.com/magazine/content/05_12/b3925608.htm (accessed 24 February 2007).

have to satisfy health and safety requirements. A cook would not have to be hired. The breakfast costs of £3 per person would also be saved. A caterer would supply breakfasts for £5 each and dinners for £30 each. Dinners would still be provided for £40 each and breakfast would be included as part of the room rental rate. The Stuarts assume that 2,500 breakfasts and 5,000 dinners would be served annually.

Incremental annual costs of providing breakfast and dinner (not catered):

	£
Breakfasts (£3 × 2,500)	7,500
Dinners (food and cook)	150,000
Interest forgone in remodelling kitchen (£100,000)(10%)	10,000
Total incremental costs	167,500

Catering costs:

	£
Breakfasts (£5 × 2,500)	12,500
Dinners (£30 × 5,000)	150,000
Total catering costs	162,500

Catering the breakfasts and dinners will save £167,500 − £162,500, or £5,000 per year. The Stuarts are uncertain, however, if the catering company is reliable, so they decide not to use the catering service.

■ The decision to promote a product or service

The decision to promote a product or service is also based on a comparison of incremental costs and incremental revenues. In the case of advertising, the incremental revenues are the additional sales generated by the advertising. The incremental costs are the additional advertising costs and the costs of making the additional units. If the incremental revenues are greater than the incremental costs, the advertising campaign should proceed.

Another promotion decision for an organization is persuading a customer to buy one of its products instead of another product in its product line. For example, which vehicle on the lot of a new-car dealership would the dealer want the customer to buy? Which type of ticket does the manager of a soccer team want a fan to purchase? The organization wants to sell the product that generates the most profit. The contribution margin per unit is the profit from selling one more unit of a product, if the organization is operating below capacity. The product with the highest contribution margin per unit is the product that will generate the most profit if sold. For most car manufacturers, higher priced cars with more luxury options have the higher contribution margin per unit. Therefore, most car salespeople push customers to buy more expensive cars.

Numerical **example** 5.11

A company manufactures three types of plasma televisions in separate plants. Their costs and prices are:

Type of TV	Fixed costs (£)	Variable cost per unit (£)	Price per unit (£)
MB-2000	10,000,000	500	800
MB-2400	30,000,000	700	1,300
MB-2800	40,000,000	1,000	1,500

Assume all three divisions are operating below capacity. If a customer decides to buy one of these three TVs, which model should the company promote?

→

Solution

The contribution margins per unit of the three types of televisions are:

Type of TV	Contribution margin per unit (£)
MB-2000	300
MB-2400	600
MB-2800	500

The MB-2400 has the highest contribution margin per unit and is the model that the company prefers to sell. The fixed costs are irrelevant in this decision.

Concept **review**

1 What types of costs should be considered to make a decision to add a product?

2 Why are avoidable costs used to make a decision to drop a product?

3 Why do some organizations decide to buy products rather than make the products in-house?

4 How should an organization decide whether to process a product further?

5 What types of products do organizations prefer to sell?

PRODUCT-MIX DECISIONS WITH CONSTRAINTS

Short-term decisions are influenced by the existence of capacity constraints. If organizations are operating below capacity, the variable cost approximates the marginal cost of making further units of different products. The use of the excess capacity should be directed toward making and selling more of the product with the highest contribution margin per unit. If a capacity constraint exists that affects multiple products or services, however, the problem becomes more complex. For example, suppose a machine that is used to process more than one product is operating at capacity. If the organization has some flexibility in determining which product uses the machine more frequently, how should the organization make that decision?

The product with the highest contribution margin per unit is not necessarily the product that should have priority on a machine that is a constrained resource. Instead, the organization should determine which product yields the highest contribution margin per use of the machine. If a product with a high per-unit contribution margin requires considerable machine time, the contribution margin per use of the machine would be low. A product might have a low contribution margin per unit, but can be processed quickly. Therefore, it will have a high contribution margin per use of the machine. The following demonstrates this relation (CM is the contribution margin):

Product	CM/Unit (£)	Units/Machine hour	CM/Machine hour (£)
A	8	3	24
B	3	10	30

In this example, using the machine to manufacture B, the lower contribution margin product, results in a higher contribution margin per machine hour. The machine is the constraint in the production process for both products A and B; therefore, the organization wants to use the machine in the most profitable manner until it can add capacity. Giving product B a higher priority in using the machine creates a higher profit for the organization, assuming the organization can sell as many units of B as it can produce.

Numerical **example** 5.12

Sophie Chang, CA, is a sole trader. Sophie does corporate, partnership and individual tax returns. Her major constraint and only cost is her time. On average, the revenues and time required for different types of tax returns are:

Type of tax return	Time in hours	Revenues/Tax return (£)
Corporate	20	2,000
Partnership	10	1,200
Individual	5	400

Which type of tax return should Sophie prepare, if she has plenty of opportunities to do all three types?

Solution

Since variable costs are zero (other than the opportunity cost of Sophie's time), the contribution margin of doing each type of tax return is equal to the revenue. The contribution margin per use of the scarce resource (hour of Sophie's time) for each type of tax return is:

Tax return	Contribution margin/Hour (£)
Corporate	100
Partnership	120
Individual	80

The partnership tax return has the highest contribution margin per hour of Sophie's time and is the preferred tax return to prepare. Of course, Sophie also needs to consider the long-term effects on her practice if she only prepares partnership returns.

Identifying the product that yields the highest contribution margin per use of a scarce resource requires simple calculations. If more than one constraint exists (such as a constraint on both machine time and labour time), the problem is much more difficult to solve. Linear-programming techniques can be used to choose a product mix that maximizes the contribution margin, given more than one constraint. This procedure is examined in operations management and advanced management accounting courses.

Tweedsmuir Hall (continued)

The primary constraint in operating Tweedsmuir Hall is space. Heather and Jesse could use one of the bedrooms as a private dining room. This choice should be based on a comparison of the contribution margins from alternative uses of the bedroom: room rental versus private dining room. The bedroom would be the last rented. The Stuarts estimate that they can rent the room 100 days of the year with a contribution margin of £124 if rented at £150 per night. The total contribution margin from rental is 100 × £124, or £12,400. Jesse and Heather estimate that they can sell 1,100 more dinners in a private dining room with a contribution margin per dinner of £10 if catered. The total contribution margin from using the room as a private dining room is 1,100 × £10, or £11,000. Therefore, the Stuarts decide not to use the bedroom as a private dining room.

Following this analysis, Jesse and Heather take the plunge and decide to purchase Tweedsmuir Hall. With the extra £74,800 in profit from adding the dinner service, the Stuarts can operate the remaining parts of the bed and breakfast at a loss of £34,800 and still achieve a total profit of £40,000. Also, if the bed and breakfast is not financially successful, Heather and Jesse assume that they can sell Tweedsmuir Hall to another gullible couple wanting to leave central London for the charms of the English countryside.

THEORY OF CONSTRAINTS

The process of identifying and managing constraints is called the **theory of constraints**.[2] In describing opportunity costs and the rate of output, we noted that the marginal cost of making a product increases as capacity is reached. Not all processes within an organization, however, have the same capacity. The theory of constraints focuses on capacity and the use of scarce resources. For example, the steps to make plywood include: debarking the logs, heating the logs, cutting logs into veneer (thin layers of wood), cutting the veneer into sheets, sorting the veneer, drying the veneer, layering and gluing the veneer, trimming the plywood, and sanding and patching the plywood. Each of these steps has a different capacity. In terms of tonnes of wood product processed per day, a particular plywood factory has the following constraints:

Process	Tonnes of wood product per day
Debarking log	300,000
Heating log	200,000
Cutting log into veneer	100,000
Cutting veneer	150,000
Sorting veneer	120,000
Drying veneer	130,000
Layering and gluing veneer	150,000
Trimming plywood	250,000
Sanding and patching plywood	300,000

Cutting the log into veneer has the lowest capacity and is called the **bottleneck**. Bottlenecks can usually be identified, even if the capacity of the different processes is unknown, because work-in-process (unfinished inventory) accumulates prior to the bottleneck process. The bottleneck deserves the primary attention of management, as the bottleneck inhibits the flow of the production process. Care should be taken that the bottleneck operates as many hours as possible. Maintenance of the bottleneck is extremely important and methods of increasing the capacity of the bottleneck should be considered. By increasing the capacity of the bottleneck, the organization can produce more units of its product or service. If those additional units can be sold at a price above the variable cost per unit, then the organization can increase its profit.

Dealing with bottlenecks is a continuous process. Suppose that another lathe is purchased to cut logs into veneer in the plywood example. This additional lathe

---

[2] Further details on the theory of constraints can be found in E. M. Goldratt and J. Cox (1992) *The Goal: a process of ongoing improvement*, 2nd revised edition (Great Barrington, Mass: North River Press).

increases the capacity of cutting logs to 200,000 tonnes per day, so cutting logs into veneer is no longer the bottleneck. Therefore, sorting veneer is the bottleneck at 120,000 tonnes per day. The sorting of veneer then becomes the primary focus of management attention.

The theory of constraints also has control implications. Employees are often rewarded based on the output of the particular process that they control. The more output that they can produce, the more they are rewarded. In an organization with processes that have different capacities, this reward system can lead to dysfunctional behaviour. Employees do not benefit the organization by creating more output, if they are operating a process that is not a bottleneck. Increasing the output of a non-bottleneck process simply increases work-in-process, but does not lead to more finished units. More finished units only can be made by increasing the output of the bottleneck. The excess work-in-process can actually be costly to the organization, since it causes congestion and uses resources. Just-in-time production, described in Chapter 14, examines the problem of excess work-in-process.

© Derek Croucher/Alamy

Increasing capacity to alleviate bottlenecks on major roadways often fails. Tax incentives, tolls and rapid transit encourage commuters to leave their vehicles at home instead.

Concept **review**

1 If a capacity constraint that affects multiple products exists, which product should have priority?
2 How should an organization manage a bottleneck?

SUMMARY

1 Explain why short-term decisions differ from strategic decisions. Strategic decisions involve long-term planning with the opportunity to change the existing resources of the organization, while short-term decisions assume that most of the organization's resources cannot be changed.

2 Estimate profit and break-even quantities using cost-volume-profit analysis. The break-even quantity is the level of output that generates zero profit. It can be estimated by dividing the fixed costs by the contribution margin per unit. The output level necessary to achieve a specified profit is the sum of the profit and fixed costs divided by the contribution margin per unit.

3 **Identify limitations of cost-volume-profit analysis.** Cost-volume-profit analysis assumes that costs can be approximated with fixed and variable costs. It assumes a constant sales price; cannot be used to determine optimal levels of output and price; and does not consider the time value of money.

4 **Make short-term pricing decisions considering variable cost and capacity.** If an organization is operating below capacity, the marginal cost is approximated by the variable cost. Therefore, in the short run, the variable cost should be considered as the lower boundary in making a pricing decision.

5 **Make decisions on adding or dropping products or services.** Products or services should be added, if the incremental revenues are greater than the incremental costs. Products and services should be dropped, if the lost revenues are less than the avoidable costs.

6 **Determine whether to make or buy a product or service.** A product or service should be purchased instead of produced, if the purchase price is greater than the cost of making the product or service.

7 **Determine whether to process or promote a product or service further.** A product or service should be processed further, if the incremental revenue is greater than the incremental cost. Managers that are maximizing profit prefer to sell products with higher contribution margins, if the organization is operating below capacity.

8 **Decide which products and services to provide when a constraint exists in the production process.** A manager that is attempting to maximize profit will choose to produce more of the product or service with the highest contribution margin per use of the scarce resource.

9 **Identify and manage a bottleneck to maximize output.** A bottleneck is the limiting factor of the operating rate of an organization. The bottleneck should be managed so that it is operating at its capacity, and ways of relaxing the bottleneck should be considered.

KEY TERMS

Avoidable product and service costs Costs that are no longer incurred, if a product or service is dropped.

Bottleneck The process of an organization that has the least capacity.

Break-even analysis The process of identifying the number of units that must be sold to achieve zero profit.

Contribution margin per unit The sales price minus the variable cost per unit.

Contribution margin ratio (Appendix) The ratio of the contribution margin to sales revenues.

Cost-volume-profit (CVP) analysis The process of estimating profit assuming constant fixed and variable costs and a constant price over all rates of output.

Operating leverage (Appendix) A measure of an organization's cost structure calculated as the ratio of its fixed costs to its total costs.

Theory of constraints A process of identifying and managing constraints in organizational activities.

APPENDIX
Additional aspects of CVP analysis

This appendix describes some extensions of CVP analysis that can be used to make various planning decisions. As noted in the chapter, CVP often provides an initial analysis to determine whether further study is warranted.

■ Examining the contribution margin ratio

The **contribution margin ratio** is the ratio of the contribution margin to sales revenues, generally expressed as a percentage. This ratio can be used to examine the impact of changes in sales revenues, fixed costs and the break-even quantity. For example, a firm has sales revenues of €200,000 and variable costs of €80,000. Its contribution margin is €200,000 − €80,000, or €120,000. The contribution margin ratio is €120,000/€200,000, or 60 per cent. If revenues increase by 10 per cent or €20,000, then the corresponding increase in the contribution margin is 60 per cent of €20,000, or €12,000. Similarly, if sales decline by 20 per cent, the impact on the contribution margin is a decrease of 60 per cent of €40,000, or €24,000. Examining the contribution margin ratio provides a quick analysis of the effect of fluctuations in sales revenues.

The contribution margin ratio has other applications. For instance, it provides a means to determine the break-even point when cost and revenue data are not available on a per-unit basis. The approach is similar to the break-even quantity in units, but substitutes the contribution margin ratio for the per-unit contribution margin in the break-even formula.

Numerical **example** 5.13

A firm has fixed costs of £1 million and variable costs of £750,000. Its current sales revenues are £2,000,000. At what level of sales will the firm break even?

Solution

The firm's contribution margin is £2,000,000 − £750,000, or £1,250,000. The contribution margin ratio is £1,250,000/£2,000,000, or 62.5 per cent. The break-even quantity, expressed in terms of sales revenues, is:

$$FC \div CM \text{ ratio} = £1,000,000/0.625 = £1,600,000$$

Most firms offer a basket of goods or a number of products in a product line. In these situations, the contribution margin ratio represents the average contribution margin ratio of this basket of goods. It then can be used to determine the overall sales revenues that are required to break even.

Numerical **example** 5.14

Alpha Company sells a basket of goods whose current sales revenues are £150,000. The total variable costs are £82,500. Fixed costs are £35,000. At what level of sales will the firm break even?

Solution

The firm's contribution margin is £150,000 − £82,500, or £67,500. The contribution margin ratio is £67,500/£150,000, or 45 per cent. The break-even quantity in terms of sales revenues is:

$$FC \div CM \text{ ratio} = £35,000/0.45 = £77,777.78$$

On pages 157–58 we described the use of CVP with multiple products. There, the sales price and variable cost of each product were known. If we knew instead the contribution margin ratio of each product, we could determine the break-even quantity in terms of sales revenues.

Numerical **example** 5.15

Alpha Company manufactures and sells three products in its basket of goods: X, Y, and Z. The contribution margin ratios are 45 per cent, 35 per cent and 50 per cent, respectively. The basket of goods is composed as follows: 10 per cent of X, 30 per cent of Y and 60 per cent of Z. The total variable costs are £82,500. Fixed costs are £35,000. At what level of sales will the firm break even?

Solution

The weighted-average contribution margin is $(0.10 \times 0.45) + (0.30 \times 0.35) + (0.60 \times 0.50)$, or 0.45. The break-even quantity in terms of sales revenues is:

$$FC \div CM \text{ ratio} = £35,000/0.45 = £77,777.78$$

This break-even quantity assumes that there is no change in the product mix.

The contribution margin ratio is a useful tool to determine the increase in sales revenues required to cover higher fixed expenses, such as an increase in property taxes or administrative expenditures. It also can be used to compute the additional sales revenues necessary to provide for an increase in the desired target profit. The next section outlines a further extension of CVP analysis based on the knowledge of an organization's cost structure.

Analysing operating leverage

Knowledge of the fixed and variable components of an organization's cost structure is useful planning information, especially in designing changes to the product mix, marketing campaigns or examining the effect of short-term fluctuations in operating levels. The ratio of fixed costs to total costs is known as **operating leverage**. The higher are the organization's fixed costs, the higher is the organization's risk. This high leverage means that small percentage changes in sales volume translate into large percentage changes in net cash flow and profit. Firms with low operating leverage (a low ratio of fixed costs to total costs) have less variability in cash flows and profits. These firms are less risky than are their competitors whose cost structures have a greater proportion of fixed costs. For example, a firm might outsource activities to convert certain fixed costs into variable costs, thereby reducing its operating risk.

Firms with high operating leverage experience higher net profit when sales exceed the break-even point. When sales fall below the break-even point, the impact on net profit is correspondingly greater. Firms with low operating leverage experience less impact on net profit when cash flows exceed or fall below the break-even level. To summarize, high operating leverage magnifies the effect of percentage changes in sales revenues, whereas low operating leverage reduces this impact. The degree of operating leverage is one indication of an organization's ability to withstand short-term declines in sales levels.

Consider two firms, LeBas and LeHaut. The following is a summary of the firms' revenues and costs:

	LeBas (€)	LeHaut (€)
Sales revenues	10,000	10,000
Variable costs	5,000	2,500
Fixed costs	2,000	5,000
Net profit	3,000	2,500

The operating leverage of LeBas is €2,000/€7,000, or 0.2857. The operating leverage of LeHaut is €5,000/€7,500, or 0.6667. Thus, LeHaut is more highly leveraged compared to LeBas. If sales increase or decrease by a given percentage, the impact on LeHaut's net profit will be greater than the impact on the net profit of LeBas. To illustrate, let's examine a drop in sales of 30 per cent:

	LeBas (€)	LeHaut (€)
Sales revenues	7,000	7,000
Variable costs	3,500	1,750
Fixed costs	2,000	5,000
Net profit	1,500	250

When sales decrease by 30 per cent, the net profit of LeBas falls by 50 per cent, whereas that of LeHaut drops by 90 per cent. Hence, the cost structure of LeBas, which contains a lower percentage of fixed costs, cushions the impact of decreases in the firm's operating level. This cushion has a corresponding effect when sales increase. LeBas experiences a smaller percentage increase in net profit for a percentage increase in sales revenues compared to that which LeBas receives.

■ Achieving a specified after-tax profit

This section describes how to modify the cost-volume-profit formulae in the chapter to include taxes. Not-for-profit organizations do not have to pay taxes, but other organizations do. The amount of the tax paid depends on the taxable profit and the tax rates. The profit calculated using variable and fixed costs to approximate product costs is not necessarily equal to taxable profit. For example, depreciation is often calculated differently for tax purposes. In this section, we assume that the profit determined by the variable and fixed costs is also the taxable profit and a constant tax rate (t) is used to calculate taxes. Under these circumstances, the after-tax profit is:

$$\text{After-tax profit} = [(P - VC/\text{unit})Q - FC](1 - t)$$

To determine the quantity of units necessary to achieve a specified after-tax profit, the formula can be re-arranged to solve for Q:

$$\text{After-tax profit}/(1 - t) = (P - VC/\text{unit})Q - FC$$

$$[\text{After-tax profit}/(1 - t)] + FC = (P - VC/\text{unit})Q$$

$$[(\text{After-tax profit}/(1 - t)) + FC]/(P - VC/\text{unit}) = Q$$

Our ice cream vendor earlier in the chapter had fixed costs of £100 per day, variable costs of £0.20 per ice cream cone, and a price of £1.00 per cone. If the vendor has a tax rate of 30 per cent and wants to have a profit after taxes of £50 per day, how many ice creams must she sell? Using the equation above:

$$[(\text{After-tax profit}/(1 - t)) + FC]/(P - VC/\text{unit})$$
$$= [(£50/(1 - 0.3)) + £100]/(£1.00 - £0.20) = 215 \text{ ice cream cones}$$

How many ice cream cones must she sell to break even (after-tax profit = £0)?

$$[(£0/(1 - 0.3)) + £100]/(£1.00 - £0.20) = 125 \text{ ice cream cones}$$

Notice that this is the same number of ice cream cones when taxes are ignored. Taxes are only paid when there are profits. At the break-even level, there are no profits, hence, no taxes.

Self-study problem

The Bike-2-Go Company is the brainchild of Charles Johnson. Charles has designed a portable bicycle that can be disassembled easily and placed in a suitcase. He is thinking about implementing the idea and going into production. Charles estimates that the fixed costs of producing between 1,000 and 3,000 portable bicycles will be £50,000 annually. In addition, the variable cost per portable bicycle is estimated to be £40 per bicycle. Charles could outsource the suitcase production, which would reduce the fixed costs to £40,000 annually and the variable costs to £35 per bicycle. If Bike-2-Go makes less than 2,000 portable bicycles, excess capacity would exist that could be used to make 1,000 regular bicycles. There would be no additional fixed costs and the variable costs would be £60 per regular bicycle. No other use exists for the space.

Required

a Charles would like to make £60,000 annually on this venture. If Charles makes and sells 3,000 portable bicycles (with the suitcase), what price should Charles charge for each portable bicycle?

b If Charles decides to charge £80 per portable bicycle while making the suitcase, what is the break-even number of portable bicycles?

c If Charles makes 2,500 portable bicycles, should Charles consider buying the suitcases from an outside supplier if the supplier's price per suitcase is £10?

d If Charles only makes and sells 2,000 portable bicycles because of limited demand, what is the minimum selling price that Charles should consider for 1,000 regular bicycles built with the excess capacity?

Solution

a Profit = (Price per unit − Variable cost per unit) × (Number of units) − Fixed cost

$$£60,000 = (\text{Price per unit} - £40) \times (3,000) - £50,000$$
$$\text{Price per unit} = £76.67$$

b Break-even quantity = Fixed cost/(Price per unit − Variable cost per unit)

$$\text{Break-even quantity} = £50,000/(£80 - £40) = 1,250 \text{ portable bicycles}$$

c Avoidable costs if the suitcase is not made in-house:

Reduction in fixed costs (£50,000 − £40,000)	£10,000
Reduction in variable costs 2,500 units × (£40 − £35)	£7,500
Total avoidable costs	£17,500
Cost of purchasing suitcases £10 × 2,500	£25,000

The cost to purchase the suitcases exceeds the total avoidable costs. Therefore, the suitcases should be made in-house.

d The regular bicycles do not add to the fixed costs, therefore, the variable cost per unit establishes the lower boundary for pricing the regular bicycles. As long as the price is greater than the variable cost, the company has a positive contribution margin from the regular bicycles.

Numerical exercises

NE 5.1 Break-even analysis LO 2

A taxi driver must pay €100 per day for taxi rental, insurance and licences. The taxi driver charges €0.50 per kilometre. The petrol and maintenance costs are €0.15 per kilometre. The taxi driver travels 50 kilometres per day without customers.

a Not counting tips, how many kilometres must the taxi driver carry customers to break even?

b How many kilometres must the taxi driver carry customers to make €50 plus tips?

NE 5.2 Short-term pricing decisions LO 4

Alpha plc manufactures a product that has a fixed cost of £400,000 and a variable cost of £100 per unit. The company has been making 10,000 units and selling them for £200 per unit. There is excess capacity in the plant and a buyer has asked to buy 1,000 units for £120 apiece.

What should Alpha do?

SUMMARY

1 **Balance the assignment of responsibilities, the choice of performance measures and the reward system.** The assignment of responsibilities, the choice of performance measures and the reward system should be consistent with each other, and should change simultaneously when the organizational structure changes.

2 **Link responsibilities with individuals who have the specific knowledge to make the decision.** Ideally, responsibility within an organization should reside with the individual with the best information related to that decision, or with an individual in a position to receive that information. Either the responsibilities are assigned to the person with the knowledge, or the knowledge is transferred to the person with the responsibility to make the decision. The method chosen depends on the relative costs of transferring responsibilities or transferring the knowledge.

3 **Recognize self-interest in motivating individuals within organizations.** Individuals join organizations and work within organizations to better their own welfare. The benefits each individual receives from joining the organization must exceed the costs the individual bears. Self-interested individuals do not automatically seek to further the organization's goals unless incentive systems motivate such behaviour.

4 **Identify the costs and benefits of monitoring members of an organization.** Monitoring individuals within an organization to determine if they are properly performing their duties is costly. Someone must observe their behaviour or measure the results of their actions. Without some monitoring, however, individuals will not always perform their duties to benefit the organization.

5 **Choose performance measures that reveal actions of members of an organization.** Performance measures should reveal the actions of the individuals being evaluated and be consistent with the goals of the organization. Also, the measures should not be easily manipulated by the individual being evaluated.

6 **Create a balanced scorecard to articulate the strategy of the organization.** A balanced scorecard describes objectives in a cause-and-effect sequence to achieve the strategy of the organization. Performance measures and targets are identified for each objective.

7 **Design compensation contracts based on performance measures and responsibilities assigned.** Individuals within organizations should have compensation contracts that motivate the individual to act in the best interest of the organization. The performance rewards should be matched to and co-ordinated with the performance evaluation system and the responsibilities assigned to the person. All legs of the three-legged stool must match.

8 **Design internal control systems by separating the planning process from the control process.** Responsibilities associated with making planning decisions, such as initiation and implementation, should be separated from responsibilities for control, such as ratification and monitoring.

9 **Identify control issues within an organization.** The purpose of control is to motivate individuals within the organization to act in the best interests of the organization.

KEY TERMS

Balanced scorecard An articulation of an organization's strategy through a sequence of objectives with a set of performance measures that provide a comprehensive view of the organization by recognizing the goals of shareholders and the satisfaction of customers.

Driver performance measures Input or lead measures of objectives within a balanced scorecard.

Implementation The step in the decision process to carry out the plans of the organization.

Initiation The step in the decision process to identify areas of improvement within the organization.

Internal control system A system of checks and balances within the organization that helps achieve its goals.

Monitoring The step in the decision process to make sure that plans are implemented as planned.

Monitoring costs The cost of observing members of the organization directly or indirectly.

Outcome performance measures Output measures of objectives in a balanced scorecard.

Performance measures A description of how well an individual has performed a task.

Ratification The step in the decision process to determine whether a proposal is consistent with the goals of the organization.

Self-study problem

Jennifer Whitsell had worked for men long enough. She was neither promoted nor recognized for her skills, and was paid less than her male counterparts. Jennifer decided it was time to become her own boss, so she started her own advertising agency. Her agency's primary function was to match organizations that wanted to advertise with media companies. Her agency was paid a percentage of every advertising contract that it organized.

Jennifer had had such a difficult time as a woman working for men that she attempted to give women plenty of opportunities in her organization. But recently she had a problem. One of her female employees, Liana Moreno, had just had a baby and wanted a more flexible work schedule. Instead of working from nine to five, Monday through Friday, Liana wanted to work some evenings, but take off during the afternoons to be with her new daughter. She also wanted to work at home rather than in the office. Jennifer was not sure that allowing for flexible work time would work in her company. On the one hand, flexible time and working at home meant that Jennifer would not be able to control her employees very well, as she would not be able to observe their activities. What if employees say they are going to work at home, but they end up playing with their children? On the other hand, she knows that flexible work time will improve morale and may even improve productivity.

How can Jennifer solve this problem?

Solution

Jennifer assumes that she can only control her employees by observing them. There are many ways of controlling employees other than direct observation. For example, Jennifer could use web-based reporting to have her employees check in with her. She also could have employees work in teams. Members of teams tend to control each other. If performance measures are team-based, the other members will be sure that Liana does her fair share or they will complain.

Jennifer could also use employee output as a performance measure, rather than the number of hours they work. In the case of the advertising agency, an employee that generates more advertising contracts contributes to the agency. The financial amount of contracts written by an employee could be used as a performance measure. This performance measure would indirectly measure the effort and skill of the employee. It is also consistent with the goal of maximizing profit for the agency. Hours worked is not a very good performance measure, because an employee could spend a lot of time in the office without contributing to the agency.

Analysis and interpretation problems

AIP 6.1 Monitoring LO 4

Drivers for long-haul (international and cross-country) moving companies (e.g. Allied International, Euro Transport) are often independent contractors, whereas inter-city movers are usually employees of the company.

Why are long-haul drivers often not employees of a company?

AIP 6.2 Voluntary disclosure of performance measures LO 4

The UK Companies Acts of 1900 and 1907 required public companies to issue financial statements. Increased disclosure requirements were legislated by subsequent acts in 1928–29 and, significantly, the Companies Act of 1948. Yet, prior to these legislative requirements, many other companies voluntarily issued profit and loss statements and balance sheets.

Discuss the advantages and disadvantages of such voluntary disclosures.

AIP 6.3 Separation of duties LO 1

In a bank, the employee interacting with someone seeking a loan does not have the authority to grant the loan.

Why is the employee not given the responsibility to grant the loan?

AIP 6.4 Choosing performance measures LO 1, 5, 9

Jen and Barry opened an ice cream shop in Manchester. It was a big success, so they decide to open ice cream shops in many cities including Bristol. They hire Dante to manage the shop in Bristol. Jen and Barry are considering two different sets of performance measures for Dante. The first set would grade Dante based on the cleanliness of the shop and customer service. The second set would use accounting numbers, including the profit of the shop in Bristol.

What are the advantages and disadvantages of each set of performance measures?

AIP 6.5 Compensation LO 5

Lawyers in a small practice in central Cardiff have the following compensation agreement. Each lawyer bills the client for his or her services. The lawyer pays for all direct expenses incurred in the firm, including paralegals, malpractice insurance, secretaries, supplies and equipment. Each lawyer has a stated salary cap (e.g. £100,000). For client fees collected over the salary cap, the lawyer retains 30 per cent of the additional fees less expenses. For example, if £150,000 is billed and collected from clients and expenses of £40,000 are paid, then the lawyer retains £3,000 of the excess net fees [30% × (£150,000 − 40,000 − 100,000)] and the firm receives £7,000. If £120,000 of fees are collected and £40,000 of expenses are incurred, the lawyer's net cash flow is £80,000 and the legal practice receives none of the fees.

Critically evaluate the existing compensation plan and recommend any changes.

AIP 6.6 Designing a balanced scorecard LO 6

Old Town Roasters (OTR) owns and operates a chain of 12 coffee shops around town. OTR's strategy is to provide the highest quality coffee and baked goods in a warm, friendly environment. Internet access is available along with current newspapers. Some of the shops are open 24 hours a day, especially those located around the university campus. Each shop manager is responsible for deciding the hours that the shop is open, the selection of baked goods to stock, and the number of Internet connections to provide in the shop.

Design a balanced scorecard that can be used to evaluate and reward the manager of each shop.

AIP 6.7 Identifying control issues LO 3, 9

Mary Sweet has just opened a candy shop. The store is open from 10 am to 8 pm each day, which means that Mary must work a minimum of 10 hours a day for 7 days a week. In addition to sales, she also must spend time on purchasing, paying bills and cleaning up. Mary quickly decides that she needs to hire help. Her first hire is a person to operate the cash register for five days of the week. This person will also be responsible for closing the shop on those days so Mary can spend the evenings with her family. While Mary was operating the store by herself, she did not have to worry about control issues. Now that she is hiring another person, she must consider mechanisms to control the new employee.

Describe some control problems that might arise and some mechanisms that Mary could use to help control those problems.

AIP 6.8 Linking responsibilities and knowledge LO 2

In the UK, professional football teams generally have a team manager who is responsible for selecting new talent, training the team, making decisions on game day, and also signing player contracts. The team manager is responsible for the team both on and off the field. In North America, professional teams have both a coach and a general manager. The general manager is usually responsible for the business operations of the organization, and maintains the responsibility for selecting personnel on the football team. The coach is responsible for training and decisions during the game.

In North America, many coaches have been unhappy with their relationship with the general manager. They believe that they should have more responsibilities in choosing players. Some of the top coaches are now insisting on being both the coach and the general manager. In the UK, there has been a recent shift to separate the role of team manager with the appointment of a director to take care of business affairs while the team manager focuses on the coaching aspects of the game. This approach is similar to that used on the Continent and in North America.

What are the advantages and disadvantages of the approaches used in the UK and North America to assign the management and coaching duties of the football team?

AIP 6.9 Monitoring computer use LO 4

Samson Company is an engineering firm. Many of the employees are engineers who are working individually on different projects. Most of the design work takes place on computers. The computers are connected by a network and employees can also 'surf' the Internet through their desktop computers.

The chief executive is concerned about productivity among her engineers. She has acquired software that allows her to monitor each engineer's computer work. At any time during the day, she can observe on her screen the exact task on which each engineer is working. The engineers are quite unhappy with this monitoring process. They believe that it is unethical for the chief executive to be able to access their computers without their knowledge.

Discuss the advantages and disadvantages of monitoring through observing the computer work of the engineers.

AIP 6.10 Choosing performance measures LO 5

The finance director of the Canby Insurance Company has just read an article on the balanced scorecard. A balanced scorecard is a set of performance measures that reflects the diverse interests and goals of all the stakeholders (shareholders, customers, employees and society) of the company. At present, Canby has only one performance measure for the top managers: profit. The board of directors claims that profit as the sole performance measure is sufficient. If customers are satisfied and employees are productive, then the company will be profitable. Any other performance measure will detract from the basic goal of making a profit.

Explain the costs and benefits of only having profit as a performance measure.

AIP 6.11 Performance measures and responsibilities LO 7

The new president of the Sawtooth Division of the Waterhouse Company is complaining about the limitations, which the chief executive officer (CEO) of Waterhouse Company has placed on him. The Sawtooth Division is composed of several logging mills in the Pacific Northwest of the US. These mills were designed to cut large 'old growth' logs. Recent environmental and conservation regulations and policies to address climate change have curtailed the cutting of almost all old growth forests. The mills are struggling to get a sufficient supply of logs to operate. The president is being evaluated based on the profit of the logging mills and if things continue the way they are now, a loss is inevitable. The president's main complaint is that he doesn't have the right to change the logging mills to accommodate smaller logs or move into a secondary wood-products field, such as the manufacture of wood trim or pre-fabricated houses.

Does the president of the Sawtooth Division have a reasonable complaint?

AIP 6.12 Performance measures and teams LO 3, 7, 8

Royal Motors is an auto manufacturer. Until recently, the company has operated as an assembly line. The chassis started at one end of the factory. As it moved through the plant, parts were added to the chassis until a completed car emerged from the other end of the plant.

Royal Motors has recently decided to change to a cell manufacturing approach. A cell is composed of a team that completes a whole car in a relatively small area. Parts are brought to the cell for assembly. Workers have multiple skills that allow them to perform many different operations, rather than a single operation on an assembly line.

On the assembly line, a worker was evaluated by how well he or she performed a single task. The work performed by the individual workers of the cell-manufacturing team is not as easily identifiable.

How should Royal Motors change performance measures to accommodate cell manufacturing?

AIP 6.13 Outcome versus input performance measures LO 5

The Travel Magazine executive group is very unhappy with its photographer. She had been sent to Tahiti to take some pictures of sunny beaches to entice visitors to Tahiti. Unfortunately, all the pictures taken by the photographer have a greyish tinge to them. The beaches appear to be rather ordinary in the pictures. The magazine executives are thinking about replacing the photographer. The photographer believes that it was not her fault that the photographs turned out so poorly. She worked extremely hard, but it rained almost every day while she was in Tahiti.

Why has this conflict developed? Are there ways to resolve it?

AIP 6.14 Separation of duties LO 1

The local electric utility receives thousands of payments every day from its customers. The following processes occur in handling the payments: opening the letters, recording the amount of the cheque and the customer's account, filling in a deposit slip for the bank, and depositing the cheques with the bank.

Describe methods of controlling these processes so that cheques are not misplaced or stolen.

AIP 6.15 Designing a balanced scorecard LO 6

The Pottery Store is a chain of retail shops in upscale arcades that sells pottery, woodcarvings and other craft items. The typical customer is shopping for a gift and spends between £50 and £200. Buyers located in the corporate office contact artists around the country and buy inventory for the shops. Corporate headquarters sets the final selling price for each item and determines when to mark them down for sales. Each shop manager is responsible for staffing the shop and the local shop layout. Shop managers do not have responsibility for choosing the merchandise, shop hours (as these are set by the arcade) or pricing decisions.

a Design a balanced scorecard for the shop managers.

b How would your answer to (a) change if the shop managers also had decision-making responsibilities over both the selection of merchandise to carry in the shop as well as pricing decisions?

AIP 6.16 Target costs as benchmarks for performance measures LO 7

The manufacturing division manager of a computer chip company had traditionally been evaluated based on costs. As long as she could produce computer chips more cheaply than the previous year, she received her bonus. The initial benchmark for the bonus was established based on the first year of manufacturing a new computer chip. But the company recognized that this type of reward system for the manufacturing manager would no longer work. First, the product life of the computer chips was becoming shorter and shorter. Some computer chips were only made for a year. Second, the company had switched to target costing. The company's customers would request a computer chip with certain characteristics, and at a price that the customer would be willing to pay. The engineers of the computer chip company would then attempt to design a computer chip with all the appropriate features that the customer wanted, and that also could be made cheaply enough to earn a profit. Once the engineers were satisfied that the computer chip had been appropriately designed, the company would sign the deal and turn the design over to the manufacturing division manager for production. The target cost based on the engineers' estimate became the benchmark upon which the manufacturing manager's bonus was based. If she could produce the new chip at below the target cost, she would receive a bonus.

The manufacturing manager did not like this new bonus system. She felt that the target cost was imposed on her and it did not take into account the problems of producing new chips, especially the learning process.

How could the process of choosing a target cost and using it as a benchmark for the manufacturing division affect the manager's compensation?

AIP 6.17 Performance measures and free riders LO 5, 7

China's peasants working on large farm communes in the 1970s started each day with the production team leader assigning jobs. The peasants received a fixed number of 'work points' for their day's work. The peasants got food, fuel and other necessities based on work points they accumulated. After each harvest, part of it was paid as tax to the state and the remainder divided among the peasants.

The remainder of the crop was then divided based on the number of work points each person had earned. Meetings of all the peasants determined how many points would be assigned for each work point. Most men would be given 10 points for each day worked, and women eight. Exceptionally hard workers got an extra point. Unpopular peasants received fewer points for each day worked even though they often worked just as hard and were usually assigned the worst jobs.

There was little variation across peasants of the same gender in terms of points. The number of points accumulated depended primarily on how many days each one worked, rather than how much each produced.

What predictable behaviour do you expect the Chinese agricultural system will generate?

AIP 6.18 Performance measures, responsibilities and self-interest LO 1, 3

A textbook on organization theory states:

'Drawing upon the writings of Maslow, McGregor presented his Theory X-Theory Y dichotomy to describe two differing conceptions of human behaviour. Theory X assumptions held that people are inherently lazy, they dislike work, and that they will avoid it whenever possible. Leaders who act on Theory X premises are prone to controlling their subordinates through coercion, punishment, and the use of financial rewards; the use of external controls is necessary, as most human beings are thought to be incapable of self-direction and assuming responsibility. In contrast, Theory Y is based on the assumption that work can be enjoyable and that people will work hard and assume responsibility if they are given the opportunity to achieve personal goals at the same time.'

V. K. Narayanan and R. Nath (1993) *Organization Theory: A Strategic Approach* (Richard D. Irwin, Homewood, IL), p. 403.

Using the framework presented in the text, critically analyse Theory X-Theory Y.

AIP 6.19 Three-legged stool LO 1

Jacinthe Renaud manages a revenue centre of a large national manufacturer that sells office furniture to local businesses in Lyon, France. A revenue centre is evaluated on the revenues that it earns. She has responsibility over pricing. Jacinthe's compensation is a fixed wage of €23,000 per year plus 2 per cent of her office's total sales.

Critically evaluate the organizational architecture of Ms Renaud's revenue centre.

AIP 6.20 Using a balanced scorecard LO 6

The Lunatic Fringe operates a chain of up-market hair salons. Each salon manager receives a bonus of £2,500 if he or she meets or exceeds the target set for four measures in their balanced scorecard. If they meet three targets, they get a £7,500 bonus. If they meet one target, they receive a £2,500 bonus. The following table defines the four targets:

**Lunatic Fringe
Balanced Scorecard**

Objectives	Performance measure	Target (%)
Financial perspective		
Increase shareholder wealth	Return on assets	20
Customer perspective		
Customer satisfaction	% satisfied through survey	95
Internal business process perspective		
On-time service	% customers not waiting for appointment	90
Learning and growth perspective		
Reduce employee turnover	% annual turnover	20

The West End salon of the Lunatic Fringe had the following operating statistics for the financial year:

Net income	£139,500
Total assets	£634,000
Number of customer surveys	672
Number of customer surveys 'satisfied'	646
Number of customers	915
Number of customers served on time	833
Employee turnover	5
Number of employees	15

How much bonus will Lucy Chan, the West End manager of the Lunatic Fringe, receive? Discuss the potential positive and negative effects on the business of the West End salon and of Lunatic Fringe by tying Lucy's bonus to these performance measures.

AIP 6.21 Changing the three-legged stool LO 1

In December 1996, a *Wall Street Journal* article described a series of changes at one Pratt & Whitney plant that manufactured parts for aircraft engines. In 1993, it was about to be closed, due to high operating costs and inefficiencies. A new plant manager overhauled operations. He broadened job descriptions, so inspectors did 15 per cent more work than five years ago. A 'results-sharing' plan paid hourly workers if the plant exceeded targets such as cost cutting and on-time delivery. Everyone was looking for ways to cut costs.

Hourly workers also helped design a new pay scheme that was linked to the amount of training a worker had, not seniority. This plan was designed after the plant manager drafted 22 factory-floor workers, gave them a conference room and told them to develop a new pay plan linked to learning.

Shop-floor wages varied between $9 to $19 per hour (roughly £5.40 to £11.40 at the prevailing exchange rate), with the most money going to people running special cost studies or quality projects, tasks previously held by managers.

Chapter 6 emphasizes the importance of keeping all three legs of the stool in balance. Identify the changes Pratt & Whitney made to all three legs of the stool at its manufacturing plant.

Extended **analysis** and **interpretation** problems

AIP 6.22 Woodhaven Service Station

Woodhaven Service Station is a small, independent petrol station located in the outskirts of Liverpool. The station has three petrol pumps and two service bays. The repair facility specializes in automotive maintenance (oil changes, tune ups, etc.) and minor repairs (silencers, shock absorbers, etc.). Woodhaven generally refers customers who require major work (transmission rebuilds, electronics, etc.) to shops that are better equipped to handle such repairs. Major repairs are only done in-house when both the customer and mechanic agree that this would be the best course of action.

During the 20 years that he has owned Woodhaven Service, Harold Mateen's competence and fairness have built a loyal customer base of neighbourhood residents. In fact, demand for his services has been more than he can reasonably meet, and yet the repair end of his business is not especially profitable. Most of his competitors earn the lion's share of their profits through repairs, but Harold is making almost all of his money by selling petrol. If he could make more money on repairs, Woodhaven would be the most successful service station in the area. Harold believes that Woodhaven's weakness in repair profitability is due to the inefficiency of his mechanics. The mechanics are paid the industry average of £500 per week. While Harold does not think he overpays them, he feels he is not getting his money's worth.

Harold's son, Andrew, is a philosophy student at Humanities University, where he has learned the Socratic dictum of 'to know the Good is to do the Good'. Andrew provided his father with a classic text on employee morality, the Reverend Doctor Weisbrotten's *Work Hard on Thine Job and Follow the Righteous Way*. Every morning for two months, Harold, Andrew and the mechanics devoted one hour to studying this text. Despite many lively and fascinating discussions on the rights and responsibilities of the employee, productivity did not improve one bit. Harold figured he would just have to go out and hire harder-working mechanics.

The failure of the Weisbrotten method did not surprise Lisa, Harold's daughter. A student at Commerce College, she has the training to know that Andrew's methods were rubbish. As anyone serious about business knows, the true science of productivity and management of human resources resides in Dr von Drekken's masterful *Modifying Organizational Behaviour Through Commitment to a Happy Environment.* Yes, happiness leads to greater productivity! Harold followed the scientific methods to the letter. Yet, despite giving out gold stars, blowing up balloons and wearing a smiley face button, Lisa's way proved no better than Andrew's did.

Compensation plans

Harold thinks that his neighbour, Jack Myers, owner of Honest Jack's Pre-Enjoyed Autorama, might be helpful. After all, one does not become as successful as Jack without a lot of practical knowledge. Or, maybe it is Jack's great radio jingle that does it. Jack says, 'It's not the jingle, you idiot! It's the way I pay my guys. Your mechanics make 500 quid a week no matter what. Why should they put out for you? Who cares about gold stars? My guys – my guys get paid straight commission and nothing more. They do good by me and I do good by them. Otherwise, let 'em starve. Look, it's quite simple. Pay 'em a percentage of the sales for the work they do. If you need to be a nice guy about it, make that percentage so that if sales are average, then they make their usual £500. But if sales are better, they get that percentage extra. This way they don't get hurt but have good reason to help you out.'

Straight commission, however, seemed a little radical for Harold. What if sales were bad for a week? That would hurt the mechanics.

Harold figured that it would be better to pay each mechanic a guaranteed £300 a week plus a commission rate that would, given an average volume of business, pay them the extra £200 that would bring their wage back to £500. Under this system, the mechanics would be insulated from a bad week, would not be penalized for an average week, and would still have the incentive to attempt to improve sales. Yes, this seemed more fair.

Alternatively, maybe Jack only knows about the used-car business, not about business in general. Harold figured that he should look for an incentive pay method more in line with the way things are done in the auto-repair business. Perhaps he should pay his mechanics in the same way that his customers pay him – by the job. It is standard practice for garages to charge customers a flat rate for the labour associated with any job. The number of labour hours for which the customer is charged is generally taken from a manual that outlines expected labour times for specific jobs on specific vehicles. The customer pays for these expected hours regardless of how many actual labour hours are expended on the job. Many garages also pay their mechanics by the job. Harold thinks that this approach makes theoretical sense because it links the mechanic's pay to the labour charges paid by the customer.

Required

a This question presents three popular approaches to alleviating agency costs. Although certain aspects of each of these methods are consistent with the views presented in the text, none of these methods is likely to succeed. Discuss the similarities and differences between the ideas of the chapter and:

   i Dr Weisbrotten's approach,

   ii Professor von Drekken's approach,

   iii Harold Mateen's idea of hiring 'harder-working' mechanics.

b Discuss the expected general effect at Woodhaven Service Station of the newly-proposed incentive compensation plans. How might they help Woodhaven and, assuming that Harold wants his business to be successful for a long time to come, what major divergent behaviours would be expected under the new compensation proposals? How damaging would you expect these new behaviours to be on a business such as Woodhaven's? Also, present a defence of the following propositions:

   i Harold's plan offers less incentive for divergent behaviour than Honest Jack's; and

   ii limiting a mechanic's pay by placing an upper bound of £750 per week on his earnings reduces incentives for divergent behaviour.

c Suppose that Harold owned a large car repair franchise located in a department store in a popular shopping mall. Suppose also that this department store is a heavily-promoted, well-known national chain that is famous for its good value and easy credit. How should Harold's thinking on incentive compensation change? What if Harold did not own the franchise, but was only the manager of a company-owned outlet?

d In this problem, it is assumed that knowledge and responsibilities are not linked. The mechanic who services the car decides what services are warranted. Discuss the costs and benefits of this fact for Woodhaven and the independently-owned chain-store repair shop.

AIP 6.23 Balanced scorecard[a]

In 1995, Global Oil Corporation's Marketing and Refining (M&R) Division was the fifth largest US refiner with 7,700 Global-branded service stations selling about 87 million litres per day, or 7 per cent of US petrol. All the stations were company-owned. In 1990, M&R ranked last among its peers in profitability and was annually draining $500 million of cash from the corporation.

In 1993, M&R reorganized from a centralized functional organization (Refineries, Transportation, Warehousing, Retail and Marketing) into 17 geographic business units (sales and distribution) and 14 service companies. The functional organization was slow to react to changing market conditions and the special customer needs that differed across the country. The new decentralized organization was designed to focus better on the customer. New marketing strategies could be better tailored to local markets by giving local managers more decision-making authority.

A new corporate strategy to focus on the less price-sensitive customer who would not only buy Global petrol, but also shop in its convenience petrol store outlets was implemented simultaneously with the reorganization. Global's new strategy was to redesign its convenience stores so that they would become a 'destination shop', offering one-stop shopping for petrol and snacks.

The old organization used a variety of functional measures: manufacturing cost, sales margins and volumes, and health and safety metrics. After changing its corporate strategy and organizational structure, M&R decided to change its performance metrics and began investigating the balanced scorecard.

Balanced scorecard

The balanced scorecard (BSC) is a series of performance measures that track the key elements of a company's strategy.[b] Based on the adage of 'What you measure is what you get', a company's BSC seeks to complement traditional

---

[a] This case is based on R. Kaplan (1997) 'Mobil USM&R (A): Linking the Balanced Scorecard', Harvard Business School Case 9-197-025 (May 7).

[b] R. Kaplan and N. Norton (1993) 'Putting the Balanced Scorecard to Work', *Harvard Business Review* (September–October), pp. 136–147.

financial performance measures with operational measures of customer satisfaction, internal processes, and internal innovation. After setting the company's vision and strategy, four general sets of measures are identified:

1 **Financial perspective**
   Return on capital
   Cash flow
   Earnings per share growth

2 **Customer perspective**
   Customer satisfaction
   Innovation
   Competitive price

3 **Internal processes**
   Safety
   Rework
   Time to market for new products

4 **Learning and growth**
   Rate of improvement
   Employee satisfaction
   Percentage of revenue from new products

A BSC has been compared to the instrument panel in an airplane. Each gauge provides specific information on the plane's location (altitude, speed, direction), and its operating condition (fuel, cabin pressure, temperature). Like an airplane's control panel, a BSC helps managers steer their business toward achieving its mission.

BSC at M&R

M&R formed project teams of managers to design performance metrics for their operations. Thirty-two different metrics were identified. These included Financial (return on assets (ROA), cash flow, volume, growth, etc.), Customer (share of segment, mystery shopper, etc.), Internal (safety incidents, refinery ROA, inventory level, etc.), and Learning (strategic skills acquisition, quality of information system, etc.). The 'mystery shopper' is a third-party vendor who purchases petrol and snacks at each station monthly. During each visit, the mystery shopper rates the station on 23 items related to external appearance, rest rooms, and so forth. A brochure describing the BSC was prepared and distributed to M&R's 11,000 employees in August of 1994. Extensive meetings with employees explained the new metrics and the BSC concept.

Compensation plans

All salaried employees of M&R received up to a 10 per cent bonus if Global ranked first among its seven competitors on ROA and earnings per share (EPS) growth. In addition to this existing plan, a new programme was added that awarded bonuses up to 20 per cent to managers. The size of the bonus depended on the average performance of three factors:

1 Global's competitive ranking on ROA and EPS growth;
2 M&R's balanced scorecard metrics;
3 own business unit's balanced scorecard.

In 1995, M&R generated more income per barrel of oil than the industry average, and its ROA exceeded the industry's average.

a Critically evaluate M&R's implementation of the balanced scorecard. Identify any strengths and weaknesses of the programme.
b Was the adoption of the balanced scorecard at M&R responsible for its turnaround financial performance?

CHAPTER SEVEN

Decentralized organizations
(Control)

Learning objectives

1 Use the controllability principle to choose performance measures for managers.

2 Identify responsibility centres based on the extent of each manager's responsibilities.

3 Choose performance measures for cost, profit and investment centres.

4 Identify the strengths and weaknesses of using return on investment (ROI) and residual income as performance measures for investment centres.

5 Choose transfer prices to create performance measures that reflect the activities controlled by each manager.

6 Use opportunity costs to choose transfer prices that will lead to decentralized decision making that is best for the organization.

7 Choose transfer prices to minimize taxes and overcome international obstacles.

Shah Motors

Shah Motors is a new- and used-car dealership. Jeremy Shah is the owner and president of Shah Motors. Jeremy makes long-term strategic decisions for the company and supervises three managers representing the following departments: new-car sales, used-car sales and service. The new-car sales manager advises Jeremy on orders to the plant for new cars, makes the final pricing decision on sales, is responsible for customer satisfaction and co-ordinates the new-car sales staff. The sales staff is paid solely on a commission basis, with the opportunity for a few bonuses such as free trips.

The used-car sales manager operates an area next to the new-car dealership. The used-car sales manager must accept from the new-car dealership the used cars that are traded in to purchase a new car. The used-car sales manager also purchases inventory directly from wholesalers and people wanting to sell their used cars. The used-car sales manager makes the final pricing decision and co-ordinates the used-car sales staff, who individually are rewarded based on commissions from sales.

The service manager is in charge of the service department, which provides maintenance and repair services for cars. The service manager is responsible for maintaining a parts department and co-ordinating a service crew. The service crew is paid a fixed salary.

Like most car dealerships, Shah Motors' financial success varies with the economy. When the economy is booming, the new- and used-car sales make the business very profitable. When the economy is weak, Shah Motors must rely on profits from the service department to survive. Jeremy feels that his company should not be so dependent on the economy, and is considering a new compensation scheme for the managers of Shah Motors. Presently, the managers receive a fixed salary, but Jeremy wonders if some type of bonus scheme might motivate the managers to work harder to achieve higher profits for the company.

THE CONTROLLABILITY PRINCIPLE

The idea of holding managers responsible for those decisions for which they are given authority is called the **controllability principle**. **Controllable costs** are costs affected by a manager's decisions. Managers affect controllable costs; therefore, these costs partially reveal the actions of the manager. Through the measurement of controllable costs, superiors have information about what decisions the manager has made. Therefore, controllable costs are potential performance measures for the manager who controls those costs. For example, the manager of a manufacturing plant is held responsible for the plant's costs because the manager makes decisions that affect plant costs.

A single manager generally does not have control over all of an organization's costs. Each manager has responsibilities, which are limited by the manager's job description, and which allow the manager to control only certain costs. Some costs also are affected by the organization's environment and not controlled by any managers of the organization. For example, economic forces that a plant manager cannot control affect the cost of raw materials. Uncontrollable costs generally do not reveal the actions of the manager, and are less useful performance measures.

Costs generally cannot be classified as either completely controllable or completely uncontrollable. Figure 7.1 demonstrates that costs usually are influenced by both managerial actions and uncontrollable environmental factors. For example, if a yacht-club manager is not held accountable for damage done by hurricanes, the manager has less incentive to prepare the yacht club for severe storms. While managers cannot influence the likelihood of hurricanes, they can influence the costs incurred from the impact of severe storms. Along with taking steps to safeguard the yacht club, the manager can obtain insurance to mitigate the financial impact of damages. In these cases, the manager should be responsible for the portion of costs that can be controlled. Holding managers accountable for only those costs solely under their control does not provide them with incentives to take actions that can affect the consequences of an uncontrollable event. The feedback loop from the performance measures and rewards in Figure 7.1 demonstrates the influence of the performance measurement system and the reward system on the actions of the manager.

Managers prefer to be evaluated based on controllable costs as it makes their rewards much more predictable. Generally they do not want their rewards to be uncertain. To avoid uncertainty, managers do not want performance measures which are affected by factors that they cannot control. Therefore, controllable performance measures, such as controllable costs, are preferred performance measures.

Figure 7.1 Controllability of costs

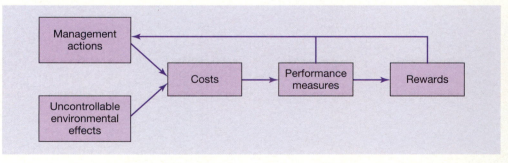

Yacht-club managers cannot control the weather but they can influence its cost impact. Managers accountable for these costs have incentives to prepare for such events.

Some performance measures, however, are partially affected by factors not under the manager's control. In the previous example, hurricanes were not controllable, but hurricanes affected costs. Managers would like to eliminate the uncontrollable portion of the costs from their performance measures.

One method of removing uncontrollable factors from a performance measure is to compare performance measures of different managers facing similar circumstances. With **relative performance measurement**, the performance of a manager is judged relative to the performance of a comparison group. The comparison group helps control for random events that affect both the person being evaluated and the comparison group. If the costs of the yacht-club manager are compared with those of other yacht-club managers adversely affected by the hurricane, the uncontrollable effects of the hurricane can be eliminated. Relative performance measurement is also used in assigning course grades. Many instructors 'curve' the grades. Instead of awarding A grades for scores of 80 to 100, the top 15 per cent of the class receives A's. Curving the grades controls for unusually easy or hard exams, and is a way to remove some of the risk for students.

Relative performance measures, however, do not recognize whether all the students or managers performed better or worse than some absolute standard. By comparing individual performances with the performance of others, approximately half of the individuals will always be graded better than average and half will be graded worse than average. No possibility exists for all individuals to be rated above average, even if all the individuals performed their duties as specified. Relative performance measures discourage co-operative effort across individuals, because individuals recognize that they will be compared with the other individuals.

In summary, each manager in an organization is given certain responsibilities. These responsibilities define the limits of the manager's control. The part of the organization within these limits is under the control of the manager. Ideally, managers are evaluated based on performance measures of activities that they also control.

Shah Motors (continued)

To analyse his organization, Jeremy Shah outlines the responsibilities that he has given to his three managers. Before designing the performance measurement and compensation system, Jeremy must determine what each manager controls.

Alice Ho: new-car sales manager. Controls product mix ordered from the factory, price, showroom facilities, sales staff and customer interactions. Does not control size of new-car inventory and showroom facility, and liabilities of the dealership.

Slick Thompson: used-car sales manager. Controls purchasing and size of inventory, used-car lot and office, sales staff and prices of used cars. Does not control acceptance of used cars from the new-car centre and liabilities of the dealership.

Grease Johnson: service department manager. Controls scheduling of maintenance, parts management and service workers. Does not control billing rates and price of parts, the size of the service shop and liabilities of the dealership.

Concept **review**

1 Why is the controllability principle used in most organizations?

2 What are the advantages and disadvantages of using a relative performance measure?

RESPONSIBILITY CENTRES

Organizations are typically composed of sub-units. For example, the firm might be organized into functional areas such as marketing, manufacturing and distribution departments. Other organizations are divided into sub-units by product or service offered. A university, for example, is divided into colleges that teach different topics. Each of these sub-units is commonly subdivided into smaller sub-units. For example, manufacturing may be further subdivided into parts manufacturing and assembly, and assembly organized by product assembled. Colleges are divided into departments, and specialized groups within departments. Each of these sub-units represents work groups and managers with specific responsibilities.

Responsibility accounting is the process of recognizing sub-units within the organization, assigning responsibilities to managers of those sub-units, and evaluating the performance of those managers. These sub-units of the organization, called responsibility centres, could be a single individual, a department, a functional area such as finance or marketing, or an entire operating division. The managers of each of these responsibility centres have different responsibilities and, accordingly, different performance measures. In each case, responsibilities should be linked with the requisite specialized knowledge. Responsibility accounting then dictates that the performance measurement system is designed to measure the performance that results from the responsibilities assigned to the managers. For example, if a manager is assigned responsibilities to sell products to customers in Rome, the performance measurement of this agent should not include sales to customers in Milan. The following sections and Table 7.1 describe different types of responsibility centres.

Table 7.1 Differences among cost, revenue, profit and investment centres

Type of responsibility centre	Responsibilities	Performance measurement
Cost centre (type 1)*	Choose output for a given cost of inputs	Output (maximize given quality constraints)
Cost centre (type 2)	Choose input mix to achieve a given output	Cost (minimize given quality constraints)
Profit centre	Choose inputs and outputs with a fixed level of investment	Profit (maximize)
Investment centre	Choose inputs, outputs, and level of investment	Return on investment, residual income (maximize)

*If output is revenue, this type of centre is often referred to as a revenue centre.

■ Cost centres

The responsibilities of a manager dictate the type of responsibility centre, and imply the appropriate performance measure for the manager. Some managers have more responsibilities than do others. Those with more responsibilities generally make more complex decisions. Managers with fewer responsibilities have less control over factors that affect organizational value. The responsibilities of a manager are commonly described in terms of the different types of responsibility centres.

Managers of **cost centres** tend to have the least responsibilities within an organization. Cost centre managers generally have control over a limited amount of assets, but usually have no right to price those assets for sale or to acquire more assets. A manager of an internal service of an organization is typically a manager of a cost centre. Managers of information technology, accounting, personnel, and research and development (R&D) are usually cost centre managers. Also, manufacturing managers usually are classified as managers of cost centres.

There are two ways cost centres can operate. Some cost centres (type 1 in Table 7.1) are given a fixed amount of resources (a budget). The cost centre is told to produce as much output as it can for the given amount of fixed resources. For example, suppose the manager of a marketing department has a fixed budget for sales staff and advertising. This manager is evaluated based on the amount of sales generated with the fixed budget. The cost centre manager usually has authority to change the mix of inputs, as long as the unit stays within the budget constraint. The marketing manager can substitute between sales staff and advertising, as long as the total cost stays within the budget.

The performance measure for the manager of a type-1 cost centre is the amount and quality of the output. Producing a large number of units, without controlling for quality, is not in the organization's best interest. Thus, quality must be monitored. The danger also exists that an output performance measure will motivate the manager to over-produce. Over-production can lead to the imposition of costs on other parts of the organization. For example, the manufacturing manager of a dishwasher plant, who makes more dishwashers than can be sold, will impose costs on the part of the organization that is responsible for storing the finished inventory.

An alternative cost centre arrangement (type 2 in Table 7.1) is the minimization of costs, while producing a fixed quantity of output. For example, the manager of a metal stamping department is told to produce 10,000 stampings per day of a fixed specification and quality. The manager is evaluated on meeting the production schedule and on reducing the cost of the 10,000 stampings, without reducing quality. The performance measure is the total cost necessary to produce the required output. Once again, however, quality must be monitored. The focus on minimizing costs can lead to a lower quality of output.

Neither type of cost centre manager has the responsibilities to set the price or scale of operations. In both cases, the cost centre manager has the responsibilities to change how inputs are combined to produce the output. Performance measures include total costs, quantity produced and quality of output.

Shah Motors (continued)

Jeremy Shah looks at his list of managers and what they control. Grease Johnson, the service manager, controls the input mix (service staff and parts) to repair a car, but doesn't control the billing rate or the price of parts. At first glance, the service department appears to operate as a cost centre. But Jeremy isn't sure how to choose the performance measure for the service department. On the one hand, output is limited to

→

the cars needing repair, therefore using the number of repairs as a performance measure doesn't appear to be appropriate. On the other hand, Jeremy is worried that using cost as a performance measure will encourage Grease to take short cuts in making repairs. To circumvent this problem, Jeremy decides to use both costs and customer evaluations as performance measures for Grease.

■ Profit centres

Some managers have responsibilities beyond the control of costs through the efficient use of resources. Typically, managers of products are ultimately responsible for both the cost and the pricing of the product. These product managers are described as managers of **profit centres**. They have some control over both revenues and expenses, which are the factors that lead to profit. As well, managers of restaurants and retail shops are typically treated as profit centre managers.

Profit centre managers are given a fixed amount of assets (for example, the restaurant or retail shop and its furnishings) and usually have the responsibility for pricing and input mix decisions. They can decide what products to produce, the quality level (given some constraints), and how to market the products. For example, the local branch of a chain of copy centres is treated as a profit centre. The branch manager does not have the responsibility to increase the size of the building of the local branch, nor to open other local branches. The branch manager, however, can change the mix of services offered in the store, and is also responsible for the marketing of those services. For example, the manager might decide to provide online order submission and to market this service via the Internet. Local branch managers have the responsibility to price the various services offered because they have the knowledge of the local competition. If pricing decisions were not assigned to them, the company could not respond quickly to changes in competitor prices.

The primary performance measure for a profit centre is the profit generated by the centre. One of the goals of a profit organization is to generate profit. Therefore, using profit as a performance measure generally will motivate the profit centre manager to act in the best interest of the entire organization. But profit centres are not always independent of other profit centres within the same organization. For example, managers of hotels belonging to the same chain can affect each other's profits. Customers who have a bad experience in one of the chain's hotels are unlikely to try other hotels of the same chain. Therefore, the evaluation of profit centre managers commonly includes other performance measures, such as quality and customer satisfaction, in addition to profits.

Profit centre managers have greater responsibilities than do cost centre managers. In many cases, several cost centres are grouped together to form a profit centre. The managers of the cost centres within the profit centre are managed by, and report to, the profit centre manager. For example, a manufacturing unit and a sales unit could be separate cost centres within a single profit centre. The profit centre manager tells the manufacturing manager what to produce, and the sales manager how much cash is available to promote and generate sales. The manufacturing and sales managers can choose the mix of resources to accomplish their tasks, but pricing responsibilities are held by the profit centre manager. The manufacturing manager is evaluated on costs necessary to produce the required output. The sales manager is evaluated on sales generated from advertising and the efforts of the sales staff. The profit manager is evaluated on the profit of the combined efforts of manufacturing and sales.

Shah Motors (continued)

Jeremy Shah believes that the new-car sales division should be treated as a profit centre. Alice Ho, the manager, controls price and the product mix, but not the size of the inventory or showroom. But using profit as the sole performance measure for Alice appears to be a little risky for both parties. Alice is worried that her performance will be affected by the state of the economy. Profits and, therefore, her reward will be depressed during economic downturns. Jeremy believes that using profits as a sole measure of performance is risky because he is not sure how long Alice will be working for Shah Motors. Some competitors have been trying to hire her. Also, Jeremy is worried that she will act in an unethical manner to entice customers to purchase cars to increase short-term profit, especially if she plans to leave the dealership. Jeremy decides to use a relative performance measure (profits compared to the industry average) in conjunction with customer surveys to evaluate Alice.

■ Investment centres

Some managers have even more responsibilities than do profit centre managers. Managers of profit centres are limited to the use of a pre-specified amount of assets. Managers of **investment centres** have all the responsibilities of a profit centre manager, plus the right to expand or contract the size of operations. Division managers who control multiple product lines normally are considered investment centre managers. Investment centre managers can request more funds from the central administration to increase capacity, develop new products, and expand into new geographical areas. If these requests are too large or inconsistent with organizational policy, they generally must be ratified by someone in the central administration. Even investment centre managers have limits on their responsibilities and some control is imposed.

Investment centres usually contain several profit centres. For example, local branches of a restaurant chain are treated as profit centres, and regional districts are treated as investment centres. Managers of the regional district are responsible for all of the locations (profit centres) within the district. In addition, the manager of the regional district has the responsibility of identifying and constructing new locations. If existing restaurant locations are not successful, the manager of the regional district also has the responsibility to close them.

The choice of responsibility centres through the granting of responsibilities reflects the hierarchy of the organization. The organization is composed of investment centres. Investment centres are composed of profit centres. Lastly, profit centres are composed of cost centres. This hierarchy of responsibility centres is illustrated in Figure 7.2.

Performance measures for investment centre managers are more difficult to identify, due to the nature of their responsibilities. Although investment managers have the opportunity to expand or contract their investment centre, they generally are not responsible for financing the expansions. Cash infusions necessary for expansion usually come from the central administration, which is responsible for issuing debt and equity. Investment centre managers generally only have control of assets and short-term liabilities, such as wages and accounts payable. The accounting reports of these investment centres have no interest expenses or dividend payments.

The absence of interest expenses in an investment centre means that profit is not a very good performance measure for a centre's manager. Investment centre managers generally can increase the profit from the assets by increasing the amount of assets. However, increasing the size of the investment centre, without recognizing the

Figure 7.2 Hierarchy of responsibility centres

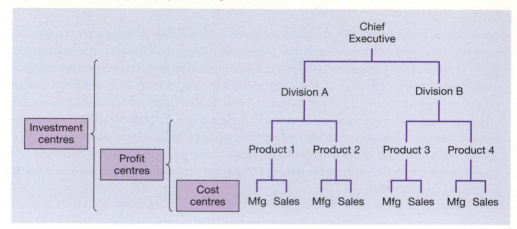

opportunity cost of having more cash invested in assets (the opportunity cost of capital), can be harmful for the entire organization.

The **opportunity cost of capital** is represented by a percentage return that reflects the forgone opportunity of using the cash. The forgone opportunity could be placing the money in a bank account and earning interest, or the cost of borrowing more money to fund other investment opportunities. The opportunity cost of capital in the former case is the interest rate earned in a bank account. The opportunity cost in the latter case is the interest rate paid to borrow money. Chapter 13 provides a more detailed description of the opportunity cost of capital. In this chapter, the opportunity cost of capital is provided but in finance, the opportunity cost of capital must be estimated.

Numerical **example 7.1**

The television division of an electronics firm requests €100 million from the central administration to develop, manufacture and sell a new flat-screen model. Central administration borrows the €100 million at a 10 per cent interest rate to provide the cash to the television division. The television division invests the €100 million to generate annual profits of €6 million. What is the net effect of these transactions on the profit of the electronics firm?

Solution

The interest expense on the €100 million is €10 million annually. Therefore, the investment in the new flat-screen television caused a €4 million loss (€6 million profit – €10 million interest expense) to the electronics firm.

Shah Motors (continued)

Slick Thompson is the manager of the used-car division at Shah Motors. Jeremy Shah has given Slick more responsibilities than the rest of the managers. Slick not only can choose the used cars for his inventory (except he must accept trade-ins for new cars from the new-car division), but he can also decide on the size of his inventory up to £1 million. When Slick expands his inventory, however, he must obtain the necessary cash from Jeremy. Unfortunately, the profit of the used-car division does not explicitly recognize the opportunity cost of holding the inventory, so Jeremy is worried that Slick will overuse the privilege of buying inventory. If Jeremy uses the profit of the used-car division, which does not recognize the opportunity cost of capital, as a performance measure for Slick, then Slick will choose to have the maximum inventory allowed. More inventory will increase the number of opportunities to make a sale, but Slick would not be penalized for holding excess inventory. Jeremy must find a different performance measure for the used-car division, which he recognizes as an investment centre.

■ Identifying responsibility centres

Although cost, profit and investment centres are identified by the responsibilities of the managers of those centres, not all managers fit exactly into one of these categories. For example, manufacturing managers are commonly treated as managers of cost centres. Yet the manufacturing managers typically influence revenues, even though they do not have responsibilities over pricing. Revenues are influenced by customer satisfaction due to timely delivery and quality. The manufacturing manager does influence timely delivery and quality, so the manufacturing manager is partially responsible for revenues.

Profit centre managers seldom control all aspects of revenues and costs. Profit centre managers, however, are usually able to make marginal adjustments to the asset size of the responsibility centre. Investment centre managers, alternatively, seldom have unlimited authority to increase asset size.

Therefore, identifying the appropriate type of responsibility centre is often difficult, as the Microsoft case below indicates. Nonetheless, the partitioning of the organization into different types of responsibility centres is important for guiding the choice of performance measures. In particular, it is important to match the performance measures chosen to the responsibilities assigned to the responsibility centre.

Concept review

1 What are the two types of cost centres?
2 Why should quality performance measures be used in conjunction with cost as a performance measure for cost centres?
3 What type of responsibilities do profit centre managers typically have?
4 Why are performance measures of investment centres difficult to determine?
5 Why is it difficult to classify some responsibility centres?

Organizational analysis

Microsoft's 'Software as a service' platform strategy

Over the last several years, in spite of constant growth and increasing profits, concerns had been expressed that Microsoft was getting sluggish. Bureaucratic delays due to layers of management were causing Microsoft to lose business in the rapidly changing, high-technology market. Important managers were leaving the company in frustration. Microsoft also needed to adapt its successful platform strategy to take advantage of the Internet and 'software as a service' delivered online. A streamlined organizational structure was implemented to enable Microsoft to

→

manage growth successfully as it implemented its strategy to remain competitive in the Internet era.

Microsoft was able to decentralize decision making because the new divisions were based on customers, rather than functional areas which required more central co-ordination. The new divisions and their customer bases were:

- *Platform Products and Services Division:* Client Group, Server and Tools Group, Online Services Group;
- *Business Division:* Information Worker Group, Microsoft Business Solutions Group, Unified Communications Group;
- *Entertainment and Devices Division:* Home and Entertainment Group, Mobile and Embedded Devices Group.

Microsoft also announced that beginning with fiscal year 2007, it would align its financial reporting

structure to reflect these organizational changes and report its financial results based on five operating segments: Client, Server and Tools, Online Services Group, Microsoft Business Division, and Microsoft Entertainment and Devices Division.

What type of responsibility centres are these centres likely to be?

What are some advantages and disadvantages of organizing Microsoft around types of customers, rather than functions or products?

Sources: www.microsoft.com/msft; Ina Fried, 'Microsoft spring cleans its Windows unit', Silicon.com, 28 February 2007, http://software.silicon.com/os/0,39024651,39166072,00.htm (accessed 5 May 2007); David Mitchell Smith, 'Microsoft Restructures for Emergence of Internet Platforms', Gartner, Inc., 23 September 2005, ID Number G00131235.

ACCOUNTING-BASED PERFORMANCE MEASURES

Managers of responsibility centres are evaluated based on performance measures. Those performance measures should be based on the controllability principle. Performance measures are either accounting-based or non-financial. Return on investment (ROI) and residual income/economic value added are accounting-based performance measures that are commonly used to evaluate managers of investment centres. These performance measures have their own strengths and weaknesses, and generally are more effective when used in conjunction with other performance measures.

■ Return on investment (ROI)

The profit (excluding the opportunity cost of capital) generated by an investment centre depends on the size of the investment centre; therefore, performance measures should reflect the size of the investment centre. The more assets in the investment centre, the greater the opportunity cost of capital wrapped up in the assets of the investment centre. **Return on investment (ROI)** adjusts for size by dividing the profit, excluding interest expense generated by the investment centre, by the total assets of the investment centre.

ROI = Earnings before interest/Total assets of the investment

ROI is the most popular investment centre performance measure. It has intuitive appeal since the comparison of ROI to the opportunity cost of capital (the interest rate of borrowing or the dividend rate of share capital) provides a benchmark for a division's performance. The ROI measure can be traced to the E.I. Du Pont de Nemours Powder Company, where it was developed to deal with the allocation of capital resources across its business operations.

Organizational **analysis**

The Du Pont Company ROI method

In the early 1900s, the E.I. Du Pont de Nemours Powder Company was the leading firm in the manufacturing of gun powder and high explosives, with geographically dispersed operations across the US. It would later grow into one of the world's largest chemical companies. To control and evaluate these operations, Du Pont managers, and Pierre Du Pont in particular, developed the concept of return on investment.

The financial staff traced the cost and revenues for each product produced. This gave management accurate information of profits which provided a more precise way to evaluate financial performance. However, they found product-line profits to be an incomplete measure of performance because it did not indicate the rate of return on capital invested. One manager said, 'The true test of whether the profit is too great or too small is the rate of return on the money invested in the business and not the per cent of profit on the cost.'

Developing a rate of return on each segment of business required accurate data on investment in fixed capital. Du Pont undertook a careful valuation of each of its plants, properties, and inventories by product line. These data along with profits allowed management to track ROI by product line. But in addition, they decomposed ROI (profits ÷ investment) into its component parts to account specifically for the underlying causes for changes in ROI. The figure below illustrates this decomposition.

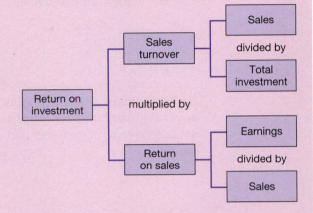

ROI is the product of sales turnover (sales ÷ total investment) and return on sales (earnings ÷ sales). Given these data, managers could determine the causes of a product's change in ROI. Du Pont managers used these data to evaluate new capital appropriations by establishing the policy that there 'be no expenditures for additions to the earnings equipment if the same amount of money could be applied to some better purpose in another branch of the company's business.'

Source: Alfred D. Chandler (1977) *The Visible Hand* (Cambridge, MA: Harvard University Press), pp. 445–449.

If the ROI is greater than the opportunity cost of capital, then the assets of the investment are increasing organizational value. An organization that can borrow £1,000 in cash for 10 per cent per year, then turn around and invest the money in assets that generate a 14 per cent annual return on the investment will increase the organization's value. At the end of the year, the organization must repay the loan (£1,000) and the interest (£1,000 × 0.10), or a total of £1,100. But the organization has the investment (£1,000) and a return of (£1,000 × 0.14), or £1,140. The net gain is £1,140 − 1,100, or £40.

Numerical **example 7.2**

An organization's investment centre has the following investment opportunities:

Project	Required investment £	Annual earnings before interest £
A	500,000	50,000
B	200,000	10,000
C	100,000	20,000

The opportunity cost of capital of the organization is 8 per cent. What is the ROI of these investment opportunities and which investment would add value to the organization?

Solution

The ROI is the earnings divided by the investment.

Project	ROI
A	£50,000/£500,000 = 0.10 or 10%
B	£10,000/£200,000 = 0.05 or 5%
C	£20,000/£100,000 = 0.20 or 20%

Projects A and C would add value to the organization. The return on those investments is greater than the opportunity cost of capital of 8 per cent. Project B would not add value because its return on investment is less than the opportunity cost of capital.

Limitations of ROI

Although ROI has the advantage of controlling for the size of the investment centre, it has limitations regarding its use as a performance measure. These problems include measurement problems, not recognizing the risk of the projects and incentives to under- or over-invest.

ROI is not necessarily a measure of the division's percentage change in market value for at least two reasons. First, accounting profit (the numerator of the ROI) is not a measure of change in market value of the organization. Second, 'investment' (the denominator of the ROI) is not the market value of the division's investment. Traditionally, the profit and investment are measured using historical costs, which usually differ from the market value. Accounting depreciation, which is deducted from accounting profits, does not necessarily reflect the change in market value of fixed assets. Investment centre managers, who are evaluated based on ROI, can make inappropriate decisions due to the way in which the ROI is measured. For example, new assets cause higher depreciation expenses and lower profits (the numerator of ROI) and higher net assets (the denominator of ROI). The combined effect will reduce the short-term ROI, even though long-term benefits to purchasing the new assets may exist.

The ROI of an investment centre does not explicitly recognize the centre's risk. From finance theory, we know that risky investments should have a higher expected return to compensate for the higher risk. Therefore, a manager who generates a large ROI could be investing in riskier assets, which may not be consistent with organizational goals.

The use of ROI as a performance measure of an investment centre can also lead to an under- or over-investment in assets. Managers might attempt to increase the average ROI by investing only in assets that have ROIs above the current ROI and forgoing projects with ROIs below the current average ROI. If a project with an ROI above the current average ROI but less than the opportunity cost of capital is chosen, the organization decreases in value. Likewise, rejecting a project with an ROI above its cost of capital, but below the average ROI of the investment centre, reduces organizational value. To increase organizational value, a manager should invest in all assets that have returns greater than the opportunity cost of capital rather than projects that raise the investment centre's average ROI. For example, suppose an investment centre has an average ROI of 20 per cent and a cost of capital of 15 per cent. A proposed project has an ROI of 18 per cent. Accepting this project lowers the investment centre's average ROI, but it is still profitable because its return of 18 per cent exceeds its cost of capital of 15 per cent.

Numerical example 7.3

An investment centre manager is considering four possible investments. The required investment, annual profits (which are approximately equal to cash flows) and ROIs of each investment are as follows:

Project	Required investment (€)	Annual profits (€)	ROI (%)
A	400,000	80,000	20
B	200,000	10,000	5
C	300,000	36,000	12
D	100,000	15,000	15

The investment centre is currently generating an ROI of 18 per cent, based on €1,000,000 in assets and a profit of €180,000. The company can borrow cash at a 10 per cent annual rate. Which projects will increase the ROI of the investment centre? Which projects will increase organizational value?

Solution

Only project A will increase the ROI of the investment centre:

$$(€180,000 + €80,000)/(€1,000,000 + €400,000) = 18.57\%$$

Projects C and D also will increase the value of the entire organization. The additional profit generated by these projects is greater than the interest expense from borrowing to invest in C (€300,000 × 10% = €30,000) and D (€100,000 × 10% = €10,000).

ROI can lead to over-investment problems as well. Suppose an investment centre has an ROI of 12 per cent but its cost of capital is 14 per cent. Clearly, this investment centre is not earning its cost of capital. The investment centre manager might be tempted to invest in a new project with an ROI of 13 per cent. This new investment raises the average investment centre ROI above 12 per cent, but this investment should *not* be accepted. Its ROI of 13 per cent is below the investment centre's opportunity cost of capital of 14 per cent.

■ Residual income/economic value added

To overcome the incentive problems of ROI, such as under- or over-investment and lack of risk adjustment, some firms use **residual income** to evaluate performance. Residual income is the difference between the investment centre's profits and the opportunity cost of using the assets of the investment centre. The opportunity cost of using the assets is the opportunity cost of capital times the market value of the assets. The following equations define the relation between residual income and ROI.

Residual income = Profits − (Opportunity cost of capital × Total assets)
 = (Profits/Total assets × Total assets) − (Opportunity cost of capital × Total assets)
 = (ROI × Total assets) − (Opportunity cost of capital × Total assets)
 = (ROI − Opportunity cost of capital × Total assets)

Therefore, the residual income is positive if the ROI is greater than the opportunity cost of capital. A positive residual income number means that the investment centre manager has added value to the organization by achieving a higher return on the assets than the cost of using the assets. If residual income is used as a performance measure, the investment manager invests in all assets that have a positive residual income. There is no under- or over-investment incentive.

In measuring residual income, the profit figure does not include any interest expense. Interest expense is excluded to avoid double counting the cost of debt. The opportunity cost of capital includes a charge for the cost of both debt and equity.

Measuring residual income requires a measure of the opportunity cost of capital. The opportunity cost of capital should reflect the risk of the assets in the investment centre. Financial institutions are more reluctant to lend money to organizations that invest in high-risk projects. To compensate for the additional risk, they charge a higher interest rate. This problem is discussed in Chapter 13 and finance textbooks. By choosing the opportunity cost of capital to reflect the risk of the assets, no incentives exist to choose high-risk projects just to increase the ROI figure.

Numerical **example** 7.4

A tractor division has profits (not including interest expense) of £20 million and investment (total assets) of £100 million. The division has an opportunity cost of capital of 15 per cent. What is the residual income of the division?

Solution

The residual income is:

$$£20 \text{ million} - (15\% \times £100 \text{ million}) = £5 \text{ million}$$

As with ROI, residual income is not a perfect performance measure. The profits and total assets are commonly measured using the historical costs from the financial reporting system. If the accounting profits vary due to changes in the market value of the assets, and the book value of assets is not representative of their market value, then residual income will not function well as a performance measure. Managers will be trying to maximize accounting residual income, but the owners of the organization would prefer that managers increase the market value of the organization.

Another perceived problem in using residual income is the comparison and evaluation of performance across investment centres of different sizes. Residual income is an absolute monetary figure and is likely to be larger for larger investment centres. For example, consider the example in Table 7.2 of two investment centres, Divisions A and B:

Table 7.2 Comparison of residual income to ROI (€000)

	Division A	Division B
Net assets	€100	€1,000
Net profit	€30	€250
Cost of capital (20%)	€20	€200
Residual income	€10	€50
ROI	30%	25%

Division A has a larger ROI, but Division B has a larger residual income because Division B is bigger. Which division's manager is performing better? If both managers have control over the size of their divisions (that is, they are investment centres), then the manager of Division B is performing better. Although the manager of Division A is operating efficiently with a smaller amount of net assets, he or she is not able to find as many profitable opportunities as can the manager of Division B. Division B's manager adds more value to the organization and should be rewarded accordingly. Residual income is appropriate for evaluating managers of investment centres of different sizes, since the manager has control of the size of the investment centre. If the manager does not have control over size and the division is more like a profit centre, then ROI is more appropriate as a relative performance measure of managers of differently sized divisions.

A variant of residual income is the *economic value added (EVA)*.[1] EVA is calculated in the same manner as is residual income, but differences in the general formula are noted in practice. First, EVA often makes a series of adjustments to accounting profit. For example, research and development costs often are included as an asset and amortized over the estimated useful lives of these expenditures. Second, the opportunity cost of capital is calculated as the weighted-average cost of debt and equity. Third, EVA has been linked more frequently to managerial compensation contracts. This linkage increases the manager's risk, but creates incentives to maximize organizational value.

◼ Multiple performance measures

As in the case of cost and profit centres, the manager of an investment centre should not be evaluated by a single performance measure. An organization generally has multiple goals. A single performance measure will not motivate the manager to consider all of these goals. For example, investment centre managers are usually constrained in terms of the quality of products that they can sell and the market niches that they can enter. The reason for these constraints is to prevent these investment centre managers from debasing the firm's brand-name capital (the firm's reputation). For example, Marks & Spencer Group plc (M&S) is recognized for offering quality products at competitive prices, with a focus on service, value and trust in the M&S brand. M&S executives receive bonuses for meeting profit targets and increasing long-term shareholder value. Store management receive bonuses based on improved sales, profits and customer service. One way M&S managers could meet their profit targets would be to reduce costs by offering products of lower quality than expected by customers. Over time, customers would come to learn of the lower-than-expected quality. M&S managers might exceed their short-term

Ferruccio/Alamy

Quality, competitive prices, service and trust are part of M&S brand-name capital; key criteria in rewarding managers and encouraging a focus on long-term shareholder value.

---

[1]EVA is a registered trademark of Stern Stewart & Company. EVA is described more fully in G. Bennett Stewart (1991), *The Quest for Value: the EVA management guide* (New York: Harper Business).

profit targets, but their actions would lower expectations of quality and value for all M&S products. To control this problem, M&S continually monitors costs, quality and sales levels, and rewards management based on these criteria.[2]

Shah Motors (continued)

Jeremy Shah is considering the use of ROI as a performance measure for Slick Thompson. He is not concerned with problems in measuring profit and net assets. Most of the assets of the used-car division are in the form of used cars. These used cars are normally sold within four months of acquisition, so book value should not differ much from market value, and the accounting profit of the used-car division should be a close approximation of change in economic value. Jeremy is also not concerned about the risk of the used-car division. The sale of used cars tends to be less sensitive to changes in the economy. He is concerned, however, about the under-investment problem. He thinks that Slick Thompson may be able to increase ROI by only buying and selling foreign used cars, which generally have a higher profit margin than do domestic cars. But good foreign used cars are hard to find, and Slick would operate with a substantially reduced inventory. Jeremy feels that the domestic used-car market is still profitable and doesn't want Slick to focus on foreign cars. Therefore, Jeremy concludes that residual income is a better performance measure because it would encourage Slick to invest in all used cars that have ROIs greater than the opportunity cost of capital. Jeremy uses the interest rate on his debt to approximate the opportunity cost of capital.

Concept review

1 What are the benefits and problems with using ROI as a performance measure?
2 What are the benefits and problems of using residual income as a performance measure?

TRANSFER PRICING

Most organizations contain multiple responsibility centres. Responsibility centres within the same organization can interact in many ways and can create adverse or favourable impacts on other responsibility centres. A manufacturing department's operating efficiency can be affected by the quantity and timing of the orders that it receives from the marketing department. A purchasing department can affect the manufacturing department's operations by the timing and quality of the raw materials purchased. The sharing of a newly-discovered, cost-saving idea or R&D by one responsibility centre with other centres is an example of a favourable interaction. Managing these interactions (eliminating the negative ones and encouraging the positive ones) is critical to the successful partitioning of responsibilities to the different managers of the organization. The firm's management accounting system often plays a powerful role in either encouraging or discouraging these interactions. The management accounting system recognizes the interactions of different responsibility centres through **transfer pricing**.

---

[2] Information about Marks & Spencer Group plc adapted from www.marksandspencer.com and Hoovers, Inc. (www.hoovers.com).

Figure 7.3 The external and internal transfer of products

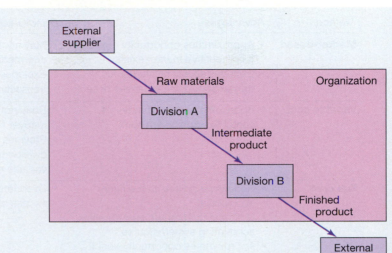

◼ Reasons for transfer pricing

When goods or services are transferred from one responsibility centre to another, an internal price or transfer price is attached to the units transferred. Figure 7.3 presents a typical scenario with an internal transfer of a product or service. Division A of an organization purchases raw materials from an external supplier. Division A converts these raw materials into an intermediate product used by Division B. Division B converts the intermediate product into a finished product for sale to an external customer. The purchase price of the raw materials and the sales price of the finished product are determined by external market forces. External market forces do not directly affect the 'price' of the intermediate product, which is transferred between divisions within the organization. Therefore, some flexibility exists in setting that internal 'price' for the product transferred.

For example, BMW manufactures engines in one of its UK plants that are installed in its vehicles in assembly plants located in Germany. The transfer price in this case is the internal charge that the BMW assembly plants pay to the BMW engine plant. The transfer payment may not involve any cash flows between the two divisions, but an accounting entry is made to reflect a cost to the assembly division and a corresponding revenue to the engine division.

Transfer prices are much more prevalent in organizations than most managers realize. Consider the charge that the advertising department receives from the maintenance department for janitorial service, or the monthly charge for telephones, security services, information technology or legal and personnel services. Most firms distribute the costs of services provided by one part of the organization to the departments that use the services. These cost distributions are internal transfer prices.

The three main reasons for transfer pricing within firms are control (incentives and performance measures), decentralized planning decisions and international/tax reasons. All of these factors should be considered in setting transfer prices. Table 7.3 outlines four common transfer-pricing methods. These methods are discussed in the following sections in terms of control and planning. The choice of one method over

Table 7.3 Summary of transfer-pricing methods

Method	Advantages	Disadvantages
Market-based	• Approximates opportunity cost if competitive market exists • Excludes effects of internal transaction costs on transfer price	• May not have external market for intermediate good • Excludes effects of internal transaction costs on transfer price
Variable cost	• Approximates opportunity cost if fixed costs are sunk	• Does not allow selling division to recover fixed costs • Provides incentive for selling division to convert fixed costs to variable costs
Full cost	• Reduces disputes as the figure is objective • Is simple to compute as it parallels accounting system figures • Approximates opportunity cost if division operating at capacity	• Overstates opportunity cost, if excess capacity exists
Negotiated	• Maintains managerial autonomy • Preserves upper-management time	• Is time consuming and relies on negotiation skills of divisional managers • May not be the optimal transfer price for the firm as a whole • Can lead to conflicts among responsibility centres

another usually reflects a compromise in terms of its effectiveness for control versus planning purposes.

■ Transfer pricing for control

Transfer prices are used for control purposes in a decentralized organization. Decentralization involves transferring certain responsibilities to subordinates, which is accomplished by partitioning the organization into responsibility centres, and by designing performance measurement and compensation systems for the responsibility centres. Firms create profit and investment centres primarily to link specialized knowledge and responsibilities, and to increase the motivation for local managers. Moreover, profit centres also improve response time, conserve central management's time and facilitate training of local managers.

Measuring the performance of profit or investment centres requires the use of transfer prices, when one profit or investment centre transfers goods or services to another unit. Transfer-pricing systems should reflect the controllability principle by assigning costs to the responsibility centre managers who are responsible for the costs. Transfer prices should lead to performance measures that discriminate between good and bad managers. In other words, managers of responsibility centres should not be rewarded or penalized by transfer prices that are affected by the performance of managers of other responsibility centres. For example, the manager of an engineering department should not be able to charge the manager of the production department for cost over-runs due to mistakes made by the engineering department.

Numerical **example** 7.5

The Parts division of an organization manufactures parts that it sells to the Assembly division of the same organization. The cost to the Parts division of providing a particular set of parts is £10 per unit. The Assembly division, at a cost of £4 per unit, assembles the parts purchased from the Parts division and sells the assembled product to another organization for £23 per unit.

a What is the profit per unit of the two divisions, if the transfer price is £12 per unit?
b What is the profit per unit of the two divisions, if the Parts division's cost of £10 per unit is used as the transfer price?
c If the Parts division operates inefficiently and the cost of parts rises to £11 per unit, and that cost is used as the transfer price, what is the profit of the two divisions?
d What is wrong with the solution in part c?

Solution

a If the transfer price is £12 per unit, the profit per unit of the two divisions is:

Parts division	£	Assembly division	£
Revenue per unit	12	Revenue per unit	23
Cost per unit	10	Parts cost per unit	12
Profit per unit	2	Assembly costs	4
		Profit per unit	7

b If the transfer price is £10 per unit, the profit of the two divisions is:

Parts division	£	Assembly division	£
Revenue per unit	10	Revenue per unit	23
Cost per unit	10	Parts cost per unit	10
Profit per unit	0	Assembly costs	4
		Profit per unit	9

Notice that the larger transfer price shifts profit from the Assembly division to the Parts division. With each transfer price, the total profit of both divisions is £9 per unit.

c If the transfer price is £11 cost per unit due to inefficiencies in the Parts division, the profit of the two divisions is:

Parts division	£	Assembly division	£
Revenue per unit	11	Revenue per unit	23
Cost per unit	11	Parts cost per unit	11
Profit per unit	0	Assembly costs	4
		Profit per unit	8

d The additional cost of £1 per unit, due to inefficiencies in the Parts division, does not affect the profit of the Parts division, but adversely affects the profit of the Assembly division. The Parts division is responsible for the extra £1 per unit cost; therefore the performance measure of the Parts division, not the Assembly division, should reflect that responsibility.

■ Transfer pricing for decentralized planning purposes

Managers also use transfer prices for decentralized planning purposes. In a decentralized organization, managers of responsibility centres are given responsibilities to make certain input and output decisions. For some inputs and outputs, however, the managers may not have the right to go outside the organization. For example, the manager of BMW's assembly division is required to purchase engines from BMW's engine division. The manager of the assembly division does not have the right to go to Toyota or Ford to purchase engines. Under these circumstances, a transfer price does not affect the choice of the supplier or buyer, but it will influence the level of output of both divisions. For example, if the transfer price is too high, the internal buyer will tend to purchase less of the internally-supplied service or product than would be optimal for the entire organization. The problem is choosing a transfer price that leads to decentralized decisions consistent with the entire organization's goals.

imagebroker/Alamy

The BMW brand indicates that the vehicle is not a Ford or Toyota. Divisions make transfers within BMW but cannot purchase from market competitors.

Numerical **example 7.6**

A company that makes large earth-moving machines has a Parts division and an Assembly division. The Parts division supplies the Assembly division with a set of parts which are assembled and sold. The sales price per machine declines because the demand for the machine is sensitive to the final selling price. The following are the costs and company revenues for different levels of output:

Output per week	Parts division costs (€)	Assembly division costs (€)	Selling price per unit (€)	Total revenues (€)	Company profits (€)
1	100,000	50,000	200,000	200,000	50,000
2	180,000	100,000	170,000	340,000	60,000
3	240,000	150,000	160,000	480,000	90,000

What problems will the company encounter if it uses a transfer price of €100,000 per set of parts and allows the manager of the Assembly division to make the choice of how many sets of parts to assemble? The Assembly division manager is evaluated based on divisional profits.

Solution

With a transfer price of €100,000, the following are the profits of the Assembly division:

Output per week	Transfer cost of parts (€)	Assembly division costs (€)	Total revenues (€)	Assembly division profit (€)
1	100,000	50,000	200,000	50,000
2	200,000	100,000	340,000	40,000
3	300,000	150,000	480,000	30,000

The Assembly division's profits are highest when it assembles one set of parts per week. The division's manager, therefore, will choose to assemble one set of parts, even though the company's profit would be maximized if it made and assembled three sets of parts.

Managers of some responsibility centres are given the opportunity to buy or sell outside the organization, even though there is an internal supplier of the responsibility centre's inputs or an internal buyer of the responsibility centre's outputs. Allowing managers to go outside the organization forces the responsibility centres within the organization to compete with outside suppliers and buyers. Competitive markets provide the discipline to encourage the efficient operation of responsibility centres; inefficient responsibility centres will not survive under these circumstances. Once again, the transfer-pricing system should be designed to motivate managers to make input and output decisions that are consistent with the organization's goals, such as maximizing profits.

To motivate managers to make decentralized input and output decisions (choices of quantity, supplier and customer) consistent with maximizing the profit of the entire organization, the transfer price should be set equal to the opportunity cost of providing the product or service being transferred. If insufficient capacity exists to sell both inside and outside the firm, this opportunity cost is composed of the opportunity cost of using raw materials, labour and the facilities, along with the forgone profit of not being able to sell the product or service to an outside party. Cash outlays, alternative uses of the material, labour and facilities, and forgone profit should be considered in establishing the transfer price. The opportunity cost of providing the product or service may be difficult to estimate so the following sections describe some useful heuristics for doing so.

Existence of a competitive market for the intermediate product or service

Suppose that a competitive market exists for the product or service being transferred between the two responsibility centres. The responsibility centre providing the product or service could sell it to someone outside the organization, and the responsibility centre using the product or service could purchase it from an outside supplier. The sale to an outside buyer or the purchase from an outside supplier would occur at a market price determined by competitive forces.

The general rule of transfer pricing is to use the external market price of the intermediate product or service, if a competitive market exists. The market price approximates the opportunity cost of providing the product or service. The market price is equal to the cost of making the product or service plus the forgone profit of not selling the product or service to an outside party.

In some cases, the external market price does not exactly equal the opportunity cost of providing the intermediate product or service. Sometimes additional opportunity costs of dealing with external customers exist. For example, external customers may require more negotiating and accounting effort to complete the deal. Also, additional transaction and customer service costs may be incurred when dealing with an external customer. Therefore, the opportunity cost of selling to external customers is the market price less these additional costs, which should be reflected in the transfer price. A transfer price below the market price will encourage the internal customer to purchase the intermediate product, and allow the company to avoid the costs of dealing with the external customer.

Numerical **example 7.7**

The restaurant division of a hotel provides a catering service for the convention centre of the hotel and for external organizations. The restaurant charges £20 per person to cater events for external clients. But to cater these non-convention events, the restaurant incurs additional costs of £1 per person. These additional costs include the cost of transporting and re-heating the food. What transfer price should be used between the restaurant division and the convention centre to encourage decentralized decision making that will maximize total profit for the hotel?

Solution

The transfer price should be the market price of £20 less the additional transaction and contracting costs of £1, or £19 per person. The restaurant is indifferent at that transfer price between catering internally or externally. The £19 transfer price will encourage the convention centre to buy from the restaurant division. Otherwise the convention centre would have to pay a price of about £20, reflecting additional costs if the convention centre purchases from an outside supplier.

Producing internally (even though 'cheaper' external markets exist) may also make sense, if timeliness of supply and quality control is important. When these factors are included in the analysis, the external market may no longer be less expensive. The market price should be adjusted for these other factors to determine the transfer price.

Sometimes an internal supplier of a service or product cannot compete with external suppliers, even after adjusting for transportation costs, quality and timely delivery. Under these circumstances, the internal supplier will be forced to improve efficiency or shift to providing other services or products.

Numerical **example 7.8**

The Kali Company has two divisions. The Paper division makes paper that costs £1,000 per tonne. The Paper division makes 10,000 tonnes of paper each year. The Paper division can either sell all of the paper in the market for £1,500 per tonne, or transfer all of the paper to the Printing division of Kali Company. The Printing division converts the paper into gift wrap at an additional cost of £4,000 per tonne. The gift wrap can be sold for £5,200 per tonne.

a What is the profit of the company, if all the paper is transferred to the Printing division?

b What is the profit of the company, if all the paper is sold in the market and the Printing division is closed?

c How does the use of the market price as the transfer price cause managers of the division to achieve the highest profit for the company?

Solution

a The following is the profit of the company if all the paper is transferred to the Printing division:

	£
Revenues (10,000 tonnes × £5,200/tonne)	52,000,000
Paper costs (10,000 tonnes × £1,000/tonne)	(10,000,000)
Printing costs (10,000 tonnes × £4,000/tonne)	(40,000,000)
Profit	2,000,000

b The following is the profit of the company if all the paper is sold in the market and the Printing division is closed:

	£
Revenues (10,000 tonnes × £1,500/tonne)	15,000,000
Paper costs (10,000 tonnes × £1,000/tonne)	(10,000,000)
Profit	5,000,000

c If the market price of £1,500 is used as the transfer price, the Printing division's costs (£1,500 tonne + £4,000/tonne) will be greater than its revenues (£5,200/tonne). Rather than operating at a loss, the manager can close the Printing division or look for a more profitable opportunity. This example assumes that the costs of the two divisions are opportunity costs and reflect alternative uses of the inputs to the process.

No competitive market exists for the intermediate product or service

If no external market exists for the intermediate product or service, there is no alternative of selling the product or service to another buyer. The intermediate service or product can be sold only internally. There is no forgone profit opportunity, and the opportunity cost is limited to the cost of using the raw materials, labour and facilities to supply the product or service. The cost of each input of the product or service should be considered in terms of cash outlays and alternative uses of the assets. For example, if the existing facilities already have been purchased and no alternative use of these facilities exists, the opportunity cost of using them is limited to the incremental costs of operating the facilities. Opportunity costs are approximated by the variable cost, if the fixed costs are sunk. If fixed costs are sunk and included in the transfer price, the purchasing responsibility centre will tend to purchase less of the intermediate product or service than is best for the entire organization.

Numerical **example** 7.9

The HD DVD division of a large computer company manufactures and sells HD DVD players to the Laptop division of the same firm. The variable cost to the HD DVD division to provide the product is €100 per unit and the fixed, sunk cost is €50 per unit. The HD DVD division has excess capacity and no alternative use of this capacity. The Laptop division, at an additional variable cost of €60 per unit,

→

modifies the product purchased from the HD DVD division. The Laptop division then sells the modified product to another computer firm for €180 per unit. What is the contribution margin per unit for the organization, if the transfer price is the variable cost? What happens if the full cost is used as the transfer price?

Solution

If the variable cost of the HD DVD division (€100) is used as the transfer price, HD DVD's contribution margin is €100 − €100, or €0. The Laptop division's contribution margin is €180 − €100 − €60, or €20 per unit. The contribution margin of the entire firm is €20 per unit. The transfer price based on the full cost of the HD DVD division is the sum of the fixed cost (€50) and variable cost (€100), or €150. If the full cost of €150 is used as the transfer price, HD DVD's contribution margin is €150 − €100, or €50. The Laptop division's contribution margin is €180 − €150 − €60, or −€30. Under these circumstances, the manager of the Laptop division receives €50 less in contribution margin compared to the contribution margin received when the variable cost is used as the transfer price. Therefore, the Laptop manager would not want to purchase HD DVD players from the HD DVD division. The Laptop manager receives €0 in contribution margin by not selling modified HD DVD players, rather than purchasing them from the HD DVD division. This amount (€0) is greater than the loss in contribution margin (−€30) that the manager receives when the transfer price is full cost. The firm overall would lose the chance of earning a €20 contribution margin per unit.

Numerical example 7.9 makes an important point. Think of the firm's total profit as a pie. The choice among transfer-pricing methods not only changes how the pie is divided among the profit or investment centres, but also the size of the pie to be divided. Many managers think that changing transfer-pricing methods merely shifts profit among responsibility centres (as was illustrated in Numerical example 7.5); except for relative performance evaluation, nothing else is affected. Unfortunately, this is not true. The level of the firm's output and overall firm-wide profitability may change with different transfer prices.

One problem with using the variable cost as a transfer price is that the selling responsibility centre does not recover its fixed costs. If *all* the selling division's output is transferred internally, the only revenue that the seller receives is its variable cost, and its fixed costs are not recovered. Thus, sellers show losses and appear to be losing money. One solution is to treat the selling division as a cost centre or as part of the purchasing division.

Any transfer-pricing scheme that involves calculating variable costs creates incentives for selling division managers to classify costs as variable. Classifying costs into variable and fixed is somewhat arbitrary, thus managers in the selling and buying divisions and senior managers waste their time debating the nature of costs. Moreover, the manager of the selling division manager has incentives to convert fixed costs into a greater amount of variable costs, even though this reduces the value of the firm. For example, the selling division may choose to replace a £1 fixed machine cost with a £2 variable labour cost. The buying division pays the extra cost, not the selling division, and the selling division is relieved of the burden of the fixed cost.

To avoid wasteful disputes that distract operating managers from operating and strategic decisions, managers often adopt simple, objective transfer-pricing rules such as full accounting cost. Since full cost is the sum of fixed and variable cost, the full cost

Table 7.4 Transfer prices for decentralized planning decisions

Circumstance	Transfer price
Market price exists	Market price
No market price exists; supplying division has no alternative use of capacity	Variable cost
No market price exists; supplying division has alternative use of capacity	Full cost*

*The full cost is intended to be a rough approximation of the forgone opportunity of using the facilities of the supplying division to do something else.

cannot be changed by simply reclassifying a 'fixed' cost as 'variable' cost. Using a full cost transfer price results in better *control* by reducing the producer division's incentives to reclassify fixed costs as variable costs. Full cost transfer pricing comes at a price, however: *decision making* is impaired because the buying unit purchases too few units. Thus, the trade-off between *making planning decisions* and *control* is observed again.

To improve decentralized planning decisions, the transfer price should equal the opportunity cost of providing the intermediate product or service. If the selling responsibility centre is operating at capacity and has alternative uses of that capacity, then the opportunity cost of providing a product or service should include the forgone profit of using the facility for some other purpose. Although the fixed cost of using the facility does not change with the number of units produced, the fixed cost is often a close approximation of the forgone profit of using the facility. Under these circumstances, the full cost (including variable and fixed costs) is a reasonable approximation of the opportunity cost.

To summarize the discussion of transfer pricing, firms decentralize and form responsibility centres to take advantage of the division manager's specialized knowledge of local conditions. Responsibility centre managers are given responsibilities to make certain local decisions, and are held responsible for the performance of the responsibility centre. Transfer-pricing systems offer desirable mechanisms for permitting local managers to exploit specialized information that they possess about local opportunities.

Table 7.4 describes the appropriate transfer prices for decentralized planning decisions. In each case, the transfer price is intended to be equal to the opportunity cost of providing the intermediate product or service.

■ Choosing transfer prices: control and making planning decisions

Accounting numbers frequently are used in setting internal transfer prices. The conflict between 'planning decisions' and 'control' discussed in Chapter 1 also applies to transfer prices. In setting the transfer price that maximizes firm value, one must often compromise between transfer pricing for planning decisions and control. The transfer price that most accurately measures the opportunity cost to the organization of transferring one more unit inside the organization might not be the transfer-pricing method that motivates internal managers to maximize organizational value. For example, if the transfer-pricing method that most accurately measures the opportunity cost of units transferred also requires managers producing the units to reveal privately-held and hard-to-verify knowledge of their costs, then these managers have much discretion over the transfer prices. If these prices are important in rewarding managers, the producing managers can distort the system to their benefit and to the detriment of maximizing firm profits. Alternatively, a transfer-pricing scheme that less accurately measures opportunity cost but is less subject to managerial discretion might produce a higher firm value than a transfer-pricing scheme that more closely approximates opportunity costs.

Another control problem arises when actual costs are used as a transfer price. The selling responsibility centre manager does not have an incentive to control costs, since any increase in cost is passed on to the buying responsibility centre through the transfer price. The manager of the buying responsibility centre will be penalized for the inefficiencies of the selling responsibility centre. To overcome this problem, an estimated cost should be used as the transfer price, instead of the actual cost. Any variation between the actual cost and the estimated cost will be attributed to the manager of the selling responsibility centre.

In some organizations, transfer prices are negotiated by the managers of the selling and buying responsibility centres. Negotiation, however, is time-consuming and leads to conflicts among responsibility centres. Divisional performance measurement becomes sensitive to the relative negotiating skills of the two division managers. Negotiated transfer prices are more successful when managers have a fall-back position, such as an external market for the intermediate product. In this case, the external market acts as a check on opportunistic management behaviour.

Chapter 6 outlines the relation between responsibilities and knowledge and the role of accounting. Transfer prices are one way in which knowledge is transferred in decentralized organizations. A recent study has suggested that firms are more likely to prefer negotiated transfer prices when the cost of transferring knowledge from divisions to top management is high, for example, in firms operating in unrelated businesses. Negotiated transfer prices are preferred in settings where specialized education is required to understand division operations; when divisions are located far from headquarters; in dynamic markets; and when firms lack sophisticated resource-planning systems. All else being equal, firms with high knowledge-transfer costs earn higher profits with negotiated transfer pricing versus cost-based transfer pricing. Firms must take into account, however, the opportunity cost of management time and potential organizational conflict due to the negotiation process.[3]

Given the many different factors that influence the choice of transfer prices, it is not surprising that different organizations choose different transfer-pricing methods. Table 7.3 (earlier) summarizes the advantages and disadvantages of the various transfer-pricing methods. Research studies also have examined the transfer-pricing methods used by domestic and multinational companies. Cost-based transfer pricing is more prevalent than are market-based methods for domestic transfers, whereas market-based transfers are more prevalent than are cost-based transfers for international transactions. The higher use of market price for international transfers is presumably due to tax and customs regulations that frequently require the use of market price as the transfer price for calculating income taxes. In selecting a transfer-pricing method, multinationals need to trade off tax-minimization objectives with restrictions on profit repatriation, and consider the effects of the selected method on performance evaluation.[4]

---

[3] Shane S. Dilolli and Igor Vaysman (2006) 'Information Technology, organizational design, and transfer pricing,' *Journal of Accounting and Economics*, Vol. 41, pp. 203–236.

[4] Susan C. Borkowski, (1996) 'An Analysis (Meta- and Otherwise) of International Transfer Pricing Research', *The International Journal of Accounting*, Vol. 31, No. 1, pp. 39–53; Canri Chan (2007) 'An Experimental Examination of the Effect of Tax Rates on Transfer Pricing Decisions', *Journal of American Academy of Business*, Vol. 10, No. 2 (March), pp. 1–6.

Concept **review**

1 How should transfer pricing be used to improve decision control?

2 How should transfer prices be chosen to improve decentralized planning decisions?

Shah Motors (continued)

In Shah Motors, the three divisions have considerable interactions. Both the new- and used-car divisions use the service department to make final preparations of cars sold to customers. All the divisions use the accounting services of the central administration. But the primary interaction that is causing problems at Shah Motors is the transfer of used cars from the new-car division to the used-car division. Alice Ho, the new-car sales manager, gives very generous trade-in allowances to buyers of new cars. She would like to pass these costs on to the used-car division, but Slick Thompson claims that he would operate at a loss, if he had to buy the used cars at their inflated trade-in price. Under present policy, Slick must buy all the used cars received by the new-car division at the trade-in allowance offered by Alice Ho. To solve this problem, Jeremy decides to use published lists of used-car prices as the transfer price. If Alice decides to give a trade-in allowance greater than the list price of the used car, she will have to bear the cost.

At the end of the year, Jeremy Shah of Shah Motors decides to calculate the profit of each of the three departments of his company. He allocates his central administration costs, which are mostly interest costs at 10 per cent annually, to the three managers based on total sales. Transfers of trade-ins from the new-car department to the used-car department occur at a list price published by an outside source.

	New-car sales (£)	Used-car sales (£)	Service department (£)
Revenues	8,000,000	2,000,000	1,500,000
Sale of trade-ins	1,000,000		
Total revenues	9,000,000	2,000,000	1,500,000
Controllable costs	(5,000,000)	(700,000)	(1,200,000)
Cost of trade-ins		(1,000,000)	
Profit before allocation	4,000,000	300,000	300,000
Allocated administration costs	(2,160,000)	(480,000)	(360,000)
Profit (Loss)	1,840,000	(180,000)	(60,000)
Average net assets	20,000,000	1,900,000	300,000

Alice Ho, the new-car sales manager is most pleased with this segment reporting. She is evaluated based on profit and the new-car sales department shows a profit of £1,840,000.

Slick Thompson of the used-car sales department is not happy with the profit analysis of the segments. Slick is supposed to be evaluated based on residual income. The profit calculated in the segment reports includes interest charges allocated from central administration. Slick argues that the residual income of his department is the profit before the allocation of administration costs less the opportunity cost of capital, i.e. £300,000 − (10% × £1,900,000), or £110,000.

Grease Johnson is also unhappy with the analysis. He has provided good quality service at a low cost. He has no control over the pricing of his department's services. Also, the allocated administrative costs appear excessive, given that they are mostly interest costs and the net assets of his department are relatively small.

Jeremy Shah agrees with most of his managers' arguments. He is still concerned, however, about the allocation of administration costs to the different departments. If he cannot cover those administration costs with profits from the different departments, his business will incur a loss. Jeremy decides that he had better read Chapter 9 on allocating costs.

■ Globalization and transfer pricing

In a purely domestic firm, the choice of the 'best' transfer price involves looking at how transfer pricing affects the selling and buying divisions' incentives. If the price is set too high, the buyer purchases too few units. Alternatively, if the price is set too low, the seller produces too few units. Transfer pricing, which is already a complicated choice problem, becomes even more complicated for a multinational organization. Internal incentives aside, domestic and foreign taxes and political considerations are affected. This section outlines some of the more important international aspects of transfer pricing.

Tax minimization

If a multinational firm transfers products between two countries with different tax rates, the multinational will try to set a transfer price to minimize its total tax liability in the two countries. One way to do this is to recognize more of the profits in the country with the lowest tax rate. If the country of the supplying division has the lowest tax rate, a higher transfer price shifts profit to the supplying division and lowers after-tax profit. If the country of the purchasing division has the lowest tax rate, a lower transfer price shifts profit to the purchasing division and lowers after-tax profit.

Numerical **example 7.10**

Suppose Fizzi Bottling ships 5,000 units of syrup from the US to a foreign subsidiary, where carbonated water is added and the mixture is bottled and sold. Suppose the US corporate tax rate is 40 per cent and the foreign country's tax rate is 20 per cent. The cost to manufacture and ship the syrup is €14 per unit. It costs the foreign subsidiary €10 per unit to add the water, bottle and sell the drink for €80 per unit. The following table summarizes the tax rates, final sales price, operating costs and units transferred. To simplify the example, all sales have been converted to euros.

	US	Foreign subsidiary
Tax rate	40%	20%
Units transferred and sold	5,000	5,000
Incremental costs/unit	€14	€10
Incremental costs	€70,000	€50,000
Selling price per unit		€80
Revenue from final sales		€400,000

Suppose Fizzi can select a transfer price of €16 per unit or €18 per unit. Which one should it select?

Solution

The following table calculates the total tax liability of Fizzi, if the syrup is transferred at €16 per unit.

	US (€)	Foreign subsidiary (€)	Total (€)
Revenue from transferring syrup @ €16	80,000		
Revenue from final sales		400,000	
Cost of syrup transferred		80,000	
Incremental costs	70,000	50,000	
Profit before taxes	10,000	270,000	
Taxes	4,000	54,000	58,000

From the preceding table, Fizzi's total tax liability is €58,000 if the transfer price is set at €16 per unit. The following table shows that the total tax liability rises to €60,000 if the transfer price is set at €18 per unit.

	US (€)	Foreign subsidiary (€)	Total (€)
Revenue from transferring syrup @ €18	90,000		
Revenue from final sales		400,000	
Cost of syrup transferred		90,000	
Incremental costs	70,000	50,000	
Profit before taxes	20,000	260,000	
Taxes	8,000	52,000	60,000

Fizzi's taxes are higher with the €18 transfer price because profits are shifted out of the low-tax foreign subsidiary to the high-tax US parent.

Transfer pricing is an effective way for multinational organizations to shift taxes to lower tax jurisdictions. Therefore, government officials closely monitor firms' transfer-pricing methods. For example, in 2006, Glaxo-Smith Kline (GSK) reached a $3.1 billion (£1.6 billion) out-of-court settlement with the US Internal Revenue Service for transfer-pricing arrangements between its UK parent and US subsidiary – the largest single payment in such cases. The dispute related to where the profits of its Zantac product should be earned and how much of the product value should be attributed to operations in the US and the UK. Transfer-pricing cases like this one are time-consuming and expensive.[5] For example, the GSK case covered transactions from 1989 to 2000 and has been cited as a reason for mandatory arbitration to resolve transfer-pricing disputes in global markets. Arbitration has been adopted by the European Union and the Organization for Economic Co-operation and Development (OECD).[6] Tax authorities in both the importing and exporting countries scrutinize the transfer-pricing schemes used. Moreover, numerous tax treaties exist between countries that specify the general transfer-pricing methods that companies in the two countries covered by the treaty can use when conducting business. In general, these treaties specify the use of the market price as the transfer price. The OECD's international transfer-pricing guidelines are based on the arm's length principle: transfer prices should be established as if the two firms were independent businesses and not part of the same corporate structure.[7] Thus, while firms have some discretion in setting transfer prices, they are constrained by existing tax laws and treaties. Governments are co-operating increasingly to share information in order to ensure tax compliance and reduce tax abuses, such as using tax havens. Firms' transfer-pricing policies, therefore, must comply with the various governments' complex tax laws.

Globalization affects transfer pricing as firms organize themselves across borders to maintain their international competitiveness. Increasing trade in services and via the Internet makes it more difficult to determine where a transaction has taken place. Some countries, such as those in the European Union, are examining the benefits of

---

[5] A summary of legal cases dealing with transfer pricing can be found at www.transferpricing.com.

[6] Vanessa Houlder (2007), 'Proposal to cut tax disputes across borders', *Financial Times* (London), 8 February, p. 5; 'Improving the Resolution of Tax Treaty Disputes', (2007) OECD Centre for Tax Policy and Administration, February.

[7] *Transfer Pricing Guidelines for Multinational Enterprises and Tax Administrations* (2001) (Paris: OECD); see also Dale C. Hill (2007) 'Transfer Pricing 101', *CMA Management*, Vol. 81, No. 1 (March), pp. 36–39; and 'Transfer Pricing: industry challenges', *CMA Management*, Vol. 81, No. 2 (April), pp. 26–29.

greater harmonization of taxes to reduce the cost of scrutinizing transfer-pricing mechanisms. Tax harmonization also would reduce firms' non-value-added activities devoted to transfer-pricing and taxation disputes and eliminate the need to interpret the differing and changing policies across multiple jurisdictions.

Political considerations

Taxes and tariffs are important considerations in setting transfer prices of goods shipped among global operations. Political considerations also can influence the transfer-pricing decision. If the local government is threatening to expropriate the assets of high-profit, foreign-owned companies, these companies may want to choose high transfer prices to reduce the apparent profitability of their foreign subsidiaries. This action might reduce the attractiveness to the government of seizing the foreign-controlled company. Also, high transfer prices, which lower reported profits, might forestall entry by local competitors. For example, the Russian government investigated sales by major oil firms of crude oil. The firms sold the oil at less than the prevailing market price to trading companies. The trading companies, controlled by the oil firms and often registered in tax-free or lower-tax zones, then sold the oil at market prices and retained the profits. The Russian government put pressure on such firms to restructure their operations to eliminate lost tax revenues and to avoid confiscation of their assets.[8]

Governments frequently engage in tax competition, offering lower tax rates to lure firms to locate in their jurisdictions. Tax authorities recently have focused their attention on domestic firms that have shifted operations to countries offering lower tax rates. Studies have found that firms are increasingly influenced by these taxation policies and choose to locate where taxation is lowest.[9]

Trade-offs with planning decisions and control

As discussed earlier, domestic organizations try to set transfer prices for performance evaluation purposes to get the buying and selling divisions to exchange the number of units that maximize the organization's overall profits. However, in multinational firms, tax and political considerations force managers to choose a transfer price that trades off planning for taxes and political purposes with control. One solution is to choose a transfer price that partially satisfies planning and control functions within the multinational, but is optimal for neither purpose. If multinationals choose transfer prices solely to minimize taxes, they must devise alternative measures of performance to motivate managers of foreign subsidiaries. Instead of relying on accounting profits affected by transfer prices to measure and reward the performance of its subsidiary managers, organizations might want to use revenues, production costs and market share as performance measures.

If income taxes and political considerations have a significant effect on the choice of transfer-pricing methods, organizations may change their structure. Some firms may become more centralized because they cannot rely on transfer prices to create appropriate decentralized incentives.

---

[8] Neil Buckley, 'TNK-BP settles its back taxes in Russia', *Financial Times* (London 3rd Edition: 11 November 2006), p. 15; Arkady Ostrovsky, 'TNK-BP to commence restructuring', *Financial Times* (London: 15 January 2005), p. 8; Arkady Ostrovsky, 'TNK-BP in move to resolve dispute', *Financial Times* (London: 23 June 2004), p. 28.

[9] 'The mystery of the vanishing taxpayer,' and 'Gimme shelter,' in 'Survey: Globalization and Tax', *The Economist*, 29 January 2000, pp. 1–22; *Tax Administration Goes Global*, Ernst & Young Global Limited (London: 2007).

Concept **review**

1 For a product transferred between two subsidiaries of a multinational firm operating in two foreign countries, how would you set the transfer price to minimize the combined income tax liability?

2 How do international taxation and political considerations affect multinational organizations' decision management and control systems?

SUMMARY

1 **Use the controllability principle to choose performance measures for managers.** Managers should be evaluated based on the activities that they control. Performance measures should reflect those controllable activities.

2 **Identify responsibility centres based on the extent of each manager's responsibilities.** Managers who have responsibilities only over the input mix of their activities are managers of cost centres. Managers who have responsibilities only over the input and output mix of their activities are managers of profit centres. Managers who have the additional responsibilities to change the size of their responsibility centre are managers of investment centres.

3 **Choose performance measures for cost, profit and investment centres.** Managers should be evaluated by multiple performance measures to control for quality and other organizational goals. For cost centres, the primary accounting performance measure is cost; for profit centres, profit; and for investment centres, ROI or residual income.

4 **Identify the strengths and weaknesses of using return on investment (ROI) and residual income as performance measures for investment centres.** ROI provides a return measure that controls for size and is comparable to other return measures. However, the measurement of ROI can be difficult, and does not explicitly correct for differences in risk. ROI also leads to under- and over-investment. The residual income measure, however, corrects for the under-

and over-investment problem, but requires an estimate of the opportunity cost of capital.

5 **Choose transfer prices to create performance measures that reflect the activities controlled by each manager.** Transfer prices are used to charge responsibility centres for products or services that they receive from other responsibility centres within the same organization. The transfer price should be chosen so that each party of the internal transaction is rewarded or penalized for the activities that they control.

6 **Use opportunity costs to choose transfer prices that will lead to decentralized decision making that is best for the organization.** To allow decentralized managers to make the most profitable input and output decisions for the entire organization, the transfer price should reflect the opportunity cost. If a market price exists for the intermediate product or service, the market price, adjusted for transaction and contracting costs, is the appropriate transfer price. If no market exists for the intermediate product, the opportunity cost depends on alternative use of raw materials, labour and facilities.

7 **Choose transfer prices to minimize taxes and overcome international obstacles.** Profits can be transferred among countries through the use of transfer prices. Besides transfer pricing, political considerations also might affect the profits of organizational units in different countries.

KEY TERMS

Controllable costs Costs that are affected by a particular manager's decisions.

Controllability principle Holding managers responsible for only those decisions for which they are given authority.

Cost centres Areas of responsibility within the organization where responsibilities are limited to maximizing output given a certain level of cost, or minimizing cost given a certain level of output.

Investment centres Areas of responsibility within the organization where responsibilities include choices affecting costs, revenues and the amount invested in the centre.

Opportunity cost of capital The forgone opportunity of using cash for another purpose, such as earning interest in a bank account.

Profit centres Areas of responsibility within the organization where responsibilities include choices affecting costs and revenues, but not size of investment.

Relative performance measurement Performance is judged relative to how some comparison group performed.

Residual income A performance measure for investment centres that subtracts the opportunity cost of the investment from the profit (excluding interest expense) generated by the assets of the investment.

Responsibility accounting The process of recognizing sub-units within the organization, assigning responsibilities to managers in those sub-units, and evaluating the performance of those managers.

Return on investment (ROI) A performance measure calculated by dividing the profit (excluding interest expense) from an investment by the size of the investment.

Transfer pricing A system of pricing of products and services transferred from one responsibility centre to another within the same organization.

Self-study problem

Tasty Burger has grown to over 200 restaurants within the past five years, 80 per cent of which are franchised (independently owned). Two of the company-operated units, Merseyside and Southampton, are among the fastest-growing restaurants. Both are considering expanding their menus to include pizza. Installation of the necessary ovens and purchase of the necessary equipment would cost £180,000 per restaurant. The current investment in the Merseyside location totals £890,000. Restaurant revenues are £1,100,500 and expenses are £924,420. Expansion of Southampton's menu should increase profits by £30,600. The current investment in the Southampton restaurant totals £1,740,000. Its revenues are £1,760,800 and expenses are £1,496,680. Adding pizza to Southampton's menu should increase its profits by £30,600.

Tasty Burger evaluates its managers based on ROI. Managers of individual locations have responsibilities over the pizza expansion.

Required

a Calculate the ROI for both restaurants using current numbers, for the expansion project and for the restaurants after expansion.

b Assuming a 14 per cent cost of capital, calculate residual income for both restaurants, before and after the potential expansion.

c Will the Tasty Burger restaurants choose to expand? How would your answer change if the locations were franchised units and owned by value-maximizing investors?

Solution

a ROI before and after the pizza expansion.

	Merseyside	Southampton
ROI before pizza:		
Revenue	£1,100,500	£1,760,800
Expenses	924,420	1,496,680
Net profit	£ 176,080	£ 264,120
Assets	890,000	1,740,000
ROI	19.78%	15.18%

ROI of pizza only:

Increased profits from pizza	£ 30,600	£ 30,600
Expansion cost	180,000	180,000
ROI of project	17.00%	17.00%

ROI after pizza:

Total profit	£ 206,680	£ 294,720
Total assets	1,070,000	1,920,000
Total ROI	19.32%	15.35%

b Residual income before and after the pizza expansion.

	Merseyside	Southampton
Cost of capital	14.00%	14.00%

Residual income before pizza:

Net profit	£176,080	£264,120
Assets × 14%	124,600	243,600
Residual income	£ 51,480	£ 20,520

Residual income of pizza only:

Increased profits from pizza	£30,600	£30,600
less: 14% × expansion cost	(25,200)	(25,200)
Residual income	£ 5,400	£ 5,400

Residual income after pizza:

Net profit	£206,680	£294,720
14% × assets	149,800	268,800
Residual income	£ 56,880	£ 25,920

c The two units currently have different ROIs. The smaller Merseyside restaurant is earning an ROI of just under 20 per cent, while the larger Southampton restaurant is earning an ROI of just over 15 per cent. Since the ROI of the project is 17 per cent, adding the project to the Merseyside location lowers its average ROI, while adding the project to the Southampton location raises its average ROI. Therefore, the Merseyside manager will not want to add pizza to the menu since the restaurant's average ROI would drop as a result. The Southampton manager, however, would want to add pizza since the restaurant's ROI would subsequently rise.

   If the restaurants were franchised units, the owners definitely would expand. The ROI of the pizza is higher than the cost of capital. Thus a positive residual income for the project is assured. As long as the residual income is positive, any franchise owner would jump at the opportunity. Franchise owners would not care if the restaurant's average ROI dropped, as long as the residual income increased.

Numerical exercises

NE 7.1 ROI and investment centres LO 4

An investment centre of an organization has the following investment opportunities:

Project	Required investment (£)	Annual earnings before interest (£)
X	250,000	12,500
Y	100,000	15,000
S	50,000	10,000

The opportunity cost of capital of the organization is 8 per cent.

   What is the ROI of these investment opportunities and which investment would add value to the organization?

NE 7.2 ROI and residual income LO 4

A manager has control of a division with €10,000,000 in assets and no debt. The division's profit is €500,000 for the year. The cost of capital is 8 per cent.

   What is the ROI of the division? What is the residual income of the division? How is the division performing?

NE 7.3 Selecting performance measures LO 4

The ROI of three potential investments is 20 per cent, 15 per cent and 10 per cent respectively. The cost of capital is 12 per cent and the ROI of existing assets is 18 per cent.

Which investment(s) will the manager choose if the manager is evaluated based on ROI? Which investment(s) will increase organizational value?

NE 7.4 Choosing transfer prices for planning and control LO 5

Division A makes 100 units of a product. The fixed cost is £200, and the variable cost is £5 per unit. Division B of the same company purchases the product from Division A. It adds £3 per unit and sells the product to an outside buyer for £13 per unit.

What is the profit of the two divisions with respect to this product if the transfer price is £8 per unit?

NE 7.5 Choosing transfer prices LO 5

Division A makes 100 units of a product for a fixed cost of £200 and a variable cost of £5 per unit. Division B of the same company purchases the product from Division A. It adds £3 per unit and sells the product to an outside buyer for £13 per unit. Division A can sell the 100 units of the intermediate product to an outside buyer for £11 per unit.

What should be the transfer price? What decentralized decision does Division B reach? Show why this is the correct decision for the entire organization.

NE 7.6 Selecting transfer prices LO 5

Division A makes 100 units of a product for a fixed cost of £200 and a variable cost of £5 per unit. Division B of the same company purchases the product from Division A. It adds £3 per unit and sells the product to an outside buyer for £9 per unit. There is no other buyer for the intermediate product and the fixed cost is sunk.

What happens if the full cost is used as the transfer price? What happens if the variable cost is used as the transfer price?

NE 7.7 Residual income LO 4

The computer division of Acme Inc. located in France has profits (not including interest expense) of €15 million and investment (total assets) of €120 million. The division has an opportunity cost of capital of 10 per cent.

What is the division's residual income?

NE 7.8 Transfer prices and decentralized decision making LO 6

Food services at Oxbridge University provides meal services to Oxbridge's conference facility. It also provides catering to off-campus organizations at an average cost of £30 per person. Off-campus events require additional services to transport staff, food and equipment to these locations. The cost of these services is £4 per person.

What transfer price should be used between Oxbridge's conference facility and food services to encourage decentralized decision making that will best benefit the university?

NE 7.9 ROI and residual income LO 4

The following data summarizes the operating performance of your company's wholly-owned Spanish subsidiary for 2006 to 2008. The opportunity cost of capital for this subsidiary is 10 per cent.

	(€m)		
	2006	2007	2008
Subsidiary net profit	14.0	14.3	14.4
Total assets in subsidiary	125	130	135

Calculate the ROI and residual income of the subsidiary for each year.

NE 7.10 Transfer prices and divisional profit LO 5

A chair manufacturer has two divisions: framing and upholstering. The framing costs are £100 per chair and the upholstering costs are £200 per chair. The company makes 5,000 chairs each year, which are sold for £500.
a What is the profit of each division if the transfer price is £150?
b What is the profit of each division if the transfer price is £200?

Numerical problems

NP 7.1 ROI and residual income LO 4

The following investment opportunities are available to an investment centre manager:

Project	Investment (£)	Annual Earnings (£)
A	800,000	90,000
B	100,000	20,000
C	300,000	25,000
D	400,000	60,000

a If the investment manager were currently making a return on investment of 16 per cent, which project(s) would the manager want to pursue?

b If the cost of capital is 10 per cent and the annual earnings approximate cash flows excluding finance charges, which project(s) should be chosen?

c Suppose only one project can be chosen and the annual earnings approximate cash flows excluding finance charges. Which project should be chosen?

NP 7.2 ROI and residual income LO 4

Suppose a division of a company is treated as an investment centre. The division manager is currently getting an ROI of 15 per cent from existing assets of €1 million. The cost of capital (corporate discount rate) is 10 per cent. The manager has the option of choosing among the following projects, which are independent of existing operations and the other alternative projects.

Project	Investment (€)	ROI (%)
A	100,000	14
B	400,000	20
C	200,000	14
D	300,000	12
E	500,000	8

a Given the current investment in existing assets, in which additional projects should the division manager invest if the objective is to maximize ROI?

b Which projects yield a positive net present value?

c Which projects have a negative residual income?

d Using this example, explain why under-investment is a problem when using ROI for evaluation purposes.

NP 7.3 Transfer prices LO 6

The Alpha Division of the Carlson Company manufactures product X at a variable cost of £40 per unit. Alpha Division's fixed costs, which are sunk, are £20 per unit. The market price of X is £70 per unit. Beta Division of Carlson Company uses product X to make Y. The variable costs to convert X to Y are £20 per unit and the fixed costs, which are sunk, are £10 per unit. Product Y sells for £80 per unit.

a What transfer price of X causes divisional managers to make decentralized decisions that maximize Carlson Company's profit if each division is treated as a profit centre?

b Given the transfer price from (a), what should the manager of the Beta Division do?

c Suppose there is no market price for product X. What transfer price should be used for decentralized decision making?

d If no market exists for product X, are the operations of the Beta Division profitable?

NP 7.4 Dropping a division LO 6

Scoff Division of World-Wide Paint is currently losing money so senior management is considering selling or closing Scoff. Scoff's only product, an intermediate chemical called Binder, is used principally by the Latex Division of the firm. If Scoff is sold, Latex Division can purchase ample quantities of Binder in the market at sufficiently high quality levels to meet its requirements. World-Wide Paint requires all of its divisions to supply product to other World-Wide Divisions, before servicing the external market.

Scoff's statement of operations for the latest quarter is:

Scoff Division Profit/Loss
Last Quarter
(€ thousands)

Revenues		
Inside	200	
Outside	75	275
Operating expenses		
Variable costs	260	
Fixed costs	15	
Allocated corporate overhead	40	315
Net profit (loss) before taxes		(40)

Notes:

1 World-Wide Paint has the policy of transferring all products internally at variable cost. In Scoff's case, variable cost is 80 per cent of the market price.

2 All of Scoff's fixed costs are avoidable cash flows if Scoff is closed or sold.

3 10 per cent of the allocated corporate overhead is caused by the presence of Scoff and will be avoided if Scoff is closed or sold.

Should the Scoff Division be sold?

NP 7.5 ROI using market values LO 4

Your firm uses ROI to evaluate investment centres and is considering changing the valuation basis of assets from historical cost to current value. The historical cost of the asset is updated using a price index to approximate replacement value. For example, a metal-fabrication press, which bends and shapes metal, was bought seven years ago for £522,000. The company will add 19 per cent to this cost, representing the change in the wholesale price index over the seven years. This new, higher cost figure is depreciated using the straight-line method over the same 12-year assumed life (no salvage value).

a Calculate depreciation expense and book value of the metal press based upon both historical cost and the change in the wholesale price index.

b In general, what is the effect on ROI of changing valuation bases from historical cost to current values?

c The manager of the investment centre with the metal press is considering replacing the press, as it is becoming obsolete. Will the manager's incentives to replace the metal press change if the firm shifts from historical cost valuation to the proposed price-level adjusted historical cost valuation?

(Contributed by L. Harrington, R. Lewis, P. Siviy and S. Spector.)

NP 7.6 Transfer price and capacity LO 6

Microelectronics is a large electronics firm with multiple divisions. The Circuit Board Division manufactures circuit boards, which it sells externally and internally. The Phone Division assembles mobile telephones and sells them to external customers. Both divisions are evaluated as profit centres. The firm has the policy of transferring all internal products at market prices.

The selling price of mobile telephones is £40 and the external market price for the mobile telephone circuit board is £20. The outlay cost for the Phone Division to complete a telephone (not including the cost of the circuit board) is £25. The variable cost of the circuit board is £13.

a Will the Phone Division purchase the circuit boards from the Circuit Board Division? (Show calculations.)

b Suppose the Circuit Board Division is currently manufacturing and selling externally 10,000 circuit boards per month, and has the capacity to manufacture 15,000 boards. From the standpoint of Microelectronics, should 3,000 additional boards be manufactured and transferred internally?

c Discuss what transfer price should be set for (b) above.

d List the three most important assumptions underlying your analysis in (b) and (c).

NP 7.7 Transfer prices and capacity LO 6

Disraeli Company has two divisions: Disraeli Bottles and Disraeli Juice. Disraeli Bottles makes glass containers, which it sells to Disraeli Juice and other companies. Disraeli Bottles has a capacity of 10 million bottles a year. Disraeli Juice currently has a capacity of 3 million bottles of juice per year. Disraeli Bottles has a fixed cost of £100,000 per year and a variable cost of £0.01/bottle. Disraeli Bottles can currently sell all of its output at £0.03/bottle.

a What should Disraeli Bottles charge Disraeli Juice for bottles, in order that both divisions make appropriate decentralized planning decisions?

b If Disraeli Bottles can only sell 5 million bottles to outside buyers, what should Disraeli Bottles charge Disraeli Juice for bottles in order that both divisions make appropriate decentralized planning decisions?

NP 7.8 Planning decisions and transfer prices LO 6

A hotel company is divided into two divisions: construction and management. The construction division builds the hotels and the management division operates the hotels. The construction division borrows money to cover the cost of construction. The construction division charges the management division an annual price per room to use the hotel. The transfer price is used by the construction division to make the annual debt payments.

The estimated costs of both divisions and the estimated revenues for the management division for different sizes of hotels follow:

Room size	Construction division Annual debt costs (£)	Management division Annual costs (£)	Management division Annual revenues (£)
150	2,000,000	10,000,000	15,000,000
200	2,400,000	11,000,000	16,500,000
250	2,600,000	12,000,000	18,000,000
300	2,700,000	13,000,000	18,500,000

a What room size of the new hotel maximizes the value of the company?

b If the transfer price is set at £15,000 per year per room, what is the profit of each division?

c What size of hotel will the management division choose if the transfer price is £15,000 per year per room?

d Why is this transfer price not working for the company?

NP 7.9 ROI and residual income LO 4

The Aberdeen Fishing Company operates five trawlers (fishing boats) out of Aberdeen, Scotland. The boats are of different sizes and incur different operating expenses during the year. The following table describes the operating data and value of each boat.

	Boats				
	A (£)	B (£)	C (£)	D (£)	E (£)
Revenues	5,500,000	8,300,000	10,400,000	12,800,000	20,400,000
Annual expenses	3,800,000	8,200,000	9,100,000	9,900,000	18,900,000
Profit	1,700,000	100,000	1,300,000	2,900,000	1,500,000
Book value	0	5,200,000	6,100,000	5,200,000	8,300,000
Market value	5,000,000	6,200,000	8,000,000	10,000,000	15,000,000

The cost of capital for the company is 10 per cent.

a What is the ROI of each boat, using the book value of the investment in each boat?

b What is the ROI of each boat, using the market value of the investment in each boat?

c What is the residual income of each boat, using the book value of each boat?

d What is the residual income of each boat, using the market value of each boat?

e Which trawler had the best year?

NP 7.10 Performance measures for cost centres LO 1, 2, 3

A soft drink company has three bottling plants throughout the country. Bottling occurs at the regional level due to the high cost of transporting bottled soft drinks. The parent company supplies each plant with the syrup. The bottling plants combine the syrup with carbonated soda to make and bottle the soft drinks. The bottled soft drinks then are sent to regional grocery stores.

The bottling plants are treated as costs centres. The managers of the bottling plants are evaluated based on minimizing the cost per soft drink bottled and delivered. Each bottling plant uses the same equipment, but some produce more bottles of soft drinks because of different demand levels. The costs and output for each bottling plant are:

	A	B	C
Units produced	10,000,000	20,000,000	30,000,000
Variable costs (€)	200,000	450,000	650,000
Fixed costs (€)	1,000,000	1,000,000	1,000,000

a Estimate the average cost per unit for each plant.

b Why would the manager of plant A be unhappy with using average cost as the performance measure?

c What alternative performance measure would make the manager of plant A happier?

d Under what circumstances might the average cost be a better performance measure?

NP 7.11 ROI and residual income LO 4

Zwann Systems develops and manufactures residential water filtration units that are installed under the sink. The filtration unit removes chlorine and other chemicals from drinking water. This Dutch company has successfully expanded sales of its units in the European market for the past twelve years. Six years ago, Zwann started a US manufacturing and marketing division and three years ago, an Australian manufacturing and marketing division. Summary operating data for the last financial year are:

Zwann Systems
Summary of Operations
Last Financial Year (€m)

	Australia	Netherlands	US	Total
Sales	50	55	75	180
Divisional expenses	38	33	58	129
Net profit	12	22	17	51

Senior management is in the process of evaluating the relative performance of each division. While the Netherlands division is the largest and generates the most profit, this division also has the largest asset investment, as indicated by the following table:

Zwann Systems
Miscellaneous Operating Data
Last Financial Year (€m)

	Australia	Netherlands	US	Total
Divisional net assets	80	195	131	406
Allocated corporate overhead*	4	4	6	14
Cost of capital	8.0%	8.0%	8.0%	

*Allocated based on divisional sales revenue.

After careful consideration, senior management has decided to examine the relative performance of the three divisions using several alternative measures of performance: ROI (return on investment as measured by net assets, total assets less liabilities), residual income (net profit less the cost of capital times net assets), and both of these measures after subtracting allocated corporate overhead from divisional profit. The cost of capital in each division is estimated to be the same (8 per cent). (Assume that this 8 per cent estimate is accurate.)

There has been much debate about whether corporate overhead should be allocated to the divisions and subtracted from divisional profit. Senior management has decided to allocate back to each division the portion of corporate overhead that is incurred to support and manage the divisions. The allocated corporate overhead items include global marketing, legal expenses, accounting and administration. Sales revenue has been selected as the allocation base. It is simple to use and best represents the cause-and-effect relation between the divisions and the generation of corporate overhead.

a Calculate ROI and residual income (1) before any corporate overhead allocations, and (2) after corporate overhead allocations for each division.

b Discuss the differences among the various performance measures.

c Based on the data presented in the case, evaluate the relative performance of the three operating divisions. Which division do you think performed the best and which performed the worst?

NP 7.12 International transfer pricing and taxes LO 7

Phipps manufactures circuit boards in Low Division located in a country with a 30 per cent corporate tax rate. Low Division transfers them to High Division located in a country with a 40 per cent corporate tax rate. An import duty of 15 per cent of the transfer price is paid on all imported products. The import duty is not deductible in computing taxable income. The circuit boards' full cost is €1,000; variable cost is €700. High Division sells them for €1,200. The tax authorities in both countries allow firms to base their transfer prices on either variable cost or full cost.

Analyse the effect of full cost and variable cost transfer-pricing methods on Phipps' cash flows.

NP 7.13 International taxation LO 7

Multi-National Enterprises (MNE) operates in two countries, X and Y, with tax rates of 40 per cent and 10 per cent respectively. Production costs are exactly the same in each country. The following summarizes the operating data for the two subsidiaries of MNE. (All data have been converted to euros to simplify the example.)

	Subsidiary in Country X	Subsidiary in Country Y
Tax rate	40%	10%
Units sold	100	200
Unit cost	€10	€10
Selling price per unit	€20	€20

a If each operating unit of MNE produces and sells only in its local country, is treated as a separate company, and each unit pays taxes only in the country of its operations, what is MNE's total tax bill?

b Suppose that MNE's subsidiary in country Y manufactures all the output sold in both countries. It ships the output to the MNE subsidiary in country X that sells the product. The transfer price is set at €20. There are no costs of shipping the units from Y to X. If each country taxes only those profits that occur within its jurisdiction, again calculate MNE's total tax liability.

c Now suppose that the MNE's subsidiary in country X manufactures all the output sold in both countries. It ships the output to the MNE subsidiary in country Y that sells the product. Again, there are no costs of shipping the units from Y to X. If each country taxes only those profits that occur within its jurisdiction, what transfer price must be set to minimize MNE's total tax liability?

NP 7.14 International transfer prices LO 7

A Bristol-based company has two divisions: Division A in Mexico and Division B in the UK. Division A makes a product at a cost of £4 per unit that it transfers to Division B. At an additional cost of £1 per unit, Division B sells the product to outside customers for £8 per unit. During the year, 100,000 units are produced, transferred, and sold. Assume that the tax rate in the UK is 30 per cent and that the tax rate in Mexico is 40 per cent.

What is the total tax liability of the company if the transfer price is £5 per unit?

Analysis and interpretation problems

AIP 7.1 Responsibility centres LO 1, 2, 3

Oakwood Golf Course is a private club that is owned by its members. It has the following managers and organizational structure:

Eric Olson: General Manager responsible for all the operations of the golf course and other facilities (swimming pool, restaurant, golf shop).

Jennifer Jones: Manager of the golf course and responsible for its maintenance.

Edwin Moses: Manager of the restaurant.

Mabel Smith: Head golf professional and responsible for golf lessons, the golf shop, and reserving times for starting golfers on the course.

Wanda Itami: Manager of the swimming pool and family recreational activities.

Jake Reece: Manager of golf carts rented to golfers.

Describe each of the managers in terms of their being responsible for a cost, profit or investment centre. Provide possible performance measures for each manager.

AIP 7.2 Transfer prices LO 5

The Bookmark Company uses cost-based transfer pricing to transfer books from the publication division to its bookstores. The transfer price is based on a budget established at the beginning of the year. At the end of the year, the publication division had a cost over-run and its manager wants to charge the bookstores for the extra costs. Under which of the following cases does the publication manager have a valid argument?

a The cost over-runs were due to equipment failure.
b The cost over-runs were due to rush orders from the bookstores.
c The cost over-runs were due to the return of defective books.
d The cost over-runs were due to lower demand for books than expected.

AIP 7.3 Evaluating a new product with ROI LO 4

An Italian wholesaler of Mexican crafts is considering the importing of rugs. The rugs are hand-woven in southern Mexico and use natural dyes. The rugs cost an average of €250 including transportation and handling. The wholesaler plans to sell them in Italy for €300. Therefore, the profit per rug should be €50. The wholesaler's cost of capital is 10 per cent annually. The wholesaler estimates an ROI on the project of €50/€250, or 20 per cent. The residual income is estimated to be €50 − (10% × €250), or €25 per rug.

What is wrong with the use of ROI and residual income in this analysis?

AIP 7.4 Responsibility centres LO 2

News Inc. owns five newspaper stands. Each stand has a manager who is responsible for ordering newspapers each day. News Inc. purchases the newspapers for each stand. Any newspapers not sold at the end of the day are thrown away.

Describe how the newspaper stands might operate as cost centres, profit centres and investment centres. Outline the advantages and disadvantages of each type of responsibility centre.

AIP 7.5 Salespeople as profit centres LO 2

Memories Company sells cosmetics door to door. The company has traditionally paid its salespeople a commission based on total sales. The company is considering making each sales representative a profit centre.

How would making each sales representative a profit centre affect his or her behaviour?

AIP 7.6 Influencing the ROI measure LO 4

The chairman of a company is trying to improve his firm's ROI. He asks a consultant for assistance. The consultant tells the chairman that he must increase either his profit margin (Profit/Sales) or asset turnover (Sales/Assets). The chairman complains that every time he tries to increase his profit margin, the asset turnover goes down.

Evaluate the consultant's advice and the chairman's complaint.

AIP 7.7 ROI and throughput LO 4

A popular book claims that manufacturing managers should always work to improve throughput (the time from starting the manufacturing process to the time of sale).

How is this philosophy related to ROI?

AIP 7.8 Transfer prices LO 6

Peaceful Valley Company owns both hotels and manufacturing companies. One hotel has a convention centre, which is leased to various groups. The manufacturing companies want to use the convention centre for a training session.

What conditions should affect the choice of the transfer price?

AIP 7.9 Transfer prices and changing from a cost to a profit centre LO 2, 5

Northern Blue Company has manufacturing plants and retail shops. The retail shops purchase products from the manufacturing plants. Currently, the manufacturing plants are operated as cost centres and only supply the company's retail shops. The transfer price is cost-based and the retail shops operate as profit centres. The chief executive is considering an increase in manufacturing capacity that will allow sales to customers outside the company. The chief executive plans to make the manufacturing plants profit centres.

Why are the managers of the retail shops unhappy with these new plans?

AIP 7.10 ROI and other performance measures LO 4

Brownside Company is highly decentralized. The divisions can issue their own debt, but they must pay their own interest. The manager of Brownside's Park Division is evaluated based on ROI. He has borrowed a considerable amount of money from the bank for expansion. A large interest expense on that debt is lowering the division's profits. Brownside Company's chairman calculates the ROI of the Park Division by using the net profit figure, which includes the interest expense, and dividing this figure by the total assets of the division.

Why does the manager of the Park Division believe this ROI measure is inappropriate? Suggest alternative performance measures for Park Division.

AIP 7.11 Transfer price LO 6

UK Pumps is a multi-divisional firm that manufactures and installs chemical piping and pump systems. The Valve Division makes a single standardized valve. Two divisions, the Valve Division and the Installation Division, currently are involved in a transfer-pricing dispute. Last year, half of the Valve Division's output was sold to the Installation Division for £40 per valve and the remaining half was sold to outsiders for £60 per valve.

The existing transfer price of £40 per valve has been set through a negotiation process between the two divisions and also with the involvement of senior management. The Installation Division has received a bid from an outside valve manufacturer to supply it with an equivalent valve for £35 each.

The manager of the Valve Division has argued that if it is forced to meet the external price of £35 per valve, it will lose money on internal sales.

The operating data for last year for the Valve Division follow:

Valve Division
Operating Statement
Last Year

	To Installation Division (£)		To outside (£)	
Sales	20,000 @ £40	800,000	20,000 @ £60	1,200,000
Variable costs	@ £30	(600,000)		(600,000)
Fixed costs		(135,000)		(135,000)
Gross margin		65,000		465,000

Analyse the situation and recommend a course of action. What should the Installation Division managers do? What should the Valve Division managers do? In your opinion, what should UK Pumps' senior managers do?

AIP 7.12 Transfer prices LO 5, 6

Lewis is a large manufacturer of office equipment, including copiers. The Electronics Division of Lewis is a cost centre. Currently, Electronics sells circuit boards to other divisions exclusively. Lewis has a policy that internal transfers are to be priced at full cost (Fixed + Variable). 30 per cent of the cost of a board is considered fixed.

The Electronics Division is currently operating at 75 per cent of capacity. Given this excess capacity, Electronics is seeking opportunities to sell boards to non-Lewis firms. The Electronics Division policy on non-Lewis sales states that each job must cover full cost and a minimum 10 per cent profit. Electronics Division management will be measured on its ability to make the minimum profit on any non-Lewis contracts which are accepted.

Copy Products is another Lewis Division. Copy Products recently has reached an agreement with Siviy, a non-Lewis firm, for the assembly of sub-systems for a copier. Copy Products has selected Siviy due to Siviy's low labour cost. The sub-system, which Siviy will assemble, requires circuit boards. Copy Products has stipulated that Siviy must purchase the circuit boards from the Electronics Division because of Electronics' high quality and dependability. The Electronics Division is anxious to accept this new work from Copy Products, as it will increase its workload by 15 per cent.

In negotiating a contract price with Siviy, Copy Products needs to take into account the cost of the circuit boards from Electronics. The financial analyst from Copy Products assumes that Electronics will sell the circuit boards to Siviy at full cost (the same as the internal transfer price). Electronics is considering adding the minimum 10 per cent profit margin to its full cost and transferring at that price to Siviy.

Copy Products is preparing to negotiate its contract with Siviy.

Develop and discuss at least three options that may be used to establish the transfer price between the Electronics Division and Siviy. Discuss the advantages and disadvantages of each.

AIP 7.13 Transfer price from shared service LO 6

Susan Byrne, the CEO of Troy Industrial Designs (TID), has called a meeting to evaluate the present method of charging the two offices at Dublin and Shannon, Ireland for the shared services of the Creative Design Group (CDG). She wants to discuss the present cost allocation system and suggest a better one.

TID is a reputable firm in the industrial design sector. It bids for design contracts from different firms. If successful, it makes prototypes based on the client's blueprints, designs new products out of existing designs, or draws designs for a product that the client has in mind. TID charges clients a fixed figure upon completion of the job and 1 per cent of sales accruing to the client every year for the first seven years, for the use of TID designs or products designed by TID.

The two offices of TID are run independently by different managers and are profit centres. Each manager assigns account executives to individual accounts. The account executives are paid a fixed salary, but a large part of their compensation is their bonus, which is based on the revenues accruing from the jobs that they manage. On receiving a job, the account executive informs Greg O'Connor, the head of CDG. They meet with the client and decide on a plan, detailing the job, expected time to complete the job and other job-specific factors. The account executive then waits for the final design before informing and discussing the design with the client. As soon as the job for a client is finished, the account executive makes a detailed report explaining the work done, the number of designers employed for the job, the number of hours worked on it, the amount billed to the client and any follow-up needed. Designing is a one-time job and it is not often that time is needed to follow up on the same job. Account executives are responsible for any follow-up on the jobs done by them. If the client comes back with another project, it is treated as a separate job.

TID centralized the design departments of the two offices to take advantage of the specialized knowledge of the designers. Although CDG is only five years old, it employs the best talent and uses the latest technology. This strategy has had a positive impact on customers so TID has grown rapidly in the past few years. The two offices have a lot of confidence in the CDG and use it for all their design needs. The rapid growth has caused top management to rethink the cost procedures and other organizational aspects of the business.

CDG is totally responsible for the design part of the job. It only interacts with the client at the design stage; all other aspects of the job are done by the appropriate account executive. CDG works in small teams. Each team is led by a supervisor who reports to Greg on a day-to-day basis. Greg is evaluated on the excess of revenues collected from the two offices over the costs of his department. The cost charged to each office is decided prior to the design job being taken by CDG. Before the client is brought in for the discussion, the account executive and Greg decide what fees CDG will charge the office for the services. Revenues for CDG come from the predetermined fees charged to the two offices.

Susan suggests that CDG should provide its services free of charge. Under this proposal, Greg would receive a fixed salary and a bonus based on overall firm profits (i.e. a percentage of the combined profits of the two offices). She believes that as the cost of the department is finally consolidated with those of the firm, there should be no allocation of costs for the department. Removal of the transfer price will help reduce the work of the accounts department and help streamline the accounts department to cope with the rapid growth of the firm. Susan says that the firm is committed to designing the best products and that cost allocations really do not matter.

Will the resources of the Creative Design Group (CDG) be efficiently utilized under the new plan? Why? What are the merits and demerits of the existing plan? Is the proposed plan better than the existing one? Why?

AIP 7.14 Transfer prices in a competitive market LO 6

Celtex is a large, successful, decentralized specialty chemical producer, organized into five independent investment centres. Each of the five investment centres is free to buy products either inside or outside the firm, and is judged based on residual income. Most of each division's sales are to external customers. Celtex has the general reputation of being one of the top two or three companies in each of its markets.

Don Horigan, President of Synthetic Chemicals (Synchem) division, and Paula Juris, President of Consumer Products division, are embroiled in a dispute. It all began two years ago when Paula asked Don to modify a synthetic chemical for a new household cleaner. In return, Synthetic Chemicals would be reimbursed for out-of-pocket costs. After spending considerable time perfecting the chemical, Paula solicited competitive bids from Don and some outside firms. Ultimately, Paula awarded the contract to an outside firm who was the low bidder. This decision angered Don, who expected his bid to receive special consideration because he developed the new chemical at cost and the outside vendors took advantage of his R&D.

The current conflict has to do with Synchem's production of chemical Q47, a standard product, for Consumer Products. Due to an economic slowdown, all synthetic chemical producers have excess capacity. Synchem was asked to bid on supplying Q47 for Consumer Products. Consumer Products is moving into a new, experimental product line and Q47 is one of the key ingredients. While the magnitude of the order is small relative to Synchem's total business, the price of Q47 is very important in determining the profitability of the experimental line. Don bid €3.20 per litre. Meas Chemicals, an outside firm, bid €3.00. Paula is mad because she knows that Don's bid contains a substantial amount of fixed overhead and profit. Synchem buys the base raw material, Q4, from the Organic Chemicals division of Celtex for €1.00 per litre. Organic Chemical's out-of-pocket costs (i.e. variable costs) are 80 per cent of the selling price. Synchem then further processes Q4 into Q47, incurring additional variable costs of €1.75 per litre. Allocated fixed overhead adds another €0.30 per litre.

Don argues that he has €3.05 of cost in each litre of Q47. If he turned around and sold the product for anything less than €3.20, he would be undermining his recent attempts to get his sales people to stop cutting their bids and start quoting full cost prices. Don has been trying to enhance the quality of the business that he is getting. He fears that if he were forced to make Q47 for Consumer Products, all of his effort the last few months would be for naught. He argues that he already gave away the store once to Consumer Products and he won't do it again. He questions, 'How can senior managers expect me to return a positive residual income, if I am forced to put in bids that don't recover full cost?'

Paula, in a chance meeting at the airport with Debra Donak, Senior Vice President of Celtex, describes the situation and asks her to intervene. Paula believes Don is trying to get even after their earlier clash. Paula argues that the success of her new venture depends on being able to secure a stable, high-quality source of supply of Q47 at low cost.

a Prepare a statement outlining the cash flows to Celtex of the two alternative sources of supply for Q47.

b What advice would you give to Debra Donak?

AIP 7.15 Identifying responsibility centres LO 1, 2

In late 2006, Ford Motor Company announced a major reorganization that would streamline decision making and lever its global assets. The company's CEO, Alan Mulally stated, 'This new leadership will enable us to work together more effectively as one Ford team to continuously improve the quality, productivity and speed of our product development process.' The key objective of this plan was to realign the organization in terms of its customers and its markets. The leaders of its three global business units would report directly to Mr Mulally, as would the newly created position responsible for global product development. The three business units were Ford the Americas, Ford Europe and Premier Automotive Group, and Ford Asia Pacific and Africa/Mazda. The Global Product Development unit would emphasize shared vehicle platforms, thereby reducing costs and improving quality through exchange of information and best practices. Ford also announced changes to its marketing and sales structure to reduce positions and streamline operations.

a Based on their responsibilities, would you classify the leaders of the global business units and of global product development as managers of cost, profit or investment centres?

b What are possible performance measures for these managers?

Sources: *Ford Motor Company 2006 Annual Report* (www.ford.com/en/company/investorInformation/companyReports/default.htm, accessed 7 May 2007); 'Ford Moves to Streamline Reporting Structure', *Wall Street Journal* (2006). (Eastern edition). New York, N.Y.: 15 December, p. A.18; 'Ford Scraps a Post, Shuffles Executives In Sales, Marketing', *Wall Street Journal* (2006) (Eastern edition). New York, N.Y.: 14 December p. B.11.

AIP 7.16 Exchange rates and performance evaluation LO 7

Monsanto is a global agricultural company. In the 1980s, Monsanto noticed that sales were declining in certain foreign markets. The local managers in these markets were asked to increase their advertising and marketing expenditures to try to stem the decline. When the senior managers in the US looked at accounting reports of advertising and marketing expenditures in these markets, these expenditures were declining. Monsanto had the accounting practice of converting all foreign currencies into US dollars, before reporting the foreign results to US senior managers. The dollar had been strengthening against the local currencies in the foreign markets. When asked why they had not increased these expenditures, the foreign managers were confused and said they had increased the expenditures. Explain the apparent inconsistency between the foreign managers and the accounting reports used by the senior US managers.

AIP 7.17 Transfer prices and responsibility centres LO 2, 5, 6

Euro Copiers manufactures a full line of copiers including desk-top models. The Small Copier Division (SCD) manufactures desk-top copiers and sells them across Europe. A typical model has a retail price of under €500. An integral part in the copier is the toner cartridge that contains the black powder used to create the image on the paper. The toner cartridge can be used for about 10,000 pages and then must be replaced. The typical owner of a SCD copier purchases four replacement cartridges over the life of the copier.

SCD buys the initial toner cartridges provided with the copier from the Toner Division (TD) of Euro Copiers. Subsequent replacement cartridges are sold by TD to distributors who sell them to European retail stores. Toner cartridges sell to the end consumer for €50. TD sells the toners to distributors for about 70 per cent of the final retail price paid by the consumer. The Toner Division manager argues that the market price to TD of €35 (70% × €50) is the price SCD should pay to TD for each toner cartridge transferred.

a Why does Euro Copiers both manufacture copiers and toner cartridges? Why do separate firms not exist that specialize in either copiers or toner cartridges, like Intel specializes in making computer chips and Dell specializes in assembling computers and selling PCs?

b You work for the chief executive of SCD. Write a memo to your boss outlining the salient issues that she should raise in discussing the price SCD should pay TD for toner cartridges included in SCD copiers.

AIP 7.18 Return on investment and economic value added (EVA) LO 4

General Motor's former Chief Financial Officer, Michael Losh converted GM's performance measure for compensation from net income to return on investment, calculated as return on assets (ROA). In explaining the move he said, 'ROA was a logical next step because all those other measures generally have focused on the income statement. Moving to ROA means that we're going to focus not only on the income statement, but on the balance sheet and effective utilisation of the assets and liabilities that are on the balance sheet as well.'

'ROA is a better measure for us than EVA. . . . EVA is simpler conceptually, because it automatically builds on growth, whereas with this approach we know that we've got to have growth as an overlying objective. EVA is more comprehensive. And that has a certain appeal to me. But, given our situation, particularly in our North American operations, it just would not have been the right measure.'

'ROA works for us and EVA doesn't because our operations have to deal with those two different kinds of starting points. Within GM, in our North American operations, you've got a classic turnaround situation, and in our international operations, you've got a classic growth situation. You can apply ROA to both; you can't apply EVA to both.'

Source: S. L Mintz (1996) 'What's good for General Motors . . . CFO', 12(8), p. 20. Document ID: 100008495. Retrieved, 18 December 2007 from ABI/INFORUM Global database.

a Explain how ROA focuses on both the income statement and the balance sheet.

b Explain why EVA is more 'comprehensive' than ROA.

c Do you agree with Mr Losh's statement that 'You can apply ROA to both; you can't apply EVA to both'? Explain.

AIP 7.19 Transfer prices and external market opportunities LO 6

KCG is a division of Metro Stores (a large retail firm) that designs and maintains websites for individual stores of Metro. It also sells its services outside the firm to other retail stores. KCG, a profit centre, has two web designers who do not have any assignment for the next month. Each designer currently is paid £4,000 per month. The Manchester Metro store wants its website updated. This work will require two designers one month each to complete the project.

a How much should the Manchester Metro store be charged for KCG's services?
b Suppose KCG expects that the two designers will be assigned to work on an outside job that will generate revenues of €15,000. What should the Manchester Metro store be charged?

Extended **analysis** and **interpretation** problems

AIP 7.20 PortCo Products

PortCo Products is a divisionalized furniture manufacturer. The divisions are autonomous segments, with each division being responsible for its own sales, costs of operations, working capital management and equipment acquisition. Each division serves a different market in the furniture industry. The markets and products of the divisions are so different; thus there have never been any transfers between divisions.

The Commercial Division manufactures equipment and furniture that is purchased by the restaurant industry. The division plans to introduce a new line of counter and chair units which feature a cushioned seat for the counter chairs. John Kline, the Commercial Division Manager, has discussed the manufacturing of the cushioned seat with Russ Fiegel of the Office Division. They both believe a cushioned seat currently made by the Office Division for use on its deluxe office stool could be modified for use on the new counter chair. Consequently, Kline has asked Fiegel for a price for 100-unit lots of the cushioned seat. The following conversation took place about the price to be charged for the cushioned seats.

Fiegel: 'John, we can make the necessary modifications to the cushioned seat easily. The raw materials used in your seat are slightly different and should cost about 10 per cent more than those used in our deluxe office stool. However, the labour time should be the same because the seat fabrication operation basically is the same. I would price the seat at our regular rate – full cost plus 30 per cent mark-up.'

Kline: 'That's higher than I expected, Russ. I was thinking that a good price would be your variable manufacturing costs. After all, your capacity costs will be incurred regardless of this job.'

Fiegel: 'John, I'm at capacity. By making the cushioned seats for you, I'll have to cut my production of deluxe office stools. Of course, I can increase my production of economy office stools. The labour time freed by not having to fabricate the frame or assemble the deluxe stool can be shifted to the frame fabrication and assembly of the economy office stool. And, you will save the cost of the framing raw materials. However, I am constrained in terms of the number of hours I have for cushion fabrication. Fortunately, I can switch my labour force between these two models of stools without any loss of efficiency. As you know, overtime is not a feasible alternative in our plant. I'd like to sell it to you at variable cost, but I have excess demand for both products. I don't mind changing my product mix to the economy model if I get a good return on the seats I make for you. Here are my budgeted costs for the two stools and a schedule of my manufacturing overhead.' [See next page for budgeted costs and overhead schedule.]

Kline: 'I guess I see your point, Russ, but I don't want to price myself out of the market. Maybe we should talk to corporate to see if they can give us any guidance.'

Office Division Budgeted Costs and Prices

	Deluxe Office Stool (€)		Economy Office Stool (€)	
Raw materials				
Framing	8.15			9.76
Cushioned seat				–
Padding	2.40			–
Vinyl	4.00			–
Melded seat (purchased)	–			6.00
Direct labour				
Frame fabrication (0.5 × €7.50/DLH)	3.75	(0.5 × €7.50/DLH)		3.75
Cushion fabrication (0.5 × €7.50/DLH)	3.75			–
Assembly* (0.5 × €7.50/DLH)	3.75	(0.3 × €7.50/DLH)		2.25
Manufacturing				
Overhead (1.5DLH × €12.80/DLH)	19.20	(0.8DLH × €12.80/DLH)		10.24
Total standard cost	45.00			32.00
Selling price (30% mark-up)	58.50			41.60

*Attaching seats to frames and attaching rubber feet.
DLH stands for direct labour hours.

Office Division Manufacturing Overhead Budget

Overhead item	Nature	Amount (€)
Supplies	Variable – at current market prices	420,000
Indirect labour	Variable	375,000
Supervision	Non-variable	250,000
Power	Use varies with activity; rates are fixed	180,000
Heat and light	Non-variable – light is fixed regardless of production while heat/air conditioning varies with fuel charges	140,000
Property taxes and insurance taxes	Non-variable – any change in amounts/rates is independent of production	200,000
Depreciation	Fixed amount	1,700,000
Employee benefits	20% of supervision, direct and indirect labour	575,000
	Total overhead	3,840,000
	Capacity in DLH (÷ 300,000)	
	Overhead rate/DLH	€12.80

a John Kline and Russ Fiegel did ask PortCo corporate management for guidance on an appropriate transfer price. Corporate management suggested that they consider using a transfer price based upon opportunity cost. Calculate a transfer price for the cushioned seat based upon variable manufacturing cost plus forgone profits.

b Which alternative transfer-pricing system – full cost, variable manufacturing cost, or opportunity cost – would be better as the underlying concept for an intra-company transfer-pricing policy? Explain your answer.

(CMA adapted)

AIP 7.21 Royal Club and Casino

The Royal Club and Casino (RCC), a publicly-quoted company, caters to affluent customers seeking plush surroundings, high quality food and entertainment, and all the 'glitz' associated with the best resorts and casinos. RCC consists of three divisions: Hotel, Gaming and Entertainment. The Hotel division manages the reservation system and lodging operations. Gaming consists of operations, security and junkets. Junkets offer complimentary airfare, lodging and entertainment at RCC for customers known to wager large sums. The Entertainment division consists of restaurants, lounges, catering, and shows. The latter books lounge shows and top-name entertainment in the auditorium. While many of those people attending the shows and eating in the restaurants are staying at RCC, customers staying at other hotels and casinos in the area frequent RCC's shows, restaurants and gaming operations. The following table disaggregates RCC's total EVA of £12 million into an EVA for each division:

Royal Club and Casino
EVA by Division (£m)

	Entertainment	Hotel	Gaming	Total
Adjusted accounting profits	5	10	30	45
Invested capital	40	120	60	220
Weighted-average cost of capital	15%	15%	15%	15%
EVA	(1)	(8)	21	12

Based on an analysis of similar companies, it is determined that each division has the same weighted-average cost of capital of 15 per cent.

Across town from RCC is a city block with three separate businesses: Big Horseshoe Slots & Casino, Nell's Lounge and Grill, and the Sunnyside Inn. These businesses serve a lower-income clientele.

a Why does RCC operate as a single firm, whereas Big Horseshoe Slots, Nell's Lounge and Grill, and the Sunnyside Inn operate as three separate firms?

b Describe some of the interdependencies that likely exist across RCC's three divisions.

c Describe some of the internal administrative devices, accounting-based measures, and/or organizational structures that senior managers at RCC can use to control the interdependencies that you describe in (a).

d Critically evaluate each of the 'solutions' that you propose in (c).

CHAPTER **EIGHT**

Budgeting
(Planning and control)

Learning objectives

1 Use budgeting for planning purposes.

2 Use budgeting for control purposes.

3 Identify the conflicts that exist between planning and control in the budgeting process.

4 Describe the benefits of having both short-term and long-term budgets.

5 Explain the responsibility implications of a line-item budget.

6 Identify the costs and benefits of budget lapsing.

7 Develop flexible budgets and identify when flexible budgeting should be used instead of static budgeting.

8 Explain the costs and benefits of using zero-base budgeting.

9 Create a master budget for an organization including sales, production, administration, capital investment and financial budgets.

10 Create pro-forma financial statements based on data from the sales, production, administration, capital investment and financial budgets.

11 Use spreadsheets to analyse monthly cash flows. (Appendix)

Mother Goose Child-Care Centre

Mother Goose Child-Care Centre (MGCC) is a not-for-profit organization that provides child care and pre-school education to children in the Selly Oak Ward in the city of Birmingham. MGCC rents space in a neighbourhood building, where both the child care and pre-school programmes are housed along with MGCC's administrative offices.

The child-care programme is for children between six months and three years of age. MGCC charges £600 monthly per child for eight hours of child care every weekday. MGCC's child-care centre is open 12 months of the year. A licensed and certified staff provides a structured set of activities tailored to the ages of the children; one assistant is required for every four children. The child-care centre has a capacity of 30 children.

The pre-school programme is four hours per day, either morning or afternoon, for nine months. Each session has a capacity of 40 children from three to five years of age. The programme costs £450 per month per child. MGCC requires one pre-school teacher for every eight children. A qualified nurse is always on call for both the pre-school and the child-care programmes.

A ten-member Board of Directors oversees and supervises the operations of MGCC. The Board of Directors hires the manager of the child-care centre, the head teacher of the pre-school programme and the office manager. The child-care manager and the head teacher hire their staff, plan their programmes and are responsible for the financial operations of their programmes. The office manager has a secretary and bookkeeper, who prepare monthly bills for users of the facility, monthly financial reports for the Board of Directors, purchase supplies and are responsible for collecting and disbursing funds.

The financial year of MGCC is from 1 July to 30 June. Prior to its beginning, the office manager asks the child-care manager and head teacher to prepare budgets to plan for the coming financial year. MGCC cannot spend more than its revenue, so the budgeting process is very important for planning the new school year. While not profit-driven, MGCC strives to create value for parents by providing quality programmes that adhere to government standards and best practices for early childhood education. This strategy ensures that organizational value is created in terms of MGCC's continued attractiveness and viability as an educator and child-care provider.

THE PURPOSE OF BUDGETS

Organizations develop strategies as a basis to compete in their operating environment. **Budgets** are a key component of the organization's planning and control system, providing the mechanism to translate organizational goals into financial terms. More specifically, budgets are forecasts of future revenues and expenditures. Once established, budgets provide a control tool to ensure that organizational members work to achieve the organizational goals that create organizational value. **Budgeting** is the process of gathering information to assist in making those forecasts. Budgeting can be a very costly process. Managers often spend up to 20 per cent of their time on budgeting. The popularity of budgeting, however, indicates that its perceived benefits are greater than its costs.

The benefits of budgeting result from making planning decisions and control. For planning purposes, the budgeting process generates and communicates information to improve co-ordination. The budgeting process is the initial step to implement change in an organization in response to changes in its environment and in customer preferences. The control benefits of budgets include assigning of responsibilities and scarce resources, providing goals to motivate managers and establishing performance measures to reward managers.

■ Budgeting for planning decisions

Budgets play an integral role in making planning decisions. One purpose of budgeting is to transfer information to the individuals making decisions within the organization. Managers near the top of an organization's hierarchy must make major, long-term planning decisions, yet some of the information necessary to make those decisions is located with managers lower in the hierarchy. To improve major, long-term decisions, the information located lower in the hierarchy must filter up to top-level management. The budgeting process attempts to fulfil this role by encouraging the 'bottom-up' flow of information. An example of the 'bottom-up' flow of information in the budgeting process is the collection of expenditure requests by a university's central administration from the various departments. The head of each department knows the needs of that department, and those needs are communicated to central administration through the budgeting process. Central administration reviews these requests and selects those with the most merit and, in the process, learns about the priorities of each department.

Lower-level managers of the organization also must make decisions. To improve their decisions, lower-level managers could use information located with top-level managers. Top-level managers have aggregated information from the various parts of the organization and the outside environment. To allow lower-level managers to make both more informed decisions and decisions that are co-ordinated with other managers within the organization, top-level management must communicate its information and plans from the 'top-down'. For example, the top managers of a bottle-manufacturing firm must communicate production requirements to the managers of the different manufacturing facilities. The top-level managers have information on global demand for bottles and use this information to determine production requirements for each of the manufacturing facilities.

■ Budgeting for control

Budgets also play an important role in control. The budget is frequently used to assign responsibilities by allocating resources to different managers. Giving a manager an advertising budget of £800,000 authorizes that manager to consume £800,000 of the firm's resources on advertising. The level of responsibility given to the manager determines how the £800,000 on advertising can be spent. If the he or she has the confidence of the top-level managers and specialized knowledge of advertising, the budget might give the advertising manager the flexibility to choose how to spend the £800,000. If the manager is new and does not have specialized knowledge, the budget might also specify how the £800,000 is to be spent. For example, it might stipulate spending £500,000 on Internet advertisements and £300,000 on print media. With more constraints in the budget, a manager has fewer opportunities to make decisions.

The numbers in the budget are also used as goals to motivate organizational members. Budgeted numbers become targets for managers. For example, the manager of a manufacturing plant producing tennis racquets is allocated £700,000 to make 10,000 racquets. The 10,000 racquets represents a goal for the plant manager, who is expected to work hard and manage well to achieve the goal.

Once the budget is set, it becomes the target by which performance is evaluated and rewarded. In setting the budget, some experts argue that the budget should be 'tight' but achievable. If budget goals are achieved too easily, they provide little incentive to expend extra effort. If budgets are unachievable, they provide little motivation. The motivation to achieve budgeted numbers results from rewards. If budgeted numbers are achieved, the manager is rewarded through bonuses or other privileges. The manager of the tennis racquet plant strives to achieve the goal of manufacturing 10,000 racquets for £700,000, knowing that rewards are based on achieving the budget.

The difference between a budgeted performance measure and an actual performance measure is called the **variance**. An **adverse variance** occurs when actual costs are greater than the budgeted costs, or actual revenues are less than budgeted revenues. A **favourable variance** occurs when actual costs are less than the budgeted

Budgets are important for planning and control, translating organizational goals into numerical targets against which managers are evaluated and rewarded.

Larry Lilac/Alamy

costs, or actual revenues are greater than budgeted revenues. Variances are commonly calculated in monthly reports to identify how successfully an organization is achieving its goals. Large favourable or adverse variances are commonly investigated to determine the reason for the variances and to correct any problems that may exist.

Numerical example 8.1

Ayala Telecom has the following budgeted and actual results for the month of July:

Ayala Telecom
July Profit Statement
Budgeted and Actual

	Budgeted (£)	Actual (£)
Revenues	450,000	453,000
Cost of goods sold	(235,000)	(248,000)
General administration	(80,000)	(132,000)
Selling expenses	(100,000)	(90,000)
Profit	35,000	(17,000)

Calculate the variances for each of the items in the monthly report and describe them as favourable or adverse. Which item appears to warrant investigation?

Solution

The variances are the difference between the budgeted and actual amounts:

Ayala Telecom
July Profit Statement
Budgeted and Actual

	Budgeted (£)	Actual (£)	Variance (£)
Revenues	450,000	453,000	3,000 F
Cost of goods sold	(235,000)	(248,000)	13,000 A
General administration	(80,000)	(132,000)	52,000 A
Selling expenses	(100,000)	(90,000)	10,000 F
Profit	35,000	(17,000)	52,000 A

The actual general administration expense account differs greatly from what was expected and has the largest variance. Large adverse variances are generally the focus of an investigation if the cause of the problem is unknown. The other accounts have smaller variances but also might be investigated.

Organizations should modify the budgeting process to meet their special planning and control needs. Avon Automotive, an industry leader in the design and manufacture of automotive components, operates in a highly volatile industry. Annual budgets did not provide meaningful targets for the company due to the rapidly changing nature of the automobile sector and the impact of these changes on demand for its products. To adapt to its operating environment, Avon Automotive adopted a system of global, rolling forecasts to update its budget each month. By continuously updating its budget, the firm, with factories in Europe, Asia and North America, is able to meet its strategic priorities of on-going product development and continuous improvement.[1]

---

[1] Paul Clarke and Rob West (2007) 'Rolling forecasts', *Financial Management* (April), pp. 38–39; see also www.avonauto.com.

Mother Goose Child-Care Centre (continued)

MGCC's budget translates its strategy into specific activities and programmes, and forms the basis for their control. Budgeting is extremely important for MGCC. Initially, the budget is used to estimate the total enrolment and revenues available. Based on estimated enrolment and revenues, MGCC determines how many teachers and assistants to hire. The budget also specifies how much the managers of the child-care and pre-school programmes and the office manager can spend on educational and office supplies. A larger budget for educational and office supplies gives the managers more responsibilities. No bonuses are based on the budget, but having greater resources makes child care and teaching less stressful and more rewarding.

CONFLICT BETWEEN PLANNING AND CONTROL

A budgeting system serves two principal purposes: planning and control. In making planning decisions, budgets communicate specialized knowledge from one part of the organization to another. For control, budgets serve as benchmarks for performance-measurement systems. Budgets serve several purposes so trade-offs must be made when designing or changing a budgeting system. The budget becomes the benchmark against which to judge actual performance. If too much emphasis is placed on the budget as a performance benchmark, then managers with the specialized knowledge will stop disclosing accurate forecasts of future events for planning decisions. Managers will tend to report budget figures that make benchmarks easier to achieve.

The conflict between planning decisions and control is particularly severe in marketing. Salespeople usually have specialized knowledge of future sales. This information is important in setting future production plans, such as how many units to manufacture. If budgeted sales are used to evaluate salespeople at the end of the year then salespeople have an incentive to under-forecast future sales, thus improving their performance evaluation. However, production plans will then be too low, and the firm will incur costs due to its inability to plan the most efficient production schedules.

To manage the conflict between planning decisions and control, many organizations put the chief executive (CE) in charge of the budgeting process. While the actual collection of data and preparation of the budget is the formal responsibility of the chief financial officer or controller, the chairman or CE has the final responsibility. The CE has immediate control for numerous reasons. First, it signals the importance of the budgeting process. Second, resolving disagreements among departments requires making trade-offs and the CE, who has an overall view of the entire firm, is best able to make these trade-offs.

In addition to placing the CE in charge of the budgeting process, many firms also use a budget committee. Such a committee consists of the major functional executives (directors of sales, manufacturing, finance, and human resources) with the CE as chairperson. The budget committee facilitates the exchange of specialized knowledge and the achievement of consensus in establishing a budget.

The budget is an informal set of contracts between the various units of the organization. By accepting the budget, the organization's managers agree to perform the responsibilities assigned and to abide by the limitations that it specifies.

Most budgets are set in a negotiation process involving lower- and higher-level managers. Lower-level managers have incentives to set easier targets to guarantee that they will meet the budget and be favourably rewarded, whereas higher-level managers have incentives to set more difficult targets to motivate the lower-level managers to exert additional effort. The conflict between making planning decisions and control is often viewed as a trade-off between 'bottom-up' budgeting versus 'top-down' budgeting. Bottom-up budgets are submitted by lower levels of the organization to higher levels and usually imply better information for planning decisions. An example of a bottom-up budget is the submission by the field sales offices of their forecasts for the next year to the marketing department. A 'top-down' budget would be the central marketing department's use of aggregate data on sales trends to forecast sales for the entire firm, and then disaggregating this firm-wide budget into field office targets. This top-down budget provides greater control; but by not soliciting input from the field offices, it forgoes assembling knowledge from its sales staff.

A bottom-up budget process, in which the person ultimately held responsible for meeting the target makes the initial budget forecast, is called **participative budgeting**. Participation enhances the motivation of the lower-level participants by motivating them to accept the targets.

The extent to which a budget is bottom-up or top-down ultimately depends on where the knowledge is located. If the knowledge is with the field salespeople, the responsibility to set the budget should be linked with the knowledge and placed in the field. If the central marketing organization has better knowledge, a top-down budget is likely to prove better. Which budgeting scheme provides better motivation depends, in the final analysis, on how the performance measurement and reward systems are designed.

In a survey of Australian manufacturing firms, managers indicated that they used participative budgeting more frequently when lower-level managers had specialized knowledge.[2] A Finnish study of 83 managers concluded that participative budgeting had a positive effect on performance when managers had a high level of cost-management knowledge.[3] Moreover, participative budgeting is more frequently used when managers' rewards are based on their performance against the budget. This evidence is consistent with budgets and performance reward systems being designed to link responsibilities and specialized knowledge.[4]

Mother Goose Child-Care Centre (continued)

The child-care manager and the pre-school head teacher are responsible for estimating how many children will be attending their programmes next year. They are closer to the parents of the children than are members of the Board of Directors and, therefore, have the specialized knowledge to make that estimate. But the child-care manager and the head teacher have a dilemma. They know that their estimated enrolment numbers will be used to allocate space, staff and supplies to their respective programmes. The higher the estimated enrolment, the greater the resources that they will receive. Recognizing this conflict, the Board of Directors decides to do its own survey of the community to verify the programme leaders' estimates.

---

[2] V. K. Chong and D. M. Johnson (2007) 'Testing a model of the antecedents and consequences of budgetary participation on job performance', *Accounting and Business Research*, Vol. 37, No. 1, pp. 3–19.

[3] A. Agbejule and L. Saarlkoski (2006) 'The effect of cost management knowledge on the relationship between budgetary participation and managerial performance', *The British Accounting Review*, Vol. 38, pp. 427–440.

[4] J. F. Shields and M. D. Shields (1998) 'Antecedents of Participative Budgeting', *Accounting, Organizations and Society*, Vol. 23, Issue 1 (January), pp. 49–76.

Concept **review**

1 What are the planning benefits of budgeting?

2 What are the control benefits of budgeting?

3 How do planning and control issues lead to conflict in the budgeting process?

HOW BUDGETING HELPS RESOLVE ORGANIZATIONAL PROBLEMS

Budgeting systems are an administrative device used to resolve organizational problems. In particular, these systems help link knowledge with the responsibility to make planning decisions and distribute responsibilities, and measure and reward performance for control. This section further analyses various budgeting devices, such as short-term versus long-term budgets, line-item budgets, budget lapsing, static versus flexible budgets and incremental versus zero-base budgets.

■ Short-term versus long-term budgets

Most organizations have annual budgeting processes. Starting in the prior year, organizations develop detailed plans of how many units of each product they expect to sell, at what prices, the cost of such sales and the financing necessary for operations. These budgets then become the internal 'contracts' for each responsibility centre (cost, profit and investment centre) within the firm. These annual budgets are *short term* in the sense that they only project one year at a time. But most firms also project two, five and sometimes ten years in advance. These *long-term* budgets are a key feature of the organization's strategic planning process.

Strategic planning, described in Chapter 4, is the process whereby managers select the firm's overall objectives and the tactics to achieve those objectives. Strategic planning is primarily concerned with how the organization can add customer value and respond to competitors. For example, British Airways is faced with the strategic question of how to respond to the environmental concerns related to air travel. Making this decision requires specialized knowledge of the various aircraft technologies and flight services on which British Airways and other market participants compete, knowledge of the future demand for air travel, along with consideration of potential regulatory changes to deal with global warming.

Long-term budgets, like short-term budgets, encourage managers with specialized knowledge to communicate their forecasts of future expected events. Such long-term budgets contain forecasts of large asset acquisitions (and financing plans) for the manufacturing and distribution systems required to implement the strategy. Research and development

Specialized knowledge of future demand, aircraft technologies, competitors and environmental regulations can assist British Airways in developing strategies to deal with global warming.

The Flight Collection/Alamy

(R&D) budgets are long-term plans of the multi-year spending required to acquire and develop the technologies to implement the strategies.

In short-term budgets, important estimates include the quantities produced and sold, and prices. All parts of the organization must accept these estimates. In long-term budgets, important assumptions involve the choice of markets to serve and the technologies to be acquired.

A typical firm integrates the short-term and long-term budgeting process into a single process. As next year's budget is being developed, a five-year budget is also produced. Year one of the five-year plan is next year's budget. Years two and three are fairly detailed, and year two becomes the base to establish next year's one-year budget. Years four and five are less detailed, but incorporate new market opportunities. Each year, the five-year budget is rolled forward one year and the process begins anew.

The short-term (annual) budget involves both planning and control functions, thus a trade-off arises between these two functions. Long-term budgets are rarely used as a control (performance evaluation) device. Rather, long-term budgets are used primarily for planning. Five- and ten-year budgets force managers to think about strategy and to communicate their specialized knowledge of potential future markets and technologies. Thus, long-term budgets have much less conflict between planning and control, since much less emphasis is placed on using the long-term budget as a performance-measurement tool.

Long-term budgets also reduce managers' focus on short-term performance. Without long-term budgets, managers have an incentive to cut expenditures, such as maintenance, marketing and R&D, in order to improve short-term performance. Alternatively, managers might seek to balance short-term budgets at the expense of the firm's long-term viability. Budgets that span five years increase the likelihood that top management and/or the board of directors are informed of the long-term trade-offs that are being taken to accomplish short-term goals.

Some organizations and studies question the usefulness of budgets and the budgeting process in today's global marketplace. This 'beyond budgeting' debate has examined the implementation of alternative approaches to budgets and their relative success compared to traditional budgeting techniques.[5] Ericsson is one of many firms that have modified their organizational strategy and structure to remain competitive in a rapidly changing telecommunications market. In conjunction with its strategic and structural changes, Ericsson has modified its accounting and budgeting system.

Organizational **analysis**

Ericsson

Ericsson, a worldwide leader in telecommunications, is headquartered in Sweden. It operates in over 175 countries and has more than 100,000 employees. Ericsson's strategy is focused on the customer and the need to react constantly to market trends. Rapid changes in technology, such as the shift to wireless communications, the Internet and the demand by

customers for total solutions, have required Ericsson to adapt not only its products, but also its organizational structure. In a highly competitive industry where market dominance is difficult to attain and sustain, Ericsson had initially been slow to ensure that its operations enhanced customer value. Recently, Ericsson re-organized to gain the requisite flexibility to be competitive in this dynamic environment. The re-organization has eliminated several levels of

---

[5] Jeremy Hope and Robin Fraser (2003) 'Who Needs Budgets', *Harvard Business Review*, Vol. 81, Issue 2 (February), pp. 108–115; further information on the Beyond Budgeting Roundtable can be found at www.bbrt.org

management and introduced management teams centred on business segments and market regions. Ericsson has also adopted a more entrepreneurial strategy with greater decentralization of decision making to its operating segments. Business segments, established by customer category, handle product range and customer responsibilities. Product units work with several business units to take advantage of potential synergies and to create organizational value through efficient use of resources.

In parallel with its re-organization, Ericsson has changed its accounting system. It has eliminated its use of annual budgets, replacing them with a system of rolling (continuously updated) financial plans and forecasts. The focus is on activities, and how cost centres consume financial resources on various activities. Along with these rolling financial forecasts, Ericsson reports quarterly operating profit and sales per business segment. Greater local responsibility has also been given for financial transactions and

spending. Ericsson has broadened its reporting to include a series of key performance indicators (KPIs) that provide non-financial measures on customers, finance, employees, internal efficiency and innovation. The forecasts and KPIs form the basis for performance evaluation of the business units, with each unit agreeing to specific targets.

How has the organizational structure at Ericsson adapted to changes in its environment and its strategy?

Why has Ericsson's management accounting system been required to evolve with these changes?

What risks and trade-offs exist in Ericsson's new reporting system?

What are some possible measures that Ericsson might use to track its key performance indicators?

Sources: www.ericsson.com

◼ Line-item budgets

Line-item budgets refer to budgets that authorize the manager to spend only up to the specified amount on each line item. For example, consider Table 8.1.

In this budget, the manager is authorized to spend £12,000 on office supplies for the year. If the supplies can be purchased for £11,000, the manager with a line-item budget is prohibited from spending the £1,000 savings on any other category (such as additional office equipment). The manager cannot spend savings from one line item on another line item without prior approval; therefore the manager has less incentive to look for savings. Moreover, if next year's line item is reduced by the amount of the savings, managers have even less incentive to search for savings.

Line-item budgets impose more control on managers – in some cases an extreme form of control. Managers responsible for line-item budgets cannot reduce spending on one item and divert the savings to items that enhance their own welfare. By maintaining tighter control over how much is spent on particular items, the organization reduces the possibility of management action that is inconsistent with organizational goals.

Line-item budgets are quite prevalent in government organizations like local councils and police authorities. (They also are used in some corporations, but with fewer

Table 8.1 **Line-item budget example**

Line item	Amount (£)
Salaries	185,000
Office supplies	12,000
Office equipment	3,000
Postage	1,900
Maintenance	350
Utilities	1,200
Rent	900
Total	204,350

restrictions.) The manager does not have the responsibility to substitute resources among line items as circumstances change.

For example, a manager given the responsibility to spend up to £3,000 on office equipment does not have the responsibility to substitute office equipment for postage. Such changes during the year require special approval from a higher level in the organization, such as the local council.

Line-item budgets, however, come at a cost. They reduce management incentives to search for cost savings and they also reduce the organization's flexibility to adapt quickly to changing market conditions.

Budget lapsing

Another common feature in budgeting is **budget lapsing**. If budgets lapse, funds that have not been spent at year end do not carry over to the next year. Budget lapsing creates incentives for managers to spend their entire budget. Not only do managers lose the benefits from the unspent funds, but next year's budget might be reduced by the amount of the under-spending.

Budgets that lapse provide tighter controls on managers than budgets that do not lapse. If budgets do not lapse, managers have the opportunity to choose when to make expenditures. When budgets lapse, managers can make the expenditure only in the current year.

One disadvantage of lapsing budgets is less efficient operations. Managers devote substantial time at the end of the year ensuring that their budget is fully expended. This action is taken, even if it means buying items of lower value (and of a higher cost) than those that would be purchased if the budget carried over to the next financial year. Often, these end-of-year purchases cause the firm to incur substantial warehousing costs to hold the extra purchases. In many organizations, including universities and governments, year-end purchases of technology and equipment can lead to bulk purchases that are not aligned to long-term plans. Vendors also take advantage of clients' need to spend their budget, by offering last-minute deliveries or, in some cases, offering to store equipment until a later date. For example, a programme manager in a women's shelter purchased a 12-month supply of non-perishable food items to spend her remaining budget. The food items were so bulky that the shelter had to reduce the space available for other activities to have adequate room to store these supplies. Managers cannot adjust to changing operating conditions during the year if budgets lapse. For example, if managers have expended all of their budget authority and the opportunity to make a bargain purchase arises, they cannot 'borrow' against next year's budget without getting special approval.

Without budget lapsing, managers could build up substantial balances in their budgets. Toward the end of their careers with the firm, these managers would then be tempted to make large expenditures on perquisites. For example, they could take their staff to the French Riviera for a 'training retreat'. Budget lapsing also prevents risk-averse managers from 'saving' their budget for a rainy day. If it were optimal for a manager to spend a certain amount of money on a particular activity like advertising, then saving part of that amount as a contingency fund would reduce organizational value. Budget lapsing is one way to prevent the occurrence of these control problems.

Static versus flexible budgets

All of the examples in this chapter have described **static budgets**, which do not vary with volume. Each line item is a fixed amount. In contrast, a **flexible budget** is stated

Table 8.2 **Flexible budget for concert**

		Ticket sales (€)		
	(Formula)	3,000	4,000	5,000
Revenues	€18N*	54,000	72,000	90,000
Band	€20,000 + 0.15(18N)	(28,100)	(30,800)	(33,500)
Auditorium	€5,000 + 0.05(18N)	(7,700)	(8,600)	(9,500)
Security	€80(N/200)	(1,200)	(1,600)	(2,000)
Other costs	€28,000	(28,000)	(28,000)	(28,000)
Profit/(Loss)		(11,000)	3,000	17,000

*N is the number of tickets sold.

as a function of some volume measure. Flexible budgets are adjusted for changes in volume. Flexible budgets and static budgets provide different incentives.

As an example of flexible budgeting, consider the case of a concert. A band is hired for €20,000 plus 15 per cent of the gate receipts. The auditorium is rented for €5,000 plus 5 per cent of the gate receipts. Security guards are hired, one for every 200 people, at a cost of €80 per guard. Advertising, insurance and other fixed costs are €28,000. Ticket prices are €18 each. A flexible budget for the concert is shown in Table 8.2.

Each line item in the budget is stated in terms of how it varies with volume, or ticket sales in this case. Then a budget is prepared at different volume levels. At ticket sales of 3,000, an €11,000 loss is projected. At sales of 4,000 and 5,000 tickets, €3,000 and €17,000 of profit are forecasted, respectively.

The major reason for using flexible rather than static budgets is to better gauge the actual performance of a person or venture after controlling for volume effects, assuming, of course, that the individual being evaluated is not responsible for the volume changes. For example, consider the following illustration. After the concert, which 5,000 people attended, the actual cost of the auditorium was €9,900. The budget for the auditorium is automatically increased to €9,500 as a result of the 5,000 ticket sales and the manager is not held responsible for volume changes. However, the manager is held responsible for the €400 adverse variance between the actual charge of €9,900 and €9,500. In evaluating the manager's performance, the cause of the variance should be investigated. For example, if the €400 had been caused by damage to the auditorium, would additional security personnel have prevented this damage?

When should a firm or department use a static budget and when should it use a flexible budget? Static budgets do not adjust for volume effects. Volume fluctuations in static budgets are passed through, and show up in the difference between actual and budgeted numbers. Thus, static budgets force managers to be responsible for volume fluctuations. If the manager has some control over volume or the consequences of volume, then static budgets should be used as the benchmark to gauge performance. Flexible budgets adjust for volume effects. Volume fluctuations in flexible budgets are not passed through, and do not show up in the difference between actual and budgeted numbers. Flexible budgets do not hold managers responsible for volume fluctuations. Therefore, if the manager does not have any control over volume, then flexible budgets should be used as the benchmark to gauge performance. Flexible budgets reduce the risk that volume changes are borne by managers.

Flexible budgets are used primarily in manufacturing settings, but they are also employed for budgeting distribution, marketing, R&D, or general and administrative expenses. Manufacturing settings offer readily available volume measures and many costs vary with volume.

Numerical **example** 8.2

Rugged Terrain plc makes mountain bikes. The company establishes a flexible annual budget. The company sells its bikes for £200 each. The fixed manufacturing costs are budgeted to be £2 million. The variable manufacturing costs are budgeted to be £80 per bike. Selling and administrative costs are expected to be fixed and are budgeted to be £1 million. There is no beginning and ending inventory.

a Prepare a budgeted profit and loss statement for Rugged Terrain plc assuming the manufacture and sale of 20,000, 30,000, and 40,000 bikes.

b The company actually produced and sold 34,000 bikes. Actual revenues are £6,500,000, actual variable costs are £2,500,000, actual fixed manufacturing costs are £2,100,000, and actual selling and administration costs are £950,000. What are the variances of each of these accounts and the profit variance?

Solution

a

Rugged Terrain plc
Budgeted Profit and Loss Statement

Number of bicycles manufactured and sold

	20,000 (£)	*30,000 (£)*	*40,000 (£)*
Revenues (× £200)	4,000,000	6,000,000	8,000,000
Variable costs (× £80)	(1,600,000)	(2,400,000)	(3,200,000)
Fixed manufacturing	(2,000,000)	(2,000,000)	(2,000,000)
Selling and administration	(1,000,000)	(1,000,000)	(1,000,000)
Profit (Loss)	(600,000)	600,000	1,800,000

b If 34,000 bikes are produced and sold, the following are the budgeted revenues and costs, actual revenues and costs, and variances:

	Budgeted (£)	*Actual (£)*	*Variance (£)*
Revenues (34,000 × £200)	6,800,000	6,500,000	300,000 A
Variable Costs (34,000 × £80)	(2,720,000)	(2,500,000)	220,000 F
Fixed manufacturing	(2,000,000)	(2,100,000)	100,000 A
Selling and administration	(1,000,000)	(950,000)	50,000 F
Budgeted profit	1,080,000	950,000	130,000 A

The adverse variance results from lower than expected prices and higher than expected fixed manufacturing costs.

■ Incremental versus zero-base budgets

Most organizations construct next year's budget by starting with the current year's budget, then adjusting each line item for expected price and volume changes. Each manager submits a budget for next year by making incremental changes in each line item. For example, the line item in next year's budget for purchases is calculated by increasing last year's purchases for inflation and including any incremental purchases due to volume changes and new programmes. Only detailed explanations to justify the increments are submitted or reviewed. These **incremental budgets** are reviewed and changed at higher levels in the organization, but usually only the incremental changes are examined in detail. The base/core budget (i.e. last year's base budget) is taken as given.

Under **zero-base budgeting** (ZBB), senior management mandates that each line item in total must be justified and reviewed each year. Each line item is reset to *zero* each year. Departments must defend the entire expenditure each year, not just the changes. In a zero-base budget review, the following questions are generally asked:

■ Should this activity be provided?
■ What will happen if the activity is eliminated?
■ At what quality/quantity level should the activity be provided?
■ Can the activity be provided in some alternative way, such as outsourcing the activity to another organization?
■ How much are other, similar companies spending on this activity (benchmarking)?

In principle, ZBB motivates managers to maximize firm value by identifying and eliminating those expenditures whose total costs exceed total benefits. Under incremental budgeting, in which incremental changes are added to the base budget, incremental expenditures are deleted when their costs exceed their incremental benefits. However, inefficient base budgets often continue to exist.

In practice, ZBB is used infrequently. ZBB is supposed to overcome traditional, incremental budgeting, but it often deteriorates into incremental budgeting. Each year under ZBB, the same justifications as those used in the previous year are typically submitted and adjusted for incremental changes. Since the volume of detailed reports rising up the organization is substantially larger under ZBB than under incremental budgeting, higher-level managers tend to focus on the changes from last year anyway. The focus on budgetary changes is especially true, if managers have been with the organization for a number of years and already know the 'base'-level budgets.

ZBB is most useful and common when new top-level managers come from outside the firm. These new managers do not have the specialized knowledge incorporated in the base budgets. New outside managers also bring changes in strategy. Prior budgets are no longer as relevant with each line item requiring justification in light of these changing goals and strategies. However, ZBB is substantially more costly to conduct and is unlikely to continue once management has gained knowledge of operations and the budgets have encompassed the new goals.

Mother Goose Child-Care Centre (continued)

The Board of Directors of the Mother Goose Child-Care Centre (MGCC) is primarily concerned about the annual budget. The purchase of a building for MGCC is the only strategic issue that the Board is examining. This long-term decision will be based primarily on demand for child care and pre-school education in the Selly Oak Ward. Long-term demand for MGCC child care and pre-school education is a function of the cost, perceived quality of care and instruction, competition from other care providers, and the future demographics of the Selly Oak Ward and the city of Birmingham more generally. Information on these factors is located with the Board of Directors, who are responsible for making this decision. Therefore, the budgeting process is not necessary to communicate the information.

The child-care manager and the head teacher of the pre-school programme are relatively new, so the Board of Directors has decided to use a line-item budget. The line-item budget relieves the child-care manager and head teacher of decisions regarding how to spend the money allocated to the programmes. The Board of Directors also uses a lapsing budget, so the novice programme leaders need not make decisions on the periods in which to spend resources.

A static budget is developed based on the original projection of enrolment. The programme leaders are responsible for the quality of their programmes, which is the determining factor in whether or not parents keep their children at MGCC. Any lost revenue due to drop-outs during the year is the responsibility of the programme leaders, so flexible budgeting would provide the wrong incentives.

MGCC's Board of Directors has been around for longer than the programme leaders. This continuity brings considerable experience in budgeting for MGCC. In addition, the operational procedures of MGCC have not changed much over the years, so the Board has budget and accounting data from past years that can be used to prepare the new budget. Therefore, MGCC uses an incremental approach to budgeting.

Concept **review**

1 How do short-term and long-term budgets relate to planning and control?

2 How do line-item budgets affect the responsibilities of a manager?

3 What are the costs and benefits of budget lapsing?

4 How do the responsibilities of the manager influence the choice between static and flexible budgets?

5 Under what conditions is zero-base budgeting useful?

COMPREHENSIVE MASTER BUDGET ILLUSTRATION

The previous sections described the basic concepts that must be considered in budgeting. This section describes how to construct a **master budget**, which integrates the estimates from each department to predict production requirements, financing, cash flows and financial statements at the end of the period. The master budget serves as a guide and benchmark for the entire organization.

To prevent the example from becoming overwhelming with respect to the amount of data, a simple firm, NaturApples, an apple processor, is used. This example describes how various parts of the organization develop their budgets. It illustrates the importance of co-ordinating the volume of activity across the different parts of the organization and how budgets are then combined for the firm as a whole.

■ Description of the firm: NaturApples

NaturApples processes apples into two products, applesauce and apple-pie filling. Apples are purchased from local growers. They are processed and packed in metal recyclable cans as either applesauce or pie filling. Principal markets are institutional buyers, such as hospitals, public schools, military bases and universities. NaturApples' market is regional and is serviced by four salespeople, who make direct calls on customers in South England.

The firm is organized into two departments, production and marketing. A director, who reports directly to the chairman, heads each department. In addition, there is a director of finance, who is responsible for all financial aspects of the firm, including collecting data and preparing budgets. The three directors and the chairman comprise NaturApples' executive committee, which oversees the budgeting process.

Independent farmers in the region grow the apples. Once harvested, the apples are purchased through the efforts of the director of finance and stored either in coolers at

Bad data like bad apples can disrupt the entire budget process; therefore, most firms retain budget responsibility at executive levels.

NaturApples or in third-party warehouses until NaturApples can process them. The processing plant operates for nine months of the year. In October, the plant starts up after a three-month shutdown. Workers first thoroughly clean and inspect all the processing equipment. The apples begin arriving in the middle of October and by the end of November, all of the apple harvest is in warehouses or in production. By June, all the apples have been processed and the plant shuts down for July, August and September. NaturApples has a financial year starting 1 October and ending 30 September.

For both applesauce and pie filling, the production process begins with the inspection, washing, peeling and coring of the apples. Next, the apples are either mashed for applesauce or diced for pie filling. The apples then are combined with other ingredients, such as spices and chemical stabilisers, and cooked in vats. Both products are immediately canned on a single canning line in five-pound cans and packed in cases of 12 cans per case. At this point, the product has a two-year shelf life and is stored until ordered by the customer.

■ Overview of the budgeting process

The budgeting process begins on 1 December, 10 months before the start of the financial year. The chairman and director of finance forecast the next year's crop harvest, which will determine the purchase cost of apples. The director of marketing begins forecasting sales of applesauce and pie filling next year. Likewise, the production director forecasts production costs and capacity. Every two months for the next 10 months, these marketing, processing, and apple procurement forecasts and budgets are revised in light of new information. All three directors and the chairman then meet for a morning to discuss their revisions. On 1 August, the executive committee adopts the final master budget for the next financial year, which begins on 1 October, and then takes it to the board of directors for final approval. The executive committee also meets weekly to review current-year operations as compared to budget and to discuss other operational issues. Figure 8.1 is a schematic diagram that illustrates the relations among the component budgets of NaturApples' master budget. The final product of the master budget is the budgeted profit and loss statement, budgeted balance sheet, and budgeted cash flows at the bottom of Figure 8.1. All the other budgets provide the supporting detail, including the various key planning assumptions underlying the master budget.

The budgeting process should yield budgets that are internally consistent. For example, the amount of apples purchased should be equated to the amount processed into sauce and pie filling. To maintain consistency, a sequential and simultaneous process, similar to Figure 8.1, is commonly used. The budgeting process normally begins with a sales estimate, but the sales estimate depends on the price of the product.

Figure 8.1 Budgeting process – NaturApples

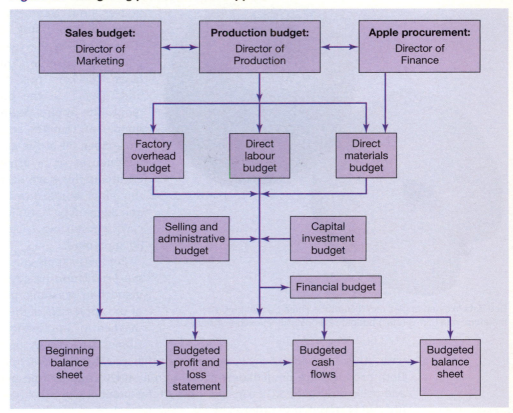

Sales quantities and prices should be chosen to maximize profits. The sales estimate also must consider production costs. The production costs depend on the availability and cost of raw materials (apples), direct labour and overhead. Thus, the sales budget, the production budget and apple procurement should be considered jointly.

The production budget includes raw materials, direct labour and factory overhead budgets. These budgets jointly affect the estimated cost of goods sold. Not all expenditures are treated as part of the cost of goods sold. Selling and administrative expenditures are treated as expenses in financial reporting and are budgeted separately.

The production budget is also used to determine whether new property, plant or equipment must be purchased to have sufficient capacity to meet production requirements. The capital investment budget reflects the estimated purchase of property, plant and equipment for the next fiscal year.

Capital expenditures require cash. If cash is not available from operations, the firm may have to borrow to make large purchases. The financial budget is used to plan for borrowing, issuing share capital, and making interest and dividend payments.

The individual budgets for sales, production, capital investments and so forth are used to estimate financial statements at the end of the financial year. The estimated profit and loss statement and cash-flow statement are used to adjust the beginning balance sheet to form an estimated ending balance sheet. The remainder of this section illustrates the preparation of these various component budgets and the estimated financial statements.

Table 8.3 is the estimated balance sheet for the beginning of the financial year. The beginning balance sheet is estimated, as the budget is determined before the end of

Table 8.3

NaturApples		
Expected Beginning Balance Sheet		
1 October 2008		
Assets	£	£
Cash		100,000
Accounts receivable		200,000
Inventory		
Sauce (13,500 cases × £58/case)	783,000	
Pie filling (2,500 cases × £48/case)	120,000	903,000
Property, plant and equipment (net)		2,300,000
		3,503,000
Liabilities and shareholders' equity		
Accounts payable		100,000
Long-term debt		1,000,000
Shareholders' equity		2,403,000
		3,503,000

the previous financial year. The beginning balance sheet represents the starting point for operations in the upcoming financial year.

■ Sales budget

The sales (revenue) budget is generally created with the help of the marketing department. Employees of the marketing department usually have more information about the nature of potential customers. Moreover, they can provide insights on the relation between the selling price and the quantity that customers will purchase. The production department also must be involved in setting the sales budget because cost information is important in setting prices.

At NaturApples, the executive committee agrees on an estimate of next year's sales and prices based on information from the marketing and production departments. The sales budget for the next financial year is given in Table 8.4. The executive committee agrees that the firm should be able to sell 140,000 cases of sauce at £68 per case and 60,000 cases of pie filling at £53. After months of exploring alternative price and quantity assumptions, these quantities and prices were finalized. In particular, the budgeted prices and quantities represent the managers' best judgement of the quantity at which marginal revenue equals marginal cost. Presumably, higher prices (and thus lower sales) or lower prices (and higher sales) will both result in lower profits than the combinations presented in Table 8.4.

Table 8.4

NaturApples			
Sales Budget			
for financial year beginning			
1 October 2008			
	Budgeted cases	*Budgeted price/case (£)*	*Budgeted revenue (£)*
Sauce	140,000	68	9,520,000
Pie filling	60,000	53	3,180,000
Total			12,700,000

■ Production budget

The second major component of the master budget is the production budget. The production volume is chosen based on the following equation:

Beginning inventory + Production = Sales + Desired ending inventory

or

Production = Sales + Desired ending inventory − Beginning inventory

The total units in beginning inventory plus the units produced during the financial year must be either sold or in ending inventory. Any units scrapped are considered part of production.

Numerical example 8.3

The SB Company manufactures soccer balls. In the next year, the company expects to sell 20,000 soccer balls. The company has 2,000 soccer balls in its beginning inventory and wants to have 1,000 soccer balls in its ending inventory. How many soccer balls should the company plan to manufacture?

Solution

Production = Sales + Ending inventory − Beginning inventory

= 20,000 + 1,000 − 2,000 = 19,000

The SB Company should manufacture 19,000 soccer balls.

To solve for the number of units to produce at NaturApples, sales estimates from the sales budget in Table 8.4 are used. In addition, the beginning inventory from the expected beginning balance sheet in Table 8.3 must be estimated and a desired ending inventory position must be projected. Table 8.5 presents the estimation of units to be produced, given a desired ending inventory level of 5,000 cases of sauce and 1,000 cases of pie filling. This ending inventory amount should cover expected sales in October, before production begins for the next financial year.

The budgeted number of units to be produced during the year is used as a basis for estimating the required amounts of direct materials, direct labour and factory overhead. This information is usually derived through discussions with the individual in charge of operations. For NaturApples, 25 kilograms of apples and 0.60 hours of direct labour are necessary to make a case of sauce. To make a case of pie filling, 20 kilograms of apples and 0.50 direct labour hours are necessary. The cost of apples is estimated to

Table 8.5

		NaturApples				
		Number of Cases to be Produced				
		1 October 2008 to 30 September 2009				
Product	Sales	+ Ending inventory	−	Beginning inventory	=	Production
Sauce	140,000	5,000		13,500		131,500
Pie filling	60,000	1,000		2,500		58,500

Table 8.6

NaturApples
Production Budget
1 October 2008 to 30 September 2009

Raw materials

Product	Kilograms per case ×	Cases =	Kilograms ×	Cost per kilogram (£) =	Cost (£)
Sauce	25	131,500	3,287,500	0.80	2,630,000
Pie filling	20	58,500	1,170,000	0.80	936,000
Total			4,457,500		3,566,000

Direct labour

Product	Hours per case ×	Cases =	Hours ×	Cost per hour (£) =	Cost (£)
Sauce	0.60	131,500	78,900	10	789,000
Pie filling	0.50	58,500	29,250	10	292,500
Total			108,150		1,081,500

Overhead

Product	Direct labour cost ×	Overhead per £ of direct labour =	Cost (£)
Sauce	£789,000	2	1,578,000
Pie filling	292,500	2	585,000
Total			2,163,000*

*Includes £400,000 of depreciation expense

Product costs

Product	Total product cost (£) (Materials + Labour + Overhead) ÷	Cases =	Cost per case (£)
Sauce	4,997,000	131,500	38
Pie filling	1,813,500	58,500	31
Total	6,810,500		

be £0.80 per kilogram, and the cost of direct labour is estimated to be £10 per hour. Factory overhead is estimated to occur at the rate of £2 for every £1 of direct labour. Table 8.6 is the production budget for NaturApples and includes the raw materials, direct labour and factory overhead budget.

The production budget in Table 8.6 determines that 4,457,500 kilograms of apples must be purchased to achieve the production target. If spoilage is a problem, then more apples to cover expected spoilage must be obtained. The production budget also provides an estimate of the direct labour requirements. To meet production targets, the company should plan on 108,150 hours of direct labour. The production budget also estimates the cost of apples, direct labour and overhead. The overhead depreciation expense is identified separately, as depreciation does not involve the use of cash. This point is important to recognize for cash-flow planning purposes.

The production budget in Table 8.6 is an annual budget. The company may want to have monthly production budgets as well. Monthly production budgets are useful for planning cash flows and material and labour requirements, especially when production is cyclical, as in the case of NaturApples.

■ Selling and administration budget

Selling and administrative expenses are treated as period expenses for financial reporting purposes, even though some of these costs can be traced to products. The generation of estimated (end-of-year) financial statements is one of the functions of the

Table 8.7

NaturApples Selling and Administration Budget for financial year beginning 1 October 2008	
Selling and administrative areas	£
Marketing	470,000
Finance	160,000
Shipping	380,000
Chairman's office	180,000
Total selling and administration	1,190,000

budgeting process. Therefore, selling and administrative expenses are frequently identified separately.

The selling and administration budget for NaturApples in Table 8.7 contains the remaining operating expenses, including the costs of the marketing department, finance, shipping, and the chairman's office. The total of all these administrative costs is £1.19 million.

■ Capital investment budget

The capital investment budget is used for major, planned purchases of property, plant and equipment. These purchases generally appear as fixed assets on the balance sheet, but could include R&D expenditures for a new product. R&D spending would be expensed for financial reporting purposes.

In the process of establishing the production budget, the executive committee of NaturApples recognizes that an additional coring machine and a dicing machine must be purchased to increase capacity. The capital investment budget in Table 8.8 includes the expected purchase price of the two machines.

■ Financial budget

One reason for budgeting is to ensure that ample cash is available for operations and major purchases. If cash shortages are expected, the organization must plan to borrow money to cover these shortages. The financial budget is used to plan for borrowing cash and to record planned interest expense, retirement of debt, issuance of stock and the payment of dividends.

Table 8.8

NaturApples Capital Investment Budget 1 October 2008 to 30 September 2009		
Capital investment project	*Purchase date*	*Cost (£)*
Coring machine	05/10/2008	40,000
Dicing machine	05/10/2008	80,000
Total		120,000

Numerical **example** 8.4

At the beginning of the month, the Trevor Book Store has cash of €1,000 and accounts receivable of €4,000. This month, the manager of the book store plans to collect 80 per cent of the beginning accounts receivable, make sales of €8,000 (€5,000 in cash and €3,000 on account due next month), and make payments of €12,000 to book publishers. How much must the book store borrow this month?

Solution

	€
Beginning cash balance	1,000
Collection of receivables (0.80 × €4,000)	3,200
Cash sales	5,000
Payments to publishers	(12,000)
Ending cash balance without financing	(2,800)

The manager must borrow at least €2,800 to cover the cash shortfall.

NaturApples must purchase both the coring machine and dicing machine early in the financial year. Given that the beginning cash balance is insufficient to cover this purchase, NaturApples must borrow an additional £100,000 from the bank. Near the end of the financial year, however, NaturApples should have enough cash to pay off the loan, resolve an additional £200,000 of long-term debt, and pay shareholders £2,000,000 in dividends. In addition, the executive committee estimates that interest costs during the financial year will be £100,000. This information is provided in the financial budget in Table 8.9.

■ Budgeted financial statements

Budgeted financial statements are the end product of the budgeting process. In a for-profit organization, these statements include the budgeted profit and loss statement, the budgeted cash-flow statement, and the budgeted balance sheet. These budgeted financial statements provide a picture of the organization's financial condition at the end of the budget period, if events happen according to plan.

Table 8.9

NaturApples
Financial Budget
1 October 2008 to 30 September 2009

Financial transactions	Date	Amount (£)
Loan from bank	05/10/2008	100,000
Repayment of bank loan	05/04/2009	(100,000)
Retirement of long-term debt	01/06/2009	(200,000)
Payment of interest	31/12/2009	(50,000)
Payment of interest	30/06/2009	(50,000)
Payment of dividends	30/09/2009	(2,000,000)
Net cash flow from financial transactions		(2,300,000)

Table 8.10

NaturApples Budgeted Profit and Loss Statement 1 October 2008 to 30 September 2009	£	£	£
Revenues (Sales budget)			12,700,000
Cost of goods sold			
Beginning inventory (Beg. balance sheet)		903,000	
+ Production costs (Production budget)		6,810,500	
− Ending inventory (Production budget)			
Sauce (£38/case × 5,000 cases)	190,000		
Pie filling (£31/case × 1,000 cases)	31,000	(221,000)	(7,492,500)
Gross margin			5,207,500
Selling and administrative expenses (Selling and admin. budget)			(1,190,000)
Interest expense (Financial budget)			(100,000)
Net profit before taxes			3,917,500
Taxes (£3,917,500 × 0.40)			1,567,000
Net profit			2,350,500
Beginning shareholders' equity (Beg. balance sheet)			2,403,000
+ Net profit (from above)			2,350,500
− Dividends (Financial budget)			(2,000,000)
Ending shareholders' equity			2,753,500

The budgeted profit and loss statement

Most elements in the budgeted profit and loss statement come from parts of the prior budgets. The cost of goods sold is the one part of the budgeted profit and loss statement that remains to be estimated. The estimation of the cost of goods sold depends on the accounting method used to record the flow of inventory costs. The first-in-first-out (FIFO) method assumes that the products sold are from the beginning inventory and early production, and that the products most recently made are in the ending inventory. Other inventory-costing methods include last-in-first-out (LIFO) and average costing. These inventory-costing methods are explained further in the Appendix to Chapter 10 and in financial accounting textbooks.

NaturApples employs the FIFO method, so the estimated cost of ending inventory is determined using the most recent product costs (£38 per case for sauce and £31 per case for pie filling).

Tax planning is also part of the budgeting process. For the next financial year, NaturApples expects to pay 40 per cent of its net profit in taxes. Table 8.10 contains the budgeted profit and loss statement for NaturApples. The numbers in the statement come from the previous budgets.

The budgeted cash-flow statement

The budgeting of cash flows is extremely important to an organization. Running out of cash is inconvenient and can lead to bankruptcy, even though the organization is profitable. Simply stated, accounting profit is not the same as cash on hand. Therefore, monthly budgeted cash-flow statements should be prepared to avoid cash shortfalls.

Cash-flow statements identify cash flows from operations, capital investments, and financial transactions. These transactions are captured in the sales, production, selling and administration, capital investment, and financial budgets.

In addition, the collection of accounts receivable and the payment of accounts payable influence cash flows. Hastening the collection of receivables and postponing the payment of payables can have a positive short-term effect on cash flows. However, such behaviour may not be consistent with the goals of the organization. For example, rather than billing customers 30 days later, requiring them to pay cash might reduce total sales. For the purpose of annual budgeting, cash-flow effects can be determined by estimating ending balances in the receivables and payables accounts and calculating the change in those balances from the beginning of the year. Decreases in accounts receivable and increases in accounts payable mean more cash available. Increases in accounts receivable and decreases in accounts payable mean less cash available.

Numerical example 8.5

The Kreuger Corporation had beginning accounts receivable and accounts payable balances of €20,000 and €10,000, respectively. The corporation estimates that ending balances for accounts receivable and accounts payable will be €30,000 and €5,000, respectively. What are the cash-flow implications?

Solution

Change in accounts receivable: €30,000 − €20,000 = €10,000
  The increase of €10,000 implies a €10,000 decline in cash available.
Change in accounts payable: €5,000 − €10,000 = (€5,000)
  The decrease of €5,000 implies a €5,000 decline in cash available.
The combined effect is a €15,000 decline in cash available.

The executive committee at NaturApples estimates that accounts receivables at the end of the next fiscal year will be £300,000 and accounts payable will be £150,000. The budgeted cash-flow statement is presented in Table 8.11.

The budgeted balance sheet

The budgeting process begins with a beginning balance sheet. These beginning balances are adjusted for expected events during the coming fiscal year. The adjusted balances of each account comprise the budgeted balance sheet for the end of the fiscal year. The budgeted balance sheet for NaturApples is shown in Table 8.12.

The budgeted financial statements (profit and loss, cash-flow, and balance sheet) are called **pro-forma financial statements**. Pro-forma financial statements provide a prediction of how financial statements will look in the future, if the expected events occur. Financial statements are used to measure performance; thus managers are very concerned about the pro-forma financial statements. If the organization's top managers do not like the pro-forma financial statements that result from the budgeting process, they will ask organizational members to repeat the budgeting process using different strategies and assumptions. This process continues until the pro-forma financial statements meet expectations, or top management is convinced that better alternative plans do not exist.

Concept review

1 What is normally the first step in the master budget process?
2 How are estimated sales and inventory levels used to estimate production requirements?
3 Why is a financial budget necessary?
4 What are pro-forma financial statements?

Table 8.11

NaturApples
Budgeted Cash-Flow Statement
1 October 2008 to 30 September 2009

	£	£
Cash flows from operations		
Profit (Profit and loss statement)		2,350,500
Depreciation (Profit and loss statement)		400,000
		2,750,500
Change in accounts receivable		
Ending accounts receivable (Predicted)	300,000	
Beginning accounts receivable (Beg. bal. sheet)	(200,000)	(100,000)
Change in inventory		
Ending inventory (Predicted)	221,000	
Beginning inventory (Beg. bal. sheet)	903,000	682,000
Change in accounts payable		
Ending accounts payable (Predicted)	150,000	
Beginning accounts payable (Beg. bal. sheet)	(100,000)	50,000
Total cash flows from operations		3,382,500
Cash flows for capital investments (Cap. inv. budget)		
Purchase of coring machine	(40,000)	
Purchase of dicing machine	(80,000)	(120,000)
Cash flows for financial transactions (Financing budget) *		
Loan from bank	100,000	
Repayment of bank loan	(100,000)	
Retirement of long-term debt	(200,000)	
Payment of dividends	(2,000,000)	(2,200,000)
Change in cash balance		1,062,500
Beginning cash balance		100,000
Ending cash balance		1,162,500

*The interest is already included in the net profit figure.

Table 8.12

NaturApples
Budgeted Balance Sheet
30 September 2009

	£	£
Assets		
Cash (Cash-flow statement)		1,162,500
Accounts receivable (Predicted)		300,000
Inventory (Predicted)		
Sauce (£38/case × 5,000 cases)	190,000	
Pie filling (£31/case × 1,000 cases)	31,000	221,000
Property, plant and equipment (Net)		
Beginning balance (Beg. bal. sheet)	2,300,000	
Capital investments (Cap. inv. budget)	120,000	
Depreciation (Profit and loss statement)	(400,000)	2,020,000
		3,703,500
Liabilities and shareholders' equity		
Accounts payable (Predicted)		150,000
Long-term debt		
Beginning balance (Beg. bal. sheet)	1,000,000	
Retirement (Financing budget)	(200,000)	800,000
Shareholders' equity (Profit and loss statement)		2,753,500
		3,703,500

Mother Goose Child-Care Centre (continued)

Mother Goose Child-Care Centre Master Budget

MGCC's Board of Directors has asked the two programme leaders to estimate the number of children that will attend their programmes next year. The child-care programme manager estimates an average of 24 children every month. The head teacher of the pre-school programme estimates 30 children for the morning session and 35 children for the afternoon session. These estimates are consistent with the survey performed by the Board of Directors. The revenue budget for MGCC is as follows:

Programme	Children	Price/month (£)	Months	Revenues (£)
Child-care	24	600	12	172,800
Pre-school	65	450	9	263,250
Total revenues				436,050

The operating (production) budget of MGCC encompasses the operations of the two MGCC programmes. Given the enrolment estimates, the child-care programme manager is given the right to hire six full-time child-care assistants. The head teacher of the pre-school programme is given the right to hire three and a half full-time instructors (three for both the morning and afternoon, and one for just the afternoon). The expected annual cost of hiring a child-care assistant is £18,000 and the expected cost of hiring a pre-school instructor is £20,000 for 9 months. Resources for educational supplies are allotted to the programmes based on the estimated number of registrations per year. The current rate is £400 for each child. The following budget also includes the programme leaders' salaries.

		£
Child-care programme		
Programme manager		20,000
Assistants	(6 × £18,000)	108,000
Educational supplies	(£400 × 24)	9,600
Total		137,600
Pre-school programme		
Head teacher		20,000
Instructors	(3.5 × £20,000)	70,000
Educational supplies	(£400 × 65)	26,000
Total		116,000
Total programme costs		253,600

MGCC also has a selling and administrative budget. This budget includes advertising, rent, insurance, and the salaries of the office manager, secretary, bookkeeper and on-call nurse.

Selling and administrative budget	£
Advertising	10,000
Rent	80,000
Insurance	15,000
Salaries	50,000
Total	155,000

The Board of Directors of MGCC decides that the coming year is a good time to update the computer equipment in the office and the classrooms. The planned expenditure is £30,000. MGCC is a not-for-profit organization. Not-for-profit organizations typically do not have profit and loss statements. MGCC operates strictly on a cash basis and does not record payables and receivables. Fixed assets, such as computers, are treated as cash expenditures and not recognized as assets. MGCC is a service organization and has no inventory. Any leftover supplies from one period are considered immaterial. Therefore, MGCC is only concerned about the cash flows, and the beginning and ending cash balance.

MGCC has an estimated beginning cash balance of £10,000. The following cash-flow statement is used to estimate the ending cash balance.

	£
Beginning cash balance	10,000
Estimated revenues	436,050
Programme costs	(253,600)
Selling and administrative costs	(155,000)
Capital investments (computers)	(30,000)
Ending cash balance	7,450

SUMMARY

1 **Use budgeting for planning purposes.** Budgeting facilitates the flow of information from the bottom up for general planning and from the top down for co-ordination.

2 **Use budgeting for control purposes.** The budget is used to allocate responsibilities to different members of the organization and to establish performance measures, which are used to reward managers.

3 **Identify the conflicts that exist between planning and control in the budgeting process.** The flow of information in the budgeting process might be inhibited or biased as the information used for planning is often the same information used for performance evaluation.

4 **Describe the benefits of having both short-term and long-term budgets.** Long-term budgets are used for long-term planning. Short-term budgets are used for both planning and control.

5 **Explain the responsibility implications of a line-item budget.** Line-item budgets constrain responsibilities by limiting the ability of managers to shift resources from one use to another.

6 **Identify the costs and benefits of budget lapsing.** Budget lapsing constrains the manager to expend resources in the budget period. This policy provides more control. However, managers are not able to use their specialized information to make more efficient decisions, and are frequently motivated to consume excess resources during the budgeted period.

7 **Develop flexible budgets and identify when flexible budgeting should be used instead of static budgeting.** Flexible budgeting adjusts for volume effects. If the manager cannot control volume, the flexible budget provides more appropriate numbers for evaluating the manager.

8 **Explain the costs and benefits of using zero-base budgeting.** Zero-base budgeting (ZBB) is costly, because each line item in total must be justified. The benefit of ZBB is the additional flow of information that might be useful to new managers and might lead to more efficient use of resources.

9 **Create a master budget for an organization including sales, production, administration, capital investment and financial budgets.** The master budget is a plan for a certain period that includes expected sales, operating costs (production and administration), major investments and methods to finance those investments.

10 **Create pro-forma financial statements based on data from the sales, production, administration, capital investment and financial budgets.** The pro-forma statements include the budgeted profit and loss statement, the budgeted cash-flow statement, and the budgeted balance sheet.

11 **Use spreadsheets to analyse monthly cash flows. (Appendix)** Monthly cash-flow analysis is extremely important to determine if a cash shortage might arise in a given month. If a cash shortage is expected, the organization can plan to arrange some financing to allow the organization to pay its bills and continue to operate. Financial forecasting tools and spreadsheets offer a means of determining the sensitivity of cash flows to the budget estimates.

KEY TERMS

Adverse variances The amount by which budgeted costs are less than actual costs, or budgeted revenues are greater than actual revenues.

Budget lapsing Budgets for one period cannot be used to make expenditures in subsequent periods.

Budgeting Process of gathering information to assist in making forecasts.

Budgets Forecasts of future revenues and expenditures which translate organizational goals into financial terms.

Flexible budgets Budgets that adjust to some measure of volume.

Favourable variances The amount by which budgeted costs are greater than actual costs, or budgeted revenues are less than actual revenues.

Incremental budgets Use of last year's budget as a base to make future budgets.

Master budget A document that integrates all the estimates from the different departments to establish guidelines and benchmarks for the entire organization.

Participative budgeting The preparation of the initial budget forecast by eliciting information from those managers responsible for meeting the budget targets.

Pro-forma financial statements Financial statements based on forecasted data.

Static budgets Budgets that do not adjust for volume.

Strategic planning The process whereby managers select the firm's overall objectives and the tactics to achieve those objectives.

Variance The difference between a budgeted and an actual number.

Zero-base budgeting A budgeting process whereby each line item in total must be justified and reviewed each year.

APPENDIX
Monthly cash-flow estimates and spreadsheets

One of the most important aspects of budgeting is to be certain that the organization has sufficient cash. Many organizations that are growing tend to under-estimate the amount of cash that will be needed. Cash is obviously needed for the purchase of long-term assets and production purposes. However, it is also needed to cover increases in inventory and other current assets. Accounts receivable, for example, tends to increase as sales increase. The organization must wait to be paid cash for sales made on credit. Sometimes the customer never pays the organization for its purchases.

An organization must estimate future cash flows carefully. If the cash balance becomes negative, the organization will not be able to pay its own bills. A cash shortfall can force a profitable organization into bankruptcy. Therefore, monthly budget predictions of cash flows are extremely important to avert an unexpected cash shortfall. If an organization can predict a cash shortfall early enough, plans can be altered to conserve cash, or the organization can plan to borrow cash.

Most events affecting future cash flows are not completely predictable. Sales, collection of accounts receivable and production costs are all difficult to predict. Yet unpredictability does not mean budgets for cash flows should not be made. Instead of making a single cash-flow budget, the organization should make multiple ones given different scenarios. These different scenarios reflect different estimates about sales and other events affecting cash flows. For example, cash flows could be estimated assuming a monthly increase in sales of 1 per cent per month, and then 2 per cent per month. By changing the estimate of the monthly growth in sales, a manager can look at the sensitivity of cash flows to sales estimates. A manager can obtain a range of plausible cash-flow estimates by varying the estimates of the different events affecting cash flows.

Analysing the sensitivity of cash flows to different estimates can be costly, if a manager must go through all the procedures of the master budget by hand for each different estimate. Financial forecasting tools and spreadsheets offer a quick means of analysing data that have specific relations. Once a spreadsheet is set up with the raw data and the functional relations, it is quite simple to change some of the parameters and obtain a new solution. In the case of cash flows, the relations among the different events have been outlined in the master budget and can be placed in spreadsheet form for analysis. Spreadsheets provide an efficient means to obtain cash-flow estimates for multiple scenarios. They also allow for simple updates of future monthly cash flows, once the outcomes of earlier months are known.

The example in Table 8.13 illustrates the functional relations that can be captured through spreadsheet analysis. The monthly cash-budgeting process begins with estimates of monthly sales. The purchase of inventory sold occurs two months prior to the sales month, but the bills for those purchases are paid in the month prior to the sale. There is a 30 per cent profit margin on sales. Other costs are estimated and paid in the month incurred. Large cash investments are identified separately. Sales are assumed to be composed of 20 per cent cash sales, 50 per cent credit sales that are collected in the following month, and 30 per cent credit sales that are collected in the second month following the sales transaction. Only sales, purchases and the accounts that affect cash flows and the cash balances are reported in this example. A typical spreadsheet analysis would have multiple, inter-related worksheets that could generate all of the pro-forma financial statements. The subscripts on the functional relations represent the month relative to month t.

The monthly cash-flow analysis in Table 8.13 indicates that the organization will have cash problems in May and June, primarily due to a large cash investment of £20,000 in fixed assets. If these estimates are accurate, the organization will have to borrow money in May, or reconsider the large cash investment.

The numbers in Table 8.13 are estimates or functions of estimates. No certainty exists that these estimates actually will occur. Suppose that in April an additional larger sale of £25,000 is possible. Spreadsheet analysis can accommodate this adjustment by simply increasing the April sales estimate of £15,000 by £25,000 to £40,000. Table 8.14 illustrates in bold the effects of this change on other accounts.

Table 8.13 Monthly cash-flow budget

Account	Functional relation	January (£)	February (£)	March (£)	April (£)	May (£)	June (£)
Sales	Estimated	10,000	20,000	25,000	15,000	10,000	20,000
Purchases	$(0.70 \times Sales_{t+2})$	17,500	10,500	7,000	14,000	21,000	15,000
Cash flow effects							
Cash sales	$(0.20 \times Sales_t)$	2,000	4,000	5,000	3,000	2,000	4,000
Collection of credit sales	$(0.50 \times Sales_{t-1}) +$ $(0.30 \times Sales_{t-2})$	10,000	10,000	13,000	18,500	15,000	12,500
Inventory payment	$Purchases_{t-1}$	(14,000)	(17,500)	(10,500)	(7,000)	(14,000)	(21,000)
Other costs	Estimated	(2,000)	(3,000)	(2,000)	(1,500)	(3,000)	(2,000)
Large cash investments	Estimated					(20,000)	
Net cash flows	Cash Sales$_t$ + Collections$_t$ − Payments$_t$ − Other costs$_t$ − Investments$_t$	(4,000)	(6,500)	(5,500)	13,000	(20,000)	(6,500)
Beg. cash balance	End. cash balance$_{t-1}$	20,000	16,000	9,500	4,000	17,500	(2,500)
End. cash balance	Beg. cash balance$_t$ + Net cash flows$_t$	16,000	9,500	4,000	17,000	(2,500)	(9,000)

Table 8.14 Monthly cash-flow budget with additional April sale

Account	Functional relation	January (£)	February (£)	March (£)	April (£)	May (£)	June (£)
Sales	Estimated	10,000	20,000	25,000	**40,000**	10,000	20,000
Purchases	$(0.70 \times Sales_{t+2})$	17,500	**28,000**	7,000	14,000	21,000	15,000
Cash flow effects							
Cash Sales	$(0.20 \times Sales_t)$	2,000	4,000	5,000	**8,000**	2,000	4,000
Collection of credit sales	$(0.50 \times Sales_{t-1}) +$ $(0.30 \times Sales_{t-2})$	10,000	10,000	13,000	18,500	**27,500**	**17,000**
Inventory payment	$Purchases_{t-1}$	(14,000)	(17,500)	**(28,000)**	(7,000)	(14,000)	(21,000)
Other costs	Estimated	(2,000)	(3,000)	(2,000)	(1,500)	(3,000)	(2,000)
Large cash investments	Estimated					(20,000)	
Net cash flows	$Cash Sales_t + Collections_t -$ $Payments_t - Other costs_t -$ $Investments_t$	(4,000)	(6,500)	(12,000)	18,000	(7,500)	(2,000)
Beg. cash balance	End. cash balance$_{t-1}$	20,000	16,000	9,500	**(2,500)**	15,500	8,000
End. cash balance	Beg. cash balance$_t$ + Net cash flows$_t$	16,000	9,500	**(2,500)**	15,500	8,000	6,000

The additional sale in Table 8.14 actually causes a cash shortage during an earlier month (March). The organization will be forced to borrow money in March. This shortage occurs because the organization must purchase the inventory before it sells it. The additional sale, however, provides sufficient cash flows in May and June to allow for the £20,000 cash investment.

Self-study problem

Joseph Chang, president of Changware Company, has developed a software program for accounting for drugstores. The firm's competitive strategy is to meet customer needs in the drugstore market by providing quality software. In the first year, sales were far greater than expected and Joseph hired additional marketing and customer service personnel. In addition, Joseph must keep up with the competition, so he has added more software engineers and programmers to create new software. This hiring increase caused Joseph to rent bigger facilities. Although Changware appears to be successful, Joseph has cash-flow problems with all the expansion activities. Joseph believes that it is time to compose a budget.

Required

a Describe the planning and control implications of the budgeting process for Changware.

b Should Changware emphasize short- or long-term budgets? Explain.

c Should Changware use line-item budgets, budget lapsing, flexible budgets or zero-base budgets? Explain.

Solution

a Changware needs a budget for two reasons: planning and control. Changware is in a state of growth and change. Rapid growth is requiring the use of additional cash, and Joseph Chang must plan to ensure that the company has sufficient cash. He must estimate cash inflows from sales and the collection of accounts receivable to determine whether sufficient cash is available to fund the expansion. If cash inflows from operations are insufficient, Joseph will have to investigate alternative methods of financing, such as bank loans or issuing stock.

  The growth in Changware also means that the firm will become more decentralized and require more control efforts. Joseph Chang will not be able to make all the decisions. The budget serves as a means to communicate organizational goals to other members of the organization, and to establish performance expectations. The budget also serves as a benchmark for rewarding individuals within the organization.

b Changware's budget probably should emphasize short-term planning and control. Organizational change and the volatile nature of the software industry make long-term budgets less valuable. The creation of organizational value depends upon Changware's ability to adapt quickly to changes in technology and the drugstore market.

c Ordinarily, the addition of many new employees would suggest the use of a line-item budget. Yet flexibility is extremely important in an industry with an average product life of about 18 months. A line-item budget might constrain the organization too much.

Budget lapsing probably will not be appropriate because the development of new software may take more than a year. Changware would not want to restrict funding to financial years. The company is more likely to budget for a project, rather than for a period of time.

Flexible budgets are appropriate if the responsible parties cannot control the volume of sales. The software-manufacturing unit is unlikely to have much control over volume, so flexible budgeting would be appropriate for that unit.

Zero-base budgeting is likely to be appropriate for the company, especially given that this is the first budget. Even subsequent budgets are not likely to be incremental due to the volatile nature of the business and the continual cycle of new products.

Numerical exercises

NE 8.1 Estimating production LO 1

The Shocker Company's sales budget shows quarterly sales for the next year as follows:

Quarter 1	10,000 units
Quarter 2	8,000 units
Quarter 3	12,000 units
Quarter 4	14,000 units

Company policy is to have a finished goods inventory at the end of each quarter equal to 20 per cent of the next quarter's sales.

Compute budgeted production for the second quarter of the next year.

(CMA adapted)

NE 8.2 Computing budgeted manufacturing costs LO 1

Candide Chocolate expects to sell 100,000 cases of chocolate bars during the next year. Budgeted costs per case are €150 for direct materials, €120 for direct labour and €75 for manufacturing overhead (all variable). Candide Chocolate begins the year with 40,000 cases of finished goods on hand and wants to end the year with 10,000 cases of finished goods inventory.

Compute the budgeted manufacturing costs of Candide Chocolate for the next year.

NE 8.3 Flexible budgets LO 7

A chair manufacturer has established the following flexible budget for the month.

	Units produced and sold		
	1,000	*1,500*	*2,000*
Sales (£)	10,000	15,000	20,000
Variable costs (£)	(5,000)	(7,500)	(10,000)
Fixed costs (£)	(2,000)	(2,000)	(2,000)
Profit (£)	3,000	5,500	8,000

a What is the sales price per chair?

b What is the expected profit if 1,600 chairs are made?

NE 8.4 Flexible budget LO 7

Tubbs Company has established the following flexible budget for the coming month.

Units produced	10,000	11,000	12,000
Total costs (£)	30,000	32,000	34,000

a What is the variable cost per unit?

b What is the fixed cost?

NE 8.5 Estimating cash collections and accounts receivable LO 11

Wolski Company expects sales in July to be €100,000. Of total sales, 20 per cent are cash and the remaining to be collected in August. Accounts receivable at the beginning of July is €70,000, which will be collected in July.

a How much cash is expected to be collected in July from accounts receivable and cash sales?
b What is the expected ending balance in July of accounts receivable?

NE 8.6 Variance analysis LO 2

A company had the following budgeted and actual results during the year:

	Budgeted (£)	Actual (£)
Revenues	200,000	210,000
Cost of goods sold	(100,000)	(75,000)
General administration	(20,000)	(18,000)
Selling expenses	(50,000)	(85,000)
Profit	30,000	32,000

Perform a variance analysis and identify variances that should be investigated.

NE 8.7 Flexible budgets LO 1

A company makes multiple products. Direct labour hours are used to measure activity. Variable costs are expected to be £40 per direct labour hour. Revenues are expected to be £60 per direct labour hour. The fixed manufacturing costs are expected to be £200,000 and the selling and administrative costs are expected to be fixed at £100,000.

Prepare a flexible budget for 20,000, 30,000 and 40,000 direct labour hours.

NE 8.8 Estimating production requirements LO 9

A company plans to sell 5,000 units and has beginning inventory equal to 500 units and plans to have 800 units in ending inventory.

How many units must be produced?

NE 8.9 Estimating direct materials LO 9

A company makes a product that requires 3 kilograms of raw material A and 5 metres of wire per unit. The cost of raw material A is £10 per kilogram. The cost of the wire is £1 per metre. There are 100 kilograms of raw material A in beginning inventory and the company would like to have 200 kilograms of raw material A in ending inventory. There are 200 metres of wire in beginning inventory and the company would like to have 500 metres of wire in ending inventory.

What is the cost of purchasing raw materials during the period if 1,000 units must be produced?

NE 8.10 Estimating cash collections and accounts receivable LO 11

A company plans to have sales of €20,000 in January, €30,000 in February and €40,000 in March. Cash sales are expected to be 20 per cent of the total and the remaining sales are sold on account and collected the month after the sales. Accounts receivable are €25,000 at the beginning of January.

How much cash from sales and the collection of accounts receivable are expected in January, February and March?

NE 8.11 Estimating cash flows LO 11

A company has the following beginning and expected ending balances:

	Beginning (£)	Ending (£)
Accounts receivable	40,000	30,000
Inventory	60,000	80,000
Accounts payable	20,000	35,000
Wages payable	10,000	12,000

What are the cash effects of these changes in the balances?

Numerical problems

NP 8.1 Estimating cash payments for inventory LO 1

The annual cost of goods sold for a company is expected to be £82,000. The beginning inventory balance is £25,000. The ending inventory balance is expected to be £21,000. All purchases are on credit. The beginning and ending balances for accounts payable are expected to be £11,000 and £8,000, respectively.

   What is the amount of cash payments made to pay accounts payable?

NP 8.2 Flexible budget LO 7

The Topper Restaurant uses a flexible budget to estimate profit in each month. The restaurant expects to charge €15 per meal on average. Some costs are assumed to vary with the number of meals served. The restaurant estimates a variable cost of €5 per meal served. The restaurant also has monthly fixed costs of €10,000.

   Prepare a monthly flexible budget of total revenue, costs and profit given that 1,000 meals, 1,500 meals, and 2,000 meals are served.

NP 8.3 Estimating production costs LO 1

The Fancy Umbrella Company makes recyclable beach umbrellas. The production process requires 3 square metres of plastic sheeting and a metal pole. The plastic sheeting costs £0.50 per square metre and each metal pole costs £1.00. At the beginning of the month, the company has 5,000 square metres of plastic and 1,000 poles in raw materials inventory. The preferred raw material amount at the end of the month is 3,000 square metres of plastic sheeting and 600 poles. At the beginning of the month, the company has 300 finished umbrellas in inventory. It plans to have 200 finished umbrellas at the end of the month. Sales in the coming month are expected to be 5,000 umbrellas.

a How many umbrellas must the company produce to meet demand and have sufficient ending inventory?
b What is the cost of materials that must be purchased?

NP 8.4 Estimating cash requirements LO 11

Humdrum Company is worried about cash flows. The company has £1,000 in cash at the start of February. January's total sales were £20,000 and total sales in February are expected to be £30,000. Sales are 30 per cent cash sales and 70 per cent account sales collected in the following month. Production costs in February are expected to be £25,000, all of which must be paid during February. The company would also like to buy equipment that costs £10,000.

   How much will the company have to borrow to have £800 in cash at the end of February?

NP 8.5 Production requirements LO 1

The Birdie Company makes badminton racquets. Beginning inventory for the coming year is 1,000 racquets. During the year, the company expects to sell 10,000 racquets and wants to have 800 racquets in inventory at the end of the year.

   How many racquets must the company produce during the year to meet demand and to have sufficient inventory at the end of the year?

NP 8.6 Pro-forma financial statements LO 9, 10

The Gold Bay Hotel is developing a master budget and pro-forma financial statements for 2009. The beginning balance sheet for the fiscal year 2009 is estimated to be as follows:

Gold Bay Hotel
Estimated Balance Sheet
1 January 2009

	£		£
Cash	20,000	Accounts payable	20,000
Accounts receivable	30,000	Notes payable	500,000
Facilities	3,010,000	Share capital	100,000
Accumulated dep.	(1,100,000)	Retained earnings	1,340,000
Total Assets	1,960,000	Total equities	1,960,000

During the year, the hotel expects to rent 30,000 rooms. Rooms rent for an average of £90 per night. Additionally, the hotel expects to sell 40,000 meals at an average price of £20 per meal. The variable cost per room rented is £30, and the variable cost per meal is £8. The fixed costs, excluding depreciation, are projected to be £2,000,000. Depreciation is expected to be £500,000. The hotel also plans to refurbish the kitchen at a cost of £200,000, which is capitalized (included in the facility account). Interest on the notes payable is expected to be £50,000, and £100,000 of the notes payable will be retired during the year. The ending accounts receivable balance is projected to be £40,000 and the ending accounts payable balance is expected to be £30,000.

Prepare pro-forma financial statements for the end of the year.

NP 8.7 Estimating direct materials purchase LO 1

The Jung Corporation's budget calls for the following production:

Quarter 1	45,000 units
Quarter 2	38,000 units
Quarter 3	34,000 units
Quarter 4	48,000 units

Each unit of product requires three kilograms of direct material. The company's policy is to begin each quarter with an inventory of direct materials equal to 30 per cent of that quarter's direct material requirements.

Compute budgeted direct materials purchases for the third quarter.

(CMA adapted)

NP 8.8 Variance analysis LO 2

August Company's budget for the current month called for producing and selling 5,000 units at £8 each. Actual units produced and sold were 5,200, yielding revenue of £42,120. Variable costs per unit are budgeted at £3 and fixed costs are budgeted at £2 per unit. Actual variable costs were £3.30 and fixed costs were £12,000.

a Prepare a variance report for the current month's operations comparing actual and budgeted revenues and costs.
b Write a short memo analysing the current month's performance.

NP 8.9 Monthly estimates of cash flows LO 11

The Corner Hardware Store is developing a budget to estimate monthly cash balances in the near future. At the end of December the cash balance is £6,000 and the accounts payable balance is £30,000 (reflecting December's purchases of inventory). The Corner Hardware Store expects £40,000 in sales in January and an increase in sales of 2 per cent per month over the next six months. All sales are on a cash basis. Inventory purchases are expected to rise at the same rate as are sales. Inventory purchases are paid in the month following the purchase. Other monthly cash outflows are expected to be £10,000 per month.

a How much money will the store have to borrow to pay £20,000 for a new computer system in May?
b How much will the store have to borrow to pay £20,000 for a new computer system in May, if sales and purchases are expected to increase by 5 per cent per month?

NP 8.10 Monthly estimates of cash flows LO 11

The Quality Auto Parts Wholesaler maintains an inventory of car parts to supply local car-repair shops. The company is making cash-flow estimates for the coming year. The monthly inventory purchases are sufficient to cover sales for a two-month period, but the bills for those purchases are paid in the month prior to their sale. There is a 20 per cent profit margin on sales. Other costs are €2,000 per month and paid in the month incurred. Sales are assumed to be composed of 10 per cent cash sales, 70 per cent credit sales that are collected in the following month and 20 per cent credit sales that are collected in the second month following the sales transaction. The cash balance at the beginning of March is €5,000. The following are the expected sales by month:

Account	January	February	March	April	May	June	July	August
Sales (€)	10,000	12,000	10,000	20,000	25,000	15,000	10,000	20,000

a What will be the cash balances for the end of March, April, May and June?
b Will the company have to borrow money during the months March through June?
c Would the firm have to borrow cash if June sales were expected to be €50,000 instead of €15,000?

NP 8.11 Master budget and pro-forma statements LO 9, 10

The Essex Eye Company (EEC) makes reading glasses. EEC's expected beginning balance sheet on 1 January 2009 follows:

The Essex Eye Company
Expected Beginning Balance Sheet
1 January 2009

Assets	£
Cash	80,000
Accounts receivable	50,000
Inventory (6,000 units at £6/unit)	36,000
Property, plant and equipment (net)	100,000
	266,000
Liabilities and shareholders' equity	
Accounts payable	100,000
Long-term debt	100,000
Shareholders' equity	66,000
	266,000

During 2009, EEC expects to sell 100,000 units (reading glasses) for £12 apiece. The reading glasses are sold on account, and the accounts receivable is expected to be £100,000 on 31 December 2009. The firm expects to have 10,000 reading glasses in inventory on 31 December 2009.

EEC uses a JIT-purchasing system with no raw materials inventory. Instead, EEC purchases raw materials only when needed immediately for the assembly of reading glasses at its Essex facility. The cost of the materials is £6 per unit. The raw materials are bought on account, and the company expects the accounts payable on 31 December 2009 to be £120,000.

Labour and overhead are treated as period expenses. The average direct labour for each pair of reading glasses is expected to be £2 per unit. The overhead is fixed and projected to be £200,000 for the year. Depreciation of £20,000 is included in fixed overhead. The remaining overhead requires cash payments.

During 2009, EEC plans to buy £50,000 in property, plant, and equipment and issue £20,000 more in long-term debt. The interest on the long-term debt for 2009 is expected to be £12,000. The firm expects to pay £10,000 in dividends in 2009.

Prepare a master budget for EEC and pro-forma statements for the period ending 31 December 2009.

NP 8.12 Flexible budgets LO 7

Hadrian Power manufactures small power supplies for car stereo systems. The company uses flexible budgeting techniques in order to deal with the seasonal and cyclical nature of the business. The accounting department provided the following data on budgeted manufacturing costs for the month of January 2009:

Hadrian Power
Planned Level of Production for
January 2009

	£
Budgeted production (in units)	14,000
Variable costs (vary with production)	
Direct materials	140,000
Direct labour	224,000
Indirect labour	21,000
Indirect materials	10,500
Maintenance	6,300
Fixed costs	
Supervision	24,700
Other (depreciation, taxes, etc.)	83,500
Total plant costs	510,000

In January 2009, actual operations are summarized below:

Hadrian Power
Actual Operations for
January 2009

	£
Actual production (in units)	15,400
Actual costs incurred:	
Direct materials	142,400
Direct labour	259,800
Indirect labour	27,900
Indirect materials	12,200
Maintenance	9,800
Supervision	28,000
Other costs (depreciation, taxes, etc.)	83,500
Total plant costs	563,600

a Prepare a report comparing the actual operating results to the flexible budget.

b Write a short memorandum analysing the report prepared in (a) above. What likely managerial implications do you draw from this report? (What are the numbers telling you?)

NP 8.13 Budgeting for a takeover LO 1

You work for a firm that specializes in mergers and takeovers, and your job is to analyse potential acquisitions. You are assigned the task to evaluate a possible merger between Europa and Italiana Airlines. These two carriers are competing in the European markets of Nice, Milan, Barcelona and Rome. Excess capacity currently exists in these two airlines. Your boss thinks that a merger of the two airlines, accompanied by cancelling some redundant flights and raising some fares, could create the 'synergy' necessary to make a positive return on the acquisition. Your boss asks you to provide her with an estimate of the first-year cost savings that would result from a combination of Europa and Italiana Airlines. You assemble the following operating data on the two airlines:

	Europa Airlines	Italiana Airlines
Passenger miles flown	72 million	80 million
Average price per passenger mile	€0.25	€0.25
Number of jets	3	4
Operating labour costs	€5 million	€6 million
Corporate office expense	€2 million	€2 million
Landing and parking fees*	€0.75 million	€1 million

*These fees are proportional to the number of jets in the fleet.

Both airlines are using the same type of jet. The annual operating costs and lease payment (including fuel, maintenance, licences and insurance) are €3 million per jet. After an analysis of the various markets served, you determine that a combination of the two airlines would result in the following operating characteristics: average price can be increased 10 per cent, some duplicate flights can be cancelled, and combined corporate office expenses can be cut by €1 million. The combination of the higher prices and reduced frequency of flights is expected to cut demand by 6 per cent. The existing flights have enough excess capacity to support a reduction in the fleet size of the combined airline by one jet.

Each firm's operating labour costs are proportional to the number of jets in the fleet. You assume that the combined firm will have operating labour costs per jet equal to that currently being incurred by Europa. However, Italiana Airlines' labour union contract specifies that employees with five or more years of service with the airline cannot be laid off in the event of a merger. Therefore, only some of the labour cost savings that could have been achieved by reducing the fleet to six jets will be achieved. An additional half million dollars of labour cost will be incurred as a result of the existing Italiana labour contract.

Prepare an analysis comparing the current profitability of the two airlines as independent firms, and of a combined firm using the planning assumptions stated above. Recommend a course of action, outlining other factors to consider in terms of the airlines' strategies and operating environment.

NP 8.14 Flexible budgets LO 7

Golf World is a 1,000-room luxury resort with swimming pools, tennis courts, three golf courses, and many other resort amenities.

The head golf course superintendent, Sandy Green, is responsible for all golf course maintenance and conditioning. Sandy also has the final say as to whether a particular course is open or closed due to weather conditions and whether players can rent motorized riding golf carts for use on a particular course. If the course is very wet, the golf carts will damage the turf, which Green's maintenance crew will have to repair. Since Sandy is out on the course every morning supervising the maintenance crews, she knows the condition of the course.

Wiley Grimes is in charge of the golf cart rentals. His crew maintains the golf cart fleet of over 200 carts, cleans them, puts oil and petrol in them, and repairs minor damage. He also is responsible for leasing the carts from the manufacturer, including the terms of the lease, the number of carts to lease and the choice of the cart vendor. When guests arrive at the golf course to play, they pay greens fees to play and a cart fee if they wish to use a cart. If they do not wish to rent a cart, they pay only the greens fee and walk the course.

Grimes and Green manage separate profit centres. The golf cart's profit centre revenues are composed of the fees collected from the carts. The revenues for the golf course profit centre are from the greens fees collected. In reviewing the results from April, golf cart operating profits were only 49 per cent of budget. Wiley argued that the poor results were due to the unusually heavy rains in April. He complained that the course was closed to golf carts for several days. Although only a few areas of the course were wet, the grounds crew was too busy to rope off these areas from carts, so that the entire course was closed to carts.

To better analyse the performance of the golf cart profit centre, the controller's office has implemented a flexible budget based on the number of cart rentals:

Golf World
Golf Cart Profit Centre
Operating Results April

	Static budget (£)	Actual results (£)	Variance from static budget (£)	Flexible budget (£)	Variance from flexible budget (£)
Number of cart rentals	6000	4000	2000	4000	0
Revenues (@ £25/cart)	150,000	100,000	50,000A	100,000	0
Labour (fixed cost)	7,000	7,200	200A	7,000	200A
Oil & petrol (@ £1/rental)	6,000	4,900	1,100F	4,000	900A
Cart lease (fixed cost)	40,000	40,000	0	40,000	0
Operating profit	97,000	47,900	49,100A	49,000	1,100A

a Evaluate the performance of the golf cart profit centre for the month of April.
b What are the advantages and disadvantages of the controller's new budgeting system?
c What additional recommendations would you make regarding the operations of Golf World?

NP 8.15 Flexible budgeting LO 7

Wielson Company employs flexible budgeting techniques to evaluate the performance of several of its activities. The selling-expense flexible budgets for three representative monthly activity levels are as follows:

Representative Monthly Flexible Budgets
for Selling Expenses

Activity measures:			
Unit sales volume	400,000	425,000	450,000
Sales volume	£10,000,000	£10,625,000	£11,250,000
Number of orders	4,000	4,250	4,500
Number of salespersons	75	75	75
Monthly expenses:	£	£	£
Advertising and promotion	1,200,000	1,200,000	1,200,000
Administrative salaries	57,000	57,000	57,000
Sales salaries	75,000	75,000	75,000
Sales commissions	200,000	212,500	225,000
Salesperson travel	170,000	175,000	180,000
Total selling expenses	1,702,000	1,719,500	1,737,000

The following assumptions were used to develop the selling-expense flexible budgets:

- The average size of Wielson's sales force during the year was planned to be 75 people.
- Salespeople are paid a monthly salary plus commissions on gross sales.
- The travel costs are best characterized as a step-variable cost. The fixed portion is related to the number of salespersons, while the variable portion fluctuates with gross dollar sales.

A sales force of 80 people generated a total of 4,300 orders, resulting in a sales volume of 420,000 units during November. The gross dollar sales amounted to £10.9 million. The selling expenses incurred for November were as follows:

	£
Advertising and promotion	1,350,000
Administrative salaries	57,000
Sales salaries	80,000
Sales commissions	218,000
Salesperson travel	185,000
Total	1,890,000

Prepare a selling expense report for November that Wielson Company can use to evaluate its control over selling expenses. The report should have a line for each selling expense item showing the appropriate budgeted amount, the actual selling expense, and the monthly dollar variation.

(CMA adapted)

NP 8.16 Flexible budgets LO 7

The coating department of a parts-manufacturing department coats various parts with an anti-rust zinc-based material. The parts to be processed are loaded into baskets, and then the baskets pass through a coating machine that sprays the zinc material onto the parts. Next, the machine heats the parts to ensure the coating bonds properly. All parts being coated are assigned a cost for the coating department based on the number of hours that the parts spend in a coating machine. Prior to the beginning of the year, cost categories are accumulated by department (including the coating department). These cost categories are classified as being either fixed or variable and then a flexible budget for the department is constructed. Given an estimate of machine hours for the next year, the coating department projected cost per machine hour is computed.

Data for the last three operating years are given below. Expected coating machine hours for 2009 are 16,000 hours.

Coating department operating data

	2006	2007	2008
Machine hours	12,500	8,400	15,200
Coating materials	€51,375	€34,440	€62,624
Engineering support	27,962	34,295	31,300
Maintenance	35,850	35,930	36,200
Occupancy costs (square metres)	27,502	28,904	27,105
Operator labour	115,750	78,372	147,288
Supervision	46,500	47,430	49,327
Utilities	12,875	8,820	16,112
Total costs	€317,814	€268,191	€369,956

a Estimate the coating department's flexible budget for 2009. Explicitly state and justify the assumptions used in deriving your estimates.
b Calculate the coating department's cost per machine hour for 2009.

NP 8.17 Preparing a master budgets LO 9

Construct a master budget using the following data:

Company C
Beginning Balance Sheet
1 January 2009

	£		£
Cash	1,000	Accounts payable	1,200
Accounts receivable	500	Notes payable	3,000
Raw materials	800		
Finished goods	3,000		
Property, plant and equipment	5,000	Share capital	100
Accumulated depreciation	(1,000)	Retained earnings	5,000
	9,300		9,300

The following events are expected to happen during 2009:

- Sales of 2,000 units at £10 per unit.
- Cost of each unit equal to £3 in raw materials and £2 in direct labour.
- Manufacturing overhead equal to £3 per unit, which includes £1 per unit of depreciation.
- The cost per unit is the same as last year.
- Purchase equipment for £1,000.
- Payment of interest of £300.
- Retire notes payable of £500.
- Pay dividends of £200.
- Selling and administrative expenses are expected to be £400.
- Final expected balances: Accounts receivable = £600, Raw materials = £900, Finished goods = £2,400, Accounts payable = £1,500.

Analysis and interpretation problems

AIP 8.1 Budget lapsing LO 6

Professors at Northampton University are given a budget of £2,000 per year for travel and research purposes. Presently, the university allows the professors to carry over unused balances from one year to the next. The university is considering a new policy of having the £2,000 lapse from year to year.

What are the advantages and disadvantages of having the travel and research budget lapse?

AIP 8.2 Different types of budgets LO 4, 5, 6, 7, 8

The Sticky Company makes a glue that is used to make the layers of wood veneer adhere to make plywood. The glue-making process has been used for many years and the customers are satisfied with the product. The Sticky Company has had very low turnover of personnel and the president and all of the managers have been with the firm for many years. Although the company appears stable today, plywood prices are rising and the construction industry is beginning to switch to a cheaper product called chipboard. Chipboard uses a different glue than the product made by the Sticky Company.

Given the present condition of Sticky Company, should the company use long-term budgets, line-item budgets, budget lapsing, flexible budgets or zero-base budgeting?

AIP 8.3 Long-term budgets LO 4

The sales manager of the T Corporation is complaining about the budget process. He notes, 'Each year the central administration asks for expected sales in each of the next three years. The first year's budget is used to determine production amounts and establish benchmarks for measuring performance and rewarding employees. The second and third year budgets, however, seem to be forgotten. Next year, management asks us again for expected sales in each of the next three years. Why does management not simply use last year's forecast, or only ask us to make sales forecasts for one year ahead?'

Does the sales manager have a legitimate complaint?

AIP 8.4 Budgeting and performance evaluation LO 3

'I've given a good deal of thought to this issue of how companies . . . go about negotiating objectives with their different business units. The typical process in such cases is that once the parent negotiates a budget with a unit, the budget then becomes the basis for the bonus. And they are also typically structured such that the bonus kicks in when, say, 80 per cent of the budgeted performance is achieved; and the maximum bonus is earned when management reaches, say, 120 per cent of the budgeted level. There is thus virtually no downside and very limited upside.

'Now, because the budget is negotiated between management and headquarters, there is a circularity about the whole process that makes the resulting standards almost meaningless. Because the budget is intended to reflect what management thinks it can accomplish – presumably without extraordinary effort and major changes in the status quo – the adoption of the budget as a standard is unlikely to motivate exceptional performance, especially since the upside is so limited. Instead it is likely to produce cautious budgets and mediocre performance.

'So, because of the perverse incentives built into the budgeting process itself, I think it's important for a company to break the connection between the budget and planning process on the one hand and the bonus systems on the other hand. The bonuses should be based upon absolute performance standards that are not subject to negotiation.'

Source: G. Bennett Stewart, III (1990) 'CEO Roundtable on Corporate Structure and Management Incentives', *Journal of Applied Corporate Finance*, Fall p. 27.

Critically evaluate the preceding quotation.

AIP 8.5 Zero-base budgeting LO 8

You currently work as a financial analyst with a large investment bank, RP Investments. Last year, there was a major scandal at one of your major competitors, CC Bank, involving manipulation of some auctions for government bonds. A number of senior partners at CC Bank were charged with price fixing in the government bond market. The ensuing investigation led four of the eight managing directors (the highest-ranking officials at CC Bank) to resign. A new senior managing director was brought in from outside to run the firm. This individual recruited three outside managing directors to replace the ones who resigned. A thorough 'house cleaning' then took place. In the following six months, 15 additional partners and over 40 senior managers left CC Bank and were replaced, usually with people from outside the firm.

RP Investments has had no such scandal and almost all of its senior executives have been with the firm for all of their careers.

a Describe zero-base budgeting (ZBB).
b Which firm, RP Investments or CC Bank, is more likely to be using ZBB and why?

AIP 8.6 Problems with budgets LO 1, 2

A *Fortune* magazine article with the title, 'Why Budgets are Bad for Business', included the following statements:

Budgets, say experts, control the wrong things, like head count, and miss the right ones, such as quality, customer service – and even profits. Worse, they erect walls between the various parts of the company and between a company and its customers.

When you're controlled by a budget, you're not controlling the business.

Reliance on budgets is the fundamental flaw in American management. That's because they assume that everything important can be translated into this quarter's or this year's dollars, and that you can manage the business by managing the money. Wrong. Just because a budget was not overspent doesn't mean it was well spent.

For tracking where the money goes, budgets are dandy. They become iniquitous when they are made to do more – when the budget becomes management's main tool to gauge performance. Managers do incredibly stupid things to make budget, especially if incentive pay is at stake. They woo marginal customers. They cut prices too deeply.

The worst failure of budgets is what they don't measure. Budgets show what you spend on customer service, but not what value customers put on it.

Source: Thomas A. Stewart and Shawn Tully (1990) 'Why budgets are bad for business', *Fortune*, Vol. 121, No. 13 (4 June), pp. 179–182.

Critically evaluate the article.

AIP 8.7 Responsibility for an unusual event LO 2

In March, a devastating ice storm struck central Scotland causing millions of dollars of damage. Mathews & Peat (M&P), a large horticultural nursery, was hard hit. As a result of the storm, £653,000 of additional labour and maintenance costs were incurred to clean up the nursery, remove and replace damaged plants, repair fencing and replace glass broken when nearby tree limbs fell on some of the greenhouses.

Mathews & Peat is a wholly-owned subsidiary of Agro Inc., an international agricultural conglomerate. The manager of M&P, R. Dye, is reviewing the operating performance of the subsidiary for the year of the ice storm. The following are the results for the year as compared to budget:

Mathews & Peat
Summary of Operating Results for the Year 2008
(£000)

	Actual results	Budgeted results	Actual as % of budget
Revenues	32,149	31,682	101
Less:			
Labour	13,152	12,621	104
Materials	8,631	8,139	106
Occupancy costs*	4,234	4,236	100
Depreciation	2,687	2,675	100
Interest	1,875	1,895	99
Total expenses	30,579	29,566	103
Operating profits	1,570	2,116	74

*Includes property taxes, utilities, maintenance and repairs of buildings, etc.

After thinking about how to present the performance of M&P for the year, Dye decides to break out the costs of the ice storm from the individual items affected by the storm and report the storm separately. The total cost of the ice storm of £653,000 consists of additional labour costs of £320,000, additional materials of £220,000, and additional occupancy costs of £113,000. These amounts are net of the insurance payments received due to the storm. The following alternative performance statement is provided:

Mathews & Peat
Summary of Operating Results for the Year 2008
(£000)

	Actual results	Budgeted results	Actual as % of budget
Revenues	32,149	31,682	101
Less:			
Labour	12,832	12,621	102
Materials	8,411	8,139	103
Occupancy costs	4,121	4,236	97
Depreciation	2,687	2,675	100
Interest	1,875	1,895	99
Total expenses	29,926	29,566	101
Operating profits before ice storm costs	2,223	2,116	105
Ice storm costs	653	0	
Operating profits after ice storm costs	1,570	2,116	74

a Put yourself in Dye's position. Write a short, concise cover memo for the second operating statement to summarize the essential points that you want to communicate to your superiors.

b Critically evaluate the differences between the two performance reports as presented.

AIP 8.8 Lapsing and multi-year budgets LO 4, 6

Roberta Esteban, manager of market planning for Viral Products of the IAIP Pharmaceutical Co., is responsible for advertising a class of products. She has designed a three-year marketing plan to increase the market share of her product class. Her plan involves a major increase in magazine advertising. She has met with an advertising agency that has designed a three-year advertising campaign, involving 12 separate adverts that build on a common theme. Each advert will run in three consecutive monthly medical magazines and then be followed with the next advert in the sequence. Up to five different medical journals will carry the advertising campaign. Direct-mail campaigns and direct-sales promotional material will be designed to follow the theme of the advert currently appearing at the time. The following data summarize the cost of the campaign:

	Year 1	Year 2	Year 3	Total
Number of adverts	4	4	4	12
Number of magazines	5	5	4	
Cost per ad (€)	6,000	6,200	6,500	
Advertising cost (€)	120,000	124,000	104,000	348,000

The firm's normal policy is to budget each year as a separate entity without carrying forward unspent funds. Roberta is requesting that, instead of just approving the budget for next year (labelled 'Year 1' above), the entire three-year project be budgeted. This approval would allow her to move forward with her campaign. Also, it would give her the freedom to apply any unspent funds in one year to the next year, or to use them in another part of the campaign. Roberta argues that the advertising campaign is an integrated project stretching over three years, and should be either approved or rejected in its entirety.

Critically evaluate Roberta's request and make a recommendation as to whether a three-year budget should be approved per her proposal. For purposes of your answer, assume that the advertising campaign is expected to be a profitable project.

AIP 8.9 Budget effects of purchasing patterns LO 1, 2, 3, 6

You are working in the office of the Vice President of Administration at International Telecon (IT) as a senior financial planner. IT is a *Fortune Global 500* firm with sales approaching €1 billion. IT provides long-distance satellite communications around the world. Deregulation of telecommunications in Europe has intensified worldwide competition. It also has increased pressures inside IT to reduce costs, in order to allow lower prices without cutting profit margins.

IT is divided into several profit and cost centres. Each profit centre is further organized as a series of cost centres. Each profit and cost centre follows IT policy regarding submitting budgets to IT's Vice President of Administration, and then is held responsible for meeting the budget. The Vice President of Administration described IT's financial control, budgeting, and reporting system as, 'pretty much a standard, state-of-the-art approach, where we hold our people accountable for producing what they forecast'.

Your boss has assigned to you the task of analysing firm-wide supplies expenditures, with the goal of reducing waste and lowering expenditures. Supplies include all consumables ranging from pencils and paper to electronic sub-components and parts that cost less than €1,000. Long-lived assets that cost under €1,000 (or the equivalent amount in the domestic currency for non-euro purchases) are *not* capitalized (and then depreciated), but rather categorized as 'supplies' and written off as an expense in the month purchased.

You first gather the last 36 months of operating data for both supplies and payroll. The supplies and payroll data are for the entire firm. The payroll data is used to help you benchmark the supplies data. You divide each month's payroll and supplies amount by revenues in that month to control for volume and seasonal fluctuations. Figure 8.2 plots the two data series.

Payroll fluctuates between 35–48 per cent of sales and supplies fluctuate between 13–34 per cent of sales. Figure 8.2 shows the past three years of supplies and payroll; the vertical lines in the graph divide the financial years. For financial and budgeting purposes, IT is on a calendar-year (January to December) financial year.

Figure 8.2 International Telecon: monthly payroll and supply expenses, past 36 months

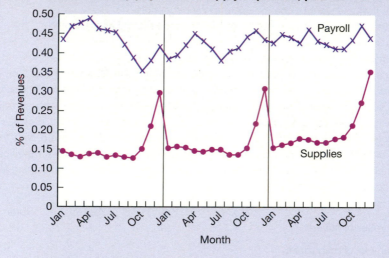

Besides focusing on consolidated firm-wide spending, you prepare disaggregated graphs like the one above, but at the cost and profit centre levels. The overall patterns observed in the consolidated graphs are repeated in general in the disaggregated graphs.

a Analyse the behaviour over time of supplies expenditures for IT. What is the likely reason for the observed patterns in supplies?

b Given your analysis in (a) above, what corrective action might you consider proposing? What are its costs and benefits?

AIP 8.10 Adjusting budgets and effect on behaviour LO 1, 2, 3, 6

Panarude Airfreight is an international air-freight hauler with over 75 jet aircraft operating in the Pacific Rim and North America. The firm is headquartered in Melbourne, Australia and is organized into five geographic areas: Australia, Japan, Korea, Indonesia and North America. Supporting these areas are several centralized, corporate function services (cost centres): human resources, finance and administration, fleet acquisition and maintenance, and information technology (IT). Each responsibility centre has a budget, negotiated at the beginning of the year with the director of finance. Any unspent funds at the end of the year do not carry over to the next financial year. The firm is on a January-to-December financial year.

After reviewing the month-to-month variances, Panarude senior management had become concerned about the large increases in spending occurring in the last three months of each financial year. In particular, in the first nine months of the year, expenditure accounts typically had shown favourable variances (actual spending was less than budget) and in the last three months, adverse variances had been the norm. In an attempt to smooth out these spending patterns, each responsibility centre now is reviewed at the end of each calendar quarter, and any unspent funds can be deleted from the budget for the remainder of the year. For example, the budget and actual spending in the Telecommunications Department for the first quarter of 2009 are as follows:

Panarude Airfreight
Telecommunications Department
2009 First Quarter Budget and Actual Spending
(A$)

	Monthly budget	Cumulative budget	Actual spending	Cumulative spending	Monthly variance	Cumulative variance
Jan.	110,000	110,000	104,000	104,000	6,000F	6,000F
Feb.	95,000	205,000	97,000	201,000	2,000A	4,000F
Mar.	115,000	320,000	112,000	313,000	3,000F	7,000F

At the end of the first quarter, IT's total annual budget for 2009 can be reduced by A$7,000, the total budget under-run in the first quarter. The remaining nine monthly budgets for IT are reduced by A$778 (A$7,000 ÷ 9). If at the end of the second quarter, IT's budget shows an adverse variance of say A$8,000 (after reducing the original budget for the first quarter under-run), management of Telecommunications is held responsible for the entire A$8,000 adverse variance. The first-quarter under-run is *not* restored. If the second-quarter budget variance is also favourable, the remaining six monthly budgets are reduced again by one-sixth of the second-quarter favourable budget variance.

a What behaviours would this budgeting scheme engender in the responsibility centre managers?
b Compare the advantages and disadvantages of the previous budget regime where any end-of-year budget surpluses do not carry over to the next financial year to the system of quarterly budget adjustments described above.

AIP 8.11 Analysing variances LO 2

Rose Manor is a horse farm in the Republic of Ireland that specializes in boarding thoroughbred breeding mares and their foals. Customers bring their breeding mares to Rose Manor for delivery of their foals and post-natal care of the mare and foal. Recently, there has been a substantial decline in thoroughbred breeding as a result of changes in the tax laws. Due to these changes in the market for thoroughbred boarding, profits have declined in the industry.

Rose Manor prepared a master budget for 2008 by splitting costs into variable costs and fixed costs. The budget for 2008 was prepared before the extent of the downturn was fully recognized. Exhibit 1 compares the actual results to the budget for 2008.

Exhibit 1

Rose Manor
Profit and Loss Statement for the
Year Ended 31 December 2008

	Budget formula (per mare per day)	Actual	Master budget	Variance
Number of mares		52	60	8
Number of boarding days		18,980	21,900	2,920
Revenues	€25.00	€379,600	€547,500	€167,900A
Less variable expenses:				
Feed and supplies	5.00	104,390	109,500	5,110F
Veterinary fees	3.00	58,838	65,700	6,862F
Blacksmith fees	0.30	6,074	6,570	496F
Total variable expenses	8.30	169,302	181,770	12,468F
Contribution margin	16.70	210,298	365,730	155,432A
Less fixed expenses:				
Depreciation and insurance		56,000	56,000	0
Utilities		12,000	14,000	2,000F
Repairs and maintenance		10,000	11,000	1,000F
Labour		88,000	96,000	8,000F
Total fixed expenses		166,000	177,000	11,000F
Profit before income taxes		€44,298	€188,730	€144,432A

Note: A (F) denotes an adverse (favourable) variance.

Evaluate Rose Manor's operating performance based on the variances in the table.

Extended **analysis** and **Interpretation** problems

AIP 8.12 Budgets and cost centres LO 1, 2, 3

The University of North-Western England publishes and distributes over 100,000 copies of its *Official Bulletin on Undergraduate Studies* to prospective students, high-school guidance counsellors, faculty and staff of the university, and other interested parties. This 250-page catalogue with four-colour pictures and state-of-the art graphics is one of the primary marketing devices for the university's undergraduate programmes. The catalogue is also available online, but the hardcopy version continues to be distributed widely as the public relations department considers it to be more effective in reaching its target audience, especially parents. Students completing school or college who express interest in attending the university receive the *Bulletin*, along with other information about the university. It lists the various programmes of studies, course offerings and requirements. Each year, it is revised and reprinted as courses and programmes change and the photographs are updated, to improve its use as a recruiting tool. The annual cost of preparing and printing the *Bulletin* is about £1 million, which includes the cost of photographers, non-university graphic designers, typesetting and printing. This figure excludes the cost of university employees who rewrite the text, proofread and manage the entire process.

The admissions office and the public relations department share the responsibility of preparing the catalogue. The admissions office co-ordinates the collection of the basic data on course and programme changes. Many of these are not known until June, after the various faculties have met and approved academic programme and course changes. These changes are edited and the overall content of the publication is determined based on the admissions office experience with applicants. Admissions then sends a draft copy of the brochure to public relations. Public relations is responsible for the overall image and publicity of the university and for ensuring that university publications present a consistent image. Public relations, using outside graphic designers, marketing specialists, typesetters and printers that it has come to know, take the changes and produce an attractive, high-quality catalogue.

The admissions office reports to the Dean of the Undergraduate College, who reports to the Vice-Chancellor. The public relations department reports to the Director of External Affairs, who reports to the Vice-Chancellor. The admissions office affects the cost of the brochure in terms of the quantity of text to be included and how many *Bulletins* must be ordered to satisfy its distribution plan. Public relations affects the cost by using more colour photographs, more expensive paper and cover materials, and elaborate layouts. Both admissions and public relations affect the cost by not meeting timely production schedules. If copy is returned late or the design is not completed on time, additional charges are incurred by typesetters and printers working overtime to meet the publication schedule. It is critically important to the admissions process that the *Bulletin* be available for distribution in late autumn to prospective students beginning their university entrance process.

Admissions and public relations are both cost centres. They have been arguing over whether the cost of the *Bulletin* should be in the admissions office budget or the public relations department budget.

a Discuss the advantages and disadvantages of placing the budget for the *Bulletin* into the public relations versus the admissions office budget.

b What are some other alternative ways of handling the *Bulletin*'s budget?

c Based on your analysis, what recommendation would you make?

AIP 8.13 Master budget

The Halifax Brewing Company is budgeting for the next year. The following is the beginning balance sheet of the company:

Halifax Brewing Company
Balance Sheet
1 January 2009

Assets	£	Liabilities and equities	£
Cash	10,000	Accounts payable	3,000
Accounts receivable	20,000	Long-term debt	50,000
Inventory	30,000		
Total current assets	60,000	Total liabilities	53,000
Fixed assets	200,000	Common shares	10,000
Accumulated depreciation	(90,000)	Retained earnings	107,000
Total assets	170,000	Total liabilities and equities	170,000

The company expects to collect the beginning balance of accounts receivable in January. In general, 30 per cent of the company's sales are on a cash basis. Of the credit sales, 40 per cent are paid in the following month and 60 per cent are paid in the second month after the sale.

The accounts payable at the beginning of the year must be paid in January. All materials are purchased on credit and paid for in the following month.

The long-term debt has an annual interest rate of 12 per cent. Interest payments of 1 per cent of the principal are made each month. The long-term debt is not due for another five years.

Halifax Brewing Company makes two different types of beer, an ale and a porter. The ale is a lighter beer that requires fewer ingredients than does the darker and heavier porter. The following are the input requirements for a case of each type of beer:

For making ale

Material	Quantity/case	Cost
Hops	5 kg	£0.30/kg
Yeast	50 grammes	£0.10/50 g
Sugar	0.5 kg	£0.40/kg
Bottles	24	£0.05/bottle

For making porter

Material	Quantity/case	Cost
Hops	10 kg	£0.30/kg
Yeast	50 grammes	£0.10/50g
Sugar	0.8 kg	£0.40/kg
Bottles	24	£0.05/bottle

The labour to make a case of beer is the same for each type of beer: 0.20 hours at £10/hour. Labour is paid in the month earned.

Monthly overhead expenses are paid in the month incurred and expected to be:

	£
Electricity	2,000
Indirect labour	20,000
Rent	5,000
Depreciation	2,000

Ale sells for £10/case and porter sells for £12/case. Estimated sales in cases for Halifax Brewing are:

	Ale	Porter
January	3,000	4,000
February	3,000	5,000
March	4,000	3,000
April	2,000	2,000

The beginning inventory includes 2,000 cases of ale and 3,000 cases of porter. The company prefers to have inventory at the end of each month equal to the expected sales in the next month. Halifax Brewing Company uses a first-in-first-out (FIFO) method of costing inventory.

Halifax Brewing Company must buy a new bottling machine for £20,000 at the end of January.

a Estimate cash flows in each of the months.

b Does the company need to borrow money in any of the months?

c Prepare a balance sheet as of the end of March and a profit and loss statement for the first three months. Assume that the company borrows cash at an interest rate of 1 per cent per month to make up any cash shortfall.

CHAPTER NINE

Cost allocations
(Planning and control)

Learning objectives

1 Describe the relation among common resources, indirect costs and cost objects.

2 Explain the role of allocating indirect costs for external financial reports, income tax reports and cost reimbursement.

3 Identify reasons for cost allocation for planning purposes.

4 Identify reasons for cost allocation for control purposes.

5 Describe how the various reasons for cost allocation can create conflict within the organization.

6 Allocate indirect costs using five basic steps.

7 Create segment reports for the organization.

8 Use direct, step-down and reciprocal methods to allocate reciprocal service department costs. (Appendix)

City Square Dental (CSD)

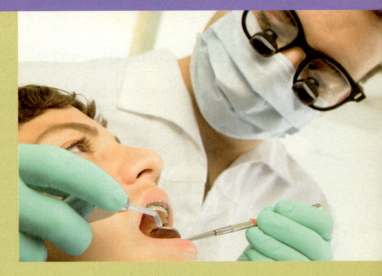

City Square Dental (CSD) is a private dental practice composed of a group of dental specialists that provide regular and cosmetic dental care services to different types of patient. Patients are categorized by the type of service provided and the method of payment. Some patients come to CSD due to its reputation for using the latest technologies and equipment, along with the ability to book appointments at convenient times and in emergencies. These patients generally adopt CSD's private dental plan. For a fixed monthly fee, patients are covered for routine examinations, x-rays and hygiene visits, plus special benefits and fees for emergencies and cosmetic services. The monthly fee varies and is customized to the patient's preferences.

Other patients come to CSD through an agreement with their employer's extended health care plan. This plan covers a portion of all the employee dental costs depending on the dental fee schedule and whether a service is deemed to be routine or cosmetic in nature. The bulk of these patients are corporate executives. Other dentists also refer patients to CSD when patients need the attention of a specialist for restorative dentistry and orthodontics, and patients can recover the cost from their employers or via private insurance plans. Individual patients must pay CSD directly and then submit their claims to their employers for reimbursement. In some instances, CSD submits the claim electronically to the plan provider, thus providing the practice with greater security of payment, while the patient must cover only the non-insured portion.

Finally, another group of patients pays its own dental costs on a fee-for-service basis. These patients are charged an amount based on the cost of services provided. These patients who tend to choose CSD for advanced restorative or cosmetic work are less price sensitive.

The partners of CSD are 12 dental specialists, who are paid based on the profit they generate individually. The dentists have hired a practice manager, who is responsible for the general operations and management of the clinic. An accountant, procurement manager and a secretary/bookkeeper provide administrative support to the manager. The costs related to this support group are treated as general administration costs. The following departments assist the dentists in performing their duties: hygienists, nurses, radiography and reception. In addition, the dental practice incurs costs related to building occupancy, such as rent, equipment maintenance and utilities. Laboratory services are performed by an outside clinic that is located in the same building. The fees for these services are billed separately to the patient.

CSD's accountant faces two primary problems: how to determine the cost of services provided by the dentists; and how to determine the profit generated by each dentist. As well, the accountant is concerned about how to report the general administration costs, the occupancy costs, and the costs related to the departments that support the dentists.

ALLOCATING INDIRECT COSTS

Cost allocation is the process of assigning indirect costs to **cost objects**. Cost objects include products, activities, sub-units of the organization, customers, suppliers and time periods. For example, cost objects in a hospital could include a patient, the paediatrics department or the first quarter of the financial year. Each of these cost objects has direct and indirect costs associated with them. Direct costs occur when resources are used for only one cost object. For example, raw materials are used by a specific product and are considered direct costs of the product. The product is the cost object. Indirect costs, however, result from the use of resources by multiple cost objects. A machine that is used by many products is an indirect cost to those products. The allocation of indirect costs to cost objects is the subject of this chapter.

In Chapter 3, the tracing of indirect product costs for planning purposes was performed using activity-based costing (ABC). Indirect product costs are part of the cost of providing a product and must be traced or allocated to the different products through the use of cost drivers. The cost drivers are chosen to reflect the cause of the indirect costs. If the product uses the cost driver, indirect costs are traced to the product. Ideally the tracing of indirect costs through cost drivers will reflect the cost of using indirect resources.

Choosing cost drivers to trace indirect costs is appropriate, if the purpose is to make a planning decision with respect to the cost object. Reasons exist, however, to allocate indirect costs to cost objects, other than to make planning decisions. This chapter also examines the allocation of indirect costs for control and external reporting purposes. Allocating indirect costs through cost drivers is not necessarily best for the organization when control and external reporting issues are considered. While ABC can be worthwhile, other indirect cost allocation mechanisms often prove more beneficial in motivating managers or influencing users of external accounting reports. The choice of the cost allocation method is subjective and ethical considerations must be taken into account. Cost allocations for control purposes can adversely affect certain managers and benefit others. Cost allocation methods for external reporting are often chosen to minimize the organization's tax liability.

The subjective nature of indirect cost allocations makes the process one of the most controversial in accounting. Inappropriate cost allocation mechanisms can lead to poor planning decisions, demoralized managers and unhappy customers. In spite of the potential problems associated with cost allocation, the practice is prevalent in organizations. For example, the costs of the human resources department are an indirect cost to other departments, and are commonly allocated to those departments. Hospitals allocate the indirect costs of shared medical equipment among departments that utilize the equipment. The costs of the Information Technology (IT) department are allocated among the IT users within the organization. The depreciation of manufacturing facilities is allocated among the products manufactured there.

For instance, Enbridge Inc., an international energy transportation and distribution company, allocates the cost

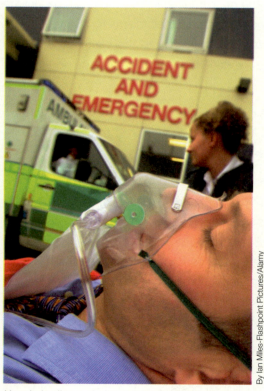

By Ian Miles-Flashpoint Pictures/Alamy

Hospitals allocate indirect costs to departments such as Accident and Emergency for planning and control, including the determination of the total cost of patient services.

of its centralized services to its business operations based on budgeted costs established during the budget process. These allocations allow management to assess the overall financial performance of each line of business. Business operations know in advance the allocated costs that they will receive in the upcoming budget year. While allocated and budgeted costs might differ, the budget process acts as a mechanism to control costs. However, conflicts over cost allocations could arise between the different user groups and between the users and the centralized services due to the greater ambiguity of these costs.

The widespread use of cost allocation implies that many benefits also result from the practice. However, an organization should identify clearly why costs are being allocated and the effect of those cost allocations on management behaviour. Each cost allocation has planning, control and external reporting implications. An organization must often make trade-offs amongst these considerations in choosing an allocation method.

City Square Dental (continued)

At CSD, the general administration, occupancy and other departments (hygienists, nurses, radiography and reception) support the dental specialists. All these departments are indirect resources for the dentists, and are used by all the dentists and by many of the patients. The dentists and the patients are the cost objects or recipients of the allocated indirect costs from the indirect resources. A method must be chosen to allocate these indirect costs.

Concept review

1 What are some examples of cost allocation?
2 What is the relation between common resources and cost objects?

REASONS FOR ALLOCATING INDIRECT COSTS

Most organizations use cost allocation, but the allocation of indirect costs remains controversial. One example is the allocation of indirect costs to responsibility centres controlled by managers. The controllability principle based on responsibility accounting suggests that managers should be held responsible for costs that they can control. Yet the allocation of indirect costs is often a distribution of costs to managers who have little or no control over those costs. Managers in many organizations complain bitterly about the allocation of certain indirect costs. While managers usually do not have complete control of indirect costs, they often partially affect the use of the indirect resource. For example, if a production department expands its workforce, greater demands are placed on the human resources department, which ultimately must expand or else provide less service to the other departments.

The allocation of some indirect costs to products is also controversial. In Chapter 5, the pricing decision that maximized profits was determined through the use of marginal costs. A product cost that includes allocated fixed costs does not appear to be a likely representation of the marginal cost of making a product.

Given the contentious nature of the allocation of indirect costs, benefits must exist from this process. These benefits fall into three categories:

1 satisfying external reporting requirements,
2 planning purposes, and
3 control purposes.

These are discussed in the following sections.

■ Satisfying external requirements

Not all management accounting decisions are based on internal demand for information for making planning decisions and control. Organizations often have responsibilities to provide certain information to outside parties. Shareholders of corporations have the right to receive financial reports from the corporation. Profit organizations must file tax returns to government bodies and not-for-profit organizations file informational returns. Also, some contracts between different organizations specify that costs incurred by one organization will be reimbursed by the other. Therefore, cost information must be communicated from one organization to the other.

Allocated indirect costs play an important role in each of these settings. In some cases, the method of allocating indirect costs is specified. In other cases, the allocation of indirect costs provides opportunities for an organization to achieve some financial objective, such as reducing taxes. The following sections describe each setting, and the corresponding cost allocation requirements and opportunities.

Financial reports to shareholders

The compilation of financial reports to shareholders is based on regulations from bodies such as the International Accounting Standards Board (IASB), the UK Accounting Standards Board (ASB), the London Stock Exchange (LSE) and the US Securities and Exchange Commission (SEC), and other authoritative professional bodies such as the Institute of Chartered Accountants in England and Wales and the International Federation of Accountants. Rules from the IASB and the ASB do not cover all aspects of financial reporting. Moreover, financial accounting and taxation rules followed in one country do not necessarily converge with those followed in other countries. When rules from the regulatory bodies do not specify the appropriate accounting method, past accounting practices provide guidelines. Rules from the regulatory bodies and guidelines based on past accounting practices comprise generally accepted accounting principles (GAAP).

The allocation of indirect manufacturing costs to products is a financial accounting procedure that has become part of GAAP as a result of past practice. Traditionally, indirect manufacturing costs, but not indirect selling and administrative overhead costs, have been allocated to products. Selling and administrative overhead costs are period costs that are expensed on the profit and loss statement.

Rob Wilkinson/Alamy

The LSE is one of several regulatory bodies that establish rules and guidelines for shareholder reporting. Globalization has encouraged harmonization of standards across different jurisdictions.

In most wholesale, retail and service organizations, no indirect costs are allocated to the product or service for financial reporting purposes.

The method used to allocate indirect manufacturing costs to products affects the calculation of profit. Indirect manufacturing costs that are allocated to products become part of the inventory cost, and remain an asset until the product is sold. The allocation of indirect manufacturing costs to products that remain in ending inventory affects the current period's financially reported profits.

Numerical **example** 9.1

A sports equipment manufacturer makes two types of balls: soccer balls and footballs. There is no beginning inventory and during the year the manufacturer makes 20,000 soccer balls and 40,000 footballs. Indirect manufacturing costs during the year are £100,000. During the year, all the soccer balls are sold and 30,000 of the footballs are sold. The company is considering two possible methods of allocating indirect manufacturing costs. The first method allocates £80,000 to the soccer balls and £20,000 to the footballs. The second method allocates £40,000 to the soccer balls and £60,000 to the footballs. Which method causes a higher reported profit this period?

Solution

10,000/40,000 or 25 per cent of the footballs are not yet sold. Therefore, indirect manufacturing costs associated with the unsold footballs remain an asset. They are not a deduction from profits. Under the first method, 25 per cent of the manufacturing overhead of £20,000, or £5,000, is not deducted from profits in the current period. Under the second method, 25 per cent of £60,000, or £15,000, is not deducted. Therefore, the second method causes reported profits to be £15,000 − £5,000, or £10,000 higher.

If management compensation is based on that earnings number, incentives exist to allocate indirect costs to influence externally reported profits. Top-level managers frequently have bonuses tied to externally reported profits, so they are concerned about how indirect manufacturing costs are allocated. There are constraints, however, in the allocation of costs for external reports. The allocation method must follow GAAP. Importantly, organizational managers cannot change the method of allocation without agreement from the organization's external auditors.[1]

Reporting of taxable profits

Tax accounting rules require that inventory be stated at cost, including an appropriate amount for indirect manufacturing costs. For example, inventory includes not only direct labour and direct material, but also a fraction of factory depreciation, property taxes and the salaries of security guards at the factory. As in the case of external financial reports, the allocation of these indirect manufacturing costs among products can influence the calculation of taxable profits.

---

[1] When the units in inventory are sold, the indirect costs allocated to these units are charged to profits. Thus, managers cannot continually increase earnings by allocating excessive indirect costs to units in inventory without building inventories.

The owners of an organization would like to allocate costs in a manner that reduces taxable profits. The lower the taxable profit figure, the lower are the tax payments. The methods of allocating indirect costs, however, are constrained by the rulings of the tax authority.

Cost reimbursement contracts

Cost reimbursement is another reason for cost allocations. Government cost-based contracts and medical reimbursements for costs give rise to cost allocations. The UK Ministry of Defence spends billions of pounds a year under cost-plus contracts. A cost-plus contract states that the customer will compensate the supplier for the cost of the product or service, plus some amount or percentage to provide the supplier with a profit. For example, a satellite-communication system contract might state that the supplier will be paid for the cost of the system, plus a 10 per cent mark-up to allow the supplier to make a profit. The Ministry's Smart Acquisition programme has reduced the value of cost-plus contracts in favour of competitive contracting and supplier partnerships to lower its costs and to shift more risk to suppliers.

Cost reimbursement contracts are frequently used when the product or service is unique, and the cost of making the product or providing the service is uncertain. With uncertain costs, suppliers may be unwilling to offer the product or service. By promising to reimburse costs, the customer removes the risk of uncertain costs from the supplier. The customer, however, must worry about incentives for the supplier to control costs. If the supplier knows that all costs will be reimbursed, the supplier will not be as careful to control costs.

Indirect cost allocation is a controversial part of cost reimbursement. If a supplier makes multiple products and some are sold on a cost-reimbursement basis, the supplier would like to allocate as many indirect costs as possible to the products that are reimbursed based on cost. The allocation of more indirect costs to products subject to cost reimbursement translates into greater revenues for the organization.[2]

Numerical example 9.2

A web-page design firm has two types of clients: those that request a cost-plus 20 per cent contract and those that request a fixed fee of €20,000 for design services. The firm completes 50 web designs of each type during the year. The average direct costs of each design are €10,000. Indirect costs for the web-page design firm are €500,000. The first method of allocating indirect costs assigns €200,000 to the cost-plus designs and €300,000 to the fixed-fee designs. The second method allocates €400,000 to cost-plus designs and €100,000 to fixed-fee designs. Which method provides a higher profit for the web-page design firm?

Solution

The reported cost for the cost-plus designs under the first method are:

	€
Direct costs (50 × €10,000)	500,000
Indirect costs	200,000
Total	700,000

---

[2] John Christensen and Joel S. Demski (2003) 'Factor Choice Distortion under Cost-Based Reimbursement', *Journal of Management Accounting Research*, Vol. 15, pp. 145–160.

The total profit of both the cost-plus and fixed fee contracts using the first method of allocating indirect costs is calculated as follows:

		€
Revenues		
Cost-plus (€700,000 × 120%)		840,000
Fixed fee (50 × €20,000)		1,000,000
Total		1,840,000
Costs		
Direct (100 × €10,000)		1,000,000
Indirect		500,000
Net profit		340,000

The reported cost for the cost-plus designs under the second method follows:

	€
Direct costs (50 × €10,000)	500,000
Indirect costs	400,000
Total	900,000

The total income of both the cost-plus and fixed fee contracts using the second method of allocating indirect costs is determined as follows:

	€
Revenues	
Cost-plus (€900,000 × 120%)	1,080,000
Fixed fee (50 × €20,000)	1,000,000
Total	2,080,000
Costs	
Direct (100 × €10,000)	1,000,000
Indirect	500,000
Net income	580,000

The second method provides a higher profit, as more reimbursable indirect costs are allocated to the cost-plus designs.

The allocation of indirect costs is such a critical aspect of cost reimbursement contracts that the contracts should specify the allowable cost allocation methods. To help regulate the cost allocations by suppliers of US government agencies, the US federal government established an independent body, the Cost Accounting Standards Board (CASB). It issues standards covering the broad areas of cost measurement, cost assignment to accounting periods and cost allocation within an accounting period. Suppliers of US government agencies with cost-plus contracts must follow the accounting procedures specified by the CASB. Similarly, in the UK, the Review Board for Government Contracts, an independent body established by the government and the Confederation of British Industry, recommends government accounting conventions related to cost allocation methods and baseline profit rates for non-competitive government contracts, primarily those with the Ministry of Defence.

In addition to defence contractors, public utilities, such as electric and gas companies, have their revenues tied to reported costs. Public utilities are often granted exclusive monopolies over service territories by their respective government authorities. In return for the monopoly, the government regulates the prices that the utility can charge its customers. In many cases, the regulated prices are based on reported costs, including allocated costs. In public-utility regulation, the major issue is deciding how to allocate the indirect costs of capacity, such as the electricity-generating plant, among the different classes of users (residential versus business customers). Cost allocation is the pre-eminent issue in many public-utility, rate-setting cases.

In 2002, the Canadian provincial government of Ontario deregulated the electricity industry and eliminated the monopoly of the public utility, Ontario Hydro. After almost a century, the market was opened to competition from independent power producers and suppliers. The government established four firms to replace its public utility. Two of these were Hydro One, which was responsible for power distribution, and Ontario Power Generation, which operated the province's existing power-generating facilities. The government faced many technical, human resources and administrative challenges in the process of opening the market to competition.

One critical issue was how to determine market rates in a deregulated retail and wholesale market, given the existence of these two large firms. The independent firms needed assurance that they would have fair access to the transmission network and the power-generating facilities at competitive prices. A mechanism was also required to prevent Hydro One and Ontario Power Generation from overcharging the independent companies by allocating an unfair proportion of their own operating costs to the new market entrants. To mitigate these potential abuses, the government established a market power mitigation agreement with short-, medium- and long-term measures to regulate prices, to cap revenues and to reduce the capacity of Ontario Power Generation. These steps included the disposal of some of its assets. The government expected that the deregulated system would increase competition and create value for customers through a wider selection of energy services, options and reduced prices.

City Square Dental (continued)

The CSD practice is not a manufacturing concern with inventory, so no cost allocation problems exist in terms of manufactured products for financial reporting or tax reporting. CSD, however, does charge the self-paying patients based on the cost of services provided. In this case, the patient is the ultimate cost object, and general administration and other service costs are allocated to the different patients. Given that the revenues generated from other patients are either fixed (CSD's dental plan) or based on pre-determined rates for the services provided (employer extended health care plans), CSD would like to allocate as many indirect costs to the self-paying patients as is ethically possible. Self-paying patients are charged for the allocated and direct costs of services that they use. The self-paying patients, however, are not restricted to coming to CSD, so limits exist on what can be charged to these patients. For example, should self-paying patients be charged for the cost of supplying services to individuals who do not pay their dental bills? In choosing cost allocation methods for patients, CSD must offset the cost of disgruntled, self-paying patients and the benefit of additional short-term revenue. A strategy of increasing revenue in the short term by charging self-paying patients more can lead to a long-term loss in revenue if those patients decide to go to other dental practices.

Different accounting systems for external and internal purposes

Using a single cost allocation method for external financial reports, tax reporting, and cost reimbursement can lead to conflicts. Management may want to choose cost allocation methods that increase present profits to receive bonuses, while owners may want to choose cost allocation methods that reduce present profits for tax purposes. In addition, increasing revenues through cost reimbursement may lead to a different cost allocation scheme. One solution is to have different accounting systems for each purpose.

In a similar fashion, the cost allocation schemes used for external reports need not affect the choice of cost allocation schemes for internal purposes. One reason for using a single accounting system is to reduce accounting costs since having multiple accounting systems is more costly. The disadvantage of having a single accounting system is the conflict that might arise from using the system for different purposes. These conflicts in external reporting can lead to lost revenues and greater profit taxes. Losses from using a single accounting system within the organization occur due to the conflict between planning and control. These issues are discussed in the next two sections.

Concept **review**

1 How is cost allocation used with external financial and tax reporting?

2 How do cost reimbursement contracts influence cost allocations?

■ Cost allocation for planning purposes

Information for planning purposes is used to make better decisions through increased understanding of the problem. The allocation of indirect costs can provide managers with information that allows them to make better decisions. For example, the allocation of indirect costs provides a better measure of all the costs of providing a product or service. The allocation of indirect costs also serves as a communication mechanism to let managers know how their actions are affecting costs in the rest of the organization.

Estimation of the cost of products and services

Managers must make planning decisions related to products and services. In particular, managers make pricing and product-mix decisions. These planning decisions should be made based on the cost of providing those products and services. The allocation of indirect costs to products improves planning decisions, if the allocated indirect costs are representative of the opportunity costs of providing those products.

The allocated indirect costs do not equate necessarily to the opportunity cost of using a resource. For external reporting purposes, all indirect manufacturing costs are allocated to products. However, the use of facilities for which no better alternatives exist does not constitute an opportunity cost. The cost of the facility allocated to products for external reporting purposes, therefore, does not reflect necessarily an opportunity cost of making the product. The estimation of the opportunity cost of the indirect resource requires a clear understanding of how a product or service uses the indirect resource, and of its alternative uses.

Communication of costs to improve planning decisions

The allocated indirect costs also serve as a communication device to inform managers of the cost of their actions to the entire organization. When managers use internal resources or services, they impose costs on other parts of the organization. For example, most universities offer advisory services to all students. The cost of advisory services is allocated to the different faculties within the university based on the number of students in each faculty. The allocated cost is intended to represent the cost of advising more students. If a faculty accepts more students, more students will use the advisory services, and the advisory office must hire more advisors. Otherwise, the quality of student advising declines. By allocating the cost of advisory services to the different faculties, the university is communicating to the faculty deans the cost of providing these services. With this additional information, the deans can make better decisions about admission levels.

Managers are not always aware of some of the costs (or benefits) that they impose on other parts of the organization. In many cases, these costs or benefits are imposed on others without their consent or without direct compensation. These costs or benefits are called **externalities**. Externalities are usually considered in a social context. For example, pollution is a negative externality or cost imposed on others. Automobile exhaust pollutes the air, yet car drivers do not pay for the costs that they impose on others by their pollution (except via petrol and user taxes). The consumers of polluted air are not paid directly for the polluted air they breathe. Education contains a positive externality because people derive benefits from having more educated citizens with whom to interact. Well-tended gardens of private homes create positive externalities by providing a pleasant view for passers-by, and by increasing the property values of neighbouring homes.

Externalities pervade organizations. Improvements in tracking materials in the supply room provide positive externalities to the manufacturing department, as material requisitions can be met more quickly. Hiring another salesperson imposes negative externalities on the human resources department and other departments that provide services to employees. Adding a new product or service can impose either positive or negative externalities on other products or services of the same organization. The communication of the costs or benefits of externalities through the allocation of indirect costs allows managers to make more informed decisions. The problem with externalities, however, is that they are difficult to identify and measure. Therefore, the allocated costs are often a proxy for the cost of an externality.

Concept **review**

1 What type of cost should cost allocations approximate, if they are used for planning purposes?

2 How are cost allocations used to resolve externality issues?

■ Cost allocation for control reasons

Motivation and control are likely explanations for the prevalence of cost allocations within many organizations. Cost allocations control managers through the allocation of resources and the effect of cost allocations on performance measures. Cost allocations also allow managers to monitor each other. The way in which indirect costs are allocated affects managers' behaviour. Therefore, the choice of the allocation method is a tool for controlling managers.

Cost allocations and the allocation of resources

The allocation of costs in some organizations coincides with the allocation of resources. For example, universities may shift resources from one college to another by allocating more general administrative costs to one college than another. The allocated costs are like a tax that is imposed on each college. The university vice-chancellor constrains the deans of the colleges by allocating costs to them and forcing them to pay a higher tax. Funds are distributed to the deans, after the allocated general administration costs are deducted.

Cost allocations and performance measures

Responsibility centres are evaluated, at least partially, based on accounting numbers. Costs, profit, and return-on-investment (ROI) are common performance measures to evaluate managers. These accounting numbers are influenced by the allocation of indirect costs from resources used by multiple responsibility centres. For example, suppose costs of the marketing department are allocated to the various responsibility centres that benefit from marketing. These marketing costs become part of the performance measures of the managers of the other responsibility centres.

As discussed in Chapter 6, performance measures should ideally reveal the actions of the manager who is being evaluated. The controllability principle, as outlined earlier, is based on the theory that managers should be evaluated on costs that they can control. Therefore, the allocation of indirect costs to responsibility centres for the purpose of measuring performance should occur only if the manager has some control over either the cause of the indirect costs, or how the indirect costs are allocated to the responsibility centre. For example, if general administrative costs over which a manager has no control are arbitrarily allocated to that manager, the manager's performance measures will be affected and the individual will be rightfully upset.

However, an organization may choose to allocate uncontrollable indirect costs through methods that can be affected by managers. In doing so, the organization can motivate managers to achieve certain organizational goals. For example, suppose an organization would like to reduce the number of employees within the organization. Its chairman chooses to allocate the uncontrollable general administrative costs based on the number of employees in each responsibility centre. To reduce the amount of general administrative costs allocated to their responsibility centre, the managers reduce the number of their employees. Therefore, the allocation of general administrative costs motivates managers to achieve the goals of the organization, even though a reduction in employees may not affect general administrative costs.

Cost allocations act like a tax system; therefore, the organization uses the allocation of general administrative costs to tax the hiring of employees. As in any tax system, individuals modify their behaviour to reduce the taxes that are imposed on them. If a characteristic of the responsibility centre, such as the number of employees, is used to allocate indirect costs, that characteristic is taxed and the manager will choose to use less of it. If multiple characteristics are used to allocate indirect costs, the manager of the responsibility centre will use less of the heavily taxed characteristics, and more of those that are taxed less or not at all.

Cost allocations change behaviour within organizations. By imposing taxes on certain characteristics used to allocate costs, the organization is motivating managers to reduce those characteristics. The organization should recognize, however, that although taxing certain characteristics might achieve short-term goals, it might lead in the long term to perverse decisions by managers. For example, Tektronix, an electronics manufacturer, used direct labour to allocate indirect costs. Engineers were encouraged to reduce the cost of the products, so they reduced the amount of direct labour required to make new products. Eventually the manufacturing plant was almost fully automated, but total costs were even higher.

To avoid such perverse behaviour, an organization should continually evaluate its cost allocation methods. If the costs of an indirect resource are being allocated at a rate different to the opportunity cost of using that indirect resource, managers will have an incentive to use either too much or too little. In the case of Tektronix, direct labour was taxed at a rate higher than the opportunity cost of using direct labour. This situation led to an excessive use of other factors, such as machines, and a correspondingly higher cost of production.

Mutual monitoring incentives

The usual method of monitoring behaviour within firms is for superiors to monitor subordinates. Monitoring can occur, however, among managers at the same level of the organization. This control, or **mutual monitoring**, can result when cost allocations are made from one responsibility centre to another. For instance, suppose the costs from an information technology (IT) department are allocated to other departments. If the allocated costs of the IT department become too high, other departmental managers will complain and urge the IT department to cut costs. Managers who have the opportunity to acquire IT services elsewhere will force the IT department to lower its costs. Otherwise, they will seek other options, such as outsourcing their IT needs. If costs from the IT department are not allocated to other departments, the other departmental managers will not be concerned about cost control in the IT department, resulting in less mutual monitoring. The discipline to control costs in the IT department will have to be imposed by higher-level management.

In order to maintain control of costs and to encourage efficiency of its support services, many universities allow faculties and departments to outsource services, such as IT, janitorial, printing and maintenance, which could be provided internally. Internal services must be cost competitive and prove that they add value to the customer on other dimensions beyond the cost of their services. Universities face a competitive market for faculty and students and must adapt their costing methods to respond to these pressures. The strategy of the University of Bath is one such approach.

Organizational **analysis**

Strategy, pricing and costing in universities

Universities worldwide are increasing their efforts to gain national and international recognition for their research and teaching. Research and teaching excellence are important factors in attracting highly qualified faculty, the best students and external support. These strategies also require universities to understand better the nature of their varied activities, the links between these activities and their cost. A better grasp of an activity's direct and indirect costs enables universities to make pricing decisions that reflect the value of their programmes and services. Better information should lead to informed decision making about which programmes to offer, which to eliminate, and promote decisions that are consistent with the universities' long-term goals.

The *Vision Statement* of the University of Bath declares its goal to be 'a world class, research university offering high quality teaching in a high technology learning environment'. The university has also declared a commitment to continuous improvement. Its *Strategy for Costing and Pricing* outlines operating and risk management objectives to achieve these goals and to

provide long-term financial stability. Financial planning is increasingly important as universities face a competitive market for higher education, reductions in public resources and greater reliance on external funding (including from students). Within this *Strategy*, the university outlines a resource allocation model to allocate central costs to its academic activities, including a variety of cost drivers to be used. The model also 'provides a transparent spreadsheet of income and expenditure by academic department' available to all department heads and deans. The *Strategy* document emphasizes transparency, accountability, awareness, and consistency to develop costing and pricing models that reflect sound business practices.

Does the University of Bath use cost allocation primarily for planning or control purposes?

Why would cost allocation for the purpose of accurate 'product costs' have been less important in the higher education market?

How does the cost allocation procedure at the University of Bath relate to its strategy?

Sources: *Corporate Plan: 2006/07 to 2008/09* and *Strategy for Costing and Pricing*, www.bath.ac.uk/vc.

City Square Dental (continued)

Cost allocation at CSD plays an important role in determining the performance measures and rewards of the dentists. Each dentist is rewarded based on the profit that he or she generates for the dental practice. Costs that are allocated to the dentists, who are the cost objects under this system, affect the profit associated with each dentist. General administration and other service department costs are allocated to the dental specialists to determine the profits generated by each of them. CSD must be careful in allocating costs to the dentists. They may have an incentive to under- or over-use a service department, if costs are allocated by certain methods. CSD is very concerned about its reputation as a place that offers high-quality, patient-friendly dental services. CSD does not want the cost allocation scheme leading dentists to make decisions that could harm its reputation and result in a loss of patients and revenues.

Concept **review**

1 How can cost allocations affect resources available to managers?
2 How can cost allocations influence the behaviour of managers?
3 What is mutual monitoring and how is it influenced by cost allocations?

BASIC STEPS OF COST ALLOCATION

All indirect cost allocation methods are composed of the same series of steps. Chapter 3 discussed the steps leading to the tracing of indirect costs through cost drivers to cost objects. The steps described in this section are the same, except the term **allocation base** is used instead of cost driver. An allocation base is a characteristic of the cost object upon which costs are allocated. A cost driver is a type of allocation base; it is the characteristic of the cost object that causes the indirect costs. Cost drivers are important for estimating the cost of a product or other cost object. Allocation bases, however, may be chosen for reasons other than cost estimation, such as control. As described in the previous section, cost allocations can motivate managers to make certain decisions.

The steps for cost allocation are:

1 defining the cost objects,
2 accumulating the indirect costs into cost pools,
3 choosing an allocation base,
4 estimating an application rate, and
5 distributing indirect costs based on usage of the allocation base.

Each of these steps is described in the following sections.

■ Defining the cost objects

The organization must decide what departments, products, customers, suppliers or processes should receive the indirect costs. For example, users of the IT centre may be defined as cost objects. Or the IT centre itself may be chosen as a cost object. The cost object can be a sub-unit of the organization, such as a cost or profit centre. As described in Chapter 3, services and products generated by an organization are treated

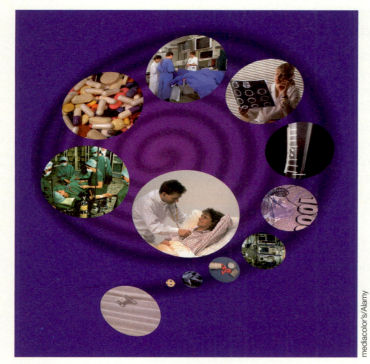

mediacolor's/Alamy

Hospitals are developing sophisticated systems to provide standardized cost data, enabling them to measure and evaluate outcomes of their patient-care services and control costs.

as cost objects. In each case, the choice of a cost object is based on the desire to obtain cost information about the cost object that is useful for planning purposes, or to influence the decisions of managers for control purposes.

Toronto's Hospital for Sick Children, fondly known across Canada as 'Sick Kids', developed a customized accounting system to provide cost information to manage its patient-care, research and teaching activities. An initial step was the development of a cost allocation methodology to combine patient, financial and administrative services into cost pools, cost centres and activities. The cost allocation system allows Sick Kids to determine the actual costs of its specialized paediatric care in terms of operating activities (e.g. admitting, medical examination, counselling, in-patient care, outpatient treatment). Information is available to meet external reporting requirements, but also provides internal management with data to analyse the cost-benefit of different programme and treatment options. Cost data are standardized to enable the hospital to measure and evaluate the outcomes of its patient-care services and its research and teaching programmes.[3]

City Square Dental (continued)

CSD has two cost objects: dentists and patients. The remaining part of this chapter analyses the allocation of costs to dentists to determine their profit share. This allocation of costs will also influence their decisions to use common resources. A similar type of analysis, but with a different goal (cost reimbursement), would have to be performed to allocate costs to patients. For example, fee-for-service patients would be billed for each treatment provided, such as consultations, hygiene treatments, x-rays, orthodontics and teeth whitening.

◼ Accumulating the indirect costs in cost pools

The common use of a resource, such as a machine, building, administrative service, or a production or service department, creates indirect costs. Costs associated with these resources are accumulated in **cost pools**. The size of the cost pool depends on how resources are aggregated. For example, each machine could have a separate cost pool, or the costs associated with all the machines could be placed in a single cost pool.

---

[3] Brian Mackie (2006) 'Merging GPK and ABC on the Road to RCA', *Strategic Finance*, (November), Vol. 88, No. 5, pp. 32–39.

Figure 9.1 **Two-stage allocation procedure**

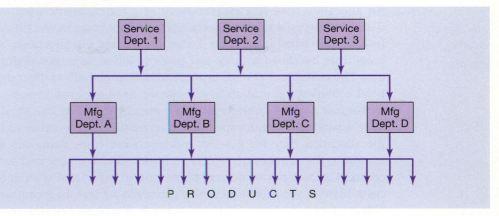

Indirect costs associated with a resource include all the costs that can be traced to the resource. For example, the indirect cost pool associated with the IT department would include direct costs to the department, such as the cost of the hardware, the labour costs of departmental employees, software and supplies.

In addition, a cost pool may contain costs that are associated only indirectly with the resource. These indirect costs are allocated to the cost pool from other cost pools that represent commonly shared resources. For example, the maintenance department is a resource that many other departments use. If the IT department uses the maintenance department, the IT department cost pool should contain allocated costs from the maintenance department cost pool.

Multi-stage cost allocation occurs when costs are allocated through a series of cost pools. Figure 9.1 is an example of a two-stage allocation procedure. Internal service department costs are allocated to production departments that use the internal service departments. Internal service departments include human resources, accounting, maintenance and computer services. Production department costs are then allocated to the different products that use the different production departments. Production departments, such as assembly departments, are directly associated with the product or service that the organization provides. In this case, the production departments are the intermediate cost objects and the products and services are the final cost objects.

City Square Dental (continued)

CSD chooses the following cost pools for allocating costs to dentists:

Cost pool	Types of costs
General administration	Salaries of practice manager, accountant, secretary/bookkeeper, supplies, insurance, financial services
Occupancy	Rent, cleaning, equipment maintenance, utilities
Hygienists	Salaries, supplies and equipment
Nurses	Salaries
Radiography	Technician salaries, radiography equipment, x-ray film, digital-imaging costs
Reception	Salaries

Choosing an allocation base

An allocation base is a measurement of a characteristic used to distribute indirect costs of a cost pool to cost objects. Each cost pool may have a different allocation base. In ABC, described in Chapter 3, cost drivers are the allocation bases that distribute costs from overhead activity cost pools to different responsibility centres and products. The cost driver chosen through ABC is intended to reflect the usage of the overhead activity. An allocation base, however, need not even be associated with the costs in the cost pools. As noted earlier, a company might choose an allocation base to reduce a particular organizational characteristic. If the number of defects is chosen as the allocation base for general administration costs, managers would be motivated to reduce the number of defects so fewer costs are allocated to their responsibility centre. The number of defects might not be associated with general administrative costs. Instead, the allocation base is chosen to achieve an organizational goal to reduce defects. Japanese firms often use simpler allocation systems based on direct labour. Less precision is accepted in order to focus management attention on direct labour, as the latter tends to be a scarce resource.[4]

The choice of the allocation base depends on the goals of the organization. Cost allocations are used internally for two primary purposes (making planning decisions and control). No single choice of an allocation base is always right or always wrong. In general, the most frequently used allocation bases are those that have the greatest association with the cost being allocated. For example, an important method for allocating executive salaries is time spent by executives in the responsibility centre. Rent is frequently allocated based on square metres occupied. Many costs are allocated based on the time spent providing services for the responsibility centre. The allocation of advertising and marketing expenses, for example, commonly utilizes as the allocation base the time spent by marketing personnel on activities and projects for individual responsibility centres.

The choice of allocation bases is diverse, reflecting different organizational objectives. Another factor in the selection of allocation bases is the ease of measurement. A particular allocation base might be closely associated with an indirect cost, but could be difficult and costly to measure. A popular allocation base for corporate salaries is the time spent by executives in each responsibility centre. To measure this time, however, is a nuisance and some organizations might choose an easier allocation base to measure. For example, Enbridge Inc. allocates a number of corporate-level expenses based on capital employed in the business unit. The key objectives of its allocation system are fairness, consistency and simplicity in terms of administration and understanding.

City Square Dental (continued)

In choosing the allocation bases for the cost pools, CSD wants to motivate the dental specialists and other staff to use common resources efficiently, but also to provide excellent service to patients. The following choices are made with those goals in mind:

---

[4] K. A. Merchant and M. D. Shields (1993), 'When And Why to Measure Costs *Less* Accurately to Improve Decision Making', *Accounting Horizons*, Vol. 7, No. 2 (June), pp. 76–81.

Cost pool	Allocation base
General administration	Number of patients
Occupancy	Number of examination rooms
Hygienists	Hours used
Nurses	Hours used
Radiography	Number of x-ray and digital-imaging patients
Reception	Number of patients

These choices are based partly on recognizing the cost of using common resources and partly on achieving the goal of good patient care. For example, insurance is a major general administration cost and is closely related to the number of patients seen by the dentist. The number of examination rooms is used as an allocation base to discourage dentists from tying up too many examination rooms while patients wait for them. Each dentist has the choice of how many examination rooms to reserve for his or her patients. The number of radiography patients, rather than the number of x-rays or digital images, is used as an allocation base for the radiography department due to the fixed cost of getting the patient prepared for these treatments. Moreover, the clinic does not want to skimp on the number of x-rays or digital images, as they can be used to detect problems early. Under the current system, however, the incremental cost of another x-ray to the dentist is zero, so dentists will tend to have too many x-rays taken on a particular patient.

The use of nurses, hygienists and receptionists is a problem at CSD. The allocation bases tend to encourage dentists to use the reception staff more and to use the nurses and hygienists less, because the allocated costs of using the latter increases by hour of use. But under this system, there is no incremental cost to the dentists of using reception staff to perform certain tasks, such as explaining treatment plans and options to patients. Given that the salaries of nurses and hygienists are greater than those of receptionists, the dentists prefer to substitute some work performed by nurses and hygienists with that of receptionists. This substitution could have a negative effect on patient care and their perception of CSD's services.

■ Estimating an application rate

Once the allocation base for a cost pool is selected, an application rate is calculated. Normally, the application rate is determined at the beginning of the year, prior to the actual incurrence of the common cost. A pre-determined application rate allows for the allocation of costs during the period before common costs are completely measured. The allocated cost information is timelier with pre-determined application rates, but might not reflect actual costs incurred. The sum of all indirect costs allocated to cost objects with a pre-determined application rate does not usually equal the actual indirect costs. This problem is discussed in Chapter 10. In this section, we assume that management can make accurate estimates of indirect costs and allocation bases. For simplicity, we also assume that no difference exists between allocated indirect costs and actual indirect costs.

The application rate for an allocation base is commonly estimated with the following ratio:

$$\frac{\textbf{Estimated cost in the cost pool}}{\textbf{Estimated total usage of the allocation base}}$$

As an example, suppose that the estimated cost pool of the IT department for the next period is €400,000. The allocation base is the number of hours that IT personnel work on projects for different responsibility centres. The managers of the responsibility centres estimate that they will use 5,000 hours of IT personnel time. Therefore, the application rate is €400,000/5,000 hours or €80/hour.

Figure 9.2 Applied and estimated costs

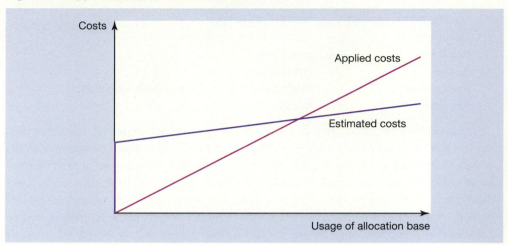

A number of problems are inherent in this application rate. First, cost allocation for planning decisions should be performed to obtain estimates of the cost of using the indirect resource. Some of the estimated IT may be sunk if estimated through an historical cost system. For example, the cost pool may contain historical cost depreciation, rather than the change in market value of a fixed asset (which is often referred to as economic depreciation).

Second, cost pools usually contain fixed costs with respect to the allocation base. For example, some of the costs of the IT department do not vary with the number of hours personnel work for other departments. The cost of using some of the hardware is likely to be fixed with respect to the number of hours that IT personnel work. All the IT costs, however, are allocated as if they varied with the number of hours that IT personnel work. After the fixed costs have been incurred, the application rate, which includes both fixed and variable costs, exceeds the variable costs of operating the IT department. This relation is shown in Figure 9.2 with the cost application curve being steeper than the total cost line. If allocated costs are higher than the incremental costs of operating the IT department, managers will tend to use less of the IT department than they should.

Numerical **example** 9.3

A motor pool allocates costs to other departments of the same organization based on the number of kilometres driven in company vehicles. The motor pool expects to incur annual fixed costs of £200,000 and variable costs of £0.20 per kilometres driven. The motor pool expects company vehicles to be driven a total of 800,000 kilometres. What is the application rate used by the motor pool? How does that application rate lead to under-use of the motor pool and costly behaviour by other departments?

Solution

The application rate is total expected costs in the motor pool divided by the total expected kilometres driven:

$$\frac{£200,000 + (£0.20/km \times 800,000 \text{ km})}{800,000 \text{ km}} = £0.45/km$$

This application rate, however, is higher than the incremental cost of operating an automobile, which is £0.20/km. The application rate acts like a transfer price. Therefore, managers in other departments will choose to use other means of transportation, if the cost per kilometre of alternative transportation is less than the application rate of £0.45/km for the motor pool. The entire organization would benefit, however, if the motor pool were used whenever the cost of the alternative means of transportation exceeded £0.20/km.

Fixed costs in the cost pool also mean that the application rate is affected by total estimated usage of the allocation base. If the cost pool contained only variable costs, a 10 per cent increase in the estimated usage of the allocation base causes a 10 per cent increase in the size of the cost pool. If the cost pool includes fixed costs, however, the size of the cost pool will increase proportionally less than the usage of the allocation base. Therefore, greater estimated usage of the allocation base causes the application rate to be lower. If the estimated usage of the allocation base declines, the application rate becomes higher. In other words, a reduction in the allocation base means that the fixed costs must be spread over fewer units of the allocation base.

Numerical *example* 9.4

Use the data in *Numerical example 9.3,* except assume that the motor pool expects company vehicles to be driven a total of 1,000,000 kilometres. What is the application rate used by the motor pool?

Solution

The application rate is total expected costs in the motor pool divided by the total expected kilometres driven:

$$\frac{\pounds200,000 + (\pounds0.20/km \times 1,000,000\ km)}{1,000,000\ km} = \pounds0.40/km$$

This rate is less than the application rate when it is assumed that 800,000 kilometres will be driven.

With fixed costs in the cost pool, one responsibility centre can affect the application rate used to allocate costs to other responsibility centres. In other words, if one department decides not to use an internal service represented by a cost pool, the application rate increases and the service becomes more costly for other departments. When managers affect the cost allocations to other managers, the controllability principle is violated. Managers prefer application rates that are insulated from the effects of other managers. If the cost pool being allocated includes fixed costs, application rates calculated by the total estimated usage of the allocation base do not insulate managers from the performance of other responsibility centres.

Numerical *example* 9.5

Use the data in *Numerical example 9.3.* Suppose that one department decides not to use the motor pool because of alternative transportation opportunities, and the total expected kilometres to be driven are reduced to 600,000 kilometres. What is the effect on the application rate?

→

Solution

The new application rate follows:

$$\frac{£200{,}000 + (£0.20/\text{km} \times 600{,}000 \text{ km})}{600{,}000 \text{ km}} = £0.53/\text{km}$$

The application rate is higher than the rate of £0.45/km in *Numerical example 9.3,* as the remaining users of the motor pool must pay a higher share of the fixed costs. The fixed costs of operating the motor pool must be spread over fewer users.

City Square Dental (continued)

The following table is used to calculate application rates at CSD:

Cost pool	Expected costs(£)	Expected allocation base	Application rate £
General administration	950,000	25,000 patients	38/patient
Occupancy	400,000	20 examination rooms	20,000/examination room
Nurses	250,000	12,500 hours	20/hour
Hygienists	360,000	30,000 hours	12/hour
Radiography	100,000	5,000 patients	20/patient
Reception	100,000	25,000 patients	4/patient

■ Distributing indirect costs based on usage of the allocation base

Once the application rate for the allocation base has been estimated, indirect costs are allocated to cost objects as they use the allocation base. For example, if hours of maintenance is the allocation base of the maintenance department cost pool, maintenance costs are allocated to cost objects when hours of maintenance are incurred by the cost object.

Numerical example 9.6

The application rate for maintenance department costs is €20 per hour of service. The use of the maintenance department by other departments is:

Department	Hours
Accounting	50
Sales	80
Manufacturing	200

How much of the maintenance department costs are allocated to these departments?

Solution

Department	Hours	Application rate (€)	Allocated costs (€)
Accounting	50	20	1,000
Sales	80	20	1,600
Manufacturing	200	20	4,000
Total costs allocated			6,600

In summary, the cost allocation procedure allows for the assignment of costs from a cost pool to cost objects. Cost objects are identified, costs are accumulated in cost pools, allocation bases are chosen, application rates are calculated, and indirect costs are allocated. These steps are repeated several times in the case of multi-stage cost allocations. A more difficult problem exists, however, when interactions exist between cost pools. As a result, one or more cost pools are the cost objects of other cost pools. For example, suppose different cost pools represent the accounting and maintenance departments, and each department provides services to the other department. In other words, the accounting department uses the maintenance department and the maintenance department uses the accounting department. The interaction of service departments leads to a special cost allocation problem. The Appendix to this chapter examines these interactions and their accounting treatment.

City Square Dental (continued)

Each CSD dental specialist acts as a profit centre and is evaluated and rewarded based on the profit that he or she generates. Dr Kim is a dentist at CSD with two examination rooms. She serves 2,000 patients who generated total revenues of £700,000 during the year. During the year, she used 3,000 hours of nurse time and 4,000 hours of hygienist services. Five hundred of her patients used radiography services. The profit associated with Dr Kim are as follows:

Revenues			£700,000
Costs			
Cost pool	*Application rate £*	*Usage*	*Costs allocated* (£)
General administration	38/patient	2,000 patients	76,000
Occupancy	20,000/patient room	2 patient rooms	40,000
Nurses	20/hour	3,000 hours	60,000
Hygienists	12/hour	4,000 hours	48,000
Radiography	20/patient	500 patients	10,000
Receptionists	4/patient	2,000 patients	8,000
Total costs			242,000
Profit			458,000

The profit of £458,000 generated by Dr Kim represents her share of the total profit of the clinic. Notice that £458,000 is Dr Kim's profit share, and her compensation for the dental services that she provided. From this amount, Dr Kim will have to pay for other expenses, such as professional and malpractice insurance and membership fees, along with any costs not included in the departmental costs.

Concept review

1 How are cost objects chosen?

2 What is a cost pool?

3 What is the purpose of an allocation base?

4 How is an application rate calculated?

5 How are common costs allocated to multiple cost objects?

6 What is the difference between a cost driver and an allocation base?

SEGMENT REPORTING

Segment reporting is the process of developing accounting reports for the separate units of the organization. The profit of each unit is measured to evaluate its performance and that of its managers. The ability to identify profitable and unprofitable segments of the business allows the president of an organization to add or withdraw resources from the segments and to reward the managers appropriately. If internal transfers occur among the units, the management accountant must use transfer prices to calculate each unit's income. The profit of each unit or segment should reflect the sales to other segments within the organization, as well as sales to external customers.

The income of each segment also includes costs of resources that are used by multiple segments. Therefore, these resource costs must be allocated to the segments. The internal purposes for allocating costs to segments are (1) to communicate information to managers of the different segments, and (2) to motivate the managers to make decisions consistent with the goals of the organization. External reports also use segment reporting. Corporations are required to report the profit of segments of the firm that correspond to different lines of business and geographic areas. For example, Bayer AG reports operating results of the following business segments: Health Care (pharmaceuticals, consumer health), Crop Science (crop protection, environmental/bio science) and Materials Science (materials, systems). Each segment is a cost object, and a recipient of costs allocated for organizational resources used by other business segments. Each business segment is also a profit centre with both internal and external sales recognized. Bayer AG reports the sales by segment and the inter-segment transfers to provide information on the profitability of these activities as well as its overall financial situation.

Companies also must report profits from different geographical regions. Bayer AG, for example, identifies profits separately for its European, North American, Asia Pacific, Latin American/Africa/Middle East regions. This process also involves transfer pricing and the allocation of costs.[5]

External reports include segment reporting to provide external users, such as investors, with more information

A neighbour's garden is an example of a positive externality. The view is yours effortlessly, while your neighbour receives no direct compensation for the work involved.

The Garden Picture Library/Alamy

---

[5] www.annualreport2006.bayer.com (accessed 13 June 2007).

about the profitability of the organization's different components. If segment reports were not included in external reports, investors would not be able to discern if a highly profitable segment is offsetting an unprofitable one.

Numerical example 9.7

The Green Corporation makes two products: chemex and citrol. The corporation has two product lines. A separate manager is responsible for each division. The Chemex Division sells 50 tonnes of chemex on the open market for £10,000 per tonne. Also, 20 tonnes of chemex are transferred to the Citrol Division. The Citrol Division sells 100 tonnes of citrol on the open market for £20,000 per tonne. The Chemex Division has variable costs of £5,000 per tonne and fixed costs of £200,000. The Citrol Division has variable costs of £8,000 per tonne, excluding the cost of chemex. The fixed costs of the Citrol Division are £400,000. The central administration allocates £100,000 of fixed costs to the Chemex Division and £500,000 of fixed costs to the Citrol Division. Calculate the profit of the two divisions, using the market price as the transfer price of chemex.

Solution

	Chemex division (£)	Citrol division (£)
Revenues		
Open market sales	500,000	2,000,000
Internal sales of chemex	200,000	
Variable costs		
Internal purchase of chemex		(200,000)
Other variable costs	(350,000)	(800,000)
Contribution margin	350,000	1,000,000
Fixed costs	(200,000)	(400,000)
Profit before allocated costs	150,000	600,000
Allocated costs	(100,000)	(500,000)
Divisional profit	50,000	100,000

If all the central administration costs have been allocated, Green Corporation's profit is the sum of the profit of the two divisions, or £150,000.

In *Numerical Example 9.7*, the allocated costs, fixed costs and internal sales are reported separately in the segment reports of the two divisions. These costs and sales are highlighted to provide managers with additional information for decision making. For example, allocated costs might be eliminated for performance evaluation purposes, if the allocated costs are not controlled by, or affect the behaviour of, the divisional manager. Reporting each division's contribution margin allows a manager to ignore fixed costs when making incremental planning decisions. Internal sales should be highlighted to identify interactions among the divisions. These interactions provide important information when considering the elimination of or changes in one of the divisions.

Segment reporting is just one of the end results of the transfer-pricing and cost allocation process. Product costs are another result. The next chapter describes different methods of allocating costs to products.

Concept review

1 What is the purpose of segment reporting?

2 How do transactions with other units of the organizations affect segment reports?

SUMMARY

1 **Describe the relation among common resources, indirect costs and cost objects.** Common resources are resources that are used by more than one sub-unit or product of the organization. Common resources generate indirect costs, which may be allocated to the users of the common resource. The recipients of allocated indirect costs are called cost objects.

2 **Explain the role of allocating indirect costs for external financial reports, income tax reports and cost reimbursement.** For external financial reporting and income tax reports, manufacturing overhead is traditionally allocated to products. Costs allocated to products sold on a cost reimbursement contract provide additional revenues for the organization.

3 **Identify reasons for cost allocation for planning purposes.** If allocated costs provide better estimates of the opportunity cost of providing a product or service, they are valuable for planning purposes. In this case, cost allocations communicate information to managers about the opportunity cost of using common resources.

4 **Identify reasons for cost allocation for control purposes.** Common cost allocation is a method to allocate scarce resources in some organizations. Cost allocation is also used for external reporting, cost reimbursement and for motivating managers to use common resources in a manner consistent with organizational goals.

Additionally, cost allocation can be used for mutual monitoring.

5 **Describe how the various reasons for cost allocation can create conflict within the organization.** Costs are allocated for external reporting, planning decisions and control purposes. A single cost allocation system will lead to conflict as each reason for cost allocation might imply a different allocation method.

6 **Allocate indirect costs using five basic steps.** Indirect costs are allocated by (1) defining the cost objects, (2) accumulating indirect costs in cost pools, (3) choosing an allocation base, (4) estimating an application rate and (5) distributing indirect costs based on the usage of the allocation base by the cost objects.

7 **Create segment reports for the organization.** Segment reports disclose the profit of the organization's sub-units. The profit of the sub-units reflects transfer prices and cost allocation.

8 **Use direct, step-down and reciprocal methods to allocate service department costs that interact. (Appendix)** The direct method ignores any interaction of service departments. The step-down method allocates service department costs in sequence, and recognizes some of the interaction of service departments. The reciprocal method solves simultaneous equations (one for each service department) to account for all interactions of service departments.

KEY TERMS

Allocation base A characteristic of the cost object used to distribute indirect costs.

Cost allocation The distribution of indirect costs among cost objects.

Cost object The subject of interest in determining the cost.

Cost pool The accumulation of costs related to an indirect activity.

Direct method (Appendix) A method of allocating service department costs that ignores any interaction of the service departments.

Externality The effect of a decision on parties other than the contracting parties.

Multi-stage cost allocation The process of allocating costs to cost objects, followed by the allocation of costs from those cost objects to other cost objects.

Mutual monitoring A process of having an organization's members monitor and control each other.

Reciprocal method (Appendix) A method of allocating service department costs that recognizes all interactions among the service departments.

Segment reporting A process of developing accounting reports for the separate units of the organization.

Step-down method (Appendix) A method of allocating service department costs that sequentially allocates the costs of the service departments.

APPENDIX
Allocating costs of service departments with interactions

In this chapter, cost allocations flow from the cost pools of indirect costs to cost objects. This flow of allocated costs could occur in multiple stages as in Figure 9.1, but costs do not flow back to any cost pools after the costs of that cost pool have been allocated. In other words, costs could be allocated from the IT department to the accounting department, but accounting costs then could not be allocated back to the IT department. In many organizations, service departments, represented by different cost pools, provide services to each other. The cost pool of each department is a cost object of the other. This interaction leads to a special cost allocation problem. How can you allocate costs from one service department to another and then back again?

With reciprocal service department costs, the service departments are not the ultimate cost objects, even though they receive services from each other. In the example in Table 9.1, the ultimate cost objects are two operating divisions, A and B, which use two service departments, Administrative Services and Engineering Maintenance. The two operating divisions are the ultimate recipients of all of the service department costs. Both service departments in Table 9.1 use the hours of their respective services as an allocation base.

Table 9.1 provides the usage of the service departments by each other, as well as by the two operating divisions. Administrative Services consumes 100 hours of its own service internally and 200 hours of engineering maintenance. Engineering Maintenance consumes 300 hours of its own service internally and 400 hours of administrative services. The goal is to assign the costs of the service departments (Administrative Services and Engineering Maintenance) to the operating divisions (A and B). Divisions A and B make the final products, and the cost of those products should include the administrative services and engineering maintenance costs.

Suppose the following total costs of the two service departments are to be allocated to Divisions A and B:

	£
Administrative Services	200,000
Engineering Maintenance	150,000
Total costs	350,000

Service department costs can be allocated to the operating divisions in several ways: direct allocation, step-down allocation, and reciprocal allocation. This Appendix uses the preceding data to illustrate the computations of the various methods, and to discuss the advantages and disadvantages of each method.

■ Direct allocation method

The first method for allocating service department costs is direct allocation. The **direct method** ignores all the internal and interactive usage of the service departments. Only

Table 9.1 Hours of use of service departments

	Administrative Services	Engineering Maintenance	Division A	Division B	Total
Administrative Services	100	400	400	100	1,000
Engineering Maintenance	200	300	600	900	2,000

Table 9.2 Direct allocation method

Calculation of the application rates

	Service Department costs	Total hours used by Divisions A and B	Application rate per hour
Administrative Services	£200,000	400 + 100 = 500	£200,000/500 = £400
Engineering Maintenance	£150,000	600 + 900 = 1,500	£150,000/1,500 = £100

Allocation of Service Department costs to Divisions A and B

	Administrative Services			Engineering Maintenance		
	Hours used	Application rate	Costs allocated	Hours used	Application rate	Costs allocated
Division A	400	£400/hour	£160,000	600	£100/hour	£ 60,000
Division B	100	£400/hour	40,000	900	£100/hour	90,000
Total costs			£200,000			£150,000

the usage of the service departments by the two operating divisions is used to allocate the costs of the two service departments.

If only usage by the two operating divisions is considered, the application rates are determined by dividing each service department's costs by its total hours of service supplied to the two operating divisions. These application rates are calculated in the first panel of Table 9.2. Once the application rates are estimated, the service department costs are allocated in the second panel of Table 9.2.

Table 9.2 demonstrates the allocation of the total service department costs to the two operating divisions. Division A receives a total of £160,000 + £60,000, or £220,000. Division B receives a total of £40,000 + £90,000, or £130,000 from the two service departments.

The direct method of allocating service department costs is simple to perform, but ignores the interaction of services by the service departments. This simplification can lead to poor decision making by organizational managers. In particular, ignoring the reciprocal services means that the application rate will not reflect the opportunity cost of using the service department. Managers of the operating divisions will tend to over- or under-utilize the service departments, depending on whether the application rate is lower or higher than the opportunity cost of the service department.

Another problem with direct cost allocation is that each service department will over-use the other service departments. The cost of each service department is only allocated to the operating departments; thus the service departments view the usage of other service departments as being free. They are not charged for other service departments and, therefore, have no monetary incentive to limit their usage. Accordingly, other administrative mechanisms must be implemented to control the utilization of each service department by the others. Such controls could include a constraint in the budget limiting the number of hours that can be used among service departments, or a priority system in providing services.

■ Step-down allocation method

The **step-down method** recognizes some of the interaction of service departments, but not all of the reciprocal uses. The procedure begins by choosing a service department and allocating all of its costs to the remaining service and operating departments.

Figure 9.3 **Flow of costs using the step-down method**

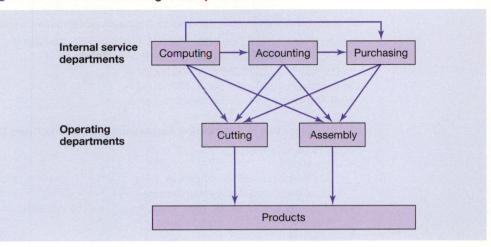

Then, a second service department is chosen and all of its costs (including its allocated costs from the first service department) are allocated to the remaining service and operating departments. This process continues until all service department costs are allocated. In this way, all service department costs cascade down through the service organizations and eventually are allocated to the operating departments.

Figure 9.3 describes the flow of costs through service departments and operating departments. Computing costs are allocated to the remaining service departments (Accounting and Purchasing) and the two operating departments (Cutting and Assembly). Accounting costs, which now include some allocated computing costs, are allocated to Purchasing, Cutting and Assembly. Then purchasing costs, which include some Computing and Accounting costs, are allocated to Cutting and Assembly. In this manner, all of the costs of the service department are allocated to the operating departments. The cost pools of Cutting and Assembly, which included allocated costs from the internal service departments, are then allocated to the different products to determine product costs.

Using the example in Table 9.1, assume that the first service department costs to be allocated are Administrative Services. Administrative Services' costs are allocated to Engineering Maintenance and Divisions A and B in the first step-down. In the second step, Engineering Maintenance costs plus its share of Administrative Services costs are allocated to Divisions A and B. The step-down method recognizes the use of Administrative Services by Engineering Maintenance, but not the use of Engineering Maintenance by Administrative Services. Internal use by each service department of its own services is also ignored. The step-down allocation method is demonstrated in Table 9.3.

The total costs allocated to Divisions A and B (£183,445 + £165,555, or £350,000) equal the original service department costs to be allocated. The costs allocated to each division using the step-down method differ considerably from the costs allocated by the direct method. The difference occurs because some of the interactions are considered.

Like the direct method, the step-down method also has some drawbacks. One is deciding the order of service departments to be allocated. A general rule of thumb is to allocate first the department that provides the greatest level of services to other users, in either monetary or percentage terms (or a combination). However, this procedure need not be followed and the order of the service departments will ultimately affect

Table 9.3 Cost allocation by the step-down method

Allocation of Administrative Services to Engineering Maintenance and Divisions A and B

Application rate = £200,000/(400 + 400 + 100 hours) = £222.222/hour

To Engineering Maintenance (£222.222/hour × 400 hours) =	£ 88,889
To Division A (£222.222/hour × 400 hours) =	88,889
To Division B (£222.222/hour × 100 hours) =	22,222
Total Administrative Services costs allocated	£200,000

Allocation of Engineering Maintenance to Division A and Division B

Costs to be allocated

Original costs	£150,000
Costs from Administrative Services	88,889
Total costs of Engineering Maintenance	£238,889

Application rate = £238,889/(600 + 900 hours) = £159.2593/hour

To Division A (£159.2593 × 600 hours) =	£ 95,556
To Division B (£159.2593 × 900 hours) =	143,333
Total Engineering Maintenance costs allocated	£238,889

Total service department costs allocated to Divisions A and B

	To Division A	To Division B
From Administrative Services	£ 88,889	£ 22,222
From Engineering Maintenance	95,556	143,333
Total costs allocated	£183,445	£165,555

the total costs that are allocated to the final cost objects. This flexibility might result in conflicts between managers whose departmental allocations depend upon the selected order. For example, if Engineering Maintenance were allocated first, the total service department costs allocated to Divisions A and B, respectively, would be approximately £227,062 and £122,941.

The order of the service departments also affects the application rates of the service departments. Service departments that are allocated early have lower application rates than under the direct method, and service departments that are allocated late have higher application rates than under the direct method. For example, the application rates under the direct and step-down methods are:

	Administrative Services (£)	Engineering Maintenance (£)
Direct method	400.00	100.00
Step-down method		
Administrative Services first	222.22	159.26
Engineering Maintenance first	435.29	88.24

If these application rates are different from the opportunity costs of using the service departments, managers will tend to use too much or too little of these services. The ordering of the service departments, however, allows the organization to put greater weight on certain allocation bases as opposed to others. By allocating a service department's costs last under the step-down method, the organization is taxing the allocation base of that service department more heavily and discouraging its use.

■ The reciprocal method

The **reciprocal method** of allocating service department costs recognizes all the interactions among service departments. The reciprocal method begins with establishing an equation for each service department. This equation includes the cost of the service department and the proportional use of the service department by other service departments and itself. In the example demonstrated in Table 9.1, Administrative Services (AS) uses 100/1,000 or 0.100 of its own services and 200/2,000 or 0.10 of Engineering Maintenance (EM). Engineering Maintenance uses 300/2,000 or 0.15 of its own services and 400/1,000 or 0.40 of Administrative Services. These proportions are used to establish the following equations, which represent the 'total' cost of operating the service departments. This total cost equals each service department's costs, plus a proportion of its own and other service department costs based on its usage of the allocation base:

$$AS = £200,000 + 0.10AS + 0.10EM$$
$$EM = £150,000 + 0.15EM + 0.40AP$$

These two equations have two unknown variables, the cost of Administrative Services (AP) and the cost of Engineering Maintenance (EM). By substituting one equation into the other, AP and EM can be calculated as £255,172 and £296,552, respectively. These costs are considerably higher than the original costs of the two service departments; they represent costs to be allocated to each other as well as the ultimate cost objects, Divisions A and B. The proportion of divisional usage of the service department to total usage of the service department is used to allocate costs to Divisions A and B. Table 9.4 demonstrates this allocation.

The total allocated costs to Divisions A and B (£191,035 + £158,965 or £350,000) equal the original costs of the two service departments, so the reciprocal method is consistent with complete cost allocation. The reciprocal method also recognizes the interaction of service departments. It will provide a cost allocation equal to the opportunity cost of using the service department, if the costs being allocated are the opportunity costs to operate the service departments and vary with the allocation base. If costs other than opportunity costs are being allocated, users of the service departments are likely to misuse the service department no matter which method is used for cost allocation. Also, if fixed and variable costs of operating the service department are allocated together, no method of cost allocation will approximate the incremental opportunity cost of using the service department. To take full advantage of the reciprocal method's ability to estimate opportunity costs, only the variable costs in each service department should be allocated using the system of equations. The fixed costs in each service department either should not be allocated or should be allocated based on another allocation base, such as each operating division's planned use of the service department's capacity.

Although the reciprocal method has advantages over the direct and step-down method it is more difficult to use. If there are 20 service departments, the solution

Table 9.4 The reciprocal method

	£
To Division A	
From Administrative Services (£255,172 × 400/1,000)	102,069
From Engineering Maintenance (£296,552 × 600/2,000)	88,966
Total Allocated Costs to Division A	191,035
To Division B	
From Administrative Services (£255,172 × 100/1,000)	25,517
From Engineering Maintenance (£296,552 × 900/2,000)	133,448
Total Allocated Costs to Division B	158,965

requires the solving of 20 equations with 20 unknown variables. Before computers, organizations had to use the direct or step-down method; the continued popularity of these methods is evident today.

Self-study problem

Incentives created by overhead allocations

Blackburn Springs plc is a bottler/supplier of bottled spring water to both commercial and residential customers. Blackburn Spring's corporate headquarters is located in Manchester. It operates distribution centres (DCs) in three territories throughout Lancashire and Merseyside. Customers pay a one-time subscription fee of £100 and then £11 per canister. The company began by selling to residential areas and small businesses in the region. In recent years, its sales have moved toward larger businesses. The Lancashire Centre was the first DC established and is the oldest of the three. The newest centre, Lancashire North, was established four years ago and continues to show great growth potential.

Bottling and distribution operations are treated as separate entities. The costs associated with each are easily tracked and charged to the appropriate division. There have been no problems related to the accounting systems between the two divisions. However, the managers in the distribution division have recently started to raise some questions regarding the accounting systems in place within their division.

Distribution centre operations are relatively straightforward. Bottled water shipments are taken from the main bottling plant and stored at the DCs for delivery to customers at later dates. Most subscribing customers take delivery once every two weeks. Expenses associated with DC operations can be seen in the quarterly profit and loss statement (See Table 9.5). DC overhead includes lease, building maintenance, security and other costs related to running the warehouse facility. Staff and administrative expenses include salaries of sales and support staff, as well as the cost of materials used in running the office (i.e. office supplies, forms, etc.).

Each distribution centre has its own sales staff. The corporate office handles the subscription process, and provides the drivers and delivery employees with the information regarding delivery type and schedule. The majority of corporate overhead allocated to distribution centres results from the processing and maintenance of subscriptions and schedules. Blackburn Springs allocates these overhead costs based on the proportion of the book value of trucks at each DC facility to the total book value of the entire Blackburn Springs Park delivery fleet. This allocation scheme was implemented at the time the company was founded to relate costs to the most significant cost item. Each DC is treated as a profit centre and DC management is evaluated based upon its territory's net profit performance.

Lorries are requested by distribution centres and purchased by the corporate offices under a corporate fleet contract with a major lorry manufacturer. Like interest expense, the lease expense is shown as a separate corporate level expense and is not allocated to the DCs. (See Table 9.6 for relevant data.)

Table 9.5 Quarterly Profit and Loss Statements for Blackburn Spring's Three Distribution Centres (£000)

	Lancashire Centre		Merseyside		Lancashire North	
Revenues		865.0		928.0		766.4
Expenses:						
Delivery wages	34.2		40.0		33.6	
Overtime wages	4.2		3.2		4.4	
Staff and administrative	150.0		120.0		125.0	
DC overhead	75.0		80.0		125.0	
Petrol	24.0		28.1		26.0	
Lorry maintenance	105.0		65.0		75.0	
Corporate overhead	235.7	(628.1)	283.0	(619.3)	391.3	(745.3)
Net profit		236.9		308.7		21.1

Table 9.6 Data for Blackburn Springs analysis

	Lancashire Centre	Merseyside	Lancashire North
Delivery employees	80	70	50
Delivery employee wages (£ per hour)	8	8	8
Total subscriptions	8,533	7,200	5,040
Deliveries per quarter	51,198	43,200	30,240
Canisters delivered per quarter	75,000	78,000	62,400
Average kilometres driven per delivery	4	4.5	5.2
New subscriptions this quarter	400	700	900
Lorries based at distribution centre	70	65	60
Lorry value (£)	700,000	690,000	670,000
Accumulated depreciation (£)	350,000	270,000	90,000
Allocation base (£)	350,000	420,000	580,000
Overhead allocation percentage	26	31	43

Additional Notes:
Lorry average is 16l/100km
Petrol cost is £1.20/litre
Delivery charge is £11 per canister delivered
Subscription fee is £100 per subscription

The bottled-water industry is experiencing strong growth, as is Blackburn Springs. While Blackburn Springs' business seems to be profitable, all is not well within the ranks of the organization. Corporate has been pressuring DCs to expand their territories and increase delivery volume, but DCs have been reluctant to meet this request. Some DC managers are beginning to question the amount of overhead being charged to them. They complain that increased deliveries will only cause overhead costs to rise. DC drivers are also unhappy; they complain about being overburdened by their ever-expanding routes and the pressure to meet difficult delivery schedules.

Judy Tsai, Assistant to the Controller, has been assigned the task of examining the situation and developing alternatives if, indeed, a solution is needed.

Required

a Describe the problems, if any, at Blackburn Springs. Specifically, discuss items related to decision making, cost allocation and incentives.

b Describe some alternative ways to allocate corporate overhead.

c Which allocation system would you choose? What effects do you believe that it would have upon Blackburn Springs's distribution operations?

d Calculate net profit for the three DCs under the system you have chosen and compare these results with those found under the present system.

e How does total profit of the three DCs compare across the original allocation and your proposed allocation scheme?

(Contributed by D. Lonczak, R. Bingham, M. Eisenstadt and B. Sayers.)

Solution

a The current overhead allocation system at Blackburn Springs is creating tremendous incentive problems with distribution centre managers. Corporate overhead is allocated based on the book value of delivery lorries; therefore, an internal tax is created when new vehicles are acquired by the distribution centres. This system provides incentives for DC managers to attempt to make more and more deliveries with their current number of lorries. In addition, these managers have incentives to keep older, less reliable vehicles in their delivery fleet. The growing number of driver complaints and the high percentage of overtime pay found in the respective profit and loss statements are further indications of these problems.

Other problems in the accounting system include the fact that the cost of bottled water and the cost of lorries are not being charged to the distribution centres. Since both of these are 'free' (except for corporate overhead being allocated based on the depreciated cost of lorries), DC managers are likely making the wrong decisions.

b **Equal overhead allocation**. Since corporate overhead results from functions which are necessary for the survival of each distribution centre, this expense could be allocated equally among the three centres.

Allocation based on profits. To take into account the profitability levels of each of the centres, corporate overhead could be allocated based on the net profits of each DC. This allocation scheme leads to some degree of monitoring and co-operation among the centres, because other divisions' profits affect allocated overhead.

Allocation based on total subscriptions. Since most of the corporate overhead expense results from the maintenance of subscriptions, corporate overhead can be tied to the total number of subscriptions held by each distribution centre.

c Blackburn Springs should allocate corporate overhead based on total subscriptions. Since much of corporate expense results from the processing and maintenance of subscriptions, this allocation scheme ties the distribution of these costs to a more accurate cost driver. This method removes the disincentive for DC managers to request additional lorries, use older vehicles for deliveries and force drivers to work overtime. While this method imposes an 'internal tax' on the sale of subscriptions, the new allocation encourages distribution centres to sell subscriptions to customers who buy larger quantities.

d Table 9.7 presents profit and loss statements for the three distribution centres under the proposed allocation scheme. Under the current allocation, Lancashire North is being unfairly penalized because of the high book value of its newer lorries. Alternatively, the Lancashire Centre, with lower lorry book values, appears more profitable due to the fact that it is not receiving a large enough portion of the corporate overhead expense. The proposed allocation method provides each distribution centre with improved incentives for growth and profitability.

However, such a change substantially alters the relative profitability of the three divisions. Lancashire Centre is the big 'loser' and Lancashire North the big 'winner'. Corporate headquarters should adjust the compensation formulas of the DC managers to ensure that bonuses are insulated from the new cost allocation scheme.

Table 9.7 Quarterly Profit and Loss Statements for Blackburn Spring's Three Distribution Centres Under Proposed Allocation Scheme (£000)

	Lancashire Centre		Merseyside		Lancashire North	
Revenues		865.0		928.0		766.4
Expenses:						
Delivery wages	34.2		40.0		33.6	
Overtime wages	4.2		3.2		4.4	
Staff and administrative	150.0		120.0		125.0	
DC overhead	75.0		80.0		125.0	
Petrol	24.0		28.1		26.0	
Lorry maintenance	105.0		65.0		75.0	
Corporate overhead*	373.1		315.8		221.1	
		(765.5)		(652.1)		(575.1)
Net profit		99.5		275.9		191.3

* Corporate overhead allocated based on subscriptions.

Supporting notes:

	Lancashire Centre	Merseyside	Lancashire North
Total subscriptions	8,533	7,200	5,040
Percentage of total	41.0%	34.7%	24.3%

e Total profit of the three DCs is the same (£566.7) for both allocation methods. The reason is that the total corporate overhead cost of £910 does not vary with the allocation method used. The same amount is being allocated, and thus the total profit of the three DCs is invariant to the allocation method. The allocation method affects how the total pie is distributed to the DCs, not the size of the pie.

Numerical exercises

NE 9.1 Cost allocation and profit LO 2

A company makes 200 units of A and 500 units of B. All the units of B are sold and one-half of the units of A are sold. There was no beginning inventory, but 100 units of A are in ending inventory. Product A sells for £5 per unit and Product B sells for £10 per unit. The variable cost of making Product A is £2 per unit and the variable cost of making Product B is £6 per unit. There are no fixed costs other than £900 of costs that are allocated to the two products.

Calculate the profit with £600 allocated to Product A and £300 allocated to Product B. Calculate the profit with £300 allocated to Product A and £600 allocated to Product B.

NE 9.2 Effect of allocation on profit LO 2

A company has an agreement to sell Product A for 20 per cent above cost. The company also sells Product B for £10 per unit. The variable cost of Product A is £4 per unit and the variable cost of Product B is £6 per unit. The company makes and sells 1,000 units of Product A and 2,000 units of Product B. The company has £5,000 of common costs to allocate to the two products.

What is the profit if all the common costs are allocated to Product A? What is the profit if all the common costs are allocated to Product B?

NE 9.3 Basic steps of cost allocation LO 6

The maintenance department of a firm has fixed costs of €40,000 and variable costs of €15 per maintenance hour supplied to other divisions. The maintenance department expects to supply 1,000 hours of maintenance during the coming year.

What is the application rate per maintenance hour supplied? What is the marginal cost of another maintenance hour?

NE 9.4 Basic steps of cost allocation LO 6

What is the application rate in *Question NE 9.3*, if 2,000 maintenance hours are supplied and there is no effect on fixed costs?

NE 9.5 Basic steps of cost allocation LO 6

Use the data in *Question NE 9.3*. How are maintenance costs allocated to production departments A, B and C, which use 200, 300 and 500 hours of maintenance, respectively?

NE 9.6 Segment reporting LO 7

Company C is composed of Divisions A and B. Division A has sales of £200,000 to outside buyers and £50,000 to Division B. Division B has sales of £300,000 to outside buyers. The costs of Division A are £120,000. The costs of Division B are £200,000 excluding the purchases from Division A. Company C headquarters allocates costs of £30,000 to Division A and £10,000 to Division B.

What is the profit of the two divisions?

NE 9.7 Allocation of service department costs LO 8, Appendix

Alpha Company has two service departments, A and B. The costs of these service departments are allocated to two production departments, C and D. The following table describes the use of the allocation base of the service departments by the service and production departments:

	Service Dept. A	Service Dept. B	Production Dept. C	Production Dept. D	Total
Service Dept. A	500	100	800	600	2,000
Service Dept. B	1,000	2,000	3,000	4,000	10,000

Service Department A has costs of €100,000 and Service Department B has costs of €200,000.

Allocate these costs to production departments C and D using the direct, step-down (Service Department A first), and reciprocal method.

NE 9.8 Cost reimbursement and cost allocation LO 2, 6

A consultant has an agreement with Worldwide Foods that all her costs while working on its project would be reimbursed in addition to her being paid £100 per hour. Other clients pay her a fee of £150 per hour with no cost reimbursement. During the year, she expects to have overhead costs of £150,000 and expects to work 2,000 hours for clients. Of those 2,000 hours, 400 hours are expected to be on the Worldwide Foods project. The overhead costs are the only expected costs and are allocated based on hours working for clients.

What does the consultant expect to earn during the year?

NE 9.9 Cost allocations and performance measures LO 4

The Harrison Corporation manufactures a variety of small toys popular with children and their parents. It allocates indirect costs to different products using the following allocation bases and application rates:

Allocation base	Application rate
Direct labour hours (DLH)	£10/DLH
Machine hours (MH)	£20/MH

Yue Lee is responsible for manufacturing toy trucks at the lowest possible cost. The direct material costs of making toy trucks are £4 per unit. Yue has no control over the cost of the direct materials but can influence how the toy trucks are made. The toy trucks could be made using 10 minutes of direct labour and 20 minutes of machine time. Another option is to use 30 minutes of direct labour and 5 minutes of machine time. The direct cost of labour is £12 per hour.

Which manufacturing method will minimize the total cost of the toy trucks?

Numerical problems

NP 9.1 Effect of allocation base choice on profit LO 6

Beach Chair Corporation makes two types of beach chairs, reclining and straight-back. The direct costs per unit of the two chairs are as follows:

	Reclining (£)	Straight-back (£)
Direct materials	3	5
Direct labour	5	2

The company has no beginning inventory. During the year, the company plans and makes 10,000 reclining chairs and 20,000 straight-back chairs. The company sells all of the reclining chairs for £20 each, but only half of the straight-back chairs for £18 each. Budgeted and actual manufacturing overhead costs during the year are £150,000.

a Calculate the operating profit, using direct material cost as the allocation base for the manufacturing overhead.
b Calculate the operating profit, using direct labour cost as the allocation base for the manufacturing overhead.

NP 9.2 Choosing allocation bases with cost reimbursement LO 2, 6

The Pure Water Company operates as the municipal water supplier for North Country Town. The town allows the Pure Water Company to charge consumers of the town water the costs to provide the water plus 10 per cent. The Pure Water Company also sells bottled water to grocery stores. These sales are not regulated, and the Pure Water Company can charge what the market will bear. The costs of the two types of water per litre are:

	Municipal water (£)	Bottled water (£)
Direct labour	0.001	0.10
Direct materials	0.001	0.01

The overhead costs to provide water are £2 million per month. Each month, the Pure Water Company sells 10 million litres of water to its municipal customers. It also sells 10,000 litres of bottled water for £1 litre.

a What is the company's profit if overhead costs are allocated by direct labour cost?
b What is the company's profit if overhead costs are allocated by direct material cost?

NP 9.3 Allocation and external reporting LO 2, 6

A building contractor started and finished a 20-unit condominium complex during the year. The direct costs per unit were £100,000, and the indirect costs per unit were £50,000. The indirect costs are manufacturing overhead, and are considered product costs. By the end of the year, the contractor had sold 12 units for £200,000 apiece. The contractor had additional indirect expenses of £500,000 that were considered period expenses.

a What is the profit of the building contractor for the year?
b What is the contractor's ending inventory?
c What is the profit of the contractor if all indirect costs are considered period expenses?

NP 9.4 Cost allocation and contingency fees LO 2, 6

A lawyer allocates overhead costs based on her hours working with different clients. The lawyer expects to have £200,000 in overhead during the year and expects to work on clients' cases 2,000 hours during the year. In addition, she wants to pay herself £50 per hour for working with clients. The lawyer, however, does not bill all clients based on covering overhead costs and her own salary. Some clients pay her on contingency fees. If the lawyer works with a client on a contingency-fee basis, the lawyer receives half of any settlement for her client. During the year, the lawyer works

1,200 hours that are billable to clients. The remaining hours are worked on a contingency basis. The lawyer wins £300,000 in settlements for clients of which she receives half. Actual overhead was £210,000.

What does the lawyer earn during the year after expenses?

NP 9.5 Fixed costs and allocated costs LO 1, 6

The maintenance department's costs are allocated to other departments based on the number of hours of maintenance used by each department. The maintenance department has fixed costs of €500,000 and variable costs of €30 per hour of maintenance provided. The variable costs include the salaries of the maintenance workers. More maintenance workers can be added if other departments demand greater maintenance, without affecting the fixed costs of the maintenance department. The maintenance department expects to provide 10,000 hours of maintenance.

a What is the application rate for the maintenance department?
b What is the additional cost to the maintenance department of providing another hour of maintenance?
c What problem exists if the managers of other departments can choose the amount of maintenance to perform?
d What problem exists if the other departments are allowed to outsource their maintenance services?

NP 9.6 Fixed costs and cost allocation LO 4, 6

The Human Resources department's costs are allocated to the other departments based on the number of direct labour hours. The department's expected fixed costs are £400,000 and its variable costs are £0.25 per direct labour hour. The Human Resources department has sufficient capacity such that fixed costs will not change with increased direct labour. The expected annual usage of direct labour by other departments is:

	A	B	C	D
Direct labour hours	100,000	500,000	250,000	150,000

a What is the application rate for the Human Resources department's costs?
b What would the application rate be if Department B were closed?
c Why would the managers of Departments A, C and D be upset with the closure of Department B?

NP 9.7 Cost allocation and dropping a unit LO 3

Cosmo operates two retail novelty shops, the Mall Shop and the Town Shop. Condensed monthly operating profit data for Cosmo Ltd for November follows. Additional information regarding Cosmo's operations follows the statement.

	Total (£)	Mall Shop (£)	Town Shop (£)
Sales	200,000	80,000	120,000
Less variable costs	116,000	32,000	84,000
Contribution margin	84,000	48,000	36,000
Less direct fixed expenses	60,000	20,000	40,000
Store segment margin	24,000	28,000	(4,000)
Less indirect fixed expenses	10,000	4,000	6,000
Operating profit	14,000	24,000	(10,000)

- One-fourth of each shop's direct fixed expenses would continue through December of next year, if either shop were closed.
- Cosmo allocates indirect fixed expenses to each shop on the basis of sales revenues.
- Management estimates that closing the Town Shop would result in a 10 per cent decrease in Mall Shop sales, while closing the Mall Shop would not affect Town Shop sales.
- The operating results for November are representative of all months.

a A decision by Cosmo Ltd to close the Town Shop would result in a monthly increase (decrease) in Cosmo's operating profit during next year of how much?
b Cosmo is considering a promotional campaign at the Town Shop that would not affect the Mall Shop. Increasing monthly promotional expenses at the Town Shop by £5,000 in order to increase Town Shop sales by 10 per cent would result in a monthly increase (decrease) in Cosmo's operating profit next year of how much?
c One-half of Town Shop's sales are from items sold at variable cost to attract customers to the store. Cosmo is considering the deletion of these items, a move that would reduce the Town Shop's direct fixed expenses by 15 per cent

and result in the loss of 20 per cent of the remaining Town Shop's sales volume. This change would not affect the Mall Shop. A decision by Cosmo to eliminate the items sold at cost would result in a monthly increase (decrease) in Cosmo's operating profit next year of how much?

(CMA adapted)

NP 9.8 Direct and indirect costs LO 3, 6

Nixon & Ross, a regional law firm, is about to install a new accounting system that will improve the tracking of overhead costs to individual cases. Currently, overhead is allocated to individual client cases based on billable professional staff salaries. Lawyers who work on client cases charge their time to 'billable professional staff salaries'. Time spent by lawyers in training, law firm administrative meetings, and the like is charged to an overhead account titled 'unbilled staff salaries'. Overhead is allocated to clients based on billable professional hours.

A summary of the costs for 2008 is given below:

	£
Billable professional staff salaries	4,000,000
Overhead	8,000,000
Total costs	12,000,000

The overhead costs were as follows:

	£
Secretarial costs	1,500,000
Staff benefits	2,750,000
Office rent	1,250,000
Telephone and mailing costs	1,500,000
Unbilled staff salaries	1,000,000
Total costs	8,000,000

Under the new accounting system, the firm will be able to trace secretarial costs, staff benefits, and telephone and mailing costs to its clients.

The following costs are incurred on the Lawson Company case:

	£
Billable professional staff salaries	150,000
Secretarial costs	25,000
Staff benefits	13,500
Telephone and mailing costs	8,000
Total costs	196,500

a Calculate the 2008 overhead application rate under the current cost accounting system.
b How would this application rate change, if the secretarial costs, staff benefits, and telephone and mailing costs were reclassified as direct costs instead of overhead, and overhead were assigned based on direct costs (instead of staff salaries)? Direct costs are defined as billable staff salaries plus secretarial costs, staff benefits, and telephone and mailing costs.
c Use the overhead application rates from (a) and (b) to compute the cost of the Lawson case.
d Nixon & Ross bill clients 150 per cent of the total costs of the job. What would be the total billings to the Lawson Company if the current overhead application scheme were replaced with the new overhead scheme?
e Steve Nixon, managing partner, has commented that replacing the current allocation system with the direct charge method of the new accounting system will result in more accurate costing and pricing of cases. Critically evaluate the new system.

NP 9.9 Allocation of central corporate overhead LO 6, 7

Eurlandia Wood Products is one of the world's largest integrated timber grower and wood processors. The Forest Group manages and harvests timber from company-owned and public forests. The Lumber Group buys cut trees from either the Forest Group or other timber companies, and processes the trees into a full line of wood products, including plywood, lumber and veneers. The Building Products Group buys wood products (from the Lumber Group and other companies) as well as other building supplies, such as dry wall and roofing products, and distributes these products worldwide to retailers. The senior managers in each group receive a bonus based on their group's profit before taxes.

Central corporate overhead is allocated to each group on the basis of actual sales revenues in each division. The current year's corporate overhead allocated to the three groups is:

	€
Corporate salaries and other	50,000,000
Research and development	600,000,000
Interest	850,000,000
Corporate overhead	1,500,000,000

Operating data for the last financial year (in millions of euros) follows:

	Forest Group (€)	Lumber Group (€)	Building Products Group (€)	Total (€)
Revenues	5,000	8,000	12,000	25,000
Operating expenses	3,500	7,000	11,500	22,000
Gross margin	1,500	1,000	500	3,000
Corporate overhead	300	480	720	1,500
Profit (loss) before taxes	1,200	520	(220)	1,500
Group assets	5,000	2,000	1,000	8,000

Instead of allocating €1.5 billion of overhead to the groups on the basis of revenues, the controller is proposing that each of the overhead categories be allocated using a different allocation base. In particular:

Overhead category	Allocation base
Corporate salaries and other	Sales revenue
Research and development	Gross margin
Interest	Group assets

a Calculate each group's profits before taxes, using the controller's proposed allocation scheme.
b What are the pros and cons of allocating corporate overhead to operating divisions?
c What are the advantages and disadvantages of the controller's proposed change relative to the existing method?

NP 9.10 Allocating service department costs LO 8

A manufacturer has two service departments (Power and Maintenance) and two production departments (Parts and Assembly). The following table indicates costs, the allocation bases and the use of the allocation bases (budgeted = actual) of the two service departments by each other and the production departments.

			Usage of the allocation base			
Service department	Cost (£)	Allocation base	Power	Maintenance	Parts	Assembly
Power	30,000	KWH	5,000	8,000	15,000	20,000
Maintenance	40,000	Square metres	5,000	10,000	80,000	40,000

a Use the direct method to allocate service department costs to the Parts and Assembly production departments.
b Use the step-down method, beginning with the Power department, to allocate service department costs to the Parts and Assembly production departments.
c Use the reciprocal method to allocate service department costs to the Parts and Assembly production departments.

NP 9.11 Estimating application rates LO 3, 4, 5, 6

Mutual Fund Company (MFC) is considering centralizing its overnight mail function. Five departments within MFC use overnight mail service: Trades Processing, Trades Verifications, Securities Processing, Accounts Control, and Customer Service. Although these departments send different types of packages (weight and content), often different departments send packages to the same destinations. Currently, each of these departments independently contracts for overnight mail service. The five departments' present rates are as in Table 9.8.

Table 9.8 **Present rates per package (£)**

	Number of kilograms in package				
	1	2	3	4	5
Department					
Trades Processing	7.25	8.50	9.75	11.00	12.25
Trades Verifications	7.75	8.75	9.75	10.75	11.75
Securities Processing	8.00	9.50	11.00	12.50	14.00
Accounts Control	10.00	12.00	14.00	15.50	16.50
Customer Service	16.00	18.00	20.00	22.00	24.00

MFC has requested each of the five departments to submit an estimate of its overnight mail for the coming year. The departments' estimates are as in Table 9.9.

Table 9.9 **Estimated usage**

	Packages per day	Annual number of packages*	Average weight per package	Kilograms per year
Trades Processing	100	25,000	5 kg	125,000
Trades Verifications	100	25,000	3 kg	75,000
Securities Processing	100	25,000	2 kg	50,000
Accounts Control	50	12,500	5 kg	62,500
Customer Service	10	2,500	1 kg	2,500
Total	360	90,000		315,000

*Based on 250 days per year.

Using these volume estimates, MFC was able to negotiate the corporate rates shown in Table 9.10 with EXP Overnight Express:

Table 9.10 **Corporate rates per package**

Weight (kilograms)	Rate (£)
1	7.75
2	8.70
3	9.65
4	10.65
5	11.60
6	12.55
7	13.55
8	14.50
9	15.45
10	16.45

The centralized overnight mail unit would be run as a cost centre. All expenses would be charged back to the five departments. The charge-backs would be comprised of two components:

1 The corporate rate per package charged by EXP (based on weight).
2 An overhead allocation per package.

MFC plans to use a 'prospective' overhead rate. Kilograms per package would be used as the allocation base. As each package comes in, overhead is charged. The rate is set at the beginning of the year and allows the overnight mail service to be costed as it is used. The common costs that comprise overhead (labour, supervision and other expenses) are as in Table 9.11.

Table 9.11 Overhead expenses

	£
3 employees @ £11,000 per person, per year	33,000
1 supervisor @ £18,000 per year	18,000
Other costs (rent, utilities, etc.)	24,000
Total overhead	75,000

At this time, the centralization of the overnight mail function has resulted in much controversy and scepticism. The managers of Trades Processing and Trades Verifications are the two managers who are most opposed to the proposed system. They claim that this proposed centralized system is unfair, and also that its annual cost savings do not justify a change.

a Calculate the overhead allocation rate that would be used with the centralized system.

b Calculate the estimated cost overall and per department of MFC's overnight mail service, under both the present system and the proposed centralized system.

c Discuss why the managers of the Trades Processing and Trades Verifications are opposed to the proposed centralized system. Do you agree with their criticisms?

d Evaluate the proposed method of allocating overhead under the centralized system. Does a better method to allocate cost exist? If so, what is it?

e Do you think the proposed centralized system can be improved? If so, how?

(Contributed by A. DiGabriele, M. Perez, N. Rivera, C. Tolomeo and J. Twombly.)

NP 9.12 Allocating service department costs LO 8

Donovan Steel has two profit centres, Ingots and Stainless Steel. These profit centres rely on services supplied by two service departments, Electricity and Water. Ingots' and Stainless' consumption of the service departments' outputs (in millions) is given in the following table:

	Service departments		Profit centres		
Service departments	Electricity	Water	Ingots	Stainless steel	Total
Electricity	2,500 kwh	2,500 kwh	2,500 kwh	2,500 kwh	10,000 kwh
Water	1,000 litres	800 litres	1,600 litres	1,400 litres	4,800 litres

The total operating costs of the two service departments follow:

	£m
Electricity	80
Water	60
Total cost	140

a Service department costs are allocated to profit centres using the step-down method. Water is the first service department allocated. Compute the cost of electricity per kilowatt-hour using the step-down allocation method.

b Critically evaluate this allocation method.

NP 9.13 Allocating corporate overhead to sales districts LO 3, 7

World Imports buys products from around the world for import into the UK. The firm is organized into a number of separate regional sales districts that sell the imported goods to retail stores. The North Eastern Sales District is responsible for selling the imports in the North Eastern region of the country. Sales districts are evaluated as profit centres and have authority over what products they wish to sell and the price they charge to retailers. Each sales district employs a full-time direct sales force. Salespeople are paid a fixed salary, plus a commission of 20 per cent of revenues on what they sell to the retailers.

The North Eastern District sales manager, J. Krupsak, is considering selling an Australian T-shirt that the firm can import. Krupsak has prepared the following table of his estimated unit sales at various prices and costs. World Imports corporate offices provided the cost data for the imported T-shirts.

World Imports
North Eastern Sales District
Proposed Australian T-Shirt
Estimated Demand and Cost Schedules

Quantity (000s)	Wholesale price (£)	T-shirt imported cost (£)
10	6.50	2.00
20	5.50	2.20
30	5.00	2.50
40	4.75	3.00

The unit cost of the imported shirts rises because the Australian manufacturer has limited capacity, and will have to add overtime shifts to produce higher volumes.

Corporate headquarters of World Imports is considering allocating corporate expenses (advertising, legal, interest, taxes and administrative salaries) back to the regional sales districts based on the sales commissions paid in the districts. It estimates that the corporate overhead allocation rate will be 30 per cent of the commissions (or for every £1 of commissions paid in the districts, £0.30 of corporate overhead will be allocated). District sales managers receive a bonus based on net profits in their districts. Net profits are revenues less costs of imports sold, sales commissions, other costs of operating the districts, and corporate overhead allocations.

The corporate controller, who is proposing that headquarters costs be allocated to the sales regions and included in bonus calculations, argues that all of these costs must ultimately be covered by the profits of the sales districts. Therefore, the districts should be aware of these costs and must price their products to cover the corporate overhead.

a Before the corporate expenses are allocated to the sales districts, what wholesale price will Krupsak pick for the Australian T-shirts, and how many T-shirts will Krupsak sell? Show how you derived these numbers.

b Does the imposition of a corporate overhead allocation affect Krupsak's pricing decision on the Australian T-shirts? If so, how? Show calculations.

c What are the arguments for and against the controller's specific proposal for allocating corporate overhead to the sales districts?

NP 9.14 Incentives of make-buy decisions in cost-plus contracts LO 2

BFR is a shipbuilding firm that has just won a government contract to build 10 high-speed patrol boats for the French Coast Guard for drug interdiction and surveillance. Besides building ships for the government, BFR operates a commercial vessel division that designs and manufactures commercial fishing and commuting ships. The commercial division and government division are the only two divisions of BFR. The Coast Guard contract is the only work in the government division.

The Coast Guard contract is a cost-plus contract. BFR will be paid its costs plus 5 per cent of total costs to cover profits. Total costs include all direct materials, direct labour, purchased sub-assemblies (engines, radar, radios, etc.), and overhead. Overhead is allocated to the Coast Guard contract based on the ratio of direct labour expense on the contract to firm-wide direct labour.

BFR can either purchase the engines from an outside source or build the engines internally. The following table describes the costs of the Commercial Division and the Coast Guard contract, if the engines are built by BFR versus purchased outside.

BFR
Cost structure (€m)

	Commercial Division	Coast Guard Contract – engines manufactured internally	Coast Guard Contract – engines purchased externally
Direct labour	14.600	22.800	18.200
Direct material		32.900	25.900
Purchased engines		0.000	17.000

Overhead for BFR is €83.5 million and does not vary if the engines are purchased outside or manufactured inside BFR. Overhead consists of corporate-level salaries, building depreciation, property taxes, insurance and factory administration costs.

a How much overhead is allocated to the Coast Guard contract if:
  i the engines are manufactured internally, and
  ii the engines are purchased outside?
b Based on the total contract payment to BFR, will the Coast Guard prefer BFR manufacture or purchase the engines?
c What is the difference in net cash flows to BFR of manufacturing versus purchasing the engines?
d Explain how cost-plus reimbursement contracts affect the make-or-buy decision for sub-assemblies.

NP 9.15 Allocating the cost of shared resource and incentives LO 1, 4

Grove City Broadcasting owns and operates a radio and a television station in Grove City. Both stations are located in the same building and are operated as separate profit centres with separate managers who are evaluated based on station profits. Revenues of both the radio and television station are from advertising spots. The price of a standard 30-second advert is based on audience size, which is measured by an independent outside agency. The radio station sells a 30-second advert for £100. (Assume that all 30-second adverts sell for £100 irrespective of the time of day the advert is aired.) The £100 price is based on an expected audience size of 20,000 listeners. If the listener audience were doubled, the 30-second advert would sell for £200. Or, each radio listener is worth £0.005 (£100 ÷ 20,000) of advertising revenue per 30-second advert. Television viewers are worth £0.008 per 30-second advert.

The radio station sells 3,550 30-second adverts per month and the TV station sells 3,200 30-second adverts per month.

The Sports Wire has approached both the radio and television managers about subscribing to its online service (which brings all sports scores, sports news and sports analyses to the station via standard telephone lines). The radio or TV station's sports announcers could download scores and news directly into their sports announcing scripts that can be read over the air. Sports Wire is more comprehensive, offers up-to-the-moment news, and contains more sports stories than the current general news wires that Grove City receives. If one of the two stations bought the Sports Wire, the price would be £30,000 per month. For an extra £5,000 per month, both the radio and TV stations could utilize the Sports Wire. If both stations used the Sports Wire, the £5,000 additional fee would include an extra online link that would allow two users to be on the system at the same time without interfering with each other.

The Sports Wire would not increase the number of adverts each month, just the revenue per advert. The Grove City radio manager believes that purchasing the Sports Wire would allow him to increase his audience by 1,500 listeners per advert. The television manager believes her audience size would increase by 500 viewers per advert.

a If the two managers did not co-operate, but rather, each made the decision, assuming they were the sole user of the system, would either buy the Sports Wire? Support your answer with detailed calculations.
b If the owner of Grove City Broadcasting had all the facts available to the two managers, would the owner buy the Sports Wire?
c The cost of the current wire services Grove City purchases are allocated to the two stations based on the number of stories aired each month from the wire service. The owner of Grove City Broadcasting decides to purchase the Sports Wire for both stations, and to allocate its £35,000 cost based on the number of Sports Wire stories aired each month. At the end of the first month, the radio station used 826 Sports Wire stories and TV used 574. Allocate the Sports Wire cost to the radio and TV stations.
d What is the allocated cost per Sports Wire story in the first month?
e Given the allocation of the Sports Wire cost, what behaviours can you predict will occur from the radio and TV station managers?
f Design an alternative allocation scheme that avoids the problems identified in (e). Discuss the advantages and disadvantages of your allocation scheme.

NP 9.16 Segment reporting LO 7

The Morris Corporation has two divisions, Engineering and Consulting. Both divisions charge customers by the hour of work performed. Engineering charges £100 per hour and Consulting charges £200 per hour. Engineering bills 10,000 hours during the year to outside customers and 2,000 hours to the Consulting Division of Morris Corporation. Consulting bills 5,000 hours. Engineering's variable costs are £40 per billable hour and annual fixed costs are £500,000.

Consulting has variable costs of £60 per billable hour, not counting the services purchased from Engineering, and annual fixed costs of £400,000. Engineering services are transferred to Consulting based on the market rate. Central administration allocates £200,000 to each division.

Calculate the profit of each division using transfer prices and allocated costs.

NP 9.17 Allocation of service department costs LO 8, Appendix

Misericordia Hospital has two service departments (Building Services and Food Service), and three patient-care units (Intensive Care, Surgery and General Medicine). Building Services provides janitorial, maintenance and engineering services as well as space (utilities, depreciation, insurance and taxes) to all departments and patient-care units. Food Service provides meals to both patients and staff members. It operates a cafeteria and also serves meals to patients in their rooms. Building Services costs of €6 million are allocated based on square metres, and Food Service costs of €3 million are allocated based on number of meals served. The following two tables summarize the annual costs of the two service departments and the utilization of each service department by the other departments.

	Annual cost* (€m)
Building Services	6.0
Food Service	3.0
Total overhead	9.0

*Before allocated service department costs

Utilization Patterns

	Allocation base	Building Services	Food Service	Intensive Care	Surgery	General Medicine	Total
Building services	Square metres	2,500	15,500	10,000	20,000	40,000	88,000
Food service	Meals	12,000	10,000	3,000	4,000	98,000	127,000

The following table summarizes the allocation of service department costs using the step-down method, with Food Service as the first service department to be allocated:

Step-down method (Food Service first) (€m)

	Intensive care	Surgery	General medicine
Food service	0.09	0.09	2.52
Building services	0.88	1.83	3.59
Total	0.97	1.92	6.11

(Round all allocation rates and all euro amounts to two decimal places.)

a Allocate the two service department costs to the three patient-care units using the direct method of allocating service department costs.

b Same as (a) except use the step-down allocation method where Building Services is the first service department allocated.

c Write a short, non-technical memo to management explaining why the sum of the two service department costs allocated to each patient-care unit in (b) differs from those computed using the step-down method starting with Food Service.

NP 9.18 Allocation of service department costs LO 8, Appendix

Fidelity Bank has five service departments (Telecom, Information Management, Building Occupancy, Training & Development and Human Resources). The Bank uses a step-down method of allocating service department costs to its three lines of business (Retail Banking, Commercial Banking and Credit Cards). Table 9.12 contains the utilization rates of the five service departments and three lines of business. Also included in this table are the direct operating

Table 9.12

		Service departments						Lines of business		
	Direct op. exp.	Tele-com	Info. mgmt	Building occ.	Training & dev.	Human res.		Retail banking	Comm. banking	Credit cards
1. Telecom	£3.5	–	0.15	0.05	0.05	0.05		0.20	0.15	0.35
2. Information Mgmt.	9.8	0.20	–	0.05	0.10	0.10		0.20	0.20	0.15
3. Building Occupancy	6.4	0.05	0.10	–	0.05	0.10		0.50	0.10	0.10
4. Training & Dev.	1.3	0.15	0.15	0.05	–	0.05		0.10	0.30	0.20
5. Human Resources	2.2	0.10	0.10	0.20	0.05	–		0.20	0.20	0.15

Fidelity Bank
Utilization Rates and Direct Operating Expenses of the Service Departments (£m)

expenses of the service departments (in millions of pounds). Direct operating expenses of each service department do not contain any allocated service costs from the other service departments. For example, Telecom spent £3.5 million and provided services to other units within Fidelity Bank. Information Management consumed 15 per cent of Telecom's services. The order in which the service departments are allocated is also indicated in the table. Telecom is the first department's costs allocated, followed by Information Management; Human Resources is the last department's costs allocated.

a Using the step-down method and the order of departments specified in Table 9.12, what is the total allocated cost from Information Management to Credit Cards, including all the costs allocated to Information Management?

b Information Management costs are allocated based on gigabytes of hard disk storage used by the other service departments and lines of business. If, instead of being second in the step-down sequence, Information Management became fifth in the sequence, does the allocated cost per gigabyte increase or decrease? Explain as precisely as you can why it increases or decreases.

c If instead of using the step-down method of allocating service department costs, Fidelity uses the direct allocation method, what is the total allocated cost from Information Management to Credit Cards, including all the costs allocated to Information Management? (Note: Information Management remains second in the list.)

Analysis and interpretation problems

AIP 9.1 Choosing allocation bases for levying taxes LO 2
The town of Seaside has decided to construct a new sea aquarium to attract tourists. The cost of the measure is to be paid by a special tax. Although most of the townspeople believe that the sea aquarium is a good idea, disagreement exists about how the tax should be levied.

Suggest three different methods of levying the tax and the advantages and disadvantages of each.

AIP 9.2 Methods of applying overhead LO 3
Rose Bach has recently been hired as Controller of Empco Inc., a sheet-metal manufacturer. Empco has been in the sheet-metal business for many years and is currently investigating ways to modernize its manufacturing process. At the first staff meeting that Bach attended, Rob Keller, Chief Engineer, presented a proposal to automate the Drilling Department. Keller recommended that Empco purchase two robots that would have the capability of replacing the eight direct labour workers in the department. The cost savings outlined in Keller's proposal included the elimination of direct labour cost in the Drilling Department, plus a reduction of manufacturing overhead cost in the department to zero, because Empco charges manufacturing overhead on the basis of direct labour costs using a plant-wide rate.

The president of Empco was puzzled by Keller's explanation of the cost savings, believing it made no sense. Bach agreed, explaining that as firms become more automated, they should rethink their manufacturing overhead systems. The president then asked Bach to look into the matter and prepare a report for the next staff meeting.

To refresh her knowledge, Bach reviewed articles on manufacturing overhead allocation for an automated factory and discussed the matter with some of her peers. She also gathered the historical data presented below on the manufacturing overhead rates experienced by Empco over the years. Bach also wanted to have some departmental data to present at the meeting and, using Empco's accounting records, was able to estimate the annual averages presented below for each manufacturing department since 2000.

Historical data

Date	Average annual direct labour cost (€)	Average annual manufacturing overhead cost (€)	Average manufacturing overhead application rate (%)
1960s	1,000,000	1,000,000	100
1970s	1,200,000	3,000,000	250
1980s	2,000,000	7,000,000	350
1990s	3,000,000	12,000,000	400
2000–08	4,000,000	20,000,000	500

Annual averages

	Cutting Department (€)	Grinding Department (€)	Drilling Department (€)
Direct labour	2,000,000	1,750,000	250,000
Manufacturing overhead	11,000,000	7,000,000	2,000,000

Required

a Disregarding the proposed use of robots in the Drilling Department, describe the shortcomings of the current system used by Empco Inc. to apply overhead.

b Do you agree with Rob Keller's statement that the manufacturing overhead cost in the Drilling Department would be reduced to zero, if the automation proposal were implemented? Explain.

c Recommend ways to improve Empco Inc.'s method to apply overhead by describing how it should revise its overhead accounting system:

   i in the Cutting and Grinding Departments, and
   ii to accommodate the automation of the Drilling Department.

(CMA adapted)

AIP 9.3 Cost reduction in service departments LO 4

Increased global competition has spurred most firms to take a hard look at their costs, and to become 'lean and mean'. Rochco, a large industrial complex, has seen off-shore competition erode its market share. Over the past few years, this industrial site of over 100 functional departments, some cost centres and other profit centres, has undergone several restructuring and labour reduction programmes to become more cost competitive.

Five years ago, the many service groups supporting Rochco's manufacturing operations were broken up into well-defined business centres. Top management encouraged all divisions to take over more decentralized decision making, and mandated that the service groups create value to the firm beyond that provided by outside contractors, or be shut down. Tom Etemad, manager of Building Services Department (BSD), was asked by Jane Corrado, General Manager of Rochco operations, to describe how he would take his unit from its then-dismal position vis-à-vis outside cleaning contractors to being the cleaning service of choice for its customers. An aggressive five-year plan was developed with break-even to be achieved in the third year. This task was not an easy one, considering that BSD's costs exceeded its competitor' prices by 53 per cent when using those of outside cleaners as a benchmark.

The majority of Rochco properties are cleaned daily by BSD, which runs as a cost centre. BSD allocates its expenses at full cost, based on the hours of service consumed by site customers. Over 80 per cent of BSD's cost is labour, not uncommon for a cleaning service. However, BSD's wage rates historically have been higher than those of its competitors due to Rochco's policy of paying in the upper bracket of local industry to attract good people. Tom Etemad's operating budget two years ago was £17 million.

Labour turnover is higher in BSD than the Rochco average (20 per cent versus 5 per cent annually). The primary reason is that BSD is one of the few departments to hire labour from outside the company. The manufacturing departments tend to recruit personnel from BSD before looking externally, for two reasons: BSD provides basic safety training and Rochco culture orientation to its people; and BSD people represent 'screened' employees to the hiring departments, inspiring greater confidence that the employee is a good, reliable worker.

The manufacturing departments also use BSD workers to fill in when normal production workers are on vacation.

Last year, BSD reduced its full costs to less than 29 per cent over market prices, ahead of the forecast of 37 per cent. BSD's costs are now £15 million annually. There is more pressure than ever on all Rochco managers to reduce costs. In June, William Laurri, a Manufacturing Manager and one of BSD's largest customers, told Tom Etemad that he was seriously considering going outside for cleaning services based on price. William Laurri manages another cost centre with challenging cost reduction goals and represents 50 per cent of BSD's customer base. Tom Etemad is concerned that the loss of William Laurri will irreparably damage BSD's progress toward its five-year break-even goal, and raise costs to other departments to such an extent that most of Tom's customers will switch to contract cleaners. Although BSD is still not competitive at full cost, it is almost competitive (within 2 per cent) on a direct-cost basis.

a Describe the cost accounting and control issues in this situation, which are driving Tom Etemad, Jane Corrado and William Laurri.

b Tom Etemad is confident that his cost-cutting programme will succeed by the target date, if BSD keeps its current accounts. Should he discount BSD's services in order to keep William Laurri?

c Should Jane Corrado insist that managers of the operating units continue to use BSD's services? What are the pros and cons of this approach?

(Contributed by S. Usiatynski, H. Merkel and M. J. Joyce.)

AIP 9.4 Cost allocation of tuition benefits in universities LO 3, 4, 5

Eastern University, located in central Canada, prides itself on providing faculty and staff a competitive compensation package. One aspect of this package is a tuition benefit of C$4,000 per child per year, for up to four years, to offset the cost of college education. The faculty or staff member's child can attend any Canadian university, including Eastern University, and receive the tuition benefit. If a staff member has three children in university one year, then the staff member receives a C$12,000 tuition benefit. This money is not taxed to the individual staff or faculty member.

Eastern University pays the benefit directly to the other university where the faculty/staff member's child is enrolled (or reduces the amount of tuition owed by the faculty/staff, if the student is attending Eastern University) and then charges this payment to a benefits account. This benefits account then is allocated back to the various faculties and departments based on total salaries in the faculty or department.

Critically evaluate the pros and cons of Eastern University's present method to account for tuition benefits. What changes would you recommend?

AIP 9.5 Effect of allocation bases on behaviour LO 4

Portable Phones, plc. manufactures and sells mobile, wireless telephones for residential and commercial use. Portable Phones' plant is organized by product line, five telephone assembly departments in total. Each of these five telephone assembly departments is responsible for the complete production of a particular telephone line, including manufacturing some parts, purchasing other parts and assembling the unit.

Each of the five assembly department managers reports to a product-line manager, who has profit responsibility for his or her product. These five product-line managers have authority over pricing, marketing, distribution and production of their product. Each of the five assembly departments is a cost centre within its respective product-line profit centres.

A key component of each telephone is the circuit board(s) containing the integrated circuit chips. Each assembly department purchases from outside vendors the basic boards and chips to be attached to its board(s). The Board Department of the plant receives the boards and chips in kits from each assembly department, and assembles them into completed boards ready for assembly into the telephones. The Board Department (with a cost structure that is 80 per cent fixed and 20 per cent variable) uses a single, highly-automated assembly line of robotic-insertion machines to precisely position each chip on the board, and soldering machines to solder the chips onto the board. The Board Department is a common resource for the plant; all five of the assembly departments use the Board Department to assemble some or all of their boards. Since the Board Department has a single assembly line, it can assemble boards for only one type of telephone at a time. The assembly departments have authority to seek the most competitive supplier for all their parts and services, including circuit-board assembly.

The Board Department's assembly schedule is determined at the beginning of each month. The five assembly departments request a time during the month when they plan to deliver particular kits to the Board Department and the number of boards to be assembled. The manager of the Board Department then takes these requests and tries to satisfy the assembly departments' requests. However, the Board Department manager finds that she has a peak load problem; the assembly departments tend to want their boards assembled at the same time. The only way to satisfy these requests is to work overtime shifts during these peak periods, even though the Board Department has excess capacity at other times of the month.

The total monthly costs of the Board Department (equipment depreciation, maintenance, direct labour, supervision, and engineering support) are assigned to the telephone assembly departments based on an hourly rate. The Board Department's total monthly costs are divided by the number of hours of capacity in the month (e.g. if a particular month has 22 working days, this is equivalent to 352 hours or 22 days × 2 shifts × 8 hours per shift) to arrive at a charge per hour. To provide the assembly departments with incentives to have its kits (boards and chips) delivered to the Board Department in a timely manner, the assembly department is charged for the time from when the last job (a batch of boards assembled for an assembly department) was finished by the Board Department until when the next job is finished. For example, suppose Telephone Assembly Department A's telephones were finished at 9:00 a.m., Department B delivered its kits at 1:00 p.m., and they were completed at 7:00 p.m. the same day. Department B would be charged for 10 hours of the Board Department's costs, even though the Board Department was idle for four of the 10 hours.

When first installed, the Board Department was expected to be operating at full capacity, two shifts per day, six days per week. Due to overseas outsourcing of some models and increased competition, the Board Department is now operating at about 70 per cent of the initial planned capacity.

a If you manage a telephone assembly department, everything else being held constant, when during the month would you tend to request your circuit boards be assembled by the Board Department? Explain why.
b Identify various dysfunctional behaviours likely to be occurring among the telephone assembly departments and the Board Department.
c What management changes would you suggest? In particular (but not limited to), what changes would you make to the accounting system? Explain why each change should be made. What would you hope to accomplish by the change?

Extended **analysis** and **interpretation** problems

AIP 9.6 Developing application rates

Marfrank Corporation is a manufacturing company with six functional departments – Finance, Marketing, Human Resources, Production, Research and Development (R&D) and Information Systems – each administered by a vice president. The Information Systems Department (ISD) was established two years ago, when Marfrank decided to acquire a new centralized computer and develop a new information technology network.

While systems development and implementation is an on-going process at Marfrank, many of the basic systems needed by each of the functional departments were operational at the end of 2007. Thus, calendar year 2008 is the first year when the ISD costs can be estimated with a high degree of accuracy. Marfrank's president wants the other five functional departments to be aware of the magnitude of the ISD costs in the reports and statements prepared at the end of the first quarter of 2008. The allocation of ISD costs to each of the departments was based on their actual use of ISD services.

Jon Werner, vice president of ISD, suggested that the actual costs of ISD be allocated on the basis of the pages of actual computer output. This basis was suggested since reports are what all of the departments use to evaluate their operations and to make decisions. The use of this basis resulted in the following allocation:

Department	Percentage	Allocated cost (€)
Finance	50	112,500
Marketing	30	67,500
Human Resources	9	20,250
Production	6	13,500
R&D	5	11,250
Total	100	225,000

After the quarterly reports detailing the allocated costs were distributed, the Finance and Marketing Departments objected to this allocation method. Both departments recognized that they were responsible for most of the output in terms of reports. However, they believed that these output costs might be the smallest of ISD costs, and requested that a more equitable allocation basis be developed.

After meeting with Werner, Elaine Jergens, Marfrank's controller, concluded that ISD provided three distinct services – systems development, computer processing represented by central processing unit (CPU) time and report generation. She recommended that a pre-determined rate be developed for each of these services from budgeted annual activity and costs. The ISD costs then would be assigned to the other functional departments, using the pre-determined rate times the actual service provided. Any difference between actual costs incurred by ISD and costs allocated to the other departments would be absorbed by ISD.

Jergens and Werner concluded that systems development could be charged based on hours devoted to systems development and programming, computer processing based on CPU time used for operations (exclusive of database development and maintenance), and report generation based on pages of output. The only cost that should not be included in any of the pre-determined rates would be purchased software; these packages were usually acquired for a specific department's use. Thus, Jergens concluded that purchased software would be charged at cost to the department for which it was purchased. In order to revise the first quarter allocation, Jergens gathered the information on ISD costs and services shown in Tables 9.13 and 9.14.

Table 9.13 Information Systems Department Costs

| | Estimated annual costs (€) | Actual first quarter costs (€) | Percentage devoted to | | |
			Systems development	Computer processing	Report generation
Wages and benefits					
Administration	100,000	25,000	60	20	20
Computer operators	55,000	13,000		20	80
Analysts/programmers	165,000	43,500	100		
Maintenance					
Hardware	24,000	6,000		75	25
Software	20,000	5,000		100	
Output supplies	50,000	11,500			100
Purchased software	45,000	16,000*	—	—	—
Utilities	28,000	6,250		100	
Depreciation					
Central computer system	325,000	81,250		100	
Printing equipment	60,000	15,000			100
Building improvements	10,000	2,500		100	
Total department costs	882,000	225,000			

* Note: All software purchased during the first quarter of 2008 was for the benefit of the Production Department

Table 9.14 Information Systems Department Services

Annual capacity	Systems Development 4,500 hours	Computer Operations (CPU) 360 CPU hours	Report Generation 5,000,000 pages
Actual usage during first quarter, 2008	Hours	CPU Hours	Pages
Finance	100	8	600,000
Marketing	250	12	360,000
Human Resources	200	12	108,000
Production	400	32	72,000
R&D	50	16	60,000
Total usage	1,000	80	1,200,000

a **i** Develop pre-determined rates for each of the service categories of ISD, i.e. systems development, computer processing and report generation.

  ii Using the pre-determined rates developed in (i), determine the amount that each of the other five functional departments would be charged for services provided by ISD during the first quarter of 2008.

b With the method proposed by Elaine Jergens for charging the ISD costs to the other five functional departments, a difference might exist between ISD's actual costs incurred and the costs assigned to the five user departments.

  i Explain the nature of this difference.

  ii Discuss whether this proposal by Jergens will improve cost control in ISD.

  iii Explain whether Jergens' proposed method of charging user departments for ISD costs will improve planning and control in the user departments.

(CMA adapted)

AIP 9.7 Allocating computer costs

The Independent Underwriters Insurance Co. (IUI) established a Systems Department two years ago to implement and operate its own information processing and storage systems. IUI believed that its own system would be more cost effective than the service bureau that it had been using.

IUI's three departments – Claims, Records and Finance – have different requirements with respect to hardware and other capacity-related resources and operating resources. The system was designed to recognize these differing demands. In addition, the system was designed to meet IUI's long-term capacity. The excess capacity designed into the system would be sold to outside users until needed by IUI. The estimated resource requirements used to design and implement the system are shown in the following schedule.

	Hardware and other capacity-related resources (%)	Operating resources (%)
Records	30	60
Claims	50	20
Finance	15	15
Expansion (outside use)	5	5
Total	100	100

IUI currently sells the equivalent of its expansion capacity to a few outside clients.

At the time the system became operational, management decided to redistribute total expenses of the Systems Department to the user departments based upon actual computer time used. The actual costs for the first quarter of the current fiscal year were distributed to the user departments as follows:

Department	Percentage utilization	Amount (£)
Records	60	330,000
Claims	20	110,000
Finance	15	82,500
Outside	5	27,500
Total	100	550,000

The three user departments have complained about the cost distribution since the Systems Department was established. The Records Department's monthly costs have been as much as three times the costs experienced with the service bureau. The Finance Department is concerned about the costs distributed to the outside user category, as these allocated costs form the basis for the fees billed to the outside clients.

Melinda Poon, IUI's Controller, decided to review the distribution method by which the Systems Department's costs have been allocated for the past two years. The additional information she gathered for her review is reported in Tables 9.15 to 9.17.

Melinda has concluded that the method of cost distribution should be changed to reflect more directly the actual benefits received by the departments. She believes that the hardware and capacity-related costs should be allocated to the user departments in proportion to the planned, long-term needs. Any difference between actual and budgeted hardware costs would not be allocated to the departments, but remain with the Systems Department.

The remaining costs for software development and operations would be charged to the user departments based upon actual hours used. A pre-determined hourly rate based upon the annual budget data would be used. The hourly rates that would be used for the current fiscal year are as follows:

Function	Hourly rate (£)
Software development Operations	30
Computer-related	200
Input/output-related	10

Melinda plans to use first-quarter activity and cost data to illustrate her recommendations. The recommendations will be presented to the Systems Department and the user departments for their comments and reactions. She then expects to present her recommendations to management for approval.

a Prepare a schedule to show how the actual first-quarter costs of the Systems Department would be charged to the users, if Melinda Poon's recommended method were adopted.
b Explain whether Melinda Poon's recommended system for charging costs to the user departments would:
  i improve cost control in the Systems Department,
  ii improve planning and cost control in the user departments, and
  iii be a more equitable basis for charging costs to user departments.

Table 9.15 Systems department costs and activity levels

| | Annual budget | | First quarter | | | |
| | | | Budget | | Actual | |
	Hours	£	Hours	£	Hours	£
Hardware and other capacity-related costs	–	600,000	–	150,000	–	155,000
Software development	18,750	562,500	4,725	141,750	4,250	130,000
Operations –						
Computer-related	3,750	750,000	945	189,000	920	187,000
Input/output-related	30,000	300,000	7,560	75,600	7,900	78,000

Table 9.16 Historical utilization by users (percentage figures)

| | Hardware and other capacity needs | Software development | | Operations | | | |
| | | | | Computer-related | | Input/output-related | |
		Range	Average	Range	Average	Range	Average
Records	30	0–30	12	55–65	60	10–30	20
Claims	50	15–60	35	10–25	20	60–80	70
Finance	15	25–75	45	10–25	15	3–10	6
Outside	5	0–25	8	3–8	5	3–10	4
	100		100		100		100

Table 9.17 Utilization of Systems Department's services (in hours), first quarter

| | Software development | Operations | |
		Computer-related	Input/output-related
Records	425	552	1,580
Claims	1,700	184	5,530
Finance	1,700	138	395
Outside	425	46	395
Total	4,250	920	7,900

(CMA adapted)

Absorption costing systems

(Planning and control)

Learning objectives

1. Identify different types of production systems and corresponding absorption costing systems.

2. Understand a job-order cost system.

3. Identify how costs flow through different accounts.

4. Calculate over- and under-absorbed overhead.

5. Account for over- and under-absorbed overhead.

6. Use activity-based costing (ABC) to allocate overhead in a job-order system.

7. Use multi-stage allocation methods and departmental cost pools to allocate overhead.

8. Calculate product costs using process costing.

9. Prepare schedules for cost of goods manufactured and cost of goods sold. (Appendix)

Orion Belts

Orion Belts is a manufacturer of leather belts. Although belts can be made from pigskin, lambskin or exotic animals such as crocodiles and sharks, the primary material used by Orion Belts and most belt manufacturers is cowhide. The cowhide is composed of two layers: the top grain, which is the outer layer, and the split leather, which is the inner one. The top grain is the preferred material for belts because it is the most durable and beautiful. The split leather does not have a natural grain, although a grain may be embossed on the split leather to more closely resemble top grain.

The construction of a belt begins with the purchase of dyed cowhides. Orion Belts buys both top grain for the production of expensive belts, and split leather for cheaper belts. The first activity in making a belt is the cutting of the leather into strips equal to the length and width of the desired belt size. Cutting is performed to minimize waste and to avoid bruises or brands on the leather.

Most belts have two layers, an outside layer of leather and an inside liner to help them maintain their shape. Naturally, the nicest leather is used for the outside layer. Some belts use top grain on the outside and split leather as a liner. The second activity of making the belt includes laminating and combining the two layers with glue. In addition, the edges of the leather strips are bevelled and dyed. This activity is referred to as combining.

The third activity in belt production is the punching of holes and making the loop. Belts typically have five to seven holes with an additional hole for the buckle.

The fourth and final activity includes adding the buckle, stitching the belt and stamping the belt with the company logo and size. Buckles are typically made of silver-plated zinc, but brass, steel, copper, nickel and aluminum are also used. The fourth activity is referred to as finishing.

Orion Belts has two manufacturing plants. Plant A makes belts to order. These belts tend to use top grain leather and are more expensive. The plant receives the design specifications from the customer and makes the belts accordingly. Machines and procedures must be modified for each order. The plant manager, Bert Stone, is responsible for negotiating a price for these special orders.

Plant B makes a standard belt from split leather that is sold to department stores. All machines in Plant B are dedicated to making the standard belt. Purchases from these stores tend to be large and unpredictable, so the plant maintains a relatively large inventory to meet customer demand. The plant manager, Katrina Gill, is responsible for inventory levels.

Each plant is divided into the four activities described earlier: cutting, combining, punching and finishing. Each plant also identifies direct material, direct labour and overhead costs. Direct labour and overhead also can be identified with each activity. Costs are used for planning (pricing and product-mix decisions) and control (motivating, evaluating and rewarding managers).

PRODUCT COSTING PROCEDURES IN ORGANIZATIONS

Chapter 3 introduced activity-based costing (ABC) as a method to estimate the cost of products and services. Costs estimated through ABC are useful for making planning decisions related to product mix and pricing. Costs related to products must not only be estimated for planning purposes, but also recorded when incurred. As we will see later in this chapter, ABC can also be used to record product costs when incurred. The initial examples of this chapter, however, use a single allocation base to record indirect product costs, to facilitate the learning of product costing procedures.

Chapter 9 described the procedures for allocating indirect costs to cost objects. In this chapter, the cost object of interest is the product or service of the organization. This chapter describes a particular, widely-used, cost allocation system called **absorption costing**. Absorption costing is the process of allocating variable and fixed overhead costs to products. In manufacturing facilities, all manufacturing (variable and fixed) overhead is commonly allocated to the goods produced by the facility. If it costs £32 million to operate a factory, and 28,000 units are manufactured (including units still in inventory), then the absorption cost system allocates the £32 million among the 28,000 units. Absorption cost systems lead to the same trade-offs between making planning decisions and control as other accounting method choices do, but we defer most of the discussion of this trade-off to Chapter 11. This chapter focuses on the mechanics of these cost systems.

Absorption cost systems are widely used in financial reporting to determine inventory valuation and the cost of goods manufactured. These systems initially were developed in manufacturing firms, and we will use this setting to describe these systems. However, the same concepts can be applied to the service sector, including financial institutions and professional services organizations (such as advertising agencies, law firms and public accounting firms). The chapter does not describe absorption cost systems in service industries, although several problems at the end of this chapter and other chapters illustrate absorption costing in non-manufacturing settings. Non-manufacturing settings tend to have simpler absorption costing systems as they do not have tangible work-in-process and finished goods inventories.

The two basic types of absorption cost systems are **job-order systems** and **process cost systems**. Job-order systems are used in departments that produce output in distinct jobs (job-order production) or batches (batch manufacturing). A 'job' might consist of a single unit, such as the construction of an office building, or a batch of units, such as 200 windscreen-wiper motors for automobiles. (In a service organization, a 'job' might be handling a client's lawsuit or processing a loan application at a bank.) The cost of each job is tracked separately, and job-order cost systems accumulate costs by jobs. Alternatively, in some assembly processes and continuous-flow production processes, process cost systems are used. Production in these settings is continuous (e.g. an oil refinery), and distinct batches do not usually exist. Under process costing, manufacturing overhead is allocated equally to all the units produced.

In practice, great diversity exists in how firms' accounting systems allocate costs to products, jobs, or activities. Even within batch manufacturing, no two systems are exactly alike. Many plants use hybrids of job-order and process costing. Each accounting system is tailored to the peculiarities of the department or plant. Accounting systems also adapt and change as firms modify their production processes. However, this chapter focuses on the similarities across all these systems. The central issue in cost systems is how to allocate indirect costs to products, jobs or services.

nagelestock.com/Alamy

Oil refineries operate round the clock with production on a continuous-flow basis. Emphasizing average costs, they tailor their accounting systems to the production process.

Concept **review**

1 What are the two different types of production processes?

2 What types of absorption cost systems are appropriate for different production processes?

Orion Belts (continued)

Although both Orion Belt plants make belts and have the same processes and machines, their operating methods are very different. Plant A makes belts as ordered from customers. Each order specifies the design and number of belts that are required. The plant treats each order as a batch. Each batch goes through the same four processes but may require different types of material, amounts of direct labour and machine time. Given the way this plant operates, management has decided to use job-order costing to identify the direct costs of each batch and to allocate overhead costs to those batches.

Plant B processes belts as a continuous flow. The factory only makes the standard belt; batches are not distinguishable as they move through the plant. This plant uses process costing to determine the cost of the belts.

JOB-ORDER COSTING

Job-order costing is the process of recording and accumulating the cost of making an identifiable product or batch of the same or similar products. A plant that manufactures different types of metal boxes in batches is used to illustrate job-order costing. Each box is produced in a batch requiring several different raw material inputs, and several different classes of direct labour. Moreover, the boxes utilize various combinations of common resources such as machines, supervisors, shipping docks and plant space. Each batch is referred to as a job. Every job passes through a common machining process. The time spent in this machining centre is recorded for each job and is used to allocate overhead costs to the job. In other words, the allocation base is machine hours and jobs are the cost objects. Each job in the plant has a job-order cost sheet that records the costs associated with the products manufactured in the batch, and the number of machine hours spent to process the job. A typical job-order cost sheet is shown in Table 10.1.

Job #5167 in Table 10.1 was started on 13 March and completed on 23 May. The job sheet records all direct materials issued for the job, including the date, the type of materials (represented by codes), the cost of the materials, and the quantity of materials. Direct labour related to Job #5167 is also recorded on the job-order sheet. This information is either obtained from workers' time cards, or directly recorded on the job sheet by the worker, frequently via online systems. Note that different types of labour (represented by codes) with different labour rates worked on the job. Job #5167 accumulated £13,375 of direct materials costs and £10,749 of direct labour costs. Also recorded on the job sheet is the number of machine hours used by the job. In this plant, machine hours are used to allocate overhead costs at the rate of £25 per machine hour. The £25 per machine hour is a pre-determined application rate. Chapter 9 discussed the calculation of application rates. Job #5167 used 213 hours of machinery. Multiplying 213 machine hours times £25 per machine hour yields £5,325 of overhead costs charged to this job. The total costs for this job are £29,449. With 1,550 units produced in this batch, the average cost is £19.00 per unit.

Table 10.1 Job-order cost sheet

Job number: 5167

Date started: 13/03
Date completed: 23/05

	Raw materials					Direct labour			
Date	Type	Cost (£)	Quantity	Amount (£)	Machine hours	Type	Rate (£)	Hours	Amount (£)
13/3	103a	30	205	6,150	13	a65	13	15	195
14/3	214	50	106	5,300	111	a68	15	20	300
1/4	217	15	52	780	45	b73	10	81	810
23/4	878	5	229	1,145	28	c89	12	368	4,416
23/5					16	c89	12	419	5,028
Totals				13,375	213				10,749

Total direct materials	13,375
Total direct labour	10,749
Overhead (213 machine hours @ £25/hour)	5,325
Total job cost	**29,449**
Divided by: Number of units in batch	1,550
Average cost per unit produced	19.00

Kitt Cooper-Smith/Alamy

Hand-held computers, RFID chips and real-time systems have replaced manual records in many firms, making job-order costing more efficient, timely and less costly.

The allocation base for indirect manufacturing costs accumulated in the overhead account is machine hours. As discussed in Chapter 9, the use of machine hours as the allocation base is similar to a tax on machine hours. This 'tax' creates incentives to economize on machine hours. The example of Job # 5167 illustrates several important features of job-order costing:

- All direct costs of manufacturing the job are traced directly to the job.
- Each job is charged for some indirect manufacturing overhead.
- At least one allocation base (such as machine hours) is used to distribute (allocate or absorb) overhead costs to jobs.
- The application rate for overhead (here, the rate per machine hour) is set at the beginning of the year, before the first jobs are started. This overhead rate is based on an estimate of what factory overhead costs and machine hours will be for the coming year.
- Reported product costs are average, not variable or marginal, costs. Each job is assigned a portion of the overhead. Since overhead contains some fixed costs, overhead distributed to jobs includes some of the fixed costs.

Numerical **example** 10.1

A customer orders a special tool (Job #676) that requires 5 units of part 103 at a cost of £40/unit, 4 units of part 244 at a cost of £20/unit, and 1 unit of part 566 at a cost of £100/unit. The tool also requires 5 hours of direct labour at £18/hour. Overhead is allocated to the job at a rate of £15/direct labour hour. The job is started and finished on 6 May. Prepare a job-order sheet for the tool.

Solution

Job number: 676

Date started: 06/05
Date completed: 06/05

		Raw materials				Direct labour	
Date	Type	Cost (£)	Quantity	Amount (£)	Rate (£)	Hours	Amount (£)
06/05	103	40	5	200	18	5	90
	244	20	4	80			
	566	100	1	100			
				380			

Total direct materials	380
Total direct labour	90
Overhead (5 direct labour hours @ £15/hour)	75
Total job cost	**545**

Concept **review**

1 What costs are recorded on a job-order cost sheet?

2 How are overhead costs added to the job-order cost sheet?

Orion Belts (continued)

In developing its job-order cost system, Plant A of Orion Belts must design a job cost sheet, train employees to make appropriate entries on the job cost sheet, and decide how to allocate overhead to the different batches. To keep its accounting system simple, Jane Chang, the plant accountant, decides to accumulate overhead in a single cost pool, and to allocate costs by direct labour hours. The application rate for the year is determined by dividing the estimated overhead costs (£800,000) for the year by the estimated direct labour hours (80,000). Therefore, an application rate of £800,000/80,000 hours, or £10/direct labour hour, is used. The overhead costs include supplies such as dye, thread, hangers and labels.

An example of a completed job-order cost sheet for Orion Belts is as follows.

Job-Order Cost Sheet

Job number: 543
Job description: 1,000 belts using design #456G

Date started: 30/06
Date completed: 05/07

Direct material costs

Date	Process	Part	Quantity	Unit cost	Total (£)
30/06	Cutting	Top grain leather	75 m^2	£33/m^2	2,475
05/07	Finishing	Buckle (#356)	1,000	£0.80/buckle	800
Total direct materials cost					3,275

Direct labour costs

Date	Process	Hours	Cost (£)/hour	Total (£)
30/06	Cutting	10	10/hour	100
02/07	Combining	15	8/hour	120
03/07	Punching	5	12/hour	60
05/07	Finishing	15	12/hour	180
Totals		45		460

Total cost of job

Direct materials	3,275
Direct labour	460
Overhead (45 hours × £10/hour)	450
Total costs	4,185
Number of units	1,000
Manufacturing cost per belt	4.185

COST FLOWS THROUGH THE ACCOUNTS

The job sheet illustrated in Table 10.1 is the underlying source document in the job-order cost system. For many years, manufacturing firms maintained job-order cost sheets manually with paper and ink. Today, job-order cost sheets are electronic records in computer systems. Costs are commonly recorded through the use of bar codes, RFID (radio-frequency identification) chips and hand-held computers. Job-order costing systems are frequently used where complex specifications and details need to be tracked and recorded. CAE is one example of the use of job-order costing in an advanced manufacturing environment.

Organizational *analysis*

CAE and job-order costing

CAE is the global leader in the specialized markets of simulation and modelling technologies and integrated training services. Its training network serves approximately 3,500 airlines, aircraft operators and manufacturers in more than 20 facilities worldwide. CAE's flight simulation products are recognized for their reality, quality and reliability, and for being the closest thing to the actual flight experience. The company also provides military training services for pilots, maintenance and crew members across the world. From its corporate headquarters in Montreal, Canada, the company builds its strength by focusing on its customers, innovation and quality. CAE seeks to create organizational value through the leverage of its products and services into related and emerging markets in the aerospace and defence industries, along with civil and domestic markets, such as urban simulation.

To achieve these goals, CAE must provide solutions that match customer preferences. This customer focus is one way in which CAE can maintain a competitive edge in the global marketplace. CAE also must be mindful of costs. Therefore, CAE designs, develops and manufactures its products in terms of 'mass customization' and modularization. While products might share common features to permit some economies of scale, CAE customizes them to meet the requirements of individual clients. It also reduces costs by shortening manufacturing cycle times. Working with its customers to meet current and anticipated market demand allows CAE to remain both competitive and innovative. In the long run, this ability to meet customer preferences translates into sustained shareholder value.

For example, CAE's Simulation Products group maintains its niche by customizing simulation systems to meet the specifications of global customers as diverse as the British Royal Air Force, Singapore Airlines, Ryanair, Boeing, Airbus and the US Navy. In terms of its costing system, CAE employs a detailed job-order system to accumulate and record costs for each specific contract. The system must also track complex contracts that span an extended time frame from initiation to completion.

Why does CAE use a job-order costing system instead of a much simpler process costing system?

How does the costing system at CAE operate to support CAE's strategy and its goals to create customer and organizational value?

Source: www.cae.com

While Table 10.1 illustrates the job-order cost sheet for one job, manufacturing plants can have hundreds, or even thousands, of jobs in various stages of completion on the plant floor at any one time. The accounting system tracks the costs charged to each job. As costs are charged to individual jobs, the costs are entered simultaneously in a work-in-process inventory account, which contains all of the costs of all unfinished jobs in the organization. Each job cost sheet can be thought of as a subsidiary account for the work-in-process account. The sum of the costs on the job cost sheets is equal to the balance of the work-in-process account.

The job-order cost sheet is not the original source document for product-related costs. Figure 10.1 diagrams the flow of costs from the original documents to the job-order cost sheet (as represented by work-in-process), to finished goods, and finally to cost of goods sold. Labour costs are recorded based on the amount of time the employee works times a labour rate, which includes national insurance contributions and pension costs. When an employee works on a job, she records the time spent on the job and her labour rate on the job cost sheet. At the same time, labour costs are recorded by the same amount. Not all labour costs eventually appear on job cost sheets. Employees have down time when they are not working on any job but are still getting paid. Also, some employees do not work directly on jobs. Any labour costs that do not end up on job cost sheets, often called 'indirect labour', become part of the overhead account.

Figure 10.1 Schematic of a job-order cost system

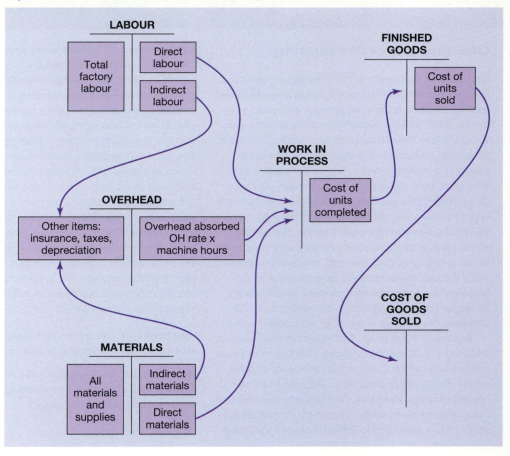

At the time of purchase, material costs initially are recorded as raw materials. The manager of the inventory warehouse controls the inventory; requisition slips are necessary to move raw materials from the warehouse to the factory floor. At the time of requisition, the raw materials are recorded on the job-order cost sheet and eliminated from the raw materials inventory account. Some raw materials are not used directly on jobs but are used indirectly by multiple jobs. For example, raw materials used to check the settings of a machine are not directly related to a specific job. The cost of these raw materials is treated as overhead.

Overhead indirect manufacturing costs are also recorded in various overhead accounts (such as Insurance, Property Taxes, Depreciation, Accounting, Purchasing, Security, General Plant Management, and Utilities) before being allocated to job-order cost sheets through the use of allocation bases. In Figure 10.1, the overhead accounts are aggregated into a single cost pool and allocated by a single allocation base. When overhead is allocated to a job-order cost sheet, the overhead account is reduced by an equivalent amount. The application rates of the allocation bases are estimated at the beginning of the time period. Estimates of the application rate do not always accurately reflect the actual usage of the allocation base and the actual overhead costs; therefore, the overhead allocated to jobs usually does not equal the total costs in the overhead account. The next section explains procedures to account for any differences between allocated (applied or absorbed) overhead and actual overhead.

When a job is finished and transferred to finished goods inventory, the total job cost from the job-order cost sheet is transferred out of the work-in-process account and into the finished goods account. Similarly, when the goods are sold, the costs flow out of the finished goods account and into the cost of goods sold account.

The cost structures of manufacturing firms differ considerably across industries and are influenced by factors such as firm size, product diversity and the intensity of competition. The ratio of direct to indirect costs has also changed over the years as firms have implemented more sophisticated costing systems. A review of European research into cost structures reported that the cost of direct materials tended to be higher than that of indirect costs, while direct labour costs represented the smallest proportion of total costs. A recent study of 87 UK manufacturing firms found that direct labour represented about 14 per cent of total costs, direct materials about 52.2 per cent, and manufacturing overhead costs about 10.3 per cent. Non-manufacturing costs (both direct and indirect) were about 23.5 per cent of the total costs.[1] However, these percentages can vary widely. In some cases, direct labour can be as low as 1 to 5 per cent of total manufacturing costs, and overheads as high as 80 per cent. An earlier US study of manufacturing overhead costs in the electronics, machinery and automobile-components industries reported that manufacturing overhead is approximately three times the direct labour cost. Manufacturing overhead represented 26 per cent of total manufacturing costs, direct labour 8 per cent and direct material 65 per cent in the electronic plants studied.[2]

Numerical **example** 10.2

The job cost sheet for a special product is as follows:

Job number: 711

Date started: 26/05
Date completed: 15/06

		Raw materials			Direct labour		
Date	Type	Cost (€)	Quantity	Amount (€)	Cost (€)	Hours	Amount (€)
26/5	130	30	6	180	18	5	90
15/6	248	10	20	200	15	10	150
				380		15	240

Total direct materials	380
Total direct labour	240
Overhead (15 direct labour hours @ €10/hour)	150
Total job cost	**770**

Overhead is allocated based on direct labour hours (DLH). The parts were in the raw materials inventory before being used on Job #711. The product is sold on 10 July. Identify the cost flows on 26 May, 15 June and 10 July.

→

[1] J. A. Brierley, C. J. Cowton and C. Drury (2001) 'Research into product costing practice: a European perspective', *The European Accounting Review*, Vol. 10, No. 2, pp. 215–256; M. Al-Omiri and C. Drury (2007) 'A survey of factors influencing the choice of product costing systems in UK organizations', *Management Accounting Research,* doi:10.1016/j.mar.2007.02.002.

[2] R. Banker, G. Porter and R. Schroeder (1995) 'An Empirical Analysis of Manufacturing Overhead Cost Drivers', *Journal of Accounting and Economics*, Vol. 19 (February), pp. 115–137.

Solution

Cost flows:

On 26/05:   €180 from raw materials inventory to work-in-process
€90 from labour to work-in-process
€50 from overhead to work-in-process for overhead related to direct labour hours (5 DLH × €10/DLH)

On 15/06:   €200 from raw materials inventory to work-in-process
€150 from labour to work-in-process
€100 from overhead to work-in-process for overhead related to direct labour hours (10 DLH × €10/DLH)

When finished: €770 from work-in-process to finished goods

On 10/07:   €770 from finished goods to cost of goods sold.

Concept **review**

1 When production begins, which account receives costs?

2 When production ends, which account receives costs?

3 Which account reflects the production costs of a product that is sold?

Orion Belts (continued)

Plant A has an inventory of leather and buckles. When an order arrives, the manager of the cutting process requisitions the leather necessary to make the belts. Similarly, the manager of the finishing process requisitions the buckles when the partially completed belts arrive in the finishing department. The manager of the raw materials inventory uses the requisition slips to verify the reduction in raw materials and their cost. The recipients record the cost and amount of raw materials used in their department on the job cost sheet. When the raw materials are recorded on the job cost sheet, they become part of the cost of work-in-process. In a similar fashion, direct labour and overhead become part of work-in-process when recorded on the job cost sheet. Upon completing the batch of belts, the total cost of the batch is recorded as part of finished goods inventory. When delivered to the customer, the cost of the batch is recorded as cost of goods sold.

Orion Belts has a financial year ending 30 June. Job-order number 543 (described on page 366) is the only partially completed batch in Plant A. The work-in-process as of 30 June follows:

	£
Direct materials	2,475
Direct labour	100
Overhead (10 hours × £10/hour)	100
Total work-in-process	2,675

ALLOCATING OVERHEAD TO JOBS

Chapter 9 outlined the following steps to allocate overhead (indirect product) costs: (1) defining the cost objects, (2) accumulating indirect costs in cost pools, (3) choosing an allocation base, (4) estimating an application rate, and (5) allocating indirect costs based on use of the allocation base. In this section, the cost objects are jobs, which are composed of individual or batches of products. The accumulation of indirect costs includes costs that are both fixed and variable with respect to the allocation base. The allocation base is some input into the production process, such as direct labour hours machine hours or material costs.

As described in Chapter 9, the allocation base is chosen for making planning decisions and control reasons. The application rate is pre-determined based on budgeted overhead costs and the predicted use of the allocation base. The pre-determined application rate allows for the allocation of overhead costs to jobs throughout the period, based on usage of the allocation base. For instance, a firm's digital camera manufacturing department estimates its overhead costs for the upcoming year to be £1,000,000. The allocation base is machine hours used by the manufacturing jobs. It is predicted that 50,000 machine hours will be used next year. The pre-determined application rate is established as £1,000,000/50,000, or £20 per hour. For each hour of machine time used by a job, overhead costs of £20 will be allocated.

These steps create an absorption cost system. If budgeted overhead costs and usage of the allocation base in the application rate are accurate predictions of the actual overhead costs and the actual allocation base usage, all manufacturing costs are absorbed by the jobs. Yet the predictions are not usually perfectly accurate; hence, applied (allocated or absorbed) overhead costs do not equal actual overhead costs. In this section, we examine reasons why the application rate under- or over-allocates the overhead costs, why we should be concerned about having applied overhead different from actual overhead allocated to jobs, and how to account for these differences.

■ Over- and under-absorbed overhead

The application rate is a ratio of budgeted overhead costs to budgeted usage of the allocation bases. As long as the actual overhead costs divided by the actual usage of the allocation base (the actual application rate) equals the budgeted application rate, the allocated overhead costs equal the actual overhead costs. In reality, however, the estimated application rate rarely if ever equals the actual application rate. Therefore, the allocated overhead does not equal the actual overhead. If applied overhead costs are greater than actual overhead costs, the difference is called **over-absorbed overhead**. If allocated overhead costs are less than actual overhead costs, the difference is called **under-absorbed overhead**.

Numerical example 10.3

A tool manufacturer uses machine hours (MH) to allocate overhead costs. The company expects to use 1,000 machine hours during the month and overhead costs are expected to be £100,000. Therefore, the application rate of £100,000/1,000 MH or £100/MH is used.

a If the actual overhead costs during the month are £90,000 and actual machine hours are 900, what is the difference between applied and actual overhead?
b If the actual overhead costs during the month are £98,000 and actual machine hours are 950, what is the difference between applied and actual overhead?

Solution

		£
a	Actual overhead costs	90,000
	Applied overhead costs (£100/MH × 900 MH)	90,000
	Difference	0

→

There is no difference between applied and actual costs because the actual application rate (£90,000/900 MH = £100/MH) is equal to the estimated application rate.

b

	£
Actual overhead costs	98,000
Applied overhead costs (£100/MH × 950 MH)	95,000
Difference (under-absorbed)	3,000

The actual application rate (£98,000/950 MH = £103.16/MH) is higher than the estimated application rate (£100/MH). As a result, the overhead is under-absorbed.

The actual application rate differs from the predicted application rate for a variety of reasons. This difference results in a discrepancy between actual and allocated overhead costs. One reason is illustrated in Figure 10.2. The predicted and actual overhead cost functions are assumed to have a fixed cost component. The allocated overhead costs, however, are applied through the usage of an allocation base. If the allocation base is not used, no overhead costs are allocated, so the allocated cost function goes through the origin. The application rate is estimated by dividing the predicted overhead costs by the predicted usage of the allocation base. Therefore, the allocated cost line in Figure 10.2 goes through the point where the predicted overhead costs and the predicted usage of the allocation base meet. The allocated cost line has a slope equal to the application rate. If the actual usage of the allocation base turns out to be less than predicted, less overhead costs are allocated than the predicted amount. This relation can be seen on the vertical axis of Figure 10.2. Although actual costs are as predicted, the incorrect estimate of the usage of the allocation base causes under-absorbed overhead. Over-absorbed overhead occurs if the actual usage of the allocation base is greater than the predicted usage of the allocation base.

Figure 10.2 Cost allocation with fixed costs

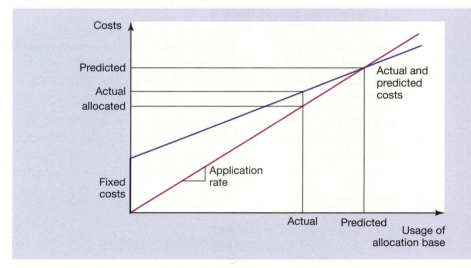

Numerical **example** 10.4

A bicycle manufacturer estimates that the company will use 3,000 direct labour hours (DLH). Direct labour hours are used to allocate overhead. The company estimates that fixed overhead costs will be €30,000, and variable costs will be €20/direct labour hour. At the end of the year, the company finds that it estimated fixed overhead and variable overhead per direct labour hour correctly, but used 4,000 direct labour hours. What is the relation between actual overhead costs and allocated overhead costs?

Solution

The company estimates the following overhead costs:

	€
Fixed costs	30,000
Variable costs (€20/DLH × 3,000 DLH)	60,000
Total estimated overhead costs	90,000

The application rate is €90,000/3,000 DLH, or €30/DLH. The company actually uses 4,000 DLH, so (4,000 DLH × €30/DLH), or €120,000 of overhead is allocated to the products. The actual overhead, however, is as follows:

	€
Fixed costs	30,000
Variable costs (€20/DLH × 4,000 DLH)	80,000
Total actual overhead costs	110,000

Therefore, the allocated overhead costs are €120,000 − €10,000, or €10,000 greater than the actual overhead costs. The overhead costs are over-absorbed.

Another reason for under- or over-absorbed overhead is simply an imprecise estimate of the overhead cost. Even if the expected usage of the allocation base is accurate, a wrong estimate of expected overhead will lead to allocated overhead not being equal to actual overhead.

Numerical **example** 10.5

An Internet bookseller allocates equal overhead to each book sold. At the beginning of the year, the bookseller estimates that 1 million books will be sold and that overhead will be £2 million. What is the over- or under-absorbed overhead, if 1 million books are sold and overhead is £2.1 million?

Solution

The application rate is £2,000,000/1,000,000 books, or £2/book. If 1 million books are sold, the bookseller allocates (1,000,000 books × £2/book), or £2,000,000. The under-absorbed overhead is £2,100,000 − £2,000,000, or £100,000.

■ Why worry about over- and under-absorbed overhead?

Differences between allocated and actual overhead exist due to inaccurate expectations about costs and cost-driver usage. One option is to ignore the differences, but there are planning, control and external-reporting reasons for adjusting product costs for over- and under-absorbed overhead.

Many of the products have been sold by the time over- and under-absorbed overhead has been identified at the end of the period. Therefore, little opportunity exists to adjust prices of the products already manufactured. The organization, however, can use product costs adjusted for over- and under-absorbed overhead to make future pricing and product-mix decisions. If the over- and under-absorbed overhead occurred due to mistakes in estimates, these mistakes should be corrected before making subsequent planning decisions. If the over- and under-absorbed overhead results from a one-period aberration, no adjustments to product costs are necessary for planning purposes.

For instance, suppose a firm has a significant amount of under-absorbed overhead at the end of the year. If the under-absorbed overhead indicates a change in market demand for its products, the firm should investigate its products and those of its competitors to determine how best to adapt to its environment and create customer value. Alternatively, if the under-absorbed amount reflects excess capacity, management should evaluate whether or not this situation is short- or long-term in nature. If it is the latter, management must decide whether to eliminate the excess capacity, or find alternative uses for it. Therefore, organizations should use the warning signs provided by over- and under-absorbed overhead to improve their future planning decisions. In this way, they can better ensure that their activities continue to create organizational value.

Over- and under-absorbed overhead costs also have control implications. Allocated costs are used as performance measures, creating incentives to influence the overhead cost allocations. One way to affect allocated overhead costs is to influence the calculation of the application rate. If the application rate is calculated with biased estimates of overhead costs and allocation base usage, managers can avoid the allocation of some overhead costs. Unless the allocated overhead is adjusted for under-absorbed overhead, managers will be tempted to influence application rates with biased estimates. These biased estimates not only will affect control, but also will harm planning efforts. For example, managers frequently are evaluated based on the profit of their responsibility centres. If they can influence the overhead rate, they would prefer to estimate their usage of an allocation base in terms of the final impact on their centre's profit. Inaccuracies could lead to poor planning, if the firm used these figures for pricing and product-mix decisions. Control also would be affected if the managers could influence reported profit to their advantage. One way to mitigate these biased estimates is to reward managers for the accuracy of their predictions.

External reports to shareholders or tax authorities are based on actual costs, not on estimated costs. Allocated overhead costs reflect estimates of actual overhead costs. Ultimately, however, these estimates must be replaced by actual overhead costs for external reporting purposes. Therefore, some adjustment for over- and under-absorbed overhead must be made to the external reports. Also, cost reimbursement contracts frequently are based on actual costs, not estimated costs. Therefore, adjustments for over- and under-absorbed overhead are commonly made to determine the final invoice for a cost reimbursement contract.

When allocated overhead costs are different from actual overhead costs, some decision must be made on accounting for the difference. The next section describes alternate procedures for dealing with over- and under-absorbed overhead.

■ Accounting for over- and under-absorbed overhead

At the end of the accounting period, an accounting adjustment must be made to eliminate any over- or under-absorbed overhead for the reasons just described. The three methods of accounting for over- and under-absorbed overhead are: (1) adjust cost of goods sold, (2) prorate among work-in-process, finished goods, and cost of goods sold, or (3) recalculate the application rate and apply to all the jobs during the year. Each method has a different impact on current earnings. If net profit is used as a performance measure for some managers, they will be concerned about the method of accounting for over- and under-absorbed overhead. Managers are not usually free to select any of the three methods. In general, if the over- or under-absorbed overhead is a material amount, managers cannot use the first method of simply adjusting cost of goods sold.

The choice of the methods also depends on how the allocated over- and under-absorbed costs are being used. If the purpose of the allocation is to communicate costs for planning purposes, the method that most closely approximates the cost of using indirect resources should be used. If the purpose of the allocation is to control managers, then the over- and under-absorbed overhead allocation should reflect controllability by the managers. The superiority of any of the following methods depends on the circumstances surrounding the allocation.

Adjustment to cost of goods sold

The simplest method of accounting for over- or under-absorbed overhead is to adjust cost of goods sold. If overhead is over-absorbed, the cost of goods sold account is reduced by the amount of over-absorption. If overhead is under-absorbed, the cost of goods sold account is increased. No adjustments are made to the work-in-process or finished goods inventory at the end of the period. This method, however, cannot be used for external reporting if the over- and under-absorbed overhead has a material impact (usually more than 3 to 5 per cent) of cost of goods sold.

Proration

Through **proration**, the over- or under-absorbed overhead is allocated to the work-in-process, finished goods, and cost of goods sold accounts proportionally to the size of those accounts at the end of the period. For example, if the ending balances of work-in-process, finished goods, and cost of goods sold are £10,000, £15,000, and £25,000, respectively, 20 per cent of the over- or under-absorbed overhead would be allocated to work-in-process, 30 per cent allocated to finished goods and 50 per cent to cost of goods sold.

Recalculation of the application rate

Recalculating the application rate and reallocating overhead to all the products manufactured during the year is the most costly in terms of accounting efforts. The actual application rate is calculated and used to reallocate the entire overhead to the products. Recalculating the application rate and reallocating overhead may be required in some cost reimbursement contracts.

Numerical **example** 10.6

At the end of the accounting period, a window manufacturer has the following account balances:

	Direct costs (£)	Allocated overhead (£)	Balance (£)
Work-in-process	10,000	2,000	12,000
Finished goods	25,000	5,000	30,000
Cost of goods sold	85,000	13,000	98,000
Total	120,000	20,000	140,000

→

The amount of overhead allocated to these accounts during the period was £20,000, based on an application rate of £5 per direct labour hour (DLH), but actual overhead costs were £25,000.

a What adjustments are made to the account balances, if the under-absorbed overhead is completely allocated to cost of goods sold?

b What adjustments are made to the account balances, if the under-absorbed overhead is prorated?

c What are the new balances, if the overhead application rate is recalculated?

Solution

a The under-absorbed overhead is £25,000 − £20,000, or £5,000. If the entire under-absorbed overhead were allocated to the cost of goods sold account, the adjusted account balances would be as follows:

	Original (£)	Allocation (£)	Adjusted (£)
Work-in-process	12,000	0	12,000
Finished goods	30,000	0	30,000
Cost of goods sold	98,000	5,000	103,000
Total	140,000	5,000	145,000

b If the entire under-absorbed overhead were prorated, the adjusted account balances would be as follows:

	Original (£)	Percentage	Allocation (£)	Adjusted (£)
Work-in-process	12,000	8.57	429	12,429
Finished goods	30,000	21.43	1,071	31,071
Cost of goods sold	98,000	70.00	3,500	101,500
Total	140,000	100.00	5,000	145,000

c The actual number of direct labour hours to produce the items in each account can be calculated by dividing the allocated overhead by the application rate of £5/DLH:

		DLH
Work-in-process £2,000/(£5/DLH)	=	400
Finished goods £5,000/(£5/DLH)	=	1,000
Cost of goods sold £13,000/(£5/DLH)	=	2,600
Total		4,000

The actual application rate is £25,000/4,000 DLH, or £6.25/DLH. The overhead allocated in the following table is calculated by multiplying the actual application rate times the actual number of direct labour hours:

	Direct costs (£)	Allocated overhead (£)	Balance (£)
Work-in-process	10,000	2,500	12,500
Finished goods	25,000	6,250	31,250
Cost of goods sold	85,000	16,250	101,250
Total	120,000	25,000	145,000

Concept **review**

1 Why do actual overhead costs generally not equal overhead allocated based on a pre-determined application rate?

2 Why should an organization be concerned about over- and under-absorbed overhead?

3 What three methods can be used to deal with over- and under-absorbed overhead?

Orion Belts (continued)

The management of Plant A had predicted that overhead costs would be £800,000, and that the number of direct labour hours would be 80,000 hours. The actual overhead costs, however, are £765,000, and actual direct labour hours are 75,000 hours. The under-absorbed overhead is:

	£
Actual overhead	765,000
Allocated overhead (£10/hour × 75,000 hours)	750,000
Under-absorbed overhead	15,000

The actual overhead application rate is £765,000/75,000 hours, or £10.20/hour. Orion Belts could use this actual application rate to recalculate the overhead allocated to each batch of belts. Jane Chang recommends that this procedure would be costly and without obvious benefits, given that Orion Belts cannot recapture any costs from its customers. Instead, she decides to increase the Cost of Goods Sold account by £15,000 to account for the under-absorbed overhead.

ABC AND MULTIPLE ALLOCATION BASES

Until this point in the chapter, all overhead costs have been accumulated first in a single overhead account and then allocated to products using a single overhead rate. Figure 10.3 illustrates this overhead allocation procedure. When a single overhead rate is used, all of the overhead is accumulated in a single cost pool. A cost pool is a collection of accounts accumulated for the purpose of allocating the costs in the pool to other cost objects. These cost objects include departments, processes, products and services.

From Chapter 3 and the discussion of ABC, we know that indirect costs have varying relations with products. For example, some indirect product costs vary with the

Figure 10.3 Single overhead cost pool and application rate

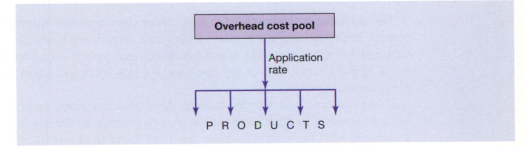

number of units produced; others vary with the number of batches. To adapt to an organizational environment with different types of indirect costs, costs can be accumulated in multiple cost pools related to different activities. A cost driver then is selected for each activity cost pool to allocate the indirect costs to the different products.

ABC can be used in a job-order costing system. Direct material and direct labour costs are recorded in a similar fashion. Overhead, however, would be added to the job cost sheet based on the use of multiple cost drivers.

Numerical example 10.7

A printing company has received an order (Job #234) to print 20 books written by Sara Windsor on her family history. The company will charge her based on cost plus 30 per cent. The company uses 10 reams of paper at £15 per ream, and 20 covers at £5 per cover. To complete the job, 15 hours of labour at £10 per hour were used. The job was started on 4 June and finished on 8 June. Overhead is allocated to the job based on ABC. The job used the following activities and cost drivers:

Activity	Cost driver	Usage	Application rate
Printing	Number of pages	4,000 pages	£0.05/page
Cropping	Number of pictures	80 pictures	£6/picture
Binding	Number of bindings	20 bindings	£10/binding
General	Direct labour hours	15 hours	£12/direct labour hour

a Construct a job-order cost sheet for Job #234.
b What price should Sara Windsor be charged?

Solution

Job number: 234

Date started: 04/06
Date completed: 08/06

Raw materials				Direct labour		
Type	Cost (£)	Quantity	Amount (£)	Rate (£)	Hours	Amount (£)
Paper	15	10	150	10	15	300
Cover	5	20	100			

Total direct materials	250
Total direct labour	150
Overhead	
Printing (4,000 pages × £0.05/page)	200
Cropping (80 pictures × £6/picture)	480
Binding (20 bindings × £10/binding)	200
General (15 hours × £12/hour)	180
Total job cost	**1,560**
Price to S. Windsor: (£1,560 × 1.3) =	**2,028**

The advantages of using ABC in a job-order system include improved planning and control. Improved planning occurs as the cost drivers are more likely to capture the different ways that cost objects use overhead resources. If each cost driver is proportional to the activity costs in the cost pool, the job-order cost sheet will report a relatively accurate product cost.

Using multiple cost drivers through ABC also has some control benefits. When using only one allocation base, managers will overuse all the overhead resources not associated with the allocation base. By using more than one allocation base or cost driver, the organization can tax multiple overhead resources. With multiple cost drivers, managers would have to make trade-offs in using overhead resources in the different activity cost pools. For example, if all of the costs of the department supporting web pages are allocated based on the number of web pages, managers will attempt to reduce the allocated costs by increasing the amount of information on each web page. At the same time, the managers may use extra plug-in and add-on software and other expensive web-page services, if no allocated costs are associated with them.

Improved control also can occur if an organization has multiple goals. An organization can use multiple allocation bases or cost drivers to achieve these multiple goals more effectively. For example, if an organization is trying to decrease both defects and the use of direct labour, both the number of defects and the number of direct labour hours can be used as allocation bases for different cost pools. Allocation bases are taxed through the allocation of overhead, so managers will be motivated to reduce defects and reduce direct labour.

The adoption of ABC systems has been less than anticipated given its perceived benefits. In firms with a high proportion of direct costs, an investment in an ABC system might not be beneficial. A simpler system often is adequate without distorting cost figures to any significant extent. A UK study examined adoption of ABC systems and found that the use of and interest in ABC had not grown and averaged about 15 per cent of manufacturing firms over the period. Additionally, firms frequently adopted ABC in parallel with their previous costing system. The financial sector had a much higher adoption rate of over 40 per cent, while the adoption rate in the service sector had dropped to about 12 per cent.[3] Higher education is one service sector in which the use of ABC has been considered. Universities have a high level of fixed and indirect costs and the analysis of their activities using ABC could contribute to a better understanding of their costs and benefits

Andrew Fox/Alamy

Universities track performance in many ways including graduation rates. ABC is one method used to determine the costs and benefits of research and teaching programmes.

Organizational **analysis**

Activity-based costing in a business school

How much does it 'cost' to teach an undergraduate student for one year? Is it more expensive to teach Ph.D. students, MBAs, or undergraduates? Most universities do not have good answers to these questions, despite complex and detailed accounting systems. Also, unlike manufacturing organizations, universities do not have products in the typical sense. Many interrelated costs and benefits result from the activities that a university undertakes. ABC is one way that can provide insights into the cost and benefits of the outputs of a university system.

A case study at a large business school developed an ABC model of its accounting department. As in the

→

---

[3] J. Innes, F. Mitchell and D. Sinclair (2000) 'Activity-based costing in the U.K.'s largest companies: a comparison of 1994 and 1999 results', *Management Accounting Research*, Vol. 11, pp. 349–362.

manufacturing sector, the objective was to allocate overhead costs in a manner that captured how different cost objects consumed resources. The study determined that the business school, like most universities, had a number of features that made cost management more difficult:

- Decentralized decision making with critical decisions taken at lower levels.
- Complex accounting and budget systems geared to compliance reporting.
- A lack of clearly defined outcomes and products.
- Many interconnected activities (e.g. teaching, research, administration).
- The consumer and the producer of activities frequently being the same.
- Interrelated costs and revenues in that certain activities are only undertaken due to the receipt of specific funds tied to the activity.
- The impact of capacity constraints on cost and quality of activities.

The ABC model focused on the accounting department of the business school. The first stage developed a set of cost objects and cost pools. The cost objects were the various programmes, research outputs, service outputs and unused capacity. The cost pools were the faculty resource costs and non-faculty resource costs. Faculty costs (compensation, travel and research allowances, etc.) were subdivided into four pools: teaching, research, service and advising of doctoral students. Non-faculty costs were placed into three pools: teaching support, research support and general administration. In the second stage, costs of the business school were identified and allocated in the same manner. These costs included the career centre, computer technology, media services and the costs of administrative offices. Once the costs of the various cost pools were assigned to the cost objects,

the study examined specific cost objects to determine if the ABC model provided insights not available from the existing approach to costing.

The following points summarize the results of the study:

- Significant differences exist in the per-student cost of the various academic programmes. For instance, the cost of a Ph.D. student per year is approximately 3.5 times that of student in a combined undergraduate/masters programme.
- Unused capacity represents a major cost. This unused capacity results from a number of factors ranging from under-subscribed classes and inefficient course scheduling.
- Space is a costly commodity at the business school, often comparable to the sum of all other costs.
- Programmes and activities do not make uniform use of support services, but the cost of the latter tends to be spread uniformly across all areas based on head count.
- ABC offers one way to focus on the cost-benefit of activity spending, and a better way to determine the efficiency in delivering teaching, research and service outputs.

What factors might contribute to the greater annual total cost per student in the Ph.D. programme compared to the five-year combined undergraduate/masters programme?

Why would the cost of capacity tend to be overlooked in a university environment?

Why would university faculty and staff be hesitant perhaps about efforts to cost their activities?

Source: M. H. Granof, D. E. Platt and I. Vaysman (2000) 'Using Activity-Based Costing to Manage More Effectively', Grant Report to The PricewaterhouseCoopers Endowment for The Business of Government, January.

MULTI-STAGE ALLOCATION PROCESSES

Overhead costs might be allocated to products through multiple stages. A common approach is to allocate general overhead costs first to departments that directly provide products and services, and then to allocate the departmental costs to the various products and services. Figure 10.4 illustrates this two-stage allocation process.

The allocation bases and application rates used to allocate costs from the departments to the products are specific to that department. One department might use machine hours and another department might use the number of engineering hours to allocate the departmental overhead costs. Alternatively, the allocation base for each department could be the direct labour hours specific to that department.

Figure 10.4 Two-stage cost allocation with departmental application rates

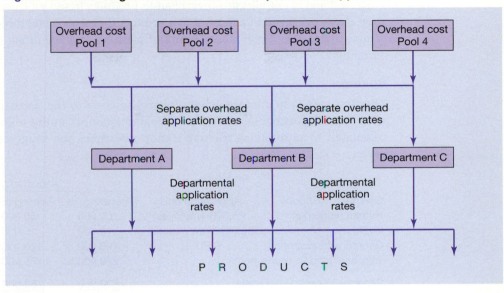

Multi-stage allocation schemes also can be used in conjunction with ABC. The general overhead cost pools would represent general activities. Cost drivers that reflect usage of the general activities would be selected to allocate costs to departmental or more specific activity cost pools. An additional set of cost drivers to allocate costs to products then would be identified for the departments or specific activities.

Control reasons exist for allocating general overhead initially to departments. Managerial responsibility is often oriented around departments. Departmental managers, who are responsible for controlling the cost of their departments, will want to control costs allocated to them. Therefore, managers will make careful use of the allocation bases upon which costs from the general overhead accounts are allocated to their departments.

Numerical **example** 10.8

A factory has three general overhead cost pools representing Human Resources, Inventory and General Administration. Their costs, allocation bases and application rates are:

Cost pool	Allocation base	Application rate
Human Resources	Number of employees	€5,000/employee
Inventory	Cost of raw materials used	€0.05/€ of raw materials
General Administration	Direct labour hours	€8/direct labour hour

The factory contains three departments: Machining, Painting and Assembly. These departments have the following costs (before allocated costs from general overhead cost pools) and usage of allocation bases:

Department	Internal department costs (€)	Raw materials (€)	Employees	Direct labour hours (DLH)
Machining	900,000	200,000	20	20,000
Painting	750,000	100,000	10	15,000
Assembly	850,000	100,000	30	25,000

→

Each department allocates overhead to products based on direct labour hours. How much overhead is allocated to a product that uses 1,000 direct labour hours of machining, 800 direct labour hours of painting and 500 direct labour hours of assembly?

Solution

The first step is to allocate general overhead costs to the departments to determine total departmental costs. The allocated amounts in the following panel are calculated by multiplying the application rate times the usage of the allocation base:

		Allocated to:		
Overhead cost pool	Application rate	Machining (€)	Painting (€)	Assembly (€)
Human resources	€5,000/employee	100,000	50,000	150,000
Inventory	€0.05/€ raw material	10,000	5,000	5,000
General administration	€8/DLH	160,000	120,000	200,000
Total allocated to departments		270,000	175,000	355,000
Separate departmental costs		900,000	750,000	850,000
Total departmental costs		1,170,000	925,000	1,205,000

The next step is to determine the application rates for the different departments:

Department	Costs (€)	Direct labour hours	Application rate (€)
Machining	1,170,000	20,000	58.50/DLH
Painting	925,000	15,000	61.67/DLH
Assembly	1,205,000	25,000	48.20/DLH

The last step is to allocate the overhead from the different departments to the products, based on the use of direct labour hours by the products. For the product in question, the allocated overhead follows:

Department	Application rate (€)	Direct labour hours	Overhead costs (€)
Machining	58.50/DLH	1,000	58,500
Painting	61.67/DLH	800	49,336
Assembly	48.20/DLH	500	24,100
Total allocated overhead costs			131,936

Concept review

1 Under what conditions will multiple allocation bases yield more accurate product costs than a single allocation base?

2 What is a control reason for first allocating costs to departments and then to products?

Orion Belts (continued)

Orion Belts is under pressure to change the cost allocation system. At Plant A, the pricing of specially ordered belts is based, in part, on the expected cost of making the belts. Some customers, who order special belts that require a great deal of finishing labour, believe that the product that they order is burdened too heavily with overhead from other departments. Jane Chang decides to reallocate overhead using departmental application rates. This allocation procedure requires her to estimate overhead costs and direct labour in each department. She makes the following estimates:

Department	Overhead costs (£)	Direct labour hours	Application rate (£)
Cutting	250,000	10,000	25.00/hour
Combining	320,000	40,000	8.00/hour
Punching	50,000	5,000	10.00/hour
Finishing	180,000	25,000	7.20/hour
Totals	800,000	80,000	

She tests the departmental allocation method on Job #543 (on page 366). The following cost allocation occurs:

Department	Direct labour hours	Application rate (£)	Allocated overhead (£)
Cutting	10	25.00/hour	250
Combining	15	8.00/hour	120
Punching	5	10.00/hour	50
Finishing	15	7.20/hour	108
Total allocated overhead			528

When using only one cost pool, the overhead allocation to Job #543 is £450. The difference of £78 appears to be large enough to warrant further testing. If sufficiently large differences do exist across different orders, the company will have to consider allocating costs by department.

PROCESS COSTING

Job-order cost systems are built around distinct jobs or batches in the manufacturing plant. In contrast, some manufacturing processes have continuous-flow production. For example, a car manufacturer, dedicated to making a single model, operates a continuous production line. A vegetable canning company operates a continuous process of cleaning, chopping, cooking and canning vegetables. A cement manufacturer continuously mixes the ingredients of cement and packages the mix. Each of these companies is devoted to making a single product (at least for a period of time) in a continuous process. Service organizations also have continuous-flow processes. For instance, fast-food restaurants often maintain a continuous production of ready-to-go items.

Since the production process is a continuous-flow operation, discrete batches do not exist. In process costing, costs are assigned to identical products that are produced in a continuous flow through a series of manufacturing steps or processes. These processes are usually organized as separate cost centres for control purposes.

For product-costing purposes, all the costs are associated with the same product. The cost allocation is not among different products, but among units still in work-in-process inventory and units transferred out of the process, or out of the plant to finished goods inventory or cost of goods sold. Work-in-process and finished goods are assets, while cost of goods sold is an expense. Therefore, the allocation will affect the organization's profit.

On the one hand, process costing is inherently simpler and less costly to maintain than job-order costing. It requires no tracking and accounting for separate units or batches. On the other hand, the information provided is far more aggregated and less useful for decision making. In particular, costs for individual units or batches are not available; hence cannot be used to evaluate cost trends across different jobs of similar products.

The simplest example of process costing can be illustrated by dividing total manufacturing costs (including indirect and direct costs) of the period by the number of units produced. For example, if the car manufacturer makes 5,000 cars during a month and incurs £50,000,000 of manufacturing costs, the average cost per car is £50,000,000/5,000 cars, or £10,000/car. The £10,000 is an average cost containing both variable and fixed costs. Therefore, the average cost provides no information about the incremental cost of making additional cars. The £10,000 average cost, however, can be used in external financial reports to indicate the cost of inventory and the cost of goods sold.

Process costing becomes more difficult when work-in-process exists at the end of the accounting period. If there is work-in-process at the end of the accounting period, some units have been partially processed, but are not yet finished. Partially completed units have consumed some of the period's manufacturing costs. Dividing total manufacturing costs during the period by the number of units finished during the period ignores the resources consumed by partially completed units.

To recognize the partial completion of some units at the end of the period, the concept of **equivalent units** is used. An equivalent unit is a measure of production during a period of time. An equivalent unit is based on the percentage of completion. This percentage of completion is used to determine the equivalence in terms of finished units completed during the period. For example, completing 40 per cent of the work to make 50 cars is equivalent to completing (0.40 × 50), or 20 cars. By recognizing the percentage of completion of ending work-in-process, the work performed during the period can be described in terms of equivalent units.

Numerical **example** 10.9

A computer workstation manufacturer began and completed 500 workstations during the period. In addition, another 50 workstations were worked on during the period. On average, these units were 60 per cent completed. There was no beginning work-in-process. Manufacturing costs during the period were €5,000,000. How many equivalent units of work were performed during the period? What was the average cost of a completed workstation?

Solution

The total equivalent units completed during the period were:

Units 100% completed	500
Partially completed units (0.60 × 50)	30
Total equivalent units	530

The average cost per computer workstation is €5,000,000/530, or €9,434.

Once the average cost per unit is determined, the average cost can be used to partition the period's production costs into costs associated with goods that are finished and goods that are still in work-in-process. In the case of the workstations in *Numerical example 10.9*, the cost of the finished workstations is 500 workstations × €9,434/workstation, or €4,717,000. The cost of the workstations in work-in-process at the end of the period is 30 workstations × €9,434/workstation, or approximately

€283,000. The original €5,000,000 in manufacturing costs are allocated to the finished goods and work-in-process accounts. Costs allocated to finished goods are transferred to the cost of goods sold account when the product is sold.

Additional complications in process costing arise when there is beginning work-in-process. With beginning work-in-process, the equivalent units of work performed during the period also must include the work necessary to complete the beginning work-in-process. The number of equivalent units of work performed during the period would include three components: (1) work to complete beginning work-in-process, (2) work on units that are both started and completed during the period, and (3) work on units that are started during the period but not completed (ending work-in-process).

Numerical **example** 10.10

A television manufacturer had 1,000 units in beginning work-in-process that were 30 per cent completed at the end of last year. This year, the remaining 70 per cent of the work on the 1,000 units was completed, and 10,000 more units were started and completed. In addition, 500 more units were started this period, but only 60 per cent completed. Manufacturing costs during the period were £2,000,000. What was the cost per equivalent unit during the period?

Solution

The number of equivalent units of work performed during the period was as follows:

	Units
Work to complete beginning work-in-process (0.70×1000)	700
Work on units started and completed	10,000
Work on ending work-in-process (0.60×500)	300
Total equivalent units	11,000

The cost per equivalent unit is £2,000,000/11,000, or £181.82.

The allocation of costs between units that are finished and units still in work-in-process is complicated when beginning work-in-process exists. In addition to the production costs in the current period, the cost of the beginning work-in-process due to work performed in the previous period also must be allocated. The cost allocation procedure depends on the accounting cost flow assumption. The FIFO, weighted-average cost and LIFO procedures lead to different cost allocations. Those procedures are explained briefly in the Appendix to this chapter and, in detail, in financial accounting and cost accounting textbooks.

Process costing yields cost numbers for work-in-process, finished goods, and cost of goods sold for external financial reporting. The use of process costs for planning purposes is limited if process costs include fixed and variable costs. Dividing total process costs by the number of equivalent units produced yields an average cost. In general, an average cost does not represent the variable cost of making the product.

Process costing is used for control, because externally reported accounting numbers are frequently used to evaluate managers. If managers are evaluated based on the cost per equivalent unit, then minimizing the average cost per unit and maximizing profit are not necessarily consistent. Minimizing the average cost can lead to production levels beyond that which can be sold. This excess production creates non-value-added costs, such as inventory holding costs. Problems related to absorption costing systems, such as job-order or process costing systems, are discussed in Chapter 11.

Concept **review**

1 What is the primary purpose of process costing?

2 How does the concept of equivalent units enable the calculation of the average cost per unit?

Orion Belts (continued)

Plant B of Orion Belts uses a process costing system, as the standard belt is its only product with no distinguishable batches. Instead of keeping track of the cost of each belt as it is processed, the plant tracks only total manufacturing costs as they occur. At the end of each month, the total manufacturing costs are divided by the number of belts produced to determine the average cost per belt. For example, in January, total manufacturing costs are £40,000, and the number of standard belts manufactured during January is 10,000. The average cost per belt in January is £40,000/10,000 belts, or £4/belt.

The chairman of Orion Belts, Vince Greco, uses the £4/belt cost to make pricing decisions for standard belts, and to evaluate and reward Katrina Gill, the plant manager, and other staff at Plant B. However, problems are arising in both areas.

The £4/belt cost is an average cost and includes fixed costs. Mr Greco would like to know the variable cost of making standard belts, but the process costing system does not reveal any information about variable costs.

Accounting reports are indicating an increase in inventory at Plant B. Mr Greco wonders if rewarding Katrina based on reducing the belt's average cost is affecting inventory decisions. He decides to read the next chapter on problems with absorption costing systems.

SUMMARY

1 **Identify different types of production systems and corresponding absorption costing systems.** Job shops and batch manufacturers tend to use job-order cost systems, and assembly processes and continuous-flow processes tend to use process costing.

2 **Understand a job-order cost system.** A job-order cost system is used to record the direct labour, direct material and overhead costs related to a particular product or batch of products. Costs are separately accumulated on the job cost sheet while work is being performed on the product or batch.

3 **Identify how costs flow through different accounts.** Costs flow from raw materials, labour and overhead accounts to work-in-process accounts during production; to finished goods accounts upon completion of production; and to cost of goods sold when sold.

4 **Calculate over- and under-absorbed overhead.** Over- and under-absorbed overhead occurs when the actual overhead costs are not equal to the applied overhead costs.

5 **Account for over- and under-absorbed overhead.** Over- and under-absorbed overhead can be (1) charged directly to cost of goods sold, (2) prorated among work-in-process, finished goods and cost of goods sold, or (3) eliminated by recalculating the application rate using the actual overhead costs and allocation base usage.

6 **Use activity-based costing (ABC) to allocate overhead in a job-order system.** Overhead is divided into different activity cost pools, and allocated to different products using different cost drivers and application rates for each cost pool.

7 Use multi-stage allocation methods and departmental cost pools to allocate overhead. Overhead is allocated initially to departmental cost pools; then allocated to products based on usage of the department's allocation base.

8 Calculate product costs using process costing. With process costing, the production costs are divided by the number of units to determine an average cost per unit. If units are partially completed during the period, equivalent units are used to divide into production costs.

9 Prepare schedules for cost of goods manufactured and cost of goods sold. (Appendix) The cost of goods manufactured schedule includes raw material used (Beginning raw materials + Purchases − Ending raw materials), direct labour and manufacturing overhead to determine total manufacturing costs. The cost of goods manufactured is equal to the total manufacturing costs plus beginning work-in-process less ending work-in-process. The cost of goods sold is equal to the cost of goods manufactured plus the beginning finished goods inventory less the ending finished goods inventory.

KEY TERMS

Absorption costing The inclusion of variable and fixed overhead in the product cost.

Equivalent units A measure of production, recognizing partial completion, that is used in process costing to identify work performed during a period of time.

First-in-first-out (FIFO) (Appendix) An inventory flow that assumes that the oldest units in inventory are sold first.

Job-order systems A system of recording costs for a particular job, which could be a single unit or a batch.

Last-in-first-out (LIFO) (Appendix) An inventory flow that assumes that the newest units in inventory are sold first.

Over-absorbed overhead The amount by which applied overhead is greater than actual overhead cost incurred.

Process cost systems A system of determining product costs by dividing total costs by the number of equivalent units produced.

Proration The process of dividing over- or under-absorbed overhead into finished inventory, cost of goods sold and work-in-process.

Specific identification inventory valuation method (Appendix) The ending inventory is determined by identifying the specific units of the raw materials, work-in-progress and finished goods, and their respective historical costs.

Under-absorbed overhead The amount by which applied overhead is less than actual overhead cost incurred.

Weighted-average cost (Appendix) A per-unit product cost determined by taking the weighted-average cost of all units in inventory.

APPENDIX
Cost of goods manufactured, the cost of goods sold and alternative cost flow methods for inventory

This chapter examines the flow of costs for a particular job from raw materials, work-in-process, finished goods inventory, and cost of goods sold. The jobs are specifically identified. The manufacturing costs of a particular job move from account to account as the job is manufactured, finished and sold. This flow of costs determines the cost of the goods manufactured and the cost of goods sold. This cost flow, in turn, affects net profit. These relations are captured in two schedules, cost of goods manufactured and cost of goods sold.

The cost of goods manufactured schedule identifies the manufacturing resources used to determine the total cost of goods manufactured during the period. Table 10.2 is an example of a cost of goods manufactured schedule. In this schedule, the raw

Table 10.2

Western Company
Schedule of Cost of Goods Manufactured
Month of May, 2008

	£	£
Direct material		
Raw material inventory, 1 May	40,000	
May purchases of raw materials	100,000	
Available raw materials	140,000	
Raw material inventory, 31 May	50,000	
Raw materials used in May		90,000
Direct labour		100,000
Manufacturing overhead		
Indirect labour	30,000	
Utilities	10,000	
Depreciation	5,000	
General administration	15,000	
Total		60,000
Total manufacturing costs		250,000
Work-in-process, 1 May		10,000
Work-in-process, 31 May		(15,000)
Cost of goods manufactured		245,000

materials used are calculated indirectly by using beginning and ending raw material balances and the purchases during the period:

Raw materials used = Beginning raw materials + Purchases
− Ending raw materials

In a similar manner, the cost of goods manufactured is calculated indirectly, using beginning and ending work-in-process and total manufacturing costs of the period:

Cost of goods manufactured = Beginning work-in-process
+ Total manufacturing costs
− Ending work-in-process

The cost of goods manufactured in Table 10.2 represents the cost of finished units transferred to the finished goods inventory. The cost of goods sold schedule in Table 10.3 uses the £245,000 cost of goods manufactured to calculate the cost of goods

Table 10.3

Western Company
Schedule of Cost of Goods Sold
Month of May, 2008

	£
Finished goods inventory, 1 May	180,000
Cost of goods manufactured (from Table 10.2)	245,000
Cost of goods available for sale	425,000
Finished goods inventory, 31 May	150,000
Cost of goods sold	275,000

sold. The cost of goods sold is calculated indirectly by using the beginning and ending finished goods inventory and the cost of goods manufactured during the month:

$$
\begin{aligned}
\textbf{Cost of goods sold} = \ &\textbf{Beginning finished goods inventory} \\
&+ \textbf{ Cost of goods manufactured} \\
&- \textbf{ Ending finished goods inventory}
\end{aligned}
$$

The cost of goods sold in Table 10.3 is used to calculate the net profit for the period.

In the cost of goods manufactured and cost of goods sold schedules, the cost of the ending balances of the raw materials, work-in-process, and finished goods inventory accounts are used in determining the cost of goods sold. There are several external reporting methods that are acceptable in calculating the cost of ending inventories. Under the **specific identification inventory valuation method**, the ending inventory is determined by identifying the specific units of the raw materials, work-in-process and finished goods, and their respective historical costs. This procedure has been used implicitly in this textbook. However, the specific identification method might be expensive to implement, as management must keep track of the batches from which each item came.

Alternative ways of measuring the cost of ending inventory and the cost of goods sold exist. Under **first-in-first-out (FIFO)**, the ending inventory is assumed to be the items produced most recently, and is valued based on the cost of producing the most recent batches. The cost of goods sold, therefore, is based on the costs of the beginning inventory and items produced earlier in the period. Under **last-in-first-out (LIFO)**, the ending inventory is assumed to be composed of items produced initially. The valuation of ending inventory under LIFO is based on the costs of items produced at the beginning of the accounting period and the costs of the beginning inventory. Therefore, the cost of goods sold is based on the cost of items most recently produced. The **weighted-average cost method** uses a weighted average of the cost of beginning inventory items and the cost of items produced during the accounting period to determine the cost of ending inventory and cost of goods sold. These methods are described in more detail in financial accounting textbooks.

Different inventory costing methods only provide different accounting numbers, when ending inventory exists and inventory costs (either manufacturing or wholesale) are changing over time. During periods of stable costs, the inventory costing method has no effect on accounting reports. If prices are changing rapidly, however, the inventory costing method can have a big effect on the valuation of inventory and the earnings reported by the organization. The choice of an inventory cost method is important, as it affects external financial statements, taxes and contracts based on the external financial statements.

During periods of rising costs, the FIFO method generally results in higher ending inventory costs. If an inventory costing method makes the cost of the ending inventory higher, the cost of goods sold is lower, and the net profit is higher. During periods of rising costs, the LIFO method generally reports a lower cost of ending inventory, a higher cost of goods sold and a lower net profit figure. A lower net profit is advantageous to reduce taxes, so LIFO is popular for tax reporting but not allowed in many jurisdictions.

If external financial statements are used for performance evaluation, the inventory costing method also will affect internal decision making and control. For the remainder of this text, we assume that organizations use the specific identification inventory valuation method but the use of other inventory costing methods should be recognized.

Numerical **example** 10.11

The BCM Company makes stereo headphones. The company had the following bi-monthly manufacturing output during the year:

Month	Output in units	Manufacturing costs (£)	Cost per unit (£)
January/February	3,000	60,000	20.00
March/April	3,500	71,750	20.50
May/June	2,500	52,500	21.00
July/August	3,000	63,000	21.00
September/October	3,200	67,200	21.00
November/December	3,300	72,600	22.00
Totals	18,500	387,050	20.92

Beginning inventory = 5,000 units at £20.00 each, or a total of £100,000
Ending Inventory = 6,000 units

a What is the cost of the ending inventory under the FIFO, LIFO and weighted-average cost methods?

b What is the cost of goods sold under each of the methods?

Solution

a *FIFO:* The 6,000 units in ending inventory include 3,300 from November/December and 2,700 from September/October. These headphones cost (3,300 units × £22/unit) + (2,700 units × £21/unit), or £129,300.

LIFO: The last 6,000 units include 5,000 units from beginning inventory and 1,000 units from January/February. These headphones cost (5,000 units × £20/unit) + (1,000 units × £20/unit), or £120,000.

Weighted-average cost: The average cost per unit including beginning inventory and manufacturing this year is (£100,000 + £387,050)/(5,000 + 18,500), or £20.72553/unit. The cost of the 6,000 units in ending inventory is (£20.72553/unit × 6,000 units), or £124,353.

b *FIFO:*

	£
Beginning inventory, 1 January	100,000
Manufacturing costs	387,050
Ending inventory, 31 December	(129,300)
Cost of goods sold	357,750

LIFO:

	£
Beginning inventory, 1 January	100,000
Manufacturing costs	387,050
Ending inventory, 31 December	(120,000)
Cost of goods sold	367,050

Weighted-average cost:

	£
Beginning inventory, 1 January	100,000
Manufacturing costs	387,050
Ending inventory, 31 December	(124,353)
Cost of goods sold	362,697

Concept **review**

1 How does the schedule for cost of goods manufactured relate to the cost of goods sold?

2 How do FIFO, LIFO and the weighted-average cost methods affect the cost of ending inventory and cost of goods sold?

Self-study problem

Over- and under-absorbed overhead

IPX is a specialized packaging company that packages other manufacturers' products. Other manufacturers ship their products to IPX in bulk. IPX then packages the products using high-speed, state-of the-art packaging machines and ships the packaged products to wholesalers. A typical order involves packaging small toys in see-through, plastic, and cardboard packaging.

IPX uses a flexible budget to forecast annual plant-wide overhead, which is then allocated to jobs, based on machine hours. The annual overhead budget is forecasted to be €6 million of fixed costs plus €120 per machine hour. The expected number of machine hours for the year is 20,000. The estimated application rate includes both fixed and variable overhead costs.

At the end of the year, 21,000 machine hours were used and actual overhead incurred was €9.14 million.

Required

a Calculate the application rate set at the beginning of the year.
b Calculate the amount of over- or under-absorbed overhead for the year.
c The company policy is to write off any over- or under-absorbed overhead to the cost of goods sold account. Will net profit rise or fall this year when the over- or under-absorbed overhead is written off to cost of goods sold?

Solution

a The application rate equals the forecasted overhead divided by the forecasted usage of the allocation base (machine hours (MH)):

$$(€6,000,000 + (€120/MH \times 20,000\,MH))/20,000\,MH = €420/MH$$

b

	€
Actual overhead	9,140,000
Absorbed overhead (€420/MH × 21,000 MH)	8,820,000
Under-absorbed overhead	320,000

c The under-absorbed overhead will increase the cost of goods sold, and decrease net profit.

Numerical exercises

NE 10.1 Job-order cost sheet LO 2

Marlborough Accounting is performing an audit for the Chandra Company. Marlborough Accounting uses a cost sheet to record the cost of each audit. Only professional services (by associates, managers and partners) and overhead are recorded on the cost sheet. The cost sheets then are compared with the bid price of the audit to determine if the audit was profitable, and to improve future bids prices. Marlborough Accounting had bid £10,000 to do the Chandra Company audit. During the month of January, the following work was performed on the Chandra Company audit: 10 hours of associate work at £30 per hour, 4 hours of manager work at £50 per hour, and 1 hour of partner time at £100 per hour. During February, the following work was performed at the same rates as in January to finish the audit: 100 hours of associate time, 50 hours of manager time, and 8 hours of partner time. Overhead is allocated at £20 per professional service hour provided.

a Make a cost sheet for the Chandra Company audit.
b Was the Chandra Company audit profitable for Marlborough Accounting?

NE 10.2 Estimated, actual, and allocated overhead LO 4

The Philbrick Company makes recreational equipment. Overhead is allocated to the different products based on machine hours. At the beginning of the year, the company estimates that overhead will be £4 million and machine hours will be 200,000. During the year, the company actually has £4.3 million of overhead and 190,000 machine hours.

a How much overhead is allocated?
b What is the over- or under-absorbed overhead?

NE 10.3 Estimated, actual and allocated overhead LO 4

The Dunrobin law firm allocates overhead to different clients based on hours of work performed by Mr Dunrobin. At the start of the year, Mr Dunrobin estimates that the total overhead of the coming year will be £100,000. He also estimates that he will perform 2,000 hours of work for clients. During the year, he works 2,100 hours for clients and incurs £110,000 of overhead.

a How much overhead is allocated?
b What is the over- or under-absorbed overhead?

NE 10.4 Over- and under-absorbed overhead LO 4

The Alphonse Company allocates fixed overhead costs by machine hours and variable overhead costs by direct labour hours. At the beginning of the year, the company expects fixed overhead costs to be €600,000 and variable costs to be €800,000. The expected machine hours are 6,000 and the expected direct labour hours are 80,000. The actual fixed overhead costs are €700,000 and the actual variable overhead costs are €750,000. The actual machine hours during the year are 5,500 and the actual direct labour hours are 90,000.

a How much overhead is allocated?
b What is the over- or under-absorbed overhead?

NE 10.5 Equivalent units LO 8

The White Flour Company mills wheat into flour. The equivalent units are measured in terms of tonnes of flour produced. At the beginning of the year, the mill contained 20 tonnes of flour that was 30 per cent milled. During the year, another 500 tonnes of flour were completely milled. At the end of the year, the company has 40 tonnes of flour 80 per cent milled.
  How many equivalent tonnes of flour has the White Flour Company milled during the year?

NE 10.6 Cost per equivalent unit LO 8

An appliance manufacturer has an assembly line for making refrigerators. At the beginning of the year, the company had 300 refrigerators on the assembly line that were 40 per cent complete on average. The appliance manufacturer started and completed another 5,000 refrigerators. At the end of the year, another 500 units were still on the assembly line and 30 per cent complete on average. During the year, the appliance manufacturer had costs of £2 million.

a How many equivalent units were produced during the year?
b What is the cost per equivalent unit of refrigerators worked on during the year?

NE 10.7 Over- and under-absorbed overhead LO 4

A company allocates overhead using direct labour hours. The expected number of direct labour hours is 4,000 for the coming year and the expected overhead is £80,000. During the year, the company uses 3,600 direct labour hours and the actual overhead was £82,000.
  What is the over- or under-absorbed overhead?

NE 10.8 Over- and under-absorbed overhead LO 4

Anacom Company has expected overhead fixed costs of £100,000. The estimated variable overhead costs are £400,000, assuming the allocation base is 50,000 machine hours. Anacom has one overhead application rate that includes both variable and fixed costs. The actual machine hours are 60,000 and the actual overhead is £550,000.
  What is the over- or under-absorbed overhead?

NE 10.9 Use of multiple application rates LO 6

Multifirm has three different types of production departments: A, B and C. Each department allocates overhead costs to products based on direct labour cost. The production departments had the following expected overhead costs and direct labour cost:

Department	Expected overhead costs (€)	Direct labour cost (€)
A	400,000	40,000
B	200,000	10,000
C	800,000	50,000

A product P requires €2,000 of direct labour in Department A, €1,000 in Department B, and €3,000 in Department C. How much overhead is allocated to the product from the three production departments?

NE 10.10 Equivalent units and process costing LO 8

A company has no beginning work in process. During the year, the company starts and completes 1,000 units and has 100 units in ending inventory that are 60 per cent complete. The costs related to this product during the period are £10,000.

How many equivalent units were produced during the period? What was the average cost per equivalent unit?

NE 10.11 Equivalent units and process costing LO 8

A manufacturer has 500 units in beginning inventory that are 30 per cent complete. During the year, the firm starts 5,000 units. It completes the 500 units in the beginning inventory and 4,200 of the 5,000 units started. The ending inventory is 80 per cent complete.

How many uncompleted units are in ending work-in-process? How many equivalent units are produced during the year?

NE 10.12 Cost of goods manufactured and cost of goods sold schedules LO 9, Appendix

Prepare a Cost of Goods Manufactured schedule for July from the following data:

	£
Work-in-Process Inventory, 1 July	10,000
Work-in-Process Inventory, 31 July	20,000
Raw Materials Inventory, 1 July	40,000
Raw Materials Inventory, 31 July	30,000
Raw materials purchased in July	100,000
Direct labour used in July	200,000
Manufacturing overhead in July	150,000

Numerical problems

NP 10.1 Job-order sheet LO 2

The Talbott Company has received an order (#324) for 100 electronic widgets. On 20 January, the shop foreman requisitioned 100 units of part 503 at a cost of £5 per unit and 500 units of part 456 at a per-unit cost of £3 to begin work on the 100 widgets. On the same day, 20 hours of direct labour at £20 per hour were used to work on the widgets. On 21 January, 200 units of part 543 at £6 per unit were requisitioned, and 10 hours of direct labour at £15 per hour were performed on the 100 widgets to complete the job. Overhead is allocated to the job based on £5 per direct labour hour.

Prepare a job-order cost sheet for the 100 electronic widgets.

NP 10.2 Job-order cost systems LO 2

Mevellec Company uses a job-order cost system to track its production costs. The following activities have been performed for Job number 515:

- Requisition of 3 units of part #34 at €40 per unit, and 2 hours of direct labour at €10 per hour on 16 May.
- Requisition of 5 kg of raw material #45 at €10 per kilogram and direct labour of 3 hours at €12 per hour on 3 June.
- Direct labour of 4 hours at €15 per hour on 10 June, and the job is finished.
- Overhead is applied at €12 per direct labour hour.
- The job is sold on 7 July.

a Prepare a job-order cost sheet for the activities.
b Describe the changes in the account balances during May, June and July for raw materials, work-in-process, finished goods, and cost of goods sold.

NP 10.3 Job-order cost flows LO 2, 3

The job-order cost sheet for 1,000 units of toy trucks is:

Job number: 555

Date started: 13/04
Date completed: 18/06

		Raw materials			Direct labour		
Date	Type	Cost (£)	Quantity	Amount (£)	Cost (£)	Hours	Amount (£)
13/04	565	3	1,000	3,000	18	20	360
24/05	889	1	4,000	4,000	12	10	120
18/06	248	2	1,000	2,000	15	100	1,500
				9,000		130	1,980

Total direct materials	9,000
Total direct labour	1,980
Overhead (130 direct labour hours @ £10/hour)	1,300
Total job cost	**12,280**

All of the materials for the job were purchased on 10 April. The batch of 1,000 toy trucks is sold on 10 July.

What are the costs of this job order in the raw materials, the work-in-process, the finished goods inventory accounts, and the cost of goods sold account at the end of April, May, June and July?

NP 10.4 Job-order cost flows LO 2, 3

The Tip Tap Company receives an order for 10,000 units of taps (a tool used to make threads in a block of steel). The taps require considerable machining on a blank (Part #14) to make. Blanks are sometimes ruined in the machining process, but the cost of the ruined blanks is treated as a part of the cost of the job. Direct labour hours are used to allocate overhead. Each blank, spoiled or good, requires the same amount of direct labour hours. The job-order cost sheet for the order is as follows:

Job number: 43

Date started: 20/04
Date completed: 20/06

		Raw materials			Direct labour		
Date	Type	Cost (£)	Quantity	Amount (£)	Cost (£)	Hours	Amount (£)
20/04	14	1	3,500	3,500	18	200	3,600
14/05	14	1	4,000	4,000	18	220	3,960
20/06	14	1	3,300	3,300	18	200	3,600
			10,800	10,800		620	11,160

Total units worked on	10,800
Good units	10,000
Spoiled units	800
Total direct materials	10,800
Total direct labour	11,160
Overhead (620 direct labour hours @ £10/hour)	6,200
Total job cost	**28,160**

All of the blanks for the job were purchased on 10 March. The batch of 10,000 taps was sold on 15 July.

What are the costs of this job order in the raw materials, the work-in-process, the finished goods inventory accounts, and the cost of goods sold account at the end of March, April, May, June and July?

NP 10.5 Proration of over- and under-absorbed overhead LO 5

A computer manufacturer has the following account balances at the end of the year.

	€
Work-in-process	100,000
Finished goods	800,000
Cost of goods sold	2,000,000
Total	2,900,000

These accounts contain €800,000 of allocated overhead. Actual overhead, however, is €1,000,000.

a What are the account balances after prorating the under-absorbed overhead?

b If the manufacturing manager's performance bonus is based on earnings, what is the effect of proration on the manager's bonus?

c If the manager had the discretion to prorate the under-absorbed overhead, or to write it off to the cost of goods sold account, which choice would the manager prefer?

NP 10.6 Allocating over- and under-absorbed overhead LO 5

A custom furniture manufacturer uses direct labour to allocate overhead. At the end of the year, the company had the following account balances with and without allocated overhead.

Account	Direct costs (£)	Direct labour hours	Allocated overhead (£)	Ending balance (£)
Work-in-process	10,000	100	5,000	15,000
Finished goods	40,000	300	15,000	55,000
Cost of goods sold	200,000	1,600	80,000	280,000
Totals	250,000	2,000	100,000	350,000

Actual overhead during the year was £80,000. Estimated and actual direct labour hours are equal.

a What are the ending account balances, if the cost of goods sold account is adjusted for the over- or under-absorbed overhead?

b What are the ending account balances, if the over- or under-absorbed overhead is prorated?

c What are the ending account balances, if the application rate is recalculated to reflect actual overhead costs?

d If the manager's performance is evaluated, in part, in terms of net profit, which method to adjust for the over- or under-absorbed overhead would the manager prefer? Explain your answer.

NP 10.7 Multiple overhead rates LO 6

A house-building contractor has the following three overhead cost pools:

	£
General administration	500,000
Utilities	100,000
Equipment	1,000,000
Total overhead	1,600,000

Costs from each of these cost pools then are allocated to housing contracts using the following allocation bases:

Overhead item	Allocation base	Expected usage
General administration	Direct labour cost	£2,000,000 in direct labour
Utilities	Number of houses	40 houses
Equipment	Cost of house	£16,000,000 in total costs

How much overhead is allocated to a house that uses £20,000 of direct labour and has a total cost of £300,000?

NP 10.8 Allocation of overhead by departments LO 7

The Old Masters Puzzle Company makes jigsaw puzzles primarily sold in museum gift shops. The manufacturing process includes using the departments related to gluing, cutting and boxing. Each type of jigsaw puzzle must go through these departments. The overhead costs in each of these departments are allocated by direct labour hours. Expected overhead costs and direct labour hours that are used to determine an allocation rate are as follows:

Department	Expected dept. costs (£)	Expected dept. direct labour hours
Gluing	90,000	10,000
Cutting	200,000	40,000
Boxing	110,000	50,000
Total overhead	400,000	100,000

A job of 5,000 jigsaw puzzles requires 10 hours of gluing, 15 hours of cutting and 12 hours of boxing.

a How much overhead is allocated to the job, if overhead is allocated by department?

b How much overhead is allocated to the job, if overhead is allocated by a single company-wide application rate?

NP 10.9 Job-order costing and incremental costs of outsourcing LO 2

Bella Cucina is considering outsourcing the production of a steel chassis that is used in a kitchen appliance. Two thousand chassis are produced per month. An outside vendor will supply an identical chassis for €9.90. The chassis is manufactured in two steps. A stamping press punches out the part from sheet metal, bends the sides, and cuts holes in it – all in one operation. Then a welding machine welds the corners. Both the welding and stamping machines are only used to produce this one chassis. The following job-order cost sheet summarizes the costs of producing a single chassis.

	Cost per unit (€)
Steel plate	4.75
Direct labour	
Stamping (€20/hour)	1.60
Welding (€30/hour)	2.50
Overhead:	
Stamping (depreciation)	3.60
Welding (lease payment)	2.15
General plant	5.90
	20.50

The stamping machine is old and has little economic value. A used equipment dealer is willing to remove the machine and haul it away at no cost. The stamping machine was purchased 13 years ago for €1,728,000. For both tax and reporting purposes, it is being depreciated using a 20-year life, straight-line method, and zero salvage value. The welding machine is leased for €4,300 per month, and the lease can be cancelled at any time and the machine returned. However, an early termination penalty of €1,800 per month for the next 42 months must be paid.

General plant overhead consists primarily of the allocated cost of depreciation on the plant, property taxes, and fire insurance on the plant. Bella Cucina currently has excess plant space. The manufacturing space freed up if the chassis is outsourced has no other use.

Employees are unionized and have a clause in their contract that prevents the firm from firing workers if their jobs are eliminated due to outsourcing. The employees working on the stamping machine will be placed on indefinite leave at 75 per cent of their current pay. The employees operating the welding machine can be reassigned to other positions in the firm as job openings occur. Given the high demand for welders, these reassignments will occur within a few weeks of outsourcing the chassis.

Bella Cucina has a tax loss for the current and the previous two years.

Should Bella Cucina outsource the chassis? Support your recommendation with a clear financial analysis of the situation.

NP 10.10 Choosing allocation base for job-order costing LO 2

Hurst manufactures custom replacement carpets for elevators in government and commercial office buildings. The elevator carpets are made of spun nylon on highly automated, expensive machinery. Hurst manufactures two styles, Plush and Deluxe. Hurst's workforce is unionized, making it difficult for the firm to compete on price. To date, Hurst has been able to successfully compete on quality, innovative design and delivery schedule. However, its union leaders are aggressive and are seeking additional work-related job guarantees. Hurst management would like to reduce its dependence on unionized labour.

Hurst's manufacturing process is overhead driven. Most of the overhead arises from the common machinery that produces the Plush and Deluxe carpets. Non-unionized engineers and technicians maintain the equipment. The machinery requires expensive lubricants and filters to operate and uses large amounts of electricity and natural gas. Each carpet style is produced in batches that consist of 10 carpets per batch. Plush and Deluxe do not put differential demands on the equipment other than through the amount of machine time required to produce each batch. The following table summarizes the operating data for each carpet style.

	Plush	Deluxe
Machine minutes per batch of 10 carpets	12	9
Direct labour per batch of 10 carpets	£4	£6
Direct material per batch of 10 carpets	£7	£5
Number of batches per year	14,000	9,000

Overhead is allocated to the two mat styles using a pre-determined overhead rate estimated from a flexible budget at the beginning of the year. Fixed overhead is estimated to be £680,000, and variable overhead is estimated to be £1.50 per machine minute. Management is debating whether to use machine minutes or direct labour cost as the overhead allocation base to allocate overhead to the two carpet styles.

a Calculate two overhead rates. The first overhead rate uses machine minutes as the allocation base and the second uses direct labour cost as the allocation base. Round both overhead rates to two decimal places.

b Calculate the *total* product cost per batch of Plush and Deluxe carpets using the two overhead rates calculated in (a).

c Discuss the advantages and disadvantages of using machine minutes or direct labour cost as the allocation base for assigning overhead to the two styles of carpet.

NP 10.11 Over-absorbed overhead and overhead rate LO 4

Jacklin Stampings allocates overhead to products based on machine hours. It uses a flexible overhead budget to calculate a pre-determined overhead rate at the beginning of the year. This rate is used during the year to allocate overhead to the various stampings produced. The following table summarizes operations for the last year.

Budgeted fixed overhead	£3,800,000
Over-absorbed overhead	£220,000
Actual machine hours	46,000
Variable overhead per machine hour	£100
Actual overhead incurred	£8,750,000

In setting the overhead rate at the beginning of the year, what budgeted volume of machine hours was used?

NP 10.12 Equivalent units LO 8

Department 100 is the first step in the firm's manufacturing process. Data for the current quarter's operations are:

	Units
Beginning work-in-process (70% complete)	30,000
Units started this quarter	580,000
Units completed this quarter and transferred out	550,000
Ending work-in-process (60% complete)	60,000

How many equivalent units were completed during the current quarter in Department 100?

NP 10.13 Recalculating overhead allocation with the actual application rate LO 5

Avion Industries makes an assortment of aircraft parts. The company allocates overhead based on direct labour costs in euros (DL€). At the beginning of the year, the company estimated that overhead costs would be €400,000 and direct labour costs would be €250,000. The application rate was estimated to be €400,000/€250,000, or €1.60/DL€. The actual overhead costs were €420,000 and the actual direct labour costs €210,000. A batch of parts that used €10,000 of direct labour was completed during the year. It was sold based on contract terms of actual costs plus 20 per cent. The original invoice was sent to the customer using the estimated application rate to calculate the overhead portion of the contract.

How much higher would the invoice have been using actual overhead and direct labour costs?

NP 10.14 Over- and under-absorbed overhead LO 2, 4

The Rosen Company has two manufacturing departments, Production and Assembly. Each department has separate application rates. The Rosen Company made the following estimates for its Production and Assembly departments for the calendar year 2008.

	Production	*Assembly*
Factory overhead	£300,000	£100,000
Direct labour cost	£1,000,000	£500,000
Machine hours	1,500	6,250
Direct labour hours	5,000	10,000

The company uses a budgeted application rate for the application of overheads to orders. Machine hours are used to allocate overhead in the Production Department and direct labour hours are used to allocate overhead in the Assembly Department.

a What is the application rate for each department?

b What are the overhead costs for Job 77? A summary of this job follows:

	Production	Assembly
Direct materials used	£3,000	£2,000
Direct labour costs	£7,000	£2,500
Machine hours	100	250
Direct labour hours	500	750

c Actual operating results for January 2008 are as follows:

	Production	Assembly
Factory overhead	£325,000	£65,000
Direct labour cost	£900,000	£600,000
Machine hours	1,550	6,250
Direct labour hours	5,000	7,500

Calculate the over- or under-absorbed overhead for each department.

NP 10.15 Work-in-process, finished goods, and cost of goods sold LO 3

Ware Paper Box manufactures corrugated paper boxes for use in the produce industry. It uses a job-order costing system. Operating data for February and March are as follows:

Job no.	Date started	Date finished	Date sold	Total manufacturing cost as of 28/02 (£)	Total manufacturing cost in March (£)*
613	28/01	05/02	15/02	12,500	
614	05/02	17/02	20/02	17,200	
615	20/02	27/02	05/03	18,500	
616	25/02	10/03	20/03	10,100	13,400
734	21/02	15/03	01/04	4,300	8,200
735	27/02	01/04	09/04	9,100	2,400
736	02/03	22/03	19/04		16,300
617	15/03	20/03	26/03		19,200
618	22/03	05/04	15/04		14,400

*Manufacturing costs incurred only in March. Does not include any manufacturing costs incurred in prior months.

Calculate the following amounts:

a Work-in-process inventory as of 28 February

b Work-in-process inventory as of 31 March

c Finished goods inventory as of 28 February

d Finished goods inventory as of 31 March

e Cost of goods sold for February

f Cost of goods sold for March

NP 10.16 Cost per equivalent unit LO 8

DeJure Scents manufactures an after-shave. In May, it started 15,000 litres. There was no beginning inventory. May's ending work-in-process inventory of 2,000 litres was 50 per cent complete. Manufacturing costs in May were €75,000.

a Calculate the equivalent units.

b Calculate the cost per equivalent unit.

c Calculate the cost of the ending work-in-process inventory and the cost transferred to finished goods inventory.

NP 10.17 Equivalent units LO 8

Chemtrex is an agricultural chemical producer. Process costing is used in its Mixing Department. At the beginning of July, it had 700,000 litres 70 per cent complete in work-in-process. During July, it started another 4,000,000 litres and finished 3,700,000 litres. One million litres of ending work-in-process were 60 per cent complete at the end of July.

Calculate the number of equivalent units of conversion work performed during July.

NP 10.18 Work-in-process and proration of over- and under-absorbed overhead LO 2, 4, 5

The following figures were taken from the records of Wellington Co. for the year 2008. At the end of the year, two jobs were still in process. Details about the two jobs are given below:

	Job A	Job B
Direct labour	£10,000	£28,000
Direct materials	£32,000	£22,000
Machine hours	2,000	3,500
Direct labour hours	1,000	2,000

Wellington Co. applies overhead at a budgeted rate, calculated at the beginning of the year. The budgeted rate is the ratio of budgeted overhead to budgeted direct labour costs. Budgeted figures for 2008 were as follows:

	£
Budgeted direct labour costs	250,000
Budgeted overhead	187,500

Actual figures for 2008 were:

	£
Direct labour	350,000
Overhead	192,500
Finished goods inventory	75,000
Cost of goods sold	550,000

There were no opening inventories. It is company practice to prorate any over- or under-absorbed overhead to finished goods inventory, work-in-process, and cost of goods sold based on the total costs in these accounts.

a Compute the cost of work-in-process before prorating over- or under-absorbed overhead.
b Prepare a schedule of finished goods inventory, work-in-process and cost of goods sold after prorating over- or under-absorbed overhead.
c What is the difference in the operating profit if the over- or under-absorbed overhead is charged to cost of goods sold, instead of being prorated to finished goods inventory, work-in-process, and cost of goods sold?
d The manager's compensation is partially based on net profit. What is the effect on the manager's compensation if the over- or under-absorbed overhead is charged to cost of goods sold instead of prorated? What managerial incentives could this system create if the manager were allowed to influence the application rate and/or the year-end adjustment of any over- or under-absorbed overhead?

NP 10.19 Work-in-process and proration of over- and under-absorbed overhead LO 2, 4, 5

Beaver Company has the following account balances after allocating overhead based on the pre-determined application rate of €10 per machine hour:

	€
Work-in-process	40,000
Finished goods	60,000
Cost of goods sold	300,000
Total	400,000

The work-in-process used 1,000 machine hours. The balance in finished goods was calculated using 1,500 machine hours. Cost of goods sold was calculated using 10,000 machine hours. The actual overhead was €115,000.

a What is the over- or under-absorbed overhead?
b What are the final account balances for the work-in-process, finished goods inventory and cost of goods sold accounts if the over- or under-absorbed overhead is (1) allocated completely to cost of goods sold; (2) prorated among the three accounts; and (3) allocated based on a recalculation of the application rate using actual data?

NP 10.20 Activity-based costing in a job-order system LO 6

A specialty ice cream company has identified the following overhead activities and calculated the following application rates:

Activity	Application rate (£)
Cleaning equipment	100/batch
Purchasing ingredients	50/purchase
Advertising	500/advertisement
Renting factory space	1,000/flavour

a What level of overhead is each of these overhead activities?

b How much overhead would a new flavour receive if it were made in 5 batches, required 20 purchases, and advertised twice?

c If plenty of factory space is available for the production of more ice cream flavours, will the company likely choose too many or too few?

NP 10.21 Use of activity-based costing to allocate overhead LO 6

GAMMA produces over a hundred different types of residential water taps at its plant in Le Mans, France. This plant uses activity-based costing to calculate product costs. The following table summarizes the plant's overhead for the year and the cost drivers used for each activity centre.

Summary of Plant Overhead and Activity Centres

Activity centre	Cost (€m)	Cost driver	Total amount of cost driver	Activity cost per unit of cost driver (€)
Material handling	20.8	Direct materials	€130m	0.16
Purchasing	13.8	Part numbers	800	17,250
Set-up labour	6.8	Batches	500	13,600
Engineering	10.9	Number of products	125	87,200
Occupancy	16.2	Direct labour	€90m	0.18
Total Plant Overhead	68.5			

Gamma manufactures an Explorer model. Its total product cost is:

	€	€	€
Direct labour			121,700
Direct material			90,500
Material handling	€90,500	0.16	14,480
Purchasing	9	17,250	155,250
Set-up	8	13,600	108,800
Engineering	1	87,200	87,200
Occupancy	€121,700	0.18	21,906
Total cost			599,836
Number of units manufactured			12,500
Product cost per unit			47.99

Calculate the product cost per unit of the Explorer model using absorption costing. Plant overhead is assigned to products based on direct labour dollars.

NP 10.22 Use of multiple application rates LO 6

Frames, Inc. manufactures two types of metal frames, large and small. Steel angle iron is first cut to the appropriate sizes and the pieces are then welded together to form the frames. The process involves a high degree of automation. Considerable indirect labour by skilled technicians and engineers is required to maintain the automated equipment. There are two manufacturing departments, Cutting and Welding. The following reports detail the actual costs of production for the year:

FRAMES, INC.
Year Ending 31 December

Direct costs

Frame type	Units produced	Direct labour (£)	Direct materials (£)
Large	10,000	480,000	950,000
Small	30,000	1,140,000	800,000

Overhead costs by department

Overhead costs	Cutting (£)	Welding (£)	Total (£)
Utilities	58,000	174,000	232,000
Indirect labour	430,000	480,000	910,000
General factory costs			150,000
Total overhead costs			1,292,000

Kilowatt hours (000s)

Frame type	Cutting	Welding	Total
Large	530	1,040	1,570
Small	910	1,200	2,110
Total	1,440	2,240	3,680

a Compute the unit costs of large frames and small frames for the year using a single, factory-wide overhead rate. The factory-wide overhead allocation base is direct labour cost.

b Compute the unit costs of large frames and small frames for the year using different overhead rates for utilities, indirect labour and general factory costs. Utility costs and indirect labour costs are allocated to frames using kilowatt hours. General factory costs are allocated to frames using direct costs (the sum of direct labour and direct materials).

c Compute the unit costs of large frames and small frames for the year using departmental overhead rates for the Cutting and Welding departments. General factory overhead costs are evenly divided between the two departments before departmental overhead is allocated to the frames. Cutting Department overhead costs are allocated based on the amount of direct materials costs. Welding Department overhead costs are allocated based on kilowatt hours in the Welding Department.

d Analyse why different unit costs result from the different methods of allocating overhead costs to the products. Which method is best?

NP 10.23 Departmental rates to allocate overhead LO 7

MumsDay Corporation manufactures a complete line of fibreglass attaché cases and suitcases. MumsDay has three manufacturing departments (Moulding, Component and Assembly) and two service departments (Power and Maintenance).

The sides of the cases are manufactured in the Moulding Department. The frames, hinges, locks, etc. are manufactured in the Component Department. The cases are completed in the Assembly Department. Varying amounts of materials, time and effort are required for each of the various cases. The Power Department and Maintenance Department provide services to the three manufacturing departments.

MumsDay has always used a plant-wide overhead rate. Direct labour hours are used to assign the overhead to its product. The pre-determined rate is calculated by dividing the company's total estimated overhead by the total estimated direct labour hours to be worked in the three manufacturing departments.

Whit Portlock, Manager of Cost Accounting, has recommended that MumsDay use departmental overhead rates. Portlock has developed the planned operating costs and expected levels of activity for the coming year. These figures by department are presented in the schedules (000 omitted) below.

	Manufacturing departments		
	Moulding	Component	Assembly
Departmental activity measures			
Direct labour hours	500	2,000	1,500
Machine hours	875	125	–
Departmental costs			
Raw materials	£12,400	£30,000	£ 1,250
Direct labour	3,500	20,000	12,000
Variable overhead	3,500	10,000	16,500
Fixed overhead	17,500	6,200	6,100
Total departmental costs	£36,900	£66,200	£35,850
Use of service departments			
Maintenance			
Estimated usage in labour hours for coming year	90	25	10
Power (in kilowatt hours)			
Estimated usage for coming year	360	320	120
Maximum allotted long-term capacity (in kilowatt hours)	500	350	150

	Service departments	
	Power	Maintenance
Departmental activity measures		
Maximum capacity	1,000 KWH	Adjustable
Estimated usage in coming year	800 KWH	125 hours
Departmental costs		
Materials and supplies	£5,000	£1,500
Variable labour	1,400	2,250
Fixed overhead	12,000	250
Total service department costs	£18,400	£4,000

a Calculate the plant-wide overhead rate for MumsDay Corporation for the coming year using the same method as used in the past.

b Whit Portlock has been asked to develop departmental overhead rates for comparison with the plant-wide rate. The following steps are to be followed in developing the departmental rates.

 i The Maintenance Department costs should be allocated to the three manufacturing departments using labour hours.

 ii The fixed costs in the Power Department should be allocated to the three manufacturing departments according to long-term capacity and the variable costs according to planned usage.

 iii Calculate departmental overhead rates for the three manufacturing departments using a machine hour base for the Moulding Department and a direct labour hour base for the Component and Assembly Departments.

c Should MumsDay Corporation use a plant-wide rate or departmental rates to assign overhead to its products? Explain your answer.

(CMA adapted)

NP 10.24 Multiple cost drivers LO 6

Astin Car Stereos manufactures and distributes four different car stereos. The following table summarizes the unit sales, selling prices and manufacturing costs of each stereo.

Astin Car Stereos
Summary of Operations
Fiscal Year 2009

	A90	B200	B300	Z7
Sales price	£100	£120	£140	£180
Manufacturing cost (all variable)	£80	£90	£100	£120
Units sold	15,000	13,000	12,000	9,000

Selling and distribution (S&D) expenses are £1,270,000. They are treated as a period cost and written off to the profit and loss statement. To assess relative profitability of each product, S&D expenses are allocated to each product based on sales revenue.

Upon further investigation of the S&D expenses, one-half of them are for marketing and advertising. Each product has its own advertising and marketing budget, which is administered by one of four marketing managers. Z7, the premier product, is advertised heavily. Forty per cent of the marketing and advertising budget goes towards Z7, 30 per cent to B300, 20 per cent to B200, and 10 per cent to A90.

The other half of the S&D expenses are composed of distribution and administration costs (25 per cent) and selling costs (25 per cent). The distribution and administration department is responsible for arranging shipping and billing customers. (Customers pay transportation charges directly to the common carrier.) It also handles government licensing of the car stereos. Upon analysis of the work in the distribution and administration department, each of the four products places even demands on the department and each consumes about the same resources as the others. Selling costs consist primarily of commissions paid to independent sales people. The commissions are based on gross margin on the product (sales revenue less manufacturing cost).

a Allocate all S&D expenses based only on sales revenue. Identify the most and least profitable products.
b Allocate all S&D expenses based only on the advertising and marketing budget. Identify the most and least profitable products.
c Allocate all S&D expenses using the advertising and marketing budget for advertising and marketing costs, the distribution and administration costs using the demand for these resources by the products, and the selling costs based on commissions. Identify the most and least profitable products.
d Discuss the managerial implications of the various schemes. Which products are the most/least profitable under each of the three allocation schemes? Why do the different schemes result in different product line profits? Which product is really the most/least profitable?

NP 10.25 Job-order costing, over- and under-absorbed overhead and departmental rates
LO 2, 4, 7

Media Designs is a marketing firm that designs and prints customized marketing brochures for companies such as Matsui. The design department designs the brochure and the printing department prints and binds it. Each department has a separate overhead rate. The following estimates for the two departments were made for the upcoming calendar year.

	Design	Printing
Overhead	£800,000	£500,000
Direct labour cost	£3,250,000	£410,000
Direct material cost	£8,500	£250,000
Direct labour hours	50,000	10,000

Media Design uses a budgeted overhead rate to apply overheads to jobs. Direct labour hours are used to allocate overhead in the design department and direct material cost is used to allocate overhead in the printing department.

a What are the overhead rates for the Design and Printing departments?
b A summary of the Matsui job follows:

	Design	Printing
Direct materials used	£3,000	£12,000
Direct labour costs	£46,200	£28,500
Direct labour hours	700	750

What are overhead costs for the Matsui job?
c Actual operating results for the year are as follows:

	Design	Printing
Overhead	£802,000	£490,000
Direct labour cost	£3,193,000	£451,500
Direct material cost	£11,550	£230,000
Direct labour hours	51,500	10,500

Calculate the over- or under-absorbed overhead for each department.

NP 10.26 Cost of goods manufactured and cost of goods sold schedules LO 9, Appendix

Marion Company had the following bi-monthly output:

Month	Output in units	Manufacturing costs (£)	Cost per unit (£)
Jan/Feb	200	4,000	20
Mar/Apr	250	5,000	20
May/June	300	6,300	21
July/Aug	240	5,280	22
Sept/Oct	300	6,900	23
Nov/Dec	200	4,800	24
Total	1,490	32,280	

The beginning inventory had 100 units at a cost of £18 per unit or a total cost of £1,800.
The ending inventory had 300 units.

a What is the cost of the ending inventory under FIFO, LIFO and weighted-average cost methods?
b What is the cost of goods sold under each of the methods?

NP 10.27 Cost of goods manufactured and cost of goods sold LO 9, Appendix

The Williams Company manufactures automatic garage-door openers. At the beginning of November, the company had the following inventory accounts:

	£
Raw materials	20,000
Work-in-process	15,000
Finished goods	30,000

At the end of November, the company had the following inventory accounts:

	£
Raw materials	10,000
Work-in-process	25,000
Finished goods	50,000

During the month of November, the company made purchases of raw material equal to £100,000. The company also incurred direct labour costs of £200,000 and overhead of £50,000.

a Make a schedule calculating the cost of goods manufactured during November.
b Make a schedule calculating the cost of goods sold during November.

NP 10.28 Cost of goods manufactured and cost of goods sold LO 9, Appendix

The McIvor Company has the following inventory balances at the beginning of 2008:

	£
Raw materials	50,000
Work-in-process	75,000
Finished goods	100,000

At the end of 2008, the controller calculates the cost of goods sold to be £700,000 and the cost of goods manufactured as £750,000. Ending work-in-process for 2008 was estimated to be £95,000. During 2008, the company purchased £200,000 of raw materials and used £190,000 of raw materials. Manufacturing overhead during 2008 was £300,000.

a What was the ending raw materials balance in 2008?
b What amount of direct labour was paid during 2008?
c What was the ending balance of finished goods in 2008?

NP 10.29 Cost of goods sold and different cost flow methods for inventory LO 9, Appendix

The City Gravel Company has the following outputs, costs, and ending inventory for its five years of operation:

Year	Output in tonnes	Manufacturing costs (£)	Cost per tonne (£)	Ending inventory (tonnes)
2004	300,000	300,000	1.00	20,000
2005	400,000	500,000	1.25	30,000
2006	500,000	750,000	1.50	50,000
2007	400,000	600,000	1.50	70,000
2008	800,000	1,400,000	1.75	80,000

a What is the cost of goods sold in each year using FIFO?
b What is the cost of goods sold in each year using LIFO?
c What is the cost of goods sold in each year using weighted-average cost?

Analysis and **interpretation** problems

AIP 10.1 Using job-order cost sheets LO 2

The shop foreman is complaining to the controller about all the time her workers are wasting in filling out job-order cost sheets. She estimates that 10 per cent of her employees' time is spent recording labour hours spent on different jobs. Given that the direct labour costs of the factory are £2 million per year, the foreman estimates that the company is losing £200,000 a year completing the job-order cost sheets.

What alternatives exist to using worker time to complete job-order cost sheets?

AIP 10.2 Job-order and process costing LO 1

A management accounting professor was trying to explain the difference between job-order costing and process costing to her class. She pointed out that a job-order costing system is generally used when distinct batches or 'jobs' can be identified. Alternatively, process costing is used for the continual processing of homogenous products. A student suggested another difference between job-order and process costing. He noted that on the one hand, job-order costs are determined at the time the job is being performed by using pre-determined overhead rates. On the other hand, process costs are normally determined at the end of the period based on the number of equivalent units produced and actual overhead costs.

What does the timing difference between job-order costing and process costing say about how job-order costs and process costs are used for planning purposes?

AIP 10.3 Modified job-order and process costing LO 1, 2

The Trophy Company makes medallions for sporting events including the upcoming Olympic Festival. All of the medallions are exactly the same, except for the type of metal that is stamped into the medallion. The company makes gold, silver and bronze medallions. Each of these medallions goes through the same steps of cutting, stamping, polishing and packaging. The controller is uncertain about whether to use a job-order system or a process costing system to determine the costs of the different types of medallions.

Provide arguments for the use of both types of costing systems. Suggest a hybrid costing system that would be suitable for the Trophy Company.

AIP 10.4 Application rates for departments LO 7

The Glass Key Company manufactures hand-blown glass pieces. The company has three glass-blowing departments (A, B and C) that revolve around three different furnaces. The work performed in each of these departments can be replicated by any of the other departments, but department C has newer and more expensive equipment that has a higher depreciation expense. Overhead costs are allocated to the different batches of glassware based on the direct labour hours. Each of the glass-blowing departments has its own application rate, with the rate in department C being the largest. Glass Key prices its product based on absorbed costs, so customers have been asking that their special orders be performed in departments A or B. As a result, department C, with the best equipment, is being used the least.

What is wrong with Glass Key's operations? What are some remedies for this problem?

AIP 10.5 Under-absorbed overhead LO 5

The end of the year has arrived and its bonus time for the successful managers of Crescent Company. Divisional managers are evaluated by the profit of their respective divisions, after the allocation of costs from headquarters. One of these allocations is the cost of data management, which is provided centrally for all divisions. The data-management services are allocated to the divisions based on the number of transactions processed. The application rate was calculated at the beginning of the year based on estimated costs and the estimated transactions to be processed by all of the divisions. Near the start of the year, however, one of the divisions was unexpectedly sold to another company and did not use very much of this central service before being sold. At the end of the year, all of the data-management costs have not been allocated. The company president has decided to allocate the under-absorbed costs to the remaining divisions based on each division's actual usage of data-management services during the year. In allocating the under-absorbed overhead to the divisions, some division managers cannot achieve their profit targets and will not receive their bonuses.

Is this type of cost allocation appropriate?

AIP 10.6 Process costing and under-absorbed overhead LO 5, 8

Process costing can be performed with estimated cost and production data and actual cost and production data. A company estimated total manufacturing costs to be €4,000,000 and estimated equivalent units to be 20,000. Therefore, the estimated cost per equivalent unit was €200. Inventory costs were adjusted for completed units based on this €200 estimated cost per equivalent unit. At the end of the year, the actual manufacturing costs were €5,000,000 and the equivalent units produced were actually 22,000.

How would you determine and account for the under-absorbed overhead?

AIP 10.7 Application rates and depreciation methods LO 2

The frame-welding department of a large automotive company welds car frames as they pass down the assembly line. Four computer-controlled robots make the welds on each frame simultaneously. When installed last year, each robot was expected to have a five-year useful life before becoming obsolete and being replaced by newer, faster models with more advanced electronics. Over its useful life, each robot is expected to make 100 million welds. Each robot cost £8 million and has no salvage value at the end of its useful life, after taking into consideration the cost of dismantling and removing it.

The firm has an absorption costing system that costs each frame as it is produced. The accounting system supports both decision making and control. Straight-line depreciation is used for both internal and external reporting. Accelerated depreciation is used for tax purposes. As frames move through the welding stations, they are charged based on the number of welds made on each frame. Different car frames require different numbers of welds, with some frame models requiring up to 1,000 welds. Welds cost £0.11 each. This charge is set at the beginning of the year by estimating the fixed and variable costs in the Welding Department. The expected number of welds projected for the year is determined by taking the forecasted number of frames times the number of welds per frame. The expected number of welds is used to estimate total costs in the Welding Department. The cost per weld is then the ratio of the projected welding costs and the expected number of welds. Seventy-two million welds were projected for the current year.

The following statement illustrates the computation of the charge per weld:

Frame Welding Department
Charge per Weld
Current Year

	Variable costs (£) (at 72 million welds)	Fixed costs (£)	Total costs (£)
Depreciation*		6,400,000	6,400,000
Welding rods	700,000		700,000
Engineering services	300,000	200,000	500,000
Electricity	180,000		180,000
Factory overhead	85,000	55,000	140,000
Total	1,265,000	6,655,000	7,920,000
÷ Expected number of welds	72,000,000	72,000,000	72,000,000
Cost per weld	0.0176	0.0924	0.1100

*Depreciation per year = (4 robots × £8 million per robot) ÷ 5-year useful life

After reviewing this statement, Amy Miller, manager of the Body Fabricating Division, which includes the Welding Department, made the following remarks:

'I know we use straight-line depreciation to calculate the depreciation component of the cost per weld now. But it would seem to make a lot of sense to compute robot depreciation using units-of-production depreciation. Each robot cost £8 million and was expected to perform 100 million welds over its useful life. That comes to eight pence per weld. Thus, we should charge each weld at eight pence plus the remaining fixed and variable costs as calculated on this statement. If I back out the £6.4 million depreciation from these figures and recompute the fixed costs per weld at 72 million welds, I get £255,000 divided by 72 million, or £0.00354. Add this to the variable cost per weld of £0.0176 plus the 8 pence depreciation and our cost per weld is £0.1011 per weld, not the 11 pence now. This reduces our costs on our complicated frames by as much as £10.

'The real advantage of using units-of-production depreciation, in my opinion, is that depreciation is no longer a fixed cost but becomes a variable cost. This has real advantages because when you lower your fixed costs, your break-even point is lower. Operating leverage is lower and, thus, the overall risk of the company is reduced.

'I think we should go to the plant controller and see if we can convince him to use a more realistic basis for calculating depreciation costs of the robots.'

Evaluate Amy Miller's proposal.

Extended **analysis** and **interpretation** problems

AIP 10.8 Flow of costs and over- and under-absorbed overhead

Targon plc manufactures lawn equipment. Targon manufactures its products in a batch, rather than a continuous-flow, process. Therefore, a job-order cost system is used. The firm employs a full absorption accounting method for cost accumulation. The balances in selected accounts for the 11-month period ended 31 August 2008, are as follows:

	£
Stores inventory	32,000
Work-in-process inventory	1,200,000
Finished goods inventory	2,785,000
Factory overhead	2,260,000
Cost of goods sold	14,200,000

The work-in-process inventory consists of two jobs:

Job no.	Units	Items	Accumulated cost (£)
3005-5	50,000	Estate sprinklers	700,000
3006-4	40,000	Economy sprinklers	500,000
			1,200,000

The finished goods inventory consists of five items:

Items	Quantity and unit cost	Accumulated cost (£)
Estate sprinklers	5,000 units @ £22 each	110,000
Deluxe sprinklers	115,000 units @ £17 each	1,955,000
Brass nozzles	10,000 gross @ £14 per gross	140,000
Rainmaker nozzles	5,000 gross @ £16 per gross	80,000
Connectors	100,000 gross @ £5 per gross	500,000
		2,785,000

The factory cost budget prepared for the 2007–08 financial year is presented below. Targon applied factory overhead on the basis of direct labour hours.

The activities during the first eleven months of the year were quite close to budget. A total of 367,000 direct labour hours have been worked through 31 August 2008.

Factory Cost Annual Budget
For the Year Ending 30 September 2008

	£
Direct materials	3,800,000
Purchased parts	6,000,000
Direct labour (400,000 hours)	4,000,000
Overhead	
Supplies	190,000
Indirect labour	700,000
Supervision	250,000
Depreciation	950,000
Utilities	200,000
Insurance	10,000
Property taxes	40,000
Miscellaneous	60,000
Total factory costs	16,200,000

The September 2008 transactions are summarized as follows:

1 All direct materials, purchased parts and supplies are charged to Stores inventory. The September purchases were as follows:

	£
Materials	410,000
Purchased parts	285,000
Supplies	13,000

2 The direct materials, purchased parts and supplies were requisitioned from Stores inventory as shown in the following table:

	Purchased parts (£)	Materials (£)	Supplies (£)	Total requisitions (£)
3005-5	110,000	100,000	–	210,000
3006-4	–	6,000	–	6,000
4001-3 (30,000 gross rainmaker nozzles)	–	181,000	–	181,000
4002-1 (10,000 deluxe sprinklers)	–	92,000	–	92,000
4003-5 (50,000 ring sprinklers)	163,000	–	–	163,000
Supplies	–	–	20,000	20,000
	273,000	379,000	20,000	672,000

3 The payroll summary for September is as follows:

	Hours	Cost (£)
3005-5	6,000	62,000
3006-4	2,500	26,000
4001-3	18,000	182,000
4002-1	500	5,000
4003-5	5,000	52,000
Indirect	8,000	60,000
Supervision	–	24,000
Sales and administration	–	120,000
		531,000

4 Other factory costs incurred during September follow:

	£
Depreciation	62,500
Utilities	15,000
Insurance	1,000
Property taxes	3,500
Miscellaneous	5,000
	87,000

5 Jobs completed during September and the actual output were as follows:

Job no	Quantity	Items
3005-5	48,000 units	Estate sprinklers
3006-4	39,000 units	Economy sprinklers
4001-3	29,500 gross	Rainmaker nozzles
4003-5	49,000 units	Ring sprinklers

6 The following finished products were shipped to customers during September:

Items	Quantity
Estate sprinklers	16,000 units
Deluxe sprinklers	32,000 units
Economy sprinklers	20,000 units
Ring sprinklers	22,000 units
Brass nozzles	5,000 gross
Rainmaker nozzles	10,000 gross
Connectors	26,000 gross

a Calculate the over- or under-absorbed overhead for the year ended 30 September 2008. Be sure to indicate whether the overhead is over- or under-absorbed.

b Calculate the balance in the work-in-process inventory account as of 30 September 2008.

c Calculate the balance in the finished goods inventory as of 30 September 2008, for the estate sprinklers using a FIFO basis.

(CMA adapted)

AIP 10.9 Departmental rates, ABC and product costs in a job-order system

Joe Bell, President and Chief Executive Officer of Dyna Golf, called a meeting of the Executive Committee of his Board of Directors. He is concerned about the price competition and declining sales of his golf wedges line of business. Mr Bell summarizes the current situation by saying:

'As you know, we set target prices to maintain a gross margin on sales of 35 per cent. On some products, such as our drivers we have been able to achieve the target price. We have been able to achieve higher prices than a target 35 per cent gross margin would dictate on our putters. But wedges are a totally different story.

'Our factory is among the most efficient in the world. I think that some foreign companies are dumping wedges in the UK market, driving down prices and unit sales. We've been reluctant to further cut our prices for fear of what this will do to our gross margins. Fortunately, we have been able to offset the decline in sales of wedges by significantly raising the price of our putters. We were pleasantly surprised when our customers readily accepted the price increases of our putters and we have not experienced much reaction from our competitors on the putter price increases.'

Sophie Barber, an outside director on the board asks:

'Joe, I don't pretend to know a lot about the golf club business, but how confident are you in your cost data? If your costs are off, won't your prices be off as well?'

Joe Bell responds:

'That's a good point Sophie, and one I have been worried about. We have been modernizing our production facilities and I have asked our controller, Phil Meyers, to look into it and report back after he has undertaken a thorough analysis. My purpose for calling this meeting was to update you on our current situation and let you know what we are doing.'

Background

Dyna Golf has been in business for 15 years. Its one plant manufactures three different types of golf clubs: drivers, wedges and putters. Dyna does not produce a complete club with a shaft and grip. It makes the metal head, which is sold to other companies that assemble and market the complete club. Dyna holds four patents on a unique golf club head design that forges together into one club head three different metals: steel, titanium, and brass. It also has a very distinctive appearance. These three metals weigh different amounts, and by designing a club head with the three metals Dyna produces a club with unique swing and feel properties. While the Dyna club is unique and covered by patents, other manufacturers recently have introduced similar technology using comparable manufacturing methods.

The Dyna driver is sold to a single distributor that adds the shaft and grip and sells the driver to retail golf shops. Dyna first made its reputation with its driver. It became an 'instant hit' with amateurs after a professional golfer won a major tournament using the Dyna driver. Based on its name recognition from its driver, Dyna introduced a line of putters and then wedges. The wedges are sold to three different distributors and the putters to six different distributors. Specialty, high-end putters, like Dyna's, have a retail price of £120 to £180 and drivers have a retail price of £350 to £500. Golfers like to experiment with new equipment, especially when they are playing badly. Therefore, it is not uncommon for golfers to own several putters and switch among them during the year. Putter manufacturers seek to capitalize on this psychology with aggressive advertising campaigns. It is less common for players to switch among wedges like they do with putters. Since it takes several rounds of golf playing a new wedge to get its feel and distance control, most players do not experiment as much with wedges as with putters, or even drivers.

Production process

All three clubs (drivers, wedges and putters) use the same manufacturing process. Each of the three clubs consists of between five and 10 components. A component is a precisely-machined piece of steel, brass, or titanium that Dyna buys from outside suppliers. The components are positioned in a jig which is placed in a specially designed, computer-controlled machine. This machine first heats the components to a very high temperature that fuses them together, then cools them, and polishes the finished club.

The factory is organized into five departments: Receiving, Engineering, Set-up, Machining and Packing. Before a production run begins, Receiving issues a separate order for each component comprising the club head and inspects each order when it arrives. Engineering ensures that the completed club heads meet the product's specifications and maintains the operating efficiency of the machines. Due to the preciseness of the production process, Engineering constantly has to issue engineering change orders in response to small differences in purchased components. Set-up first cleans out the machine and jigs, adjusts the machine to the correct settings to produce the desired club head, and then makes a few pieces to ensure the settings are correct. Machining contains several machines, any of which can be used to manufacture drivers, wedges, or putters once it is equipped with the proper jigs and tools. Packing is responsible for packaging and shipping completed units.

Table 10.4 summarizes the basic product information for the three products: production, shipments, target prices and actual prices. For example, Dyna manufactured all 10,000 drivers in a single production run and shipped them all out in a single shipment. The 5,000 putters were manufactured in 10 separate runs and shipped in 20 shipments. Dyna set the target price for drivers to be £162.61 (wholesale price) and achieved it. However, it was not able to achieve its target price for wedges (£134.09 versus £125.96), but it exceeded its target price for putters (£105.70 versus £81.31).

Table 10.4

Dyna Golf Basic Product Information			
	Drivers	*Wedges*	*Putters*
Production	10,000 units in 1 run	15,000 units in 3 runs	5,000 units in 10 runs
Shipments	10,000 units in 1 shipment	15,000 units in 5 shipments	5,000 units in 20 shipment
Selling prices:			
Target	£162.61	£134.09	£81.31
Actual	£162.61	£125.96	£105.70

Accounting system

Table 10.5 summarizes material, set-up labour, and run labour for each of the three products. Each product is produced in the machining department by assembling together the metal components. Drivers require five components, whereas wedges and putters require six and 10 components, respectively. Before the production begins, the machine must be set up, requiring set-up labour. Then to produce clubs, operating the machines requires both machine time and run labour time. Both set-up and run labour costs £20 per hour. Machining has a total budget of £700,000 consisting of the depreciation on the machine, electricity, and maintenance.

Table 10.5

Dyna Golf **Production Information**			
Raw material	*Drivers* 5 components @ £4 each = £20	*Wedges* 6 components @ £5 each = £30	*Putters* 10 components @ £1 each = £10
Labour (£20/hr) Set-up labour	10 hrs per production run	10 hrs per production run	11 hrs per production run
Run labour	$\frac{1}{2}$ hr per driver	$\frac{1}{3}$ hr per wedge	$\frac{1}{4}$ hr per putter

Table 10.6 summarizes the overhead accounts.

Table 10.6

Dyna Golf **Other Overhead**	
	£
Receiving Department	300,000
Engineering Department	500,000
Machining Department	700,000
Packing Department	200,000
Set-up Department	3,000
	1,703,000

Phil Meyers, Dyna's Controller, and Joe Bell meet a week after the Executive Committee meeting of the Board of Directors. Joe Bell asks Phil to report on what he has found. Phil begins,

'Joe, as you know our current accounting system assigns the direct material costs of the components and the direct labour for run time to the three products. Then it allocates all overhead costs, including set-up time and machine costs, to the three products based on direct run labour costs. Set-up labour is considered an indirect cost and is included in overhead. Based on these procedures, we calculate our product costs for drivers, wedges, and putters to be £105.70, £87.16 and £52.85, respectively.

'I have been looking at our system and have become worried that our overhead rate is getting out of line. It is now over 750 per cent of direct labour cost. Since we have introduced more automated machines, we are substituting capital or overhead costs for labour costs. (Each driver now takes $\frac{1}{2}$ hour per club, wedges take $\frac{1}{3}$ hour per club, and putters take $\frac{1}{4}$ hour per club of machine time.) The Engineering Department schedules its people based on change orders they receive. Drivers are pretty standard and only generate 25 per cent of the change orders; wedges about 35 per cent. Putters are our most complex production process and require the remainder of the change orders.

'I'm thinking we should refine our accounting system along the following lines. First, we should break out set-up labour from the general overhead account and assign that directly to each product. We know how much time we are spending setting up each machine for each club-head run. Second, we should stop allocating receiving costs based on direct labour costs but rather on raw material costs. And third, the remaining overhead (excluding set-up and receiving) should be allocated based on machine hours. If we make these three changes, I think we'll get a more accurate estimate of our products' costs.'

Joe Bell responded,

'These seem to be some pretty major changes in our accounting system. I'll need some time to mull these over. Let me think about it and I'll let you know in a few days how to proceed.'

What advice would you offer Mr Bell in examining changes to the accounting system? How does the accounting system affect pricing and product decisions at Dyna Golf?

CHAPTER ELEVEN

Variable costing and capacity costs

(Planning and control)

Learning objectives

1. Identify the problems with absorption costing systems.

2. Use variable costing to generate profit and loss statements, and recognize its advantages and disadvantages.

3. Identify problems in selecting the capacity of a fixed cost resource.

4. Use the organization's practical capacity to allocate overhead, and recognize its advantages and disadvantages.

5. Describe trade-offs for decentralized managers to provide accurate information to make a decision on the capacity of a common resource and on the efficient use of the resource.

6. Make decisions regarding the production and further processing of joint products. (Appendix)

Gorzów Electronics

Gorzów Electronics, located in Poland, owns a group of warehouses in an industrial park with a total of 2,500,000 square metres. The company purchases parts and assembles different electronic consumer products. Currently, Gorzów Electronics is operating assembly lines for computer modems, mobile telephones and other small electronic items. Gorzów Electronics has a very small engineering department and views its primary competitive edge to be low-cost assembly. Almost all of its production is exported to other European countries; thus, Gorzów reports in euros and not Polish zlotys. The organizational structure is closely tied to the products with a product manager for each major line. The product manager is responsible for purchasing, assembly and sales, and is evaluated based on profit of the product line. Most overhead allocated to the product manager comes from warehouse space, which is allocated based on the square metres used by the product manager.

Emilia Symanski is the product manager for the assembly lines dedicated to wireless telephones. She spends time locating more dependable and cheaper suppliers of parts, improving efficiency on the assembly line, and making sure that her customers (mostly discount stores) are satisfied. Making and selling wireless telephones is a very competitive business with increased competition coming primarily from Asia and Eastern Europe. Emilia is working hard to create a profit for the product line. Year-end bonuses for her and her managers are dependent on generating a profit of €1,000,000. The profit goal for this year looks elusive due to the loss of an important customer. In addition, she must bear the burden of the cost of warehouse space, which is allocated to her at a cost of €8 per square metre per year. Emilia is considering dropping a few wireless models in order to further conserve on space and reduce the allocation of overhead. Based on estimated sales of 200,000 units at €14 per unit, Emilia expects this year's income to be the following:

	€
Sales (€14 per unit × 200,000 units)	2,800,000
Cost of goods sold (€8 per unit × 200,000 units)	(1,600,000)
Selling and other expenses	(500,000)
Expected profit	700,000

The cost of goods sold is estimated by calculating an average cost per unit, and assuming that 200,000 units are assembled and sold:

	€ per unit
Parts	2
Direct labour	1
Variable overhead	1
Fixed overhead (€8/m² × 100,000m²)/200,000 units	4
Cost per unit	8

CRITICISMS OF ABSORPTION COST SYSTEMS

Chapter 10 described two absorption cost systems, job-order costing and process costing. These systems have been widely used for several decades. These systems have been traced back to the Industrial Revolution. For as long as these systems have been used, they have been criticized for producing misleading information and creating incentives that are inconsistent with maximizing organizational value. Despite these criticisms, absorption cost systems are the predominant systems used by manufacturing firms today. Service firms are not prone to many of these problems, since they do not manufacture a product or hold inventories. We analyse absorption costing systems by examining some common criticisms and alternative approaches to deal with them.

As described in Chapter 1, cost systems serve numerous functions, including making planning and control decisions and external reporting and taxes. No single system can satisfy all the requirements of each function so trade-offs among the requirements must be made. Costing systems are constantly being revised and updated as technology and firms' organizational structures change. The examination of the well-known problems in absorption cost systems and alternative costing systems provides increased knowledge of how to implement such systems successfully. Also, one must be careful not to reject a particular type of cost system (e.g. absorption costing versus variable costing) on the grounds that a particular firm or industry does not implement it well.

■ Incentive to overproduce

Absorption cost systems include both variable and fixed costs in the product cost. The average cost of making the product is determined by dividing the variable and fixed costs by the number of units produced. This procedure occurs in both job-order and process costing.

Hotel restaurants incur fixed and variable costs. More patrons reduce average costs but total costs increase due to the cost of food, beverages and other items.

The average product cost, however, exhibits certain qualities that are not necessarily consistent with the opportunity cost of making the product. For example, as long as the variable cost per unit is constant, the average cost per unit falls as more units are produced. This decrease is due to fixed costs being 'spread' over more units. For example, if the fixed costs of operating a hotel restaurant are £50,000 per month, the fixed cost per meal declines as more meals are served. If 5,000 meals are served during the month, the fixed cost per meal is £50,000/5,000, or £10 per meal. If 8,000 meals are served during the month, the fixed cost is £50,000/8,000, or £8 per meal. As the number of meals increases, the decline in the fixed cost per unit has nothing to do with a change in fixed costs. It simply reflects the increase in the number of meals served. Notice that the total costs of operating the hotel restaurant do not decrease as more meals are served. Rather, total costs increase to the extent that additional variable costs for waiting staff, food and beverages, maintenance, and other expenditures exist. Thus, declining average costs do not mean that total costs are falling.

Therefore, managers, who are evaluated based on the average cost per unit produced, have an easy way to reduce the average cost per unit. They simply increase the number of units produced, as long as no capacity constraints exist and the variable costs per unit do not increase. Increasing the number of units produced is not necessarily bad for the organization. As long as all the units are sold and the contribution margin of each unit is positive, the organization should encourage greater production.

A problem arises, however, if all the units produced cannot be sold. Excess units in inventory can lead to increased storage, handling costs and redundancy. In *Numerical example 11.1*, inventory handling costs are recognized.

Numerical **example** 11.1

A plant with €1 million of fixed overhead costs makes universal smart drives (USDs). Most of its customers are marketing agencies which customize the storage devices for promotional use by their clients. The USDs have a variable cost per unit of €1.00. The plant only makes USDs and allocates all the fixed costs to the product by the number produced. The firm can sell 200,000 units a year for €10.00 each. There is no beginning inventory. The plant manager has the opportunity to make 200,000 units, 220,000 units, or 240,000 units. Handling excess inventory costs €0.30 per unit. Handling costs are expensed in the year that they are incurred. Which production level yields the highest reported profit for the year?

Solution

	Production levels		
	200,000	220,000	240,000
Fixed costs	€1,000,000	€1,000,000	€1,000,000
Variable costs (€1 per unit)	200,000	220,000	240,000
Total costs	€1,200,000	€1,220,000	€1,240,000
Average cost per USD	€6 per unit	€5.55 per unit	€5.17 per unit
Revenues (200,000 USDs × €10 per unit)	€2,000,000	€2,000,000	€2,000,000
Cost of goods sold			
(200,000 USDs × €6 per unit)	(1,200,000)		
(200,000 USDs × €5.55 per unit)		(1,110,000)	
(200,000 USDs × €5.17 per unit)			(1,034,000)
Excess inventory handling costs	0		
(220,000 − 200,000) × €0.30 per unit		(6,000)	
(240,000 − 200,000) × €0.30 per unit			(12,000)
Net profit	€800,000	€884,000	€954,000

The production of 240,000 USDs results in the highest net profit. The cost of goods sold is lower with excess production because some of the fixed costs are left in the ending inventory account. The fixed costs are not treated as an expense in the current period. As a result of producing 240,000 USDs, the average cost of a USD is €5.17, of which €4.17 is a fixed cost. Therefore, the ending inventory would have €4.17/USD × (240,000 − 200,000 USDs), or €166,800 of fixed costs in inventory. The cost of the ending inventory, including the fixed cost portion, remains an asset and will not become an expense until the units are sold in the future. When the inventory is sold, the fixed costs in inventory will be part of the cost of goods sold and will reduce future income. Increased production, however, also harms the organization because additional handling costs are incurred (€12,000 for the 40,000 USDs if 240,000 are made). In addition to the extra handling costs, the firm also incurs additional variable costs (€1/USD) to produce the extra inventory.

Numerical example 11.1 demonstrates that managers can increase short-term reported profit and harm the organization at the same time. In the long term, reported profit will be lower as the higher inventory costs are passed on to subsequent years.

However, not all managers remain with the organization long enough to bear the costs of earlier overproduction. As long as managers are evaluated based on short-term profits and have the potential to leave the organization, absorption costing creates an incentive to overproduce. Managers, who are evaluated based on long-term performance and committed to the organization for the long term, have less incentive to overproduce.

In addition to the increased storage and handling costs of excess inventory, the cash invested in excess inventory represents an opportunity cost. The cash used to make the excess inventory could be invested more profitably elsewhere, or it could be paid to the owners or shareholders. The opportunity cost of capital, however, is not commonly reflected in managerial performance measures unless residual income is used to evaluate performance.

Overproduction is another example of the trade-off between planning and control. The organization would prefer that managers use resources efficiently and not overproduce. However, short-term net profit is commonly used to evaluate managers; thus, they have an incentive to overproduce.

Several methods exist to mitigate the incentive to overproduce. The first is to charge managers for holding inventory. The net profit reported in financial statements does not consider explicitly the opportunity cost of using cash to hold inventory. The residual income performance measure is one example of a charge for holding inventory because the manager is responsible for the opportunity cost of capital.

A second method is a strict senior management policy against adding to or building inventories. Compensation plans can contain a clause stating that bonuses tied to net profit will not be paid if inventories exceed a certain amount. However, such strict constraints are cumbersome and difficult to monitor. In some circumstances, such as new product introduction and unexpected orders, the organization prefers higher inventory levels.

A third approach is to choose performance measures other than short-term reported profit to evaluate managers. Long-term profit, the change in share price, total sales, or percentage of defects also could be used as measures of managerial performance.

A fourth possibility is to use just-in-time (JIT) production systems to reduce inventory levels. In a JIT system, manufacturing typically does not begin until a customer orders the part or the final product. Intermediate products flow immediately from one stage of production to another without waiting in work-in-process inventories. If the production schedule is determined by customer demand, the plant manager or product-line manager does not have the discretion to set production levels in excess of demand. In essence, a JIT system removes the responsibility from managers to set production levels. These responsibilities are replaced by demand-driven market orders. Typically, JIT systems reduce inventories and thus the incentive to overproduce to increase short-term reported profits. JIT systems and their accounting implications are discussed in Chapter 14.

A final option is to change the costing system. Variable costing systems, discussed in the next section, reduce the incentives to overproduce.

■ Under-utilization of the allocation base used to allocate fixed costs

In absorption costing systems, fixed and variable overhead costs are allocated to products through an allocation base. The allocation of overhead costs simulates a tax on the allocation base. Managers, who are evaluated based on product costs, will use the allocation base sparingly since allocated costs increase product costs and act as a tax on the manager.

The organization, however, may not benefit from the reduced usage of the allocation base. Cost allocations lead to good planning decisions, if the allocated costs approximate the opportunity cost of using the allocation base. The allocation of fixed costs to products through the usage of allocation bases is unlikely to approximate the incremental cost of using the indirect resources. By definition, fixed costs of the indirect resource do not change with the usage of the allocation base. For example, suppose the Information Technology (IT) department uses the number of networked computers as an allocation base to allocate computer centre costs to other departments. The IT department costs contain fixed costs that do not change with the number of networked computers. Yet these fixed costs are allocated to departments based on the number of networked computers. Therefore, the allocated cost of adding another networked computer is higher than the incremental cost of having the IT department support this computer. If the allocated cost is too high, departments will restrict their usage, compromising their operations by having too few networked computers. *Numerical example 11.2* demonstrates this problem:

Numerical **example 11.2**

The expected fixed costs of operating the IT department are £1,000,000 per year. The expected variable costs, which reflect the incremental cost of additional computer workstations, are £5,000 per workstation. Each workstation includes a state-of-the-art computer, monitor, printer and engineering software. The number of workstations in each department is used to allocate the IT department costs. The application rate, based on expected usage of 200 workstations, is [£1,000,000 + (200 × £5,000)]/200, or £10,000 per workstation. The Engineering department estimates the following benefits of having workstations in the department:

Number of workstations	Expected benefits (£)	Marginal benefits (£)
1	15,000	15,000
2	27,000	12,000
3	35,000	8,000
4	41,000	6,000
5	44,000	3,000

What number of workstations would the Engineering department choose if the allocation rate of £10,000 per workstation were used? What is the net loss to the organization of using £10,000 as the application rate, instead of the variable cost per workstation?

Solution

The Engineering department will use only two workstations. The marginal benefit of using the third workstation is £8,000, which is less than the allocated cost. To maximize the profit of the organization, the Engineering department should be using 4 workstations, because the marginal benefit of using the fourth workstation (£6,000) is still greater than the variable cost (£5,000). The additional benefit of having the third and fourth workstations in the Engineering department is £41,000 − £27,000, or £14,000. The incremental cost of having 2 additional workstations is £5,000 × 2, or £10,000. The net loss of not having the 2 additional workstations is £14,000 − £10,000, or £4,000.

■ Misleading product costs

The allocation of fixed costs does not represent the incremental cost of using the allocation base if the allocation base has excess capacity. Product costs generated through an absorption costing system will not approximate the marginal cost of making the

Dropping a product when full cost exceeds price can result in a death spiral: distributing fixed costs over other products until no profitable ones remain.

© Peter Stone/Alamy

products. Therefore, managers who rely on product costs from an absorption costing system are likely to misprice products and choose inappropriate product mixes.

A common result of the misuse of product costs from full absorption cost systems is the **death spiral**. The death spiral occurs when an organization drops a product because its full cost exceeds its price. Once the product is eliminated, the fixed overhead that had been allocated to it is redistributed to the remaining products. This redistribution might make other products appear to be unprofitable due to the increased overhead that these products now must bear. When these products are dropped, more overhead is again allocated to the remaining products. So the cycle continues until the organization has no profitable products left.

The death spiral is a threat to many traditional businesses, such as retail banks. Bricks-and-mortar banks face significant costs to set up and maintain retail branch networks. Internet-based banks have low start-up costs and can choose the most lucrative parts of the banking business. With the loss of customers to the Internet, traditional banks must cover their infrastructure costs with fewer fee-paying customers. If the banks increase fees, more customers leave, and service costs rise again. This continuing cycle creates the danger of a death spiral for traditional banks. *Numerical example 11.3* describes the death spiral.

Numerical **example** 11.3

A company makes two types of refrigerators, compact and full-size. Excess capacity exists for which there is no alternative use. Fixed overhead costs are allocated based on direct labour costs. The product profitability of each product is as follows:

	Compact (£)	Full-size (£)
Revenues	500,000	1,000,000
Direct costs	(300,000)	(450,000)
Allocated fixed costs	(240,000)	(360,000)
Profit	(40,000)	190,000

Management decides to drop the compact model because it appears to be unprofitable. What is the impact on the profitability of the full-size model?

Solution

By dropping the compact model, all of the fixed overhead is shifted to the full-size refrigerator. Its profitability is now as follows:

	Full-size (£)
Revenues	1,000,000
Direct costs	(450,000)
Allocated fixed costs	(600,000)
Profit	(50,000)

Absorption costing systems do not lead necessarily to erroneous product costs. If a fixed cost resource is operating at capacity, profitable alternatives to use the facility might exist but have not been utilized due to limited capacity. In this case, the allocation of the fixed costs could represent the opportunity cost of not being able to use the facility for an alternative purpose. This allocation could lead to more accurate product costs. If an organization is not operating at capacity, variable costing can overcome the planning and control problems described in this section. We examine this alternative costing system next.

Concept review

1 Why does an incentive to overproduce exist with an absorption costing system?

2 What alternatives are available to discourage overproduction?

3 Why does the allocation of fixed costs lead to under-utilization of its allocation base?

4 What causes the death spiral?

Gorzów Electronics (continued)

Emilia Symanski would like to meet the profit goal of €1,000,000 for her product line of mobile telephones so that she and many of her employees would receive a bonus. After further analysis, her sales estimate for the year appears to be accurate and further sales do not seem possible. A closer look at operations indicates no opportunities for easy cost savings. She could squeeze operations into a smaller space and be charged less overhead. A 40 per cent reduction in space used to 60,000 square metres would lower fixed overhead allocation and increase expected profit to €1,020,000. Emilia worries, however, that the reduced use of space would cause other costs to increase. Also, it makes little sense to reduce the use of space when the company already has excess warehouse capacity.

Another possibility is to increase production to transfer some fixed overhead to ending inventory. If Emilia were able to make 320,000 mobile telephones, the per-unit cost would be reduced as follows:

	€/unit
Parts, direct labour and variable overhead	4
Fixed overhead (€8/m² × 100,000m²)/320,000 units	2.50
Cost per unit	6.50

This increases the expected profit to €1,000,000:

	€
Sales (€14 per unit × 200,000 units)	2,800,000
Cost of goods sold (€6.5 per unit × 200,000 units)	(1,300,000)
Selling and other expenses	(500,000)
Expected profit	1,000,000

Emilia does not feel good about this option because she might have to bear the storage costs of the extra inventory. Also, she does not believe that the making of excess inventory is ethically appropriate, so she is still in a quandary on how to achieve the €1,000,000 profit goal.

VARIABLE COSTING

The product cost under **variable costing** includes only the variable costs of making the product. The variable costs include direct material, direct labour and variable overhead. The fixed overhead costs are treated as period costs and expensed in the period incurred. Therefore, the difference between absorption costing and variable costing is the treatment of fixed manufacturing costs. Fixed costs are included as part of product costs under absorption costing and are written off as period expenses under variable costing.

Variable costing has several advantages. The variable cost per unit approximates the marginal cost of making another unit, if the organization is operating below capacity. This information is useful in pricing and product-mix decisions. Prices above the variable cost per unit provide a positive contribution margin. The contribution margin per unit (price less variable cost per unit) also is used to direct scarce resources among products. Organizations prefer to make and sell products with higher per-unit contribution margins, assuming excess capacity in the production process.

Variable costing also reduces the dysfunctional incentive to overproduce. With all fixed costs treated as period expenses, increased production will not spread the fixed costs across more units and allow fixed costs to reside in the inventory account at the end of the period. The incremental cost of making additional units will approximately equal the recorded inventory cost. Overproduction of inventory will have a negative effect on reported profit due to additional handling and storage costs.

Numerical **example** 11.4

A factory making electric fans has estimated and actual fixed costs of £50,000. Variable costs per unit total £6. The allocation base is the number of units produced. The sales price of the electric fan is £10 per unit. There is no beginning inventory. During the year, the factory makes and sells 20,000 electric fans. In December, the factory manager has the opportunity to make another 5,000 units, but these 5,000 units can not be sold this year. What is the profit of the factory with and without the additional 5,000 units, under the absorption and variable costing systems? (Assume no handling and storage costs.)

Solution

Under the absorption costing system without the additional 5,000 units, the application rate is [£50,000 + (£6 per unit × 20,000 units)]/20,000 units, or £8.50 per unit. The profit is as follows:

	£
Sales (£10 per unit × 20,000 units)	200,000
Cost of goods sold (£8.50 per unit × 20,000 units)	(170,000)
Profit	30,000

Under the absorption costing system with the additional 5,000 units, the application rate is [£50,000 + (£6 per unit × 25,000 units)]/25,000 units, or £8.00 per unit. The profit is as follows:

	£
Sales (£10 per unit × 20,000 units)	200,000
Cost of goods sold (£8.00 per unit × 20,000 units)	(160,000)
Profit	40,000

The cost of the ending inventory of 5,000 units is (£8.00 per unit × 5,000 units), or £40,000.

→

Under the variable costing system without the additional 5,000 units, the application rate is the variable cost of £6 per unit and fixed costs are expensed. The profit is as follows:

	£
Sales (£10 per unit × 20,000 units)	200,000
Cost of goods sold (£6.00 per unit × 20,000 units)	(120,000)
Fixed costs	(50,000)
Profit	30,000

Under the variable costing system with the additional 5,000 units, the application rate is still the variable cost of £6 per unit and fixed costs are expensed. The profit is still as follows:

	£
Sales (£10 per unit × 20,000 units)	200,000
Cost of goods sold (£6.00 per unit × 20,000 units)	(120,000)
Fixed costs	(50,000)
Profit	30,000

The cost of making the additional 5,000 units is (£6 per unit × 5,000 units), or £30,000, which is recorded as the ending inventory cost.

Numerical example 11.4 indicates that the reported profit under both absorption and variable costing is the same when there is no beginning or ending inventory. When ending inventory is added, the variable costing method still reports the same income, but the absorption costing system has a higher income because it allocates some of the fixed costs to the ending inventory. The fixed costs allocated to the ending inventory are included in the costs of goods sold in the next period. Absorption costing just postpones the expense. Therefore, absorption costing may cause a lower reported profit in the next period depending on the amount of ending inventory that remains.

A variable costing system also does not have product costs that fluctuate as the output volume changes. The per-unit product cost is the variable cost per unit, which should not vary with normal fluctuations in output. The absorption costing system, alternatively, results in an average product cost. The average cost will decline with higher levels of output as fixed costs are spread over more units.

The disadvantages of variable costing include misleading product costs, if there is an opportunity cost of using fixed overhead resources. An opportunity cost exists if the fixed overhead resources are operating at capacity and there are alternative, profitable uses of the overhead resources. The allocation of these fixed costs provides a means to represent the opportunity cost of using the fixed overhead resources. If the cost of fixed overhead resources are sunk and without alternative use, however, the variable cost more closely approximates the cost of making the product.

If managers are evaluated based on product costs and are not responsible for fixed overhead costs, they will tend to over-utilize the overhead resources generating the fixed costs. Managers will avoid using variable overhead resources, which affect product costs, and attempt to use fixed overhead resources instead. This substitution will lead to dysfunctional behaviour for the whole organization, if an opportunity cost exists in using those fixed overhead resources. For example, facility costs are often considered fixed. If these fixed costs are not allocated to managers, managers will want to use more space because the space is free to them. Yet space probably is not free to the whole organization. Extra space could be rented or sold.

An implementation problem with variable costing is the choice of allocation base to allocate variable overhead costs. In *Numerical example 11.4*, the allocation base is the output measure of the number of units produced. If the manufacturing facility makes multiple products that share common variable overhead resources, some input measure such as direct labour hours is frequently used as an allocation base. As long as an allocation base uses only one input metric, overhead can be classified as variable or fixed with respect to that allocation base. If multiple allocation bases are used, however, the definition of variable and fixed becomes less clear. For example, batch-level costs are fixed with respect to the number of units or other unit-level costs, but vary with the number of batches and allocation bases such as the number of set-ups. Should batch-level costs be treated as variable and included in product costs, or should they be treated as fixed and excluded from product costs? These definitional problems become more acute when different levels of costs are recognized in activity-based costing.

Variable costing attracted much attention in the 1950s and 1960s. During this period, increased budgetary control through standard costing,[1] the introduction of computer systems and the greater focus on tax reporting had important effects on internal costing systems.[2] Some companies experimented with variable costing and some still use it, but only for internal reporting. Since 1975, SSAP 9 in the UK has required the use of absorption costing as do International Accounting Standards. The adoption of International Accounting Standards also affects companies in geographic regions where the use of variable costing has been more prevalent, such as Scandinavia. Absorption costing remains the predominant method of costing in manufacturing organizations, although all firms treat some overhead as a period expense rather than a product cost.

For income-tax calculations, absorption costing generally is the required method. A recent UK study of manufacturing firms indicated that profits under variable costing would have been lower in the majority of firms, on average, than those reported under absorption costing.[3] Tax authorities have been wary to allow methods that reduce taxable income and taxes payable. Thus, firms which use variable costing for internal purposes must maintain two costing systems. This duplication increases their costs of doing business.

The preference for absorption costing implies that the benefits of switching to variable costing for some organizations are not as great as the costs. Most organizations have retained their absorption costing system even when potential problems with planning decisions and control exist. Cost management at National Bank of Canada is an example of the use of two systems to provide information to support its organizational strategy.

Concept **review**

1 How are fixed costs treated with variable costing?

2 What are the advantages of using variable costing?

3 Why is variable costing not more widely used?

---

[1] Chapter 12 discusses standard costing in detail.

[2] D. Dugdale and T. Colwyn Jones (2003) 'Battles in the costing war: UK debates, 1950–1975', *Accounting, Business and Financial History*, Vol. 13, No. 3 (November), pp. 305–338.

[3] C. Pong and F. Mitchell (2006) 'Full costing versus variable costing: Does the choice still matter? An empirical exploration of UK manufacturing companies 1988–2002', *The British Accounting Review*, Vol. 38, pp. 131–148.

Gorzów Electronics (continued)

Emilia is glad that she did not produce extra inventory in order to improve the reported profit. For internal reporting and performance compensation, corporate headquarters has announced a change in the way profit is calculated for the different product lines. By requiring reports based on variable costing, overproduction is no longer an advantage. All fixed costs are to be reported in the period that they are incurred. No opportunity would exist to spread fixed costs over both products sold and products held in inventory in order to improve income.

Organizational **analysis**

Cost management at National Bank of Canada

National Bank of Canada is the sixth largest of Canada's chartered banks. In order to compete with the other major players, National Bank uses its cost management system to support its strategy of product differentiation and personalized customer service. In its credit card sector, the bank's cost management system reports costs on a product basis. This method contrasts with the more general approach in the banking industry to report costs on a functional or departmental basis.

Cost assignment in the banking sector is complicated, especially as many costs are fixed, semi-fixed or shared across products. For example, the cost of head-office operations and customer service representatives are not assigned easily to an individual credit card. With new products and card features constantly being added, it is more difficult to identify how a particular item affects the overall cost behaviour of credit cards.

National Bank developed a full cost system to allocate costs to credit card products. First, costs were assigned to more than 30 different activity centres. Next, costs were allocated to products based on a variety of cost drivers. These drivers included the number of cards outstanding, the number of cards in use, and bad debt levels. These allocated costs were used to determine product profitability, whether or not to launch a new product, relative profitability, marketing programmes, etc.

The cost system also provided a mechanism for the marketing and accounting groups to work together to ensure that new initiatives met National Bank's strategic objectives and financial goals. To compensate for the potential loss of information from the fully-allocated cost system, National Bank supplemented these data with a direct (variable) cost model. The direct cost model was used to evaluate the short-term impact of new products on resource consumption. Both models motivated managers to challenge cost figures from the perspective of their own experience and conventional wisdom. While managers might have had different ideas and expectations, the accounting system ensured that decisions taken were based on reasonable and realistic figures.

How did the management accounting system at National Bank support organizational strategy and its implementation?

What are the advantages and disadvantages of National Bank's full cost system?

What are the potential effects of the system on management behaviour?

Sources: A. Mersereau (1999), 'Controlling the cost of plastic', *CMA Management*, Vol. 73, No. 6 (July–August), pp. 26–30; www.nbc.ca

CAPACITY COSTS

Absorption and variable costing provide alternative ways of accounting for fixed costs. Fixed costs primarily derive from prior decisions on capacity. Capacity decisions include decisions on the size of plants and the amount of equipment purchased. These fixed costs include depreciation of buildings and equipment, property taxes, security and utilities. Other capacity decisions include the size of service units within the organization, such as information technology, accounting, maintenance and marketing. Each of these capacity decisions generates fixed costs that are usually allocated to other units within the organization.

How much capacity should the firm acquire? This decision is difficult because the future demand for an organization's products is uncertain and tends to vary over time. The cost of too much capacity (acquiring more plants and equipment, and hiring more employees) must be weighed against the cost of too little capacity (overtime pay, wear on facilities and lost sales). The capacity decision for a common overhead resource becomes even more difficult when knowledge about future demand for the overhead resource is decentralized. Product managers likely have better information about the future demand for their products than do centralized decision makers. However, the latter usually are responsible for capacity decisions. Therefore, the organization should gather information from all the potential users of the resource before making a capacity decision.

Gathering information for making a capacity decision leads to trade-offs between planning decisions and control. In particular, the organization would like to receive accurate information from decentralized managers to make the appropriate resource capacity decision. It also would prefer that decentralized managers use the resource in an efficient manner. Adding capacity, however, generates fixed costs that are allocated to the decentralized managers. For example, the decision to expand the warehouse generates additional depreciation expense and utilities that are fixed costs; therefore, the capacity decision influences their performance measures. This influence on managerial performance evaluation and rewards might lead managers to provide inaccurate estimates and to use the capacity in a less than optimal manner.

As described in the previous sections of this chapter, the allocation of fixed costs can lead to under-utilization of the allocation base used to allocate the fixed costs. This problem occurs when an organization is operating below capacity. If resource capacity is set and is not flexible, no opportunity cost exists in using the excess capacity. Yet managers will choose to control their use of the resource because of the allocation of fixed costs. In the extreme, under-utilization of the allocation base can lead to the death spiral. Not allocating fixed costs can resolve the under-utilization problem when operating below capacity.

Not allocating the fixed costs of a resource when operating below capacity, however, leads to problems with the capacity decision. Managers overstate their future resource requirements and request additional capacity that satisfies all potential future resource needs. Therefore, the allocation of fixed costs related to capacity prevents managers from overstating their capacity needs. The allocation of fixed costs to managers also commits them to recovering a share of the capacity costs.

Once the capacity decision has been made, however, the efficient use of the resource becomes the important issue. If excess capacity exists, the organization would want to encourage use of the resource by allocating little or no costs. When excess capacity exists, the opportunity cost of using the resource is zero; therefore, use of the resource should be encouraged.

In deciding whether to allocate the fixed costs of a capacity resource to its users, the firm makes a trade-off between the efficient investment in the common resource and its efficient utilization after acquisition. Allocating fixed costs helps control the problem of over-investment in capacity, but at the expense of the possible under-utilization of the asset after acquisition.

The following two sections provide methods to allocate fixed costs related to capacity.

■ Allocation of overhead based on practical capacity

In Chapter 10, the pre-determined application rate for overhead is calculated by dividing the expected overhead costs by the expected usage of the allocation base. By using the expected usage of the allocation base, the total overhead allocated should approximate the total actual overhead.

An alternative to a full absorption costing system is a partial absorption costing system. Under this system, all variable overhead is allocated, but only the fixed cost of overhead resources used is allocated. The fixed costs of unused overhead resources (excess capacity) are treated as expenses of the period and not allocated to products. To allocate overhead based on capacity used, a fixed cost application rate is calculated by dividing the expected fixed overhead costs by the **practical capacity** of the shared resource. The practical capacity is the maximum level of operations that can be achieved without increasing costs due to congestion. For example, the practical capacity of a paper mill operating 24 hours a day is estimated to be 2,000 tonnes per week. The paper mill could produce 2,300 tonnes per week by increasing the speed of the machines, but that would lead to higher maintenance and replacement costs.

When the application rate to allocate fixed costs is based on practical capacity, the under-absorption of fixed overhead costs generally occurs. The capacity level of the allocation base is usually greater than the expected level, so the application rate will be lower. A lower application rate leads to the allocation of less overhead. For example, suppose the practical capacity of the paper mill described earlier is 2,000 tonnes per week, but only 1,600 tonnes are used. Suppose the fixed costs of the mill are €300,000 per week. Using practical capacity, the application rate is €150 per tonne (€300,000 divided by 2,000 tonnes). An amount of €240,000 is allocated to the paper produced, because only 1,600 tonnes are manufactured. Any fixed cost that is not allocated is the cost of having excess capacity. The unallocated overhead is not absorbed in inventory, but is treated as a separate period expense. In the paper mill example, the remaining €60,000 is the cost of excess capacity and is a period cost.

Numerical example 11.5

The fixed costs of operating an online retail operation result primarily from the cost of the facility. The expected and actual annual cost of the facility is £200,000. The fixed cost of the facility of 20,000 square metres is allocated to the marketing and inventory divisions, which share the facility. The inventory division uses 10,000 square metres, and the marketing division uses 4,000 square metres. Currently, 6,000 square metres are unoccupied. What is the application rate using square metres as the capacity measure? How much of the fixed costs are allocated to the marketing and inventory divisions? How much is treated as the cost of excess capacity?

Solution

The application rate is as follows:

$$£200,000 \text{ per } 20,000\text{m}^2 = £10 \text{ per m}^2$$

Cost object	Usage (m²)	Application rate per m² (£)	Allocation (£)
Inventory	10,000	10	100,000
Marketing	4,000	10	40,000
Excess capacity	6,000	10	60,000
Totals	20,000		200,000

The £60,000 allocated to unused capacity is a period expense.

Using the practical capacity of the allocation base to determine the application rate has several advantages. The allocation of the fixed costs of a resource to a particular product or organizational unit is not affected by the use of the resource by other products or units. With full absorption costing systems, less use of the shared resource by some products or units means more fixed costs allocated to the other units and products that share the resource. A death spiral is less likely to occur because the cost of unused capacity is not imposed on the remaining units and their products.

Another advantage is having a measure of the cost of unused capacity. Under a full absorption costing system, the cost of unused capacity is not easily identified. Knowledge about the cost of unused capacity is valuable in making decisions to change capacity.

Using practical capacity to allocate fixed costs has some disadvantages. This procedure does not alleviate the incentive to overproduce. By producing more units than can be sold, some fixed costs remain in ending inventory at the end of the year instead of being expensed. Overproduction has a short-term, positive impact on profit.

Another disadvantage of using practical capacity occurs, if economies of scale exist. In this case, managers still have incentives to over-invest by building too large a facility. Knowing that the cost of the excess capacity is not allocated to them, they can lower their future allocated fixed costs. For example, suppose a paper mill with practical capacity of 2,000 tonnes a week can be built. The mill generates weekly fixed costs of €300,000. Due to economies of scale, a mill with a capacity of 3,000 tonnes per week can be built that generates €400,000 of fixed costs per week. The product managers know that they only need 2,000 tonnes of capacity per week. By building the larger mill, the product managers can lower their allocated fixed cost from €150 per tonne to €133.33 per tonne (€400,000 divided by 3,000 tonnes).

Managers also tend to under-utilize the allocation base even if only some fixed costs are being allocated. If the organization is not operating at full capacity, the usage of the allocation base is taxed at a higher rate than the opportunity cost of using the overhead resource. In effect, the opportunity cost is zero. When allocation rates are higher than the opportunity cost of using the indirect resource, managers are motivated to use less of the indirect resource than they would if the opportunity cost of the indirect resource were allocated. This problem is described in *Numerical example 11.2*.

■ Allocation based on the capacity decision

Capacity decisions frequently are long-term in nature and require significant capital investment. To obtain accurate information on the capacity decision, the organization must provide appropriate incentives to encourage managers to reveal truthfully their future expected demand for a resource. If the managers are not charged for the resource, they will prefer a larger resource capacity. However, if capacity costs are allocated to managers, under-utilization of the capacity occurs when excess capacity exists.

An alternative fixed-cost allocation system allocates fixed costs based on requests for the resource at the time the capacity was acquired. Decentralized managers are charged a fixed amount for the resource based on capacity requested, rather than on the resource used, as long as resource consumption is less than requested. Any use of the resource more than the requested amount is charged to the manager at a much higher rate. This rate discourages managers from requesting too little of the resource when the capacity decision is made.

This cost allocation procedure has several benefits. It encourages managers to reveal their expected use of the resource. If managers request too much of the resource when capacity decisions are made, they will be burdened with a large allocated cost for that resource. If the managers request too little of the resource, they will face stiff penalties for its over-use.

This cost allocation procedure also tends to provide decentralized managers with the correct incentives in using the resource. Once the capacity decision has been made and the fixed cost allocation has been pre-determined, managers treat the resource as free until usage of the resource reaches the requested amount. After reaching the requested amount, managers are charged considerably more for additional use. This cost allocation scheme approximates the opportunity cost of using the fixed resource. However, it too is not without problems. What charge should new users receive years after the capacity has been built? Or suppose a new technology makes it more efficient for current users to update their operating capacity. If they continue to be charged for their previous share of the existing capacity, they will not make the shift. The organization must decide if they should be excused from their previous capacity commitment.

Concept **review**

1 How are application rates calculated using practical capacity?

2 What portion of the fixed overhead is allocated to products when application rates are calculated using practical capacity?

3 What are the advantages and disadvantages of using practical capacity to allocate fixed costs?

4 What other methods might be used to manage both the capacity decision and the efficient use of fixed resources?

Gorzów Electronics (continued)

To get a clearer understanding of how overhead is allocated to her product line, Emilia Symanski has asked the corporate headquarters for an explanation of fixed overhead allocation. The following calculations were provided:

Total annual fixed costs related to all of the facilities = €16,000,000
Total area of all facilities = 2,500,000m^2
Total area expected to be used during the year = 2,000,000m^2
Application rate = €16,000,000 per 2,000,000m^2 = €8 per m^2
Applied to mobile telephone assembly = €8 per m^2 × 100,000m^2 = €800,000

Emilia recognizes that she is being charged for the cost of the unused capacity. She was not part of the capacity decision; therefore, she responds to corporate headquarters that the following allocation based on practical capacity is more appropriate:

Application rate = €16,000,000 per 2,500,000m^2 = €6.4 per m^2
Applied to mobile telephone assembly = €6.4 per m^2 × 100,000m^2 = €640,000

If corporate headquarters agrees with her argument, she will be €160,000 closer to reaching the goal of €1,000,000 profit for the assembly and sales of mobile telephones. However, she is not certain that corporate management will accept her view as these costs must be covered somewhere and will not be eliminated by this change. If she is not charged for this capacity, someone else likely will be. If it is written off as a period expense, it will reduce the firm's profit and affect bonuses of those evaluated on overall firm performance. However, the use of practical capacity does provide upper management with the cost of excess capacity.

SUMMARY

1 **Identify the problems with absorption costing systems.** Absorption costing systems can cause overproduction, under-utilization of allocation bases, and misleading product costs.

2 **Use variable costing to generate profit and loss statements, and recognize its advantages and disadvantages.** With variable costing, only variable costs are treated as part of the product cost. Fixed costs are expensed in the period incurred. Variable costing reduces the incentive to overproduce and provides product costs closer to the opportunity cost, when excess capacity exists. The disadvantages include the excessive use of fixed overhead resources and the exclusion of fixed opportunity costs in the product cost.

3 **Identify problems in selecting the capacity of a fixed cost resource.** In selecting the capacity of a fixed cost resource, the organization is committing resources for a period of time. If capacity is set too high, the organization will incur excessive fixed costs. If the capacity is set too low, it will incur additional overtime costs and excess wear on the facilities. The organization also may lose sales. Information about future demand for the organization's products is critical in making the capacity decision.

4 **Use the organization's practical capacity to allocate overhead, and recognize its advantages and disadvantages.** The application rate is calculated by dividing fixed costs by the practical capacity of the allocation base. Allocated costs only include the cost of capacity used. Advantages include an allocated cost which is not affected by other users of the resource and the identification of the cost of unused capacity. Disadvantages include the incentive to overproduce and the under-utilization of the allocation base.

5 **Describe trade-offs for decentralized managers to provide accurate information to make a decision on the capacity of a common resource and on the efficient use of the resource.** At the time when the capacity decision for a common resource is being made, decentralized managers would prefer extra capacity, if they were not charged for it through the allocation of costs. However, the allocation of the fixed costs of a common resource likely leads to under-utilization of the resource, especially if significant excess capacity exists.

6 **Make decisions regarding the production and further processing of joint products. (Appendix)** A process that produces joint products is profitable if the joint costs are less than the sales value of all the joint products. A joint product should be processed further if the incremental revenues are greater than the incremental costs.

KEY TERMS

By-products (Appendix) Joint products of relatively low value compared to other joint products.

Death spiral The process of dropping products when full cost exceeds price without lowering overhead costs previously allocated to them.

Joint costs (Appendix) The costs of the input and the processing of the input to generate joint products.

Joint products (Appendix) Products generated from the splitting of a single material input.

Net realizable value method (Appendix) A procedure of dividing joint costs based on the sales value less the finishing costs of the joint products.

Physical measure method (Appendix) A procedure of dividing joint costs based on a physical characteristic of the joint products.

Practical capacity The highest rate at which an organization can operate without increasing costs due to congestion.

Relative sales value method (Appendix) A procedure of dividing joint costs based on the gross sales value of the joint products.

Variable costing Determining product costs based only on the variable cost of making the product. The fixed costs are treated as period costs and written off directly to the profit and loss statement.

APPENDIX
Joint costs

Joint products are produced from a single input. This input is generally some raw material that is split into joint products. For example, minced meat and liver are joint products of a butchered cow. In a mining operation, gold and silver are joint products of the processed ore. Usually, but not always, joint products are produced in fixed proportions, meaning that more gold cannot be produced by making less silver. The production of joint products is demonstrated in Figure 11.1.

Joint costs refer to the cost of the input and the cost of processing the input to generate the joint products. The cost of petroleum and its refining costs are joint costs of making paraffin oil, petrol, tar and the other joint products that are separated through the distillation process. Joint costs are obviously part of the production cost of joint products, but there are no obvious ways of tracing joint costs to specific joint products. In other words, what part of the cost of a barrel of petroleum can be traced to the petrol distilled from the petroleum? All of the joint costs are necessary to make each of the joint products. This problem of 'jointness' can be illustrated as follows:

> Suppose my fare for a trip to London is £10. Can this cost be rationally split between my various doings while in London, for example, sightseeing and shopping? I might suggest, perhaps using time as basis, that £3 is the cost of sightseeing and £7 of shopping. My arithmetic is no doubt perfect, but my figures do not have a cause-and-effect relation, and therefore lack rational sense; the £3 would have meaning only if the fare would have been cut by £3 on condition that I did no sightseeing – that is the real test. This example suggests that where jobs, etc. share the benefits of an item of overhead, there may be no rational way in which to split the joint cost of the item between them.[4]

The inability to trace joint costs to joint products does not mean that joint costs cannot be allocated to joint products. To the extent that joint costs are manufacturing costs, generally accepted accounting principles (GAAP) suggests that these joint costs should be allocated to the joint products for financial reporting and tax purposes. Joint costs also may be allocated for cost reimbursement contracts.

Figure 11.1 Production of joint products

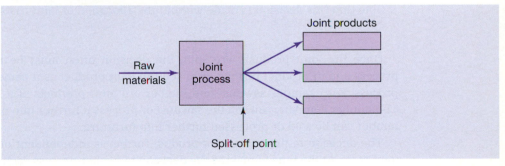

---

[4] This illustration is provided by W. T. Baxter (2005) 'Direct Versus Absorption Costing: A Comment', *Accounting, Business and Financial History*, Vol. 15, No. 1 (March), pp. 89–91. While the example speaks of joint *overhead* costs, the focus of the article is on costs in general and the choice of variable versus absorption costing systems.

Many ways exist to allocate joint costs to joint products. For example, in an oil refinery, petroleum is split into numerous joint products including petrol, paraffin oil, and bitumen. The cost of each barrel of petroleum can be allocated to the joint products based on physical measures (weight, volume, etc.), relative sales value or net realizable value. These methods are described later. The important point to remember, however, is that any joint cost allocation to a joint product is arbitrary. Joint cost allocations should not be used for pricing or product-mix decisions.

Why are allocated joint costs arbitrary and useless for planning purposes? In Chapter 2, opportunity costs were identified as the critical costs for making planning decisions. The opportunity cost of making only petrol from petroleum cannot be separated from the opportunity cost of making the other joint products. The opportunity cost of the whole joint process, however, can be determined. In the case of distilling petroleum, the opportunity cost is the forgone benefit of not purchasing the petroleum and using the oil refinery for other purposes. Therefore, a cost-benefit analysis can be performed with respect to the whole joint process. The joint opportunity costs can be compared with the total sales value of the joint products. In other words, the opportunity cost of purchasing and using the oil refinery should be compared with the total revenues generated from selling the petrol, paraffin oil, tar and other joint products.

Numerical **example** 11.6

Apples are purchased for £0.10 per kilogram, crushed, and pressed to make apple cider. The processing costs £0.03 per kilogram of apples. Every kilogram of apples generates 700 grams of apple cider and 300 grams of mash. The apple cider is sold for £0.18 per kilogram and the mash is sold as fertilizer for £0.02 per kilogram. Is the joint process profitable?

Solution

The joint costs are the sum of the raw materials and the processing: £0.10 + £0.03, or £0.13 per kilogram of apples. The benefits are the sum of the revenues generated from all the joint products. Each kilogram of apples creates the following sales value:

	£
Apple cider (£0.18 per kg × 700g)	0.126
Mash (£0.02 per kg × 300g)	0.006
Total sales value per kg of apples	0.132

The sales value is greater than the cost, so the joint process is profitable. Note that this decision is made without the allocation of joint costs.

Once the joint products are split, the decision often must be made whether to process a joint product further, or to sell the joint product as it comes out of the joint process. For example, sawdust and lumber are joint products of a lumber company. The lumber company can sell the sawdust or process it further into particle board. The lumber can be sold or processed further into furniture.

The decision to process a joint product further is independent of the allocation of joint costs. At the time of making the decision to further process each joint product, the joint costs are sunk. The joint products have already been divided and the joint costs already have been incurred. The decision to process a joint product further is based again on opportunity costs. The cost of processing the joint product (sawdust) further is the forgone revenue from selling the unprocessed joint product. The cost of selling the unprocessed joint product is the net profit forgone by not processing the joint product further and selling the processed joint product (particle board).

Another way to look at the decision to process further or not is to compare two revenue streams. The first amount is the incremental revenues of selling the processed joint product net of the incremental costs of further processing. The second amount is the revenue received from selling the unprocessed joint product. If the first revenue stream is greater than the second, then the joint product should be processed further. Of course, there may be situations where no ready market exists for the joint product unless processed further. In this case, the second amount is zero, but the first amount must be greater than zero to make further processing worthwhile. For example, the sales price of a tonne of sawdust is £200 and the sales price of particle board made from a tonne of sawdust is £2,500. The incremental cost of converting a tonne of sawdust to particle board is £2,000. Therefore, the incremental revenue (£2,500 − £200 = £2,300) is higher than the incremental costs, so the sawdust should be processed further.

Numerical **example** 11.7

A salmon-processing plant purchases salmon for £1 per kilogram from a fishing fleet. The processing plant separates the salmon into fillets and 'parts'. A kilogram of salmon yields 70 per cent fillets and 30 per cent parts. The separation process costs £0.20 per kilogram of salmon. The fillets can be sold directly after separation, or processed further and canned. The 'parts' can be sold directly as fertilizer, or processed further into canned cat food. The sales prices and processing costs are as follow:

	Unprocessed sales price (£) per kg	Further processing costs (£) per kg	Processed sales price (£) per kg
Fillets	2.50	0.50	4.00
Parts	0.10	0.30	0.35

Which joint products should the salmon processing plant process further?

Solution

The decision should be made based on a comparison of incremental revenues and costs:

	Incremental costs (£) per kg	Incremental revenues (£) per kg
Fillets	0.50	4.00 − 2.50 = 1.50
Parts	0.30	0.35 − 0.10 = 0.25

The fillets should be processed further because the incremental revenues are higher than the incremental costs. The parts should be sold for fertilizer because the incremental revenues of making cat food are less than the incremental costs. Note that the joint costs of buying and separating the salmon are not relevant to the decisions regarding further processing.

Some joint products are sometimes called **by-products**. By-products are joint products of relatively low value compared to other joint products. By-products might even have a negative value if disposal of the by-product is costly. Nestlé's Cagayan de Oro factory in the Philippines had considered spent coffee grounds as a by-product of its soluble coffee manufacturing process. These spent coffee grounds had to be disposed of in approved landfill sites. Now used as supplemental fuel to minimize waste materials, their recycling reduces the use of non-renewable resources and landfill space. The process also has been adopted in other Nestlé factories.[5] Whether a joint

---

[5] Coffee Grounds Case Study, http://nestle.com/SharedvalueCSR/Environment/Topics (accessed 25 July 2007).

product is called a by-product or joint product, however, should not affect the decisions described in this section.

■ Allocating joint costs

Although allocated joint costs should not be used for making planning decisions, external reporting requirements usually require joint costs to be allocated to joint products. For example, GAAP suggests allocating joint manufacturing costs to joint products. Also, the payment by customers for joint products on a cost-reimbursement basis would lead to the allocation of joint costs.

The choice of an allocation base is arbitrary, as it is not a question of which allocation base is most closely associated with the joint cost. The following allocation bases are commonly used: physical measure, gross sales value at time of split-off and net realizable value.

The **physical measure method** is convenient because physical measures such as weight or volume are easily observed. For example, if weight were used to allocate the joint costs of purchasing and butchering a cow, each of the joint products (steaks, roasts, minced beef, cowhide, entrails and bones) would receive joint costs proportional to their weight. One feature of allocating joint costs by physical measure is that joint products that have little value may receive the bulk of the joint costs. In the case of butchering a cow, the value of the bones is relatively small, but given their weight, the bones would receive a high proportion of the joint costs. If the allocated joint costs were greater than the value of the bones, the bones would appear to be unprofitable. The profitability of the joint products after joint cost allocation, however, is not relevant in making product-mix decisions. A meat processing plant cannot stop producing cow bones.

The **relative sales value method** allocates joint costs to joint products based on the sales value of each of the joint products when they are split into separate products. If the relative sales value method is used, the joint products with the higher sales value would receive more of the joint costs. In the case of butchering a cow, the steaks would receive a higher proportion of the joint cost because their relative sales value is higher. The relative sales value method is less likely than the physical measure method to cause some joint products to be profitable and others to be unprofitable. However, market prices used to determine the sales value often are not easily determined and change over time.

The **net realizable value method** uses the net realizable value of each joint product to allocate joint costs. The net realizable value is the difference between sales revenue and the additional costs required to process the joint products from the split-off point until they are sold. Suppose that the meat processing plant chooses to tan the cowhide to make leather. The leather's net realizable value of the leather is the sales value of the leather less the tanning costs. If market prices of unprocessed joint products are difficult to determine, the net realizable value method is easier than the relative sales value method to implement. Another feature of the net realizable value method is that all the processed joint products are either profitable or unprofitable after the allocation of joint costs.

Designating a joint product as a by-product also can lead to different joint cost allocations. One method of treating by-products is to allocate no joint costs to the by-products. All of the joint costs are allocated to the joint products that are not designated as by-products. For example, a meat-processing company might consider all non-meat parts of the cow to be by-products. In this case, only the steaks, roasts, minced beef, and other meat products would receive joint costs by one of the methods previously mentioned. The cowhide, bones and entrails would receive no joint costs.

Another way to deal with by-products is to allocate joint costs to them equal to the net realizable value of the by-products. By definition, the by-products would have a profitability equal to zero. The remaining joint costs would be allocated to the joint products not designated as by-products by one of the methods mentioned previously. Allocating joint costs equal to the by-product's net realizable value is commonly used if the by-product has a negative net realizable value. For example, a by-product of producing electric power from a nuclear plant is spent radioactive fuel rods. These fuel rods have a negative net realizable value because disposal and storage costs are incurred. Allocating joint costs equal to a negative net realizable means that joint costs are increased by the amount of the negative net realizable value. Therefore, the joint costs allocated to the electric power of a nuclear plant include the cost of disposing of the spent fuel rods.

Numerical **example** 11.8

A chicken processor pays £1.60 for a 1.5 kilogram chicken. The cost of processing the chicken into parts is £0.40 per chicken. The processor treats the feathers and the entrails as by-products. The feathers can be sold for £0.01 per chicken to a pillow manufacturer. The processor pays someone £0.05 per chicken to dispose of the entrails. The remaining parts can be sold without further processing to a cat-food manufacturer or cleaned, inspected, and packaged for human consumption. Table 11.1 provides sales prices and costs of the parts per chicken. Allocate the joint costs to the joint products by three methods: weight, relative sales value and net realizable value. By-products should receive joint costs equal to their net realizable value.

Solution

For each chicken part, the incremental revenue from selling to grocery stores is greater than the incremental costs of further processing the parts, so none of the chicken will be sold to the cat-food manufacturer. The by-products receive joint costs equal to their net realizable value; therefore, the joint costs allocated to the remaining joint products are as follows:

	£
Cost of chicken	1.60
Cost of killing and processing	0.40
Allocated to feathers	(0.01)
Allocated to entrails	0.05
Total	2.04

Table 11.1 **Sales prices and costs of parts of a chicken (per chicken)**

Part	Weight (g)	Sales price for cat food (£)	Cost of cleaning, Inspecting and packaging (£)	Sales price to grocery stores (£)	Net realizable value (£)
Back	175	0.10	0.10	0.22	0.12
Breasts	550	0.15	0.20	1.50	1.30
Thighs	350	0.12	0.15	0.80	0.65
Wings	125	0.03	0.10	0.30	0.20
Totals	1500*	0.40	0.55	2.82	2.27

* The entrails and the feathers make up the remaining weight

→

Joint cost allocation using weight:

	Back	Breasts	Thighs	Wings
Weight (g)	175	550	350	125
% of total weight (1500g)	14.58	45.83	29.17	10.42
Allocated joint costs of £2.04 (£)	(0.30)	(0.93)	(0.60)	(0.21)
Further processing costs (£)	(0.10)	(0.20)	(0.15)	(0.10)
Sales price (£)	0.22	1.50	0.80	0.30
Profitability (£)	(0.18)	0.37	0.05	(0.01)

Joint allocation using relative sales value:

	Back	Breasts	Thighs	Wings
Sales value after split-up (£)	0.10	0.15	0.12	0.03
% of sales value (£0.40)	25.00	37.50	30.00	7.50
Allocated joint costs of £2.04 (£)	(0.51)	(0.77)	(0.61)	(0.15)
Further processing costs (£)	(0.10)	(0.20)	(0.15)	(0.10)
Sales price (£)	0.22	1.50	0.80	0.30
Profitability (£)	(0.39)	0.53	0.04	0.05

Joint allocation using net realizable value:

	Back	Breasts	Thighs	Wings
Net realizable value (NRV) (£)	0.12	1.30	0.65	0.20
% of total NRV (£2.27)	5.29	57.27	28.64	8.81
Allocated joint costs of £2.04 (£)	(0.11)	(1.17)	(0.58)	(0.18)
Further processing costs (£)	(0.10)	(0.20)	(0.15)	(0.10)
Sales price (£)	0.22	1.50	0.80	0.30
Profitability (£)	0.01	0.13	0.07	0.02

Note that the net realizable method is the only joint-cost allocation method in which all the joint products generate a positive profit. In general, the net realizable method causes all the joint products to show either a positive or negative profit.

Self-study problem

The Heathshire Textile Company makes two types of fabric, cotton and polyester. The company had no beginning inventory and manufactured 300,000 metres of cotton cloth and 500,000 metres of polyester. During the year, the company sold 250,000 metres of cotton cloth for £3 per metre and 400,000 metres of polyester for £2 per metre. The manufacturing costs during the year are:

	£
Direct materials	
Cotton fibre	250,000
Polyester fibre	200,000
Direct labour	
Cotton	100,000
Polyester	60,000
Weaving machine (capacity = 5,000 hours)	100,000
(3,000 hours for cotton; 1,000 hours for polyester)	
Utilities	50,000
Set-ups of weaving machine for new production runs	400,000
Factory rental	200,000
Total	1,360,000

The weaving machine costs and utilities vary with the number of machine hours. The set-up costs are fixed with respect to the number of units produced but vary with the number of set-ups: 30 for cotton and 50 for polyester. The factory rental costs are fixed with respect to the number of units produced but vary with the number of square metres dedicated to each product: 30,000 square metres for cotton and 70,000 square metres for polyester. No raw materials remain at the end of the year.

Required

a What is the company's profit with absorption costing and machine hours used to allocate all overhead items?

b What is the company's profit if practical capacity costing and machine hours are used to allocate all overhead items? The set-up and factory rental costs are considered fixed.

c What is the company's profit if variable costing is used and machine hours are used to allocate the weaving machine costs and the utility costs? The set-ups and factory rental are considered fixed costs.

d What is the company's profit under activity-based costing (ABC)? Machine hours are used to allocate the weaving machine costs and the utility costs, the number of set-ups is used to allocate set-up costs, and factory rental costs are allocated based on the square metres of space used.

e What are the advantages and disadvantages of each method?

Solution

a The average costs per metre using absorption costing are as follows:

	Cotton (£)	Polyester (£)
Direct labour	250,000	200,000
Direct materials	100,000	60,000
Machine costs ($\frac{3}{4}$ cotton, $\frac{1}{4}$ polyester)	75,000	25,000
Utilities ($\frac{3}{4}$ cotton, $\frac{1}{4}$ polyester)	37,500	12,500
Set-ups ($\frac{3}{4}$ cotton, $\frac{1}{4}$ polyester)	300,000	100,000
Factory rental ($\frac{3}{4}$ cotton, $\frac{1}{4}$ polyester)	150,000	50,000
Total	912,500	447,500
Number of metres manufactured	300,000	500,000
Average cost per metre	£3.04167	£0.895

The profit using absorption costing follows:

	£
Revenues	
Cotton (250,000m × £3/m)	750,000
Polyester (400,000m × £2/m)	800,000
Cost of goods sold	
Cotton (£3.04167/m × 250,000m)	(760,417)
Polyester (£0.895/m × 400,000m)	(358,000)
Profit	431,583

b The average costs per metre using practical capacity costing are as follows:

	Cotton (£)	Polyester (£)
Direct labour	250,000	200,000
Direct materials	100,000	60,000
Machine costs ($\frac{3}{4}$ cotton, $\frac{1}{4}$ polyester)	75,000	25,000
Utilities ($\frac{3}{4}$ cotton, $\frac{1}{4}$ polyester)	37,500	12,500
Set-ups ($\frac{3}{5}$ cotton, $\frac{1}{5}$ polyester)	240,000	80,000
Factory rental ($\frac{3}{5}$ cotton, $\frac{1}{5}$ polyester)	120,000	40,000
Total	822,500	417,500
Number of metres manufactured	300,000	500,000
Average cost per metre	£2.74167	£0.835

→

The profit using practical capacity costing is as follows:

	£
Revenues	
Cotton (250,000m × £3/m)	750,000
Polyester (400,000m × £2/m)	800,000
Cost of goods sold	
Cotton (£2.74167/m × 250,000m)	(685,417)
Polyester (£0.835/m × 400,000m)	(334,000)
Capacity costs $\frac{1}{5}$ (400,000 + 200,000)	(120,000)
Profit	410,583

c The variable costs per metre are as follows:

	Cotton (£)	Polyester (£)
Direct labour	250,000	200,000
Direct materials	100,000	60,000
Machine costs ($\frac{3}{4}$ cotton, $\frac{1}{4}$ polyester)	75,000	25,000
Utilities ($\frac{3}{4}$ cotton, $\frac{1}{4}$ polyester)	37,500	12,500
Total	462,500	297,500
Number of metres manufactured	300,000	500,000
Average cost per metre	£1.54167	£0.595

The profit using variable costing is as follows:

	£
Revenues	
Cotton (250,000m × £3/m)	750,000
Polyester (400,000m × £2/m)	800,000
Cost of goods sold	
Cotton (£1.54167/m × 250,000m)	(385,417)
Polyester (£0.595/m × 400,000m)	(238,000)
Fixed costs (200,000 + 400,000)	(600,000)
Profit	326,583

d The average costs per metre using ABC are as follows:

	Cotton (£)	Polyester (£)
Direct labour	250,000	200,000
Direct materials	100,000	60,000
Machine costs ($\frac{3}{4}$ cotton, $\frac{1}{4}$ polyester)	75,000	25,000
Utilities ($\frac{3}{4}$ cotton, $\frac{1}{4}$ polyester)	37,500	12,500
Set-ups ($\frac{30}{80}$ cotton, $\frac{50}{80}$ polyester)	150,000	250,000
Factory rental ($\frac{30,000}{100,000}$ cotton, $\frac{70,000}{100,000}$ polyester)	60,000	140,000
Total	672,500	687,500
Number of metres manufactured	300,000	500,000
Average cost per metre	£2.24167	£1.375

The profit using ABC is as follows:

	£
Revenues	
Cotton (250,000m × £3/m)	750,000
Polyester (400,000m × £2/m)	800,000
Cost of goods sold	
Cotton (£2.24167/m × 250,000m)	(560,417)
Polyester (£1.375/m × 400,000m)	(550,000)
Profit	439,583

e The absorption costing method using a single allocation base has little advantage other than being simple and consistent with GAAP. Fixed and variable costs are mixed; therefore, the average cost gives little indication of the opportunity cost of making more units of either product. Machine hours are taxed higher than their opportunity costs and may be under-utilized relative to other indirect resources. Fixed costs reside in inventory and may encourage overproduction.

The practical capacity costing procedure has the advantage of identifying the cost of unused capacity. Some fixed costs, however, are still mixed with the variable costs leading to the same problems as absorption costing.

Variable costing provides a cost that should represent the cost of making additional units, as long as no further set-ups or square metres are required. No incentive for overproduction exists, but all non-unit-level costs are treated as fixed.

ABC has the advantage of recognizing different levels of overhead costs. ABC, however, is an absorption costing method and can lead to overproduction incentives. Users of ABC also must be concerned about the under-utilization of the cost drivers.

Numerical exercises

NE 11.1 Absorption costing systems LO 1
A firm makes a product with variable manufacturing costs equal to £3 per unit and fixed manufacturing costs of £10,000. The product cost is based on an average cost per unit. The company plans to sell 1,000 units for £15 apiece.

What is the profit for the company if 1,000, 1,200, and 1,400 units are made, but only 1,000 are sold? (Assume no beginning inventory.)

NE 11.2 Absorption costing systems LO 1
A production department is allocated costs from the maintenance department based on number of maintenance hours used. The maintenance costs are allocated at a rate of €20 per hour, which includes both variable and fixed costs. The variable cost per hour is €12. The maintenance department has plenty of excess capacity. The benefits to the production department of having maintenance service are estimated in the following table:

Number of hours	Expected benefits (€)
1,000	30,000
2,000	45,000
3,000	58,000
4,000	65,000

What level of maintenance will the production department choose if the production department is allocated maintenance costs at €20 per hour? What level of maintenance benefits the entire organization the most?

NE 11.3 Death spiral LO 1
Central administration allocates its costs of £1,000,000 to the two operating divisions (A and B) of the company. These costs are not avoidable if one division is dropped. With an equal allocation of these costs to both divisions, Division A has a profit of £300,000 and Division B has a loss of £100,000.

What is the profit effect of the company if Division B is dropped and all other division costs are avoidable?

NE 11.4 Misleading product costs LO 1
Computer Shack makes two types of laptop computers: slim-line and palm-size. Excess capacity exists for which no alternative use exists. Fixed overhead costs are allocated based on direct material cost. The product profitability of each product is:

	Slim-line (£)	Palm-size (£)
Sales revenues	500,000	250,000
Direct costs	(225,000)	(180,000)
Fixed costs	(180,000)	(120,000)
Profit	95,000	(50,000)

The palm-size model does not seem profitable and management decides to drop it.

What is the impact on the profitability of the slim-line model?

NE 11.5 Product costing using practical capacity LO 4

A company uses machine hours to allocate overhead. The company has the practical capacity to use 100,000 machine hours. The fixed overhead is expected to be £1,000,000 and the expected usage of machine hours is 70,000.

What is the application rate for fixed overhead if the company uses practical capacity as the allocation base? What proportion of fixed overhead is likely to be allocated?

NE 11.6 Absorption and variable costing LO 1, 2

A company makes a product that has a variable manufacturing cost of £4 per unit and fixed manufacturing costs of £50,000. The product sells for £10 per unit.

Using variable and absorption costing, what is the profit from the product if 10,000 units are made, but only 8,000 units are sold?

NE 11.7 Absorption and variable costing LO 1, 2

A manufacturer of ergonomically-designed computer keyboards has actual and estimated fixed costs of €1,000,000. Variable costs per unit are €18. The allocation base is the number of units produced. The sales price of the keyboard is €50 per unit. There is no beginning inventory. During the year, the manufacturer makes and sells 60,000 keyboards. In December, the plant manager is considering the opportunity to make another 15,000 units, but these 15,000 units cannot be sold this year.

What is the manufacturer's profit with and without the additional 15,000 units, under the absorption and variable costing systems? (Assume that inventory costs are zero.)

NE 11.8 Allocating overhead based on practical capacity LO 4

The cost of rental space is the major fixed cost at Mattress Mart, a discount mattress store in a warehouse mall. The annual rental cost (actual and expected) is £360,000. The store occupies 60,000 square metres of space. The warehouse department occupies 30,000 metres, and the retail department occupies 20,000 metres. The remaining space is unoccupied. Using square metres as the capacity measure, what is the application rate? Allocate the fixed costs to the warehouse and retail departments. How much of the fixed costs are treated as the cost of excess capacity?

NE 11.9 Joint costs LO 6, Appendix

Refina divides petroleum into three types of fuel (A, B, and C) and tar. Tar is considered a by-product. The joint cost of processing 1,000 barrels is £35,000. The joint products have the following characteristics:

Joint product	Number of barrels	Price per barrel (£)
A	100	150
B	300	70
C	200	30
Tar	400	2

Is the joint process profitable?

NE 11.10 Joint costs LO 6, Appendix

If product B in *Numerical exercise 11.9* can be further processed at a cost of £20 per barrel and sold for £85 per barrel, should product B be processed further?

NE 11.11 Joint costs LO 6, Appendix

Suppose tar is treated as a by-product and the net realizable value of tar in *Numerical exercise 11.9* is £2 per barrel.

What is the profit of each product and by-product for petroleum if the joint costs are allocated by number of barrels and the by-product is allocated joint costs equal to its net realizable value?

Numerical problems

NP 11.1 Cost allocation and overproduction LO 1

The Scantron Company makes bar-code scanners for major supermarkets. The sales staff estimates that the company will sell 500 units next year for £10,000 each. The production manager estimates that fixed costs of making the scanners are £2 million, and the variable cost per unit is £4,000. Assume that there are no storage costs for unsold scanners, and that Scantron uses absorption costing.

a What is Scantron's profit, if the firm actually makes and sells 500 units?

b What is Scantron's profit, if the firm makes 600 units but sells 500 units?

NP 11.2 Death spiral LO 1

An insurance company has the following profitability analysis of its services:

	Life insurance (€)	Auto insurance (€)	Home insurance (€)
Revenues	5,000,000	10,000,000	3,000,000
Commissions	(1,000,000)	(2,000,000)	(600,000)
Payments	(3,000,000)	(7,300,000)	(2,000,000)
Fixed Costs	(500,000)	(500,000)	(500,000)
Profit	500,000	200,000	(100,000)

The fixed costs are distributed equally among the services and are not avoidable if one of the services is dropped.

What is the profitability of the remaining services if all services with losses are dropped?

NP 11.3 Allocating costs using practical capacity and variable costing LO 2, 4

The Card Company makes playing cards and trading cards. The primary cost of making the cards is the use of printing machines. Therefore, overhead is allocated based on machine hours. The Card Company has sufficient machines to operate 20,000 hours during the year. The fixed costs of making all types of cards are £2 million. The variable costs (including direct costs) of making a deck of playing cards are £0.10 per deck. The variable costs of making a pack of trading cards are £0.30 per pack. The company makes 2 million decks of playing cards using 8,000 machine hours. The sales price of a deck of playing cards is £1.00 and the company sells 1.8 million decks. The company also makes 1 million packs of trading cards using 7,000 machine hours. The sales price for a pack of trading cards is £1.50 and the company sells 900,000 packs. There was no beginning inventory.

a What is the profit of the company, if the company uses practical capacity to allocate fixed costs?

b What is the profit of the company, if the company uses variable costing?

NP 11.4 Processing further LO 6

Walters Company produces 15,000 kilograms of Product A and 30,000 kilograms of Product B each week by incurring a joint cost of £400,000. These two products can be sold as is, or processed further. Further processing of either product does not delay the production of subsequent batches of the joint product. Data regarding these two products are as follows:

	Product A (£)	Product B (£)
Selling price per kilogram without further processing	12.00	9.00
Selling price per kilogram with further processing	15.00	11.00
Total separate weekly variable costs of further processing	50,000	45,000

To maximize Walters Company's manufacturing contribution margin, how much total separate variable costs of further processing should be incurred each week?

NP 11.5 Variable and absorption costing LO 1, 2

Varilux manufactures a single product and sells it for £10 per unit. At the beginning of the year, there were 1,000 units in inventory. Upon further investigation, you discover that units produced last year had £3.00 of fixed manufacturing cost and £2.00 of variable manufacturing cost. During the year, Varilux produced 10,000 units of product. Each unit produced generated £3.00 of variable manufacturing cost. Total fixed manufacturing cost for the current year was £40,000. There were no inventories at the end of the year.

Prepare two profit and loss statements for the current year, one on a variable cost basis and the other on an absorption cost basis. Explain any difference between the two net income numbers. Provide calculations to support your explanation of the difference.

NP 11.6 Profit and absorption costing LO 1

The MAPICS Company uses full absorption costing and has the following cost structure:

Variable costs per unit	£0.30
Fixed costs	£2.0 million
Normal production	1.0 million units
Selling price	£2.50 per unit

In the first year of production, MAPICS produced 1.4 million units and sold 1.0 million units. In the second year, MAPICS sold 1.0 million units but produced 0.8 million units. There was no beginning inventory in year 1. FIFO is used to value inventories.

a Analyse the change in profitability between years 1 and 2.

b What would profits have been, if 0.6 million units had been produced in the second year?

NP 11.7 Further processing of joint products and allocation of joint costs LO 6

A production department produces two joint products, X and V, using a common input. These are produced in batches. The common input costs €8,000 per batch. To produce the final products (X and V), additional processing costs beyond the split-off point must be incurred. There are no beginning inventories. The following data summarize the operations.

	Products	
	X	V
Quantities produced per batch	200 kg	400 kg
Additional processing costs per batch beyond split-off	€1,800	€3,400
Unit selling prices of completely-processed products	€40 per kg	€20 per kg
Ending inventory	2,000 kg	1,000 kg

a Compute the full cost of the ending inventories using both the net realizable value and the kilograms to allocate joint costs.

b If the selling prices at the split-off point (before further processing) were €35 and €1.00 per kilogram of X and V, respectively, what should the firm do regarding further processing? Show calculations to support your answer.

NP 11.8 Allocating joint costs and processing further LO 6

Sonimad Sawmill manufactures two lumber products from a joint milling process. The two products developed are mine support braces (MSB) and unseasoned commercial building lumber (CBL). A standard production run incurs joint costs of €300,000 and results in 60,000 units of MSB and 90,000 units of CBL. Each unprocessed unit of MSB sells for €2 per unit and each unprocessed unit of CBL sells for €4 per unit.

If the CBL is processed further at a cost of €200,000, it can be sold at €10 per unit but 10,000 units are unavoidably lost (with no discernible value). The MSB units can be coated with a preservative at a cost of €100,000 per production run and then sold for €3.50 each.

a If no further work is done after the initial milling process, calculate the cost of CBL using physical quantities to allocate the joint cost.

b If no further work is done after the initial milling process, calculate the cost of MSB using relative sales value to allocate the joint cost.

c Should MSB and CBL be processed further or sold immediately after initial milling?

d Given your decision in part c, prepare a schedule computing the completed cost assigned to each unit of MSB and CBL, as charged to finished goods inventory. Use net realizable value to allocate joint costs.

(CMA adapted)

NP 11.9 Allocating joint costs LO 6

Metro Blood Bank, a for-profit firm, collects whole blood from donors, tests it, and then separates it into two components: platelets and plasma. Three pints of whole blood yield two pints of platelets and one pint of plasma. (Blood donations usually are measured in pints although they are about 470 ml, roughly equal to one pint.) The cost of collecting the three pints, testing them, and separating them is €300.

The platelets are sold for €165 per pint. Before they are sold, they must be packaged, labelled and frozen. The variable cost of this additional processing is €15 per pint. Plasma is sold for €115 per pint after incurring additional variable processing costs of €45 per pint.

Market forces set the selling prices of the platelets and plasma. The prices of platelets and plasma quoted above are the current market prices. However, these prices vary widely depending on supply and demand conditions. Metro Blood Bank ships its products nationwide to maximize profits and to meet regional blood requirements. It has three operating divisions: Blood Collection and Processing, Platelets and Plasma. Collection and Processing is a cost centre; Platelets and Plasma are profit centres.

Neither platelets nor plasma has any commercial value without further processing.

a Prepare two statements showing the profits per pint of platelets and plasma, where the collection and processing costs are assigned to platelets and plasma using the following:
  i the number of pints of platelets and plasma produced from whole blood, and
  ii the net realizable value of platelets and plasma.
b Discuss the advantages and disadvantages of each of the methods in (a) for assigning the collection and processing costs to the blood products.

NP 11.10 Allocating joint costs LO 6

The Doe Company sells three products: sliced pineapples, crushed pineapples, and pineapple juice. The pineapple juice is a by-product of sliced pineapple; while crushed pineapples and sliced pineapples are produced simultaneously from the same pineapple.

The production process is as follows:

- 100,000 kilograms of pineapples are processed at a cost of £120,000 in Department 1. Twenty per cent of the pineapples' weight is scrap and discarded during processing. Twenty per cent of the processed pineapple is crushed and is transferred to Department 2. The remainder is transferred to Department 3.
- In Department 2, a further cost outlay of £15,000 is required to pack the crushed pineapple. Here a further 10 per cent is lost while processing. The packed product is sold at £3 per kilogram.
- In Department 3, the material is processed at a total additional cost of £40,000. Thirty per cent of the processed pineapple turns into juice and is sold at £0.50 per kilogram after incurring £3,500 as selling costs. The remaining 70 per cent is transferred to Department 4.
- Department 4 is used to pack the sliced pineapples into tins. Costs incurred here total £25,500. The cans then are ready for sale at £4 per kilogram.

Prepare a schedule showing the allocation of the processing cost of £120,000 between crushed and sliced pineapple using the net realizable value method. The net realizable value of the juice is added to the sales value of the sliced pineapples.

NP 11.11 Absorption costing and overproduction LO 1

Zipp Cards buys sports trading cards in bulk from the companies producing the cards. Zipp buys the cards in sheets of 48 cards. It then cuts the sheets into individual cards and sorts and packages them, usually by team. Zipp then sells the packages to large discount stores. The following table provides information regarding the operating results for 2008 and 2009:

Zipp Cards
Summary of Operations
2008 and 2009
(one unit = 48 cards)

	2008	2009
Unit sales (of 48 cards)	50,000	48,000
Price	£5.00	£4.90
Production in units (Budgeted = Actual)	50,000	75,000
Variable cost	£1.00	£1.00
Fixed manufacturing overhead	£160,000	£160,000

Volume is measured in terms of 48-card sheets processed. Budgeted and actual production in 2008 was 50,000 units. There were no beginning inventories on 1 January 2008. In 2009, budgeted and actual production rose to 75,000 units.

After concluding the 2009 year, the owner of Zipp was pleasantly surprised when the accountant showed him the profit and loss statement for the 2009 year. The owner remarked, 'I'm surprised we made more money in

2009 than 2008. We had to cut prices and we didn't sell as many units, but yet we still made more money. Well, you're the accountant and these numbers don't lie.'

a Prepare profit and loss statements for 2008 and 2009 using absorption costing.

b Prepare a statement reconciling the change in net income from 2008 to 2009. Explain to the owner why the firm made more money in 2009 than in 2008.

NP 11.12 Absorption costing and overproduction LO 1

The Medford Mug Company is an old-line maker of ceramic coffee mugs. It imprints company logos and other sayings on mugs for both commercial and wholesale markets. The firm has the capacity to produce 50 million mugs per year, but a downturn has cut production and sales in the current year to 15 million mugs. The operating statement for 2008 follows:

Medford Mug Company
Profit and Loss Statement
Year Ending 2008 (£m)

	£	£
Sales (15 million @ £2)		30.0
Less: Cost of goods sold		
Variable cost (15 million @ £0.50)	(7.5)	
Fixed cost	(20.0)	(27.5)
Gross margin		2.5
Less: Selling and administration		(4.0)
Operating profit		(1.5)

At the end of 2008, there is no ending inventory of finished goods.

The Board of Directors is very concerned about the £1.5 million operating loss. It hires an outside consultant who reports back that the firm suffers from two problems. First, Medford Mug's chief executive receives a fixed salary, and since she owns no share capital, she has little incentive to worry about firm profits. The second problem is that Medford Mug has not marketed its product aggressively and has not kept up with changing market preferences. The current chief executive is 64. The Board of Directors makes her an offer to retire one year early so that Medford Mug can appoint a new chief executive to turn the firm around. The current chief executive accepts the offer to retire and the Board immediately hires someone with a proven track record as a 'turnaround' specialist.

The new chief executive's employment contract pays him a fixed salary of £50,000 a year plus 15 per cent of the firm's operating profits (if any). Operating profits are calculated using absorption costing. In 2009, the new chief executive doubles the selling and administration budget to £8 million (which includes his salary of £50,000). He designs a new line of 'politically correct' sayings to imprint on the mugs and expands inventory and the number of distributors handling the mugs. Production is increased to 45 million mugs and sales climb to 18 million mugs at £2 each. In 2009, variable costs per mug remain at £0.50 and fixed costs at £20 million.

At the end of 2009, the chief executive meets with the Board of Directors and announces that he has accepted another job. He believes that he has successfully got Medford Mug back on track and thanks the board for giving him the opportunity. His new job will be to turn around another struggling company.

a Calculate the chief executive's bonus for 2009.

b Evaluate the performance of the new chief executive for 2009. Did he do as good a job as the 'numbers' in (a) suggest?

NP 11.13 Absorption and variable costing using FIFO LO 1, 2

Smidt & Sons produces a single product and has the following operating data:

	2006	2007	2008
Units produced	22,000	16,000	15,000
Units sold	20,000	15,000	18,000
Fixed manufacturing overhead (€)	800,000	880,000	950,000
Variable manufacturing cost (€)	3.00	3.10	3.20
Variable selling costs (€)	0.25	0.30	0.35
Selling price (€)	45.00	50.00	53.00

The firm uses FIFO inventory costing, and there was no beginning inventory in 2006.

a Calculate net profit in each year using absorption costing.
b Calculate net profit in each year using variable costing.
c Reconcile the annual differences between the two costing methods.

NP 11.14 Absorption and variable costing LO 1, 2

BBG Corporation is a manufacturer of a synthetic chemical. Gary Voss, president of the company, has been eager to get the operating results for the just-completed financial year. He was surprised when the profit and loss statement revealed that profit before taxes had dropped to €885,500 from €900,000, despite an increase in sales volume of 100,000 kg. The drop in net profit occurred even though Voss had implemented two changes during the past 12 months to improve the profitability of the company:

- In response to a 10 per cent increase in production costs, the sales price of BBG's product was increased by 12 per cent. This action took place on 1 December 2008, the first day of the 2009 financial year.
- The managers of the Selling and Administrative departments were given strict instructions to spend no more in financial year 2009 than in 2008.

BBG's Accounting Department prepared and distributed to top management the comparative profit and loss statements presented below.

BBG Corporation
Statements of Operating Profit
For the years ended 30 November 2008 and 2009 (€000s)

	2008 (€)	2009 (€)
Sales revenue	9,000	11,200
Cost of goods sold	7,200	8,320
Under(over)-absorbed overhead	(600)	495
Adjusted cost of goods sold	6,600	8,815
Gross margin	2,400	2,385
Selling and administrative expenses	1,500	1,500
Profit before taxes	900	885

The Accounting staff also prepared related financial information, presented in the schedule below, to assist management in evaluating the company's performance. BBG uses the FIFO inventory method for finished goods.

BBG Corporation
Selected Operating and Financial Data
for 2008 and 2009

	2008	2009
Sales price	€10.00 per kg	€11.20 per kg
Material cost	€1.50 per kg	€1.65 per kg
Direct labour cost	€2.50 per kg	€2.75 per kg
Variable overhead cost	€1.00 per kg	€1.10 per kg
Fixed overhead cost	€3.00 per kg	€3.30 per kg
Total fixed overhead costs	€3,000,000	€3,300,000
Normal production volume	1,000,000 kg	1,000,000 kg
Selling and administrative (all fixed)	€1,500,000	€1,500,000
Sales volume	900,000 kg	1,000,000 kg
Beginning inventory	300,000 kg	600,000 kg
Production	1,200,000 kg	850,000 kg

a Explain to Gary Voss why BBG Corporation's net profit decreased in the current financial year, despite the sales price and sales volume increases.

b A member of BBG's Accounting Department has suggested that the firm adopt variable costing for internal reporting purposes.

   i Using the variable costing method, prepare BBG Corporation's statement of operating profit before taxes for the year ended 30 November 2009.

   ii Present a numerical reconciliation of the difference in profit before taxes using the absorption costing method as currently employed by BBG and the proposed variable costing method.

c Identify and discuss the advantages and disadvantages of using the variable costing method for internal reporting purposes.

(CMA adapted)

NP 11.15 Absorption and variable costing LO 1, 2

Matson manufactures a single metal dog cage that has a variable cost of £50 per cage. Budgeted and actual fixed overhead costs are £900,000. Cages sell for £60 each.

Calculate net profit under both variable costing and absorption costing for each of the following independent cases:

a Sales and production are 100,000 cages.
b Sales are 90,000 cages and production is 100,000 cages.
c Sales are 100,000 cages and production is 90,000 cages. The beginning inventory consists of 20,000 units manufactured last year. Last year 100,000 units were manufactured, 80,000 were sold, variable costs were £50 per cage, and fixed manufacturing overhead costs were £900,000. For inventory valuation purposes, all of this year's production is sold and 10,000 units in the beginning inventory are sold. LIFO is used for inventory valuation.

NP 11.16 Absorption costing and variable costing LO 1, 2

Alliance Tooling produces a single product in its plant. At the beginning of the year, there were no units in inventory. During the year, Alliance produced 120,000 units and sold 100,000 units at £26.75 per unit. Variable manufacturing costs are £13.50 per unit. Alliance pays £2.70 per unit for sales commissions and shipping. It has fixed costs of £720,000 for selling and administration. The tax rate is 40 per cent.

a Prepare a profit and loss statement for Alliance Tooling using absorption costing.
b Prepare a profit and loss statement for Alliance Tooling using variable costing.
c Explain why the net profit figures computed in (a) and (b) differ.

NP 11.17 Joint products LO 6, Appendix

New View is a chemical processor. Two chemicals, V7 and AC, are produced from a decomposition of M68JJ. Each batch of M68JJ costs €22,000 and yields 300 kilograms of V7 and 400 kilograms of AC. Each unit of V7 can be sold for €35 and each unit of AC can be sold for €25. Either intermediate product can be processed further. It costs €2,000 to convert 300 kilograms of V7 into 240 kilograms of V7HX. Likewise, it costs €1,500 to convert 400 kilograms of AC into 320 kilograms of AC92. Each kilogram of V7HX can be sold for €50 and each kilogram of AC92 can be sold for €45. The €22,000 batch cost is allocated to the two intermediate products using kilograms.

a Prepare a financial statement assuming V7 and AC are sold and not processed further. Calculate the profit per batch of each intermediate product that includes the allocated batch cost.
b If neither V7 nor AC is processed further, should New View produce V7 and AC?
c Should New View further process V7 into V7HX and/or AC into AC92? Justify your answer with supporting calculations.

Analysis and interpretation problems

AIP 11.1 Average costs and variable costs as performance measures LO 1, 2

The manager of the manufacturing unit of a company is responsible for the costs of the manufacturing unit. The president is in the process of deciding whether to evaluate the manufacturing manager based on the average cost per unit or the variable cost per unit. Quality and timely delivery would be used in conjunction with the cost measure to reward the manager.

What problems are associated with using the average cost per unit as a performance measure?
What problems are associated with using the variable cost per unit as a performance measure?

AIP 11.2 Allocating overhead using practical capacity LO 4

The president of Celestial Printing has decided to use the practical capacity of the firm's printers to determine the application rates per machine hour for overhead. She believes that the cost of unused capacity would be valuable information. As the controller begins to calculate application rates for the coming year, he is surprised to find that several more printers were purchased during the previous year despite there being considerable excess capacity.

How does the cost allocation system affect the behaviour of managers?

AIP 11.3 Using allocated joint costs LO 6

The Green Packing Company has discovered an increasing demand for frozen boneless chicken breasts. The frozen chicken breasts can be thawed and cooked quickly. This product is becoming very popular with people who do not want to deal with the bones and other parts of the chicken that have less meat. The company recently received an offer to buy frozen boneless chicken breasts for £1 per kilogram. The Green Packing Company, however, is not sure that the company should accept the new offer, because the cost of chicken breasts is greater than £1 per kilogram as the following indicates:

Joint costs purchasing and butchering a chicken	
Cost of a chicken	£0.30
Butchering costs per chicken	0.10
Cost of de-boning, freezing and packaging breasts per chicken	
(0.50 kg. per chicken)	0.15
Cost of chicken breasts per chicken (0.50 kg)	£0.55
Cost of chicken breasts per kilogram (2 × £0.55)	£1.10

All of the joint costs of purchasing and butchering the chicken are allocated to the chicken breasts in this analysis because the chicken breasts are specially ordered.

How should the company analyse this special order for chicken breasts?

AIP 11.4 Allocating the cost of scrap LO 6

ITI Technology designs and manufactures solid-state computer chips. In one of its production departments, a six-inch circular wafer is fabricated by laying down successive layers of silicon and then etching the circuits into the layers. Each wafer contains 100 separate solid-state computer chips. After a wafer is manufactured, the 100 chips are cut out of the wafer, initially tested, mounted into protective covers and electrical leads attached. A final quality control test then is performed.

The initial testing process consists of successive stages of heating and cooling the chips and testing how they work. If 99 per cent of each chip's circuits work properly after the testing, it is classified as a high-density (HD) chip. If between 75 per cent and 99 per cent of a chip's circuits work properly, it is classified as a low-density (LD) chip. If fewer than 75 per cent of the circuits work, it is discarded. Twenty wafers are manufactured per batch. In each batch, 50 per cent of the chips are HD, 20 per cent are LD, and 30 per cent are discarded. HD chips are sold to defence contractors and LD chips to consumer electronic firms. Chips sold to defence contractors require different types of mountings, packaging, and distribution channels than chips sold to consumer electronic firms do. HD chips sell for £30 each and LD chips sell for £16 each.

Each batch of 20 wafers costs £29,100: £8,000 to produce, test, and sort; £21,100 for mounting, attaching leads, final inspection and distribution costs (£14,500 for HD chips and £6,600 for LD chips). The £29,100 total cost per batch consists of direct labour, direct materials and variable overhead.

The following report summarizes the operating data per batch:

ITI Technology
Operating Cost Summary for HD and LD Chips

	Total	HD Chips	LD Chips	Scrap
Per cent of chips	100	50	20	30
Total costs (£)	29,100	14,550	5,820	8,730
Revenue (£)	36,400	30,000[a]	6,400[b]	0
Total costs (£)	29,100	14,550	5,820	8,730
Profit per batch (£)	7,300	15,450	580	(8,730)

[a] £30,000 = 50% × 20 wafers × 100 chips per wafer × £30 per chip.
[b] £6,400 = 20% × 20 wafers × 100 chips per wafer × £16 per chip.

The cost of scrap is charged to a plant-wide overhead account, which then is allocated directly to the lines of business based on profits in the line of business.

a Critically evaluate ITI's method of accounting for HD and LD chips.
b What suggestions would you offer ITI's management?

AIP 11.5 Variable costing LO 2

You are working as a loan officer at TransOceana Bank. While analysing a loan request for a client, you come across the following footnote in the client's annual report:

Inventories are priced at the lower of cost or market of materials plus other direct (variable) costs. Fixed overheads of £4.2 million this year and £3.0 million last year are excluded from inventories. Omitting such overhead resulted in a reduction in net profit (after taxes) of £720,000 for this year. Our tax rate is 40 per cent.

You are preparing your presentation of the loan application to TransOceana's loan committee. Write a brief paragraph in non-technical terms describing what this footnote means and how it affects the bank's decision regarding the evaluation of the borrower's financial condition.

AIP 11.6 Variable and absorption costing LO 1, 2

National Mixing is a division of National Chemicals; a large diversified chemical company. National Mixing (NM) provides mixing services for both outside customers and other National divisions. NM buys or receives liquid chemicals and combines and packages them according to the customer's specifications. NM computes its divisional net profit on both a fully absorbed and variable costing basis. For the year just ending, it reported:

	Net profit (£)
Absorption costing	13,800,000
Variable costing	12,600,000
Difference	1,200,000

Overhead is assigned to products using machine hours.

There is no finished goods inventory at NM, only work-in-process (WIP) inventory. As soon as a product is completed, it is shipped to the customer. The beginning inventory was valued at £6.3 million and contained 70,000 machine hours. The ending WIP inventory was valued at £9.9 million and contained 90,000 machine hours.

Write a short, non-technical note to senior management explaining why the net profit amounts under variable costing and absorption costing differ.

Extended **analysis** and **interpretation** problems

AIP 11.7 Overhead costs from a new factory

Karsten is one of the premier carpet manufacturers in the world. It manufactures carpeting for both residential and commercial applications. Home sales and commercial sales each account for about 50 per cent of total revenues. The firm is organized into three departments: Manufacturing, Residential Sales and Commercial Sales. Manufacturing is a cost centre and the two sales departments are profit centres. The full cost of each roll of carpeting produced (including fully-absorbed overhead) is transferred to the sales department ordering the carpet. The evaluation of the sales departments includes the fully-absorbed cost of each roll as the transfer price.

The current manufacturing plant is operating at capacity. A new plant is being built that will more than double capacity. Within two years, management believes that its businesses will grow such that most of the excess capacity will be eliminated. When the new plant comes online, the plan is for one plant to produce exclusively commercial carpeting and the other to produce exclusively residential carpeting. This change will simplify scheduling, ordering, and inventory control in each plant. It also will create some economies of scale by producing longer mill runs. Nevertheless, it will take a couple of years before these economies of scale can be realized.

Each mill produces carpeting in four-metre-wide rolls of up to 100 metres in length. The output of each mill is measured in terms of metres of four-metre rolls produced. Overhead is assigned to carpet rolls using carpet metres produced in the mill. The cost structure of each plant is as follows:

	Old plant	New plant
Normal machine hours per year	6,000	5,000
Normal carpet metres per hour	1,000	1,400
Normal capacity	6 million metres	7 million metres
Annual manufacturing overhead costs		
excluding accounting depreciation	€15,000,000	€21,000,000
Accounting depreciation per year	€6,000,000	€21,000,000

Karsten's new mill will run at higher speed and thereby, produce more metres of carpet per hour. Moreover, the new mill will use 15 per cent less direct materials and direct labour because the new machines, being more automated, produce less scrap and require less direct labour per metre. A job sheet run at the old mill is as follows:

Carpet No. A6106: (100-metre roll)

Direct materials (€)	800
Direct labour (€)	600
Direct costs (€)	1,400

Although the new mill has lower direct costs of carpet production than the old mill does, the new facility's higher overhead costs per metre have the sales department managers worried. They already are lobbying senior management to have the old mill assigned to produce their products. The Commercial Sales department manager argues: 'More of my customers are located closer to the old plant than are Residential Sales' customers. Therefore, to economize on transportation costs, my products should be produced in the old plant.' The Residential Sales department manager counters with the argument, 'Transportation costs are less than 1 per cent of total revenues. The new plant should produce commercial products because we expect new commercial products to use more synthetic materials and the latest technology at the new mill is better able to adapt to the new synthetics.' Senior management is worried about how to deal with the two sales department managers' reluctance to have their products produced at the new plant. One suggestion put forth is for each plant to produce about half of Commercial Sales products and about half of Residential Sales products. However, this proposal would eliminate most of the economies of scale that would result from specializing production in each plant to one market segment.

a Calculate the overhead rates for the new plant and the old plant, where overhead is assigned to carpet based on normal metres per year.
b Calculate the expected total cost of Carpet No. A6106, if run at the old mill and if run at the new mill.
c Put forth two new potential solutions that overcome the desire of the Residential and Commercial Sales department managers to have their products produced in the old plant. Discuss the pros and cons of your two solutions.

AIP 11.8 Overhead costs and dropping a product with joint costs

Carlos Sanguini S.p.a. makes Italian premium wines and table wines. Grapes are crushed and the free-flowing juice and the first-pressing juice are made into the premium wines (bottles with corks). The second- and third-pressing juices are made into table wines (bottles with screw tops).

Table 11.2 (overleaf) summarizes operations for the year.
Table 11.3 provides a breakdown of the manufacturing overhead expenses into General Winery costs and Production Facilities costs.

Based on Tables 11.2 and 11.3, the Accounting Department prepared the report shown in Table 11.4.

Senior management was concerned that the table wines had such a low margin and some managers urged that these lines be dropped. Competition kept the price down at the €7.00 per case level. This information caused some managers to question how the competition could afford to sell the wine at this price.

Before making a final decision, senior management asked for an analysis of the fixed and variable costs by product line and their break-even points. When they saw Table 11.5, the President remarked, 'Well, this is the final nail in the coffin. We'd have to almost triple our sales of table wines just to break even. But we don't have that kind of capacity. We'd have to buy new tanks, thereby driving up our fixed costs and break-even points. This looks like a vicious circle. By next month, I want a detailed set of plans on what it will cost us to shut down our table wines.'

Table 11.6 summarizes the shutdown effects.
Based on the data, what should management do?

Table 11.2 Summary of operations for the year

| | Tonnes of grapes | 10,000 | |
| | Average cost per tonne | €190 | |

	Premium wines	Table wines
Number of cases produced and sold	400,000	70,000
Selling price per case	€11.00	€7.00
Revenues	€4,400,000	€490,000
Grape costs[a]	1,650,000	250,000
Packaging costs	1,000,000	140,000
Labour	200,000	35,000
Selling and distribution[b]	400,000	35,000
Manufacturing overhead	400,000	87,500
Operating profit (loss)	€750,000	(€57,500)

[a] Grape costs represent the cost of the juice placed into the two product categories and are calculated as:

	Litres of juice used in each product	×	Total % of juice	=	Grape costs (€)	Grape cost per product (€)
Premium wines	52,800,000		86.84		1,900,000	1,650,000
Table wines	8,000,000		13.16		1,900,000	250,000
TOTAL	60,800,000		100			1,900,000

Note: A greater quantity of juice is required per case of premium wine than per case of table wine because there is more shrinkage in the premium wines than in table wines.

[b] Each product has its own Selling and Distribution (S&D) organization. Two thirds of Selling and Distribution expenditures vary with cases produced. The remainder of the expenditures does not vary with output.

Table 11.3 Manufacturing overhead by products

	Premium wines (€)	Table wines (€)	Total (€)
General winery costs[a]	212,800	37,200	250,000
Production facilities costs[b]			
(depreciation and maintenance)	187,200	50,300	237,500
Manufacturing overhead	400,000	87,500	487,500

[a] General winery costs do not vary with the number of cases or number of product lines. These costs are allocated based on cases produced.
[b] One-fourth of total production facilities costs varies with cases produced. The remainder is fixed costs previously incurred to provide the production capacity.

Table 11.4 Product-line cost structure

	Cost structure per case			
	Premium wines (€)		Table wines (€)	
Net sales		11.00		7.00
Variable costs				
Grapes	4.13		3.57	
Packaging	2.50		2.00	
Labour	0.50		0.50	
Selling and distribution	1.00	8.13	0.50	6.57
Margin		2.87		0.43
Less manufacturing overhead		1.00		1.25
Operating profit (loss)		1.87		(0.82)

Table 11.5 Fixed and variable costs per product and product break-even points

	Premium wines (€)		Table wines (€)	
Sales		11.00		7.00
Less variable costs				
Grapes	4.13		3.57	
Packaging	2.50		2.00	
Labour	0.50		0.50	
Selling and distribution	0.67		0.33	
Manufacturing overhead	0.13	7.93	0.13	6.53
Contribution margin		3.07		0.47
Less unitized fixed costs per unit				
Selling and distribution	0.33		0.17	
Manufacturing overhead	0.87	1.20	1.12	1.29
Profit (loss)		1.87		(0.82)
Break-even:				
Fixed costs	(400,000 × €1.20)	€480,000	(70,000 × €1.29)	€90,300
Divided by contribution margin		€3.08		€0.47
Number of cases to break even		156,000		192,000

Table 11.6 Effects of discontinuing table wines

1 No effect on the sale of premium wines is expected.
2 The juice being used in the table wines can be sold to bulk purchasers to use in fruit juices for €150,000 per year.
3 The table wine production facilities (tanks, refrigeration units, etc.) have no use in premium wine production. These facilities can be sold for €350,000, net of disposal costs.

CHAPTER TWELVE

Standard costs and variance analysis

(Control)

Learning objectives

1. Provide reasons for using standard costs.

2. Describe planning and control issues in setting standards.

3. Calculate direct labour and direct material variances.

4. Identify potential causes of different favourable and adverse variances.

5. Recognize incentive effects of standard costs.

6. Measure expected, standard and actual usage of an allocation base to apply overhead and determine overhead variances.

7. Identify factors that influence the decision to investigate variances.

8. Summarize the costs and benefits of using standard costs.

Erin Castor, Custom Design Homes

Erin Castor started her career as an architectural designer with a major architectural firm. She soon tired of the long hours and the lack of creativity and decided to start her own custom home business. She did most of the design work, adhering to the latest standards for sustainable construction. Erin sub-contracted the finishing and interior work on the new houses but maintained her own crew to do the wood framing. Erin was successful while the local economy was doing well but new housing starts are very sensitive to interest rates and the economy. At times she had to lay off her crew due to lack of work, especially in bad weather or when mortgage rates began to move upwards. Erin believed that there must be something to do with the crew during down time in the local economy, so she approached a local developer that produced affordable, eco-friendly, modular homes. Erin also returned to university to take a short course to learn more about modular housing and how it might be a way to match her concern for sustainability at a price that new homeowners could afford.

Home construction traditionally has been done on site, one house at a time. But recently demand has increased for modular housing solutions which offer lower-cost, quality units that can be built in factory-controlled conditions. Components, such as walls and roofs, are shipped and assembled at their final location saving time and cost. Erin obtained a contract to partner with the local developer to build wall panels for delivery to the developer's main factory. These panels would be placed onto its production line before being shipped to the building lot where the house would be erected. Erin's crew would have steady work and she would have a new way to provide innovative solutions in the housing market.

Erin received an initial order for 1,000 wall sections. The wall sections were 4 metres (height) by 3 metres (width) with plasterboard on one side. Erin leased suitable warehouse space and began construction. The first order was a real learning experience for her and her crew. The wall panels were relatively easy to make but moving and shipping them led to many problems given their size and weight. Also, the local developer would accept only wall panels made of softwoods, such as clear fir (no knots), even though the vertical studs and horizontal rails would be hidden eventually behind the panel sheathing, plasterboard and exterior cladding. Erin lost money on this first order but the developer was interested in future ones if Erin could guarantee that the delivered panels would meet its quality and delivery standards.

Erin believed that she could do better the next time with a little more control of the manufacturing process. In particular, she was certain that she could save costs by reducing excess scrap and slack time for her crew. She had heard that standard costing systems might help her achieve those goals and make the new orders more profitable.

Erin re-organized the business. She placed Karim Sharma in charge of buying lumber, plasterboard and other supplies. Barbara Kaplan was delegated responsibility for the timber framing and David Walker was assigned to manage the panel plasterboard lining. Erin remained in charge of administration and marketing.

STANDARD COSTS

Historical costs are useful for satisfying financial reporting requirements, such as deriving unit product costs for valuing inventories (balance sheet) and cost of goods sold (profit and loss statement). Historical costs also can be a useful starting point for estimating opportunity costs. Yet historical costs do not provide any built-in controls or benchmarks as to what costs should be. They only state what the costs actually were. An over- or under-absorbed overhead number conveys some information about whether or not the plant has met expectations with respect to overhead. However, no benchmarks exist as to whether direct labour or direct materials are too high or too low, except by comparing the actual results to the same numbers from prior periods.

Standard costs provide these benchmarks. They represent the expected future cost of a product, service, process or sub-component. Once standards are set, managers can gauge performance by comparing actual operating results against the standards. The difference between an actual and standard cost is called a **variance**. Variances provide useful information for senior management in determining whether the production system is operating efficiently. Variances are an important part of the control process. Like budget variances discussed in Chapter 8, standard cost variances are attention-getters, alerting senior managers that something is not going according to plan. Variances also provide information for performance evaluation. In addition to their role in control, standard costs are useful in making planning decisions such as product pricing, make-versus-buy, and plant resource allocation. While this chapter primarily examines standard costs in production settings, standard costing is used in service organizations and other non-manufacturing activities, such as public accounting, legal services, marketing and sales. For example, audit firms typically have standard hours and rates to conduct audit services for clients and to establish fees. Standard costing techniques assist organizational members in creating customer and organizational value by meeting cost and quality objectives.

This chapter describes the use of standard costs for planning and control. The conflict between planning and control, which you have seen in previous chapters, also exists in standard cost systems. The focus of this chapter is on the costs and benefits of standard cost systems.

■ Reasons for standard costing

Historical costs often can prove misleading for planning purposes. They can be out of date if operating conditions, material prices or labour rates have changed or are expected to change. Operating conditions in the past might not provide a valid basis for forecasting the future, especially when new products are introduced or a new manufacturing process is implemented.

Organizations frequently use standard costs instead of historical costs in a wide variety of planning decision contexts: product pricing, contract bidding, outsourcing decisions and assessing alternative production technologies. Standard costs are part of the budgeting system, which organizations utilize to co-ordinate their operating plans for the coming year. The estimated product cost at the beginning of the year is a standard cost. Standard costs convey information about product costs among the different parts of the organization. For example, marketing managers generally rely on standard costs to make pricing and selling decisions.

Standard costs also provide information for control. As part of the budgeting process, standard costs might be the basis for contracts among the organization's managers.

Manufacturing managers agree to supply a certain number of units of the product at a standard cost. Service department managers agree to supply their services at a standard cost. Managerial performance is evaluated based on the success of managers in achieving these standard costs. Achieving standard costs can lead to bonuses and rewards and, in some cases, promotions.

Large variances between actual and standard costs indicate that a particular activity differs significantly from what was expected when the standard was set. Variances are treated as signals that activities might be out of control and corrective action might be necessary. Not all variances necessarily indicate a problem, however; they might also indicate that the environment has changed and the standards are no longer appropriate. The variance itself does not tell the manager exactly what is wrong. Further investigation is usually necessary to determine the cause. **Management by exception** is a management strategy that focuses management effort on significant variances. When actual costs are close to the standard costs, managers assume that the activity is operating as planned and no further investigation is necessary.

Surveys indicate that most large manufacturing firms use standard costs. Standard cost systems are common in large organizations, but some managers question their costs and benefits especially in advanced manufacturing settings and dynamic markets. Some firms are scaling back on their reliance on standard costs, changing how they estimate them, or even abandoning their standard cost systems. Despite criticisms, studies indicate that standard costing remains widely used for planning decisions and control. Many organizations have adapted their standard cost systems to respond to globalization and competitive challenges, supplementing their standard cost reports with non-financial performance indicators instead of abandoning them.[1] The problems generally reflect the trade-off between using standard costs for planning decisions and control. We outline this trade-off in the next section.

Setting and revising standards

No commonly accepted method for deriving standard costs exists. Some experts argue that standard costs should be attainable, meaning the cost that is achievable if normal effort and environmental effects prevail. Others argue that the standards should be those that will occur with extra effort. How difficult the standards should be to attain and how much weight to place on their achievement for performance evaluation purposes are important issues in the design of the firm's organizational structure. These issues involve trading off the costs and benefits of tight versus loose standards. One survey of UK firms reported that 44 per cent of the firms indicated that they set standards to be achievable, yet difficult to attain, 46 per cent said that standards were set based on average past performance, and 5 per cent said that they set the standard as the maximum theoretical efficiency level (5 per cent indicated other approaches).[2]

If the standard cost is to reflect the cost of using a resource, standard setting and revision require communication with individuals who have specific knowledge. The standard cost should contain all the specific knowledge pertaining to the resource.

[1] M. Sulaiman, N. Nazli Nik Ahmad and N. Mohd Alwi (2005) 'Is standard costing obsolete? Empirical evidence from Malaysia', *Managerial Auditing Journal*, Vol. 20, No. 2, pp. 109–124; C. Guilding, D. Lamminmaki and C. Drury (1998) 'Budgeting and standard costing practices in New Zealand and the United Kingdom', *The International Journal of Accounting*, Vol. 33, No. 5, pp. 569–588.

[2] C. Guilding, D. Lamminmaki and C. Drury, *op cit*. An earlier but frequently referenced article on this topic is W. Cress and J. Pettijohn (1985) 'A Survey of Budget-Related Planning and Control Policies and Procedures', *Journal of Accounting Education*, Vol. 3, Issue 2 (Autumn), pp. 61–78.

Standards that are the most accurate estimates of costs are the most useful in conveying information within the firm about alternative resource utilization.

The accuracy of the standard as a cost measure, however, is often compromised for control reasons. Usually managers with the specific knowledge for updating the standard will be evaluated, at least in part, based on the difference between their actual performance and the standard. Managers are reluctant to reveal information that might be used later to penalize them. This issue was described in Chapter 8 in terms of motivating managers to reveal private knowledge in setting next year's budget, when their performance would be judged relative to the budget.

Planning decisions require assembling the specialized knowledge that often resides only with the person or unit of the firm that later will be judged by the standard. For example, the purchasing department has the specialized knowledge to set the purchase price standard. If the purchasing department also has the responsibility to set the standard, then it becomes less useful in evaluating the performance of the purchasing department manager. One solution is to separate the setting of the standard from approving, ratifying and monitoring it.

Usually, the accounting or industrial engineering department has the responsibility to set or change standards. Individuals responsible for the standard cost variance have some ability to influence the standards. Standards then are reviewed and revised each year as part of the annual budgeting cycle. In the study referred to earlier, design/engineering studies were the most popular approaches to setting standards. However, the study also noted the use of a variety of methods including work study techniques, observations based on trial runs, and the average of historical usage.[3] Many groups participate in setting standards reflecting the cross-functional approach of organizations: industrial engineering, purchasing, human resources, accounting, top management and line managers with specific cost responsibility.[4] The involvement of different functional areas in the standard-setting process is also one way to capture and communicate specialized knowledge across the organization.

A common approach to derive standard costs is a bottom-up technique. The manager who will be held responsible for meeting the standard usually submits an initial estimate of it. Industrial engineers, controllers, and higher-level managers then review and ratify the standard. Sometimes industrial engineers submit the initial estimate of the standard. In all cases, setting and revising standards involve assembling specific knowledge from various individuals in the firm. The standard cost of each type of labour, material and overhead is estimated and the standard cost of the complete product is built up from the sum of these individual costs.

Target costing is a top-down approach. It starts with the long-run price, estimated by marketing, required to achieve a desired market share. The required return on investment (profits) is subtracted from this price to derive a total target product cost. This total target cost then is divided into sub-component costs, including selling and distribution costs. These sub-component costs become the targets or standards to be achieved if the firm is to meet its goals for market penetration, cost reduction and return on capital. Target costs then become part of the performance evaluation system.[5] Chapter 4 discussed target costing in more detail.

[3] C. Guilding, D. Lamminmaki and C. Drury, p. 581.
[4] W. Cress and J. Pettijohn, p. 74.
[5] See S. Ansari, S. Swenson and J. Bell (2006) 'A Template For Implementing Target Costing', *Cost Management* (September/October), pp. 20–27; T. W. Lin, K. A. Merchant, Y. Yang and Z. Yu (2005) 'Target Costing and Incentive Compensation', *Cost Management* (March/April), pp. 29–42; K.-H. Yook, I.-W. Kim and T. Yoshikawa (2005) 'Target Costing in the Construction Industry: Evidence from Japan', *Construction Accounting & Taxation,* Vol. 15, No. 3, (May/June), pp. 5–18.

Jeremy Sutton-Hibbert/Alamy

Target costing is prevalent in the auto industry. Total target cost is divided into sub-component costs that become part of the performance evaluation system.

Once standards are set, they are used to judge performance by calculating the variance between the actual cost and the standard cost. In general, firms produce three sets of standard cost variances: direct labour variances, direct materials variances and overhead variances. Since their calculations and incentive effects are quite similar, we discuss direct labour and direct materials variances together in the next two sections. Overhead variances are more complicated and are described generally in the section *Standard overhead costs and variances*. We describe their specific calculation in the Appendix to this chapter.

The variances described in this chapter are generic to a wide cross-section of applications. Not every department, plant and company will use all of them. Some organizations develop others variances; for example, many firms also calculate sales and marketing variances. Variances and their analysis are tailored to the organization's specific requirements. The following discussion illustrates the types of variances possible and their advantages and disadvantages.

Concept **review**

1 Why do organizations use standard costing?

2 How are standards set?

Erin Castor, Custom Design Homes (continued)

Erin Castor believes that standard costing could be quite beneficial to her business. The business of making wall panels requires a series of repetitive actions by workers and the material requirements are fairly easy to measure. She hopes the standard costs will do three things for her:

1 determine product costs for the different sizes of wall panels so she can do a better job of pricing;

2 encourage managers and workers to use the materials and their time more efficiently; and

3 provide a final product that meets stringent quality and environmental standards.

To implement the standard costing system, Erin calls in her managers to discuss the current problems. To encourage them to pay attention to the standards, she tells them that she will give them bonuses if their department performs better than the standards. Karim will be responsible for the material price variances and Barbara and David will be responsible for the direct labour variances and the material quantity

→

variances. Then she asks them for input on establishing the standards. Karim believes that lumber prices are going up in the future, so the standard price of the lumber should be higher than the current market price. Barbara and David think the standards should recognize some scrap, crew training and slack labour time.

Erin realizes that her managers are not going to be completely forthcoming in establishing standards. Therefore, she decides to set the standards based on her knowledge of prices and the process of making wall panels. The following standards for direct labour and direct materials are used for making one wall panel:

Direct labour cost	£20 per hour
Direct labour time per unit	3 hours
Material costs	
Lumber	£40 per timber length
Plasterboard	£20 per sheet
Material per unit	
Lumber	6 lengths
Plasterboard	3 sheets

The estimated direct costs per unit are as follows:

	£
Direct labour (£20 per hour × 3 hours)	60.00
Direct materials	
Lumber (£20 per length × 6 lengths)	120.00
Plasterboard (£20 per sheet × 3 sheets)	60.00
Total direct costs per unit	360.00

DIRECT LABOUR AND DIRECT MATERIALS VARIANCES

Within an organization, variances are used primarily to identify problems in following a prescribed plan. Variances are calculated to help managers determine the cause and responsibility for the problem. By partitioning variances into component variances, cause and responsibility become easier to identify. This section describes how standard cost variances for direct labour and materials are decomposed and calculated.

Direct labour and materials costs are composed of a price per unit and a quantity. In other words, the cost of direct labour is the labour rate per hour (price per unit) times the number of hours worked (quantity). The cost of direct materials used is the purchase price per unit of the materials times the quantity of units used. Any variance between the actual and standard costs is due to the actual price per unit and/or actual quantity differing from the standard price or quantity. Recognizing the dual effect of price and quantity on costs allows the direct labour and materials variances to be decomposed into two parts: (1) variance due to the actual price per unit differing from the standard price per unit and (2) variance due to the actual quantity differing from the standard quantity.

■ Direct labour variances

The **direct labour variance** is the difference between the actual direct labour costs and the standard direct labour costs for a period of time. The direct labour variance can be decomposed into a **labour rate variance** and a **labour efficiency variance**.

The following equations define the labour rate and labour efficiency variances such that the sum of the two variances is equal to the direct labour variance:

Direct labour variance = Actual cost of labour − Standard cost of labour
= (Actual labour rate × Actual hours)
− (Standard labour rate × Standard hours)

Labour rate variance = (Actual labour rate − Standard labour rate) × Actual hours

Labour efficiency variance = (Actual hours − Standard hours) × Standard labour rate

Direct labour variance = Labour rate variance + Labour efficiency variance

The labour rate variance focuses on the difference between the actual labour rate and the standard labour rate. The labour efficiency variance highlights the difference between the actual direct labour hours and the standard direct labour hours.

To demonstrate the calculation of direct variances, an example of the printing costs of the Smith Art Book is used. The standard costs to make a batch of 1,000 books are shown in Table 12.1.

The standard costs to make the 1,000 copies of the Smith Art Book are used as benchmarks for comparison with actual costs. Table 12.2 shows the actual costs.

Table 12.1 Standard cost sheet

Smith Art Book: 1,000 copies

Direct materials				Direct labour			
Type	Quantity	Price (£)	Amount (£)	Type	Hour	Wage (£)	Amount (£)
Paper	800 kg	2	1,600	Typesetters	80	15	1,200
Covers	2,000	3	6,000	Printers	55	40	2,200
Binding	500 kg	4	2,000	Binders	70	20	1,400
Totals			9,600				4,800

Total direct materials	£9,600
Total direct labour	4,800
Total overhead*	5,500
Total cost	£19,900
Number of copies	÷1,000
Cost per book	£19.90

*Overhead is charged at the rate of £100 per printer hour.

Table 12.2 Actual cost sheet

Smith Art Book: 1,000 copies

Direct materials				Direct labour			
Type	Quantity	Price (£)	Amount (£)	Type	Hour	Wage (£)	Amount (£)
Paper	810 kg	2.10	1,701	Typesetters	85	15.40	1,309
Covers	2,010	2.90	5,829	Printers	53	41.00	2,173
Binding	490 kg	4.20	2,058	Binders	72	19.50	1,404
Totals			9,588				4,886

Total direct materials	£9,588
Total direct labour	4,886
Total overhead*	5,300
Total cost	£19,774
Number of copies	÷1,000
Cost per book	£19.77

*Overhead is charged at the rate of £100 per printer hour.

The actual costs are £19,774, which is £126 less than the standard cost of £19,900. The £126 is called a **favourable variance**. A favourable variance occurs when the actual costs are less than the standard costs. An **adverse variance** occurs if actual costs are greater than standard costs.

The existence of a £126 favourable variance for the printing of the 1,000 copies of the Smith Art Book does not tell the manager much about the cause of the variance. To better understand the total cost variance, the cost variance can be broken into parts representing the prices and quantities of each of the inputs of the manufacturing process. For example, the direct labour variance for typesetters can be decomposed into a labour rate variance and a labour efficiency variance:

$$\text{Labour rate variance} = (\text{Actual labour rate} - \text{Standard labour rate}) \times \text{Actual hours}$$

Typesetters: (£15.40 − £15.00) × 85 =	£34 Adverse
Printers: (£41.00 − £40.00) × 53 =	£53 Adverse
Binders: (£19.50 − £20.00) × 72 =	£36 Favourable
Total	£51 Adverse

$$\text{Labour efficiency variance} = (\text{Actual hours} - \text{Standard hours}) \times \text{Standard labour rate}$$

Typesetters: (85 − 80) × £15.00 =	£75 Adverse
Printers: (53 − 55) × £40.00 =	£80 Favourable
Binders: (72 − 70) × £20.00 =	£40 Adverse
Total	£35 Adverse

Notice that the sum of the labour variance and the efficiency variance (£51 + £35 = £86) is the difference between the total standard labour costs (£4,800) and the actual labour costs (£4,886). The relation among the direct labour variances is described in Table 12.3.

The variance analysis indicates that the adverse labour variances are primarily due to typesetter labour costs. The sum of the labour rate variance and the labour efficiency variance for printers is favourable and for binders only slightly adverse. The typesetter labour costs exceeded standard because (a) £0.40 more per hour was paid than expected and (b) 5 hours more typesetter hours were used than expected. If management believes that the standards are correct, then the typesetter labour variances indicate that the person responsible for assigning typesetters to the Smith Art Book assigned typesetters with a higher actual labour rate per hour than expected. Also, the typesetters' supervisor allowed more typesetting hours than expected. The costs of

Table 12.3 Relations among direct labour variances

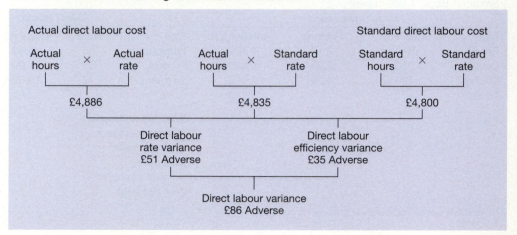

Figure 12.1 Direct labour variances

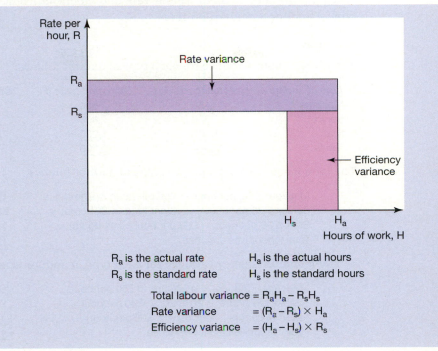

R_a is the actual rate H_a is the actual hours
R_s is the standard rate H_s is the standard hours

Total labour variance = $R_aH_a - R_sH_s$
Rate variance   = $(R_a - R_s) \times H_a$
Efficiency variance   = $(H_a - H_s) \times R_s$

these two 'errors' are £34 for paying too much per hour and £75 for using too many hours. Clearly, management's ability to draw these inferences depends on its belief that the standards are indeed accurate forecasts of what the typesetting labour rates should have been and how many hours of typesetting should have been used.

The foregoing analysis is illustrated graphically in Figure 12.1. In Figure 12.1, the rectangle $R_s \times H_s$ represents what the labour should have cost and the rectangle $R_a \times H_a$ represents what the labour actually cost. The total typesetting labour variance is the difference between what the typesetting actually cost and what it should have cost, $R_aH_a - R_sH_s$. This difference is the shaded areas in Figure 12.1. The shaded areas are decomposed into a labour variance (the top shaded rectangle) and an efficiency variance (the shaded rectangle on the right).

Numerical **example 12.1**

A public accounting firm estimates that an audit will require the following work:

Type of auditor	Expected hours	Cost per hour (£)	Standard costs (£)
Manager	10	50	500
Senior	20	40	800
Staff	40	30	1,200
Totals	70		2,500

The following were the actual hours and costs:

Type of auditor	Actual hours	Actual cost per hour (£)	Actual costs (£)
Manager	9	52	468
Senior	22	38	836
Staff	44	30	1,320
Totals	75		2,624

→

Calculate the direct labour, labour rate and labour efficiency variances for each type of auditor and interpret them.

Solution

The direct labour variance for each type of auditor follows:

Type of auditor	Actual costs (£)	Standard costs (£)	Direct labour variance (£)
Manager	468	500	(32)
Senior	836	800	36
Staff	1,320	1,200	120
Totals	2,624	2,500	124 Adverse

The labour rate variance for each type of auditor follows:

Manager (£52 per hour − £50 per hour × 9 hours) =	£18
Senior (£38 per hour − £40 per hour × 22 hours) =	£(44)
Staff (£30 per hour − £30 per hour × 44 hours) =	0
Total labour rate variance	(£26) Favourable

The labour efficiency variance for each type of auditor is as follows:

Manager (9 hours − 10 hours × £50 per hour)	(£50)
Senior (22 hours − 20 hours × £40 per hour)	£80
Staff (44 hours − 40 hours × £30 per hour)	£120
Total labour efficiency variance	£150 Adverse

Note that the direct labour variance equals the sum of the labour rate and labour efficiency variances. The favourable labour rate variance means that, on average, the auditors were paid less than expected, although managers were paid more than expected. The adverse labour efficiency variance means that, on average, the auditors took longer to complete the audit than expected. The manager, however, spent less time on the audit than expected.

Large variances, either favourable or adverse, can mean that the activity is out of control. An accounting variance can indicate that either the operating unit deviated from an appropriate standard, or faulty assumptions were used to develop the standard. In the first case, direct labour supervisors did not operate at the levels assumed in the standards. Direct labour was used more or less efficiently than expected. In the second case, the standards were set at a level that could not be attained, even if the supervisor used the direct labour as efficiently as possible. The reporting of a large adverse variance does not mean necessarily that the person responsible is performing below expectations.

Large favourable variances are not necessarily good news, as they could signal that quality is being reduced. For example, one way to generate favourable labour efficiency variances is to use too few labour hours and produce lower-quality products. Likewise, favourable labour rate variances might mean that lower-skilled, lower-paid workers were employed, a decision that could compromise product quality. Managers and supervisors do not investigate all variances, since the cost to investigate and gather further information may be greater than any additional benefits from doing so. Variance investigation is examined in more detail later in the chapter.

The human resources department is held responsible for the labour rate variance, if that department has the responsibility for hiring workers with specific job skills at a given standard labour rate. In other cases, the shop-floor supervisor is held responsible for labour rate variances if the supervisor can schedule different workers with varying skills and labour rates to produce the product. A supervisor who can change the mix of workers and, thus, the cost of the job by substituting more or less skilled workers at different labour rates is usually assigned the total direct labour variance. In this case, there is no reason to compute separately a labour variance and an efficiency variance, except to provide information about what caused the labour variance.

The extent to which labour and efficiency variances are used to measure performance depends on the reliability of the underlying standards, the inherent variability of the labour rates and hours due to random fluctuations, and how much of the variance is potentially controllable by the manager. Some organizations place large weight on variances in performance evaluation, others place little or no weight on them.

Numerical **example** 12.2

The public accounting firm in *Numerical example 12.1* awards bonus compensation to managers based on the audit manager's ability to meet budgeted costs. The manager's bonus is adjusted for the direct labour variance by adding or deducting 50 per cent of the direct labour variances, excluding those related to managerial labour, to the performance bonus.

What is the manager's bonus for the audit engagement?

Solution

The direct labour variance for senior and staff auditors is as follows:

Type of auditor	Actual costs (£)	Standard costs (£)	Direct labour variance (£)
Senior	836	800	6
Staff	1,320	1,200	120
Totals	2,624	2,500	156 Adverse

The labour rate variance for senior and staff auditors follows:

Senior (£38 per hour − £40 per hour × 22 hours) =	(£44)
Staff (£30 per hour − £30 per hour × 44 hours) =	0
Total labour rate variance	(£44) Favourable

The labour efficiency variance for senior and staff auditors follows:

Senior (22 hours − 20 hours) × £40 per hour	£80
Total labour efficiency variance	£200 Adverse

The direct labour variance is £156 Adverse. Therefore, 50 per cent of £156, or £78, is deducted from the audit manager's bonus. This bonus scheme motivates the manager to control costs. The manager used more senior and staff hours than anticipated. However, these additional hours were not offset by the lower salary paid to senior auditors. The system is effective if the manager has the ability to change the mix of the audit team members to meet the budget. The audit manager still might consider that the bonus scheme is unfair, if the firm's human resources department establishes salary scales.

■ Direct materials variances

Direct materials variances are similar to those computed for direct labour. As with direct labour, the total direct materials variance can be decomposed into a **material price variance** and a **material quantity variance**. The calculations are identical to those for direct labour.

Figure 12.2 Direct materials variances (materials uses as purchased)

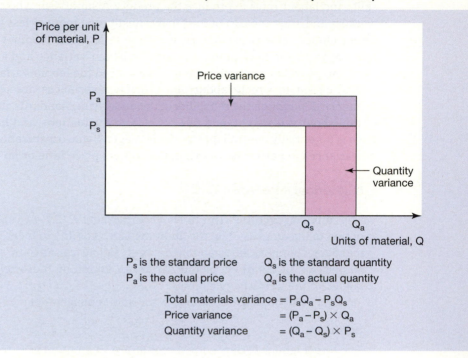

P_s is the standard price $\quad$ Q_s is the standard quantity
P_a is the actual price $\quad$ Q_a is the actual quantity

Total materials variance $= P_a Q_a - P_s Q_s$
Price variance $= (P_a - P_s) \times Q_a$
Quantity variance $= (Q_a - Q_s) \times P_s$

Direct material variance = **Actual cost of material** − **Standard cost of material**
= **(Actual price × Actual quantity)**
− **(Standard price × Standard quantity)**
Price variance = **(Actual price − Standard price) × Actual quantity**
Quantity variance = **(Actual quantity − Standard quantity) × Standard price**
Direct material variance = **Price variance + Quantity variance**

Figure 12.2 illustrates how the total materials variance is decomposed into a material price variance and a material quantity variance, under the assumption that *all materials purchased are used immediately in production.* As in Figure 12.1, this difference is the shaded areas in Figure 12.2.

The material price variance typically is reported to the purchasing manager and is one measure of the purchasing manager's performance. To be timely, the price variance should be calculated at the time of purchase. The time of purchase may be different from when the material is used. Other performance measures for the purchasing department or manager include the percentage of on-time delivery of materials, raw materials inventory turnover and material quality.

The quantity variance is reported to the manager responsible for the efficient use of materials (usually the shop supervisor) and is one performance measure of this manager. Other performance measures for the shop supervisor include quality of output, defect rates and cycle time.

The calculation of material price variances is demonstrated using the standard cost data for the Smith Art Book in Table 12.1 and the actual cost data in Table 12.2. The total direct material variance is £9,588 − £9,600, or £12 favourable. This variance can be decomposed into the material price variance and the material quantity variance.

The following are the material price variances for each of the materials for the Smith Art Book:

Material price variance = (Actual price − Standard price) × Actual quantity

Paper (£2.10 per kg − £2.00 per kg) × 810kg	£81 Adverse
Covers (£2.90 − £3.00) × 2,010	£(201) Favourable
Binding (£4.20 − £4.00) × 490kg	£98 Adverse
Total material price variance	(£22) Favourable

The material quantity variance for each of the materials is as follows:

Material quantity variance = (Actual quantity − Standard quantity) × Standard price

Paper (810kg − 800kg) × £2 per kg	£20 Adverse
Covers (2,010 − 2,000) × £3	£30 Adverse
Binding (490kg − 500kg) × £4 per kg	£(40) Favourable
Total quantity variance	£10 Adverse

Table 12.4 demonstrates the relation among the direct material variances.

In a standard cost system, materials are recorded in the raw material inventory account at standard cost. That is, inventory is stated at standard price, not actual price. The material price variance is recorded in a separate ledger account. This variance usually is written off to cost of goods sold at the end of the year, instead of flowing through inventory and product costs. For example, suppose 100 kilograms of copper are purchased for £12 per kilogram when the standard price is £10 per kilogram. The purchase is recorded in the raw material inventory account at £1,000 and the £200 difference is recorded separately in a materials price variance account (at the time of purchase). Future products using this copper are charged £10, not £12, per kilogram. By recording the £200 in a separate account and writing it off directly to cost of goods sold, the unit cost of the products using the copper is not distorted by the price variation of £2 per kilogram.

The advantage of recording raw materials at standard cost is that downstream users in the plant only see standard costs. Likewise, labour is charged to products and jobs at standard cost. If standard costs are unbiased forecasts of future costs, using standard costs gives downstream managers more accurate information regarding the opportunity cost of the raw material. Of course, this discussion assumes that standard raw material prices are more accurate predictors of opportunity costs than are actual raw

Table 12.4 Relation among direct material variances

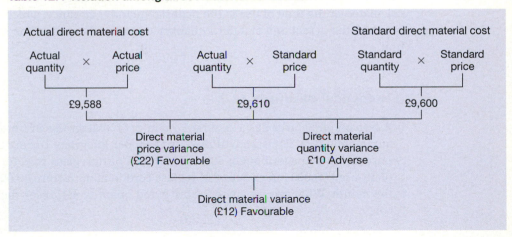

Figure 12.3 Direct materials variances (materials purchased but not used yet)

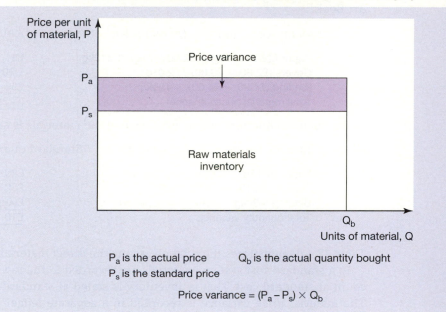

P_a is the actual price Q_b is the actual quantity bought
P_s is the standard price

Price variance $= (P_a - P_s) \times Q_b$

material prices. Using standard costs also reduces the risk borne by downstream 'purchasers' of the product, such as the marketing department. At the beginning of the year, downstream users know what they will be charged for raw materials throughout the year. Price changes or inefficient use of materials do not affect the downstream users. The use of standard costs thus removes uncontrollable factors from the performance measures of downstream users.

Figure 12.3 depicts the more usual case in which raw material is bought, placed in raw materials inventory, and then used at a later date. In Figure 12.3, the material price variance is isolated as soon as the raw material is purchased. The raw materials inventory is stated thereby at the standard cost per unit. The price variance is reported as soon as the material is bought and not when the material is used at some later date. Once the material price variance is isolated at purchase, all the remaining withdrawals from the raw material inventory account are stated at the same standard cost per unit.

Given that the direct material is recorded at standard cost at the time it is used, there is no further material price variance. The only direct material variance that is calculated at the time of use is the material quantity variance, which is the difference between the actual and standard quantity of materials used at the standard cost per unit

Numerical **example** 12.3

A tyre manufacturer has a standard quantity of 3 kilograms of fibreglass cord per automobile tyre. The standard price is €1.00 per kilogram. During the month, the purchasing manager bought 98,000 kilograms of fibreglass cord for €102,000. The plant used 95,000 kilograms of fibreglass cord to manufacture 30,000 tyres during the month. What are the material price and quantity variances for the fibreglass cord?

Solution

The material price variance is calculated at the time of purchase. The actual purchase price per kilogram is €102,000/98,000 or €1.04082 per kg. Therefore, the material price variance is (€1.04082 per kg − €1.00 per kg) × 98,000kg, or €4,000, adverse.

The material quantity variance is calculated when the material is used. In this case, 95,000 kilograms were used. But (3 kg per tyre × 30,000 tyres), or 90,000 kilograms should have been used according to the standard. The material quantity variance is (95,000kg − 90,000kg) × €1 per kg, or €5,000 adverse.

The material price and quantity variances often are interrelated. For example, if substandard materials are purchased at a price below the standard price, usually an adverse material quantity variance is generated because more material than standard is used. If a less expensive exterior house paint is purchased, probably more of it will be required to provide the same coverage as a higher-quality, higher-priced paint would provide. A variance in one area is likely to be related to other variances. A favourable material price variance might cause an adverse material quantity variance, or a favourable labour efficiency variance from one type of labour might be the result of another adverse labour efficiency variance, if another type of labour is substituted. A favourable materials price variance and a resulting adverse materials quantity variance can cause adverse labour efficiency variances, if extra material and labour are used due to the sub-standard materials. Therefore, as a performance measurement system of the manufacturing process, the variances must be analysed as an integrated whole.

Concept **review**

1 What are the two components of direct labour and material costs?
2 What is the relation between standard and actual costs when the variance is favourable?
3 What type of manager is likely to be responsible for labour rate and efficiency variances?
4 What type of manager is likely to be responsible for material price and quantity variances?
5 Under what conditions would the material quantity variance be adverse?

Erin Castor, Custom Design Homes (continued)

Erin Castor's latest order for wall panels is for 3,000 units. Given the standards that she has set for constructing the panels, Erin has estimated that the total direct costs of making the 3,000 wall sections would be 3,000 units × £360 per unit, or £1,080,000. Erin is pleased to find that the actual direct costs of completing the order are only £1,059,000. The total direct cost variance for the order is £1,080,000 − £1,059,800, or £20,200 favourable. She figures that the standard costing system is working, at least in terms of her costs. The following information used to calculate direct cost variances, however, makes her wonder what is happening.

Purchases:
    Lumber: 24,000 lengths at £19.00 per length
    Plasterboard: 15,000 sheets at £18.00 per sheet

→

Actual labour used: 10,000 hours at £17.50 per hour

Standard labour: (3,000 units × 3 hours per unit) = 9,000 hours

Actual direct material used:

    Lumber: 19,600 lengths

    Plasterboard: 9,100 sheets

Standard material:

    Lumber: (3,000 units × 6 lengths per unit) = 18,000 lengths

    Plasterboard: (3,000 units × 3 sheets per unit) = 9,000 sheets

The variances for direct costs for the order are:

Labour rate variance: (£17.50 − £20.00) × 10,000 hours	(£25,000) Favourable
Labour efficiency variance: (10,000 − 9,000) × £20.00 per hour	£20,000 Adverse
Material price variance for materials used for order:	
Lumber (£19.00 − £20.00) × 19,000 lengths	£(19,000) Favourable
Plasterboard (£18.00 − £20.00) × 9,100 sheets	£(18,200) Favourable
Material quantity variance:	
Lumber (19,000 − 18,000) × £20.00 per length	£20,000 Adverse
Plasterboard (9,100 − 9,000) × £20 per sheet	£2,000 Adverse
Total direct cost variance	(£20,200) Favourable

Karim Sharma, the purchasing manager, is especially pleased with himself. The material price variances for both the lumber and plasterboard are favourable. Karim estimates that the material price variance would be even higher, if the material price variance were calculated based on the amount purchased rather than the amount used. Both Barbara Kaplan and David Walker report favourable labour rate variances to offset adverse labour efficiency and material quantity variances. They both claim that the adverse quantity variances are due to low-quality materials.

The variance analysis worries Erin. The total cost of making the order is less than the total standard cost but certain aspects of the analysis make her feel that her problems are not over. The managers' concerns about the quality of materials are especially bothersome, given the developer's stringent quality standards. Also, Barbara and David apparently have hired lower-paid workers to complete the order. Are these workers capable of producing work to meet the customer's quality requirements? Also, why did Karim purchase far more materials than were needed for the order? Eventually they will use the materials but holding the inventory is costly. Standard costing is proving to be more complex than Erin expected.

INCENTIVE EFFECTS OF DIRECT LABOUR AND MATERIALS VARIANCES

Standard costs and variances, when used as part of the performance evaluation system, create incentives for managers to control costs. Standards are part of the performance evaluation system, as described in Chapter 6. However, if the standard cost system is not designed properly and is not integrated consistently with the other parts of the organizational structure including assignment of responsibilities, performance measures and compensation, dysfunctional behaviour can ensue.

When used as performance measures, standard cost variances create subtle incentive effects. This section describes five:

1 the incentive to build inventories and/or lower quality,
2 externalities,

3 unco-operative effort,

4 mutual monitoring incentives, and

5 satisficing behaviour.

■ Incentive to build inventories

The evaluation of purchasing managers based on direct materials price variances creates incentives for these managers to build inventories. Price discounts often are granted for large volume purchases. Therefore, one way to generate favourable price variances is to purchase raw materials in lot sizes larger than necessary for immediate production and to hold these inventories until they are needed. However, it is costly to hold inventory due to warehousing, material handling, obsolescence and financing costs.

The incentive to hold large inventories can be reduced by charging the purchasing department for the cost of holding inventories. For example, suppose the firm's opportunity cost of capital is 8 per cent per year and warehousing and handling costs are 12 per cent of the cost of the inventory per year. Then charging the purchasing department 20 per cent per year of the average monetary balance in the raw materials inventory account reduces the incentive to purchase in large lots. In other words, the inclusion of inventory holding costs in the purchasing department's performance report reduces incentives to buy large lots just to get price concessions.

Most firms do not charge purchasing managers for inventory holding costs since many holding costs are not part of the external reporting system. An alternative mechanism for controlling inventory-building behaviour is to adopt techniques such as just-in-time (JIT) manufacturing described in Chapter 14. That is, the purchasing department can order materials only as they are needed for production.

■ Externalities

Externalities occur within an organization when the behaviour of one individual affects other individuals within the organization. Purchasing managers can impose externalities on production by purchasing sub-standard materials. The lower quality materials frequently cause more labour hours and more skilled workers (paid higher wages) to process the sub-standard materials. The sub-standard materials impose downstream costs on the production managers due to the consumption of additional production resources for rework or machine down time.

To offset the purchasing manager's incentive to acquire low-quality raw materials, purchases are inspected when received, engineering specifications are set for each product, and purchasing is not allowed to buy materials that deviate from these standards. Alternatively, part of the purchasing manager's performance evaluation can be tied to the amount of rework generated in production and/or the raw material quantity variance. The purchasing manager then has incentives to reduce rework and quantity variances by purchasing higher-quality products. However, purchasing managers cannot control all reasons for rework and quantity variances, so they might not consider including the variances in the performance evaluation scheme to be appealing or fair.

Production managers also can impose externalities on purchasing by requesting that materials be purchased on short lead times and in small lot sizes to reduce the quantity of materials in storage. Also, engineering can increase the actual price of the purchases by making frequent design changes. These examples are just a few of the types of externalities that purchasing and production can impose on each other.

■ Unco-operative effort

Evaluating individuals within an organization based on different variances can discourage co-operative effort. In some firms, every employee is evaluated based on a labour efficiency variance. In other words, the output of each individual is measured and compared with a standard to determine how the employee is rewarded. The employees in these settings frequently are reluctant to support others if their evaluation only reflects what they produce individually.

An alternative is to measure variances for a team or department within the organization. Team performance measures encourage co-operative effort but can lead to shirking on the part of some individuals. For example, a team project for a class is given a single grade that is shared by all the students in the group. Some students take advantage of the group grading system by shirking their duties because they know that other responsible team members will complete the group task.

To encourage co-operative effort and avoid shirking, many organizations calculate variances and measure performance at multiple levels. For example, an individual worker would be evaluated based on an individual labour efficiency variance and a departmental labour efficiency variance. Bonuses would be paid for both individual and group accomplishments.

■ Mutual monitoring incentives

The usual method of monitoring behaviour within firms is for superiors to monitor subordinates. Another important form of monitoring occurs between managers who are not in a direct reporting relationship with each other. Monitoring can occur between managers at the same level in the same sub-unit or between managers in different sub-units. Mutual monitoring occurs when managers or workers at the same level monitor each other.

If the purchasing department manager is held responsible for materials variances (including the quantity variance), the purchasing manager has the incentive to monitor the production supervisor's usage of materials. Likewise, the production supervisor monitors the quality of the materials that the purchasing manager buys. A purchasing manager rewarded on the basis of both the price and quantity variance will try to devise ways in which the production manager can economize on the use of materials. Also, the production manager will try to devise ways in which the purchasing manager can purchase materials to reduce purchase costs. Therefore, in designing the performance evaluation and reward systems, organizations can create mutual monitoring incentives that encourage managers to acquire and utilize their specialized knowledge to improve the performance of other managers.

■ Satisficing behaviour

If standards are used as a benchmark for evaluating managers, the reward system often is tied to achieving the standard. If the manager works sufficiently hard to achieve the standard, the manager is paid a bonus. In this type of reward system, managers have incentives to achieve the standard but go no further. This drawback is called **satisficing behaviour**. A further disincentive exists to perform beyond the standard. Next year's standards usually are based on past performance and would be harder to achieve if raised due to exceptional performance. The organization, of course, would like managers to improve continually and not stop when the standard is met.

Digital Vision/Alamy

Call centre employees prefer short calls to meet cost and time standards. This behaviour may put customer satisfaction and service quality at risk.

Satisficing behaviour also can affect quality if employees are motivated to meet production quotas, but sacrifice quality to do so. For example, a metal refiner realized that its cost system created incentives for employees to meet or exceed its yield target – the ratio of raw materials to saleable product – by disregarding quality. While production targets were met, the refinery was producing both high-grade and low-grade metals. To mitigate this dysfunctional behaviour, management changed its system to measure only the yield of high-grade products to hold employees responsible for attaining the refiner's real goal of producing metals that met its quality standard.[6] Satisficing behaviour also arises in the service sector. Call centres, for example, are evaluated on a number of measures including quality, time and cost of service. Call centre employees often keep calls short to maintain cost and time standards but at the expense of resolving the situation to the customer's complete satisfaction.[7]

Managers also need to react to competitors. If the manager focuses only on the internal standard instead of the competition, the organization will not change to meet new market preferences. Rewarding managers for simply achieving the standard encourages them to think that the status quo is appropriate. Rewards of this nature do not promote innovation. Therefore, management rewards based on achieving the standard are less appropriate in rapidly changing industries with new, innovative products. However, the problem is not the use of standards as performance measures, but rather the way in which the compensation schemes reward performance. Compensation schemes should motivate managers to continuously improve beyond the standard by providing higher payments for greater improvement.

Concept **review**

1 How do standard cost variances encourage the creation of excess inventory?

2 How does standard costing create externalities and discourage co-operative effort?

3 How can mutual monitoring be encouraged?

4 What is satisficing behaviour and how is it related to standard costs?

Erin Castor, Custom Design Homes (continued)

Erin realizes that her standard costing system has affected the behaviour of her managers but some behaviour was perverse. Karim Sharma was able to obtain favourable material price variances because he received discounts by purchasing more raw materials than required. To overcome this problem, Erin decides

➔

---

[6] M. Hammer (2007), 'The 7 Deadly Sins of Performance Measurement and How to Avoid Them', *MIT Sloan Management Review*, Vol. 48, No. 3 (Spring), pp. 19–28.

[7] A. E. Raz and E. Blank (2007), 'Ambiguous professionalism: managing efficiency and service quality in an Israeli call centre', *New Technology, Work and Employment*, Vol. 22, No. 1, pp. 83–96.

to charge Karim for the average amount of raw materials in inventory. The quality of the raw materials and the workmanship is another issue that Erin has to reconsider. Henceforth, incoming raw materials will have to pass a quality inspection. This step will reduce the externalities imposed by Karim on the other two managers. Also, Erin will retain the responsibility for hiring and training workers to try to improve the quality of workmanship.

Erin also decides to encourage co-operative behaviour by tying part of each manager's bonus to the profit of the entire company. Bonuses will be a percentage of total profit, rather than a fixed amount, if a certain level of profit is achieved. By making the bonuses a percentage of total profit, satisficing behaviour on the part of managers should be less likely.

With these adjustments, Erin hopes that her standard costing system will lead to less perverse behaviour. She still wants to control direct costs but not at the risk of reduced quality, excess inventory costs and management dissension.

STANDARD OVERHEAD COSTS AND VARIANCES

The previous discussion described standards for direct labour and direct materials. Standards also are established for overhead costs. Overhead standard costs are used for both planning and control purposes and provide information about the cost of using overhead resources. Standard product costs used for pricing decisions include standard overhead costs. Standard overhead costs also provide benchmarks for evaluating managers who control overhead resources.

Overhead cost variances are more difficult to calculate and interpret than are the direct material and labour variances, because 'quantity' and 'price' are not inherent characteristics of overhead. Instead, quantity and price are defined in terms of the allocation base used to allocate overhead costs. The *quantity* of overhead is defined as the level of usage of the allocation base. The *price* of overhead is the application rate of the allocation base. The next section describes different measures of quantity for the allocation base. The subsequent section describes variances in terms of budgeted, applied and actual overhead. We defer the calculation of specific overhead variances to the Appendix to this chapter.

■ Expected, standard and actual usage of the allocation base

Before describing overhead variances, it is useful to review some terminology involving the concept of volume. Most plants or departments within plants do not produce a single homogeneous product but a diverse set of outputs. In this case, volume is not measured in terms of output but in terms of a common input such as direct labour cost, machine time or raw materials cost.

Once an input measure, such as machine time, is selected as the definition of plant or departmental volume, three different ways are used to quantify input volume: expected usage, standard usage and actual usage of the input. The first volume measure, **expected usage**, is set at the beginning of the year based on the amount of production expected to occur during the year. Greater expected output volume implies greater expected input usage. If a car repair shop measures volume using direct labour hours, the expected direct labour hours are estimated at the beginning of the year based on the estimated number of vehicles to be repaired during the year.

Expected usage of the allocation base is estimated for budgetary purposes. The overhead application rate generally is calculated by dividing the expected overhead costs by the expected usage of the allocation base.

Standard usage is the amount of the input used if each unit of product actually manufactured consumed precisely the standard units of input allowed. Given the output actually produced, standard usage measures how much input should have been used. For example, suppose the allocation base selected is direct labour hours. After each job is manufactured, the number of units actually produced times the standard number of direct labour hours per unit is the standard usage. Standard usage relates inputs to outputs.

The third input volume concept is **actual usage**. This volume measure is the actual amount of an allocation base used (e.g. actual machine hours, actual direct labour hours, actual direct labour cost). Actual usage focuses simply on inputs.

The three input volume measures (expected, standard and actual usage) differ in terms of when they are computed. Expected usage is estimated before the fiscal year begins and before production starts. Both standard and actual usage are computed after production is completed.

Numerical **example** 12.4

Pizzazz Pizza makes two types of frozen pizzas, pepperoni and cheese. The company allocates overhead to these two products based on the number of direct labour hours. The direct labour hours per unit to make a pepperoni pizza is 5 minutes, or $\frac{1}{12}$ of an hour. The direct labour hours per unit to make a cheese pizza is 4 minutes, or $\frac{1}{15}$ of an hour. At the start of the year, Pizzazz Pizza expected to make 12,000 pepperoni pizzas and 6,000 cheese pizzas. During the year, the firm actually made 9,000 pepperoni pizzas and 7,500 cheese pizzas. The payroll system indicates that direct labourers worked for 1,300 hours. What are the total expected direct labour hours, standard direct labour hours and actual direct labour hours?

Solution

Expected number of direct labour hours	
Pepperoni (12,000 × $\frac{1}{12}$)	1,000
Cheese (6,000 × $\frac{1}{15}$)	400
Total	1,400
Standard number of direct labour hours	
Pepperoni (9,000 × $\frac{1}{12}$)	750
Cheese (7,500 × $\frac{1}{15}$)	500
Total	1,250
Actual number of direct labour hours	1,300

■ Budgeted, applied and actual overhead

The previous section described three measures of usage of an allocation base. There are also three equivalent measures of overhead costs: budgeted, applied, and actual. **Budgeted overhead costs** (expected overhead costs) are the overhead costs expected at the beginning of the period. Budgeted overhead costs are estimated using the expected level of operations of the organization during the coming period. Budgeted overhead costs are divided by the expected usage of the allocation base to calculate the application rate for the allocation base.

Applied overhead costs are the overhead costs that are applied to cost objects through the standard usage of the allocation base. In Chapter 10, the allocation of overhead occurs with the actual usage of the allocation base. With standard costing, however, the standard usage of the allocation base is used to allocate overhead costs. A standard costing system pre-determines all the components (direct labour, direct materials and overhead) of the product cost. If 3 direct labour hours (DLH) are the standard for making a particular product and the allocation base is direct labour hours, the overhead allocated to the product is 3 DLH times the application rate per DLH. Even though the product actually may have required 4 DLH, the standard number of 3 is used to apply the overhead.

The **actual overhead costs** are the actual costs of overhead resources consumed. These costs include cash outlays and non-cash expenses such as the depreciation of fixed assets.

Budgeted, applied and actual overhead costs usually differ. Budgeted and applied overhead costs differ when the actual output (and, thus, the standard input usage) and the expected output are not equal. Only if the expected usage of the allocation base equals to the standard usage of the allocation base will the budgeted and applied overhead costs be equal.

The difference between applied (allocated) overhead costs and actual overhead costs is described in Chapter 10 as under- or over-absorbed overhead. In a standard costing system, the difference between the applied and actual overhead costs is called the **total overhead variance**. Many factors can cause the total overhead variance; for example, the adoption of JIT often alters the firm's operations such that the existing overhead allocation base does not measure accurately how overhead resources are consumed. Unexpected price changes for overhead items also contribute to the overhead variance. Moreover, multiple managers frequently are responsible for overhead resources. Overhead is incurred in many parts of the organization, and different management levels make decisions that influence these overhead costs. For instance, the human resources department frequently negotiates the labour rates for workers in production areas. Top management generally determines plant capacity. In both cases, lower-level managers might be held responsible for the overhead costs related to these decisions. Therefore, partitioning the total overhead variance into components can allow for better identification of the cause and responsibility for the total overhead variance. The Appendix to this chapter describes one method of partitioning the total overhead variance.

Numerical **example** 12.5

A company makes two types of plastic pipe, 2.5 centimetre and 5 centimetre diameter. Overhead is allocated based on kilograms of plastic in the pipe. The standards for the two types of pipe are as follows:

Type	Standard kilograms/unit	Expected units	Expected kilograms of plastic
2.5cm	2	500,000	1,000,000
5cm	3	600,000	1,800,000
Totals			2,800,000

The budgeted overhead for the period is €1,400,000. During the period, 450,000 units of 2.5cm pipe are made using 1,050,000kg of plastic. As well, 650,000 units of 5cm pipe are made using 1,900,000kg of plastic. Actual overhead costs are €1,300,000. The application rate is €1,400,000/2,800,000kg, or €0.50 per kg. What is the total overhead variance?

→

Solution

The total overhead variance is the difference between the actual overhead costs (€1,300,000) and the applied overhead costs. To calculate the applied overhead costs, the standard kilograms of plastic first must be determined. The standard kilograms times the application rate (€0.50 per kg) is equal to the overhead applied.

Type	Standard kilograms/unit	Actual units	Standard kilograms of plastic	Overhead applied (€)
2.5cm	2	450,000	900,000	450,000
5cm	3	650,000	1,950,000	975,000
Totals			2,850,000	1,425,000

The total overhead variance is €1,300,000 − €1,425,000, or €125,000 over-absorbed (favourable).

■ Incentive effects of overhead standards and variances

Managers of overhead resources are responsible for providing quality services to the organization at the lowest possible cost. Standard costs for overhead are established, in part, to provide benchmarks for evaluating the managers of the overhead resources. If overhead standards are used to evaluate and reward managers, they will have an effect on managerial behaviour.

The preferred effect of standard overhead costs is the reduction in overhead costs. The manager of the overhead resources can create favourable overhead variances by reducing overhead costs below the standard levels. Of course, maintaining the quality of the overhead service is still important to the organization, so a danger exists that the manager will trade off cost savings and quality inappropriately.

Increasing output also can create favourable overhead variances. More output increases the standard usage of the allocation base, which results in more applied overhead. If actual overhead costs do not increase proportionally with the allocation base, a favourable overhead variance occurs with higher output levels. For example, applied costs increase more rapidly than actual costs if some costs are fixed with respect to the allocation base.

One organizational mechanism to overcome this overproduction incentive is the separation of responsibilities such that overhead resource managers do not control output levels. If the managers do not control output levels, they should be evaluated only on the portion of the overhead variance caused by cost savings or overruns. The Appendix to this chapter examines the partitioning of the overhead variances to identify responsibility for different portions of the overhead variance.

Concept **review**

1 How do expected, standard and actual usage of the allocation base differ?

2 Why are standard overhead costs different from budgeted overhead costs?

3 What are some incentive effects of using overhead standards and variances for control?

Erin Castor, Custom Design Homes (continued)

Once Erin has designed a standard costing system to control the direct costs, she turns to overhead costs. Overhead costs were small when she was only running a small design business for custom homes and was able to work out of her house. The building of wall panels, however, has forced her to rent a warehouse that offers a controlled environment for panel construction. In addition, she has more manager salaries and other indirect costs to pay. Overhead costs are rising more rapidly than her direct costs; she needs some mechanisms to control overhead spending.

During the budgetary process for the year, Erin estimated the total overhead costs for the company to be £600,000. She decided to use standard direct labour hours to allocate overhead to the various types of wall panels, because direct labour hours were related to the number of managers, a major overhead expense. She estimated that the company would use 100,000 standard direct labour hours based on expected production. The standard application rate, therefore, was £600,000/100,000 standard direct labour hours, or £6 per standard direct labour hour.

Given that each wall panel had a standard of 3 direct labour hours per unit, the total standard hours for the order of 3,000 units was (3,000 units × 3 direct labour hours per unit), or 9,000 hours. Other orders during the year have caused an additional use of 86,000 standard direct labour hours for a total of 95,000 standard direct labour hours. Therefore, during the year, 95,000 standard direct labour hours × £6 per direct labour hour, or £570,000 of overhead have been applied to products. The actual overhead for the year, however, is £605,000. Therefore, the overhead variance is £605,000 − £570,000, or £35,000 under-absorbed (adverse).

Erin is unsure about what to do with this variance. It is not clear who is responsible. Many of the overhead decisions were actually her own. She is also not sure whether the overhead costs are variable or fixed. The overhead variance requires further investigation.

VARIANCE INVESTIGATION

The management accounting system routinely reports variance calculations in both monetary terms and as a percentage of the standard cost. These reports are only the first step in the decision-making process in a standard costing system. Variances provide information for planning and control purposes. In both cases, the variance figures alone rarely provide sufficient information for making good decisions.

Variances are intended to identify problems in existing processes that require attention but variances often occur when processes are operating correctly. Random fluctuations in the costs of materials, labour, or overhead can cause a variance. A manager is seldom certain whether a problem or a random fluctuation caused the variance. Large variances, however, are more likely to indicate a problem than are small ones.

Small deviations between actual costs and standard costs are expected and unavoidable. Moreover, random variances tend to offset each other over time. Positive random variances approximately equal negative random variances, so aggregating random variances over time should lead to actual costs being close to standard costs. If variances do not offset each other over time, some factor other than randomness likely caused the variances. Aggregating variances over time provides supervisors with more confidence about the origins of the variance.

Even if managers know that a problem other than random variation underlies a variance, they seldom can identify the nature of the problem by just looking at the figures. Looking at all of the variances provides more information. Certain combinations of variances are indicative of certain problems. For example, favourable material price variances with adverse material quantity and labour efficiency variances are consistent with the purchase of cheap, low-quality materials. However, an analysis of all the variances does not reveal the complete story.

To understand the cause of a variance, a manager must investigate its source. Investigations include questioning responsible parties and looking at non-cost data, such as the percentage of defects and quality measures of raw materials. As noted earlier, call centres are evaluated on both financial and non-financial measures. Call centres track the cost per call and compare it to the budgeted cost. Non-financial measures include call time (average duration of each incoming call), call abandonment rates (the percentage of callers who do not wait in the queue), process accuracy (the accuracy of customer data entered into the system), and call quality (whether the agent is polite and friendly as measured through random call monitoring). Call centres frequently supplement both sets of measures with customer surveys to establish a customer satisfaction index. Firms summarize and compare these data to budget estimates, to the results of other call centres, and to industry benchmarks. If a significant variance is noted in the reported data, managers can investigate further by requesting additional information. For example, an increase in the cost per call might be related to calls of longer duration. These items might signal that the call centre was handling more complex inquiries requiring a higher level of service and more skilled customer service representatives. The variances are one way that call centres determine whether or not they are meeting the goal of customer satisfaction, an important strategic focus in these organizations.[8]

The decision to investigate is a decision in itself. Variance investigations are often costly, involving labour, engineering time and sometimes the shut-down of processes during the investigation. Therefore, not every non-zero variance should be investigated. The manager frequently uses a decision rule based on the size of the variance to determine when to investigate. Large variances are less likely the result of random fluctuations and, therefore, often deserve further study. The decision problem is determining how large the variance must be to make an investigation worthwhile. Organizations frequently establish benchmarks or rules-of-thumb for variance investigation. These decision rules include, for example, investigating variances that are more than 10 per cent of the standard cost, or more than a specific monetary value, say €500. As well, firms investigate variances that have continued over a period of time, using control charts to track variances over time. Statistical models, discussed in advanced management accounting and operations management courses, can be helpful in determining when a variance should be investigated.

Factors that affect the decision rule to investigate variances include the size of the random fluctuations, the cost of investigation, the cost of not investigating, and the ease of correcting the problem if it exists. If random fluctuations tend to be high, only very large variances would distinguish a variance caused by randomness from a variance caused by a problem. If an investigation is costly, the manager is much less likely to investigate smaller variances. If the cost of not investigating is high, however, smaller variances are more likely to be investigated. For example, if the material quantity variance is caused by theft, a lack of investigation in all likelihood leads to further theft and a high cost to the organization. Therefore, small variances probably are investigated. The ease of correcting the problem, if it exists, also influences the investigation

---

[8] M. M. Cheng, P. F. Luckett and H. Mahama (2007) 'Effect of perceived conflict among multiple performance goals and goal difficulty on task performance', *Accounting and Finance*, Vol. 47, pp. 221–242; A. E. Raz and E. Blank, *op cit*; G. Robinson and C. Morley (2006) 'Call centre management: responsibilities and performance', *International Journal of Service Industry Management*, Vol. 17, No. 3, pp. 284–300.

decision. High correction costs mean that even if the problem is discovered, the organization may not fix the problem as the benefits of doing so are less than the costs. Therefore, less reason exists to investigate the problem. Instead, the organization may choose to revise the standard. The new standard recognizes the existence of the problem, so the manager no longer is responsible for the variance that is considered too costly to fix.

Innovations in process technologies make production problems easier to detect and even correct. These innovations also affect variance investigation, as it is increasingly possible to avoid future problems with timely intervention and preliminary variance information. The decision to investigate a variance relates to the opportunity cost concept outlined in Chapter 2. The organization must weight the value of the increased information against the cost of producing it. In the current environment, technologically-advanced expert systems can correct problems detected by the variance. These systems thus separate the variance-investigation decision from the correction of the detected problem. Other models of variance investigation collapse these actions into one and might not lead to the correct cost-benefit decision in today's environment.[9]

Concept review

1 Why are investigations of variances often appropriate?

2 What are some factors that influence the decision to investigate?

Erin Castor, Custom Design Homes (continued)

To investigate the £35,000 overhead variance, Erin must use the services of Pat Shaw, her staff accountant, for 10 days. Pat has some free time and is paid a fixed salary, so Erin figures that the cost of Pat's time will be only about £600. The potential cost savings from correcting a problem with overhead could be much larger but Erin is not sure that a problem exists. The variance could have been caused by not estimating the overhead costs or the number of standard direct labour hours correctly. Erin decides to go ahead with the investigation. Pat determines that much of the variance is caused by mis-estimates but does find a way to save £2,000 per year by more careful use of electricity. Therefore, Erin's decision to investigate is expected to save £2,000 less the £600 investigation cost, or £1,400.

COSTS AND BENEFITS OF USING STANDARD COSTING SYSTEMS

Standard cost systems are expensive to implement and operate. Detailed standards must be maintained for each labour and material input (standard prices and quantities). These standards also must be revised in a timely fashion. Rapid technological change and continuous improvement initiatives (total quality management (TQM) programmes are described in Chapter 14) make standards quickly obsolete. In addition, investigating cost variances is expensive in terms of the cost of the manager's time.

---

[9] These issues are examined in P. K. Sen (1998) 'Another Look at Cost Variance Investigation', *Issues in Accounting Education*, Vol. 13, No. 1 (February), pp. 127–137. Variance investigation models are provided for a variety of production settings.

Standard cost systems also create incentive problems. Workers tend to focus on existing standards, rather than seeking continuous cost reductions. In addition, standard cost systems can cause overproduction and lower quality, and can discourage co-operative effort.

Standard cost variances also are not particularly timely; they usually are reported monthly or quarterly. This information may be too late to correct problems. However, advanced technology and diagnostic systems make it possible to report and act upon variance information in real time.

For many organizations, the benefits of standard costs through improved control and planning decisions exceed the costs of using standard costs. As mentioned earlier, most large companies are maintaining their use of standard costs.[10] Many firms combine these systems with other techniques such as activity-based costing, JIT and TQM. For example, results of a survey of 121 manufacturing firms reported that firms in advanced manufacturing environments were adding supplementary measures to their standard costing systems instead of replacing them. These findings suggest that firms experience benefits from the continued use of their standard costing systems that outweigh their costs.[11]

While some organizations might be abandoning their detailed standard cost systems, they often maintain some standard costs. These firms still see opportunities to use standard costs for planning and control purposes. A standard cost system must be designed and implemented carefully to maximize firm value. Burn Stewart Distillers Ltd provides an example of one firm whose system is intended to do so. Carelessly designed standard cost systems, which serve as performance evaluation schemes, can lead to dysfunctional behaviour.

Organizational **analysis**

Burn Stewart Distillers Ltd

The production of spirits and whiskies conjures up images of the master brewer and age-old recipes. However, the global business environment has brought changes to this image and introduced the need for sophisticated planning and control systems to supplement mystery and tradition.

Burn Stewart Distillers Ltd, based in East Kilbride, Scotland, operates three distilleries; Deanston in Perthshire, Bunnahabhain on the Isle of Islay and Tobermory on the Isle of Mull. It sells several million litres of cased and bulk whisky each year in the UK and to export markets.

Burn Stewart utilizes an integrated planning and costing system to manage its inventories and optimize the efficiency of its distilling processes. The system provides the firm with up-to-date information to ensure that it achieves consistent output. While consistency is important, cost also is critical, especially in the blended whisky market where Burn Stewart must compete for the price-conscious consumer who prefers low cost and supermarket convenience. The planning system allows the management team to monitor the cost of its blended products from the beginning to the end of the distilling process. For example, the firm might opt to purchase whisky from another producer rather than draw down its own inventory when a cost advantage exists.

Burn Stewart's master blender creates a recipe for each blend. The standard cost of the blend is determined from this standard 'bill of materials'. Costs are calculated in real time, providing management information to make informed decisions about markets

→

---

[10] The survey by Guilding *et al.* reported that 76 per cent of the UK firms and 73 per cent of the New Zealand firms used standard costing systems.

[11] R. R. Fullerton and C. S. McWatters (2004) 'An Empirical Examination of Cost Accounting Practices', *Advances in Management Accounting*, Vol. 12, pp. 85–113.

and prices. If the standard cost of the blend is deemed to be too high relative to market demand, the blender can use this information to alter the recipe to reduce costs without affecting product quality.

What factors caused Burn Stewart to adopt its integrated planning and control system?

How does the firm's use of standard costing enable it to meet customer preferences and also to maximize organizational value?

Sources: www.burnstewartdistillers.com; www.ssi-world.com/gencontent/casestudies/burnstewart.htm

Concept review

1 Why are standard costs difficult to implement in a rapidly changing business environment?
2 What evidence indicates that for many organizations, the benefits of using standard costs outweigh the problems of using standard costs?

SUMMARY

1 Provide reasons for using standard costs. Standard costs are used for planning purposes by communicating expected costs to members of the organization. Standard costs also are used for control by establishing benchmarks to evaluate processes and managers.

2 Describe planning and control issues in setting standards. For planning purposes, the person with the best knowledge of a process should establish standards. Conflict exists, however, if that individual also is evaluated based on those standards.

3 Calculate direct labour and direct material variances. Direct labour and material variances are divided into variances related to differences between actual and standard prices, and variances related to differences between actual and standard quantities.

4 Identify potential causes of different favourable and adverse variances. All variances are potentially due to incorrect standards. Favourable price variances (standard prices greater than actual prices) also are caused by purchasing large amounts of materials to obtain discounts or by purchasing lower-quality items. Adverse price variances (actual prices more than standard prices) could result from rush orders or paying for higher-quality materials or labour. Efficient use of labour or materials or the use of

higher-quality labour or materials could cause favourable quantity variances (actual quantity used less than the standard quantity). Adverse quantity variances (actual quantity used greater than the standard quantity) could be the result of the inefficient use or theft of direct resources or the use of lower-quality labour or materials.

5 Recognize incentive effects of standard costs. Standard costs have the potential to cause overproduction and lower quality, externalities to other parts of the organization, unco-operative effort, mutual monitoring, and satisficing behaviour.

6 Measure expected, standard and actual usage of an allocation base to apply overhead and determine overhead variances. At the beginning of the period, the expected usage of the allocation base and the application rate are calculated based on budgeted numbers. Standard usage is the standard input per unit times actual units produced and is used to apply overhead. Actual usage is measured throughout the period based on the observed usage of the allocation base. The total overhead variance is the difference between the actual overhead and the overhead applied.

7 Identify factors that influence the decision to investigate variances. The decision to investigate a variance is based on the size of the random variation, the cost of investigation, the cost of not investigating, and the ease of correcting the problem if one exists.

8 **Summarize the costs and benefits of using standard costs.** Standard costs can improve planning and control, but standard costing

systems are expensive to implement and adjust if the product mix is changing rapidly. As well, standard costs potentially cause adverse incentive effects such as overproduction and satisficing behaviour, depending on how the performance reward systems use the standard costs.

KEY TERMS

Actual overhead costs Indirect costs actually incurred by the organization.

Actual usage The number of times an allocation base actually is used.

Adverse variance The result when actual costs are higher than standard costs.

Applied overhead costs The monetary amount of overhead allocated to different products or other cost objects.

Budgeted overhead costs The expected indirect costs used to establish application rates.

Direct labour variance The difference between actual and standard labour costs.

Direct materials variance The difference between actual and standard material costs.

Expected usage The number of times an allocation base is expected to be used.

Favourable variance The result when actual costs are less than standard costs.

Fixed overhead budget variance (Appendix) The difference between budgeted and actual fixed overhead.

Fixed overhead variance (Appendix) The difference between applied and actual fixed overhead.

Fixed overhead volume variance (Appendix) The difference between applied and budgeted fixed overhead.

Labour efficiency variance The difference between actual and standard direct labour hours times the standard labour rate.

Labour rate variance The difference between the actual labour rate and the standard labour rate times the actual hours.

Management by exception A management style that focuses management effort on large cost variances.

Material price variance The difference between the actual price and standard price of raw materials times the actual quantity used or purchased.

Material quantity variance The difference between the actual and standard quantity of materials used times the standard price.

Satisficing behaviour Behaviour of employees seeking to achieve satisfactory levels of performance measures but not trying to excel.

Standard costs Benchmarks based on expected future costs.

Standard usage The number of times a cost driver should have been used given the actual number of units of output.

Target costing Choosing a cost goal given a competitive sales price and an expected profit margin.

Total overhead variance The difference between total actual and applied overhead.

Variable overhead efficiency variance (Appendix) The difference between actual and standard usage of the allocation base times the standard application rate for variable overhead.

Variable overhead spending variance (Appendix) The difference between actual and standard application rates for variable overhead times the actual usage of the allocation base.

Variable overhead variance (Appendix) The difference between the actual and applied variable overhead.

Variance The difference between actual and standard costs.

APPENDIX
Overhead variances

The total overhead variance is the difference between the overhead allocated and the actual overhead. Many reasons exist for a non-zero overhead variance. Standards and application rates could be wrong, the production level could be higher or lower than expected, or overhead departments might not be operating efficiently. Decomposing the total overhead variance into its components provides information about the cause of the total overhead variance.

A common procedure is to partition the total overhead variance into variances related to variable and fixed overhead. The **variable overhead variance** is defined as the actual variable overhead less the applied variable overhead; it is calculated as follows:

Actual variable overhead − Applied variable overhead

$$U_a VR_a \qquad\qquad U_s VR_s$$

where U_a = Actual usage of the allocation base
VR_a = Actual variable overhead application rate (Actual variable overhead cost ÷ Actual usage of the allocation base)
U_s = Standard usage of the allocation base
VR_s = Standard variable overhead application rate

The equation for the variable overhead variance is similar to the variance equations for the direct costs. The usage of the allocation base is a quantity measure. The application rate is a price for using the allocation base. Therefore, the variable overhead variance also can be divided into a price and quantity variance.

The **variable overhead spending variance** is a price variance caused by the actual application rate being different than the standard application rate:

$$\text{Variable overhead spending variance} = U_a(VR_a - VR_s)$$

For managers responsible for the efficient provision of variable overhead resources, the standard application rate is a benchmark for evaluating performance. An adverse variable overhead spending variance indicates that the actual variable costs are higher per unit of the allocation base than expected. An adverse variance does not mean that the manager of the overhead resources is doing a poor job. Overhead resources might have become more expensive than expected or the quality of the overhead services provided higher. An unusual variance, however, can be interpreted as a signal to investigate. For example, the prices of overhead items might change unexpectedly, such as sudden increases in the price of oil that affects the cost of petrol and lubricants used in equipment. Labour rates of supervisory staff might rise as a result of revised labour contracts. Upon investigation, these changes might signal that existing standards are no longer appropriate.

The **variable overhead efficiency variance** is a quantity variance related to the usage of the allocation base:

$$\text{Variable overhead efficiency variance} = VR_s(U_a - U_s)$$

The standard usage of the allocation base determines the amount of variable overhead that is applied. If actual usage of the allocation base is greater than the standard usage, variable overhead is under-absorbed and the variable overhead efficiency variance is adverse. In general, the responsibility for the variable overhead efficiency variance should rest with the users of the allocation base. For example, the variable overhead costs of the human resources department frequently are allocated to production departments based on standard direct labour hours. The manager of the production department is generally responsible for the difference between the actual and standard direct labour hours. The human resources manager, however, could be responsible if the quality of the people hired led to the inability to achieve direct labour standards. The variable overhead efficiency variance and the direct labour efficiency variance must be in the same direction (favourable or adverse) when the allocation base is direct labour hours. Once again, a further investigation is necessary to determine if a problem exists and who is responsible. In some cases, adoption of automated equipment makes direct labour hours inappropriate as the allocation base.

The **fixed overhead variance** is the actual fixed overhead less the applied fixed overhead. Fixed overhead, unlike variable overhead, should not change with the allocation base. The fixed overhead variance can be decomposed into two more variances: the **fixed overhead budget variance** and the **fixed overhead volume variance**. Managers responsible for fixed overhead resources generally are evaluated based on the difference between actual fixed overhead expenditures and budgeted fixed overhead, which is the **fixed overhead budget variance**. An adverse fixed overhead budget variance indicates that more resources than expected were expended on fixed overhead. For instance, fixed expenses, such as property taxes, and equipment leases, might be more than expected.

The fixed overhead variance is decomposed using the following equations:

$$\text{Fixed overhead variance} = \text{Actual fixed overhead} - \text{Applied fixed overhead}$$
$$= (\text{Actual fixed overhead} - \text{Budgeted fixed overhead})$$
$$+ (\text{Budgeted fixed overhead} - \text{Applied fixed overhead})$$
$$= \text{Fixed overhead budget variance}$$
$$+ \text{Fixed overhead volume variance}$$

The fixed overhead volume variance also can be written as follows:

$$\text{Budgeted fixed overhead} - \text{Applied fixed overhead} = U_e FR_s - U_s FR_s$$
$$= FR_s(U_e - U_s)$$

where U_e = Expected (or budgeted) usage of the allocation base
FR_s = Standard fixed overhead application rate
U_s = Standard usage of the allocation base

The difference between the expected usage (U_e) and the standard usage (U_s) of the allocation base is due to the volume of output being different than expected. Therefore, the fixed overhead volume variance is an estimate of unused or overused capacity. If the number of units produced is less than expected, the standard usage of the allocation base is less than expected. Less fixed overhead costs are applied than expected and the volume variance is adverse. Given that the volume variance depends on the output of the organization, the manager responsible for fixed overhead resources should not be held responsible for the volume variance. Instead, the manager in control of output levels should be responsible for the volume variance. This manager has an incentive to overproduce because increased output makes the volume variance more favourable as more fixed costs are applied to units produced. The volume variance, however, is not a measure of the opportunity cost of unused capacity. The opportunity cost is estimated by the contribution margin on products and services that could have been sold but were not. Therefore, performance based on the volume variance encourages managers to build inventories that might not be sold. Organizational value is decreased instead of increased.

Numerical **example** 12.6

A company that services office machines applies variable and fixed overhead to jobs based on standard labour hours. The company has the following budget numbers related to the allocation base:

Type of service	Expected service units	Standard labour per service unit	Total expected labour hours
Photocopiers	5,000	1 hour per unit	5,000
Fax machines	1,000	2 hours per unit	2,000
Total			7,000

The standard numbers related to the allocation base given actual output follow:

Type of service	Actual service units	Standard labour per service unit	Total standard labour hours
Copiers	4,500	1 hour per unit	4,500
Fax machines	1,100	2 hours per unit	2,200
Total			6,700

The actual number of labour hours used to service the copiers and fax machines was 6,800 hours. Budgeted and actual variable and fixed overhead costs were as follows:

Overhead	Budgeted costs (£)	Actual costs (£)
Variable	20,000	22,000
Fixed	15,000	14,000

Calculate the application rates for variable and fixed overhead, the amount of variable and fixed overhead applied, the variable overhead spending and efficiency variances, and the fixed overhead budget and volume variances.

Solution

The application rates are calculated by dividing the budgeted (or expected) overhead by the expected usage of labour hours:

$$\text{Variable overhead application rate} = £20,000/7,000 \text{ hr} = £2.857 \text{ per hr}$$
$$\text{Fixed overhead application rate} = £15,000/7,000 \text{ hr} = £2.143 \text{ per hr}$$

The applied fixed and variable overhead are calculated by multiplying the application rates times the standard hours:

$$\text{Variable overhead applied} = (6,700 \text{ hr} \times £2.857 \text{ per hr}) = £19,142$$
$$\text{Fixed overhead applied} = (6,700 \text{ hr} \times £2.143 \text{ per hr}) = £14,358$$

The variable overhead variance is the difference between the actual variable overhead (£22,000) and the applied variable overhead (£19,142), or £2,858 adverse. The variable overhead variance can be further decomposed into the variable overhead spending variance and the variable overhead efficiency variance. The actual application rate for variable overhead is the actual variable overhead costs (£22,000) divided by the actual labour hours (6,800), or £3.235 per hr.

$$\text{Variable overhead spending variance} = U_a(V_a - V_s)$$
$$= 6,800 \text{ hr} (£3.235 \text{ per hr} - £2.857 \text{ per hr}) = £2,570 \text{ adverse}$$

$$\text{Variable overhead efficiency variance} = V_s(U_a - U_s)$$
$$= £2.857 \text{ per hr} (6,800 \text{ hr} - 6,700 \text{ hr}) = £286 \text{ adverse}$$

The sum of these two variances equals £2,856, which differs slightly from the variable overhead variance of £2,858 due to rounding error.

The fixed overhead variance is the difference between the actual fixed overhead (£14,000) and the applied fixed overhead (£14,358), or £358 favourable. The fixed overhead variance can be decomposed into the fixed overhead budget variance and the fixed overhead volume variance.

$$\text{Fixed overhead budget variance} = \text{Actual} - \text{Budgeted fixed overhead}$$
$$= £14,000 - £15,000 = £1,000 \text{ favourable}$$

$$\text{Fixed overhead volume variance} = \text{Budgeted} - \text{Applied fixed overhead}$$
$$= £15,000 - £14,358 = £642 \text{ adverse}$$

The sum of the fixed overhead budget and volume variances equals the total fixed overhead variance.

Self-study problem

Killarney Canoes makes fibreglass canoes. The fibreglass resin is moulded initially to the shape of a canoe and then is sanded and painted. Metal or wooden seats and frames are added for stability. Killarney Canoes was started several years ago in the owner's garage. The owner, Jordan Fitzpatrick, did a lot of the initial manual labour with the help of a few friends. The company has since expanded into a large warehouse and new employees have been hired. As a result of the expansion, Jordan is no longer directly involved with production and is concerned about his ability to plan for and control the company. He is considering the implementation of a standard cost system.

a Describe the procedures Jordan should use in setting standards for direct labour and direct materials.
b Describe how Jordan could use standards for planning purposes.
c Describe how Jordan could use standards for motivating employees as well as the problems in using standards as performance measures.
d Why are some of Jordan's friends, who worked with him from the beginning, not excited about a change to a standard cost system?

Solution

a Direct material standards should be established for the fibreglass resin and the wood and metal for the seats and the frame. For planning purposes, the standards for quantity and price should reflect expectations, but Jordan is no longer familiar with production and must ask some employees about expected quantities and prices. The purchasing manager has information on prices, and the manufacturing manager has information on quantities. The direct labour standards are based on expectations from the personnel manager and the manufacturing manager.
b If accurate estimates of prices and quantities are provided, Jordan can use the information to plan for cash flows. The standards also can be used to plan for appropriate inventory levels given planned manufacturing efforts.
c The standards can be used as benchmarks to evaluate the performance of employees. One problem with using standards as performance measures is the difficulty of obtaining accurate standards from the individuals being evaluated. Standards also can provide incentives to increase inventories, discourage co-operative behaviour, and lead to satisficing behaviour.
d Some of Jordan's friends, who are still working in the expanded organization, probably will be unhappy with the standard costing system. They will no longer be judged directly by their friend Jordan but through standards that appear impersonal and lacking in trust. Jordan's friends, however, must recognize that he cannot observe directly what is happening in the company given the expanded operations. Standard costing systems are not established because of a lack of trust; their use conveys information among the different members of the organization.

Numerical exercises

NE 12.1 Direct labour variances LO 3

A web page consultant estimates the following hours to create a web page for a small retail store:

Staff member	Expected hours	Cost per hour (€)	Standard costs (€)
Senior designer	10	25	250
Junior designer	20	20	400
Secretarial staff	10	10	100
Totals	40		750

The actual hours and costs were as follows:

Staff member	Actual hours	Actual cost per hour (€)	Actual costs (€)
Senior designer	9	30	270
Junior designer	22	18	396
Secretarial staff	12	11	132
Totals	75		798

Calculate the direct labour, labour rate and labour efficiency variances for each staff member.

NE 12.2 Direct labour variances and compensation LO 3

The web page consultant in *Numerical exercise 12.1* receives a bonus based on the direct labour variances. If the labour rate variance is adverse, 50 per cent of this amount is deducted from the bonus. If it is favourable, 100 per cent is added to the bonus received. The labour efficiency variance is added or deducted in total from the bonus.

What is the impact of the variances calculated in *Numerical exercise 12.1* on the consultant's bonus?

NE 12.3 Direct materials variances LO 3

Muffin Mania Bakery has a standard quantity of 1 kilogram of flour for one batch of muffins. The standard price is £0.50 per kilogram. During the month, the bakery manager bought 3,000 kilograms of flour for £1,600. The bakery used 2,500 kilograms of flour to produce 2,400 batches of muffins during the month.

What are the material price and quantity variances for the flour?

NE 12.4 Direct labour variances LO 3

Microchip makes two types of microchips for mobile telephones, Supra and Magna. Microchip allocates overhead to these two products based on the number of direct labour hours. The direct labour hours per unit to make a Supra chip is 5 minutes, or $\frac{1}{12}$ of an hour. The direct labour hours per unit to make a Magna chip is 4 minutes, or $\frac{1}{15}$ of an hour. At the start of the year, Microchip expected to make 12,000 Supra chips and 24,000 Magna chips. During the year, Microchip actually made 15,000 Supra Chips and 18,000 Magna Chips. The payroll records indicate that direct labourers worked for 2,500 hours.

What are the total expected direct labour hours, standard direct labour hours, and actual direct labour hours?

NE 12.5 Overhead variances LO 6

A company makes two types of pasta sauce, Primavera and Bolognese. Overhead is based on kilograms of tomatoes in the sauce. The standards for the two types of sauce are as follows:

Type	Standard kilograms per unit	Expected units	Expected kilograms of tomatoes
Primavera	1	500,000	500,000
Bolognese	1.5	600,000	900,000
Totals			1,400,000

The budgeted overhead for the period is €700,000. During the period, 450,000 units of Primavera are made using 525,000 kilograms of tomatoes. As well, 650,000 units of Bolognese are made using 1,000,000 kilograms of tomatoes. Actual overhead costs are €800,000. The application rate is €700,000/1,400,000 kilograms, or €0.50 per kg.

What is the total overhead variance?

NE 12.6 Raw materials variances LO 3

Medical Instruments produces a variety of electronic medical devices. Medical Instruments uses a standard cost system and computes price variances at the time of purchase. One product, a digital thermometer, measures patient temperatures orally. It requires a silver lead with a standard length of 12 centimetres per thermometer. To make the leads, hollow silver tubing is purchased at £4 per centimetre, cut into the required length, and then assembled into the thermometer.

No silver tubing was in inventory when a batch of 200 thermometers was scheduled for production. Thirty metres (3,000 centimetres) of silver tubing were purchased for £4,680 by the purchasing department for this 200-unit batch of thermometers, and 27.50 metres were used in production.

Compute the materials price and quantity variances for silver tubing and comment on the meaning of each variance.

NE 12.7 Direct material variances LO 3

During November, Todco planned to produce 3,000 units of its single product, Teragram. The standard specifications for one unit of Teragram include six kilograms of material at £0.30 per kilogram. Actual production in November was 3,100 units of Teragram. The accountant computed a favourable materials purchase price variance of £380 and an adverse materials quantity variance of £120.

Based on these data, calculate how many kilograms of material were used in the production of Teragram during November.

(CMA adapted)

NE 12.8 Direct material and labour variances LO 3

An ice cream producer manufactures 10,000 litres of strawberry ice cream in a month. The standard hours of direct labour per 1,000 litres are 40 hours at a standard labour rate of £10 per hour. The standard quantities and prices of ingredients per 1,000 litres of ice cream are 1,200 litres of cream at £1 per litre, 30 kilograms of strawberries at £0.50 per kilogram, and 1,000 containers at £0.05 per container. During the month, the ice cream maker produced 11,000 litres of strawberry ice cream. The labour rate of direct labour was £12 per hour for 420 hours. The actual price of the cream was £0.90 per litre and 13,000 litres were used. The actual price of strawberries was £0.60 per kilogram and 300 kilograms were used. The quantity of containers used was 11,200 and the actual price was £0.06 per container.

Calculate all of the direct material and labour variances.

NE 12.9 Direct material and labour variances LO 3

To manufacture its main product, a firm requires a standard of 10 direct labour hours per unit. The standard labour rate is €20 per hour. The product requires a standard of 25 kilograms of material. The standard price of materials is €5 per kilogram. The actual production of 100 units uses 900 direct labour hours at a total direct labour cost of €16,200 and 2,300 kilograms of material at a total direct material cost of €9,200.

Calculate all of the direct labour and material variances.

NE 12.10 Application of overhead LO 6

At the beginning of the year, a university sets standards for processing 1,000 admissions applications with 10,000 direct labour hours. The application rate for overhead is £40 per standard direct labour hour. During the year, the university actually processes 1,200 applications.

How much overhead is applied?

NE 12.11 Overhead variances LO 6, Appendix

A company uses machine hours to apply both variable and fixed overhead. Budgeted variable overhead is €100,000. Budgeted fixed overhead is €200,000. The budgeted machine hours are 1,000. During the period, 1,200 machine hours are used but only 1,100 standard hours occurred. The actual variable overhead is €105,000 and the actual fixed overhead is €205,000.

Calculate all of the overhead variances.

Numerical problems

NP 12.1 Direct variances LO 3

Arrow Industries employs a standard cost system in which direct materials inventory is carried at standard cost. Arrow has established the following standards for the direct costs of one unit of product.

	Standard quantity	Standard price	Standard cost (£)
Direct materials	8 kilograms	£1.80 per kilogram	14.40
Direct labour	0.25 hour	£8.00 per hour	2.00
			16.40

During May, Arrow purchased 160,000 kilograms of direct material at a total cost of £304,000. The total factory wages for May were £42,000, 90 per cent of which were for direct labour. Arrow manufactured 19,000 units of product during May using 142,500 kilograms of direct material and 5,000 direct labour hours.

a Calculate the direct materials price variance for May.
b Calculate the direct materials quantity variance for May.
c Calculate the direct labour rate variance for May.
d Calculate the direct labour efficiency variance for May.
e The production manager's bonus is based, in part, on the direct labour variance and the direct material quantity variance. The manager's bonus is adjusted (increased or decreased) by 10 per cent of the direct labour variance and the direct material quantity variance. What is the impact of the variances on the manager's bonus?

(CMA adapted)

NP 12.2 Raw material variances LO 3

A company purchased 36,000 kg of plastic pellets for £8,640. These pellets are used in injection moulding machines to produce plastic parts. The pellets have a standard cost of £0.25 per kg. Thirty thousand kilograms of these pellets were used in two jobs. The first job called for 14,000 kg of pellets, but actually used 15,000 kg. The second job also used 15,000 kg, but it called for 15,500 kg. The company uses a standard cost system, calculates price variances at purchase, and had no beginning inventory of this plastic pellet.

At the end of the two jobs and before any more of the plastic pellets are used (and before proration or write-off of variances), prepare a table that indicates the financial disposition of the historical cost of the pellets (i.e. account for the £8,640).

NP 12.3 Direct labour variances LO 3

Hospital Software sells and installs performance management software used by hospitals for patient admissions, tracking and billing. For each client engagement, Hospital Services takes its proprietary software and modifies it for the specific demands of the client. Prior to each installation, Hospital Software estimates the number of hours of programming time that each contract will require and the cost of the programmers. Programmers record the amount of time that they spend on each engagement and at the end of each installation, variance reports are prepared.

For the Midhurst Hospital account, Hospital Software estimates the following labour standards:

	Standard hours	Standard rate per hour
Junior programmer	85	£23
Senior programmer	33	£31

After the job was completed, the following costs were reported:

Junior programmer (98 hours)	£2,352
Senior programmer (36 hours)	£1,044

a Calculate the labour efficiency and labour rate variances for the junior and senior programmers on the Midhurst Hospital account.

b The manager of the project receives a bonus based on labour cost and efficiency. The bonus is adjusted (increased or decreased) by 50 per cent of the total direct labour variance. What is the impact of this project on the manager's bonus?

c What incentives might this bonus system create?

NP 12.4 Standard costs LO 1, 2, 3

Ogwood Company is a small manufacturer of wooden toys. The corporate controller plans to implement a standard cost system for Ogwood. The controller has information from several co-workers that will assist him in developing the standards.

One of Ogwood's products is a small wooden racing car. Each car requires 1.25 lengths of lumber and 12 minutes of direct labour time to prepare and cut the lumber. The wooden cars are inspected after they are cut. The cars are made of a natural material that has imperfections; therefore, one car is normally rejected after cutting for each five that are accepted. Four rubber wheels are attached to each good toy. A total of 15 minutes of direct labour time is required to attach all four wheels and finish each racing car. The lumber for the racing cars costs £3.00 per length and each wheel costs £0.05. Direct labour is paid at the rate of £8.00 per hour.

a Develop the standard cost for the direct cost components of the wooden racing car. For each direct cost component of the toy, the standard cost should identify the following:
  i Standard quantity.
  ii Standard rate.
  iii Standard cost per unit.
b What are the advantages of standard cost systems?
c Explain the role of each of the following people in developing standards:
  i Purchasing manager.
  ii Industrial engineer.
  iii Plant accountant.

(CMA adapted)

NP 12.5 Direct materials variance LO 3, 4

Howard Binding manufactures two types of notebooks, large and small. Both types of notebooks are made of the same cloth cover (direct material) but they require different quantities. The following is the standard cost sheet for each notebook:

	Large	Small
Cloth covering	3 metres @ £0.30 per m	2 metres @ £0.30 per m
Ring holder	1 @ £0.12 each	1 @ £0.12 each
Direct labour	0.15 hour @ £6.00 per hr	0.10 hour @ £6.00 per hr

At the beginning of the month, the purchasing department bought 35,000 metres of cloth for £10,850. There were no beginning inventories. During the month, 5,000 large and 8,000 small notebooks were produced. The production records for the month indicate the following actual production quantities:

	Large	Small
Cloth covering	16,000 m	15,500 m
Ring holders	5,000 @ £0.12 each	8,000 @ £0.12 each
Direct labour	800 hours @ £5.80 per hr	780 hours @ £6.10 per hr

a Calculate the cloth covering price variance (1) at purchase and (2) when the materials are actually used.
b Discuss why the two price variances calculated in (a) differ and which is superior (and why).

NP 12.6 Overhead variances LO 6, Appendix

The information technology (IT) department of Asterix Company services the firm's computers and printers. It applies variable and fixed overhead to jobs based on standard labour hours. The IT department has the following budget numbers related to the allocation base:

Type of service	Expected service units	Standard labour per service unit	Total expected labour hours
Computers	1,000	1 hour per unit	1,000
Printers	3,000	2 hours per unit	6,000
Total			7,000

The standard numbers related to the allocation base given actual output are as follows:

Type of service	Actual service units	Standard labour per service unit	Total standard labour hours
Computers	850	1 hour per unit	850 hours
Printers	3,500	2 hours per unit	7,000 hours
Total			7,850 hours

The actual number of labour hours used to service the computers and printers was 7,800 hours. Budgeted and actual variable and fixed overhead costs were as follows:

Overhead	Budgeted costs (€)	Actual costs (€)
Variable	14,000	12,000
Fixed	28,000	26,000

Calculate the application rates for variable and fixed overhead, the amount of variable and fixed overhead applied, the variable overhead spending and efficiency variances, and the fixed overhead budget and volume variances.

NP 12.7 Budgeted, standard and actual machine hours LO 6

The Turin Engine Plant of Este Italia SpA. manufactures engine blocks for automobiles. The firm produces three types of engine blocks, three, four and six-cylinder. An engine block is the basic component of an automobile engine and contains the cylinders into which the pistons are fitted. After assembling the block with the head, pan, pistons, spark plugs, rods, camshaft and valves, the motor is ready to be fitted with the fuel and exhaust systems and installed in the automobile. The engine block is cast from a single block of steel. The cylinders are bored by high-precision, computer-controlled machine tools. Then other machine tools tap and thread the block to attach the other engine components. The cylinder-boring department is the key process after the engine block is cast.

Overhead is tracked to departments. The allocation base in the cylinder-boring department is machine hours, or the number of hours each block spends in the computer-controlled machine tool having its cylinders bored. Each of the three motor blocks requires the following standard machine hours per block:

3-cylinder blocks	0.50 machine hours
4-cylinder blocks	0.70 machine hours
6-cylinder blocks	0.90 machine hours

Each block requires some set-up time to mount and correctly position the block in the computer-controlled machine tool. Hence, a six-cylinder block does not require twice the machining time of a three-cylinder block. Also, a cylinder in a three-cylinder block is larger and requires more boring time than does a cylinder in a four- or six-cylinder block.

At the beginning of the year, management forecasts the number of blocks to be manufactured based on the projected unit sales of car models requiring three-, four- and six-cylinder engines. The plant plans to produce 95,000 engine blocks using 67,500 machine hours. The expected production by block type and the standard machine hours per block are given in the following table.

Calculation of expected usage of machine hours
Turin Engine Plant's Cylinder-Boring Department

Product	Expected production	Standard machine hours per block
3-cylinder blocks	25,000	0.50
4-cylinder blocks	40,000	0.70
6-cylinder blocks	30,000	0.90
Expected machine hours	95,000	

During the year, production plans change as customer preferences become known. An unexpected increase in petrol taxes causes consumers to shift toward smaller, more fuel-efficient automobiles with smaller engines. Fewer six-cylinder engines are made and more three- and four-cylinder engines are manufactured. The following table presents the actual operating results for the year.

Calculation of actual and standard machine hours
Turin Engine Plant's Cylinder-Boring Department

Product	Actual blocks produced	Actual machine hours
3-cylinder	27,000	14,200
4-cylinder	41,000	29,000
6-cylinder	28,000	25,000
	96,000	68,200

What are the budgeted, standard, and actual machine hours?

NP 12.8 Expected, standard, and actual volume and volume variance LO 6, Appendix

Printers plc manufactures and sells a mid-volume colour printer (MC) and a high-volume colour printer (HC). MCs require 100 direct labour hours to manufacture each printer and HCs require 150 direct labour hours. At the beginning of the year, the production schedule includes 700 MCs and 500 HCs. At the end of the year, 720 MCs and 510 HCs were produced. In producing MCs, 1,400 hours too many were used and 3,000 hours less than standard were used to manufacture HCs. The flexible overhead budget is £2.9 million of fixed costs and £10 per direct labour hour.

Calculate
a Expected volume.
b Standard volume.
c Actual volume.
d Overhead rate.
e Fixed overhead volume variance and discuss its meaning.

NP 12.9 Direct variances LO 3, 4

ColdKing is a small producer of fruit-flavoured frozen desserts. For many years, ColdKing's products have had strong national sales on the basis of brand recognition. However, other companies have begun marketing similar products, and price competition has become increasingly aggressive. Sara Evans, the company's controller, is planning to implement a standard cost system for ColdKing. She has gathered considerable information from her co-workers on production and materials requirements for ColdKing's products. Sara believes that the use of standard costing will allow ColdKing to improve cost control and make better pricing decisions.

ColdKing's most popular product is frozen raspberry mousse. The mousse is produced in 40-litre batches, and each batch requires six litres of good raspberries. The fresh raspberries are sorted by hand before entering the production process. Due to imperfections in the raspberries and normal spoilage, 1 litre of berries is discarded for every 4 litres of acceptable berries. Three minutes is the standard direct labour time for sorting that is required to obtain 1 litre of acceptable raspberries. The acceptable raspberries then are blended with the other ingredients. Blending requires 12 minutes of direct labour time per batch. After blending, the frozen mousse is packaged in 1-litre containers. Sara has gathered the following pricing information:

- ColdKing purchases raspberries at a cost of £0.80 per litre. All other ingredients cost a total of £4.50 per 40-litre batch.
- Direct labour is paid at the rate of £9.00 per hour.
- The total cost of material and labour required to package the mousse is £0.38 per litre.

a Develop the standard cost for the direct cost components of a 40-litre batch of frozen raspberry mousse. The standard cost should identify the following for each direct cost component of a batch of frozen raspberry mousse.
  - Standard quantity.
  - Standard rate.
  - Standard cost per batch.

b As part of the implementation of a standard cost system at ColdKing, Sara plans to train those responsible for maintaining the standards in the use of variance analysis. She is particularly concerned with the causes of adverse variances.
  i Discuss the possible causes of adverse materials price variances and identify the individual(s) who should be held responsible for these variances.
  ii Discuss the possible causes of adverse labour efficiency variances and identify the individual(s) who should be held responsible for these variances.

(CMA adapted)

NP 12.10 Overhead variances LO 6, Appendix

Turow Trailers assembles horse trailers. Two models, G7 and V8, are manufactured. While labour intensive, the production process is not very complicated. The single plant produces all the trailers. Forty-eight work teams of two or three workers assemble entire trailers; 16 supervisors oversee the work teams. Material handlers deliver all the parts needed for each trailer to the work team. Human resources, accounting, inspection, purchasing, and tools are the other major overhead departments. Some operating statistics for 2007 and 2008 follow:

	2007	2008
Expected denominator volume (direct labour hours)	1 million	1 million
Flexible budget:		
Fixed overhead	£2.1 million	£2.2 million
Variable overhead per direct labour hour	£7	£8
Units produced:		
G7	11,000	8,000
V8	12,000	6,000
Standard direct labour hours per unit of:		
G7	40	40
V8	50	50
Actual overhead incurred	£9.0 million	£8.1 million
Actual direct labour hours	1 million	0.7 million

a Calculate all the overhead variances for both 2007 and 2008.

b Discuss who in the plant should be held responsible for each of the overhead variances.

NP 12.11 Direct materials variances LO 3

A pharmaceutical firm plans to make a new drug. The drug requires 4.5 grams of compound AN7-X1 per batch of 250 tablets. AN7-X1 has a standard price of €2 per gram. An initial inventory of 8,000 grams of AN7-X1 is purchased for €17,200. The firm produces 1,000 batches of the new drug and use 4,600 grams of AN7-X1. All variances are calculated as soon as possible.

Calculate the price and quantity variances for AN7-X1.

NP 12.12 Direct labour variances LO 3

Software Associates (SA) is a computer software consulting firm that specializes in designing and implementing integrated marketing database warehousing programs. Humboldt Catalogue is a client. In preparing its bid for Humboldt, SA estimates its total labour cost for this project to be £222,500 broken down as follows:

	Budgeted hours	Budgeted wage (£)	Budgeted cost (£)
Partner	100	175	17,500
Associate	300	120	36,000
Senior analyst	600	90	54,000
Analyst	1,000	40	40,000
Programmer	3,000	25	75,000
Total			222,500

After the completion of the Humboldt contract, the following data are reported:

	Actual hours	Actual cost (£)
Partner	90	15,750
Associate	280	35,000
Senior analyst	750	63,750
Analyst	1,400	49,000
Programmer	3,600	82,800
Total		246,300

a Prepare a performance report (variance analysis) for the Humboldt Catalogue project.

b Analyse the variances and provide a plausible explanation for SA's performance on the Humboldt project.

NP 12.13 Direct labour variances LO 3

Centre Hospitalier is a large hospital system in the French department of Gironde that offers both hospitalization (inpatient) and clinic (out-patient) services. It has a centralized admissions office that admits and registers patients, some of whom are seeking in-patient hospital services and others out-patient clinic services. Centre Hospitalier uses a standard cost system to control its labour costs. The standard labour time to admit an in-patient is 15 minutes. Out-patient admissions have a standard labour time of 9 minutes. The standard labour rate for admissions agents is €14.50 per hour. During the last week, the admissions office admitted 820 in-patients and 2,210 out-patients. Actual hours worked by the admissions agents last week were 540 hours and their total wages paid were €8,235.

a Prepare a financial report that summarizes the operating performance (including the efficiency) of the admissions office for last week.

b Based on the financial report you prepared in part (a), write a short memo summarizing your findings and conclusions from this report.

NP 12.14 Overhead variances LO 6, Appendix

The milling department uses standard machine hours to allocate overhead to products. Budgeted volume for the year was 36,000 machine hours. A flexible budget is used to set the overhead rate. Fixed overhead is budgeted to be £720,000 and variable overhead is estimated to be £10 per machine hour.

During the year, two products are milled. The following table summarizes operations:

	Product 1	Product 2
Units milled	10,500	12,000
Standard machine hours per unit	2	1
Actual machine hours used	23,000	13,000

Actual overhead incurred during the year was £1.1 million of which £750,000 was fixed and the remainder variable. Calculate all the relevant overhead variances for the department. Write a memo that describes what each one means.

NP 12.15 Overhead variance and capacity LO 6

You work in the Strategy Analysis department of On-Call, a world-wide digital-paging firm offering satellite-based digital communications through sophisticated personal digital assistants (PDAs). On-Call is analysing the possibility of acquiring AtlantiCom, a competitor located in the Republic of Ireland.

AtlantiCom's latest quarterly report disclosed a total overhead variance (under-absorbed overhead) of €1.3 million. The engineering staff of On-Call, familiar with AtlantiCom's network, estimates that AtlantiCom has quarterly overhead costs of €6.5 million that can deliver 800,000 message-packets per quarter. A message packet is the industry standard of delivering a fixed amount of digital information within a given time period.

In valuing AtlantiCom, senior management at On-Call wants to know whether AtlantiCom has excess capacity, and, if so, how much.

As a percentage of AtlantiCom's current capacity of 800,000 message packets, estimate AtlantiCom's over- or under-capacity last quarter.

NP 12.16 Variance calculations LO 3, 4, 6, Appendix

Betterton Corporation manufactures automobile headlamp lenses and uses a standard cost system. At the beginning of the year, the following standards were established per 100 lenses (a single batch):

	Input	Amount (£)
Direct material	100 kilograms @ £2.00 per kg	200
Direct labour	5 hours @ £18 per hr	90
Factory overhead:		
Fixed overhead	£4 per direct labour hour	20
Variable overhead	£6 per direct labour hour	30
Total cost per batch of		
100 headlamp lenses		340

Expected volume per month is 5,000 direct labour hours for January and 105,000 headlamp lenses were produced. There were no beginning inventories. The following costs were incurred in January:

		£
Fixed factory overhead		39,000
Variable factory overhead		20,000
Direct labour	5,400 hours	99,900
Direct material used	102,000 kg	
Direct material purchased	110,000 kg	209,000

a Calculate the following variances:
  i Variable overhead spending variance
  ii Fixed overhead volume variance
  iii Fixed overhead budget variance
  iv Variable overhead efficiency variance
  v Direct labour rate variance
  vi Direct materials price variance at purchase
  vii Direct labour efficiency variance
  viii Direct materials quantity variance.
b Discuss how the direct materials price variance computed at purchase differs from the direct materials price variance computed at use. Outline the advantages and disadvantages of each method.

NP 12.17 Fixed overhead volume variance LO 6, Appendix

Shady Tree produces two products, M1s and M2s. It has no beginning inventories or ending work-in-process inventories of either M1s or M2s. A single plant-wide overhead rate is used to allocate overhead to products using standard direct labour hours. This overhead rate is set at the beginning of the year based on the following flexible budget: fixed factory overhead is forecast to be £3 million and variable overhead is projected to be £20 per direct labour hour. Management expects plant volume to be 200,000 standard direct labour hours. The following are the standard direct labour hours for each product:

Shady Tree Manufacturing
Direct labour standards per product

	M1	M2
Standard direct labour hours per unit	3	5

The variable overhead variances and fixed overhead budget variance for the year were zero. The following table summarizes operations for the year:

Shady Tree Manufacturing
Summary of operations for the year

	M1	M2
Units produced	30,000	12,000
Units sold	20,000	10,000

a Calculate the plant-wide overhead rate computed at the beginning of the year.

b Calculate the fixed overhead volume variance for the year.

c What is the monetary impact on accounting earnings, if the fixed overhead volume variance is written off to the cost of goods sold account?

d What is the monetary impact on accounting earnings of prorating the fixed overhead volume variance to inventories and cost of goods sold compared to writing it off to cost of sales?

e Suppose that *at the beginning of the year,* management at Shady Tree Manufacturing wants to increase accounting earnings in a particular year, *without changing production or sales levels.* Describe how it might do this (assuming its external auditors would allow such action). Use the facts presented above to illustrate your answer.

NP 12.18 Variances and absorption and variable costing LO 3, 4, 6, Appendix

Mopart Division produces a single product. Its standard cost system assigns indirect costs on the basis of standard direct labour hours. At the expected volume of 4,000 direct labour hours, the standard cost per unit is as follows:

	(€)
Selling price	38.00
Direct materials, 3 kg @ €5 per kg	15.00
Direct labour, 0.4 hr @ €20 per hr	8.00
Variable indirect costs, 0.4 hr @ €6 per hr	2.40
Fixed indirect costs, 0.4 hr @ €4 per hr	1.60
Total	27.00

For the month of March, the following actual data were reported:

Units produced	9,000
Number of direct labour hours	3,800
Actual labour rate	€20.50
Direct materials used (kg)	28,000
Average price of materials used	€5.50
Average selling price	€38.75
Number of units sold	8,800
Variable indirect costs	€21,500
Fixed indirect costs	€15,800
Variable selling and administrative costs	€34,500
Fixed selling and administrative costs	€28,000

There was no beginning inventory.

a Analyse the results of operations for the month of March. Support your analysis with both reasoned arguments and data. Exposition and easy-to-follow tables are important.

b Present two profit and loss statements in good format using absorption costing and variable costing net profit.

c Reconcile any difference in net profit between the two statements.

d What is the opportunity cost of the unused normal capacity?

NP 12.19 Variance calculations LO 3, 4, 6, Appendix

Anpax, Inc. manufactures two products, L7 and Q2. Overhead is allocated to products based on machine hours. Management uses a flexible budget to forecast overhead. For the current year, fixed factory overhead is projected to be £2.75 million and variable factory overhead is budgeted at £20 per machine hour. At the beginning of the year, management developed the following standards for each product and made the following production forecasts for the year:

Anpax, Inc.
Current Year Standards and
Production Forecasts

	Products	
	L7	*Q2*
Budgeted number of units produced	25,000	35,000
Production standards:		
Direct labour per unit	10 hours @ £15 per hr	12 hours @ £15 per hr
Direct materials per unit	85 kg @ £1 per kg	95 kg @ £1 per kg
Machine hours per unit	4 hrs	5 hrs

There were no beginning or ending inventories. Actual production for the year was 20,000 units of L7 and 40,000 units of Q2. Other data summarizing actual operations for the year are given below:

Direct labour	700,000 hrs	£9.8 m
Direct materials	5.0 m kg	£5.5 m
Machine hours	270,000 hrs	
Fixed overhead	£3.4 m	
Variable overhead	£5 m	

a Calculate the overhead rate for the current year.

b Calculate materials and labour variances. Report only quantity (efficiency) variances and price (rate) variances.

c Calculate the overhead variances.

d Your boss (a non-accountant) asks you to explain in non-technical terms the meaning of each overhead variance.

Analysis and interpretation problems

AIP 12.1 Criticism of standard costs LO 1, 2

Critically evaluate the following quotation:

'The simple standard cost model of materials, labour, and allocated overhead, however, used for nearly a century, is at its heart like the economist's cost curve, based on a single product cost model. The standard cost model, developed 100 years ago, was probably the right engineering design at the time, given the low percentage of overhead, relative to direct labour and materials, the limited diversity in most firms, and the high cost of information collection and processing. By the end of the 20th century, however, this same model represented a bad engineering tradeoff. Information collection and processing costs were much lower (thanks to Moore's Law) and the simple standard cost model no longer represented well contemporary companies' cost structure in the presence of high product variety, process complexity, and customer proliferation.'

Source: Robert S. Kaplan (2006) 'The Competitive Advantage of Management Accounting', *Journal of Management Accounting Research*, Vol. 18, p. 130.

AIP 12.2 Labour efficiency ratio LO 2, 5

A number of companies use the following ratio to measure operating efficiency:

$$\frac{\text{Earned direct labour cost}}{\text{Actual direct labour cost}}$$

Earned direct labour cost is the number of units produced times the standard direct labour cost per hour. For example, the machine department produced the following four jobs today:

Job #	Number of units produced	Standard labour cost per unit (£)	Earned direct labour cost (£)
101	100	3	300
102	200	2	400
103	150	1	150
104	100	2	200
Total earned direct labour cost			1,050

Actual direct labour cost for today is £1,350.

$$\frac{\text{Earned direct labour cost}}{\text{Actual direct labour cost}} = \frac{1,050}{1,350} = 0.777$$

The higher the ratio, the more output per actual unit of direct labour cost (£ in this example). Operating managers are rewarded for high values of this ratio. Discuss the advantages and disadvantages of using this ratio to measure and reward performance of factory management.

AIP 12.3 Setting standard costs LO 2

Associated Media Graphics (AMG) is a rapidly expanding company involved in the mass reproduction of instructional materials. AMG is organized into a number of production departments responsible for a particular stage of the production process, such as copy-editing, typesetting, printing and binding. Ralph Davis, owner and manager of AMG, has made a concentrated effort to provide a quality product at a competitive price with delivery on the promised due date. Expanding sales have been attributed to this philosophy. Davis is finding it increasingly difficult to supervise personally the operations of AMG and is beginning to institute an organizational structure that would facilitate management control.

One change recently made was the designation of operating departments as cost centres, with control over departmental operations transferred from Davis to each departmental manager. However, quality control still reports directly to Davis, as do the finance and accounting functions. A materials manager was hired to purchase all raw materials and to oversee the inventory handling (receiving, storage, etc.) and record-keeping functions. The materials manager is also responsible for maintaining an adequate inventory based upon planned production levels.

The loss of personal control over the operations of AMG caused Ralph to look for a method of efficiently evaluating performance. Dana Cress, a new management accountant, proposed the use of a standard cost system. Variances for material, labour and manufacturing overhead then could be calculated and reported directly to Ralph.

a Assume that Associated Media Graphics (AMG) is going to implement a standard cost system and establish standards for materials, labour and manufacturing overhead. Identify and discuss for each of the following cost components:
  i Who should be involved in setting the standards.
  ii The factors that should be considered in establishing the standards.
b Describe the basis for assignment of responsibility under a standard cost system.

AIP 12.4 Standard overhead rates LO 6, Appendix

Spectra plc produces 42-inch, plasma screens with the following cost structure:

Direct materials	£220
Direct labour	£150

Due to the rapidly-changing market for plasma screens, standard costs, overhead rates and prices are revised quarterly. While the direct labour component of standard cost has been relatively constant over time, direct material costs, especially the cost of the circuit boards, fluctuate widely. Therefore, for pricing purposes, management reviews costs each quarter and forecasts next quarter's costs using the current quarter's cost structure. It also uses this method for revising overhead costs each quarter. Overhead is applied to product using direct labour cost. Fixed overhead is incurred fairly uniformly over the year. The overhead rate next quarter is the ratio of actual overhead costs incurred this quarter divided by this quarter's direct labour cost. Data for the last six quarters follow:

	2007				2008		
	Q1	Q2	Q3	Q4	Q1	Q2	Q3
Actual unit sales	200	200	190	180	190	250	
Total direct (£) Labour	30,000	30,000	28,500	27,000	28,500	37,500	
Actual overhead (£)	101,000	102,000	98,000	95,000	97,000	118,000	
Overhead rate (£)	3.35	3.37	3.40	3.43	3.52	3.40	3.15

The chairman of the company, responding to the auditor's suggestion that it set its projected costs on an annual basis, replied: 'Annual budgeting is fine for more static companies like automobiles. But the home entertainment industry, especially peripherals, changes day by day. We have to be ahead of our competitors in terms of revising our product price in response to cost changes. If we waited eight months to react, we'd be out of business.'

Do you agree with the chairman or the auditor? Critically evaluate Spectra's costing system. What changes would you suggest, and how would you justify them to the chairman?

AIP 12.5 Overhead variances LO 2, 6, Appendix

Europa Sugar processes sugar beets into granulated sugar that is sold to food companies. It uses a standard cost system to aid in the control of costs and for performance evaluation. To compute the standards for next year, the actual expense incurred by expense category is divided by the number of tonnes of sugar beets processed to arrive at a standard cost per tonne. These per-tonne standards then are increased by the expected amount of inflation forecast for that expense category. This year, Europa Sugar processed 6.3 million tonnes of beets. The calculation of next year's standard costs is as follows:

Western Sugar
Standard costs
for next year (€000)

	This year's cost (€)	Cost per tonne (€)	Inflation adjustment (%)	Standard cost per tonne (€)
Direct labour	33,000	0.524	4	0.544
Sugar beets	58,000	0.921	3.5	0.953
Variable overhead	24,000	0.381	5	0.400
Fixed overhead	43,000	0.683	2	0.696
Total	158,000	2.509		2.593

Next year, actual production is 6.8 million tonnes. At the end of next year, the following report is prepared:

Western Sugar
Actual results compared to standard
next year (€000)

	Actual cost (€)	Standard cost per tonne (€)	Standard cost (€)	Variance (€)
Direct labour	38,100	0.544	36,992	1,108A
Sugar beets	64,829	0.953	64,804	25A
Variable overhead	28,211	0.400	27,200	1,011A
Fixed overhead	45,227	0.696	47,328	2,101F
Total	176,367	2.593	176,324	43A

Senior management was not surprised at the small variances for labour and sugar beets. The processing plant has good operating controls and there had been no surprises in the sugar beet market or in the labour market. Its initial forecasts proved to be good. Management was delighted to see the favourable total overhead variance (€1,090F = €1,011A + €2,101F). Although variable overhead was over budget, fixed overhead was below budget and more than offset the over-budget variable overhead. No major change had taken place in the plant's production technology to explain this shift (such as increased automation). Therefore, senior management was prepared to attribute the favourable total overhead variance to better internal control by the plant manager.

a What do you think is the reason for the overhead variances?
b Is it appropriate to base next year's standards on last year's costs?

Extended **analysis** and **interpretation** problems

AIP 12.6 Volume measures

The gear-cutting department of Universal Transmissions cuts the teeth into gears. These gears then are finished in other departments and assembled into farm and construction equipment transmissions (tractors, combines, bulldozers). The department contains three identical cutting machines that were purchased two years ago. Each machine is expected to be used 2,400 hours a year. The production budget for the year is as follows:

Gear-Cutting Department
Budgeted production for
1 January 2008 to 31 December 2008

Gear type	Budgeted production (No. of gears)	Standard minutes/gear	Budgeted minutes
A7474	965	36	34,740
B7682	290	21	6,090
C4983	993	24	23,832
D7575	514	44	22,616
F8390	733	39	28,587
H6363	547	54	29,538
H8983	989	32	31,648
J3839	354	33	11,682
K9828	546	52	28,392
L2738	922	48	44,256
L7378	494	26	12,844
L9383	313	11	3,443
M7483	199	52	10,348
M8992	950	50	47,500
Q2839	423	52	21,996
R093	588	37	21,756
S2829	719	45	32,355
S2882	488	25	12,200
T8390	373	57	21,261
U1920	185	34	6,290
Y7382	647	37	23,939
Total			475,313

The operating budget for the Gear-Cutting Department for 2008 is as follows:

Gear-Cutting Department
operating budget for
1 January 2008 to 31 December 2008

	Fixed costs (£)	Variable costs/ machine hour (£)
Cutting oil		3.21
Depreciation	632,000	
Engineering	232,890	
Maintenance	69,840	4.56
Operators	25,400	36.34
Plant overhead	124,400	1.20
Utilities	26,800	2.21
Total	1,111,330	47.52

Costs in the Gear-Cutting Department are assigned to gears based on standard gear-cutting machine minutes. At the beginning of the year, the cost per minute on the gear-cutting machines is set by dividing budgeted costs in the department (budgeted fixed costs plus budgeted variable costs per machine minute times projected minutes for the year) by projected minutes for the year. The following table summarizes actual operations by gear type:

Gear-Cutting Department
Summary of operations for
1 January 2008 to 31 December 2008

Gear	Actual production	Standard minutes/gear	Standard minutes of volume	Actual minutes of volume	% variance actual from standard
A7474	1,041	36	37,476	41,528	11
B7682	304	21	6,384	6,160	−4
C4983	937	24	22,488	24,671	10
D7575	543	44	23,892	26,359	10
F8390	724	39	28,236	29,546	5
H6363	544	54	29,376	26,970	−8
H8983	958	32	30,656	29,631	−3
J3839	331	33	10,923	10,142	−7
K9828	596	52	30,992	28,823	−7
L2738	1,007	48	48,336	49,494	2
L7378	536	26	13,936	14,484	4
L9383	335	11	3,685	3,936	7
M7483	208	52	10,816	10,657	−1
M8992	1,020	50	51,000	55,543	9
Q2839	462	52	24,024	23,125	−4
R093	603	37	22,311	22,761	2
S2829	675	45	30,375	28,110	−7
S2882	447	25	11,175	12,371	11
T8390	351	57	20,007	19,989	0
U1920	191	34	6,494	6,332	−2
Y7382	585	37	21,645	20,167	−7
Total			484,227	490,799	

a Identify the various measures of volume (e.g. actual volume) that can be used in the Gear-Cutting Department for 2008. For each volume measure identified, provide the 2008 empirical magnitude.

b Calculate the cost per minute in the Gear-Cutting Department for 2008.

c An outside company offers to provide gear cutting for gear A7474 for £63 per gear. This price includes pick-up and delivery, and it guarantees the same quality and timeliness of delivery as the Gear-Cutting Department does. Analyse the outside offer and make a recommendation as to whether or not the offer should be accepted. Be sure to identify any assumptions underlying your recommendation.

AIP 12.7 Direct material variance analysis

Maidwell Company manufactures washers and dryers on a single assembly line in its main manufacturing plant. The market has deteriorated over the last five years and competition has made cost control very important. Management has been concerned about the materials cost of both washers and dryers. No model changes have been made in the past two years and economic conditions have allowed the company to negotiate price reductions for many key parts.

Maidwell uses a standard cost system in accounting for materials. Purchases are charged to inventory at a standard price, and purchase discounts are considered an administrative cost reduction. Production is charged at the standard price of the materials used. Thus, the price variance is isolated at time of purchase as the difference between gross contract price and standard price multiplied by the quantity purchased. When a substitute part is used in production rather than the regular part, a price variance equal to the difference in the standard prices of the materials is recognized at the time of substitution in the production process. The quantity variance is the actual quantity used compared to the standard quantity allowed with the difference multiplied by the standard price.

The materials variances for several of the parts that Maidwell uses are adverse. Part No. 4121 is one of the items that have an adverse variance. Maidwell knows that some of these parts are defective and will fail. The failure is discovered during production. The normal defective rate is 5 per cent of normal input. The original contract price of this part was

£0.285 per unit; thus, Maidwell set the standard unit price at £0.285. The unit contract purchase price of Part No. 4121 was increased £0.04 to £0.325 from the original £0.285 due to a parts-specification change. Maidwell chose not to change the standard but treated the increase in price as a price variance. In addition, the contract terms were changed from payment due in 30 days to a 4 per cent discount if paid in 10 days or full payment due in 30 days. These new contractual terms were the consequence of negotiations resulting from changes in the economy.

Data regarding the usage of Part No. 4121 during December are as follows:

- Purchases of Part No. 4121   150,000 units
- Unit price paid for purchases of Part No. 4121   £0.325
- Requisitions of Part No. 4121 from stores for use in products   134,000 units
- Substitution of Part No. 5125 for Part No. 4121 to use obsolete stock   24,000 units
  (standard unit price of Part No. 5125 is £0.35)
- Units of Part No. 4121 and its substitute (Part No. 5125)   9,665 units
  identified as being defective
- Standard allowed usage (including normal defective units) of   153,300 units
  Part No. 4121 and its substitute based upon output for the month

Maidwell's material variances related to Part No. 4121 for December were reported as follows:

	£
Price variance	7,560.00 Adverse
Quantity variance	1,339.50 Adverse
Total materials variances for Part No. 4121	8,899.50 Adverse

Rob Speck, the Purchasing Director, claims the adverse price variance is misleading. Rob says that his department has worked hard to obtain price concessions and purchase discounts from suppliers. In addition, he has indicated that engineering changes have been made in several parts increasing their price, even though the part identification has not changed. These price increases are not his department's responsibility. Rob declares that price variances no longer measure the Purchasing Department's performance.

Gillian Buddle, the Manufacturing Manager, thinks the responsibility for the quantity variance should be shared. Gillian states that manufacturing cannot control quality associated with less expensive parts, substitutions of material to use up otherwise obsolete stock, or engineering changes that increase the quantity of materials used.

The Accounting Manager, Martha Kohl, has suggested that the computation of variances be changed to identify variations from standard with the causes and functional areas responsible for the variances. Martha recommends the following system of materials variances and the method of computation for each:

Variance	Method of calculation
Economic variance	Quantity purchased times the changes made after setting standards. Standards are the result of negotiations based on changes in the general economy.
Engineering change variance	Quantity purchased times change in price due to part specification changes.
Purchase price variance	Quantity purchased times change in contract price due to changes other than parts specifications or the general economy.
Substitutions variance	Quantity substituted times the difference in standard price between parts substituted.
Excess usage variance	Standard price times the difference between the standard quantity allowed for production minus actual parts used (reduced for abnormal scrap).
Abnormal failure rate variance	Abnormal scrap times standard price.

a Discuss the appropriateness of Maidwell Company's current method of variance analysis for materials. Indicate whether the claims of Rob Speck and Gillian Buddle are valid.

b Compute the materials variances for Part No. 4121 for December using the system recommended by Martha Kohl.

c Indicate who would be responsible for each of the variances in Martha's system of variance analysis.

(CMA adapted)

CHAPTER THIRTEEN

Investment decisions
(Planning)

Learning objectives

1. Describe the steps of the capital-budgeting process.

2. Identify the opportunity cost of capital.

3. Estimate the payback period of an investment and identify weaknesses of the payback method in making investment choices.

4. Calculate the accounting rate of return (ROI) and identify its weaknesses in making investment choices.

5. Calculate the net present value (NPV) of cash flows.

6. Identify non-cash profit and loss accounts that should be excluded in calculating the net present value.

7. Adjust cash flows to reflect the additional accounts receivable and inventory required.

8. Exclude financing charges when calculating the net present value of an investment.

9. Estimate tax cash flows for capital budgeting.

10. Recognize the effect of risk on the discount rate.

11. Estimate the internal rate of return (IRR) of an investment project.

12. Identify problems with using the IRR to evaluate investment projects.

13. Use annuity tables to relate present and future values. (Appendix)

Vij's Bakery and Tea Room

Vij owns a small bakery in the centre of town. Besides his popular cakes and pastries, Vij serves a wide range of specialty teas. While his business has been profitable, Vij is concerned that many of his customers are being lured to trendy establishments, especially those that offer Italian pastries, espresso, cappuccino and caffè latte. His baked goods easily match those offered

by competitors but he thinks that investing in an Italian coffee machine might encourage new customers to frequent his business and forestall the departure of existing clients. Plenty of space exists to install the machine and the additional business could be very profitable. Vij visits a restaurant supply service and learns that an Italian coffee machine costs £10,000. The machine would last for five years. Vij could pay cash for the machine but decides to borrow the amount from his bank at 8 per cent interest.

To determine whether the Italian coffee machine would be profitable, Vij estimates the impact of the machine on his reported profit for each of the next five years:

	£
Revenues from selling specialty coffee beverages	5,000
Cost of ingredients	(1,500)
Additional utility costs	(500)
Interest expense (0.08 × £10,000)	(800)
Straight-line depreciation on machine (£10,000 ÷ 5)	(2,000)
Profit per year	£200

Although these estimates indicate that the machine will generate a profit, Vij is not sure that he has included everything in his calculations.

LONG-TERM INVESTMENT DECISIONS

Chapters 2 to 5 describe different planning decisions and how management accounting facilitates those planning decisions. Those decisions tend to have short-term implications. In other words, the cash flow is received or paid within a year of the decision. Long-term investment decisions tend to differ from short-term ones in two ways: (1) the long-term investment decision usually involves a larger cash outlay and has greater implications on the organization's strategy, and (2) the long-term investment decision has cash-flow implications for many years.

The size and strategic implications of a long-term investment decision make those decisions much more critical to the organization. Therefore, organizations carefully control the decision process for these investments. We describe the control aspects of the long-term investment decision in the next section.

The multi-year, cash-flow implications of a long-term investment decision introduce additional complications in comparing the decision's costs and benefits. Cash flows received or paid in different years are not directly comparable. The remainder of this chapter and the Appendix to this chapter describe procedures to adjust the costs and benefits from different time periods to make them comparable.

■ The capital-budgeting process

Capital budgeting is a process of evaluating and choosing long-term investments. Given the size of long-term investments, the organization should take special care in making these decisions. Typically, the capital-budgeting process includes: (1) initiation or identification of the investment proposal, (2) ratification, (3) implementation and (4) monitoring. These are the same decision-making steps described in Chapter 6. While we describe this process for one investment opportunity, organizations frequently make these decisions in conjunction with others which compete for organizational resources. Several capital-budgeting projects may be evaluated in parallel; each project might have different time horizons, costs, risks and trade-offs. Therefore, the capital-budgeting process is not only a technical one but includes consideration of the investment's fit with the organization's strategic focus in the short and long term.[1]

The initiation process begins with the identification of possible investment opportunities. Different members of the organization can make proposals, but usually individuals with the most information initiate investment proposals. These proposals include a description of the investment opportunity and the predicted effect of the investment on cash flows. Large investment proposals often include the predicted impact on the balance sheet and profit and loss statement. Initiation is a planning process.

Once the proposal has been developed, a ratification process begins. For control purposes, different individuals in the organization are likely responsible for determining which investment proposals to accept. The parties responsible for ratifying a long-term investment proposal verify the accuracy of the cash-flow estimates. They also analyse the risk of the proposal. The long-term investment proposal often involves a substantial amount of cash; therefore, the organization's economic viability may be at risk.

---

[1] Tim Baldenius, Sunil Dutta and Stefan Reichelstein (2007) 'Cost Allocation for Capital Budgeting Decisions', *The Accounting Review*, Vol. 82, No. 4 (July), pp. 837–867; Peter Miller and Ted O'Leary (2007) 'Mediating instruments and making markets: Capital budgeting, science and the economy', *Accounting, Organizations and Society,* Vol. 32, Issues 7–8, pp. 701–734.

The parties responsible for ratification also should examine competitor reaction to the proposal. Initiators of long-term investment proposals often do not identify competitor reactions and assume that competitors will not change their behaviour. In competitive markets, profitable projects are not easily found. Any investment project that appears profitable will soon have many competitors, which will drive down future cash inflows. Therefore, the effect of competition should be recognized in estimating future cash flows. Firms must have some competitive edge, such as low-cost manufacturing, excellent researchers or quality customer service, to be able to consistently find profitable investment projects. When analysing investment projects, it is important to understand the source of the expected profits.

The final aspect of ratification is to be certain that the investment is consistent with the strategic goals of the organization. An investment proposal may appear to be profitable, but could shift the organization's emphasis away from its primary purpose. Ratification is a control process.

If the investment proposal is ratified, implementation follows. Cash and other resources are invested and operations related to the investment begin. Implementation is a planning process.

During and subsequent to the implementation stage, monitoring of the investment project occurs. The monitoring process determines whether the investment proposal is meeting expectations. If it is not, the investment project may be closed down before the planned termination. Once the investment project is completed, an audit of the project is undertaken to evaluate the performance of the project's managers and to determine appropriate adjustments to the capital-budgeting process in the future. Monitoring is a control process.

In general, all organizations follow these steps in the capital-budgeting process with some minor variations. As we discuss later, small firms often adapt the process if they have limited resources or expertise in capital-budgeting techniques.

In divisionalized firms, capital-budgeting decisions may create positive and negative externalities. Firms have limited investment budgets and need to co-ordinate decisions across multiple stakeholders and assess the impact of an investment in one division on other parts of the organization. As seen in Chapter 8, budgeting can be a political process. Capital budgeting displays similar characteristics and employs similar mechanisms to motivate divisional managers to transfer knowledge about these decisions to central management. Another organizational challenge of capital budgeting is the need to update decisions and the decision-making framework with new information that alters the life cycle, risks and/or expected return of the investment. These aspects are an important facet of the monitoring process.

Capital budgeting in the public sector tends to overlook the long-term benefits of such spending due to the political nature of these expenditures and the short-term focus of government decision makers. Capital expenditures, such as those related to public welfare, defence and foreign affairs, are not readily measured in financial terms. Governments are not subject to the same market discipline as are firms in the private sector. Additionally, governments often do not have clear policies to distinguish capital spending from operating budgets. The Canadian provincial government of Ontario has developed the *Municipal Capital Budget Handbook*[2] to provide assistance to municipalities in their capital planning. The handbook also includes the following criteria to rank and evaluate projects: health and safety, cost savings or payback,

---

[2] Ministry of Municipal Affairs and Housing (2002) *Municipal Capital Budgeting Handbook* (Toronto: Queen's Printer for Ontario).

whether the project replaces or maintains an existing asset, and the project's link to municipal growth, service enhancement and community-based initiatives. In the US, the General Accounting Office has published guidelines on best practices in capital budgeting to meet the needs of citizens and taxpayers. It provides five general principles that leading organizations should follow to make capital investment decisions: (1) integrating organizational goals into the capital decision-making process, (2) evaluating and selecting capital assets using an investment approach, (3) balancing budgetary control and managerial flexibility when funding capital projects, (4) using project management techniques to optimize project success, and (5) evaluating results and incorporating lessons learned into the decision-making process.[3]

Whether in the public or private sector, management accountants perform many roles in the capital-budgeting process. A management accountant usually helps put the investment proposal together. Project approval teams generally include accounting and finance staff. Once ratified, accountants identify, measure and communicate information to assist the implementation process. Accounting reports also are used in the monitoring process. Management accountants are active participants in all phases of the capital-budgeting process.

■ Opportunity cost of capital

Chapter 2 defined *opportunity cost* as the forgone opportunity of using a resource. The opportunity cost of using a resource depends on its alternative uses. The opportunity cost is the basis for making planning decisions. If one is made better off by an action, in the sense that one is not forgoing a better alternative, the proposed action is preferred.

The Chapter 2 discussion of opportunity cost focused on decisions with short-term implications. The options to use labour or materials are assumed to occur during the same time period. No reason exists, however, to presume that all alternatives will occur in the same time period. One can defer accepting a current job offer and return to school for additional years of study prior to starting a career. The current stock of raw materials can be used in current production or else stored and used next year. In general, all decisions have a time element. At any point in time up to accepting the pending alternative, one always has the option of delaying or forgoing the alternative and continuing to search for better ones.

Many decisions explicitly involve trading off cash inflows and cash outflows over time. For example, the decision to invest in research and development (R&D) involves postponing current cash payments to investors in order to fund R&D. The investment in R&D is expected to lead to higher cash payments to investors in the future (when the R&D projects produce profitable new products). The decision to buy a government savings bond involves trading current consumption for future consumption. In fact, most decisions span several time periods and, therefore, involve cash flows over different time periods.

Opting to attend university and earn a degree involves comparing costs and benefits over time. Instead of working and earning a salary, students pay tuition in anticipation of a higher-paying job in the future than they can obtain now. Students sacrifice current income and make payments on books and tuition to invest in their human capital to earn higher salaries in the future. The sacrifices occur during their university years while the benefits of higher salaries accrue over the remainder of their working

---

[3] United States General Accounting Office (1998) *Leading Practices in Capital Decision-Making* (Washington, DC: GAO/AIMD-99-32, December), p. 19.

No matter the currency – euros, yen, or pounds, organizations around the globe consider the opportunity cost of cash invested in capital projects.

career. The opportunity cost of going to university includes making a full-time salary immediately. The cash flows from the various alternatives occur in different time periods.

Calculating the opportunity cost of alternatives that involve cash flows occurring at different points of time is complicated because a pound today is not equivalent to a pound tomorrow. Time is money! A pound received today can be invested and earn interest, and therefore, is worth more than a pound tomorrow.

The **opportunity cost of capital** is a term used to describe the forgone opportunity of using cash. Like other resources, the opportunity cost of capital depends on whether the cash has another use and whether it is replaceable. Cash always has another use. If no other investments are available, the cash can be used to retire debt or pay dividends to the owners. Cash is also replaceable. Financial markets exist for issuing debt and equity. Therefore, the opportunity cost of capital is the replacement cost of cash or the cost of borrowing or issuing shares. The cost of borrowing money is the interest payment. The cost of issuing share capital is the expected return to shareholders. The opportunity cost of capital is described in terms of a percentage return or interest rate.

Not all organizations can borrow cash at the same interest rate. Organizations that are more risky and less likely to repay the loan must pay a higher interest rate to borrow cash. The same is true with issuing shares. Shareholders of risky firms expect a higher return than do shareholders of less risky ones. The relation between risk and the cost of capital is discussed later in the chapter. In the next few sections, the opportunity cost of capital is provided as an interest rate.

The purpose of recognizing the cost of capital is to make comparisons of cash flows over different periods of time. The ability to compare cash flows over different time spans is extremely important in evaluating investment decisions. The analysis of investment alternatives involving cash flows received or paid over time is called capital budgeting.

The Appendix to this chapter describes how to compare and aggregate cash flows that occur in different time periods. In general, cash now is worth more than cash in the future. The later the cash flows, the lower their present value. To compare cash flows in the future with cash flows in the present, the future cash flows must be discounted. The discount factor for a future cash flow is $(1/(1 + r)^n)$, where r is the opportunity cost of capital and n is the number of periods until the cash flow occurs. Note that the discount factor decreases with the opportunity cost of capital and the number of time periods. For example, if r equals 10 per cent and n equals two years, the discount rate is $(1/(1 + 0.10)^2)$, or 0.826. One pound received in two years is worth 82.6 pence today if the interest rate is 10 per cent. If the opportunity cost of capital is higher, say 12 per cent, and more periods are involved, say four years, the discount rate is $(1/(1 + 0.12)^4)$ or 0.636. One pound received in four years at 12 per cent is only worth 63.6 pence today. The capital-budgeting process should consider the opportunity cost of capital and discount future cash flows for comparison with present cash flows.

The next section describes methods that treat future and present cash flows in the same manner and that do not discount future cash flows.

Concept **review**

1 What are the steps in the capital-budgeting process?

2 How does the opportunity cost of capital affect long-term investment decisions?

Vij's Bakery and Tea Room (continued)

Vij does not have a control problem in deciding to invest in the Italian coffee machine. He is the sole employee and owner and will perform all the steps of the capital-budgeting process. Vij recognizes, however, that he must include the opportunity cost of capital in his decision to invest in the new equipment.

INVESTMENT CRITERIA IGNORING THE OPPORTUNITY COST OF CAPITAL

Some managers find the discounting of future cash flows confusing or difficult. To make investment decisions, they might choose instead to use the payback method or the accounting rate of return on an investment (ROI). This section describes these methods.

■ Payback

A simple method of evaluating projects is the **payback** method. Payback is the number of years or months that it takes for cash flows from an investment to equal the initial investment cost. Suppose that a project's initial investment cost is €200,000 and subsequent yearly cash inflows are €50,000, €100,000, €100,000 and €200,000 after taxes. This project has a payback of two and one-half years. At the end of the second year, the project has returned €150,000 (€50,000 + €100,000). The third year cash flow is €100,000, or €50,000 per six months. Therefore, in two and one-half years, the cash inflows just equal the initial investment of €200,000. Home-improvement firms implicitly use this logic to entice homeowners to update their heating systems, insulation and windows. For example, salespeople often suggest that an investment of £2,000 in a new boiler will translate into yearly savings of £500 for heating costs. Thus, they claim that the project 'pays for itself' in four years. The great advantage of payback is its simplicity. It is easy to compute and to understand. One needs no assumptions about the appropriate opportunity cost of capital for the particular project. Simplicity, however, is also payback's drawback.

Payback ignores the opportunity cost of capital. Two projects with the same payback are viewed as equally attractive, even though all the return might occur in the last year for one project, while it might be spread out evenly over time for the other. For example, suppose two projects each require £300,000 investments. One pays £100,000 for each of three years, while the other pays nothing for two years and £300,000 in the third year. Each has a three-year payback, but the first is more valuable because the £100,000 payments in years one and two can be earning interest.

Payback also ignores all the cash flows beyond the payback period. Thus, it ignores the 'profitability' of the project. Two projects with the same investments and same cash flows per year up to the payback year have the same payback. However, if one investment has no cash flows beyond the payback year and the other investment does, clearly the latter investment is better.

Finally, payback lacks a benchmark for deciding which projects to accept and which to reject. What payback cut-off should the firm use as a criterion for project selection? Is a three-year payback good or bad?

Some managers believe that it is difficult to accurately forecast cash flows beyond three or four years. Thus, little weight should be placed on these cash flows. Payback simply ignores them. One criticism of corporate managers is their short-term orientation; therefore, they are not willing to take risks and to look at long-term payoffs. The exclusive use of payback to evaluate investment projects motivates managers to focus on short-term cash flows and to ignore long-term rewards.

Numerical example 13.1

A £4 million investment in a motel has expected net cash flows (cash inflows less cash outflows) of £1 million in each of the next five years. What is the investment's payback? What does the payback method ignore?

Solution

The investment has a payback of four years, but the payback method ignores the cash flows in the fifth year and the time value of money.

■ Accounting rate of return

Another method for project evaluation is the accounting rate of return, which is also called the **return on investment (ROI)**. The ROI of an investment project is the accounting profit from the investment divided by the cost of the investment.

ROI = Profit/Investment

The ROI formula looks quite simple, but some questions arise about how to measure the numerator and denominator. For example, the choice of different accounting methods will influence the profit measure. Debate exists about including interest and taxes in estimating earnings. In general, interest is not included, but there is less agreement on the treatment of taxes. The investment also can be measured in multiple ways. For example, some companies estimate ROI using only fixed assets as a measure of investment. Other companies include all assets, such as inventories and accounts receivable, as part of the investment base. The investment also can be measured at the beginning or end of the earnings period, or as an average over the investment's life.

The choice of how to measure profit and investment for calculating the ROI should depend on how the ROI is being used. If the ROI is used as a performance measure, the measures of income and investment should reflect controllability. If interest, taxes, current assets, or fixed assets are controllable, they should be included in the ROI calculation. If the ROI is being used to make a capital-budgeting decision, comparisons should be made with the opportunity cost of capital. Interest is part of the opportunity cost of capital; thus, it should be excluded from the income figure. The investment should include all assets because of the forgone opportunity of using the cash invested in the assets for other purposes.

Table 13.1 Average net income, average book value of investment and annual ROI

Year	Net profit (£)	Average book value of investment (£)	ROI (%)
1	900,000	9,000,000	10
2	900,000	7,000,000	13
3	900,000	5,000,000	18
4	900,000	3,000,000	30
5	900,000	1,000,000	90

How to estimate the ROI for an investment with profits over many years is also unclear. An ROI could be measured for each year. For example, suppose a £10,000,000 investment is expected to yield profits of £900,000 for each of the next five years. The straight-line depreciation method is used on the original investment, so the average investment declines each year. Table 13.1 shows the ROI for each year of this investment using the average investment each period.

The ROI increases from 10 per cent the first year to 90 per cent the last year. The investment is not described by a single ROI; therefore, the investment is difficult to compare to other investments.

A multi-period alternative of estimating the ROI of a project is to divide the average annual profit over all the years by the average annual investment in the project, as follows:

$$\text{ROI} = \frac{\text{Average annual profit from the project}}{\text{Average annual investment in the project}}$$

$$= \frac{£900,000}{£5,000,000}$$

$$= 18\%$$

The ROI has the advantage of being easy to calculate once income and investment have been defined. The ROI also relates to the firm's accounting statements with which managers are familiar. The problem with ROI is that its use often can lead to incorrect investment decisions.

Decisions based on ROI are incorrect as they ignore the time value of money. In calculating the ROI, the average annual profit from the project is computed. Profit received today is treated the same as profit received in the future. The fact that these returns are worth different amounts is ignored in computing accounting ROI.

ROI also relies on accounting numbers rather than cash flows. For example, depreciation is often a major component of the profit figure, but depreciation has no cash-flow implications other than its impact on income taxes. The following numerical example indicates how depreciation can influence the measurement of ROI.

Numerical **example** 13.2

An investment of €300,000 generates cash inflows of €150,000 during each of the next three years. The investment is fully depreciated using the straight-line method over the three years. There are no other accrual effects, so the annual net income of the investment is €150,000 − €100,000, or €50,000. The average investment is used as the denominator to calculate the ROI. What is the ROI for each year and what is the multi-year ROI? How would the sum-of-the-years' digits method of depreciation affect the calculation of ROI?

Solution

Using the straight-line depreciation method:

Year	Profit (€)	Average investment (€)	ROI (%)
1	50,000	250,000	20
2	50,000	150,000	33
3	50,000	50,000	100

The multi-year ROI is €50,000/€150,000, or 33 per cent.

The sum-of-the-years digits method results in depreciation of €150,000 in the first year, €100,000 in the second year and €50,000 in the third. Therefore, the ROI for each year is as follows:

Year	Profit (€)	Average investment (€)	ROI (%)
1	0	225,000	0
2	50,000	100,000	50
3	100,000	25,000	400

The average annual profit is €50,000, but the average investment over the three years is €100,000, so the multi-year ROI is €50,000/€100,000, or 50 per cent. Note that accounting methods affect the ROI, making it less desirable.

Concept **review**

1 What are the limitations of using the payback method to evaluate investments?

2 How can a multi-year ROI be calculated?

3 What are the limitations of using ROI to evaluate investments?

Vij's Bakery and Tea Room (continued)

Vij decides to try all the methods of evaluating the investment in the Italian coffee machine. To estimate the payback period, he first must estimate cash flows per year from his proposed investment. His original estimate of £200 of profit per year includes £2,000 of depreciation expense, which does not involve any cash flow (ignoring tax effects). Therefore, the cash flow per year of the £10,000 investment is estimated to be £2,200. The payback period is as follows:

Payback = £10,000/£2,200 per year = 4.55 years

The ROI of the investment is calculated by taking the average investment over the five-year investment period and dividing by the annual profit. The average investment equals £10,000/2, or £5,000. The estimated annual income of £200 includes an £800 interest expense that should be eliminated. The profit before deducting the interest expense is £1,000. Therefore, the ROI for the Italian coffee machine is as follows:

ROI = £1,000/£5,000 = 20%

Vij is not sure how to interpret either of these measures and recognizes that neither method includes the opportunity cost of capital. He decides to continue reading.

THE NET PRESENT VALUE OF CASH FLOWS

Capital-budgeting decisions should consider the opportunity cost of capital. Future cash flows should be discounted when compared with present cash flows. The discounting of future cash flows is accomplished through the following equation:

$$\text{Present value} = [1/(1 + r)^n] \times \text{Future cash flow}$$

where r is the opportunity cost of capital and n is the number of time periods that separate the present and the future cash flow. The opportunity cost of capital reflects the organization's interest rate to borrow money.

Numerical **example** 13.3

Carbon Corporation, which has an opportunity cost of capital of 10 per cent, is considering an investment project that should yield the following cash flows:

Year from now	Cash inflow ($€$)
1	44,000
2	50,000
3	20,000

What is the present value of these cash inflows?

Solution

The present value of the cash inflow is based on the equation: Present value $= [1/(1 + r)^n] \times$ Future cash flow.

Cash inflow ($€$)	Discount factor	Present value ($€$)
44,000	$1/(1 + 0.1)^1 = 0.90909$	40,000
50,000	$1/(1 + 0.1)^2 = 0.82645$	41,322
20,000	$1/(1 + 0.1)^3 = 0.75131$	15,026
Total present value of cash inflows		96,348

The purpose of discounting future cash flows is to compare them with present cash flows. The **net present value (NPV)** of an investment proposal compares all the cash inflows and outflows by discounting them to the present. An investment that has a positive NPV increases organizational value and should be made.

An investment generally involves a cash outflow in the present with subsequent cash inflows. The initial investment outflow is already in present value; therefore, no need exists to discount the outflow. The present outflow can be compared to the discounted future cash inflows. In *Numerical example 13.3*, the total present value of all the future cash inflows is €96,348. If the initial investment costs €100,000, the NPV is −€100,000 + €96,348, or −€3,652. The investment proposal has a negative net present value and accepting it reduces organizational value. The costs (initial cash investment outflow) are greater than the benefits (discounted future cash inflows).

If the initial investment for *Numerical example 13.3* is €80,000, the net present value is −€80,000 + €96,348, or +€16,348. The investment proposal has a positive net present value and would increase organizational value. The benefits exceed the costs of the investment.

The general rule for making long-term investment decisions is to accept proposals that have a positive net present value and reject proposals that have a negative net present value. Other non-quantifiable factors also should be considered such as employee welfare, competitor reaction, government actions and the organization's strategic goals.

Numerical **example** 13.4

Auto Company is considering the investment in a robotic-assembly machine at a cost of £20,000. The annual cost savings of having the new equipment are expected to be £8,000 over the next three years. At the end of the three years, the equipment is expected to be sold for £2,000. Auto Company's borrowing rate is 12 per cent. What is the net present value of this investment?

Solution

Year	Cash flows (£)	Discount factor	Present value (£)
0	(20,000)	$1/(1 + 0.12)^0 = 1.00000$	(20,000)
1	8,000	$1/(1 + 0.12)^1 = 0.89286$	7,143
2	8,000	$1/(1 + 0.12)^2 = 0.79719$	6,378
3	10,000	$1/(1 + 0.12)^3 = 0.71178$	7,118
Net present value			639

The net present value of the robotic-assembly machine is positive. Therefore, Auto Company should purchase the equipment.

■ Estimating cash flows for calculating present values

Future cash flows are discounted and compared to present cash flows to determine the net present value of an investment. If the net present value of the proposed investment is greater than zero, the investment should be undertaken. Although this concept appears straightforward, estimating future cash flows involves potential problems. Considerable information often must be gathered to make reasonable estimates of future cash flows. Cash flows beyond five years are usually difficult to predict accurately in a changing world. In addition to the uncertainty in estimating future cash flows, the factors described in this section also affect future cash-flow estimates.

■ Discount cash flows not accounting earnings

Present value analysis discounts cash flows, not accounting earnings. The focus is on cash flows, not accounting earnings, as earnings contain accounting accruals and deferrals. The accounting process keeps certain cash flows out of earnings. The purchase cost of fixed assets is not treated as an expense until depreciated; that is, earnings do not contain amounts spent until the economic benefits of the investments are received. Likewise, sales are recorded when the legal liability arises, not when the cash is collected. Therefore, pounds *earned*, as computed by accounting earnings, do not reflect the pounds actually received. We discount cash flows and not accounting earnings because cash flows can be invested in the bank and thereby generate interest. Accounting earnings, however, cannot be used to open a bank account. You cannot go to a shop and buy soft drinks and crisps with accounting earnings, only cash or its equivalent is accepted.

When Wesfarmers, an Australian home-improvement retailer, announced its bid to acquire the assets of Coles Group Limited, a supermarket chain, its shares slumped in the market, reducing the market value of its takeover bid. The offer to pay a market premium was perceived negatively by market analysts and investors. While Wesfarmers analysed improved future cash flows resulting from increased capital utilization, reduced corporate overhead and supply-chain improvements, investors apparently were wary of the potential reduction in reported accounting earnings due to roadblocks such as increased financing costs, competitor reaction and differences in the firms' corporate cultures and information systems.[4]

Adjust cash flows to reflect the need for additional accounts receivable and inventory

Many businesses carry significant amounts of accounts receivable and inventories. Accounts receivable and inventory represent cash tied up that could be earning interest if invested in the bank. Therefore, cash invested in accounts receivable and inventory should be included in the investment in the business. For example, many businesses allow customers to make purchases on credit. In these cases, additional cash must be invested to finance these outstanding accounts. Alternatively, to the extent that the firm acquires goods and services on credit, the accounts payable offsets the cash needed to finance current assets. If cash flows are estimated by adjusting earnings for depreciation and other non-cash expenses, the additional amounts invested in working capital (Current assets − Current liabilities) must be included to derive the cash flows in the period.

Investments in working capital also can decline as a result of new investments. Firms that implement advanced manufacturing technologies, including just-in-time (JIT) systems, frequently experience lower inventory levels and improvements in cash flows given the reduced need to finance these assets. For example, a study of more than 90 firms that had formally implemented JIT reported that over 80 per cent had decreased levels of raw materials and work-in-process inventories. Almost 66 per cent of the firms indicated a decline in finished goods inventories. Overall, approximately 50 per cent of the firms indicated that the decrease in work-in-process inventory had been significant since implementing JIT.[5] Mason Dixon Farms provides a further example of the adoption of innovative technologies and the capital-budgeting analysis of these investments.

Organizational **analysis**

Cow-Milking robots at Mason Dixon Farms

Mason Dixon Farms (MDF) is one of the oldest and largest dairy farms in the US state of Pennsylvania.

An industry leader in the adoption of new technologies and processes, MDF currently faces a number of challenges that potentially affect its long-term profitability. These issues include residential growth that increases the value of farmland, the owners' quality of life, the

---

[4] 'Wesfarmers to spend $5bn on Coles' (2007) *The Daily Telegraph*, www.news.com.au/dailytelegraph/story/0,22049,22254658-5001024,00.html (accessed 28 August); 'Wesfarmer Alters Coles Buyout Bid After Shares Slide' (2007) Bloomberg.com, www.bloomberg.com/apps/news?pid=newsarchive&sid=a6CFUfWKi2LA (accessed 29 August).

[5] R. R. Fullerton and C. S. McWatters (2001) 'The Impact of JIT Implementation on Production Performance', *Journal of Operations Management*, Vol. 19, No. 1 (January), pp. 81–96.

management of its growing labour force, and per-cow productivity. Some of these factors are difficult, if not impossible, to quantify in monetary terms but influence decisions made about production operations and capital investments.

MDF has been considering the purchase of 40 robotic machines to milk its dairy herd of 2,000 cows. An alternative is the investment in a carousel milking parlour. The approximate capital investment in the robots is $6 million while the milking parlour requires an investment of $1 million. Both investments exclude the cost of additional buildings and equipment needed in either case.

Robotic milking systems were developed initially in the Netherlands in the 1980s with the first commercial use in 1992. They are popular in Europe where more than 90 per cent of the farms worldwide that use robotic systems are located. They are also popular in Japan, Israel and Canada.

A key factor in MDF's decision is the impact of a robotic system on the farm's labour force. As MDF has grown in scale, its dependence on hired labour has increased substantially. The management of this labour force has added to the complexity of its operations, especially as most are migrant workers from outside the US. In turn, these complexities affect the quality of life of farm management and owners. The owners expect a reduction of 75 per cent in its labour costs with the robotic milking system.

Robotic systems also offer advantages in terms of milking time, animal welfare and performance measurement. These systems provide for the tracking of individual cow performance (production per cow, milking frequency, milk quality, etc.) and the ability to detect problems. While studies have shown that robotic systems may be profitable investments,

research suggests that non-monetary factors (less milking time, improved animal welfare) are also very important. The management of MDF's labour force is one such factor. Robotic systems are sourced in Europe; thus, exchange rate fluctuations play a role in the investment decision.

MDF's capital-budgeting decision process has followed the steps outlined in this chapter. Farm management gathered relevant data for both alternatives: purchase cost, production costs, other expenses, (e.g. labour, feed, and maintenance), anticipated inflation rates, tax rates, the price of milk, the equipments' useful life and depreciation period. MDF set its discount rate at 5 per cent for both options. The NPV of both options was determined, along with a series of sensitivity analyses related to changes in milk prices, production levels and exchange rates. After making its investment decision to adopt the robotic technology, MDF owners have continued to evaluate the project and to monitor results.

Assume that the NPVs of the two investments were equal.

Should MDF proceed with the investment in a robotic system, what conclusions could we draw about the value of non-monetary factors?

What advice would you offer MDF's owners if the expected profits from using robots were less than those from installing a carousel milking parlour?

How might MDF hedge its investment in the robotic technology?

Source: Jeffrey Hyde, James W. Dunn, Annette Steward and Ellen R. Hollabaugh (2007), 'Robots don't get sick or get paid overtime, but are they a profitable option for milking cows?', *Review of Agricultural Economics*, Vol. 29, No. 2, pp. 366–380.

Include opportunity costs but not sunk costs

As in other planning decisions, opportunity costs should be used in capital budgeting. The opportunity cost of the investment might not be limited to its purchase price. A new investment project also might impose externalities on other parts of the organization. For example, an investment in a new product could affect sales of another division's products. An investment in a new machine should consider the disposal cost of the machine being replaced. If a new investment project uses existing resources, the benefit forgone of using those resources for some other project is part of the cost of the new investment. The opportunity cost concept is still valid with capital budgeting.

Sunk costs, in contrast, should be ignored in capital budgeting. If a new investment project uses resources that already have been purchased and have no other uses, the purchase price of those resources should not be included in the investment decision.

Exclude financing costs

The interest and principal payments on debt should not be included in the discounted future cash flows. The costs of financing the project are implicitly included in discounting the future cash flows. If the project has a positive net present value, the cash flows from the project yield a return in excess of the firm's cost of capital, which more than compensates the firm for the financing costs. Dividend payments also should be excluded in calculating cash outflows.

Taxes and depreciation tax shields

Taxes are usually a significant cash-flow item in most discounted cash-flow analyses. A corporate tax rate of 34 per cent implies that about a third of any project's profitability is taxed away. Therefore, taxes and how to minimize them become an important element in capital budgets.

Many firms use different depreciation methods for external reports for shareholders and for tax authorities. HM Revenue & Customs in the UK provides a system of capital allowances to generate tax relief for investments in capital assets. This system establishes the rate of capital allowances and the depreciation basis. Similarly in Canada, the federal government's Capital Cost Allowance (CCA) system dictates the depreciation that can be taken for tax purposes. These systems, like those in other jurisdictions, are also tools of public policy. Governments encourage capital investment in selected assets and industries by providing accelerated depreciation. For example, the UK Enhanced Capital Allowance (ECA) encourages firms to invest in energy-saving plant and machinery as part of the government's broader efforts to deal with climate change. Other accounting methods also cause the earnings figure reported to shareholders to differ from the firm's taxable profit. The expected cost of product warranties, for instance, is included in financial reports to shareholders when the product is sold. However, the cost of the warranty work is deductible for tax purposes only when the actual warranty cost is incurred. When calculating a project's net present value, it is important to use the tax accounting rules rather than the external financial reporting rules to estimate tax liabilities. Taxes are a cash flow. The accounting rules used to compute taxes affect tax payments. The accounting methods used only for shareholder reports, however, do not affect tax cash flows.

The primary difference between cash flows and profit for tax purposes is **depreciation**, which is the allocation of the historical cost of a fixed asset over time. The depreciation of the fixed asset is treated as an expense in calculating taxable income, but is not a cash outflow. The cash outflow took place when the fixed asset was acquired.

The amount of depreciation that can be recognized each year is determined by the tax code. Generally, organizations would prefer to recognize as much depreciation

Rob Walls/Alamy

Governments grappling with climate change use public policy to influence capital-investment decisions. Capital allowances, for instance, provide incentives for firms to invest in green technologies.

for tax purposes as possible to reduce earnings and, therefore, reduce their present tax liability. Depreciation is not a cash flow but affects cash flow through the calculation of taxable income. The reduction in cash payments due to depreciation is called the **depreciation tax shield**.

Some simple algebra illustrates the indirect cash-flow effect of depreciation and the calculation of the tax shield.

Let

t = tax rate
R = revenue
E = all cash expenses (except depreciation)
D = depreciation (allowed for tax purposes)

Using this notation, we can write down the following familiar formulae:

$$
\begin{aligned}
\text{Net profit} = \text{NP} &= (R - E - D)(1 - t) \\
\text{Taxes} = \text{TAX} &= (R - E - D)t \\
\text{Cash flow} = \text{CF} &= R - E - \text{TAX} \\
&= R - E - (R - E - D)t \\
&= (R - E)(1 - t) + Dt
\end{aligned}
$$

Notice that the last term in the cash-flow equation, Dt, the depreciation tax shield. This amount is the annual depreciation charge, D, times the tax rate, t. The product of the two is *added* to the annual after-tax operating net cash flow, $(R - E)(1 - t)$, to arrive at the after-tax net cash flow. From the last formula, we can see that the larger the depreciation expense, the higher is the firm's cash flow because the tax liability is lower. In this sense, depreciation is said to be a tax shield since it results in lower taxes and thus, a higher after-tax cash flow. The total amount of depreciation that can be deducted from taxes is limited to the original cost of the asset. Therefore, the sooner the depreciation is taken (assuming the firm has positive taxable earnings), the higher is the present value of the depreciation tax shield. Accelerated tax depreciation methods, which allow earlier recognition of depreciation, increase a project's net present value.

Numerical **Example** 13.5

An asset is purchased for €500,000. The asset has a five-year life and no salvage value. The tax rate is 34 per cent and the interest rate is 5 per cent. What is the present value of the tax shields under the straight-line and double-declining-balance depreciation methods?

Solution

Table 13.2 displays the calculation of the present value of the tax shields under the straight-line and double-declining-balance depreciation methods.

Double-declining-balance depreciation writes off the €500,000 original cost faster than does straight-line depreciation. Therefore, its tax shield has a higher present value by €5,061. In other words, by using double-declining-balance depreciation instead of straight-line depreciation for tax purposes, the net present value of the project is increased by €5,061. This amount represents about 1 per cent of the asset's cost.

→

Table 13.2 Comparing the net present value of depreciation tax shields of straight-line to double-declining-balance depreciation
(€500,000 asset, no salvage, five-year life, 34% tax rate, 5% interest)

	Straight-line depreciation				Double-declining-balance depreciation			
Year	Depreciation expense (€)	Tax shield (Dt) (€)	PV of tax shield (€)	DDB rate*	Book value at beginning of year (€)	Depreciation expense (€)	Tax shield (Dt) (€)	PV of tax shield (€)
1	100,000	34,000	32,381	0.4	500,000	200,000	68,000	64,762
2	100,000	34,000	30,839	0.4	300,000	120,000	40,800	37,007
3	100,000	34,000	29,370	0.4	180,000	72,000	24,480	21,147
4	100,000	34,000	27,972	0.4	108,000	43,200	14,688	12,084
5	100,000	34,000	26,640		64,800	64,800	22,032	17,263
	500,000		147,202			500,000		152,263

*DDB rate (double-declining-balance rate) is twice the straight-line rate; or, 40% $= 2 \times \dfrac{1}{5}$

■ Adjusting the discount rate for risk

In the previous sections, the opportunity cost of capital is provided as an interest rate. The opportunity cost of capital is the cost of replacing cash through borrowing or issuing shares. Some organizations are less likely to repay loans; therefore, the opportunity cost of capital is higher for some organizations than for others. Organizations that are more risky have a higher cost of capital than do less risky ones. Investment projects that are more risky and, therefore, make the organization riskier should be treated as having a higher cost of capital. In other words, risky projects should be discounted at higher interest rates than safe projects.

Investment projects in developing countries often are considered to be more risky yet profitable. Many of the risks involved are difficult to quantify. For example, firms are exposed to political and government instability, potential asset expropriation, loss of firm reputation and lax standards of business conduct. These types of projects should be discounted at a higher interest rate than are similar investments in advanced economies. Some firms attempt to mitigate the risks in other ways. For example, firms purchase risk insurance, or outsource activities to organizations that specialize in the assumption of these operating risks.

The definition of risk, how it is measured, and how to choose risk-adjusted discount factors are the subject of corporate finance. We will not concern ourselves with how to derive a risk-adjusted discount rate. For any given risky cash-flow stream, we will assume that an equivalent risk-adjusted interest rate exists.

The risk of an investment occurs due to the uncertainty about future cash flows. The cash inflows of an investment depend on many factors that are not perfectly predictable. For instance, future cash flows might depend on the weather, the economy, the entry of competitors, or the fickle nature of customer preferences. Since the cash flows are uncertain, one of many possible cash flows can result. Instead of discounting the highest or lowest cash flow that can occur, we discount the **expected** (or average) **cash** flow. For example, if the cash flows next year can be either £100 or £200 with equal probability, we would discount the expected cash flow of £150. The expected cash flows should be discounted using a risk-adjusted discount rate appropriate for the risk inherent in the project.

Vij's Bakery and Tea Room (continued)

Vij now knows how to calculate the net present value of the investment in the Italian coffee machine but he must reconsider his estimate of cash flows before discounting them. Vij realizes that the machine is not the only investment that he must make to provide his customers with Italian coffee beverages. He also must have some ingredients on hand to make them. Vij estimates that the amount of extra ingredients that he will need to hold is relatively small. He decides not to worry about that cost.

Vij also realizes that the opportunity cost of capital is implicitly included in the discounting process. The annual interest payments of £800 should not be included in the discounted cash-flow estimates. The interest rate of 8 per cent does appear to be the correct risk-adjusted interest rate.

The space to be taken by the machine had no alternative use, so no facility costs are applied to the investment project. Vij, however, needs to consider the potential effect of the Italian beverages on the sales of his current menu offerings. After careful consideration, he decides that the net effect of selling Italian coffees on the sale of his baked goods and teas will be approximately zero. Some tea drinkers will switch to coffee; however, having coffee will bring in more customers, some who will buy baked goods or maybe try his teas.

Vij has forgotten to adjust his cash-flow estimates for tax effects. The taxable income is £200 and the tax rate for Vij is 30 per cent. Therefore, Vij must pay annual taxes of (£200 × 0.30), or £60. After eliminating the depreciation and interest and adding the income taxes, Vij's annual cash-flow analysis is as follows:

	£
Revenues from selling Italian coffee beverages	5,000
Cost of ingredients	(1,500)
Additional utility costs	(500)
Taxes at 30% (0.30 × £200)	(60)
Cash flows per year for five years	2,940
Initial investment	10,000

Vij then estimates the present value of these cash flows over the next five years using a discount rate of 8 per cent.

Year	Cash flows (£)	Discount factor	Present value (£)
0	(10,000)	$1/(1 + 0.08)^0 = 1.00000$	(10,000)
1	2,940	$1/(1 + 0.08)^1 = 0.92593$	2,722
2	2,940	$1/(1 + 0.08)^2 = 0.85734$	2,520
3	2,940	$1/(1 + 0.08)^3 = 0.79383$	2,334
4	2,940	$1/(1 + 0.08)^4 = 0.73503$	2,161
5	2,940	$1/(1 + 0.08)^5 = 0.68058$	2,001
Net present value			1,738

Based on the calculation of a positive net present value of £1,738, Vij is pleased to invest in the Italian coffee machine.

Concept review

1 Why should cash flows not future earnings be discounted?

2 Why should accounts receivable and inventory levels be considered when making a capital-budgeting decision?

3 Why should finance charges not be included when making a capital-budgeting decision?

4 Why does depreciation act as a tax shield?

5 How does the risk of the investment project affect the discount rate used for capital budgeting?

INTERNAL RATE OF RETURN (IRR)

The internal rate of return method finds the interest rate that equates the initial investment cost to the future discounted cash flows. In other words, the internal rate of return makes the net present value equal to zero. If the project's internal rate of return exceeds a certain cut-off rate (e.g. the project's cost of capital), the project should be undertaken. On the surface, the **internal rate of return (IRR)** method for comparing different projects appears to be similar to the net present value (NPV) method.

The IRR is quite easy to calculate if an initial cash outflow (the cost of the investment) is followed by a cash inflow in one year. For example, suppose one can invest £1,000 today and receive £1,070 in a year. The IRR sets the investment cost equal to the discounted future cash flow:

$$\textbf{Investment cost} = \textbf{(Cash inflows in one year)}/\textbf{(1 + IRR)}$$

$$£1,000 = \frac{£1,070}{1 + \text{IRR}}$$

$$(1 + \text{IRR}) = \frac{£1,070}{£1,000}$$

$$\text{IRR} = 0.07 = 7\%$$

In this simple example, the IRR on an investment of £1,000 today that generates a £1,070 payment in one year is 7 per cent. If the cost of capital is 5 per cent, this investment clearly offers a return in excess of its opportunity cost. The NPV of this investment is as follows:

$$\text{NPV} = -£1,000 + \frac{£1,070}{1.05}$$

$$= -£1,000 + £1,019.05$$

$$= £19.05$$

If the IRR exceeds the opportunity cost of capital, the NPV of the investment is positive and the investment should be undertaken. If the IRR is less than the opportunity cost of capital, the NPV of the investment is negative and the investment should be rejected.

The advantage of the IRR method is that an investment project's return is stated as an interest rate. For many people, saying a project's return is 14 per cent is clearer than saying a project has a net present value of some monetary amount such as £628,623.

However, the IRR and NPV methods do not always give consistent answers. The IRR and the NPV potentially lead to different investment decisions if investments are mutually exclusive. Mutually exclusive investments are a group of investments of which only one can be chosen. For example, a manufacturing firm usually chooses only one of many possible methods to make a part. With mutually exclusive investments, a manager would like to rank the alternative investments. Consider the following two *mutually exclusive* investments:

1 Invest £1,000 today, and receive £1,070 in one year.
2 Invest £5,000 today, and receive £5,300 in one year.

We know that investment 1 has an IRR of 7 per cent and a NPV of £19.05. The IRR of investment 2 is as follows:

$$£5,000 = £5,300/(1 + IRR)$$

$$(1 + IRR) = \frac{£5,300}{£5,000}$$

$$IRR = 0.06 = 6\%.$$

The following is the NPV of Investment 2:

$$NPV = -£5,000 + \frac{£5,300}{1.05}$$

$$= -£5,000 + £5,047.62$$

$$= £47.62$$

Which investment is best? The IRR criterion says that investment 1 is better because it has the higher IRR. The NPV criterion says investment 2 is better as it has the higher NPV. How should one decide? Which is more valuable, a rate of return or cash? Net present value indicates how much cash an investment is worth today, or the *magnitude* of the investment's return. The IRR only indicates the *relative* return on the investment. A 20 per cent return on £1,000 (£20) is preferable to a 200 per cent return on £1 (£2).

The NPV and IRR methods also may rank investment projects differently due to a difference in the length of time or duration of cash flows. Consider the following two *mutually exclusive* investments:

1 Invest £1,000 today and receive £1,200 in one year.
2 Invest £1,000 today and receive £1,500 in three years.

The NPV of these two projects for different discount rates is presented in Figure 13.1. The IRR of each of the two investments is the discount rate where each line crosses the x-axis. For the first investment, the IRR is equal to 20 per cent. For the second investment,

Figure 13.1 Comparing the NPV of two investments

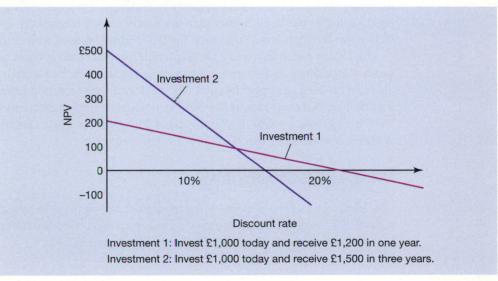

Investment 1: Invest £1,000 today and receive £1,200 in one year.
Investment 2: Invest £1,000 today and receive £1,500 in three years.

the IRR is between 1 to 4 per cent and 15 per cent. Even though the IRR of the first investment is larger, the NPV of the second investment is higher if the discount rate is below 12 per cent. Above 12 per cent, the NPV of the first investment is higher.

The net present values in Figure 13.1 decline as the discount rate rises, because only the cash inflows are affected by the change in discount rate. The cash outflows occur in the present; hence, they are not affected by the discount rate. The cash inflows, however, occur in the future and their present values will decline with an increase in the discount rate. The NPV of investment 2 declines more rapidly as the present value of cash flows in the more distant future are more sensitive to changes in the discount rate.

Perhaps the most serious limitation of the IRR method is its implicit assumption regarding the re-investment rate. The re-investment rate is the interest rate used to compound cash flows received or paid over the life of the project. In the discounted cash-flow method, each cash flow is discounted at the opportunity cost of capital. The implicit assumption is that intermediate cash flows are being re-invested at the opportunity cost of capital. If the opportunity cost of capital is expected to be higher or lower in future years, non-constant discount rates can be used. The IRR method assumes that all the intermediate cash flows are being re-invested automatically at the project's constant internal rate of return. Thus, the IRR method implicitly assumes that all the intermediate cash flows can be invested in a stock of projects identical to the one being considered, and that the same return can be achieved. If the current project is a one-time opportunity, there are no future projects like it in which to re-invest the current project's cash flows. Therefore, the IRR method overstates a project's rate of return if other investments with the same re-investment rate do not exist. This limitation of the IRR method makes its use dangerous to evaluate alternative investments.

Another drawback of the IRR method is when an organization sets a hurdle rate higher than the cost of capital. A **hurdle rate** is a benchmark that the organization establishes as an investment criterion. To be acceptable, the planned IRR must be higher than the hurdle rate. For example, an organization may establish a hurdle rate of 20 per cent but its cost of capital is 10 per cent. The organization will accept only those investment proposals with a hurdle rate higher than 20 per cent but the organization is forgoing the opportunity to invest in projects with an IRR between 10 per cent and 20 per cent, which have positive NPVs.

In summary, the IRR method provides the correct decision rule for investments if the cost of capital is used as the benchmark. If the IRR is higher than the cost of capital, then the investment should be made. The IRR fails, however, to duplicate the NPV ranking of mutually exclusive investment projects. In addition, requiring investment projects to exceed a hurdle rate that is higher than the cost of capital forgoes the opportunity to invest in positive NPV projects. Therefore, the IRR should be used with caution.

The IRR is not always easy to calculate if unequal cash inflows occur over multiple years. Calculators and computers can solve for the IRR, but a trial-and-error method also can be used to approximate it. The trial-and-error method calculates the NPV for a particular discount rate. If the NPV is positive, a higher discount rate is tried. If the NPV is negative, a lower discount is tried. This process continues until a discount rate is found that results in an NPV of approximately zero.

Numerical **example** 13.6

A company is considering an investment that requires an initial cash outlay of €100,000. The investment is expected to return €70,000 in the first year and €55,000 in the second year. What is the IRR of the investment?

Solution

An initial estimate of 10 per cent gives the following NPV:

$$-€100{,}000 + (€70{,}000/(1 + 0.1)) + (€55{,}000/(1 + 0.1)^2) = €9{,}090$$

The NPV (at 10 per cent) is positive, thus a higher estimate for the IRR, say 20 per cent, is used:

$$-€100{,}000 + (€70{,}000/(1 + 0.2)) + (€55{,}000/(1 + 0.2)^2) = -€3{,}473$$

The NPV (at 20 per cent) is negative, thus a lower estimate for the IRR, say 17 per cent, is used:

$$-€100{,}000 + (€70{,}000/(1 + 0.17)) + (€55{,}000/(1 + 0.17)^2) = €7$$

This NPV (at 17 per cent) is very close to zero, so the IRR is approximately 17%.

Concept review

1 How is the internal rate of return (IRR) determined?

2 What are some limitations in using the IRR to evaluate investments?

Vij's Bakery and Tea Room (continued)

Vij is thrilled with his new skills in using the time value of money, so he decides to calculate the IRR of the Italian coffee machine. He uses the trial-and-error method and begins with his interest rate of 8 per cent to calculate the NPV.

Discount rate (%)	Net present value (£)
8	1,738
10	1,146
12	599
14	93
16	−374

Vij determines that the internal rate of return is a little higher than 14 per cent, which exceeds his opportunity cost of capital.

CAPITAL-BUDGETING METHODS USED IN PRACTICE

The discounting of cash flows to make capital-budgeting decisions has become common practice.[6] However, the emphasis placed on these techniques varies across contexts. In one survey, differences were noted in terms of the greater strategic emphasis on the longer-term in German and Japanese firms relative to their counterparts in the UK and the US. German and Japanese firms also displayed less reliance on tight and inflexible hurdle rates. Cultural differences also appeared to affect the political nature of the

---

[6] John Graham and Campbell Harvey (2002) 'How Do CFOs Make Capital Budgeting and Capital Structure Decisions?', *Journal of Applied Corporate Finance*, Vol. 15, No. 1 (Spring), pp. 8–22.

Greg Wright/Alamy

Computers and software make capital-budgeting techniques more accessible. However, small firms may lack the expertise to use these tools and rely on simple rules-of-thumb.

capital-budgeting process.[7] This factor might prove significant as firms operate across borders and forge international alliances.

Small organizations also evaluate capital-budgeting projects differently. An entrepreneurial firm might not have the maximization of shareholder value as its main objective when the entrepreneur-owner has adopted self-employment as a life-style choice to pursue other objectives. Second, small firms often lack the management expertise to use these techniques and adopt rules-of-thumb instead. Finally, small firms do not have the same financing options as do large firms. Capital investments may be delayed due to limited borrowing capacity.[8]

Discounting methods have been criticised for their inadequacy in dealing with dynamic markets. These criticisms have led to supplementing these methods with the use of value-based techniques such as economic value-added (EVA)[9], and real-option theory to take into account market-price risk and return.[10] Nonetheless, the following reasons likely account for the continued prevalence of discounting methods: (1) discounting methods are theoretically superior, (2) they are a mainstay in business school curricula, and (3) computer technology and cheap calculators compute NPVs and IRRs quickly and easily. Finally, financial uncertainties, such as exchange rate fluctuations and interest rate increases, tend to encourage the greater use of more sophisticated capital-budgeting techniques. Discounting methods are more critical in comparing monetary values from different time periods.

SUMMARY

.1 Describe the steps of the capital-budgeting process. The steps of the capital-budgeting process include initiation, ratification, implementation and monitoring.

2 Identify the opportunity cost of capital. The opportunity cost of capital is the forgone opportunity of using cash, which is the interest rate on borrowing money to replace the cash.

3 Estimate the payback period of an investment and identify weaknesses of the payback method in making investment choices. The payback period is the time required for the investment to generate cash flows equal to the initial investment. The payback method does not consider the time value of money or cash flows beyond the payback period.

[7] Chris Carr and Cyril Tomkins (1998) 'Context, culture and the role of the finance function in strategic decisions. A comparative analysis of Britain, Germany, the U.S.A. and Japan', *Management Accounting Research*, Vol. 9, pp. 213–239.

[8] Morris G. Danielson and Jonathan A. Scott (2006) 'The Capital Budgeting Decisions of Small Businesses', *Journal of Applied Finance*, Vol. 16, No. 2 (Fall/Winter), pp. 45–56.

[9] EVA is a registered trademark of Stern Stewart & Company.

[10] Mehari Mekonnen Akalu (2003) 'The process of investment appraisal: the experience of 10 large British and Dutch companies', *International Journal of Project Management*, Vol. 21, pp. 355–362.

4 **Calculate the accounting rate of return (ROI) and identify its weaknesses in making investment choices.** The accounting rate of return, or ROI, is the average income from a project divided by the average investment cost. The ROI is an accounting measure and does not consider the time value of money.

5 **Calculate the net present value (NPV) of cash flows.** The NPV of cash flows is calculated by discounting all future cash flows to the present and comparing the present value of the cash inflows with the present value of the cash outflows.

6 **Identify non-cash profit and loss accounts that should be excluded in calculating the net present value.** Cash, not accounting profit, should be discounted to estimate the NPV of an investment. Items such as depreciation do not affect cash flows.

7 **Adjust cash flows to reflect the additional accounts receivable and inventory required.** New investments often require increased amounts of accounts receivable and inventory. Increases in accounts receivable and inventory resulting from a new investment should be treated as part of the investment cost.

8 **Exclude financing charges when calculating the net present value of an investment.** Interest and principal payments on debt should not be included in the discounting of future cash flows because the discounting implicitly includes financing charges.

9 **Estimate tax cash flows for capital budgeting.** Taxes are an important part of cash-flow estimates. Non-cash expenses, such as depreciation, do affect cash flows indirectly through their effect on taxable earnings.

10 **Recognize the effect of risk on the discount rate.** The cash flows of higher risk investment projects should be discounted at a higher interest rate.

11 **Estimate the internal rate of return (IRR) of an investment project.** The IRR is the discount rate that sets the NPV of the cash flows equal to zero.

12 **Identify problems with using the IRR to evaluate investment projects.** The IRR and NPV methods do not always rank investment projects in the same manner. The difference in rankings could be due to the relative size of the investment and the duration of the cash flows. In addition, the IRR method assumes that intermediate cash flows can be re-invested at the internal rate of return.

13 **Use annuity tables to relate present and future values. (Appendix)** The annuity tables allow for the calculation of the present value and future value of constant streams of cash over finite periods.

KEY TERMS

Capital budgeting A process of evaluating and choosing long-term investments.

Depreciation The reduction in the historical cost of a fixed asset over time.

Depreciation tax shield The reduction in taxes due to the decrease in taxable earnings from depreciation.

Expected cash flow The expected value of cash flows when cash flows are uncertain and many possible cash flows can result.

Hurdle rate A benchmark that the organization establishes as an investment criterion.

Internal rate of return (IRR) The discount rate that makes the net present value of an investment equal to zero.

Net present value (NPV) The net present value of cash flows is calculated by discounting all future cash flows to the present and comparing the present value of the cash inflows with the present value of the cash outflows.

Opportunity cost of capital A term used to describe the forgone opportunity of using cash.

Payback The time required to generate cash inflows equal to the initial investment.

Return on investment (ROI) The income divided by the assets generating the income.

APPENDIX
Interest rate mathematics

This Appendix develops the mathematical relations for converting cash flows received or paid at different times. By deriving the various formulae, the logic of the calculations is made clearer. In the following examples, the interest rate is given. Determining the appropriate interest rate to relate monetary values from different time periods is discussed in the chapter.

Future values

The **future value** of cash today is the initial amount plus interest that is earned during the interim period. If we assume an interest rate of 5 per cent and an initial investment of £1,000, the future value of the £1,000 in one year is the initial investment of £1,000 plus interest of £50 (5 per cent of £1,000), or £1,050. What is the future value of £1,000 in two years with an interest rate of 5 per cent? At the end of the first year, one has £1,050 (£1,000 principal plus £50 of interest). This amount is then re-invested to yield £1,102.50 (£1,050 principal plus interest of £52.50). Of the £52.50 of interest in the second year, £50 is interest on the original £1,000 and £2.50 is interest on the first year's interest (£50 × 5%). Or, at the end of the second year, the value of the investment is as follows:

$$£1,000 + 2(0.05 × £1,000) + [0.05 × (0.05 × £1,000)]$$
$$= £1,000 + £100 + £2.50$$
$$= £1,102.50$$

The fact that interest is earned on the interest in the second year is called *compounding*. The formulae that we derive are often called *compound interest formulae*. The future value of £1 at different interest rates for different periods of time is provided in Table 13.6 at the end of this Appendix.

We now will generalize the preceding illustration. Let PV represent the amount of money invested today at r% per year and let FV represent the amount that will be available at the end of the two years. The general formula relating present dollars to dollars in two years at r% per year is as follows:

$$PV(1 + r)^2 = PV(1 + 2r + r^2) = FV$$

The $2r$ term represents interest for two years on the original investment of PV and r^2 is the interest on the interest (compound interest). The general formula for leaving money in the bank for n years and allowing the interest to accumulate and earn interest is:

$$PV(1 + r)^n = FV \text{ (future value formula)}$$

All of the formulae of interest rate mathematics are just algebraic manipulations of this basic formula.

Numerical **example** 13.7

A mother, who recently gave birth to a daughter, has decided to put £1,000 in the bank for her daughter's university fund. The fund earns 6 per cent a year for 18 years before being withdrawn from the bank. How much will the £1,000 be worth in 18 years?

Solution

$$PV(1 + r)^n = FV$$

$$£1,000(1 + 0.06)^{18} = £2,854 = FV$$

The £1,000 will be worth £2,854 in 18 years.

■ Present values

Suppose that instead of asking how much money one will have at the end of n years, one asks how much money must be invested today at $r\%$ per year to have a defined future value at a specific future point in time? For example, how much money must be invested today, at a 5 per cent interest rate, to be able to buy a €25,000 boat in six years? The amount of money that must be invested today to equal a certain amount in the future at a given interest rate is called the *present value* (PV). In present value calculations, the future value (FV) and interest rate (r) are known, but present value (PV) is unknown. Re-arranging the future value formula yields the present value formula:

$$PV = \frac{FV}{(1 + r)^n} \qquad \text{(present value formula)}$$

To solve for the boat example,

$$PV = \frac{€25,000}{(1 + 0.05)^6}$$

$$= \frac{€25,000}{1.3401}$$

$$= €18,655$$

Therefore, if one invests €18,655 in the bank at 5 per cent and allows the principal and interest to compound, at the end of six years one will have €25,000. The present value of £1 received at different time periods in the future at different interest rates is provided in Table 13.4 at the end of this Appendix.

Numerical **example** 13.8

A recent university graduate would like to go back to school and get an MBA degree in 10 years. He estimates that a two-year MBA programme will cost £70,000 in 10 years. He can put money in a bank that will earn 5 per cent annually for the next 10 years. How much money will he have to put in the bank to have £70,000 in 10 years?

Solution

$$PV = \frac{FV}{(1 + r)^n}$$

$$= £70,000/(1 + 0.05)^{10}$$

$$= £42,974$$

The university graduate must deposit £42,974 in the bank today to have £70,000 in 10 years.

■ Present value of a cash flow stream

The future value and present value formulae (which are the same formula) allow for the comparison of cash flows from different time periods. So far, we have been dealing with a single cash flow invested today or received in the future. Now suppose one has a series of cash flows occurring *at the end of each year* for the next n years. That is, FV_1 is the cash received at the end of the first year, FV_2 is the cash received at the end of the second year, and FV_n is the cash received at the end of the nth year. What is the present value of this cash-flow stream? Apply the preceding present value formula to each cash flow and sum them together:

$$PV = \frac{FV_1}{(1 + r)^1} + \frac{FV_2}{(1 + r)^2} + \frac{FV_3}{(1 + r)^3} + \cdots + \frac{FV_n}{(1 + r)^n}$$

Suppose one is offered £500 at the end of the first year, £1,000 at the end of the second year, and £1,500 at the end of the third year. How much is this stream of cash flows worth today? Using the preceding formula:

$$PV = \frac{£500}{(1 + 0.05)^1} + \frac{£1,000}{(1 + 0.05)^2} + \frac{£1,500}{(1 + 0.05)^3}$$

$$= \frac{£500}{(1.05)} + \frac{£1,000}{1.1025} + \frac{£1,500}{1.157625}$$

$$= £476 + £907 + £1,296$$

$$= £2,679$$

Therefore, one would be indifferent between receiving the cash-flow stream of £500, £1,000, and £1,500 in the next three years and £2,678.98 today if the interest rate is 5 per cent.

Each of the cash flows, FV_t, is said to be *discounted* (or divided) by $(1 + r)^t$ where t is the year in which the cash flow is received. Notice that $1 \div (1 + r)^t$ is always less than 1 for all positive interest rates. Therefore, a pound received in the future is worth less than a pound received today. We will see that discounting is central to the concept of comparing alternatives involving cash flows received at different points of time. By discounting the future cash flows from each alternative to present values (or pounds today), we can determine which alternative is best.

Numerical **example 13.9**

An insurance company is offering Anne Leblanc a new retirement policy. The insurance company is willing to pay her €100,000 in 30 years, another €200,000 in 40 years, and a final payment of €300,000 in 50 years. What is the present value of this retirement policy to Anne, if the interest rate is 8 per cent, assuming she knows with certainty that she will live another 50 years?

Solution

$$PV = €100,000/(1 + 0.08)^{30} + €200,000/(1 + 0.08)^{40} + €300,000/(1 + 0.08)^{50}$$

$$PV = €9,938 + €9,206 + €6,396$$

$$= €25,540$$

The present value of the retirement policy is €25,540.

■ Perpetuities

A *perpetuity* is an infinite stream of equal payments received each year. Some government bonds issued by the British government promise to pay a fixed amount of cash each year forever. How much would investors be willing to pay for such bonds? All of the future payments, FV_1, FV_2, ..., FV_n are the same and equal to FV. Substituting FV into the general formula yields:

$$PV = \frac{FV}{(1 + r)^1} + \frac{FV}{(1 + r)^2} + \frac{FV}{(1 + r)^3} + \cdots$$

$$= \left(\frac{FV}{1 + r}\right)\left(1 + \frac{1}{(1 + r)^1} + \frac{1}{(1 + r)^2} + \frac{1}{(1 + r)^3} + \cdots\right)$$

From algebra, we know that the sum of an infinite series has the following expression:

$$\left(1 + \frac{1}{(1 + r)^1} + \frac{1}{(1 + r)^2} + \frac{1}{(1 + r)^3} + \cdots\right) = \frac{1 + r}{r}$$

Substituting this term into the preceding formula gives the following:

$$PV = \left(\frac{FV}{1 + r}\right)\left(\frac{1 + r}{r}\right)$$

$$PV = \frac{FV}{r} \qquad \text{(perpetuity formula)}$$

This formula is the basic one for a perpetuity, or an infinite cash-flow stream, when the interest rate is $r\%$. If the British government bonds pay £100 per year in perpetuity and the interest rate is 5 per cent, investors would be willing to pay:

$$PV = \frac{£100}{0.05}$$

$$= £2,000$$

Numerical **example** 13.10

Antonio's eccentric aunt has just died and has included him in her will. Instead of a lump sum payment, she left Antonio with an unusual contract through an insurance company. The insurance company must pay Antonio £1,000 per year beginning at the end of this year for an infinite number of years. Before Antonio dies, he can designate an heir to continue to receive these £1,000 payments. What is the present value of the contract if the interest rate is 8 per cent?

Solution

$$PV = \frac{FV}{r}$$

$$PV = £1,000/0.08$$

$$= £12,500$$

The present value of the contract is £12,500.

■ Annuities

An *annuity* is a stream of *equal* cash flows for a *fixed* number of years. Many financial instruments are annuities. For example, car loans and mortgage payments involve a fixed number of equal monthly payments. Corporate bonds pay a fixed amount twice a year over the term of the bond (usually 20 years). To derive the formula for an annuity, let FV again denote the annual cash flow received at the end of each of the next n years. The present value of an annuity of n cash flows of FV each is as follows:

$$PV = \frac{FV}{(1 + r)^1} + \frac{FV}{(1 + r)^2} + \frac{FV}{(1 + r)^3} + \cdots \frac{FV}{(1 + r)^n}$$

This formula can be rearranged into the following formula:[11]

$$PV = FV\left(\frac{(1 + r)^n - 1}{r(1 + r)^n}\right) \quad \text{(present value of annuity formula)}$$

To illustrate the application of the formula, suppose one can afford to pay £1,000 per year for 10 years. How large a loan can you borrow today? The interest rate is 5 per cent. Using our annuity formula we get the following:

$$PV = £1,000\left(\frac{(1.05)^{10} - 1}{0.05(1.05)^{10}}\right)$$

$$= £1,000\left(\frac{0.628895}{0.081445}\right)$$

$$= £7,722$$

Therefore, the bank will lend £7,722 today, with payments of £1,000 per year for 10 years.

Another useful formula is the future value of an annuity. For example, if a person invests £1,000 a year for 18 years, how much money will this individual have for a child's university education? We start with the present value of an annuity and then

---

[11] To derive the formula for this annuity stream, notice that mathematically, an annuity is equivalent to the difference between the following two streams:

Year	0	1	2	3	...	n	$n+1$	$n+2$	...
							∞		
Cash flow 1	0	FV	FV	FV	...	FV	FV	FV	...
Cash flow 2	0	0	0	0	...	0	FV	FV	...

That is, an annuity cash-flow stream = cash-flow stream 1 − cash-flow stream 2. We know how to value cash-flow stream 1 using the perpetuity formula:

$$\text{Present value of cash flow 1} = \frac{FV}{r}$$

The present value of cash-flow stream 2 is:

$$\text{Present value of cash flow 2} = \left(\frac{1}{(1 + r)^n}\right)\left(\frac{FV}{r}\right)$$

That is, the present value of cash-flow stream 2 is the present value of a perpetuity discounted back from n years because the first perpetuity payment is not received for n years. The first term in the above formula discounts the value of the perpetuity to recognize that the first payment is not received immediately. Now take the difference between the two formulae:

$$\text{PV of an annuity} = \text{PV of cash-flow stream 1} - \text{PV of cash-flow stream 2}$$

$$= \frac{FV}{r} - \left(\frac{1}{(1 + r)^n}\right)\left(\frac{FV}{r}\right)$$

$$= FV\left(\frac{(1 + r)^n - 1}{r(1 + r)^n}\right) \quad \text{(present value of annuity formula)}$$

convert this amount to a future value by taking the present value formula for an annuity and multiplying it by $(1 + r)^n$. Or,

$$\text{Future value of annuity} = \text{FV}\left(\frac{(1 + r)^n - 1}{r(1 + r)^n}\right)(1 + r)^n$$

$$= \text{FV}\left(\frac{(1 + r)^n - 1}{r}\right) \quad \text{(future value of annuity formula)}$$

To solve for how much money this will provide for a child's education, we substitute into the preceding formula:

$$£1,000\left(\frac{(1.05)^{18} - 1}{0.05}\right)$$

$$= £1,000(28.132)$$

$$= £28,132$$

Therefore, with interest left to accumulate in the bank, the individual will have over £28,000 if by investing £1,000 a year for 18 years at an interest rate of 5 per cent. The present and future values of a £1 annuity for different interest rates and different periods of time are presented in Tables 13.5 and 13.7, respectively.

Numerical **example** 13.11

Karen Wu is considering the purchase of a home. She wants to borrow £100,000 from the bank. Instead of the normal monthly mortgage payments, the bank is willing to let Karen repay the loan in equal annual payments at 12 per cent interest over the next 20 years. How much will Karen have to pay each year?

Solution

$$\text{PV} = \text{FV}\left(\frac{(1 + r)^n - 1}{r(1 + r)^n}\right) \quad \text{or} \quad \text{FV} = \text{PV} \div \left(\frac{(1 + r)^n - 1}{r(1 + r)^n}\right)$$

$$\text{FV} = £100,000/((1 + 0.12)^{20} - 1)/(0.12(1 + 0.12)^{20}))$$

$$\text{FV} = £13,388$$

Karen will have to pay £13,388 at the end of each of the next 20 years.

Multiple cash flows per year

So far we have considered only cash flows that occur once per year. How do we handle cash flows that occur more frequently, say monthly? We could add up the monthly flows and treat them as a single annual cash flow on the last day of the year. Yet this ignores the interest that we could earn on the monthly receipts. To illustrate, consider the difference between the following two options: (1) receiving 12 monthly £1,000 payments or (2) receiving a single £12,000 payment at the end of the year. Before we can calculate which option is worth more, we first have to understand the relation between monthly and annual interest rates. If the annual interest rate is 5 per cent, what is the interest rate per month? You might be tempted to say $0.05 \div 12 = 0.004166$, but this is wrong. A pound invested at the monthly interest rate, r_m, must accumulate to the same amount at the end of the year as a pound invested at the annual interest rate, r. Therefore, the following formula must hold:

$$(1 + r_m)^{12} = (1 + r)$$
$$(1 + r_m) = (1 + r)^{1/12}$$
$$r_m = (1 + r)^{1/12} - 1$$
$$= (1.05)^{1/12} - 1$$
$$= 0.004074$$

Now we can return to the original question and value the two options. The monthly interest rate just derived is 0.004074 and the annual interest rate is 0.05. Using the present value of the annuity formula to calculate the stream of 12 monthly payments of £1,000,

$$FV\left(\frac{(1 + r)^n - 1}{r(1 + r)^n}\right) = £1,000\left(\frac{(1.004074)^{12} - 1}{0.004074(1.004074)^{12}}\right)$$
$$= £1,000\left(\frac{1.05 - 1}{0.004074(1.05)}\right)$$
$$= £1,000(11.68817)$$
$$= £11,688.17$$

The present value of the single £12,000 payment is as follows:

$$\frac{FV}{(1 + r)^n} = \frac{£12000}{(1.05)^1} = £11,428.57$$

Therefore, the 12 payments of £1,000 are worth £259.60 more today than a single £12,000 payment at an annual interest rate of 5 per cent.

The preceding example illustrates that the earlier a payment is received, the more valuable is the payment. It also introduces the notion of the *compounding interval*. The compounding interval is the period of time in which interest is calculated and then compounded in the next period. The compounding interval could be a year, a month, or a day. The key point is that the annual interest rate cannot be used to discount cash flows received more frequently than yearly. Some banks quote interest rates in annual terms, say 5 per cent, but then compound the interest monthly. In this case, the *effective* annual interest is as follows:

$$\left(1 + \frac{r}{12}\right)^{12} - 1 = \left(1 + \frac{0.05}{12}\right)^{12} - 1$$
$$= (1.0041666667)^{12} - 1$$
$$= 0.05116$$

Therefore, if the bank has a stated annual interest rate of 5 per cent but compounds monthly, the *effective* interest rate is 5.116 per cent. If the bank states that its interest rate is 5 per cent but compounds interest *daily*, the *effective* annual rate is 5.127 per cent.[12] The preceding discussion illustrates that depositors who want the highest *effective* interest rate always will choose the shortest compounding interval among banks offering the same stated annual interest rate.

It is not necessary to memorize the major formulae for converting cash-flow streams into either present or future values. Tables at the end of this Appendix contain the present and future values that correspond to the formulae. These tables greatly

---

[12] $0.05127 = \left(1 + \dfrac{0.05}{365}\right)^{365} - 1$

Table 13.3 **Example of using compound interest tables (interest rate = 5%)**

	Cash flow in (£)	Discount factor	Source of factor	Present value (£)
Years 1–20	1,000	12.462	Table 13.5	12,462
Years 1–10	1,000	7.722	Table 13.5	7,722
Year 21	3,000	0.359	Table 13.4	1,077
Total present value				21,261

simplify the computation of present values. Also, computer spreadsheet programs and calculators compute present values and future values. For example, suppose one wants to compute the present value of the following cash flows (at $r = 5\%$): £2,000 for the first ten years, £1,000 for the next ten years, and £3,000 at the end of year 21. Table 13.3 outlines the calculations:

The first thing to note is that to simplify the calculations, the £2,000 stream for years 1–10 and the £1,000 stream for years 11–20 are equivalent to a £1,000 stream for the first 20 years and a £1,000 stream for the first 10 years. The discount factors for these two streams are taken from the annuity table. The single £3,000 payment in year 21 is discounted using the present value factor from the present value table. Adding the three discounted cash flows together yields a present value of £21,261. Recall that £21,261 is the *opportunity cost* or value of the three cash-flow streams (£2,000 for the first 10 years, £1,000 for the next 10 years, and then £3,000 at the end of year 21) when the market rate of interest is 5 per cent.

Numerical **example** 13.12

Juan Perez has €5,000 to invest for two years. One bank offers 5 per cent annual rate compounded monthly while another bank offers 6 per cent compounded annually. Which is the better investment?

Solution

A 5 per cent annual rate is equivalent to a monthly rate of $(1 + 0.05)^{1/12} - 1$, or 0.0040741. The value of €5,000 over 24 months at 0.40741 per cent is €5,000$(1 + 0.0040741)^{24}$, or €5,512. The value of €5,000 over two years at an annual rate of 6 per cent is €5,000$(1 + 0.06)^2$, or €5,618. Investing the €5,000 at 6 per cent annually has the higher future value.

Numerical **example** 13.13

Judy Radski is considering returning to university to get a master's degree in finance. Her current wages are £25,000. Tuition, books, and fees will cost £20,000 per year for two years. Upon completing the degree, her starting salary will be £80,000. She expects that the degree will add £55,000 to her annual salary until retirement. However, she must give up two years of current salary while in graduate school plus pay tuition, books, and fees. At a current age of 31 and with an expected retirement age of 60, does it make sense for Judy to go back to university? The market rate of interest is 5 per cent.

→

Table 13.5 **Present value of an annuity**

Present value of a stream of £1s received at the end of each of the next n periods at an interest rate of r%

Periods	3%	4%	5%	6%	7%	8%	9%	10%	12%	14%	16%	18%	20%	25%	30%	35%	40%
1	0.971	0.962	0.952	0.943	0.935	0.926	0.917	0.909	0.893	0.877	0.862	0.847	0.833	0.800	0.769	0.741	0.714
2	1.913	1.886	1.859	1.833	1.808	1.783	1.759	1.736	1.690	1.647	1.605	1.566	1.528	1.440	1.361	1.289	1.224
3	2.829	2.775	2.723	2.673	2.624	2.577	2.531	2.487	2.402	2.322	2.246	2.174	2.106	1.952	1.816	1.696	1.589
4	3.717	3.630	3.546	3.465	3.387	3.312	3.240	3.170	3.037	2.914	2.798	2.690	2.589	2.362	2.166	1.997	1.849
5	4.580	4.452	4.329	4.212	4.100	3.993	3.890	3.791	3.605	3.433	3.274	3.127	2.991	2.689	2.436	2.220	2.035
6	5.417	5.242	5.076	4.917	4.767	4.623	4.486	4.355	4.111	3.889	3.685	3.498	3.326	2.951	2.643	2.385	2.168
7	6.230	6.002	5.786	5.582	5.389	5.206	5.033	4.868	4.564	4.288	4.039	3.812	3.605	3.161	2.802	2.508	2.263
8	7.020	6.733	6.463	6.210	5.971	5.747	5.535	5.335	4.968	4.639	4.344	4.078	3.837	3.329	2.925	2.598	2.331
9	7.786	7.435	7.108	6.802	6.515	6.247	5.995	5.759	5.328	4.946	4.607	4.303	4.031	3.463	3.019	2.665	2.379
10	8.530	8.111	7.722	7.360	7.024	6.710	6.418	6.145	5.650	5.216	4.833	4.494	4.192	3.571	3.092	2.715	2.414
11	9.253	8.760	8.306	7.887	7.499	7.139	6.805	6.495	5.938	5.453	5.029	4.656	4.327	3.656	3.147	2.752	2.438
12	9.954	9.385	8.863	8.384	7.943	7.536	7.161	6.814	6.194	5.660	5.197	4.793	4.439	3.725	3.190	2.779	2.456
13	10.635	9.986	9.394	8.853	8.358	7.904	7.487	7.103	6.424	5.842	5.342	4.910	4.533	3.780	3.223	2.799	2.469
14	11.296	10.563	9.899	9.295	8.745	8.244	7.786	7.367	6.628	6.002	5.468	5.008	4.611	3.824	3.249	2.814	2.478
15	11.938	11.118	10.380	9.712	9.108	8.559	8.061	7.606	6.811	6.142	5.575	5.092	4.675	3.859	3.268	2.825	2.484
16	12.561	11.652	10.838	10.106	9.447	8.851	8.313	7.824	6.974	6.265	5.668	5.162	4.730	3.887	3.283	2.834	2.489
17	13.166	12.166	11.274	10.477	9.763	9.122	8.544	8.022	7.120	6.373	5.749	5.222	4.775	3.910	3.295	2.840	2.492
18	13.754	12.659	11.690	10.828	10.059	9.372	8.756	8.201	7.250	6.467	5.818	5.273	4.812	3.928	3.304	2.844	2.494
19	14.324	13.134	12.085	11.158	10.336	9.604	8.950	8.365	7.366	6.550	5.877	5.316	4.843	3.942	3.311	2.848	2.496
20	14.877	13.590	12.462	11.470	10.594	9.818	9.129	8.514	7.469	6.623	5.929	5.353	4.870	3.954	3.316	2.850	2.497
21	15.415	14.029	12.821	11.764	10.836	10.017	9.292	8.649	7.562	6.687	5.973	5.384	4.891	3.963	3.320	2.852	2.498
22	15.937	14.451	13.163	12.042	11.061	10.201	9.442	8.772	7.645	6.743	6.011	5.410	4.909	3.970	3.323	2.853	2.498
23	16.444	14.857	13.489	12.303	11.272	10.371	9.580	8.883	7.718	6.792	6.044	5.432	4.925	3.976	3.325	2.854	2.499
24	16.936	15.247	13.799	12.550	11.469	10.529	9.707	8.985	7.784	6.835	6.073	5.451	4.937	3.981	3.327	2.855	2.499
25	17.413	15.622	14.094	12.783	11.654	10.675	9.823	9.077	7.843	6.873	6.097	5.467	4.948	3.985	3.329	2.856	2.499
26	17.877	15.983	14.375	13.003	11.826	10.810	9.929	9.161	7.896	6.906	6.118	5.480	4.956	3.988	3.330	2.856	2.500
27	18.327	16.330	14.643	13.211	11.987	10.935	10.027	9.237	7.943	6.935	6.136	5.492	4.964	3.990	3.331	2.856	2.500
28	18.764	16.663	14.898	13.406	12.137	11.051	10.116	9.307	7.984	6.961	6.152	5.502	4.970	3.992	3.331	2.857	2.500
29	19.188	16.984	15.141	13.591	12.278	11.158	10.198	9.370	8.022	6.983	6.166	5.510	4.975	3.994	3.332	2.857	2.500
30	19.600	17.292	15.372	13.765	12.409	11.258	10.274	9.427	8.055	7.003	6.177	5.517	4.979	3.995	3.332	2.857	2.500
35	21.487	18.665	16.374	14.498	12.948	11.655	10.567	9.644	8.176	7.070	6.215	5.539	4.992	3.998	3.333	2.857	2.500
40	23.115	19.793	17.159	15.046	13.332	11.925	10.757	9.779	8.244	7.105	6.233	5.548	4.997	3.999	3.333	2.857	2.500
60	27.676	22.623	18.929	16.161	14.039	12.377	11.048	9.967	8.324	7.140	6.249	5.555	5.000	4.000	3.333	2.857	2.500
120	32.373	24.774	19.943	16.651	14.281	12.499	11.111	10.000	8.333	7.143	6.250	5.556	5.000	4.000	3.333	2.857	2.500
360	33.333	25.000	20.000	16.667	14.286	12.500	11.111	10.000	8.333	7.143	6.250	5.556	5.000	4.000	3.333	2.857	2.500

Table 13.6 Future value of £1

Future value of £1 invested today at r% interest and allowed to compound for n periods

Periods	3%	4%	5%	6%	7%	8%	9%	10%	12%	14%	16%	18%	20%	25%	30%	35%	40%
1	1.030	1.040	1.050	1.060	1.070	1.080	1.090	1.100	1.120	1.140	1.160	1.180	1.200	1.250	1.300	1.350	1.400
2	1.061	1.082	1.103	1.124	1.145	1.166	1.188	1.210	1.254	1.300	1.346	1.392	1.440	1.563	1.690	1.823	1.960
3	1.093	1.125	1.158	1.191	1.225	1.260	1.295	1.331	1.405	1.482	1.561	1.643	1.728	1.953	2.197	2.460	2.744
4	1.126	1.170	1.216	1.262	1.311	1.360	1.412	1.464	1.574	1.689	1.811	1.939	2.074	2.441	2.856	3.322	3.842
5	1.159	1.217	1.276	1.338	1.403	1.469	1.539	1.611	1.762	1.925	2.100	2.288	2.488	3.052	3.713	4.484	5.378
6	1.194	1.265	1.340	1.419	1.501	1.587	1.677	1.772	1.974	2.195	2.436	2.700	2.986	3.815	4.827	6.053	7.530
7	1.230	1.316	1.407	1.504	1.606	1.714	1.828	1.949	2.211	2.502	2.826	3.185	3.583	4.768	6.275	8.172	10.541
8	1.267	1.369	1.477	1.594	1.718	1.851	1.993	2.144	2.476	2.853	3.278	3.759	4.300	5.960	8.157	11.032	14.758
9	1.305	1.423	1.551	1.689	1.838	1.999	2.172	2.358	2.773	3.252	3.803	4.435	5.160	7.451	10.604	14.894	20.661
10	1.344	1.480	1.629	1.791	1.967	2.159	2.367	2.594	3.106	3.707	4.411	5.234	6.192	9.313	13.786	20.107	28.925
11	1.384	1.539	1.710	1.898	2.105	2.332	2.580	2.853	3.479	4.226	5.117	6.176	7.430	11.642	17.922	27.144	40.496
12	1.426	1.601	1.796	2.012	2.252	2.518	2.813	3.138	3.896	4.818	5.936	7.288	8.916	14.552	23.298	36.644	56.694
13	1.469	1.665	1.886	2.133	2.410	2.720	3.066	3.452	4.363	5.492	6.886	8.599	10.699	18.190	30.288	49.470	79.371
14	1.513	1.732	1.980	2.261	2.579	2.937	3.342	3.797	4.887	6.261	7.988	10.147	12.839	22.737	39.374	66.784	111.120
15	1.558	1.801	2.079	2.397	2.759	3.172	3.642	4.177	5.474	7.138	9.266	11.974	15.407	28.422	51.186	90.158	155.568
16	1.605	1.873	2.183	2.540	2.952	3.426	3.970	4.595	6.130	8.137	10.748	14.129	18.488	35.527	66.542	121.714	217.795
17	1.653	1.948	2.292	2.693	3.159	3.700	4.328	5.054	6.866	9.276	12.468	16.672	22.186	44.409	86.504	164.314	304.913
18	1.702	2.026	2.407	2.854	3.380	3.996	4.717	5.560	7.690	10.575	14.463	19.673	26.623	55.511	112.455	221.824	426.879
19	1.754	2.107	2.527	3.026	3.617	4.316	5.142	6.116	8.613	12.056	16.777	23.214	31.948	69.389	146.192	299.462	597.630
20	1.806	2.191	2.653	3.207	3.870	4.661	5.604	6.727	9.646	13.743	19.461	27.393	38.338	86.736	190.050	404.274	836.683
21	1.860	2.279	2.786	3.400	4.141	5.034	6.109	7.400	10.804	15.668	22.574	32.324	46.005	108.420	247.065	545.769	1,171.356
22	1.916	2.370	2.925	3.604	4.430	5.437	6.659	8.140	12.100	17.861	26.186	38.142	55.206	135.525	321.184	736.789	1,639.898
23	1.974	2.465	3.072	3.820	4.741	5.871	7.258	8.954	13.552	20.362	30.376	45.008	66.247	169.407	417.539	994.665	2,295.857
24	2.033	2.563	3.225	4.049	5.072	6.341	7.911	9.850	15.179	23.212	35.236	53.109	79.497	211.758	542.801	1,342.797	3,214.200
25	2.094	2.666	3.386	4.292	5.427	6.848	8.623	10.835	17.000	26.462	40.874	62.669	95.396	264.698	705.641	1,812.776	4,499.880
26	2.157	2.772	3.556	4.549	5.807	7.396	9.399	11.918	19.040	30.167	47.414	73.949	114.475	330.872	917.333	2,447.248	6,299.831
27	2.221	2.883	3.733	4.822	6.214	7.988	10.245	13.110	21.325	34.390	55.000	87.260	137.371	413.590	1,192.533	3,303.785	8,819.764
28	2.288	2.999	3.920	5.112	6.649	8.627	11.167	14.421	23.884	39.204	63.800	102.967	164.845	516.988	1,550.293	4,460.109	12,347.670
29	2.357	3.119	4.116	5.418	7.114	9.317	12.172	15.863	26.750	44.693	74.009	121.501	197.814	646.235	2,015.381	6,021.148	17,286.737
30	2.427	3.243	4.322	5.743	7.612	10.063	13.268	17.449	29.960	50.950	85.850	143.371	237.376	807.794	2,619.996	8,128.550	24,201.432
35	2.814	3.946	5.516	7.686	10.677	14.785	20.414	28.102	52.800	98.100	180.314	327.997	590.668	2,465.190	9,727.860	36,448.688	130,161.112
40	3.262	4.801	7.040	10.286	14.974	21.725	31.409	45.259	93.051	188.884	378.721	750.378	1,469.772	7,523.164	36,118.865	163,437.135	700,037.697

Table 13.7 Future value of an annuity of £1

Future value of a stream of n £1s invested today at r% interest and allowed to compound for n periods

Periods	3%	4%	5%	6%	7%	8%	9%	10%	12%	14%	16%	18%	20%	25%	30%	35%	40%
1	1.000	1.000	1.000	1.000	1.000	1.000	1.000	1.000	1.000	1.000	1.000	1.000	1.000	1.000	1.000	1.000	1.000
2	2.030	2.040	2.050	2.060	2.070	2.080	2.090	2.100	2.120	2.140	2.160	2.180	2.200	2.250	2.300	2.350	2.400
3	3.091	3.122	3.153	3.184	3.215	3.246	3.278	3.310	3.374	3.440	3.506	3.572	3.640	3.813	3.990	4.173	4.360
4	4.184	4.246	4.310	4.375	4.440	4.506	4.573	4.641	4.779	4.921	5.066	5.215	5.368	5.766	6.187	6.633	7.104
5	5.309	5.416	5.526	5.637	5.751	5.867	5.985	6.105	6.353	6.610	6.877	7.154	7.442	8.207	9.043	9.954	10.946
6	6.468	6.633	6.802	6.975	7.153	7.336	7.523	7.716	8.115	8.536	8.977	9.442	9.930	11.259	12.756	14.438	16.324
7	7.662	7.898	8.142	8.394	8.654	8.923	9.200	9.487	10.089	10.730	11.414	12.142	12.916	15.073	17.583	20.492	23.853
8	8.892	9.214	9.549	9.897	10.260	10.637	11.028	11.436	12.300	13.233	14.240	15.327	16.499	19.842	23.858	28.664	34.395
9	10.159	10.583	11.027	11.491	11.978	12.488	13.021	13.579	14.776	16.085	17.519	19.086	20.799	25.802	32.015	39.696	49.153
10	11.464	12.006	12.578	13.181	13.816	14.487	15.193	15.937	17.549	19.337	21.321	23.521	25.959	33.253	42.619	54.590	69.814
11	12.808	13.486	14.207	14.972	15.784	16.645	17.560	18.531	20.655	23.045	25.733	28.755	32.150	42.566	56.405	74.697	98.739
12	14.192	15.026	15.917	16.870	17.888	18.977	20.141	21.384	24.133	27.271	30.850	34.931	39.581	54.208	74.327	101.841	139.235
13	15.618	16.627	17.713	18.882	20.141	21.495	22.953	24.523	28.029	32.089	36.786	42.219	48.497	68.760	97.625	138.485	195.929
14	17.086	18.292	19.599	21.015	22.550	24.215	26.019	27.975	32.393	37.581	43.672	50.818	59.196	86.949	127.913	187.954	275.300
15	18.599	20.024	21.579	23.276	25.129	27.152	29.361	31.772	37.280	43.842	51.660	60.965	72.035	109.687	167.286	254.738	386.420
16	20.157	21.825	23.657	25.673	27.888	30.324	33.003	35.950	42.753	50.980	60.925	72.939	87.442	138.109	218.472	344.897	541.988
17	21.762	23.698	25.840	28.213	30.840	33.750	36.974	40.545	48.884	59.118	71.673	87.068	105.931	173.636	285.014	466.611	759.784
18	23.414	25.645	28.132	30.906	33.999	37.450	41.301	45.599	55.750	68.394	84.141	103.740	128.117	218.045	371.518	630.925	1,064.697
19	25.117	27.671	30.539	33.760	37.379	41.446	46.018	51.159	63.440	78.969	98.603	123.414	154.740	273.556	483.973	852.748	1,491.576
20	26.870	29.778	33.066	36.786	40.995	45.762	51.160	57.275	72.052	91.025	115.380	146.628	186.688	342.945	630.165	1,152.210	2,089.206
21	28.676	31.969	35.719	39.993	44.865	50.423	56.765	64.002	81.699	104.768	134.841	174.021	225.026	429.681	820.215	1,556.484	2,925.889
22	30.537	34.248	38.505	43.392	49.006	55.457	62.873	71.403	92.503	120.436	157.415	206.345	271.031	538.101	1,067.280	2,102.253	4,097.245
23	32.453	36.618	41.430	46.996	53.436	60.893	69.532	79.543	104.603	138.297	183.601	244.487	326.237	673.626	1,388.464	2,839.042	5,737.142
24	34.426	39.083	44.502	50.816	58.177	66.765	76.790	88.497	118.155	158.659	213.978	289.494	392.484	843.033	1,806.003	3,833.706	8,032.999
25	36.459	41.646	47.727	54.865	63.249	73.106	84.701	98.347	133.334	181.871	249.214	342.603	471.981	1,054.791	2,348.803	5,176.504	11,247.199
26	38.553	44.312	51.113	59.156	68.676	79.954	93.324	109.182	150.334	208.333	290.088	405.272	567.377	1,319.489	3,054.444	6,989.280	15,747.079
27	40.710	47.084	54.669	63.706	74.484	87.351	102.723	121.100	169.374	238.499	337.502	479.221	681.853	1,650.361	3,971.778	9,436.528	22,046.910
28	42.931	49.968	58.403	68.528	80.698	95.339	112.968	134.210	190.699	272.889	392.503	566.481	819.223	2,063.952	5,164.311	12,740.313	30,866.674
29	45.219	52.966	62.323	73.640	87.347	103.966	124.135	148.631	214.583	312.094	456.303	669.447	984.068	2,580.939	6,714.604	17,200.422	43,214.343
30	47.575	56.085	66.439	79.058	94.461	113.283	136.308	164.494	241.333	356.787	530.312	790.948	1,181.882	3,227.174	8,729.985	23,221.570	60,501.081
35	60.462	73.652	90.320	111.435	138.237	172.317	215.711	271.024	431.663	693.573	1,120.713	1,816.652	2,948.341	9,856.761	32,422.868	104,136.251	325,400.279
40	75.401	95.026	120.800	154.762	199.635	259.057	337.882	442.593	767.091	1,342.025	2,360.757	4,163.213	7,343.858	30,088.655	120,392.883	466,960.385	1,750,091.741

Self-study problem

Avroland is an amusement park in Belgium. It currently uses a central computer system to perform general accounting functions, including the tracking of ticket sales and payroll, as well as employee and maintenance scheduling functions. The original system, when purchased two years ago, cost €300,000 and has been depreciated for tax purposes using straight-line depreciation with an expected useful life of four more years and a zero salvage value. However, due to recent expansion, the computer system is no longer large enough. Upgrading the system to increase the storage capacity and processing speed to accommodate the extra data processing demands would cost €65,000. The system would become obsolete in four years. These system additions also would be depreciated using straight-line depreciation and would have a zero salvage value. The company's accountant estimates that the firm will increase operating spending by €28,000 per year after taxes for data processing, payroll (including Avroland personnel), and annual updates of software for the upgraded system. Alternatively, the firm could outsource payroll to a local payroll-processing firm at the cost of €40,000 a year after taxes. This outsourcing would free up enough computer capacity to prevent having to upgrade the system. Assume a real cost of capital of 4 per cent and a tax rate of 40 per cent.

What should Avroland do?

Solution

The relevant costs to Avroland for processing payroll internally are the cost of upgrading the computer system plus the variable cost of processing the information minus the tax savings from depreciating the upgraded system. The relevant cost for outsourcing payroll is the cost of the outside service firm. Over the next four years, Avroland's cash flows would be as follows under the two possibilities:

Keep payroll inside

	Year 0	Year 1	Year 2	Year 3	Year 4	NPV
Cost of upgrade	€65,000					
Labour plus software		€28,000	€28,000	€28,000	€28,000	
Tax savings from depreciation*		(6,500)	(6,500)	(6,500)	(6,500)	
Total cash outflows	€65,000	€21,500	€21,500	€21,500	€21,500	
Discount rate	1.000	0.962	0.925	0.889	0.855	
Present value at 4%	€65,000	€20,683	€19,878	€19,113	€18,383	€143,067

Outsource payroll

	Year 0	Year 1	Year 2	Year 3	Year 4	NPV
Annual cost of service		€40,000	€40,000	€40,000	€40,000	
Discount rate	1.000	0.962	0.925	0.889	0.855	
Present value at 4%		€38,480	€37,000	€35,560	€34,200	€145,240

*€65,000 ÷ 4 years × 40% tax rate = €6,500

Note: The depreciation of the original system will remain whether the system is upgraded or payroll is outsourced. Therefore, it is not relevant to the decisions under consideration.

Since the net present value of the cash outflows are lower by keeping the payroll inside rather than outside the firm, the computer system should be upgraded.

Numerical exercises

NE 13.1 Estimating the payback period LO 3

An investment opportunity that costs £40,000 generates £20,000 in cash inflows each of the next four years.

What is the payback period for the investment?

NE 13.2 Calculating the accounting rate of return LO 4

An investment that costs £100,000 generates £20,000 in income over the next five years. The original cost of the investment is depreciated using straight-line depreciation over the five years with no salvage value.

What is the multi-year ROI for the investment?

NE 13.3 Net present value of cash flows LO 5

What is the net present value of cash inflows of €30,000 in one year, €40,000 in two years, and €80,000 in three years if the opportunity cost of capital is 8 per cent?

NE 13.4 Net present value of cash flows LO 5

What is the net present value of an investment that costs €50,000 and generates €20,000 in cash inflows in the first year and €40,000 in the second year given a 10 per cent cost of capital?

NE 13.5 Depreciation tax shields LO 9

A company buys a machine for £60,000 that is fully depreciated over three years using the straight-line method.
    What is the value of the depreciation tax shield if the tax rate is 40 per cent?

NE 13.6 Internal rate of return LO 11

What is the IRR for an investment of £1,000 that yields £1,300 in one year?

NE 13.7 Internal rate of return LO 11

What is the IRR of an investment of £1,000 that yields cash flows of £600 in each of the first two years?

NE 13.8 Using annuity tables LO 13

What is the value of a 10-year annuity in 10 years if the interest rate is 6 per cent and each annuity payment is €100?

NE 13.9 Using annuity tables LO 13

What is the present value of a twelve-year annuity if the interest rate is 8 per cent and the annuity payment is €1,000?

NE 13.10 Future value of an annuity LO 5, 13

A mother wants to put sufficient money in the bank to cover university expenses for her daughter in 15 years. She estimates that in 15 years £100,000 will be necessary to pay for university. The bank pays 8 per cent compounded annually.
    How much does she need to deposit today to have sufficient money in 15 years?

NE 13.11 Compounding interest LO 5, 13

Your grandfather put £1,000 in the bank for you 48 years ago. The bank paid 6 per cent interest compounded annually during this time period.
    How much is your grandfather's deposit worth today?

Numerical problems

NP 13.1 Decision with discounting cash flows LO 5

A law firm is considering the dismissal of one of its junior lawyers. The law firm presently has enough space for more lawyers and a growing legal practice but considers this junior lawyer to be a net loss to the firm. To dismiss him, the firm would have to pay £100,000 to sever his employee contract early. The lawyer has a salary of £80,000 and currently brings in £200,000 per year in revenues. The law firm, however, estimates that indirect costs related to the lawyer are £180,000 per year. The alternative is to wait two more years to dismiss him at the end of his contract and not have to pay any severance costs. The discount rate is 10 per cent.
    What should the law firm do?

NP 13.2 Annuity LO 5, 13

Suppose the opportunity cost of capital is 10 per cent and you have just won a €1 million lottery that entitles you to €100,000 at the end of each of the next 10 years.

a What is the minimum lump sum cash payment that you would be willing to take now in lieu of the 10-year annuity?
b What is the minimum lump sum that you would be willing to accept at the end of the 10 years in lieu of the annuity?

c Suppose that three years have passed and you have just received the third payment. You have seven years left when the lottery promoters approach you with an offer to 'settle-up for cash'. What is the minimum you would accept (at the end of year three)?

d How would your answer to (a) change if the first payment came immediately (at $t = 0$) and the remaining payments were at the beginning instead of at the end of each year?

NP 13.3 Retirement decision and annuities LO 5, 13

Mr Wang intends to retire in 20 years at the age of 65. As yet he has not provided for retirement income and he wants to set up a periodic savings plan to do this.

If he makes equal annual payments into a savings account that pays 4 per cent interest per year, how large must his payments be to ensure that after retirement he can draw £30,000 per year from this account until he is 80?

NP 13.4 Present value of interest and principal LO 5, 13

You are thinking about borrowing £100,000 for 10 years at 12 per cent. Annual interest payments are required at the end of each year and the principal (£100,000) is to be repaid at the end of the 10 years.

What is the present value of the principal payment and what is the present value of the interest payments?

NP 13.5 Net present value and internal rate of return LO 5, 9, 11

A company is considering buying a corporate jet for €5,000,000. The jet will save employee time and eliminate the need to purchase plane tickets. These benefits are worth approximately €800,000 per year. The cost of operating the plane is €100,000 per year. The plane will last for 10 years and be sold for €1,000,000 at the end of the tenth year. Assume an interest rate of 10 per cent and no taxes.

a What is the NPV of this project?

b What is the IRR of this project, if the jet had zero value at the end of the tenth year?

c Assume that the jet is depreciated €500,000 per year for the 10 years and is sold for €1,000,000 at the end of the tenth year. Also, assume that the tax rate on income is 40 per cent. What is the NPV of the jet?

NP 13.6 Decision to sell division LO 5, 13

Several years ago, your firm paid £25,000,000 for Clean Tooth, a small, high-technology company that manufactures laser-based, tooth-cleaning equipment. Unfortunately, due to extensive production line and sales resistance problems, the company is considering selling the division as part of a 'streamlining programme'. Based on current information, the following are the estimated accounting numbers if the company continues to operate the division:

Estimated sales revenues – next 10 years	£500,000/year
Estimated cash expenses – next 10 years	£450,000/year
Current offer for the division from another firm	£250,000

Assume:

1 The firm is in the 0 per cent tax bracket (no income taxes).
2 No additional expenses are associated with the sale.
3 After year 10, the division will have sales (and expenses) of 0.
4 Estimates are completely certain.

Should the firm sell the division for £250,000?

NP 13.7 Present value of payments LO 5, 13

River Valley farmers are subject to occasional flooding when heavy rains cause the river to overflow. They have asked the government to build a dam upstream to prevent flooding. The construction cost of this project is to be re-paid by the farm owners without interest over a period of years. The cost of the dam is £30,000. No payments at all are to be made for the first five years. Then £1,000 is to be paid at the end of each year for 30 years to pay off the £30,000.

Are the farmers receiving a subsidy? Why? If the interest rate is 10 per cent, what is the approximate present value of the subsidy (if any)? Show all calculations.

NP 13.8 Mortgage payments and refinancing LO 5, 13

You have just purchased a house and have obtained a 30-year, £200,000 mortgage with an interest rate of 10 per cent.

a What is your annual mortgage payment, assuming you pay equal amounts each year?

b Assuming you bought the house on 1 January, what is the principal balance after one year? After 10 years?

NP 13.9 Replacing or modifying equipment LO 5, 6, 13

PQR Coal Company has several conventional and strip mining operations. Recently, new legislation has made strip mining, which produces coal of high sulphur content, unprofitable so those operations will be discontinued. Unfortunately, two years ago PQR purchased £1 million of earth-moving equipment for the strip mines. This equipment is not particularly well suited to conventional mining.

Mr Big, the president, suggests that since the equipment can be sold for £500,000 it should be scrapped. In his words, 'I learned a long time ago that when you make mistakes, it's best to admit them and take your lumps. By ignoring sunk costs, you aren't tempted to throw good money after bad. The original value of the equipment is gone.'

A new employee, Ms Embay, has suggested that the equipment should be adapted to the conventional operations. She argues, 'We are about to spend £800,000 on some new conventional equipment. However, for a smaller expenditure of £250,000, we can adapt the old equipment to perform the same task. Of course, it will cost about £20,000 per year more to operate over the assumed 10-year life of each alternative. But at an interest rate of 10 per cent, the inclusion of the present value of £20,000 per year for 10 years and the initial £250,000 are still less than £800,000 for new equipment. While it's true that we should ignore sunk costs, at least this way we can cut our losses somewhat.'

Who is correct? Why?

NP 13.10 Student loan payments and subsidies LO 5, 13

Student loan programmes allow university and college students to borrow funds from various levels of government. These plans vary widely depending upon the jurisdiction. For example, in Canada, student loans are offered by both the federal and provincial governments and frequently are integrated. The typical contract stipulates a 'grace period' during which the annual per centage rate of interest is 0 per cent until six to 12 months after the student ceases his or her formal education (defined as at least half-time enrolment). After this time period, the interest rate for loan repayments is set as a percentage addition to the bank prime lending rate. For the purposes of the questions below, assume the following: the student borrows $10,000 in the beginning of her first year of university and completes her education in four years. Loan repayments at an interest rate of 4% begin one year after graduation. The maximum repayment period is 10 years and the grace period is 12 months.

a Assuming that the student elects the maximum payment period, what are the uniform annual loan repayments? (Assume that all repayments occur at the end of the year.)

b If the rate of interest on savings deposits is 6 per cent, what is the minimum amount that the student has to have in a bank account one year after graduation to make the loan payments calculated in (a)?

c Are recipients of student loans receiving a subsidy? If so, what is the present value of the subsidy when the loan is taken out?

NP 13.11 Value of a home with an assumable mortgage LO 5, 13

A house in your neighbourhood identical to your home sold last week for £150,000. Your home has a £120,000 assumable, 8 per cent mortgage (compounded annually) with 30 years remaining. An assumable mortgage is one that the new buyer can assume at the old terms and continue to make payments at the original interest rate. The house that recently sold did not have an assumable mortgage; that is, the buyers had to finance the house at the current market rate of interest, which is 15 per cent.

What selling price should you ask for your home?

NP 13.12 Mortgage department decisions LO 5, 13

Suppose that you are the manager of a mortgage department at a savings bank. Under the usury law, the maximum interest rate allowed for mortgages is 10 per cent compounded annually.

a If you granted a €50,000 mortgage at the maximum rate for 30 years, what would be the equal annual payments?

b If the bank's cost of capital is 12 per cent, how much money does the bank lose by issuing the mortgage described in (a)?

c The usury law does not prohibit banks from charging 'points'. One 'point' means that the borrower pays 1 per cent of the €50,000 loan back to the lending institution at the inception of the loan. That is, if one point is charged, the repayments are computed as in (a) above, but the borrower receives only €49,500. How many points must the bank charge to earn 12 per cent on the 10 per cent loan?

NP 13.13 Decision to make or buy electricity LO 5, 13

A firm that purchases electric power from the local utility is considering the alternative of generating its own electricity. The current cost of obtaining the firm's electricity from its local utility firm is £42,000 per year. The cost of a steam generator (installed) is £140,000 and the annual maintenance and fuel expenses are estimated at £22,000 per year. The generator is expected to last for 10 years, at which time it will be worthless. The cost of capital is 10 per cent and the firm pays no taxes.

a Should the firm install the electric generator? Why or why not?
b The engineers have calculated that with an additional investment of £40,000, the excess steam from the generator can be used to heat the firm's buildings. The current cost of heating the buildings with purchased steam is £21,000 per year. If the generator is to be used for heat as well as electricity, additional fuel and maintenance costs of £10,000 per year will be incurred. Should the firm invest in the generator and the heating system? Show all calculations.

NP 13.14 Internal rate of return LO 5, 11, 12

Jasper plc is considering two mutually exclusive investments, A and B. Alternative A has a current outlay of £300,000 and returns £360,000 next year. Alternative B has a current outlay of £165,000 and returns £200,000 next year.

a Calculate the IRR for each alternative.
b Which alternative should Jasper take, if the required rate of return for those projects in the capital market is 15 per cent?
c Why do the IRR and NPV methods rank the projects differently?

NP 13.15 Decision to sell or keep an asset LO 5, 13

Rich Landlord owns a dilapidated 30-year-old apartment building in Bristol. The net cash flow from renting the apartments last year was £200,000. He expects those net cash flows from renting the apartments to continue for the remaining useful life of the apartment building, which is 10 years. In 10 years, the value of the property is expected to be £100,000. A developer wants to buy the apartment building from Rich, demolish it, and construct luxury condominiums. He offers Rich £1,500,000 for the apartments. Rich's opportunity cost of capital is 16 per cent. Assume that Rich pays no taxes.

Evaluate the developer's offer and make a recommendation to Rich.

NP 13.16 Decision to replace a machine LO 5, 9, 13

The Baltic Company is considering the purchase of a new machine tool to replace an older one. The machine being used for the operation has a book value for tax purposes of €80,000 with an annual depreciation expense of €8,000. The older machine tool is in good working order and will last, physically, for at least an additional 10 years. It can be sold today for €40,000, but will have no value if kept for another 10 years. The proposed new machine will perform the operation so much more efficiently that Baltic Company engineers estimate that labour, material and other direct costs of the operation will be reduced €60,000 a year if it is installed. The proposed machine costs €240,000 delivered and installed, and its economic life is estimated to be 10 years with zero salvage value. The company expects to earn 14 per cent on its investment after taxes (14 per cent is the firm's cost of capital). The tax rate is 40 per cent. The firm uses straight-line depreciation.

Should Baltic buy the new machine?

NP 13.17 Investment in pollution control devices LO 5, 6, 13

Lachine Steel operates a coal-burning steel mill in eastern France. Changes in the government's air quality-control laws will result in the firm's incurring a €1,000 per-day fine, which is paid at the end of the year, if the mill continues to operate. The mill currently operates 365 days a year.

The mill was built 20 years ago at a cost of €15 million and has a remaining undepreciated book value of €3 million. The mill's remaining useful life is 30 years.

Lachine Steel can sell the mill to a developer who wants to build a shopping centre on the site. The buyer would pay €1 million for the site, if the company demolishes and prepares the site for the developer. Demolition and site preparation costs are estimated at €650,000.

Alternatively, Lachine Steel could install pollution control devices and other advanced technologies at an initial outlay of €2.75 million. These improvements do not extend the useful life or salvage value of the plant but they do reduce net operating costs by €25,000 per year in addition to eliminating the €1,000 per-day fine. Currently, the net cash flows of sales less the cost of operating the mill are €450,000 per year before any fines.

Assume the following:

1 The opportunity cost of capital is 14 per cent.
2 There are no taxes.
3 The annual cash-flow estimates given above are constant over the next 30 years.
4 At the end of the 30 years, the mill has an estimated salvage value of €2 million whether or not the pollution equipment is installed.

Evaluate the alternatives available to management and make a recommendation as to which one is preferable. Support your conclusions with neatly labelled calculations where possible.

NP 13.18 Depreciation and taxes LO 5, 9

Scottie Corporation has been offered a five-year contract to produce 100 castings a year at a price of £200 per casting. Producing the castings will require an investment in the plant of £35,000 and operating costs of £50 per casting produced. For tax purposes, depreciation will be on a straight-line basis over five years with a full year's depreciation being taken in both the beginning and ending years. The tax rate is 40 per cent and the opportunity cost of capital is 10 per cent.

Should Scottie accept the contract?

NP 13.19 Decision to replace a machine LO 5, 9

Ace Company has in use a punch press with a current book value of £1,800. The press needs design modification totalling £16,200, which would be capitalized at the present time and depreciated. The press could be sold for £2,600 now. Alternatively, it could be used for three more years if the necessary modifications were made. At the end of three years, it would have no salvage value.

Ace can purchase a new punch press at an invoice price of £26,900 to replace the present equipment. Freight-in will amount to £800, and installation will cost £500. These expenses will be depreciated, along with the invoice price, over the life of the machine. Due to the nature of the product manufactured, the new machine also will have an expected life of three years and will have no salvage value at the end of that time.

Using the old machine, the operating profits before taxes and depreciation (revenues less costs) are £10,000 in the first year and £8,000 in each of the next two years. Using the new machine, the operating profits before taxes and depreciation (revenues less costs) are £18,000 in the first year and £14,000 in each of the next two years.

The corporate tax rate is 40 per cent, which is the same tax rate applicable to gains or losses on sales of equipment. Both the present and proposed equipment would be depreciated on a straight-line basis over three years. The opportunity cost of capital is 10 per cent.

Should Ace Company modify the old machine or purchase the new one?

NP 13.20 Capital-budgeting decision LO 5, 13

The town of Paisley has received a proposal to build a new multi-purpose outdoor sports stadium. The expected life of the stadium is 20 years and will be financed by a 20-year bond paying 8 per cent interest annually. The stadium's primary tenant will be the city's football team, the Cyclones. The plan's backers anticipate that the site also will be used for music concerts and university and high school sports. The town does not pay any taxes. Paisley's cost of capital is 8 per cent. The estimated costs and revenues follow:

Cash outflows	
Construction costs	£12,000,000
General maintenance (including labour)	£250,000 per year
Cash inflows	
Cyclones' minimum lease payments	£650,000 per year
Concerts	£600,000 per year
University and secondary school sports	£50,000 per year

a Should the town of Paisley build the stadium? (Assume payments are made at the end of the year.)

b The Cyclones have threatened to move out of Paisley if they do not get a new stadium. The city controller estimates that the move will cost the city £350,000 per year for 10 years in lost taxes, parking revenues and other fees. Should the town build the stadium now? State your reasoning.

NP 13.21 Payback period LO 3

Kline Corporation is evaluating two investment projects, a tennis club and a squash club. The tennis club would require £10,000,000 to build. Kline management projects annual cash inflows from the tennis club to be £2,000,000. The squash club would be smaller and would require £2,000,000 to build. Management projects annual cash inflows from the squash club to be £500,000.

a What is the payback period for each investment?

b Based on the payback period, which investment should be chosen?

c What are the drawbacks of making the investment decision based on the payback period?

NP 13.22 Accounting rate of return (ROI) LO 4

Kline Corporation in *Numerical problem 13.21* is thinking about investing in either a tennis club or a squash club. The tennis club would cost £10,000,000 and generate annual cash flows of £2,000,000 per year. The initial cost of the tennis club would be depreciated over 10 years using straight-line depreciation. The squash club would cost £2,000,000 and generate annual cash flows of £500,000 per year. The initial cost of the squash club would be depreciated over 20 years using straight-line depreciation. Depreciation is the only adjustment to cash flow for the calculation of income for both investments. Each investment would have zero salvage value after being fully depreciated.

a What is the ROI of each investment during the first year, using the investment at the beginning of the year as the denominator?

b What is the multi-year ROI for each investment?

c What are the problems with using ROI to evaluate investments?

NP 13.23 Adjusting cash flows for accounts receivables and inventory LO 7

Hammer Company is considering opening a car dealership. The business would be completely funded by borrowing. At the end of the first two years, the car dealership is expected to have accounts receivable balances of £50,000 and £75,000, and inventory balances of £300,000 and £400,000, respectively. Income for the first two years is expected to be £200,000 and £500,000, respectively.

How would the income numbers be adjusted for the accounts receivable and inventory balances if converting income into cash flows?

Analysis and interpretation problems

AIP 13.1 Capital budgeting and opportunity costs LO 6

Geico is considering expanding an existing plant on a piece of land that it already owns. The land was purchased 15 years ago for €325,000; its current market appraisal is €820,000. A capital-budgeting analysis shows that the plant expansion has a net present value of €130,000. The expansion will cost €1.73 million and the discounted cash inflows are €1.86 million. The expansion cost of €1.73 million does not include any provision for the cost of the land. The manager preparing the analysis argues that the historical cost of the land is a sunk cost, and since the firm intends to keep the land whether or not the expansion project is accepted, the current appraisal value is irrelevant.

Should the land be included in the analysis? If so, how?

AIP 13.2 Decision to drop a product LO 6

Declining Market plc is considering the problem of when to stop production of a particular product in its product line. Sales of the product have been declining and all estimates are that they will continue to decline. Capital equipment used to manufacture the product is specialized but can be readily sold as used equipment.

Discuss what is wrong, if anything, with the following decision rule for this case:

'Keep producing the product as long as its contribution to net earnings is positive.'

['Contribution to net earnings' is $(1 - t)$(Sales Variable cost − Depreciation on equipment used to manufacture product), where t is the tax rate.]

AIP 13.3 *Ex post* audit of a capital-budgeting decision LO 1

Sharp Razor Company invested in the production of a new type of razor blade three years ago. The production has been implemented and the new razor blade has been sold for two years. The company chairman has asked the controller to perform an *ex post* audit of the investment in the new type of razor blade. An *ex post* audit is an examination of an investment after it has been made. The controller is complaining that the chairman just wants her to work overtime and no reason exists for this after-the-fact analysis. She points out that the investment already has been made and is now a sunk cost.

How can an *ex post* audit of a capital-budgeting decision assist an organization?

AIP 13.4 Identifying the opportunity cost of capital LO 2

Dana Phelps recently started a dry-cleaning business. She would like to expand the business to add a coin-operated laundry. Building renovations and the laundry equipment will cost £100,000. The bank will lend the business £100,000 at a 12 per cent interest rate. Dana could get a 10 per cent interest rate loan if she uses her home as collateral. The lower interest rate reflects the increased security of the bank loan, because the bank could re-possess Dana's house if she does not repay the loan. Dana currently can put money in the bank and receive 6 per cent interest.

Provide arguments for using 12 per cent, 10 per cent and 6 per cent as the opportunity cost of capital for evaluating the investment.

AIP 13.5 Payback period and risk LO 3, 10

The controller and the president are arguing about how to adjust for risk when evaluating investments. The president thinks that the best way to evaluate risk is to measure the payback period of an investment. The shorter the payback period, the lower is the risk. The controller believes that the net present value still should be used to evaluate investments. To adjust for risk, the discount rate is simply increased.

Provide arguments for and against each of these alternative methods.

AIP 13.6 Financing charges and net present value LO 8

The managing director of ROCE Company is not convinced that the interest expense should be excluded from the calculation of the net present value. She points out that, 'Interest is a cash flow. You are supposed to discount cash flows. We borrowed money to completely finance this project. Why not discount interest expenditures?' The managing director is so convinced that she asks you, the controller, to calculate the net present value including the interest expense.

How can you adjust the analysis of net present value to compensate for the inclusion of the interest expense?

Extended **analysis** and **interpretation** problems

AIP 13.7 Davenport farms

Davenport Farms is a family-owned, fruit-growing operation. The farm currently includes 120 hectares of orchards of apples, pears and cherries, along with a warehouse for packing and storing fruit. Tom Davenport is the manager and owner of the farm, which has been in the family for several generations.

The operation of the farm requires a variety of heavy machinery including 10 tractors, eight vehicles of varying sizes, a sprayer for insecticides and a bulldozer for removing tree stumps. The warehouse also has considerable equipment for grading, sorting and packing the fruit. Part of the warehouse is dedicated to storage and is refrigerated in an atmosphere with low oxygen content to reduce spoilage.

Davenport Farms has 20 permanent employees to maintain the equipment, prune trees, apply insecticides and irrigate the trees. During picking seasons, however, large numbers of temporary workers are hired to pick fruit and to work in the warehouse.

Davenport Farms has had several successful years and Tom is considering an expansion of the farm. Recently an eight-hectare parcel adjacent to Davenport Farms has become available for sale for £100,000. The land is currently bare and would have to be developed for irrigation and planted with apple trees. Development of the land for irrigation would take several months and cost £20,000 in materials. Apple trees can be planted immediately after the land is developed. Tom assumes that his existing labour force can provide the labour for developing and planting the trees.

Tom has not decided whether he would plant dwarf apple trees or full-sized apple trees. Dwarf apple trees produce fruit earlier (in the sixth year after planting) and require less space (250 per hectare). The disadvantage is that dwarf apple trees do not last as long and will have to be replaced after 20 years. Full-sized apple trees begin producing in the 11th year after planting and are replaced after 40 years, but only 125 trees can be planted per hectare. Annual cash expenses per hectare are the same for each type of tree and each type of tree generates the same quantity of apples when producing. The cost of both types of seedling apple trees is £5 per tree. Tom plans to hold the land for 40 years and sell the land at the end of 40 years for £200,000. Tom has made the following estimates of costs and benefits of buying the land and planting either dwarf or full-sized trees for the next 40 years:

	Planting dwarfs (£)	Planting full-sized (£)
Land costs (now)	(100,000)	(100,000)
Development costs (now)	(20,000)	(20,000)
Planting costs		
Dwarf (£5 per tree × 250 per hectare)		
(8 hectares) = £10,000 (now)	(10,000)	
(in 20 years)	(10,000)	
Full-sized (£5 per tree × 125 per hectare)		
(8 hectares) = £5,000 (now)		(5,000)
Stump removal and disposal		
(in 20 years)	(100,000)	
Other cash expenses (£20,000 per year)		
(40 years) = £800,000	(800,000)	(800,000)
Cash revenues		
Dwarf: (£70,000 per year in years 6–20 and 26–40)	2,100,000	
Full-sized: (£70,000 per year in Years 11–40)		2,100,000
Sale of land	200,000	200,000
Total	1,240,000	1,275,000

Based on these estimates, the initial cash requirement to purchase and develop the land and plant dwarf trees is £130,000. If full-size trees are planted instead, the initial cost is £125,000. Tom has £40,000 of cash available to make this investment. The rest of the costs can be covered by a mortgage from the local bank. The local bank charges 10 per cent interest for mortgages of this type. Tom will need to borrow £90,000 if he plants dwarf trees and £85,000 if he plants full-size trees. Tom figures his cost of capital is the interest rate that the bank charges.

a Using net present value analysis, should Tom buy the land? If so, which type of trees should he plant?
b What other factors, which are not captured in the present value analysis, should be considered in making this land acquisition?

AIP 13.8 Performance measures and investment opportunities

Sarah Adams manages Executive Inns of London, a 200-room facility that rents furnished suites to executives on a monthly basis. The target market is people relocating to London who are waiting for permanent housing. Sarah's compensation contains a fixed component and a bonus based on the net cash flows from operations. Sarah seeks to maximize her compensation. While Sarah likes her job, and has learned a lot, she expects to be working for a financial institution within five years.

Sarah's occupancy rate is running at 98 per cent. She is considering a £10 million addition to her present building to add more rental units. She has very good private knowledge of the future cash flows. In year 1, cash flows will be £2 million and then will decline by £100,000 per year. The following table summarizes the expansion's cash flows:

Year	Net cash flow (£m)
0	(10)
1	2.0
2	1.9
3	1.8
4	1.7
5	1.6
6	1.5
7	1.4
8	1.3
9	1.2
10	1.1

Based on the preceding data, Sarah prepares the following analysis of the discounted cash flow of the addition:

Year	Net cash flow (£m)	Discount factor	Present value of cash flow (£)
0	(10)	1.000	(10)
1	2.0	0.893	1.79
2	1.9	0.787	1.51
3	1.8	0.712	1.28
4	1.7	0.636	1.08
5	1.6	0.567	0.91
6	1.5	0.507	0.76
7	1.4	0.452	0.63
8	1.3	0.404	0.53
9	1.2	0.361	0.43
10	1.1	0.322	0.35
Total			(0.72)

The discount factors are based on a weighted-average cost of capital of 12 per cent, which accurately reflects the inn's non-diversifiable risk.

Sarah's boss, Katy Judson, manages the Inn Division of Comfort Inc. which has 15 properties located across the UK. Katy does not have the same detailed knowledge of the London hotel/rental market, as does Sarah. She has some general knowledge, but neither as detailed nor as accurate as Sarah does. (For the questions below, ignore taxes.)

a The Inns Division has a very crude accounting system that does not assign the depreciation of particular inns to individual managers. Therefore, Sarah's annual net cash-flow statement is based on the operating revenues less operating expenses. Neither the cost of expansion nor the depreciation of the inn expansion is charged to her operating statement. Given the facts provided so far, what decision do you expect Sarah to make regarding building the £10 million addition? Explain why.

b Sarah prepares the following report for Katy Judson to justify the expansion project:

Year	Net cash flow (£m)	Discount factor	Present value of cash flow (£)
0	(10)	1.000	(10)
1	2	0.893	1.79
2	1.9	0.797	1.51
3	1.9	0.712	1.35
4	1.8	0.636	1.14
5	1.8	0.567	1.02
6	1.8	0.507	0.91
7	1.8	0.452	0.81
8	1.8	0.404	0.73
9	1.7	0.361	0.61
10	1.7	0.322	0.55
Net present value			0.43

Katy realizes that Sarah's projected cash flows are most likely to be optimistic. However, she does not know how optimistic, or whether or not the project even has a positive net present value. She decides, therefore, to change the performance measure used to compute Sarah's bonus. Sarah's compensation now will be based on residual income. Katy also changes the accounting system to track asset expansion and depreciation on the expansion. Sarah's profits from operations now will be charged for straight-line depreciation of the expansion using a 10-year life (assume a zero salvage value). Calculate Sarah's expected residual income from the expansion for each of the next 10 years.

c Based on your calculations in (b), will Sarah propose the expansion project? Explain why.

d Instead of using residual income as Sarah's performance measure in (b), Katy uses net cash flows from operations less straight-line depreciation. Will Sarah seek to undertake the expansion? Explain why.

e Reconcile any differences in your answers for (c) and (d) above.

CHAPTER FOURTEEN

Management accounting in a dynamic environment

Learning objectives

1 Describe factors in a dynamic environment that influence an organization.

2 Describe how the organization's strategy is related to its structure.

3 Explain the role of management accounting in the organizational structure and in making planning decisions.

4 Identify major characteristics of total quality management (TQM).

5 Use quality costs for making planning decisions and control.

6 Explain the philosophy of just-in-time (JIT) processes and accounting adjustments for JIT.

7 Identify when management accounting within an organization should change.

The Driver and Vehicle Licensing Agency (DVLA)[1]

The Driver and Vehicle Licensing Agency (DVLA) is an executive agency of the Department of Transport accountable to parliament and the public through the Secretary of State and ministers. The DVLA's mission is 'to maximise our contribution to improve road safety, reducing crime, improving public experience of Government services through the efficient provision of our statutory core activities of driver and vehicle registration'.

Its headquarters are located in Swansea. It operates 40 local offices throughout Great Britain, along with providing services through post offices. The manager of one such local office is Rashmi Rao (a fictitious person). Local managers, in turn, report to regional operations managers.

The DVLA has four major responsibilities: (1) issuing driving licences, (2) issuing registration certificates and vehicle registration marks, (3) collecting and enforcing vehicle excise duty, and (4) maintaining records of licensed drivers and registered vehicles.

When Rashmi was hired to manage the local office, her regional operations manager told her that things must change. Clients complain incessantly about long lines and unfriendly service. Other users, such as law enforcement agencies, are also unhappy about slow response times when making inquiries about licences. The DVLA is one of the most visible government agencies and some taxpayers are unhappy with what they see. Rashmi and her local staff will have to do a better job of serving the users of DVLA's services, including contributing to the government's e-services agenda.

---

[1] Information about the Driver and Vehicle Licensing Agency is available from www.dvla.gov.uk.

AN INTEGRATIVE FRAMEWORK FOR CHANGE AND MANAGEMENT ACCOUNTING

This book's major theme is that management accounting is an integral part of an organization's strategy and implementation efforts to create customer value. An organization's strategy and its management accounting system are dynamic. Organizations must continually adapt to changes in customer preferences, global competition and a rapidly evolving technological revolution. Figure 14.1 summarizes the relation between the external environment and an organization's efforts to create customer value. If the organization is successful, its value organization will increase as well.

■ External forces affecting the organization

Customer preferences

Adapting to changing customer preferences is critical for an organization. Retail clothing stores are good examples of the need to continually modify products to meet changing customer preferences. Consumers want the latest fashions and failure to update inventory is usually disastrous for a clothing store. Zara gathers information on customer preferences in its stores then quickly designs and manufactures fashions that meet these preferences. This strategy of 'fast fashion' assists Zara in remaining a global leader in the competitive, and frequently fickle, retail market.[2]

Figure 14.1 Framework for organizational change

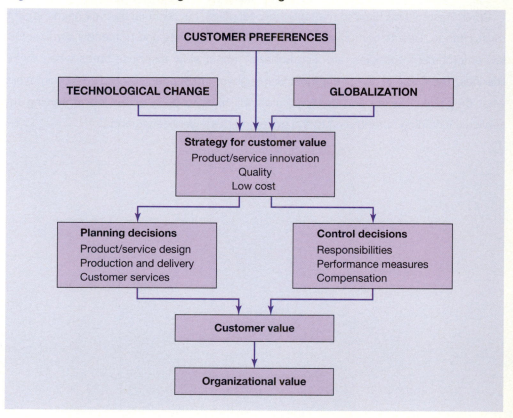

---

[2] 'Conquistadors on the beach' (2007) *The Economist*, 3 May, accessed at www.economist.com/business (29 September).

Kevin Foy/Alamy

Zara's fast-fashion strategy has made it a global leader in the retail market, offering customers the latest trends in real time.

Meeting or even exceeding customer expectations is the key to success for an organization. Total quality management (TQM) is based on meeting customer expectations. Quality is defined by the customer and designed into the product. When an organization adopts TQM, it seeks to improve continually its operations and customer services. Later in this chapter, TQM and its implications for management accounting are described more fully.

Technological innovation

Keeping up with technological innovation is critical to an organization's competitiveness. Technological innovations, such as the Internet, have redefined many consumer product markets. Technological innovation is most apparent in the electronics and communication fields, but all industries have been revolutionized by technological change in the past 30 years. Farmers have genetically altered crops. Construction firms use recently developed, advanced materials. Online music and video allow users to download their preferred listening and viewing selections on demand. Services, such as banking and share trading, have been completely revised as a result of new technology. Many bank customers prefer the convenience of online or mobile banking instead of conducting transactions at a bricks-and-mortar location. Banks have adapted their operations to meet their clients' preferences and have streamlined their retail operations.

Technological innovation has also altered the way products are designed, produced and delivered. Technology has made cost-saving procedures such as just-in-time (JIT) feasible. JIT is one of the changes in organizational philosophy described in this chapter.

TQM and JIT represent two management approaches to deal with customer preferences and technological innovation. We use these general concepts to represent a variety of tools and techniques; however, no agreement exists on their precise definition or the practices that they incorporate. Management concepts evolve and emerge over time, often as a result of new innovations or refinements. For example, TQM has been replaced in numerous firms by Six Sigma, a programme developed at Motorola yet based on many of the same underlying processes as TQM. Some organizations now refer to 'lean' manufacturing or practices to describe the set of techniques to support their strategy to create customer value. Lean manufacturing is not novel but brings together the well-known tools of TQM and JIT. In this sense, lean may be viewed as 'old wine in new bottles' and we use TQM and JIT to represent the plethora of techniques

Figure 14.2 Recent terminology

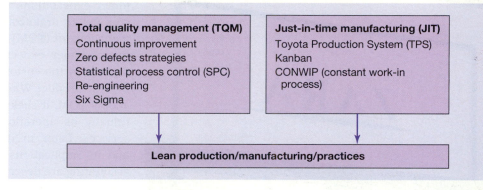

Total quality management (TQM)	Just-in-time manufacturing (JIT)
Continuous improvement	Toyota Production System (TPS)
Zero defects strategies	Kanban
Statistical process control (SPC)	CONWIP (constant work-in
Re-engineering	process)
Six Sigma	

Lean production/manufacturing/practices

seen in practice. Figure 14.2 indicates some of the recent terminology that you might encounter under the 'lean' umbrella.

Global competition

Increased global competition has forced many organizations that once faced protected domestic markets to become more cost competitive. Instead of making products domestically, organizations now outsource parts and sub-components globally. Market conditions change for a variety of reasons, including changes in government regulations and taxation policies. The World Trade Organization (WTO) is a global organization that deals with the trading rules between nations, promoting free trade and acting as an arbiter of international trade disputes. The European Union (EU) operates within the WTO's multilateral framework to provide common rules for imports and exports within the EU and to support initiatives to open up international trade based on fair

Art Kowalsky/Alamy

Globalization has positive and negative impacts. Multi-nationals provide more choice to consumers but potentially displace local firms and culture as they expand their market reach.

trading rules and a concern for social justice. In North America, The North American Free Trade Agreement (NAFTA) reduced tariffs between Canada, Mexico and the US. As a result of NAFTA, companies have relocated production sites in search of lower costs. Not only has the flow of trade increased between the three countries but also the geographic dispersion of company operations has changed. Firms, such as Bombardier Aerospace, Sanyo and Hitachi have expanded operations in Mexico to take advantage of lower labour costs and duty-free access to the North American market. Some firms have shifted operations from Asia to North America to reap the benefits of freer trade. Emerging markets in China, India, Russia and eastern Europe also set off chain reactions within organizations seeking to expand into these markets and take advantage of lower labour costs in these regions.

Organizational strategy and structure

Successful organizations are those that adapt quickly to changing customer preferences, technological innovation and global competition. New profitable investments emerge and some previously lucrative investments become unprofitable. To identify profitable investment opportunities, an organization requires an evolving strategy that recognizes the external forces affecting the organization and its own strengths and weaknesses.

An organization's strengths and weaknesses can be described in terms of its assets, its relations with suppliers and customers, and its ability to innovate and change. The assets of an organization include the current and long-term assets typically found on the balance sheet. In addition, brand-name recognition, patents and employees are important 'off-balance-sheet' assets of an organization. Brand-name recognition provides the organization with consumer name recognition that lowers the information costs of introducing new products. When Marks & Spencer introduced 'Your M&S', consumers already had an expectation of value and quality before sampling the new products. Its existing brand-name capital gives Marks & Spencer a cost advantage in introducing products that new entrants do not enjoy.

Relationships with suppliers and customers also affect the ability of an organization to adapt in a dynamic environment. Partnering with suppliers can allow the organization to move quickly into new fields if suppliers have skills and resources that otherwise would be difficult for it to acquire. Joint ventures are formal methods of partnering to compensate for weaknesses. Lufthansa AG and Deutsche Post each recognized that they lacked the strengths that the other possessed. While Lufthansa had cargo capacity and global air routes, it lacked the agility and experience in international express services that Deutsche Post's DHL Express possessed. The two firms have combined their logistics expertise to provide an expanded network for cargo services that takes advantage of their brand recognition and distribution channels. Their joint venture meets customer demands for shorter delivery times and reliability. It also includes a joint cargo airline operated through their subsidiaries DHL Express and Lufthansa Cargo.

The ability to innovate and change also differs across organizations. Studies indicate that highly educated managers are more willing to implement change. Knowledge of consumers and their preferences facilitates innovation. Flexibility in production and in the delivery of products and services is also critical to being able to innovate and change.

An organizational strategy, based on a dynamic environment and internal strengths and weaknesses, is a general plan for achieving customer and organizational value. An organization delivers customer value through innovative product/service design, high-quality products and services, and/or low-cost production and delivery. For example, much of Tesco's success results from its low cost in getting products from its suppliers to its stores. Successful organizations match their strengths with opportunities in the market to generate customer value. An organization with highly educated and creative employees is more likely to be successful in creating customer value through innovative products and service designs.

The best strategies, however, are doomed to failure if they are not matched with the appropriate organizational structure. The organizational structure is composed of the control mechanisms that motivate individuals within the organization to act in accordance with the selected strategy. The three major elements of the organizational structure are assignment of responsibilities, measurement of performance and compensation.

The assignment of responsibilities should be linked directly or indirectly to those with the specialized knowledge to make the decision. However, individuals with specialized knowledge cannot be relied upon always to make decisions that are consistent with the goals of the organization. Personal goals will influence their decisions.

One solution to this problem is to transfer the knowledge to the individual who is more likely to make decisions consistent with organizational goals. Yet information, like technical knowledge, is sometimes costly to transfer. In addition, individuals are reluctant to transfer knowledge on which their performance might be evaluated.

As described in Chapter 6, responsibilities are commonly assigned to separate planning decisions from control decisions. This separation of making planning decisions from control leads to mutual monitoring. For example, the manager responsible for approving and issuing payroll cheques is generally not the same individual who makes the payroll list. Each individual monitors the other to ensure the organization achieves its goals.

The second component of the organizational structure is the performance measurement system, which includes the accounting system. Besides using accounting-based measures of performance, organizations also develop non-accounting-based measures such as their share price, customer complaints, quality and on-time delivery percentages. Performance measures should be consistent with the assignment of responsibilities. Managers' responsibilities and performance measures should reflect controllability. The manager of a profit centre, for example, has some control over revenues and costs and is evaluated, in part, by the profit of the profit centre.

The third component of the organizational structure is the compensation system. Rewards are based on performance measures, which should be consistent with responsibilities. Rewards include compensation, promotions, titles and perquisites such as dedicated parking spaces, health-club memberships and company cars.

The three components of the organizational structure should be balanced as a three-legged stool. The balanced scorecard in Chapter 6 is one example of a comprehensive plan to link the organizational structure directly to the goals and strategy of the organization.

Planning decisions are the means of achieving organizational goals. Planning decisions include choosing organizational goals, hiring employees, creating products and service designs, selecting activities for making and delivering products and services, and providing customer services. Each of these planning decisions is made based on appropriate information. Accounting is one source of information that assists managers in making planning decisions.

The development of innovative products and services and their sale at prices in excess of their costs are key ingredients to increase organizational value. Good planning decisions based on sound information allow the organization to accomplish these goals.

Customer value and organizational value

As highlighted throughout this book, providing customer value is critical to the success of an organization. Each organization must find ways to create innovative products or services, manufacture high-quality products, and/or provide the product at a low cost. Customers purchase a product only if they perceive the value of the product and its attached services to outweigh its cost. Although the creation of customer value is necessary for organizational success, it is not sufficient.

To survive, an organization must have adequate funds to continue to operate. An organization receives funds from sales to consumers, or from donations by benefactors (in the case of many not-for-profit organizations). The inflow of funds depends on the organization's ability to create customer value. To create organizational value and survive, it must be able to supply customer value at a cost less than or equal to the inflow of funds. In the case of profit organizations, organizational value is captured in the profit concept of revenues less expenses.

The role of management accounting and change

The role of management accounting in Figure 14.1 is to assist in control through the organizational structure, and in making planning decisions. Management accounting plays an integral role in the organizational structure by assigning responsibilities through the budgeting process and by providing managerial performance measures. Management accounting also identifies the costs and benefits of different planning decisions, allowing managers to make choices that increase organizational value.

Management accounting is closely related to the organizational structure; thus, management accounting evolves as the organizational structure changes. Changes in the accounting system rarely occur in a vacuum. Alterations to the organizational structure, including changes in the accounting system, are likely in response to external shocks from technological change, political events and shifting market conditions.

The remainder of the chapter describes two concepts for implementing strategy that have become increasingly prevalent, TQM and JIT. These innovations have emerged in response to customer preferences, technological advances and global competition. They are closely tied to organizational strategy and have important implications for the management accounting system.

Concept **review**

1 What environmental forces affect organizations?

2 What should an organization consider in designing a strategy?

3 How does the organizational structure relate to strategy?

4 What is the role of management accounting in a dynamic environment?

The Driver and Vehicle Licensing Agency (DVLA) (continued)

Rashmi Rao begins her position as local manager by analysing the DVLA's local environment. Her customers are easily identified as the citizens in her local community and police services. Although the customers have not changed, their expectations have. They are no longer content with long waits and unfriendly service. Other government agencies have demonstrated that friendly and on-time service should be expected. Global competition is not Rashmi's major worry; however, she has heard rumours that failure to improve services might lead to outsourcing some of the DVLA's operations. She must take advantage of recent technological advances and management philosophies to be a success.

→

Once she understands her local environment, Rashmi is keen to develop a strategy that will enable her local office to meet customer expectations and remain a viable part of the DVLA's operations. She examines a number of alternatives, such as staff retraining, new technologies, and even the outsourcing of non-critical operations. Rashmi decides that the new strategy for her agency office must be customer-focused. Clients require prompt and courteous service. Efficiency could be improved through the adaptation of JIT techniques to the agency's services. She wonders if employees really understand that courteous service influences customer perceptions of quality. Perhaps the introduction of TQM principles would help employees to better understand what exactly quality means.

Rashmi recognizes that change at her local office is necessary but might be resisted. Her employees are committed to their work; however, they might feel threatened by changes and her novel ideas. She decides that the new strategy should take advantage of new computer technology and management approaches. Rashmi also establishes an employee team to discuss and develop plans to implement this customer-focused strategy. The team begins with small initiatives that can be successful in the short term. Team members expect that these initial projects will generate enthusiasm in the local office for further improvements and make employees more accepting of change. In particular, the team decides to update and expand its online registration process and introduce TQM and JIT techniques for service requests in its office. To accomplish this, Rashmi recognizes that she needs to re-organize the local office. Some services could be centralized to better control them but her staff have more knowledge about customer preferences. Decentralization might be more appropriate in certain areas. Consistency of service is important, so a trade-off between centralization and decentralization is necessary. In the end, she opts to give her employees more control over methods to improve face-to-face service with customers but to evaluate them based on cost and quality. Customers will be surveyed to determine satisfaction. Online licensing and registration will be centralized to ensure consistency and efficiency of service. Survey feedback will be tallied in order to evaluate these services and the achievement of the customer-focused strategy.

TOTAL QUALITY MANAGEMENT AND QUALITY MEASURES

To compete in a global market, organizations must be concerned about quality. Quality has become a major issue in both the profit and not-for-profit sectors of the economy. In attempting to improve quality, managers have had to grapple with what quality means and how to improve it. Managers also need to design measurement systems to report improvements in quality. In this section, various definitions of quality are described, followed by a discussion of some quality measurement systems.

Quality means different things to different people. Quality could mean a more luxurious product. On the one hand, a Rolls-Royce is perceived to be of higher quality than a Toyota AYGO because the Rolls-Royce has a smoother ride, leather interior and wood on the dashboard. On the other hand, the Toyota AYGO could be considered of higher quality if it reports fewer component failures than does a Rolls-Royce. Reliability is often used as a synonym for quality.

Conformity is another possible definition of quality. Using this definition, McDonald's deli sandwiches are of higher quality than are those at the local pub. McDonald's deli sandwiches taste the same no matter which outlet prepares them because of the standardization in purchasing materials and preparing sandwiches.

Quality also can be defined as having more options. A mobile phone that can provide digital video is considered to be of higher quality than one that cannot.

Meeting customer expectations is another way of defining quality. Customers have expectations with respect to all of a product's attributes: delivery schedules, operating

Motoring Picture Library/Alamy

For many, Rolls-Royce represents the ultimate in quality. Quality has many definitions; some might prefer cost and dependability over the luxury of a Rolls.

characteristics, service, etc. For example, a customer might expect a service technician to arrive on average within two hours of making the service call. If the service representative arrives in less than two hours, the organization has met the customer's expectations. Charter Mark is the UK government's national standard and certification for excellence in customer service. The Driver and Vehicle Licensing Agency, which has been granted this certification since 1993, defines one aspect of quality service as delivering your licence or vehicle registration certificate within three weeks of receiving your application.

Quality experts emphasize that quality has multiple meanings, including product performance and satisfaction. They generally define quality as meeting customer expectations, which include expectations about time to market, innovation, sustainability and cost. Quality is affected by globalization, including the increased reliance on international networks of suppliers.[3]

The traditional approach to ensure product quality was to 'inspect it in'. Inspection stations and quality assurance inspectors were added along the production line to weed out defects. Statistical sampling methods were used to draw random samples from a batch, and to reject the entire batch if a statistically large number of defective units were detected in the sample. Notice that quality was defined by the organization as meeting a certain set of technical specifications, which may or may not have been of interest to the consumer. Sections of the manufacturing plant stored defects waiting to be reworked or scrapped. Organizations built a normal allowance for scrap and rework into their operating budgets. In some cases, if market demand exceeded production in a period, marginally defective products were released. Defective products that reached the market were corrected by the field service organization under warranty arrangements.

Two key factors combined to make the traditional approach to quality obsolete in most industries. First, the cost of detecting problems and monitoring production via computer instrumentation fell relative to the cost of maintaining quality via direct labour inspectors. The cost of labour made the cost of manually detecting and correcting errors expensive relative to performing these tasks electronically. Second, global competition expanded to include non-price forms of competition such as quality. Once Japanese automobile companies had gained price competitiveness against their global counterparts, they turned their attention to achieving quality advantages. Both the lower cost of detecting defects and increased global competition have fostered the concept of zero defects. The goal of zero defects, while never achievable, has become the target. Each year, the standard becomes fewer defects than the year before.

To avoid having defective goods reach the marketplace, some organizations test their products with a sampling of potential customers. Intel distributes its computer chips to sophisticated users to 'stress' the chips and to identify any potential defects

---

[3] D. Phillips-Donaldson (2006) 'Good News – If You're Ready', *Quality Progress*, Vol. 39, No. 1 (January), pp. 37–40.

before releasing the chip to the market at large. One such user discovered a flaw in the original Pentium chip and Intel made corrections prior to its widespread use.

The movement toward improved quality and customer satisfaction is called total quality management (TQM). TQM is a management philosophy that includes involved leadership, employee participation, empowerment, teamwork, customer satisfaction and continuous improvement.

Through TQM, companies redesign their products to require fewer different part numbers, making it easier to maintain tighter controls on the quality of their suppliers. Production processes are re-engineered to reduce defects. Robots and more instrumentation are built into manufacturing to ensure more uniform production. In addition to the above changes, major changes in the organizational structure also occur, including modifying the performance evaluation and reward systems and the partitioning of responsibilities. Responsibilities are pushed lower down in the firm where the knowledge of customer preferences resides.

In summary, most TQM programmes contain the following elements:

- *Quality is a firm-wide process.* Every employee from the senior manager to the post-room employee must understand the quality work processes. Quality links customers to suppliers. The pursuit of excellence is a prime motivator in the company.
- *Quality is defined by the customer.* Customer satisfaction is a central goal of the organization. Customers expect reliability, conformity, timely delivery and customer service.
- *Quality requires organizational changes.* The organizational structure (assignment of responsibilities, performance measurement and reward systems) must encourage mutual co-operation and create incentives to improve quality. Senior managers should develop hands-on, specialized knowledge of how to improve quality. Employees are empowered (i.e. given responsibilities) to make changes that increase quality.
- *Quality is designed into the product.* Quality must be designed into the product and processes from the initial product development through manufacturing to the final delivery of a quality product to the consumer. Designers and engineers should work with manufacturers, marketers and accountants to design products that meet customer needs, are simple to manufacture, and are not too costly. Once products are designed and engineered, many of the quality attributes are pre-determined.

If the goal of the organization is to achieve customer satisfaction, some measures of quality are necessary to determine if the organization is achieving its goal and to motivate and reward managers. Many quality measures are not part of the management accounting system. Typical TQM quality measures include product design (number of new parts, number of parts), vendor rating systems (number of defects, on-time delivery), manufacturing (defect rates, scrap, rework, cycle time), and customer satisfaction (surveys, warranty expense).

Moreover, quality is often measured in terms of defects. For example, a component part must be within 0.001 millimetres of a standard or else it is termed defective. If changing the machine that produces the part decreases the defect rate from five per thousand to three per thousand, quality is said to have increased. This concept of quality is based on achieving certain specifications. One drawback of defining quality in terms of defect rates is worker opportunism. Workers can appear to improve quality if they have the responsibility to redefine the standard or benchmark against which defect rates are evaluated. For example, suppose defects are defined as being in excess of 0.0010 millimetres of a tolerance. If defects were redefined as being in excess of 0.0015 millimetres, fewer would result. If a part is produced with a tolerance of 0.0012 millimetres, under the old definition of 0.0010 millimetres, it would be classified as a defect. Under the new definition, it is not. Therefore, when installing quality improvement programmes, an organization must ensure that the definition of defects is held constant. Airlines are judged by customers and regulators based on their on-time performance. An increase in flight duration, for instance, to account for long queues on congested runways could maintain on-time performance at the expense of more time in transit overall.

Numerical **example** 14.1

A farmer of gourmet tomatoes estimates that 10 per cent of the 20,000 kilograms of tomatoes picked do not meet customers' specifications. After being picked, the tomatoes are placed on a conveyer belt for inspection and packaging. The inspection team identifies and removes 80 per cent of the defective tomatoes. How many kilograms of defective tomatoes reach the customers of the tomato farmer?

Solution

If 80 per cent of the defective tomatoes are detected, 20 per cent are not detected. Therefore, (0.20×0.10) or 2 per cent reach the customers. Of the 20,000 kilograms of tomatoes picked, $(0.02 \times 20,000 \text{ kilograms})$, or 400 kilograms of defective tomatoes are sent to the customers.

The benefits and problems of measuring quality must include the associated costs. Defect rates, cycle time, on-time delivery, and customer complaints are easy for managers to understand and easy to measure. Without a corresponding cost system, however, these diverse measures are difficult to aggregate. Managers do not know how to make trade-offs among quality decisions. For example, is it more costly to design and manufacture a product without defects or to focus on inspection and the correction of defects from initial production? Is it cheaper to buy a scanning machine for more accurate inspections or stay with manual inspections? Managers need cost data to make these comparisons for decision management purposes. Organizations can over-invest in quality if information about the costs and benefits of quality initiatives is inaccurate.

Part of the TQM philosophy is that improved quality actually can be less costly to the organization. The cost of selling defective products and not satisfying customers can be substantial. Errors must be corrected and disgruntled customers mollified. Some customers will seek other suppliers of the service or product. A reputation for shoddy workmanship is often the death knell for organizations. Even if a defect is discovered before being sent to a customer, the cost of handling and fixing the problem can be quite high. In many cases, the defective product cannot be fixed and must be disposed of. The opportunity cost of not being able to sell a product because it is defective equals the costs of making the defective product plus the forgone profit. Firms that depend on suppliers for critical components often introduce contract mechanisms to transfer responsibility for defects and on-time performance to their supplier network. However, when defects do arise, the manufacturer, not the supplier, generally bears the cost. This cost includes reputation effects. For example, the recall of Chinese-made toys sold by Mattel, Inc. damaged the firm's reputation with consumers as well as other Chinese manufacturers. Similarly, the recent recall of laptop computer batteries by Sony Corporation affected its worldwide image, as well as that of computer manufacturers which installed these batteries in their products.

If defects can be reduced through better cost prevention efforts, then organizations would no longer suffer the larger costs of fixing or throwing away defects. The philosophy of TQM is consistent with the adage 'an ounce of prevention is worth a pound of cure'. For example, further research into the demands placed on laptop computer batteries would potentially save the huge cost of product recalls to correct or prevent the defect.

Quality costs are typically categorized into four groups:

1 **Prevention costs** are incurred to eliminate defective units before they are produced. These costs include re-engineering and design, high-quality parts, improved processes, and employee training.
2 **Appraisal costs** are incurred to eliminate defective units before they are shipped. These costs include inspecting and testing of both raw material and work-in-process.
3 **Internal failure costs** are incurred when a defect is discovered before sending the product to the customer. These costs include the costs of handling and fixing the product or disposing of it. The opportunity cost of not being able to sell the disposed unit also should be included.
4 **External failure costs** are incurred when a customer receives a defective product. These costs include the cost of returns, warranty work, product liability claims and the opportunity cost of lost sales from reputation effects.

The advantage of categorizing costs is to recognize trade-offs among different activities. The shift to TQM generally is accompanied by an increase in prevention costs that is more than offset by lower internal and external failure costs. In Figure 14.3, the quality costs of a division of Texas Instruments over a six-year period after the implementation of TQM are described.[4] Notice that the failure costs have declined over this time period. Although the prevention and appraisal costs remained about the same, the decline in failure costs indicates that resources were used more effectively. The net effect is higher quality at a reduced cost.

Figure 14.3 Change in quality cost categories with TQM

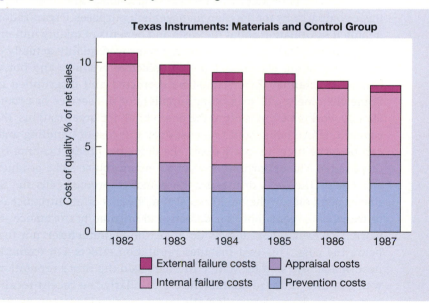

---

[4] *Texas Instruments: Cost of Quality (A)*, Harvard Business School Case 9-189-029.

Most management accounting systems do not specifically identify quality costs. Many quality expenditures are imbedded in overhead accounts. Opportunity costs are commonly not reported at all. Therefore, a quality cost system must frequently be constructed outside the cost accounting system, which makes the cost of quality more difficult to identify and measure.

One of the benefits of measuring and identifying quality costs is to bring these expenditures to the attention of senior managers. Many companies have found that their quality costs exceed 10 per cent of sales. Given that total quality costs often can be reduced through increased prevention efforts and a corresponding decline in failure costs, cost savings of a few per cent are extremely important to an organization in a globally competitive market.

Another benefit of measuring quality costs is to measure improvement in quality performance. Total quality costs should decline as an organization engages in TQM. If they do not, the organization should re-examine its TQM processes.

Numerical **example** 14.2

Yee Company decides to perform an inventory of its quality costs for 2008. The following quality costs are identified: employee training, £100,000; storing defective products, £70,000; responding to customer complaints, £50,000; lost sales due to dissatisfied customers, £110,000; inspections, £40,000; quality engineering, £40,000. Categorize the quality costs. Estimate quality costs for 2009 if a 20 per cent increase in prevention costs would result in a 30 per cent decrease in external failure costs. Appraisal and internal failure costs would remain the same.

Solution

Quality cost category	Quality costs (£) 2008		Estimated quality costs (£) 2009
Prevention			
Employee training	100,000		
Quality engineering	40,000	140,000	(1.2 × £140,000) = 168,000
Appraisal			
Inspections	40,000	40,000	40,000
Internal failure			
Storing defects	70,000	70,000	70,000
External failure			
Customer complaints	50,000		
Lost sales	110,000	160,000	(0.7 × £160,000) = 112,000
Total quality costs		410,000	390,000

The investment in prevention should be made as it results in a reduction in total quality costs.

Explicit use of quality costs is not common for planning purposes. In principle, quality costs offer an opportunity to compare and trade off different quality efforts. Quality costs should be used to identify the optimal prevention and appraisal procedures. However, some organizations seem to lack confidence in the identification and measurement of quality costs. Also, managers need to develop an understanding of the links between the cost categories. For example, how will an improved product design affect appraisal activities and reduce internal and external failures? Until senior managers can determine more confidently the advantages in tracking and using quality costs and the financial benefits, they are reluctant to invest in systems to measure and identify them.

Numerical **example** 14.3

Compty Computer Company is having problems with the hard drive for its computer. A particular part fails about 2 per cent of the time. It costs £200 each time to replace the part and to deal with customer dissatisfaction. The company could redesign the computer and leave out the part for £50,000, or perform extensive inspections on the part that would cost £2 per computer. What should the company do, if it plans to make 30,000 computers during the coming year, before the computer becomes obsolete?

Solution

The cost of not redesigning the computer or increasing inspections is 0.02 × 30,000 computers × £200 per defect, or £120,000. The cost of increasing inspections is £2 per computer × 30,000 computers, or £60,000. The cost of changing the design (£50,000) is lower than the cost of the two other alternatives and is the preferred choice.

Companies now explicitly incorporate quality-based criteria into their performance measurement systems, even if not adopting the entire TQM philosophy. Such changes in performance evaluation schemes, however, have their own problems. Quality is important and should be improved. As discussed earlier, quality is an elusive concept with many different dimensions. It is both difficult to define precisely and to measure objectively.

Much attention has been paid to quality improvement programmes in firms; nonetheless, many fail to achieve their objectives and are abandoned. TQM programmes require a difficult balance between (1) top-down control and standardized methods and (2) increased employee empowerment and responsibility for continuous improvement. Organizations often do not succeed in managing this balancing act or lose focus when management attention shifts to competing priorities and demands.[5] Although quality should be a primary goal of an organization, other goals cannot be ignored. The balanced scorecard approach described in Chapter 6 encompasses the customer perspective but also recognizes the importance of other performance dimensions (financial, internal business process, learning and growth) to increase organizational value. Trade-offs across all four dimensions are necessary as it is impossible to optimize all of these at the same time.

To summarize, if followed to the letter, TQM is very much an attempt to restructure the organization. Responsibilities must be linked with knowledge. As global competition increases, customers are able to find products more to their liking and often at lower cost. Organizations must know what product attributes consumers most desire. Employees who have day-to-day contact with customers usually possess the detailed knowledge of customer preferences. Somehow this detailed knowledge must be transferred within the organization to the product planners and manufacturing managers. Alternatively, some of the responsibility for product design and distribution must be transferred to lower-level staff who have the detailed knowledge of customer preferences. TQM programmes attempt to do both. Multi-disciplinary task forces are formed to conduct special studies and to improve quality. These task forces, composed of people from all levels of the organization, are an attempt to assemble the specialized knowledge concerning customer preferences. Sometimes these task forces are given the

---

[5] M. Beer (2003) 'Why Total Quality Management Programs Do Not Persist: The Role of Management Quality and Implications for Leading a TQM Transformation', *Decision Sciences*, Vol. 34, Issue 4 (Fall), pp. 623–642.

responsibility to change the product or processes. Employee empowerment transfers responsibilities to employees with specialized knowledge within the organization.

To successfully restructure the organization and assign responsibilities to the people with the knowledge about customer preferences, an organization must also adapt its performance evaluation and compensation systems. Empowering workers with responsibilities requires systems to evaluate and reward their performance. Firms that implement TQM often do not garner the hoped-for benefits because they overlook the need to modify their performance measurement and reward systems to support the changes in responsibilities.

Although TQM has not been universally accepted, some aspects are a part of almost every successful organization. Organizations might not completely follow TQM with all of its ramifications. However, almost every manager is aware of TQM principles and of the competitive necessity of meeting customer preferences. The Italian manufacturer, Carpigiani, highlighted in this chapter, is one firm that has risen to this challenge to maintain its competitive edge. While, TQM focuses on quality improvements to reduce costs and increase customer value, we now turn our attention to just-in-time processes which aim to eliminate non-value-added activities in the value chain. In practice, firms generally adopt TQM and JIT jointly; hence, the boundaries between the two systems are blurred.

Organizational **analysis**

Ice cream goes global

Carpigiani, a private Italian firm, is the market leader in the production and sales of ice-cream manufacturing equipment. Its machines are sold in more than 100 countries and found everywhere from specialty shops serving Italian gelato to fast-food chains selling soft-serve ice cream.

Carpigiani has experienced a major turnaround in its business fortunes in the past decade, enjoying an operating profit of more than 20 per cent of its sales revenues. Much of this turnaround is attributed to its response to threats to its competitive position as a result of globalization, and a lack of focus on customer and organizational value.

Carpigiani had begun to lose business to competitors, including those from China, who were copying its designs but also offering cheaper products. Carpigiani realized that it needed to cut costs, focus on the customer and improve its quality. Achieving all three would provide a competitive edge to match or better its competitors.

The firm re-structured and cut its workforce and outsourced some production. Quality issues were addressed through the adoption of a quality management system and the achievement of ISO 9001 certification. Carpigiani re-invested in its technical and research departments, working with nearby universities to improve its manufacturing processes and inputs. It even established Gelato University to teach ice-cream making. One example of its innovations is the introduction of self-cleaning machines that minimize human intervention, improve quality and promote health safety.

Global competitors remain but Carpigiani has taken steps to improve its competitive position, including expansion to China to provide its own machinery in a growing market for ice-cream and gelato.

What factors prompted Carpigiani to adapt its competitive strategy?

In terms of the framework for organizational change (Figure 14.1), outline briefly the steps taken by Carpigiani to compete in the global marketplace.

Source: 'A maker of ice-cream churns takes a rocky road to world domination' (2007) *The Economist*, Vol. 384, No. 8542, 18 August, pp. 55–56.

Concept **review**

1 Explain the philosophy of total quality management (TQM).
2 What are the four categories of quality costs?
3 How are prevention and appraisal costs related to failure costs?

The Driver and Vehicle Licensing Agency (DVLA) (continued)

Before implementing any changes, Rashmi and some members of her staff attend a seminar on TQM to determine how it could be used effectively at their local office. The seminar leader focuses on TQM in a manufacturing organization, but the group is convinced that TQM could work for a service organization such as the DVLA. Not only does the DVLA provide the public with services to obtain licences and registrations, it also provides the police and other legal authorities with information about registrants.

Later, Rashmi and her team puzzle over what is meant by quality at the DVLA. They can think of a number of ways to interpret quality and begin to see that it is not that easy to develop a clear definition. Perhaps this difficulty helps to explain why employees might not understand its importance. Customers do not have other sources for DVLA services so it is difficult to define quality in product terms. The local office provides a service that customers do not take away with them. They decide that what customers do take away are their perceptions of the level of service, which they currently view as unfriendly and discourteous. Thus, Rashmi and the team define quality as friendly, courteous service. To meet this quality goal, employees must take training programmes on interacting and reducing confrontation with clients. Supervisors are instructed to monitor the behaviour of clerks dealing with the public. The TQM programme appears to be a success. Both the employees and the customers at the local office are noticeably happier. As confrontations are reduced, the clerks are able to provide services more promptly.

To determine if the TQM programme is saving money, Rashmi asks the staff accountant to estimate quality costs before and after the implementation of TQM. The accountant defines quality costs as follows:

- prevention costs: employee training costs
- appraisal costs: supervisor salaries
- internal failure costs: clerk downtime while mistakes in service are corrected
- external failure costs: time spent dealing with dissatisfied and irate customers.

After implementing the TQM programme, prevention and appraisal costs have increased, but internal and external failure costs have dropped by a greater amount. Therefore, TQM appears to be cost effective.

To verify that customers are satisfied with its services, Rashmi asks customers to complete a survey either while in the local office or via the Internet. The survey results indicate that customers appreciate the smiling faces behind the counter. Nonetheless, they still are unhappy with the long queues and time necessary to obtain their licences and registrations. Online services are working well but many services still require a visit to the local office. Some people actually prefer to access services face to face; thus, Rashmi cannot improve service levels simply by switching activities to the Internet. She begins to realize that she and her team might have defined quality incorrectly. Customers are more concerned with speed of service. Rashmi decides to attend a conference on JIT.

JUST-IN-TIME (JIT) PROCESSES

As noted in Chapter 1, just-in-time (JIT) is an operating philosophy that emphasizes providing products on demand, enabling organizations to operate more efficiently and at a lower cost. With JIT processes, production and demand are synchronized by not starting production until an order is received. In this way, products are *pulled* through the plant. Non-JIT processes *push* products through the plant by a master production schedule designed to keep the plant operating at full capacity. The goal of plant managers in JIT facilities is to reduce the time that the product spends in the plant. If total production time decreases, costs will decrease as well because fewer inventories must be financed, stored, managed and secured. To accomplish these goals, the plant is

Figure 14.4 Traditional systems versus JIT systems

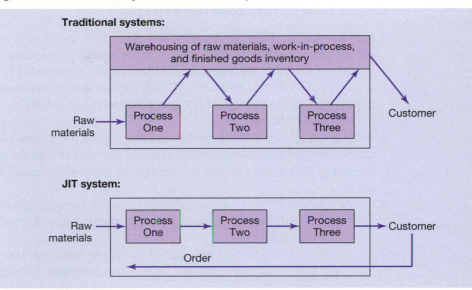

re-organized so that raw material and purchased parts are delivered to the factory right before they enter the production process. No intermediate work-in-process inventories exist. Units flow from one production cell to another with no interruptions, and all work is processed continually. Units only spend time in the manufacturing plant when actual work is being expended on them. Of course, the preceding description is that of an ideal JIT installation. Figure 14.4 compares a traditional system with a JIT system.

JIT systems seek to minimize a product's **throughput time**, which is the total time from the receipt of the order to the time of delivery to the customer. Throughput time is the sum of the following:

- processing time,
- time waiting to be moved or worked on,
- time spent in transit, and
- inspection time.

JIT now applies to everything from manufacturing to learning. For manufacturers, JIT emphasizes providing products on demand, efficiently and at a lower cost.

In a JIT manufacturing environment, the goal is to drive the last three items (waiting, transit and inspection time) to zero. The sum of the last three items is referred to as *wasted* or *non-value-added time*. The benefits of reducing throughput time include smaller in-process inventories, leading to the following:

- lower capital costs of holding inventories,
- plant and warehouse space and cost savings,
- reduced overhead costs for material movers and expediters,
- reduced risk of obsolescence, and
- faster response time to customers and reduced delivery times.

To accomplish the goal of reducing throughput time and to achieve the above benefits, the following five changes must take place:

1 *Increase quality.* To prevent production down time, the quality of raw materials and the quality of the manufacturing process must be maintained at a high level. Increased quality of materials and of the manufacturing process decreases the need to stop production due to defects. JIT and TQM share the common goal of continuous improvement. The success of JIT depends upon good quality management and production maintenance.

2 *Reduce set-up times.* If machines can be set up for a new production run very quickly (or instantaneously), then parts do not have to wait for processing to begin. Moreover, inventories do not accumulate in front of the machine while it is being set up.

3 *Balance flow rates.* The rate of production in the various manufacturing cells must be the same. Otherwise, work-in-process inventories will build up after the cells with the faster flow rates.

4 *Plant layout.* The plant is redesigned to better focus on the corporate strategy. Standardization and more efficient workflow reduce time and duplication. Machines that perform the same function are not grouped in one department, but rather are organized in terms of manufacturing cells to sequence similar parts through the machines. Dedicated JIT production lines manufacture a single type of product, sometimes called *dedicated flow lines*.

5 *Change performance measurement and reward systems.* Employees are not measured and rewarded solely on efficiency measures, such as the number of units produced or keeping machines busy. Individual manufacturing cells are no longer rewarded for maximizing output. Such efficiency measures encourage workers to build inventories and to have inventories in front of their station as buffer stocks. A key performance measure in a JIT system is throughput time divided by process time. The closer this ratio gets to one, the less non-value-added time is involved. Employees are encouraged to work as multi-functional teams to achieve this goal and to participate in decision making and problem solving. Non-financial indicators supplement financial indicators to provide for feedback that is readily understood and actionable.

Numerical **example** 14.4

Macve Motors is adopting a JIT system in order to reduce its throughput time. The current throughput time is 10 days. With a JIT system, Macve Motors believes that throughput time will fall to six days. This reduction will lower its costs of holding work-in-process inventory. The average value of its work-in-process inventory is £500,000 and the capital cost of holding inventory is 12 per cent per year. What is the impact on holding costs if the JIT system reduces throughput time as anticipated?

Solution

The annual cost of holding inventory is £500,000 × 0.12, or £60,000. With JIT, the throughput time is 60 per cent of the current throughput time. Inventory will be processed more quickly and less capital will be devoted to holding inventory. The holding cost under a JIT system is £500,000 × 0.12 × 0.60, or £36,000. Therefore, the annual cost decreases by 40 per cent, or £24,000.

One important aspect of JIT involves redesigning the firm's relations with its suppliers. In the past, managers believed that having multiple suppliers for each input increased competition and kept prices down. Firms had policies of dividing total purchases among several sources, which required each input order to be inspected to ensure quality and made it more difficult to co-ordinate timely delivery of supplies. In a JIT environment, firms drastically reduce the number of suppliers, often going to long-term, sole-sourcing contracts whereby a single supplier provides all of the firm's demand for a given input. The purchasing firm benefits from lower prices due to volume discounts, lower ordering costs (only a single-relationship contract is required), and higher quality assurance (audits of the supplier's process rather than the inspection of each shipment). Transportation costs are reduced as suppliers can establish long-term contracts with shippers. Suppliers are increasingly seen as partners, sharing both the risks and rewards of this strengthened relationship. Risks of long-term, sole-sourcing contracts include price increases and delivery problems, given the organization's dependence on a single supplier. JIT systems also impose negative externalities on society due to increased traffic congestion and pollution. Japan and parts of North America experience these problems as a result of the burden placed on the environment caused by frequent transport deliveries to manufacturing firms.

Buyers and sellers integrate their computer systems so that orders are received on a JIT basis. Online marketplaces, web exchanges and electronic data interchange (EDI) foster co-operation with suppliers, reducing costs and cycle time. Many firms have shifted their purchasing operations to the Internet. The Internet makes interactions between suppliers and purchasers easier and more flexible. Suppliers are encouraged to use the business-to-business network to remain competitive in terms of quality and cost. Automakers rely increasingly on these networks as product cycles are shortened and customers expect more customized vehicles.

Initial interest in JIT arose due to automation, information technology and global competition. Factory automation allows organizations to produce small batches of different products because setting up computer-programmed robotic systems is much simpler than doing so with traditional machinery. Robots can be set up to manufacture a different product with the insertion of different software. Short set-up times allow organizations to manufacture a variety of products to meet customized demand quickly. Robots also can be used for quality-control purposes to inspect products during the manufacturing process.

Information technology provides much better co-ordination among different departments and between suppliers and customers. Suppliers use bar coding, scanning and radio-frequency identification (RFID) chips to monitor inventory levels to provide for timely product deliveries. Information technology in the form of programs such as **materials requirement planning (MRP)** allows organizations to quickly ascertain resource requirements to make a product. An MRP system is a computerized program that makes the necessary orders for raw materials and schedules the production to facilitate a short throughput time when an order arrives. MRP systems also can be tied to the organization's accounting system. Online marketplaces in many industries are integrated into the MRP system. This integration standardizes the purchasing and production system, thereby reducing costs.

Global competition is another factor contributing to the popularity of JIT. JIT can result in lower costs and greater customer satisfaction. Ideally, manufacturing costs decline as a result of reduced inventory holding and handling costs. However, a switch to JIT does not always mean lower costs, especially in the short term. Small batch runs and reconfiguring the factory layout may cause costs to increase. JIT is a long-term strategy that takes time to have an impact on organizational performance.

An increase in customer satisfaction is anticipated as a result of more timely delivery of products. By reducing throughput time, the organization often can deliver goods more quickly. Yet lower inventory levels can have the opposite effect. If a problem develops during the production process, the organization does not have inventory on hand to satisfy immediate customer demand. As long as the organization faces shocks to either production or demand, such as labour strikes, weather-related interruptions in the flow of raw materials or changing prices for its products, satisfying customers with timely delivery can be a problem. As well, customer satisfaction should increase due to the improved quality and reliability of products.

When organizational strategy changes to incorporate the JIT philosophy, the management accounting system also must adapt to altered responsibilities, performance evaluation and reward systems. For control purposes, performance measures should coincide with the goals of JIT. Reducing throughput time is a primary performance measure for JIT organizations. Traditional performance measures to minimize input costs are inappropriate performance measures in a JIT system. These types of performance measures encourage inventory building. Instead, JIT organizations want to encourage production sufficient to cover only demand. The savings from reduced throughput time increase organizational value in the long term if they offset the costs imposed on other organizational activities.

Team effort is important in JIT environments, so performance measures should reflect co-operative goals. Employee rewards based on measures of team performance are more aligned with the JIT philosophy compared to those emphasizing individual performance. A JIT approach also lends itself to mutual monitoring to ensure that managers are aware of the costs imposed on other organizational activities when they work to decrease throughput time.

For planning purposes, the role of the accounting system changes as well. Orders come before production begins; therefore, pricing decisions must be based on estimated rather than actual costs. Once the order is accepted, no pricing reason for keeping track of the cost of filling the order exists. Product costs, however, still must be estimated for pricing purposes, so periodic cost checks should be made to ensure that pricing decisions reflect cost information.

In a JIT environment, accounting is simpler. The detailed tracking of transactions in a job-order costing system is replaced with a streamlined accounting system similar to process costing. Chapter 10 discussed these two costing systems. The elimination of job-order cost sheets for every batch shortens throughput time, because employees do not need to spend time recording costs. Having line workers complete job-order cost sheets as they work on a product is non-value-added time. Firms that adopt JIT accounting systems significantly reduce the number of accounting transactions. Some firms have reduced their journal-entry volume 20-fold because detailed payroll posting to jobs is eliminated. Also, jobs are no longer tracked through the work-in-process accounts as they move from department to department.

Inventory is in the form of work-in-process for a short time; therefore, less attention is paid to the valuation of partially completed products. The only time that an organization may want to value work-in-process is at the end of the accounting period for external reporting purposes. Balance sheets identify the assets of the organization at a particular point in time. Generally, some work-in-process exists at that point in time and its full cost must be determined.

Accounting in a JIT system is tailored to the organization's needs and circumstances. A general approach to JIT accounting is called backflushing. Backflushing simplifies the accounting system with the use of one raw materials and in-process inventory account, the elimination of work-in-process tracking, and the recording of conversion costs (labour and overhead) directly to finished goods inventory.[6]

Numerical example 14.5

Ryan plc manufactures a control assembly for Ford Motor's auto steering columns. Ryan uses a JIT production system. All conversion costs for the JIT line, such as direct and indirect labour, depreciation, and other overhead items, are budgeted at €8.8 million. Ryan expects to produce 2.2 million control assemblies this year. Each assembly has overhead of €4 per unit. Last week, factory labour was €38,000 and €59,000 of materials were purchased and used to produce 10,000 control assemblies. These units were shipped and billed to Ford Motor. Summarize the accounting entries for these activities.

Solution

The activities are summarized as follows:

Change in materials inventory	€0
Total conversion costs incurred	€78,000 [€38,000 + €4 × 10,000 units]
Change in finished goods inventory	€0
Cost of goods sold incurred	€137,000 [€78,000 + €59,000]

JIT processes and accounting systems are not without drawbacks. JIT systems take time to implement and performance can suffer in the short term as employees are trained, plants re-organized and processes changed. Research has reported mixed results from the adoption of both JIT and TQM on financial performance. Lower short-term results can reduce management interest in further investments in these systems.[7] Firms hold inventories to smooth out fluctuations in supply or demand. If a labour strike occurs, bad weather prevents delivery of raw materials, or demand increases unexpectedly, then inventories allow the firm to avoid the opportunity costs of stock-outs and lost sales. A recent strike by General Motors (GM) workers in the US immediately closed GM manufacturing plants in Canada as they relied on deliveries from sister plants south of the border. Factory re-organization, improved product and process quality, and strengthened purchasing relationships with suppliers can smooth out some of the fluctuations but they cannot eliminate all the shocks to the system. Random fluctuations beyond the control of management require the firm to carry some inventories as a buffer against lost sales. Few organizations have been able to completely eliminate raw materials inventory. Suppliers also bear the cost of buffer inventories. They must deliver more frequently and in smaller lot sizes and cannot risk late deliveries. Cross-border traffic delays have forced some firms to re-invest in inventories to avoid problems created by inventory shortages.

---

[6] The technical accounting details of backflushing are covered in cost accounting and advanced management accounting textbooks.

[7] J.L. Callen, M. Morel and C. Fader (2005) 'Productivity Measurement, Plant Performance, and JIT Intensity', *Contemporary Accounting Research*, Vol. 22, No. 2 (Summer), pp. 271–309; R. R. Fullerton, C. S. McWatters and C. Fawson (2003) 'An examination of the relationship between JIT and financial performance', *Journal of Operations Management*, Vol. 21, No. 4, pp. 383–404.

Online markets and e-commerce are important tools in competitive markets. Suppliers become partners in efforts to gain efficiencies, yet frequently bear the burden of buffer inventories.

A JIT accounting system that does not track work-in-process requires other systems to do so. In some cases, firms undertake physical counts of inventory (often daily) to supply managers with information on specific inventory levels. Inconsistent with the basic JIT philosophy, these inventory counts are non-value-added activities that disrupt the production process by forcing workers to stop production and count the inventory. To mitigate this problem, companies have installed other tracking systems. For example, Ford Motor Company uses RFID chips to track inventory through its assembly operations, replacing its manual coding system. The RFID system results in fewer errors compared to manual records and provides real-time tracking of the vehicle's production stage.[8] While simplification and lower costs are advocated as advantages of a JIT accounting system, many firms have not adapted their management accounting systems to JIT. This reluctance to simplify re-inforces that firms use their accounting systems for many decision-making and control purposes. Simplification and the lack of tracking might affect the ability to make good decisions and create weaknesses in the control system.

The Driver and Vehicle Licensing Agency (DVLA) (continued)

The JIT conference that Rashmi attends is very exciting. Once again, the emphasis is on manufacturing firms but Rashmi gains many insights that would work for her office. She decides that throughput is one concept applicable to its operations. Rashmi defines throughput as the time a customer spends in the local office. After the conference, she asks her staff for their input on the flow of customers. She believes that she can encourage managers to reduce throughput time by linking their evaluation to this measure so she decides to evaluate her managers based on the average throughput time for a customer obtaining a licence or registration. To gain the managers' enthusiasm for this new evaluation scheme, she gives them the responsibility to change procedures to achieve a quicker throughput time. Her managers come up with the following ideas:

- introducing a triage system to sort clients at arrival by type of service requested and complexity of their needs;
- using pre-filled forms, so customers have only to sign the forms if the information is correct;
- training employees across functions so staff can supplement other overburdened workers;
- hiring part-time labour during busy times;
- increasing user-friendly, website information about services and procedures; and
- encouraging licensing and registration via post and the Internet.

Throughput time declines sharply and customers are happier. The main question is whether there are also cost savings. Rashmi is eager to learn if the more efficient use of employees through JIT actually will lead to lower costs.

---

[8] D. Johnson (2002) 'RFID tags improve tracking, quality on Ford line in Mexico', *Control Engineering*, Vol. 49, No. 11 (November), p. 16.

Concept **review**

1 What are the advantages of a just-in-time (JIT) system?

2 Why is a short throughput time so important for JIT?

3 How should performance measures change with the adoption of JIT?

WHEN SHOULD MANAGEMENT ACCOUNTING BE CHANGED?

A single, ideal management accounting system that is optimum for all organizations does not exist in practice. Each organization has different circumstances that lead to different management accounting systems. For example, the balanced scorecard might be the best approach for one firm but not another. Also, management accounting must deal continually with trade-offs among internal users, who prefer information for making planning decisions and control decisions, and external users, who want information describing firm performance. Finally, each organization is continually adapting to meet the demands of a dynamic environment. Organizations are in a continual state of flux; thus, management accounting must continually adapt.

Throughout this book, we have emphasized the need for organizations to react and adapt to technological change, customer preferences and global competition. For instance, the Internet has affected many organizational activities. Organizations have shifted marketing activities to online formats. Customers want the convenience of selecting, purchasing and paying for goods and services via the Internet or their mobile phone. Organizations need to evaluate the cost and benefits of these activities. Customer-relationship management (CRM) is one value-chain approach to determine which products and services match customer preferences. Customer data provide insights into the cost and profitability of customers, and how to capture and retain customers over the long term.

Customers are also citizens and their concerns about the environment, climate change and sustainability influence their consumption patterns and firm behaviour. For example, organizations must deal with global sustainability, including the impact of their production processes on the environment and the need to cover product disposal costs. Companies are beginning to embrace the need to incorporate these factors in their planning and control processes. Capital budgeting is one area in which environmental sustainability affects the decision process as firms include the effects of their production methods, goods and services on the environment. In addition, performance measurement systems must incorporate responsibility for environmental management. Customers prefer low-cost and high-quality goods but some customers appear willing to pay more for products which are environmentally friendly. Firms need to determine how to adapt their strategies to these developments.

Oleksiy Maksymenko/Alamy

Firms are global citizens who share customer concerns for the environment and sustainability. Successful organizations are incorporating these challenges into their planning and control systems.

Global outsourcing has been one approach used by organizations to lower costs. It has brought its own problems in terms of less control over quality and concerns over of lost jobs in local markets. Recent product recalls highlight the dangers of outsourcing without adequate control mechanisms in place. Organizations need a management accounting system that alerts managers to issues of concern and motivates them to respond in a way that ensures long-term organizational value.[9]

Certain warning signals indicate that the management accounting system is not working well and must be changed. One sign is dysfunctional behaviour on the part of managers due to inappropriate performance measures. Managers make decisions to influence performance measures in a positive way. If these performance measures are not consistent with the goals of the organization, management's decisions do not coincide with organizational goals. When managers within the organization are acting at cross-purposes with each other, the management accounting system is not working and should be changed.

Another signal of deficiencies in the management accounting process is poor planning decisions. If product-mix and pricing decisions based on management accounting information are not contributing to organizational value, the management accounting system might not be estimating costs properly. One indication of a deficient management accounting system is the inability to win bids to provide goods that are the company's specialty, but the ability to win bids to provide those for which the company has no comparative advantage. John Deere Component Works, for example, had this problem and realized that its management accounting system was not allocating overhead properly.[10]

Organizations should not look necessarily to the latest management accounting trends or fads to give them direction in changing their management accounting systems. TQM, JIT and other management accounting tools discussed in this text are appropriate for certain types of organizations and in particular environments. Some features of each approach might be beneficial, while others might not contribute to the creation of organizational value in every case. Each organization must continually evaluate and improve its management accounting system to meet the challenges of a dynamic environment and an adaptive organization.

The Driver and Vehicle Licensing Agency (DVLA) (continued)

While TQM and JIT are contributing to improvements at the local office of the DVLA and to its customer-focused strategy, Rashmi Rao wonders if a more comprehensive approach might be necessary. It is difficult to determine how these techniques link together and how they contribute to the DVLA's long-term goals. She also is concerned that gaps still exist and that objectives possibly conflict. Rashmi thinks about capturing her strategy and objectives in a balanced scorecard. Is a scorecard approach the correct tool to meet her needs and those of her employees and clients? Rashmi opts to put this idea on hold for the time being. The introduction of TQM and JIT, along with their related service standards and performance metrics, has been a success to date. However, too many changes too quickly could backfire. Another new initiative might be perceived as a fad. It seems better to wait to see if the current changes really are moving her operations in the right direction before introducing another programme.

---

[9] The CIMA Global Homepage (www.cimaglobal.com) provides a useful starting point to obtain information on the role of management accounting in these emerging areas.

[10] *John Deere Component Works (A)*, Harvard Business School Case 9-187-107.

SUMMARY

1 **Describe factors in a dynamic environment that influence an organization.** Customer preferences, technology and global competition are all factors in a dynamic environment that lead to changes in organizations.

2 **Describe the way an organization's strategy is related to its structure.** The strategy of an organization determines its structure. For example, an innovative product strategy usually is best accomplished in a decentralized organization.

3 **Explain the role of management accounting in the organizational structure and in making planning decisions.** Management accounting through budgets is used to assign responsibilities. It also is used to measure performance and assists in making planning decisions.

4 **Identify major characteristics of total quality management (TQM).** TQM is a philosophy that places customer satisfaction first. Continuous improvement, involved leadership, employee participation and empowerment are all part of TQM.

5 **Use quality costs for making planning decisions and control.** The comparison of quality costs over time provides a benchmark to determine if TQM efforts are successful. Quality costs also should be used to make planning decisions comparing different quality efforts.

6 **Explain the philosophy of JIT processes and accounting adjustments for JIT.** The philosophy of JIT is to produce to order rather than produce for inventory. To be successful, the organization must have a short throughput time to meet demand. JIT has no job-order costs. Accounting performance measures should be selected to encourage faster throughput time and to discourage increased inventory.

7 **Identify when management accounting within an organization should change.** Management accounting must continually adapt to dynamic environments and organizations. Warning signals within the management accounting system are dysfunctional behaviour by managers and poor planning decisions.

KEY TERMS

Appraisal costs Costs related to the identification of defective units before they are shipped to customers.

External failure costs Costs incurred when a customer receives a defective product.

Internal failure costs Costs incurred when a defect is discovered before a customer receives it.

Material requirement planning (MRP) Computer programs that allow organizations to quickly ascertain resource requirements to make a product.

Prevention costs Costs incurred in the production process to reduce defects.

Throughput time The total time from receipt of an order to the time of delivery.

Self-study problem

Diego Morales operates a small sewing shop that makes dresses and skirts. Diego receives orders for the dresses and skirts from large clothing companies that contract with companies like his to manufacture the clothing that the companies then sell to retailers. The clothing companies provide Diego with the patterns and specifications for a clothing item. Any dresses and skirts that do not meet specifications are returned to Diego. The business is extremely competitive. Diego is forced to operate on small margins because the clothing companies are threatening to send the manufacturing to other countries. Diego has managed to keep his business operating by promising a low number of defects and timely delivery. Diego has achieved a low number of defects by careful inspection of all clothing leaving the shop. He has been less successful in achieving timely delivery.

Diego hired 20 seamstresses to do the sewing. Prior to the sewing, however, the cloth must be cut. Once the sewing has been completed, buttons and fasteners are added. The dresses and skirts then are inspected, pressed and packaged.

Required

Describe how Diego Morales might use TQM and JIT. Outline the advantages and disadvantages of each management philosophy.

Solution

Diego must maintain the quality of his product to survive, so TQM appears to be relevant for him. TQM, however, suggests a different approach to achieving fewer defects. Instead of discovering defects at final inspection, Diego should attempt to reduce defects before they happen. Providing more employee training and better sewing machines could help reduce initial defects. With fewer initial defects, Diego can save on the cost of spoiled units discovered after completion. In the long term, TQM can save on costs, but in the short term, the training and new machines will be costly.

Diego has a problem delivering his clothes on time. JIT suggests that production should start after receipt of an order rather than producing for inventory. Diego already has been following this rule, but he needs to shorten his throughput time. One method of shortening throughput time is to have small groups of seamstresses work in teams with individuals doing the cutting, adding the fasteners and buttons, pressing, and packaging. Work-in-process could be reduced, allowing defects to be identified and processes corrected more quickly. The team members could become multi-skilled to assist each other when needed. All of these actions would increase throughput. Diego would have to change the organizational structure to achieve JIT, however, and many employees might resent temporarily moving to a new evaluation system.

Numerical exercises

NE 14.1 Quality costs and defect rates LO 5

A manufacturer of recordable DVDs is concerned about the quality of a recent production run. It ships a complete batch of DVDs to the same retailer to monitor quality. In a recent batch, a retailer reported one defective disc. The firm's management believes that 1 per cent of its discs do not meet its quality specifications. Of these, it is convinced that 90 per cent are identified and removed prior to shipping.

If inspection is on a per-batch basis, what is the size of the questionable batch?

NE 14.2 Estimating quality costs LO 5

Spectra Company is examining its quality spending for the current year. It has summarized its spending as follows: prevention, £150,000; appraisal, £50,000; internal failure, £100,000; and external failure, £180,000. Next year, Spectra plans to increase its spending on prevention activities by 25 per cent. This increased spending will reduce external failure costs by 40 per cent. The costs for appraisal and internal failure will both increase by 5 per cent due to cost increases in Spectra's operations.

What is the projected cost of quality for the upcoming year? Is the increased spending on prevention activities beneficial in terms of overall costs of quality?

NE 14.3 Quality costs LO 5

For the past five years, a firm has measured (in €) the following quality costs by categories:

Category	2004	2005	2006	2007	2008
Prevention	5000	6000	7000	8000	9000
Appraisal	5000	5000	6000	7000	8000
Internal Failure	9000	9000	7000	5000	3000
External Failure	9000	8000	7000	6000	5000

a Given these costs, is it likely that the company's defective rate has gone up or down? Explain.
b If these figures reflect all the relevant quality costs, have the increased costs of prevention and appraisal yielded a net benefit to the company?

NE 14.4 An inspection decision with quality costs LO 5

A company is considering additional final inspection costs of £1 per unit before delivery to customers. The additional inspection should reduce the defective rate from 3 per cent to 1 per cent. If a defective unit is found, it is scrapped at no additional cost. The manufacturing costs before the final inspection are £200 per unit. Management believes that the external failure costs are £40 per defective unit.

Should management incur the additional inspection costs?

NE 14.5 Throughput time and inventory costs LO 6

A company has a throughput time of 32 days. It wants to reduce this time to eight days. To do so, it will need to change its layout at a cost of £150,000. It believes that its inventory level will drop by 25 per cent once these changes take effect. The capital cost of holding inventories is 10 per cent per year based on the average inventory level of £1,500,000.

Should the company adopt the new layout?

NE 14.6 JIT systems LO 6

Solarcom uses a JIT production system to manufacture its solar-powered DVD players. Solarcom has adopted back-flushing to streamline its accounting system. It accumulates all conversion costs for the JIT line in one account. These costs are estimated to be €2 million for the current year. Solarcom estimates that it will produce 500,000 DVD players this year. Last week, plant labour was €15,000, and €25,000 of materials were purchased and used to produce 10,000 DVD players. All units were shipped and billed to a major retail chain.

Provide a summary of the accounting entries for last week's production activities.

Numerical problems

NP 14.1 Defect rates and inspection LO 5

A large retailer purchases furniture directly from the manufacturer in northern Italy. The retailer insists that 99 per cent of the furniture arriving at the retail shops pass inspection. The manufacturer knows that 0.60 per cent of the furniture is damaged during shipping and 2 per cent of the furniture is defective before shipping.

In order to satisfy the retailer, approximately what percentage of defects must the manufacturer discover after production but before shipping takes place?

NP 14.2 Quality costs and benefits LO 5

A building contractor estimates the following quality costs: prevention, £100,000; appraisal, £50,000; internal failure, £40,000; external failure, £200,000. The contractor is considering one of the following two courses of action:

1 increasing prevention costs by 50 per cent, which should lead to a 10 per cent decline in internal failure costs and a 40 per cent decline in external failure costs; and
2 increasing appraisal costs by 100 per cent, which should increase internal failure costs by 20 per cent and decrease external failure costs by 50 per cent.

Which action causes the lowest quality costs?

NP 14.3 Defect rates and inspection costs LO 5

La Queue Company is experiencing problems with the handle on the carafe of its Euro-design coffeemaker. The handle breaks and must be replaced 5 per cent of the time. It costs €50 each time to replace the carafe. La Queue replaces the carafe and ships it by express courier to appease customers who cannot use their coffeemakers while awaiting a replacement. La Queue is considering the use of a specialty plastic for the handle that would not break, even under extreme use. The new plastic would increase its production costs by €10,000 per year. An alternative to the new plastic is to examine each carafe to see if the handle is defective. It would cost €3 per carafe to add this inspection. This year, La Queue plans to manufacture and sell an additional 5,000 coffeemakers. Next year, it plans to replace the model with a new design.

What should La Queue do?

NP 14.4 Scrap costs LO 5

O'Reilly Manufacturing produces three models of a product, Super, Supreme and Ultra. These models are basically the same design but different quality standards are applied in the production process. Frequent production line stops, adjustments and start-ups cause a certain amount of scrap costs. Also, scrap occurs when inspectors reject a product for not meeting its specifications. Once rejected, the product has no commercial value and is hauled away. All costs incurred to produce a scrapped product are charged to a scrap account. The scrap account is part of overhead. The firm's budgeted operating statement by product follows:

O'Reilly Manufacturing
Budgeted Operating Statement for 2008

	Super	Supreme	Ultra	Total
Unit volume	85,000	42,000	13,000	
Selling price	€205	€225	€235	
Revenue	€17,425,000	€9,450,000	€3,055,000	€29,930,000
Less:				
Raw materials	8,500,000	4,200,000	1,300,000	14,000,000
Direct labour	5,312,500	3,150,000	975,000	9,437,500
Overhead	3,478,245	2,062,395	638,360	6,179,000
Total cost	€17,290,745	€9,412,395	€2,913,360	€29,616,500
Profits	€134,255	€37,605	€141,640	€313,500

Other information:

- overhead costs are allocated to products based on direct labour cost;
- direct labour cost is €25 per hour.

Overheads consist of:

	€
Depreciation	3,500,000
Indirect labour	450,000
Scrap	1,679,000
Other	550,000
Total	6,179,000

Additional data:

	Super	Supreme	Ultra
Direct labour hours per unit	2.5 hours	3 hours	3 hours
Total scrap	€850,000	€504,000	€325,000
Profit per unit	€1.58	€0.90	€10.90

Management is concerned about the relatively low profit per unit on the Supreme line as compared to the Ultra line. It is considering a variety of marketing strategies to increase the sales of Ultras since the profit margins are substantially higher.

Critically analyse management's conclusion that profits are substantially higher on Ultra. Present supporting figures to back up your analysis and conclusions.

NP 14.5 Becoming ISO 9000 certified LO 4

The Stowbridge Division is analysing the expansion of its total quality management programme. It already has a TQM programme in place. One of its customers, Amlan Equipment, is asking all of its suppliers to become ISO 9000 qualified. ISO 9000 standards are a quality management system that certifies that the firm meets various quality standards. Once its suppliers obtain ISO 9000 certification, Amlan can reduce its inspection costs because it can depend on quality parts from its suppliers. Not all of its suppliers will receive certification. Those that do so will receive more business from Amlan.

Amlan purchases a stainless steel rotor from Stowbridge. To meet the ISO 9000 certification requirements, Stowbridge estimates that it will have to incur additional costs. The following annual incremental costs will be necessary as long as it wants to maintain its ISO 9000 certification:

**Annual incremental costs
for ISO 9000 certification**

Training	£74,000
Inspection	£96,000
Prevention	£62,000
Direct materials	10%
Direct labour	15%

To manufacture the current quality of the rotors (before receiving ISO 9000 certification), the budgeted selling price and standard cost data per rotor is provided:

	£
Selling price	14.00
Less standard costs	
Direct materials	4.30
Direct labour	2.40
Manufacturing overhead (all fixed)	2.05
Selling and administrative (all variable)	1.60
Unit cost	10.35
Unit profit	3.65

Unless Stowbridge receives ISO 9000 certification, it will lose Amlan's business of 120,000 units per year. In addition, management estimates that the higher quality of the rotor will allow Stowbridge to add 14,000 rotors to its current sales from new and existing customers. Stowbridge is currently selling 480,000 rotors per year, including the Amlan sales. The current sales of 480,000 units amount to 63 per cent of plant capacity. The additional 14,000 units sold can be manufactured without exceeding plant capacity. After receiving ISO 9000 certification, the higher quality process would apply to all the rotors produced.

Should Stowbridge seek ISO 9000 certification? Support your recommendation with an analysis of the costs and benefits of ISO 9000 certification.

NP 14.6 Allocating costs based on throughput time LO 6

Toby Manufacturing produces three different products in the same plant and uses a job-order costing system to estimate product costs. A flexible budget is used to forecast overhead costs. Total budgeted fixed factory overhead is £450,000 and variable overhead is 120 per cent of direct labour cost. There is no beginning or ending inventory.

Projected volumes, selling prices, and direct costs for the three products for the next calendar year follow:

	Product AAA	Product BBB	Product CCC
Projected number of units	6,000	3,000	1,000
Direct materials per unit	£22	£25	£30
Direct labour per unit	£11	£12	£16
Selling price	£98	£115	£140

The manufacturing process requires six operations. Between operations, intermediate products are moved and warehoused until the next production stage. Each of the three products requires 10 days of processing time to complete all six operations, but each has a different throughput time because of different waiting times between operations. *Throughput time* is defined as the total time from ordering the raw materials for the product until the product is completed and shipped. Product AAA has the shortest throughput time (20 days) because the large volume allows more accurate forecasts and more continuous scheduling of production. Total throughput time for Product BBB is 40 days, and for Product CCC is 50 days. Products BBB and CCC have longer warehousing times of work-in-process as a result of more frequent scheduling changes and more frequent supplier delays.

Half of what is currently treated as fixed overhead cost involves the warehousing function.

a Prepare a pro-forma profit and loss statement by product line for the year based on full absorption costing. Product costs should include overhead assigned on direct labour cost.

b Prepare a revised pro-forma profit and loss statement by product line using throughput time to allocate fixed overhead related to warehousing.

c Comment on the differences.

NP 14.7 Compensation and quality LO 5

Tagway 4000 is a computer manufacturer based in Shannon, Ireland. One component of the computer is an internal battery, which is used to keep track of time and date while the computer is turned off. Tagway produces the batteries in house. The division, which produces 1,000,000 batteries each year, is treated as a cost centre. The manager of the division is compensated based on her ability to keep total costs low as well as meet quality-control measures of number of defects and delivery time. She has a base salary of €144,000. She is eligible for a €34,000 bonus if total costs are less than or equal to €2,000,000 without including her compensation. She is eligible for a €40,000 bonus if there are 32 or fewer defects per 1,000,000 units produced. Finally, she is eligible for a €22,000 bonus if batteries are delivered on time. On-time delivery is defined as averaging two days between the order from the assembly department and delivery to the assembly department.

The basic cost of producing a battery is €1.55. However, current methods have an inherent defect rate of 1,032 defects per 1,000,000. The cost of improving the defect rate involves using higher quality materials and more experienced labour. Based on currently available inputs, improving the defect rate below 32 per 1,000,000 is impossible. From 1,032 defects to 32 defects per 1,000,000, the cost of removing each defect is €450. In other words, the cost to reduce defects to the desired level of 32 per 1,000,000 is €450,000. This production method also delivers the batteries in an average of four days. The cost of overtime necessary to lower the average to three days is €90,000. The cost of speeding up delivery another day is €95,000, making the cumulative cost of lowering the average to two days €185,000. The marginal cost of reducing the average delivery a third day is €115,000, making the total cost of reducing the average delivery time to one day €300,000.

a Create a table showing the production costs related to defect rates of 1,032, 500, 100, 50 and 32 per 1,000,000 and average delivery times of four, three, two and one days. Do not include the manager's salary. Note the minimum cost.

b Create a table showing the manager's compensation related to defect rates of 1,032, 500, 100, 50 and 32 and average delivery times of four, three, two and one days. Note the maximum compensation level.

c Comment on the ideal number of defects and delivery times necessary to achieve the minimum costs and the maximum compensation level.

NP 14.8 Choosing quality spending levels LO 5

Aqua Company has extremely high external failure costs for all level of defects. The company must achieve zero defects in products sent to customers through either prevention efforts or appraisal and correction efforts. The company makes 1,000 units; the following data relate to prevention efforts and costs:

Defects	Prevention costs (£)
100	1,000
50	3,000
20	10,000
10	50,000
5	100,000
0	300,000

Inspection of all the units following production costs £50,000. The cost of correcting defective units (internal failure costs) depends on the number of defective units.

Defects	Internal failure costs (£)
100	130,000
50	60,000
20	20,000
10	10,000
5	5,000
1	0

a What is the optimal level of prevention, appraisal, and correction?

b If the cost of inspecting all units is £500,000, what is the lowest cost strategy?

NP 14.9 JIT and backflush costing LO 6

Abco manufactures car radio antennas. It produces the retractable wand that other firms assemble with a motor, wiring, housing and switch for sale to the automakers. Abco receives deliveries of steel rod and tubing each day. These materials are cut, threaded, crimped, and assembled into final wands on continuous flow production lines. Twice a day, finished wands are shipped to customers who assemble the complete antenna unit.

On 16 March, rod and tubing valued at £2,040 were delivered for the 11cm antenna model. These materials were converted into wands and shipped out.

Completed units shipped in the morning:	160
Completed units shipped in the afternoon:	180

Labour and overhead on 16 March were £980. Each completed 11cm wand has a conversion cost of £4.80. Abco uses JIT accounting and backflushes raw and in-process (RIP) materials and conversion costs directly to cost of goods sold when the units are shipped because wands are not started until Abco receives an order.

What accounting entries are made on 16 March for the 11cm wands?

Analysis and interpretation problems

AIP 14.1 Factors that influence an organization LO 1

Avon (www.avon.uk.com) manufactures and sells cosmetics primarily to women using a sales force consisting of part-time (usually female) sales representatives offering the products through in-home sales parties. Sales representatives also host parties in their homes where they demonstrate the products and then take orders. Many customers also submit telephone or online orders to the sales representative or directly to the company. Other customers prefer to order by post. Avon recently began to offer its products through retail stores where customers can drop off orders for sales representatives and take delivery of products. The sales representatives are paid on a commission basis.

Discuss the factors that are currently affecting Avon's business.

AIP 14.2 Relation between organization strategy and organization structure LO 2

In the US, there have been historically many banks, each with multiple branches. Since the 1990s, numerous bank mergers occurred and branch banks have been consolidated. Discuss the factors driving US banks to change their strategy and thus, their organizational structure.

AIP 14.3 Management accounting and planning decisions LO 3

Describe various ways that the management accounting system assists in planning decisions.

AIP 14.4 Choosing TQM LO 4

Wonderful Toy Company (WTC) is celebrating its 100th anniversary this year. The company has been successful in designing and making educational toys for department stores and smaller specialty toy shops popular with doting parents and grandparents. The sales manager has recently returned from a national convention and heard that many other toy manufacturers are implementing TQM. WTC's chairman, the great grandson of the company's founder, does not think that WTC needs TQM. He states, 'We have been in business for 100 years and this company has been very profitable. Our customers must be happy with us because they are still buying our products. Why should we change the way we do business?'

Evaluate the chairman's statement.

AIP 14.5 JIT and the role of accounting LO 6

The managing director (MD) of Kelly Windows is an avid believer in JIT. Kelly Windows manufactures bay windows. The MD wants no inventory or work-in-process on the floor at the end of each day. Windows are only manufactured after being ordered and throughput time is quick enough to complete most orders during the day of the order. The MD is also trying to eliminate all non-value-added activities. She considers accounting to be non-value-added and would like to reduce accounting activities sharply if not completely.

As the financial controller, how can you defend the accounting activities that your department performs?

AIP 14.6 Measuring quality costs LO 5

The managing director of Precision Machines wants to convert to TQM. The industrial machinery produced by Precision Machines is critical to customers. If defective machinery is sold to a client, the customer incurs very high costs. Precision Machines usually has to pay these costs because of warranties or lawsuits. The managing director believes that TQM will help the organization satisfy its customers. As part of the change to TQM, he has asked you, the finance director, to devise a system for measuring the different categories of quality cost: prevention, appraisal, internal failure or external failure.

Describe the costs in each of these categories. For which categories will it be the most difficult to make cost estimates?

AIP 14.7 JIT and stock-out costs LO 6

James Industries is considering a shift to JIT. The managing director (MD) insists that reducing inventory can save considerable costs. The marketing manager is worried, however. She recognizes that the inventory holding costs, such as storage and the opportunity cost of cash consumed to hold inventory, are high and will be reduced if the company changes to JIT. She is concerned that the MD has forgotten about stock-out costs. Stock-out costs occur when customers want to purchase an item that is not immediately available and go elsewhere to make the purchase.

How should the company measure stock-out costs? What can be done to minimize them?

AIP 14.8 Identify factors suggesting management accounting change LO 7

What tell-tale signs suggest that the management accounting process requires change?

Extended **analysis** and **interpretation** problem

AIP 14.9 Quality costs

Software Development, Inc. (SDI) produces and markets software for personal computers including spreadsheet, word processing, desktop publishing, and database management programs. SDI has annual sales of €800 million.

Producing software is a time-consuming, labour-intensive process. Software quality is an extremely important aspect of success in computer software markets. One aspect of quality is program reliability. Does the software perform as expected? Does it work with other software in terms of data transfers and interfaces? Does it terminate abnormally? In spite of extensive testing of the software, programs always contain some bugs. Once the software is released, SDI stands behind the product with online and telephone customer-service consultants who answer questions and help the customer work around existing problems in the software. SDI also has a software maintenance group that fixes bugs and sends out revised versions of the programs to customers.

SDI has been tracking the relation between quality costs and quality. The quality measure that it uses is the number of documented bugs in a software package. A bug is identified when a customer calls in with a complaint and the SDI customer service representative determines that it is a new problem. The software maintenance programmers then set about to fix the program and eliminate the defect. To manage quality, SDI tracks quality costs. It has released 38 new or major revisions in existing packages in the last three years. Table 14.1 reports the number of defects (bugs) documented in the first six months following release. Also listed in Table 14.1 is total product cost and quality cost per software package release.

Product costs include all the costs incurred to produce and market the software, excluding the quality costs in Table 14.1. Quality costs consist of training, prevention and software maintenance, and customer-service costs. Training costs are those expenditures for educating the programmers and updating their technical expertise. Better educated programmers produce fewer bugs. Prevention costs include the expenditures for testing the software before it is released. Maintenance and customer service costs are those of the programmers charged with fixing the defects and re-issuing the revised software, and the customer-service representatives answering questions. The training and prevention costs are measured for the period during which the software was being developed. The number of defects, maintenance expenditures and service costs are measured in the first six months following release.

All the numbers in Table 14.1 have been deflated by lines of computer code in the particular program release. Programs with more lines of code cost more and also have more bugs. Prior studies have found that 'lines of code' is an acceptable way to control for program complexity. Thus, the numbers in Table 14.1 are stated in terms of defects and cost per 100,000 lines of code.

Figure 14.5 plots the relation between total quality cost and number of defects. SDI's Director of Quality likes to use Figure 14.5 to emphasize that costs and quality are inversely related. She is fond of saying, 'Quality pays! Our total costs are a declining function of the number of defects. The more we spend on quality, the lower our costs.'

Critically evaluate the Director's analysis.

Table 14.1 SDI defects and quality costs by program release (per 100,000 lines of computer code)

Program release	Number of defects	Product cost (€)	Training cost (€)	Prevention cost (€)	Maintenance and customer service cost (€)	Total costs (€)
1	66	3455	442	770	2160	6827
2	86	3959	428	447	2658	7492
3	14	3609	417	1167	687	5880
4	73	3948	211	655	2334	7148
5	17	3104	290	1013	544	4951
6	48	3179	253	547	1556	5535
7	80	3112	392	508	2633	6645
8	41	3529	276	577	1563	5945
9	50	3796	557	634	1666	6653
10	67	3444	365	947	2140	6896
11	42	3922	453	869	1444	6688
12	64	3846	378	1108	1942	7274
13	71	3014	555	762	2384	6715
14	1	3884	301	773	423	5381
15	18	3183	378	1080	857	5498
16	85	3475	528	1010	2572	7585
17	17	3445	357	666	631	5099
18	50	3203	285	427	1546	5461
19	22	3839	239	1080	891	6049
20	73	3060	540	1054	2309	6963
21	52	3182	329	1079	1867	6457
22	75	3075	395	832	2697	6999
23	35	3456	447	969	1518	6390
24	53	3987	355	651	2042	7035
25	25	3836	309	1160	1036	6341
26	6	3886	234	794	252	5166
27	78	3846	418	833	2800	7897
28	82	3106	409	1092	2871	7478
29	39	3506	448	899	1342	6195
30	47	3545	450	442	1450	5887
31	30	3376	456	784	1260	5876
32	17	3740	542	420	607	5309
33	67	3479	411	821	2018	6729
34	51	3773	351	1145	1873	7142
35	74	3034	497	671	2389	6591
36	25	3768	268	887	1094	6017
37	14	3168	356	645	837	5006
38	77	3561	492	1167	2597	7817
Average	48	3509	390	826	1671	6395

Figure 14.5 SDI: total costs by defect

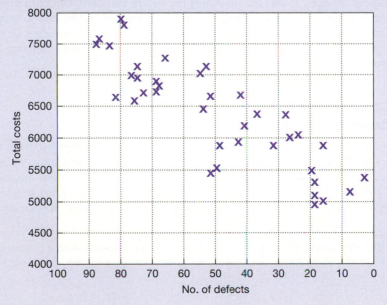

Chapter **Two**

Online securities trading with Barclays Brokers, E*Trade, Selftrade and TD Waterhouse (p. 60)

Firms with higher fixed costs, such as full-service brokerage houses, are likely to develop pricing strategies to cover the fixed and variable costs of their operations. Fixed costs relate to the higher infrastructure costs of these firms. Clients can be differentiated according to pricing schemes based on the level of service that they demand. Online trading firms have lower infrastructure costs and are more likely to pursue a low-price strategy to capture customers who will trade off higher levels of service for lower costs.

As firms try to compete in the long term, clients likely will become more demanding and expect firms to offer more at lower cost. In the long run, as commission fees drop, both existing and new firms will have more difficulty in competing successfully. Commission fees might be pushed lower to capture market share at the expense of long-run profits. In the end, successful firms will need to implement a strategy that delivers customer value in other ways, such as financial advice and banking privileges.

Chapter **Three**

Japan's DoCoMo's mobile phone services (p. 86)

Given a cost structure that is predominantly at the product, facility and batch levels, DoCoMo should enter into pricing agreements that reflect the inexpensive unit-level costs. DoCoMo could consider fixed monthly fees for unlimited long-distance telephone calls. Reducing the customer's marginal cost of a telephone call to zero, however, might have a large impact on the usage of long-distance calls. A large increase in long-distance calls could lead to capacity costs. Therefore, a fixed monthly fee for a limited number of calls during peak-use periods and an unlimited number of calls during periods of non-peak use might be an alternative pricing strategy.

DoCoMo must recognize that mobile communications could evolve in many different directions in the next five years. The company must be prepared to keep pace with technological changes. If wireless becomes the future standard, DoCoMo must be prepared with satellite networks and control over sufficient wavelengths. It also must consider ways to reach local customers through the acquisition of other companies, strategic alliances with competitors or bundling of its services with the products of other firms such as music and game providers.

Chapter **Four**

Omnicom Group Inc. (p. 119)

If an organization does not have the in-house personnel or expertise, it might prefer to outsource its advertising activity to an outside agency, such as Omnicom. Advertising agencies offer industry expertise, a broad range of services and lower costs due to economies of scale.

When making the decision to outsource, an organization must weigh the advantages and disadvantages of this choice. Advantages include the items previously mentioned, as well

---

[1] The RIM case in Chapter One does not include questions but is used to illustrate the Framework for Organizational Change.

as potential time savings by outsourcing the activity to experts. Disadvantages include not developing and maintaining this expertise within the firm (contributing to organizational growth), the potential loss of confidentiality (one reason advertising agencies generally cannot work for competing firms), and possible cost increases once the organization becomes dependent on the agency. In addition, no guarantee exists that the agency will develop a successful advertising campaign. Any decision to change agencies or revert to in-house production also could lead to lost sales if it is not carried out effectively.

Chapter **Five**

Ryanair (p. 160)

Ryanair, like other low-cost carriers, might establish its airfares by determining the marginal cost of carrying passengers, examining competitors' fares, and analysing customers' price sensitivity. Customers might be willing to pay more than the firm's marginal cost of the alternative flight is a full-cost fare with a major carrier.

The low-cost carriers must be careful not to price their flights too low such that they do not cover their long-run fixed costs. In addition, customers might react negatively to future price increases, once low prices have been established. Low-cost carriers also face threats from larger firms that enter this market and try to lure customers by offering lower fares. The larger firms might consider that they can pursue this strategy in the short run, gain passengers, and place the smaller firms in a difficult position in terms of maintaining both market share and profits. Low-cost airlines, however, often can compete better with lower fares as they have lower fixed costs, operate more efficiently and frequently have less unionized labour. They also tend to choose routes that are less popular for major carriers.

Break-even analysis provides a tool to determine the required number of passengers (or passenger revenues) for a particular flight to be potentially profitable. By using various combinations of prices and passengers, the airline can determine when it is better to add an additional flight to a specific route or enter a new market, especially when this decision might reduce the number of passengers on existing flights. Break-even analysis also provides the airline initial insights into market potential before undertaking more in-depth study.

Chapter **Six**

High-Technology Health Care (p. 205)

Ratification, such as Fallon Community Health's pre-authorization procedure, is not the only method of control available for health plans. In most decentralized organizations, only decisions with a very large impact on the organization require ratification. Control is achieved through monitoring. In the case of Fallon Community Health, medical practitioners can be monitored using performance measures. Medical practitioners could be evaluated, for example, based on the total costs of services that the patients receive. The number of referrals could be another performance measure. Given Fallon Community Health's voluntary programme to provide incentives, its system of tracking normal trends in specific imaging techniques and procedures could be adapted to reward those doctors whose usage patterns reflect best practices in the industry. Performance measures could be adjusted for doctors with different types of clientele. For example, those doctors who have predominately older patients would be expected to have patients with higher service costs.

Chapter **Seven**

Microsoft's 'Software as a service' platform strategy (p. 225)

Given that all of the responsibility centres are oriented toward external customers, each centre manager must make decisions related to sales. Therefore, the responsibility centres are either profit or investment centres, depending on the amount of discretion each manager has with respect to expansion.

Organizing around customers rather than functions or products focuses managers on customer needs. In a rapidly changing area such as technology, an organization must be ready to move quickly in generating new products and services for customers. Organizing around customers, however, means that managers must contract with centralized service departments to provide internal services such as accounting, purchasing, or maintenance. The alternative is for each centre to have its own internal service departments, which could lead to some redundancies within the organization.

Chapter **Eight**

Ericsson (p. 272)

Ericsson must react quickly to customer demands and technological change. Thus, it has adapted its organizational structure to create a firm that can react more quickly and adapt to changes. For example, the firm has reduced management levels, created teams to share market information more efficiently and effectively, and decentralized decision making. The management accounting system must support the firm's decision-making and control mechanisms and reflect the firm's need for quick decisions and up-to-date information. The management accounting system has been altered to reflect the emphasis on activities, business segments and key performance indicators. The system de-emphasizes the annual budget and uses a continuous one. In addition, Ericsson uses a series of non-financial performance indicators to measure the achievement of its strategic goals.

Ericsson's summary of Key Performance Indicators (KPIs) measure five categories: customers, finance, employees, internal efficiency and innovation. The following measures are examples of the types of indicators that Ericsson has selected:

Customers: customer satisfaction, market share, brand-name awareness
Finance: sales growth, cash flow, profitability
Employees: skill development, employee turnover
Internal Efficiency: capital turnover, reliability of deliveries to customers, reliabilities of market deliveries
Innovation: number of patent applications

These measures are reported to higher levels in the organization for review and follow up.

Chapter **Nine**

Strategy, pricing and costing in universities (p. 322)

The University of Bath uses cost allocation primarily for planning purposes. The University of Bath uses its system to better understand the relationship between its research and teaching activities and their costs. This knowledge enables the University to make informed decisions about which programmes to offer, promote or wind down.

Cost allocation for the purpose of accurate 'product costs' might have been less important in the higher education market in the past when students and their parents were less informed about programmes, universities and international study opportunities. With the Internet and other information sources, students are more demanding and universities must compete globally to attract the brightest and the best. Additionally, in some countries, universities previously received much more funding from government than they do presently, reducing the attention paid to costs and their control. In today's market, universities need information to determine the cost of their activities and to demonstrate their financial stewardship. Financial stability is important to external donors whose support is increasingly important.

The University of Bath strives to be a leading university combining teaching and research excellence. Its cost allocation procedure links activity costs to achieve this strategy to outcomes. Also, the allocation of central costs highlights to departments and units that these costs must be covered by providing programmes and research activities that attract the best students, faculty and external support. Allocated costs emphasize the need for the University to pursue its short-term objectives in a fiscally transparent and stable manner to ensure that it can achieve its long-term goals. Programmes must be both financially viable and support the University's strategy for high-quality research and teaching in a high technology learning environment.

Chapter **Ten**

CAE and job-order costing (p. 367)

CAE uses a job-order costing system to support its production process. It customizes its products to meet the requirements of individual clients. CAE also remains cost competitive by manufacturing products that share common features to permit economies of scale. A job-order costing system provides a mechanism to track these costs to individual customers, projects and contracts. In addition, the system enables CAE to track costs over extended periods of time. This system provides a mechanism for cost control and details to ensure that the project meets customer demands. Finally, job-order costing information is an important input for pricing. CAE must offer competitive pricing, technological innovation and mass customization.

CAE's job-order costing system supports the company's goals of innovation and competitiveness in that it provides both the firm and its customers detailed information regarding production costs. These details include the ability to track the cost of special features that customers require. The cost information assists CAE in setting prices competitively that at the same time cover all costs. By highlighting activity costs, the detailed tracking supports CAE's goals to create organizational value. In this way, CAE can work to eliminate non-value-added activities and their costs, increasing both customer and organizational value.

Chapter **Ten**

Activity-based costing in a business school (p. 379)

Factors that might contribute to the higher cost of Ph.D. students compared to those in a combined undergraduate/masters programme are the small size of doctoral classes, the more senior rank of faculty who teach in the doctoral programme, and special incentives and compensation for professors who teach in this programme (extra salary, reduced teaching loads, etc.). Although not included in this study, extra costs also typically include the greater financial aid given to Ph.D. students.

The cost of capacity tends to be overlooked in a university environment for a number of reasons. First, universities have no market mechanisms to highlight inefficiencies and wasteful use of capacity. Second, in most universities, space is a free good to the extent that the internal cost of this space does not reflect its full cost or comparable cost if this space were acquired in the rental market. Third, in some situations, the decision to allocate space to a specific activity is linked to other decisions, such as accommodating preferred class times and elective courses.

University faculty and staff might be reluctant about efforts to cost their activities since many of them might be difficult to measure and capture quantitatively. For example, course or research projects that are reported to be high cost might be considered unnecessary or inappropriate when the university is dealing with cost constraints. Financial measures might not reflect the contribution of these items in other ways (reputation of the university, ability to attract high-quality professors and students) and might lead to decisions that are contrary to the university's long-run mission. Finally, as in all organizations, individuals react to what is measured and might not like the focus placed on their activities. However, cost measurement might also motivate university members to better manage the costs of the resources that they consume.

Chapter **Eleven**

Cost management at National Bank of Canada (p. 423)

The management accounting system supports National Bank's strategy and the implementation of that strategy by providing critical information on the cost of delivering value to customers. For example, the system enables the bank's management to analyse the cost of different products, services and types of customers. National Bank's management accounting system has evolved to centre around the customer in conjunction with its strategic focus on personalized customer service.

National Bank's full-cost system has certain advantages. It ensures that pricing strategies and the introduction of new products consider the fixed costs of the bank's infrastructure. This system emphasizes that these full costs must be covered in the long run. Another advantage is to curb the enthusiasm of marketing personnel to develop new products without adequate attention to their long-term as well as short-term impact. A disadvantage of the system is that it requires many decisions regarding which costs are fixed and which are variable. Also, it might not fully consider that certain costs are sunk and incurred regardless of the strategy pursued. Another disadvantage is that it might create situations in which short-term, profitable initiatives are overlooked due to the full-cost analysis. National Bank's direct cost model offsets this disadvantage.

Potential effects on management behaviour are the reluctance to take risks that are beneficial in terms of the bank's strategic goals and the efforts of managers to use resources in such a way as to minimize allocated costs. A positive impact of the system is to make managers more careful in the use of resources whose costs are allocated to them.

Chapter **Twelve**

Burn Stewart Distillers Ltd (p. 477)

Burn Stewart Distillers (BSD) faced increased competition in its market, a market in which customers often are price conscious but expect a high quality product. Distillers also must meet stringent quality standards imposed by governments. BSD also wanted to address factors across its supply chain including sales forecasting, production scheduling and improved cash management, all of which can be integrated into its planning and control system.

BSD's standard cost system enables the firm to determine cost-quality trade-offs of its various blends in light of changing market preferences. Its system also provides real-time information to decide if BSD should acquire inputs from other producers or use its internal inventories to meet expected sales levels. Besides costing, BSD's system provides management with critical data to support its reporting to government especially in the area of Customs and Excise which monitors closely the movement of spirits and the valuation of inventories.

Chapter **Thirteen**

Cow-Milking robots at Mason Dixon Farms (p. 512)

If Mason Dixon Farms proceeds with the investment in the robotic milking system, we could conclude that non-monetary factors had a major influence on its decision. For example, a decrease in its labour force would reduce the need to deal with migrant labour, reducing management stress and time. Additionally, the robotic system offers advantages in animal welfare, milking time and problem identification. If the investment in robots was less profitable compared to the purchase of a carousel milking parlour, Mason Dixon Farms management would need to evaluate the importance of these non-monetary factors. Their impact, while difficult to quantify, might alter Mason Dixon Farm's decision.

Mason Dixon Farms could hedge its investment by not purchasing all 40 robots at one time. This alternative allows management to monitor their use, operating costs and savings, and the impact of exchange rates, etc. It also might leave certain options open, such as the future investment in the carousel milking parlour.

Chapter **Fourteen**

Ice cream goes global (p. 563)

Carpigiani was losing market share and customers due to low-cost rivals and concerns about the quality of its products. It had not kept pace with customer preferences, including customer demands for low-cost, high-quality and innovative products. In its market, customers expected all three.

Carpigiani focused on cost, quality and innovation. It cut costs through staff reductions and outsourcing and improvements to its production processes. It introduced a quality management system to improve its quality control (and obtained ISO 9001 certification) and invested in research and development to design and produce innovative equipment. It also opted to compete with its major competitors by opening a factory in China to make its equipment locally.

Chapter **One**

Page 10

1 Management accounting must adapt to changes in the organization, which is changing due to technological changes, customer preferences and globalization.
2 Technological innovations allow an organization to communicate information better and to operate more efficiently.
3 Globalization forces organizations to continually innovate to meet the demands of its customers.
4 If an organization cannot meet customer demand, it cannot generate revenues to remain in operation.

Page 14

1 Customer value is the well-being that occurs when a customer consumes a product or service.
2 An organization can create customer value by offering products and services at a cost that is less than the well-being generated by consuming the product or service.

Page 19

1 Organizations form to achieve goals that a person cannot attain individually.
2 The three basic processes are assigning responsibilities, measuring performance and rewarding individuals.
3 Planning decisions are made to select activities to implement the strategy. Control decisions encourage members of the organization to follow the organization's strategy.

Page 23

1 Management accounting provides information for internal users; financial reporting provides information primarily for parties outside the organization.
2 Management accounting provides information for improved planning decisions.
3 Management accounting helps align the interests of the members of the organization with the organization's goals by measuring performance.
4 The growth of large corporations and the separation of managers and owners made management accounting more important and more sensitive to a changing environment.

Page 25

1 The communication of information within the organization is affected when the same information is used to evaluate members of the organization.
2 Historical costs may differ from the market value of an asset.
3 Maximizing profit based on historical cost is not always consistent with maximizing shareholder wealth.

Page 29

1 The controllers are responsible for the organization's accounting system; the internal auditors monitor the organization to determine whether prescribed operational procedures are being followed.
2 A code of ethics provides direction for management accountants when they make a subjective decision that affects multiple stakeholders.

Chapter **Two**

Page 47

1 Only differential costs and benefits are relevant to a decision because all other costs and benefits are the same for each alternative.
2 Future costs and benefits are not known with certainty and often involve factors that are not easily quantified in monetary terms.
3 The alternative use of resources should be considered in determining the opportunity cost.
4 Sunk costs are the effect of past decisions that cannot be changed.

Page 48

1 The cost of information includes the cost of acquiring, modifying, communicating, and analysing the information. Resources, such as cash and employee time, are used in the process.
2 The benefit of information is improved decisions.

Page 52

1 The cost of starting operations and making the first few units includes the purchase and setting up of machinery and training of labour.
2 When the capacity of resources is reached, the cost of the additional use of those resources becomes very high.
3 The marginal cost identifies the cost of making one more unit and should be used for making a decision of whether to make additional units.
4 The average cost does not provide the cost of making additional units and should not be used in deciding whether to increase output.

Page 55

1 The fixed cost does not change with the rate of output.
2 Variable costs approximate the marginal cost at a normal rate of operations.

Page 59

1 The account classification method separates accounts into variable and fixed. The summation of the costs of all the fixed accounts is the fixed cost. The summation of the costs of all the variable accounts divided by the expected output is the variable cost per unit of output.
2 The high-low method uses the costs of the highest and lowest output periods to estimate variable and fixed costs.

Chapter **Three**

Page 81

1 The cost object is the recipient of traced costs. A cost object is chosen based on the decision being made.
2 The product cost can be used to determine whether a particular product is profitable. A product whose selling price is less than its cost should be dropped from the product mix.

Page 82

1 Direct product costs are traced to a single product; while indirect product costs are related to multiple products.
2 Direct product costs are normally classified as either direct labour or direct materials.
3 Direct material costs can be estimated using pricing lists of suppliers. Engineers often are called on to estimate the number of direct labour hours necessary to complete a product. The direct labour hours times the wage rate provides an estimate of direct labour costs.

Page 85

1 Indirect product costs are not specific to a single product but are related to multiple products.

2 Unit-level costs increase with the number of units produced. Batch-level costs increase with the number of batches. Product-level costs increase with the number of different products. Facility-level costs are fixed unless another facility is purchased.

Page 89

1 The six steps are to (1) identify the activities that generate indirect product costs, (2) estimate the cost of the activities, (3) select a cost driver for each activity, (4) estimate the cost-driver use by all products, (5) calculate a cost-driver application rate, and (6) apply activity costs to each product.

2 Ideally the cost-driver use should be proportional to the activity costs.

Page 95

1 The first step of ABC is to identify activities and the cost drivers for each activity. The estimated cost of each activity is divided by the estimated usage of its respective cost driver to determine an application rate for each cost driver. Costs then are applied based on the usage of the cost drivers by the different products.

2 The advantage is that ABC recognizes different levels of indirect costs and generally provides a more accurate estimate of the cost of a product. A disadvantage is that ABC is more costly to estimate.

Page 99

1 Estimated indirect costs are divided by the estimated usage of the cost driver to determine an application rate. The application rate then becomes the cost of using the cost driver.

2 The problem with tracing indirect costs using a single cost driver is that all indirect costs do not necessarily vary with the use of that cost driver. Therefore, the estimated product costs are not necessarily a good estimate.

Chapter **Four**

Page 117

1 Strategic decisions have long-term implications and recognize external forces and the organization's strengths and weaknesses. Short-term decisions assume that the organization's existing resources are fixed and only marginal changes can be made.

2 The critical success factors that add customer value are innovative product/service design, high-quality products and services, and low-cost production.

Page 121

1 Activity-based management helps identify the critical activities that lead to customer value.

2 If external parties can provide certain activities at a lower cost, those activities potentially can be outsourced.

Page 126

1 Trade-offs exist among the different phases of the product life cycle. Increased costs in one phase can lead to decreased costs in other phases.

2 Most costs are committed during the design and engineering stage.

Page 130

1 Receiving, inspecting, warehousing, purchasing, and dealing with defective parts are activities that add to the cost of working with a supplier.

2 Suppliers can be linked through EDI and e-commerce for more prompt service and lower accounting costs. Timely delivery for JIT production with appropriate packaging also can reduce costs.

Page 132

1 Customers that buy small quantities and require much service are more expensive.
2 Organizations can educate their customers as to what is costly behaviour and reward them for avoiding such behaviour with additional services or lower prices.

Page 138

1 The rule for selecting a price to maximize value is to produce the quantity at which marginal cost equals marginal benefit.
2 In a competitive environment, an organization has little opportunity to influence the price because multiple producers of similar products exist.
3 Cost-based pricing is used in regulated industries and when the supplier does not want to bear the risk of making a product with an uncertain cost.

Chapter **Five**

Page 150

1 Short-term decisions are made frequently, assume that the organization's resources are relatively fixed, and are based on incremental analysis. Strategic decisions are made infrequently, and are often tied to the annual budgeting process.
2 In the short term, most fixed costs are sunk, so the focus is on variable costs.

Page 158

1 The basic equation for CVP analysis is Profit = (Price per unit × Number of units) − (Variable cost per unit × Number of units) − Fixed costs
2 The purpose of break-even analysis is to estimate the output quantity necessary to have a zero profit to determine whether a project is potentially profitable.
3 The major assumptions of CVP analysis include a separation of costs into fixed and variable, and constant prices and variable cost per unit over the total range of output.
4 To use CVP analysis with multiple products, constant proportions or a 'basket' of the multiple goods must be assumed.

Page 159

1 Variable costs become the lower boundary for pricing in the short term when the organization is operating below capacity.
2 When an organization operates at capacity, the opportunity cost of making a product is greater than the variable cost. Therefore, the lower boundary for short-term pricing should be higher than the variable cost.

Page 166

1 Incremental costs should be considered when deciding to add a product.
2 Avoidable costs identify those costs that would be eliminated if the product were dropped.
3 If the purchase price of the product is less than the cost of making the product, the product should be purchased.
4 A product should be processed further if incremental revenues are greater than incremental costs.
5 Organizations prefer to sell products with higher contribution margins per unit.

Page 169
1 The product that yields the highest contribution margin per use of the constraint should have priority.
2 An organization should make sure that an activity that is a bottleneck is always in operation. Expanding the capacity of the bottleneck is another method to increase the rate of operation.

Chapter **Six**

Page 188
1 The two internal roles of management accounting are improving planning decisions and assisting in control.
2 Large organizations have greater control problems because they must motivate more individuals to act in the best interests of the organization.

Page 191
1 Top-level managers delegate some of their responsibilities to subordinates who delegate some of their responsibilities to their subordinates.
2 People with the best knowledge have the capabilities to make the best planning decisions.
3 By transferring knowledge to managers who will act in the best interests of the organization, the linking of knowledge with responsibilities and control are both achieved.

Page 202
1 The costs include time and effort. The benefits include monetary rewards, status and relationships with people with similar interests.
2 Monitoring costs are incurred to assist in the control of the organization.
3 Performance measures are used to evaluate individuals and sub-units of an organization.
4 A good performance measure is consistent with the goals of the organization and reveals the actions of the individual being evaluated.
5 Good performance measures should lead to extra rewards.

Page 206
1 The four steps of the decision process are initiation, ratification, implementation, and monitoring. Alternating steps are either a decision planning process (initiation, implementation) or a decision control process (ratification, monitoring).
2 Separation of planning and control activities allows for mutual monitoring.

Chapter **Seven**

Page 220
1 The controllability principle is used because it rewards and penalizes each member of an organization for those activities that they can control.
2 The advantage of a relative performance measure is that comparisons can be made across individuals facing a similar environment. The disadvantage is that there are always winners and losers no matter how all the managers did, so it may lead to competition rather than co-operation among managers.

Page 225
1 A cost centre either has a fixed set of inputs from which to maximize outputs (type 1) or a fixed output to be achieved by minimizing the cost of inputs (type 2).
2 Minimizing cost may have adverse effects on quality, so quality measures should be used in conjunction with cost measures.
3 Profit centre managers normally have control over both inputs and the sale of outputs.

4 The profit of investment centres does not normally include interest on long-term debt, so performance measures should capture the cost of capital.

5 Many responsibility centres have characteristics of more than one type of responsibility centre. For example, managers of some responsibility centres have the right to make minor expansions of their responsibility centre but do not have the right to make large expansions.

Page 232

1 ROI allows for the comparison of performances across managers of different amounts of assets and is in the form of an easily understood percentage. The problems include measurement errors resulting from the use of historical costs, manipulation, incentives to under-invest, and not including the discounting of cash flows.

2 Residual income has all of the problems of ROI except under-investment. Residual income has the advantage of explicitly recognizing the cost of capital.

Page 243

1 Transfer pricing allows decentralized managers to make transfer decisions among themselves. Transfer-pricing systems improve decision control by assigning costs to the responsibility centre managers responsible for costs.

2 Transfer prices provide managers with information on the cost of internal services so they can plan accordingly. The transfer price should equal the opportunity cost of providing the product or service to ensure that the appropriate planning decision is made to benefit the entire organization.

Page 247

1 Set the transfer price to recognize more of the profits in the country with the lower tax rate. If the country of the supplying division has the lower tax rate, a higher transfer price transfers profit to the supplying division and lowers after-tax profit. If the country of the purchasing division has the lower tax rate, a lower transfer price transfers profit to the purchasing division and lowers after-tax profit.

2 If the local government is threatening to expropriate the assets of high-profit, foreign-owned companies, these companies may want to choose high transfer prices for their imports and low transfer prices for their exports. If multinationals choose transfer prices solely to minimize taxes or for political considerations, they must devise alternative measures of performance to motivate managers of foreign subsidiaries.

Chapter **Eight**

Page 271

1 Budgeting facilitates the transfer of information within the organization to improve planning decisions. Budgeting also forces managers to plan in a periodic manner.

2 The budget is used to distribute responsibilities by specifying how much can be spent on different items. Budgeting also establishes benchmarks for evaluating performance.

3 Conflict might occur because the gathering of information for planning purposes is influenced by how the information is to be used for evaluating performance.

Page 278

1 Short-term budgets are both planning and control tools. Long-term budgets reduce managers' focus on short-term performance and are primarily used for planning purposes.

2 A line-item budget restricts the responsibilities of a manager by forcing the manager to make purchases only up to specified amounts.

3 The cost of budget lapsing is the need to continually budget for projects that span time periods and the inability of managers to make trade-offs across different time horizons. The benefit of budget lapsing is greater control on short-term spending.

4 Managers who can control the size of operations should be evaluated based on static budgets; managers who do not control the size of operations should be evaluated based on flexible budgets.
5 Zero-based budgeting is useful when there is new management resulting in a greater need of information flow.

Page 287
1 The first step of the budget process is normally the estimation of sales.
2 Production requirements are equal to sales plus expected ending inventory less beginning inventory.
3 A financial budget identifies the cash flows to and from investors and creditors of the organization.
4 Pro-forma financial statements are the expected financial statements at the end of the budgeting period.

Chapter **Nine**

Page 313
1 Cost allocation is the process of assigning indirect costs to cost objects. Examples are the assignment of the cost of internal services such as maintenance and information technology services to the users of those services such as production units, and the assignment of machinery costs to the multiple products that use the machine.
2 Common resources are used by multiple cost objects. Therefore, common resources are difficult to trace to cost objects.

Page 319
1 The allocation of all manufacturing overhead costs, but not indirect selling and administrative costs, to products traditionally is done for external financial and tax reporting. It is used to calculate the current period's financially reported profits.
2 Organizations prefer to allocate as much overhead as possible to products that are being produced under cost reimbursement contracts.

Page 320
1 Cost allocations should approximate the opportunity cost of using the overhead resource for planning purposes.
2 Cost allocations are used to communicate information to and penalize the party causing the externality (assuming it is negative).

Page 323
1 Cost allocations may coincide with the distribution of resources and limit the amount of resources that the manager controls.
2 Cost allocations affect the performance measures of managers and discourage managers from using the allocation base used to allocate the costs.
3 Mutual monitoring is monitoring that is performed by peers within the organization. Cost allocations are like prices that occur within the organization and reveal the efficiencies of other units within the organization.

Page 331
1 Cost objects are chosen depending on the type of decision being made.
2 A cost pool is an aggregation of costs related to a specific activity.
3 The allocation base is used to distribute costs of a cost pool among the different cost objects.
4 The application rate is calculated as follows: estimated size of the cost pool divided by the estimated usage of the allocation base.
5 As the cost objects use the allocation base, costs are allocated to the cost objects based on the application rate.

6 A cost driver reflects the cause of the costs in the cost pool, while the allocation base may be chosen for control reasons. Both are used to apply costs of common resources to multiple cost objects.

Page 333

1 The purpose of segment reporting is to measure the performance of the organization's different sub-units and groups of products.
2 Transactions with other sub-units of the organization affect the segment reports of the interacting sub-units. For segment reports, these transactions should be treated as if they were with external parties.

Chapter **Ten**

Page 363

1 The two types of production processes are job-order production and continuous-flow production.
2 Job-order costing is used for job-order production, and process costing is used for continuous-flow production.

Page 366

1 The job-order cost sheet records direct materials, direct labour and overhead.
2 The overhead costs are added using an allocation base.

Page 370

1 Once production begins, the work-in-process account begins receiving costs.
2 At the end of production, the costs are transferred to the finished goods account.
3 At the time of sale, the costs are transferred to the cost of goods sold account.

Page 377

1 Actual overhead costs or usage of the allocation base may be different than estimated.
2 Over- and under-absorbed overhead reflect how actual operations differed from expected operations and may be used to adjust future estimates. These future estimates are used to make product mix and pricing decisions. Over- and under-absorbed overhead may also reflect control problems.
3 Over- and under-absorbed overhead can be treated as (1) cost of goods sold, (2) prorated among the work-in-process, finished goods, and cost of goods sold accounts, or (3) eliminated by recalculating the application rate using actual numbers and reallocating the overhead.

Page 382

1 The quality of the cost drivers in reflecting the costs of the cost pools determines the accuracy of product costs. Multiple allocation bases yield more accurate product costs if products use overhead resources in different ways.
2 By allocating costs first to departments, the manager becomes responsible for those costs and has incentives to reduce them.

Page 386

1 The primary purpose of process costing is to identify the average cost of the product.
2 Equivalent unit calculation is used when partially completed units exist at the beginning and end of the accounting period.

Page 390

1 The schedule for cost of goods manufactured generates the costs transferred to finished goods. The cost of goods sold is calculated by adding the costs transferred to finished goods to the beginning inventory of finished goods less the ending inventory of finished goods.

2 FIFO assumes that cost of the early units of inventory should be transferred to cost of goods sold first. LIFO assumes that the cost of the latest units of inventory should be transferred to cost of goods sold first. The weighted-average cost method combines the costs of the beginning and recently added inventory.

Chapter **Eleven**

Page 419

1 The incentive to overproduce occurs because overproduction leads to more fixed costs being retained in inventory and a higher short-term profit.
2 To discourage overproduction, charge the cost of extra inventory to the person responsible for the inventory decision, or use JIT.
3 By definition, the marginal cost of a resource that is a fixed cost is zero. When a manager is charged through a cost allocation for using a fixed cost resource, the manager tends to use less of the resource.
4 The death spiral is caused by dropping products but not avoiding costs that then must be allocated to the remaining products.

Page 422

1 Fixed costs are treated as period expenses.
2 Variable costing removes the incentive to overproduce and identifies the contribution margin.
3 Variable costing may lead to problems in identifying fixed and variable costs. Variable costing still requires the choice of an allocation base.

Page 427

1 The application rate is equal to the estimated overhead costs divided by the usage of the allocation base when operations are at capacity.
2 The portion of fixed costs allocated is equal to the portion of capacity used.
3 The advantages are identifying the cost of unused capacity and not burdening existing products or departments with costs due to capacity decisions. The disadvantage is that using practical capacity still does not alleviate the overproduction problem.
4 Fixed costs could be allocated based on requested capacity at the time of the capacity decision. Managers would be motivated to accurately report capacity requirements by penalizing them if they used more of the capacity than they requested.

Chapter **Twelve**

Page 455

1 Organizations use standard costing to communicate expected costs for planning purposes. The primary reason, however, is to control processes and individuals by using standard costs as benchmarks.
2 No generally accepted method exists for setting standards. Some organizations set standards very tightly and others set standards that are easily attainable. Information from those with knowledge about the processes should be obtained to establish standards.

Page 465

1 The two components are quantity and unit prices.
2 A favourable variance means that standard costs are greater than actual costs.
3 The human resources manager is likely to be responsible for the labour wage variance; the operations manager should be responsible for the efficiency variance.
4 The material price variance is the responsibility of the purchasing manager, and the quantity variance is the responsibility of the operations manager.
5 The material quantity variance is adverse when more than the standard material is used. It can be caused by carelessness in using the material, or by the poor quality of the material.